TWO WEEK LOAN

Remember to return on time **or** renew at
**https://icity.bcu.ac.uk/ or
http://www0.bcu.ac.uk/library/public/**
or **24 Hour Renewals: Tel 0121 331 5278**
Items in demand may not be re

Single-Word Reading
Behavioral and Biological Perspectives

New Directions in Communication Disorders Research: Integrative Approaches

Rhea Paul, Series Editor

Rhea Paul (Ed.)
Language Disorders from a Developmental Perspective: Essays in Honor of Robin S. Chapman

Elena L. Grigorenko and Adam J. Naples (Eds.)
Single-Word Reading: Behavioral and Biological Perspectives

Single-Word Reading
Behavioral and Biological Perspectives

Edited by
Elena L. Grigorenko
Adam J. Naples

Lawrence Erlbaum Associates
Taylor & Francis Group

New York   London

Cover design by Robin S. Chapman, Ph. D.

Lawrence Erlbaum Associates
Taylor & Francis Group
270 Madison Avenue
New York, NY 10016

Lawrence Erlbaum Associates
Taylor & Francis Group
2 Park Square
Milton Park, Abingdon
Oxon OX14 4RN

© 2008 by Taylor & Francis Group, LLC
Lawrence Erlbaum Associates is an imprint of Taylor & Francis Group, an Informa business

Printed in the United States of America on acid-free paper
10 9 8 7 6 5 4 3 2 1

International Standard Book Number-13: 978-0-8058-5350-6 (Hardcover)

Library of Congress Cataloging-in-Publication Data

Single-word reading : behavioral and biological perspectives / Elena L. Grigorenko and Adam J. Naples, editors.
    p. cm.
    ISBN 0-8058-5350-2 (cloth : alk. paper) -- ISBN 1-4106-1624-X (e book)
    1. Reading, Psychology of. I. Grigorenko, Elena L. II. Naples, Adam J. III. Title.

BF456.R2S49 2007
418'.4019--dc22   2006027816

Visit the Taylor & Francis Web site at
http://www.taylorandfrancis.com

Dedication

To our immediate colleagues, junior and senior, with gratitude

Contents

Preface

Single-word reading (*aka* word recognition, word identification, single-word processing) holds unique status as a cognitive phenomenon. Unlike many other cognitive phenomena (e.g., auditory processing of a spoken word), single-word reading is a relatively new addition to the list of human competencies required by modern human culture. Additionally, it is a necessary foundation for a higher-order cognitive process, reading—a gateway to success in our complex, developed societies. As a result, cognitive mechanisms subserving reading are unlikely to be innately specified in detail, but most likely "permit" this function to form and mature. Of note is that (1) reading is typically mastered by the majority of individuals when taught systematically and by few individuals without any systematic teaching; (2) failures of successful reading mastery occur regularly and in all linguistic systems, although in a small minority of individuals; and (3) in some individuals, reading skills are preserved in the presence of otherwise impaired cognitive function. The processes leading to the emergence and maturation of successful reading competence are a fascinating constellation of intertwined cognitive phenomena and the process of single-word reading is one such phenomenon.

Whereas single-word reading bridges domains of research across multiple fields (e.g., education and psychology) and multiple subfields within psychology (e.g., developmental, cognitive, and abnormal), the concept of "representation" is an integral aspect of all areas of cognitive psychology and, correspondingly, all cognitive phenomena, including reading. Representation is the information an individual incorporates as a function of learning; representations can best be thought of as structured data in the human brain. The successful incorporation of phonological, orthographic, graphemic, and semantic information results in a set of representations suitable for the task demands of reading. Variation in reading skills and reading-related processes can often be attributed to the variation in representations for reading-related domains or the mappings between these domains. Therefore, the analysis of these representations can arguably be viewed as central to the study of reading and reading disability.

This volume includes a collection of essays systematically sampling the research on single-word reading. Such a collection will be beneficial not only for scientists working in the field of reading, but also to professionals directly linked to the teaching of reading, such as education researchers, educators, and other practitioners working with special populations. Thus, the book aims to describe the research in single-word reading to a wide audience with a sample of essays from different experimental paradigms. The book is aimed at bridging the gap between researchers in such areas as representation, performance, education, psycholinguistics, genetics, and neuroimaging.

In this fashion, this is a volume by researchers for researchers that will provide both an introduction to unfamiliar areas of research and an inspiration for future study. In addition, the book provides valuable information to educators who are looking to develop successful reading programs and the answers as to why some children experience unexpected reading difficulties. Finally, this book will help other professionals who work with children, especially children with special needs, including clinical and school psychologists, who provide the assessments, diagnosis, and recommendations for reading abilities and disabilities.

The book opens with a chapter by Philip Seymour that offers a conceptual framework for interpretation of the emergence of word recognition within a theory of literacy development as exemplified by variations of the phase model of word recognition. Although it is one of many possible accounts, it is a comprehensive model that sets up a wonderful contextual stage for connections between spoken and written word processing, the stage-based nature of their development, and the role of education. In describing the phase model, Seymour introduces the componential skills that are relevant to word recognition and comments on the communalities and specificities of the development of word recognition in different languages.

The following seven chapters expand on the themes introduced by Seymour and develop them further in depth and breadth. Specifically, the contributions by Tatjana Nazir and Anke Huckauf and by Urs Maurer and Bruce McCandliss are focused on the visual aspects of word processing. These two chapters address visual word processing from different theoretical perspectives and with different methodologies, producing, together, a comprehensive representation of modern theories and data on rapid visual word recognition. The visual word-processing chapters are followed by a chapter from Usha Goswami. This contribution considers the role of phonological representation in single-word processing in the context of the psycholinguistic grain size framework. Laurie Feldman and Dana Basnight-Brown take the reader to yet another aspect of single-word processing, the role of morphology in word recognition. The complexity of the process-based texture of word recognition becomes even more evident when Lesley Hart and Charles Perfetti consider the role of lexical representation. This set of chapters addressing different aspects of single-word processing prepares the reader for the chapters by Jonathan Grainger and Johannes Ziegler, who attempt to study both main and interactive roles of orthography, phonology, and semantics in word recognition, and the contribution by Brett Kessler, Rebecca Treiman, and John Mullennix, who consider issues of feedback on a holistic process of single-word reading.

The next two chapters, one on spelling by Tatiana Pollo, Rebecca Treiman, and Brett Kessler and the other on comprehension by Janice Keenan and Rebecca Betjemann, place word recognition into the context of other functions, such as spelling and comprehension, respectively.

The following four chapters are all focused on the biological bases of single-word reading and related processes. These contributions further crystallize references to the biological bases of single-word processing mentioned in a number of writings that appear early in the book. Specifically, Panagiotis Simos, Rebecca

Billingsley-Marshall, Shirin Sarkari, and Andrew Papanicolaou provide a comprehensive overview of studies of single-word reading using magnetic source imaging. Considering this chapter, the reader might revisit componential accounts of different aspects of single-word processing discussed earlier in the book. Richard Olson delivers an overview of behavior-genetic studies of single-word reading and related processes, attesting to the importance of genes in the etiology of these functions, and Cathy Barr and Jillian Couto illustrate Olson's general considerations with a discussion of specific examples evidencing the involvement of particular genomic regions and genes in the formation of the foundation for single-word processing. In chapter 14 by Grigorenko, she attempts to bring together findings from both brain- and gene-based studies of the biological bases of single-word processing and discuss theoretical frameworks for interpreting these findings.

The collection closes with a set of chapters on developmental dyslexia. Although many chapters throughout the book make implicit and explicit references to developmental dyslexia, only in the chapter by Piasta and Wagner is the process of single-word reading, or rather, individual differences observed on tasks requiring the engagement of this process, considered the central element of dyslexia-related identification and treatment. In addition, in describing different approaches to subtyping individuals with dyslexia, Piasta and Wagner refer to many aspects of single-word processing described in earlier chapters of the volume. The theme of the role of word recognition deficits in dyslexia is further developed by James Royer and Rena Walles, who consider different remediation approaches aimed at overcoming word-level difficulties in dyslexia and related impairments. This set of chapters is completed by a contribution from Frost and colleagues that summarizes behavioral and neuroimaging studies of both skilled and impaired reading, in an attempt, once again, to generate an appreciation of the complexity of the field of single-word processing.

Finally, the book closes with a contribution from James Magnuson, who takes a slightly different perspective from that typical for studies of printed word recognition in summarizing and discussing the main points and take-home messages of the contributors to the volume.

It is our hope that this combination of topics will appeal to a wide audience, including researchers in the cognitive and developmental sciences, educators, policy-makers, and clinicians. The sections below will describe in more detail the value of the book for the proposed audiences.

This book took about 36 months to complete, from the moment we realized the need for such a volume to the time it was actually ready. We were fortunate in generating interest among excellent scholars in the field and are grateful for their fine contributions.

—Elena L. Grigorenko
Adam J. Naples

Foreword

Rhea Paul, PhD, CCC-SLP, Series Editor

In this, the second volume in our series on New Directions in Communication Disorders Research: Integrative Approaches, we examine the role of single-word reading in the process of literacy acquisition. Elena Grigorenko and Adam Naples have assembled a broad and distinguished array of scientists who provide readers with a contemporary view of the biology, psychology, genetics and linguistics that contribute to the acquisition of this skill. In addition, issues of identification and treatment of reading disability are addressed. Current views of reading suggest that learning to read words is a complex and multi-faceted process that builds on a variety of skills that emerge and develop in early childhood. The acquisition of these skills is influenced by the individual's inherent capacities as well as the richness of input from the linguistic environment, opportunities available to observe and model literacy behaviors, and access to literacy materials and artifacts. In turn, single-word reading serves as foundation for the development of automatic, fluent reading that will allow the child to move past "learning to read" and on to "reading to learn." The ability to comprehend and derive new knowledge from written texts is the crucial development that allows children to succeed at academic pursuits, as well as to acquire higher levels of language and thinking that rely on interaction with complex texts and ideas available primarily through literate, written language.

Although it is well-known that oral language serves as a basis for the acquisition of literacy, the ability to read reciprocally influences language development. As readers are exposed to literate language they come in contact with infrequent words, synonyms, complex sentence forms, increased density of content and ideas, alternative means of expression through paraphrase, and a range of text structures and purposes. These both result in and require an increasing base of knowledge and flexibility in language processing that pushes linguistic skill forward in ways unavailable through conversation. Thus language and reading have a clearly symbiotic relationship, particularly during the school years.

For specialists in communication disorders, this synergy is particularly germane. Communication Disorders professionals are being asked increasingly often to participate in the teaching of reading, particularly at the single-word reading level. This demand stems from two sources. First, it derives from the recognition that these professionals are conversant with the concepts of phonological development and awareness, an essential element of the acquisition of single-word reading. Second, it acknowledges the foundational role played by oral language in the development of not only phonological awareness, but also the other skills that contribute to reading success, such as vocabulary knowledge, ability to comprehend grammatical structure, and understanding of basic story architecture. Communication Disorders professionals are seen as the members of the educational team who are most competent to assess the prerequisite skills for early reading development and to address deficits in these skills to prevent reading failure.

Yet, many in the field of Communication Disorders feel ill-prepared to fulfill the role for which others assume they are competent. Those who trained before the language-literacy conjunction was prominent may have had few opportunities to learn about literacy development. Even those who have trained more recently are likely to have received brief exposure to the concepts of literacy development and disorders. For this reason, our series aims to serve as a means of re-education. Our hope is that by providing readers with a ready source of information on the findings, issues, and theories that are emerging from the active and exciting research so ably summarized in this volume, the task of participating in the development of literacy and the prevention of reading disorders will become an integral area of practice.

Readers from outside the field of Communication Disorders, who we hope will also find their way to this volume, will find its content equally compelling. As the Editors point out in the Introduction, single-word reading is a unique phenomenon both cognitively and in terms of its educational implications. Unlike so many of the communication skills a child acquires, these skills necessitate direct instruction in order for the majority of children to achieve mastery. Moreover, for a substantial minority even direct group instruction needs to be supplemented with more intensive individualized assistance in order to prevent reading disability. Thus, in contrast to the myriad of language abilities children acquire effortlessly from only the normal interactions inherent in daily life, single-word reading achievement requires the application of conscious, empirically-based strategies to ensure success for the largest possible number of students. In this endeavor, both researchers and school professionals from a range of disciplines need to collaborate in order to discover and implement these strategies. One purpose of this volume is to provide a contemporary survey of what is already known that can contribute to the development and implementation of such strategies. A second is to provide a forum for additional conversations among the research and practice communities to foster additional collaborative pursuits.

We hope and expect that readers who take advantage of the compendium of information offered here will be amply rewarded for their efforts. These rewards will include both an increased depth of knowledge about the ways in which the essential cornerstone of lifelong learning emerges, and perhaps more importantly, how it can be supported by facilitating experiences and opportunities. We hope, too, that some of the wonder a child feels when he first discovers he can read will be awakened as readers come to understand the complex and multidimensional processes that build toward this moment. Finally, it is our hope that educators and Communication Disorders professionals alike will find the information here a support in their efforts to improve the reading skills of their students, and by extension, the brightness of their, and our, future.

List of Contributors

Cathy Barr
Toronto Western Research Institute, TWH

Dana Basnight-Brown
State University of New York Albany

Rebecca L. Billingsley-Marshall
University of Texas Medical School

Rebecca S. Betjemann
University of Denver

Jillian M. Couto
The Toronto Western Research Institute

Gina-Marie Della Porta
Yale University School of Medicine Department of Pediatrics

Laurie Feldman
State University of New York Albany

Stephen J. Frost
Haskins Laboratories

Usha Goswami
University of Cambridge

Jonathan Grainger
Centre National de la Recherche Scientifique, Universitè of Provence

Elena L. Grigorenko
Yale University

Lesley Hart
Yale University

Anke Huckauf
Bauhaus-Universität Weimar

Leonard Kodz
University of Connecticut & Haskins Laboratories

Jan Keenan
University of Denver

Brett Kessler
Washington University

Nicole Landi
Haskins Laboratories

James Magnuson
University of Connecticut & Haskins Laboratories

Urs Maurer
Weill Medical College of Cornell University

Bruce McCandliss
Weill Medical College of Cornell University

W. Einar Mencl
Haskins Laboratories

Dina Moore
Haskins Laboratories

John Mullennix
University of Pittsburgh at Johnstown

Adam Naples
Yale University

Tatjana A. Nazir
*Institut des Sciences Cognitives-CNRS and
Université Lyon, France*

Richard Olson
University of Colorado at Boulder

Andrew. C. Papanicolaou
University of Texas Medical School

Rhea Paul
Southern Connecticut State University

Charles A. Perfetti
University of Pittsburgh

Shayne B. Piasta
Florida State University

Tatiana Cury Pollo
Washington University

Kenneth R. Pugh
*Yale University School of Medicine, Department of
Pediatrics
Haskins Laboratories*

James Royer
University of Massachusetts

Jay G. Rueckl
University of Connecticut & Haskms Laboratories

Philip Seymour
University of Dundee

Rebecca Sandak
Haskins Laboratories

Shirin Sarkari, Ph.D.
University of Texas Medical School

Panagiotis G. Simos
University of Crete

Rebecca Treiman
Washington University

Rena Walles
University of Massachusetts – Amherst

Richard Wagner
Florida State University

Johannes Ziegler
*Centre National de la Recherche Scientifique
Université de Provence*

CHAPTER ONE

Continuity and Discontinuity in the Development of Single-Word Reading: Theoretical Speculations

Philip H. K. Seymour
University of Dundee, Scotland

The capacity to identify single written words accurately and fluently is the fundamental process in reading and the focus of problems in dyslexia. This chapter takes the form of a speculative account of the early stages of the development of word recognition and makes reference to research carried out in the literacy laboratory at the University of Dundee. It is an expression of a viewpoint and a set of hypotheses and not an attempt at a comprehensive review of the literature on the development of word recognition.

A clear sequential account is needed in order to pinpoint when and how development begins to go wrong in cases of dyslexia and to provide a rationale for remedial instruction (Frith, 1985). The basis of such an account is a *theory of literacy development*. A number of differing approaches can be identified, including: (1) theories that focus on the *causes* of reading progress or difficulty, with the assumption that development is constrained by cognitive or sensory functions or by biological or cultural factors (Frith, 1997); (2) computational models that attempt the *simulation* of development using connectionist learning networks (Seidenberg & McClelland, 1989); (3) stage models that identify a cumulative series of qualitatively distinct steps in reading development (Marsh et al., 1981; Frith, 1985); and (4) Models which identify overlapping *phases* of development, including foundational aspects (Ehri, 1992; Byrne & Fielding-Barnsley, 1989; Seymour, 1990, 1997, 1999, in press). The theoretical account proposed in this chapter falls within the purview of the phase

1

models and includes reference to causal factors in the nature of the spoken and written language, educational factors, and an interactive relationship between orthography and linguistic awareness.

PRIMITIVE PRE-ALPHABETIC VISUALLY BASED WORD RECOGNITION

Some theories propose an early stage in which word recognition is based on visual characteristics. Gough & Hillinger (1980) described this as 'associative' learning, and Marsh, Freidman, Welch & Desberg (1981) as 'rote' learning. Similarly, Frith (1985) postulated an initial 'logographic' stage, and Ehri's (1992) account of 'sight word' learning includes a preliminary 'pre-phonetic' phase. The reference here is to a developmentally early form of word recognition which occurs *in the absence of alphabetic knowledge*. Words are distinguished according to a process of 'discrimination net' learning (Marsh et al., 1980) in which the minimal visual features necessary for choice between items within a restricted set are highlighted. Learning usually involves flash cards and rapid identification of words on sight and typically includes public signs and logos as well as high interest vocabularies such as names of family members or classmates. Teachers may reinforce the approach by emphasising iconic aspects of written words, such as the two eyes in 'look' or the waggy tail at end of 'dog'.

Seymour & Elder (1986) studied a class of Primary 1 children, aged 5 yrs, in Scotland who were learning under a regime which emphasised whole word learning (flash cards and books) in the absence of teaching of the alphabet or decoding procedures. This study illustrates some characteristics of primitive pre-alphabetic word identification: Errors were always refusals or word substitutions taken from the set of learned words. Each word had a physical identifying feature, such as the "two sticks" in 'yellow'. Confusions occurred due to letter orientation and rotation (b,d,p,q; n, u; w, m). The position of the identifying feature was not critical in the early stages of learning. Thus, Seymour & Elder found that, for a particular child, the shape of the letter **K** served as a distinctive feature for the identification of the word 'black'. Tests with nonsense strings in which the 'k' was located in different positions all elicited the response "black". Thus, reading is essentially *word specific* and reliant on identifying features rather than global word shape or outline. Unfamiliar forms (either words which have not yet been taught or nonwords) cannot be read and their presentation results in refusals ("don't know" responses) or word substitution errors.

In this mode of reading, visual words will initially be treated as members of a special object class for which the semantic coding is descriptive of the identifying feature plus an associative mnemonic link to a concept. e.g.,

⊤□ ‖ □□ →	[[columns, 2] & [color, yellow]] →	"don't know"
		"two sticks"
		"yellow"
		"green"

where [] designates a semantic representation, & is an associative link, and "" is a speech code. Since, in this scheme, word selection is semantically mediated, the occurrence of semantic substitution errors is a theoretical possibility. These errors occur in the reading of deep dyslexic patients and it is of interest that a few examples were observed among the children studied by Seymour & Elder (1986). Thus, the feature [colour] could result in the production of the wrong colour name, e.g., "green". However, this process will be restricted according to the content of the word set involved. Seymour & Elder demonstrated that children possessed a rather precise knowledge of the words which were included in their "reading set" and the words which were not. This suggests the existence of a "response set" which is isolated within a store of phonological word-forms and is the sole source of possible responses. It follows that semantic errors will normally occur only to the extent that a number of words in the store share closely overlapping semantic features. Colour names may be one such case, since they are quite likely to occur in beginning reading schemes.

Some commentators have argued that this primitive form of word identification is not a *necessary* first step in learning but rather an optional development which is not observed in some languages (e.g., German or Greek) and which is seen in English only among children who lack alphabetic knowledge (Stuart & Coltheart, 1988). One possibility is that the primitive process is unrelated to subsequent reading and is effectively discarded when the formal teaching of the alphabetic principle begins (Morton, 1989). For example, Duncan & Seymour (2000) found that expertise in logo recognition in nursery school conferred no subsequent advantage in reading. The other possibility is that the primitive process, although not a basis for subsequent word recognition, is nonetheless preserved as an element in memory. An argument here is that some forms of script, such as poorly formed handwriting, may require recognition via visual features or a distinctive configuration. In addition, primitive pre-alphabetic reading shares aspects with neurological syndromes such as 'deep dyslexia' (Coltheart, Patterson & Marshall, 1980). Patients with this condition lack alphabetic knowledge, are wholly unable to read unfamiliar forms such as simple nonwords, and yet show a residual capacity for recognition of common words with concrete meaning such as predominate in early school books ('clock', 'house', etc). This preserved reading could be a surviving trace of the primitive recognition function, possibly a form of 'right hemisphere' reading which becomes visible when the normal left hemisphere reading system has been abolished. Imaging studies which suggest that right hemisphere activity which is detectable in the early stages of learning tends to reduce or disappear as development proceeds are consistent with this idea (Turkeltaub, Gareau, Flower, Zefiro & Eden, 2003).

In summary, it seems likely that a primitive mode of word recognition (sometimes called "logographic" reading) exists in a form which is functionally (and perhaps anatomically) distinct from the standard alphabetically based reading process. This function may be directly observable only in children who learn to read without alphabetic tuition or in cases where neurological factors intervene to destroy or prevent the creation of an alphabetic system.

SYMBOLIC VERSUS PICTORIAL PROCESSING

In the primitive form of reading described above a written word is treated as a visual object. The words are members of a set of objects, an object class, in which the members share various features (horizontal extension, density) much like many other object classes (faces, dogs, chairs, trees) where there may be a high level of similarity combined with variations of detail which are critical for distinguishing members of the class one from another. In earlier discussions (Seymour, 1973, 1979), I argued that there was a *pictorial* channel and memory system which was responsible for recognition of objects, colours, shapes and scenes and for mapping onto a semantic level from which a name or speech output could be selected. This is distinguished from a *symbolic* channel and memory system which develops for the restricted purpose of dealing with a sub-class of conventionally defined visual objects, most notably the written forms of the numerals and the letters of the alphabet. Various arguments can be put forward to support this distinction. In my own work, I referred to experimental studies by Paul Fraisse which were concerned with the "naming vs reading" difference. This refers to a reaction time difference (vocal RT to name a symbol is faster than RT to name a colour patch or shape or object picture) and to a differential effect of ensemble size (the effect of variation in the number of stimuli involved in a mapping task is larger for objects than for symbols). For example, Fraisse (1966) demonstrated that the shape O is named more rapidly as "oh" or "zero" within a symbol set than as "circle" within a shape set.

According to this argument, the symbol processing channel develops in a way which is functionally and neurologically distinct from the picture and object processing channel. A key aspect of this distinction is that picture processing involves semantic mapping as an initial step, so that naming an object or colour involves the sequence: object → semantic representation → name selection, whereas symbol processing may involve direct mapping to a name: symbol → name selection. A preliterate child has no symbol processing system and will treat all visual shapes and patterns as pictures to be processed in terms of their semantics. The letters of the alphabet and the arabic numerals may initially be supported by the object processing system but will normally be quite quickly segregated and referred to a new system. This specialised channel operates on members of clearly defined and bounded classes (the numerals, 0-9, and the upper and lower case letters of the alphabet), and incorporates feature definitions which allow allocation to a subset as well as discrimination within each subset and tolerance of variations which may occur due to the use of differing fonts or handwritten forms. One feature which has to be taken into account in the symbolic channel is that *orientation* is a significant issue for identification of symbols ('n' is different from 'u' and 'b' is different from 'd').

In this discussion, a key assumption is that the implementation of a segregated symbol processing channel is the critical first step in the formation of a visual word recognition system and competence in reading and spelling. Following the establishment of the symbol processing channel, there is an augmentation in the architecture of the cognitive system, so that incoming visual stimuli may be classed as pictorial or as symbolic and processed accordingly.

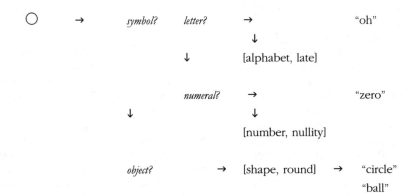

Logically, this seems to require some kind of early contextual test to decide if the input is a valid candidate for processing via the symbolic channel, and, if so, whether it is classifiable as a letter or as a numeral. Allocation to the symbol channel allows direct access to a store of symbol names. The symbols may, additionally, have a semantic representation expressing set membership, location in the conventional sequence, and aspects such as magnitude. This information might be accessed through the name or directly by an alternative pathway. If the input is not classed as a symbol it will be treated as an object and processed via the system of object semantics.

ALPHABETIC PROCESS

In line with this proposal, most theoretical accounts of reading development propose that the (optional) primitive visual phase of development is followed by a phase of alphabeticisation. Typically, this refers to the mastery of the 'alphabetic principle' of phonography according to which written words may be segregated into a left-to-right series of letters, each of which can be decoded as standing for a segment of speech. These segments correspond to the linguistic abstractions, the *phonemes*, by which the set of vowels and consonants composing the syllables of the spoken language are identified. This shift is well described in Frith's (1985) account. She proposed an initial phase, described as *logographic*, which corresponds to the primitive form of pre-alphabetic reading described above. This is followed by an *alphabetic* phase during which a new strategy involving systematic sequential conversion of letters to sounds is adopted. Frith took the view that the alphabetic process might have its origin in writing and spelling. Learning to write is naturally sequential, requiring the capacity to segment speech into a series of sounds, select a letter for each sound, and produce the graphic forms seriatim in the correct order. This strategy of proceeding in a sequential letter-by-letter manner may be transferred to reading as the model for a decoding procedure based on letters and sounds. Marsh et al.. (1981) used the term *sequential decoding* to refer to this strategy.

Letter–Sound / Decoding Distinction

For the purposes of the present discussion, it seems desirable to emphasise certain distinctions which may not have featured in the accounts provided by Marsh et al. and Frith. A first point is that a clear distinction needs to be made between (1) basic letter-sound knowledge, and (2) the mechanism or procedure of sequential decoding. Letter-sound knowledge is the foundation of the symbol processing channel described above. The reference is to a bi-directional channel in which the input of a visual symbol leads directly to the production of its spoken name and the auditory input of the spoken name leads directly to the production of the written form or to visual recognition (as in auditory-visual same-different matching). Sequential decoding is an operation which is applied to letter-sound knowledge. It requires the addition of an analytic procedure, sometimes referred to as "sounding out", which proceeds in a strict spatially oriented (left-to-right) sequence and involves the conversion of each symbol to a sound and the amalgamation of these sounds into a unified ("blended") pronunciation:

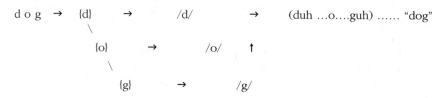

where {} is a grapheme, // is a phoneme, (..) is overt or covert letter sounding, and "" is an assembled (blended) speech output. It seems important to distinguish between this *procedure* of sequential segmentation, conversion and assembly and the *knowledge* of letter-sound correspondences which is called on by the procedure. The knowledge of the letter-sound correspondences is a pre-requisite for the implementation and application of the decoding procedure.

Decoding/Word Recognition Distinction

A second issue concerns the relationship between the decoding procedure and the recognition of familiar words belonging to a "sight vocabulary." In accounts such as those provided by Frith and Marsh it is proposed that the early visual feature based process of word recognition is effectively *replaced* by the new process of alphabetic decoding (see also Morton, 1989). According to this view, early alphabetic word recognition is founded on a process of sequential decoding. This is not the view adopted by Ehri (1992) since she speaks of a process of learning to recognise "sight words" which, while visually based in the first instance, comes to be increasingly founded on alphabetic knowledge. The establishment of this process is said to be supported by the development of decoding skill. Nonetheless, the impression is that decoding and sight word learning are separate and distinguishable processes. If this view is followed, the implication is that there may be *two* letter-based processes in early reading, one involving the recognition of already familiar "sight words," and the other the sequential decoding of unfamiliar forms. Ehri (1992) proposed that the sight word function might at first be based on partial letter-sound cues, for example the initial letter of a word, or the initial and final letters (see also Stuart & Coltheart, 1988). This proposal is reminiscent of the earlier suggestion that pre-alphabetic visual word recognition may rely on partial cues (the "two sticks" in 'yellow') rather than the whole word shape or structure. Post-alphabetic sight word learning may borrow this principle but without a reliance on visual distinctiveness and with a preference instead for the end positions of written words and the identification of letters and their partial mapping onto pronunciation:

black →   {b} {□□□} {k}   *familiar?* /b/...../k/   →   "black"

"brisk"

↓

(buh ...kuh)   →   "book?"

"bucka?"

"don't know"

In this account, sight word learning and sequential decoding are *parallel* developments (Seymour, 1990) and decoding is a back-up procedure which is implemented if the target is classified as unfamiliar.

PHONOLOGICAL AND ORTHOGRAPHIC COMPLEXITY

Sequential decoding is a simple procedure which operates on the principle that individual letters stand for individual phonemes in speech. Whether or not this basic principle is sufficient for reading depends on the extent to which the orthography of a language incorporates complex features of various kinds. It may be useful here to distinguish between two forms of complexity, to be referred to as phonological complexity and orthographic complexity, both of which differ between languages using an alphabetic script.

Phonological complexity concerns the syllabic structure of the spoken language. Relevant issues are whether the spoken language contains a significant proportion of monosyllables, as is the case for English, or whether monosyllabic words are few or absent, as is the case for many European languages where the vocabulary is largely made up of multisyllables. A second issue concerns the form of the syllables, particularly the relative proportions of *open* syllables having a consonant-vowel (CV) structure and *closed* syllables having a consonant-vowel-consonant (CVC) structure. Thirdly, the consonant structures occurring in the initial (onset) or final (coda) position of the syllable may vary in complexity, with some languages allowing numerous consonant clusters while, in others, clusters are infrequent and restricted to a limited number of possibilities. Additionally, there may be variations in the clarity with which syllables are defined and pronounced, depending on whether the placement of the boundaries between syllables is definite or ambiguous, and on whether the vowels are fully pronounced or omitted or reduced in unstressed syllables.

Orthographic complexity refers to the relationship between the written letters and the spoken form of the language. This relationship may be simple and straightforward, termed a shallow (or transparent) orthography, or complex and variable, termed a deep (or opaque) orthography. In a fully transparent alphabetic orthography it could be expected that each individual letter of the alphabet should be associated with a particular phoneme in speech in a reliable and consistent way. This correspondence should be bi-directional. Thus, it should be possible to list the phonemes of the language and to identify for each phoneme a corresponding letter. Similarly, it should be possible to list the letters of the alphabet and to identify for each letter the phoneme to which it corresponds.

/p/	↔	p		/æ/	↔	a
/b/	↔	b		/e/	↔	e
/t/	↔	t		/i/	↔	i
/d/	↔	d		.		
/k/	↔	k		.		
/g/	↔	g		:		
.				.		
. etc.				etc.		

This listing of associated phoneme-letter pairings will be exhaustive in that all the phonemes which occur in the language will be included and each one will have a corresponding letter. The size of the alphabet will, therefore, be determined by and equivalent to the size of the set of phonemic distinctions which is acknowledged. In a system of this kind, a knowledge of the set of letter-sound correspondences combined with the procedure of left-to-right sequential decoding will be sufficient to enable the reading or spelling of any legitimate spoken form from the language.

Departures from this *principle of transparency* will complicate the relationship between graphemes and phonemes. These departures can arise for various reasons. The most obvious is that there is a mismatch between the size of the set of phonemes required to speak the language and the size of the set of letters contained in the alphabet. For example, spoken English is based on 40+ phonemes while the alphabet contains only 26 letters. It follows that the transparency principle of one letter/one sound cannot be fully applicable and that it will be necessary to allow either that different phonemes may be represented by the same letter or that letter combinations must be assembled to cover some phonemes (complex graphemes):

/θ/	↔	th		/i./	↔	ee
/ʃ/	↔	sh		/ai/	↔	igh
.				.		
. etc.				etc.		

TABLE 1.1

Hypothetical Classification of European Languages Relative to the Dimensions of
Syllabic Complexity (Simple, Complex) and Orthographic Depth
(Shallow to Deep)

	Orthographic Depth			
Syllabic Structure	*Shallow. ....:....................:.................:..................Deep*			
Simple	Finnish	Greek Italian Spanish	Portuguese	French
Complex		German Norwegian Icelandic	Dutch Swedish	Danish	English

Note. From "Foundation Literacy Acquisition in European Orthographics" by P. H. K. Seymour, M. Aro, and J. M. Erskine, 2003, *British Journal of Psychology*, *94*, p.146 Copyright 2003 by The British Psychological Society. Reprinted with permission.

Further complexity arises if the mappings between graphemes and phonemes are allowed to vary, so that a given grapheme may be pronounced in different ways (one-to-many grapheme-phoneme mapping), possibly under constraint by surrounding context (e.g., {c} → /k/ or /s/ depending on the following vowel), and a given phoneme may be written using a variety of letters or letter groups (one-to-many phoneme-grapheme mapping) (e.g., the diphthong /ei/ → {a}, {a .. e}, {ay}, {ei}, {ai}, {eigh}, {aigh}, {ey}, etc.). In addition, spelling may signal lexical or morphological features, as in the distinction between 'wait' and 'weight' or the identity of the past tense morpheme {ed} in 'toured', 'walked' and 'started'.

If an orthography contains a sufficiently large number of violations of the principle of transparency it may be classed as *deep* or opaque. However, there is no exact definition of how widespread these departures must be in order to merit this classification, or, indeed, whether or not some lexical and morphological features have to be present. The question here is whether the shallow-deep distinction is dichotomous or whether it may be more appropriate to think of a continuous dimension ranging from an extreme of transparency to an extreme of complexity with many orthographies occupying intermediate positions. This was the approach adopted by Seymour, Aro & Erskine (2003) in an investigation of European orthographies undertaken within the context of a European research network, COST Action A8. Languages were classified on a phonological dimension, concerning the complexity of the syllabic structure, and on an orthographic dimension, reflecting intuitive estimates of depth (see Table 1.1). This scheme reflects the phonological contrast between the Romance and Germanic language groups and a variation in depth ranging from the very transparent orthography of Finnish to the deep and complex orthography of English.

In the context of models of reading acquisition, the relevance of this discussion is to establish that learning to read involves mastery of orthographic complexities above and beyond the simple correspondences postulated for the alphabetic phase. This is usually held to implicate a further phase during which the complex features are established, referred to as *hierarchical decoding* by Marsh et al. (1981), as an *orthographic* phase by Frith (1985), and as a *consolidation* phase by Ehri (1997). A general feature of these proposals is the suggestion that the advanced phase of learning involves the mastery of multiletter structures of various kinds, including complex onset and coda clusters, contextually determined patterns, rime segments, syllables, lexical forms, and morphemes. A possible limitation of these accounts is that they do not specify whether there is a hierarchy of complex features which may be assimilated over time and at differing rates. A further issue is that higher-order phonological structures, such as the onset-rime or the syllable, are not properly distinguished from lexical structures (words, root morphemes) and morphological structures (inflections, prefixes, derivational suffixes). Finally, although it is apparent that languages differ greatly in both phonological and orthographic complexity (see Table 1.1), and given that these variations may have large effects on learning to read, the models do not accommodate these cross-linguistic variations.

FOUNDATION LITERACY MODEL

An alternative developmental phase model has been outlined by Seymour (1990, 1997; Seymour & Duncan, 2001; Seymour, 2005, 2006). This scheme identifies an early phase of *foundation literacy* acquisition during which the basic post-alphabetic processes of simple decoding and familiar sight word recognition are established. It is supposed that these basic processes are contingent on the prior establishment of letter-sound knowledge. The foundation also provides the basis for more advanced developments during which the complex features of the orthography are internalised. A distinction is made between a phase of *orthographic literacy* involving the internalisation of the conventions for writing the syllables of the language, and a phase of *morphographic literacy* during which the conventions for writing free and bound morphemes are established. The proposed phases can be summarised in the terms shown in Table 1.2.

The phases are envisaged as being broadly successive and cumulative, such that letter knowledge must precede the establishment of foundation literacy, orthographic literacy depends on the availability of an adequate foundation, and morphographic literacy requires that basic orthographic knowledge should have been acquired. However, the model allows for some temporal overlap in the development of successive phases. It can be noted that this account refers to alphabetic literacy and, as such, does not include the primitive visual word recognition process described earlier. As already noted, the primitive process is pre-alphabetic and might be allocated to Phase 0 – 1 in the model.

Metalinguistic Awareness

Literacy acquisition is seen as a process of learning about the orthographic structures which correspond to *linguistic units* of differing sizes and characteristics. This proposition is in line with the well-documented evidence of a close relationship between literacy

TABLE 1.2

Hypothetical Phases in Reading Acquisition and Associated
Elements of Metalinguistic Awareness.

Phase	Name	Description	Metalinguistic awareness
0	Letter–sound knowledge	Alphabet of symbols Dominant correspondences	Letters Phonemes
1	Foundation literacy	Familiar sight-word recognition Simple decoding	Lexemes Phonemes
2	Orthographic literacy	Abstract model of spellings of monosyllables	Multiletter graphemes Onset-peak-coda Onset-rime, syllable
3	Morphographic literacy	Multisyllables, Morphologically complex words	Multiletter segments Syllables Morphemes

and awareness of linguistic structure. As originally formulated by Mattingly (1972), the concept of linguistic awareness admits of two levels of definition. There is firstly a natural competence in the use of spoken language in communication which may be encapsulated and inaccessible to conscious inspection or mental manipulation. This level may be referred to as *implicit* or, to use Gombert's (1992) term, *epilinguistic*. The second level is achieved when this implicit information is extracted and brought into the open where the elements can be paraded and manipulated. This level is designated as *explicit* or *metalinguistic*. According to Mattingly, reading is a secondary language skill which requires the development of an awareness of the operation of the primary skills of speaking and listening. In essence, this means that literacy acquisition depends on a capability to become aware of the segments of spoken language which correspond to the alphabetic symbols and groups which are contained in the written language.

The assumption of the phase model is that the elevation of structures to a metalinguistic level is normally achieved by a process of *interaction* between the learning of written forms and the definition of the corresponding spoken segments. In previous discussions (Duncan, Seymour & Hill, 1997, 2000), this process was interpreted according to Gombert's (1992) suggestion that encounters with written forms may create a cognitive "demand" for the establishment of explicit (metalinguistic) representations of the corresponding segments in speech. Thus, while it is supposed that all children possess implicit representations of relevant linguistic structures, the formation of explicit representations may occur primarily in the context of literacy instruction. Empirical tests of this argument depend on the possibility that measures of phonological awareness can be classified according to whether the task can be performed on the basis of implicit knowledge alone or whether explicit representations are required. Duncan et al. (1997, 2000; also Duncan & Seymour,

2001) argued that some tasks, such as language production, similarity detection or odd-man-out detection, might be performed successfully on the basis of implicit representations. Other procedures, including standard methods such as phoneme deletion or transposition, require an explicit level of representation, allowing that language structures can be isolated and manipulated.

Duncan et al. (1997, 2000) used a "common unit" task to assess the explicit level. In this procedure, the child hears pairs of spoken words which share a segment of sound and is instructed to report back the shared segment. An advantage of the method is that it is possible to test for explicit awareness of linguistic units of differing size – for example phonemes, onsets and rimes, and syllables – within a constant task structure. Taking the rime as an example, Duncan et al. found that young children might show an implicit awareness of rhyming (they could give a rhyme on demand, decide that rhyming words sounded similar, detect a rime-based oddity) while being at the same time unable to perform an explicit task (they were unable to report that "oat" is the segment shared by the words "boat" and "goat"). A notable feature of Duncan et al.'s (1997) study was the finding that beginning readers who possessed excellent implicit rhyming skills did not begin learning to recognise words using onset and rime segments. Instead, their early word learning was characterised by a "small unit" approach based on letter sounds. This was thought to be a direct consequence instruction which emphasised letter-sounds and decoding as well as the learning of a sight vocabulary. The trend was reflected in performance on the explicit common unit task. Thus, as reading developed during the first school year, children were able to report shared phoneme-sized units ("boat – bill" → "buh"; "book – sick" → "kuh") with near perfect accuracy while remaining unable to report the larger rime units. Duncan et al. (2000) found that capacity to report shared rime units did not appear until reading age was quite well advanced. According to the interactive model, this could be at a more advanced stage when the organisation of the orthographic lexicon in terms of onset and rime structures creates a demand for the formation of explicit rime representations.

These ideas are incorporated into the model as a proposition that the phases of literacy development differ with respect to their demands for the formation of explicit metalinguistic representations. Table 1.2 contains suggestions regarding the linguistic entities which might be emphasised (and hence raised from implicit to explicit status) at each phase. The argument is that, in an alphabetic orthography, this development broadly follows a *small - to - large unit progression*. It can be noted that this is the opposite to the commonly formulated proposal in favour of a large - to small progression in phonological development, encompassing syllables, then onset-rimes, and finally phonemes (Treiman & Zukowski, 1991). This latter progression may be characteristic of implicit (epilinguistic) phonological representations but not of explicit (metalinguistic) representations which depend very directly on the way in which literacy develops. Hence, it is argued that, at the beginnings of literacy (Phases 0 and 1), when letter knowledge and sequential decoding are emphasised, the primary demand is for the emergence of explicit *phonemic* representations. At the same time, a parallel emphasis on sight word learning from flash cards and texts is expected to enhance metalexical representation (making explicit what entities constitute *words* in the language).

In line with the proposal that the later stages of development involve the *consolidation* of multi-letter structures of various kinds (Ehri, 1997), it is supposed that Phases 2 and 3 involve the emergence of larger linguistic structures. At Phase 2 (orthographic literacy) learning focuses on the internal structure of the syllable. This incorporates single and multi-letter spellings used to represent the onset, peak and coda elements of the syllable and accommodates variations and alternatives which may be arbitrary or contextually constrained. Accordingly, it is expected that learning will be paralleled by the emergence of explicit representations of these structures (possible onset and coda clusters, vowels and diphthongs) and by higher-order combinations, such as the onset-rime division. In the case of English monosyllables, constraints operate which improve the coherence of spelling when rime (peak + coda) structures are treated as units (Treiman et al., 1995) and this feature is expected to encourage the formation of explicit representations of rime units (Duncan et al., 2000). In Phase 3 (morphographic literacy) learning involves the coordination of large segments (for example, syllables or morphemes) to establish legitimate combinations and orthographic conventions for attaching elements one to another. This will entail making explicit the phonological segments (syllables) or, more pertinently, the morphological segments (free and bound morphemes) out of which complex words are composed.

A controversial feature is the proposal that the emergence of explicit awareness of the *syllable* is linked to Phase 2 or 3 and is consequently seen as a later development. This conflicts with the long standing assumption that syllable awareness is an early development which may be present before the beginnings of reading (Liberman, Shankweiler, Fischer & Carter, 1974). Part of the issue here is the distinction between implicit and explicit representations, so that, in agreement with the results for rimes, implicit awareness may be demonstrable in an early pre-literate phase whereas explicit awareness is apparent only much later. Extensions of the "common unit" method to bisyllables have tended to support this argument. When presented with spoken word pairs such as "window – winter" children were unable to isolate and report the shared syllabic segment "win". This was the case for pre-readers and for post-literate children who had been reading for some time and contrasted with performance on implicit tasks (e.g., indicating that "window" and "winter" sound similar). However, this difficulty in performing explicit syllable manipulation tasks may be a special feature of English. Implementation of the task with groups of French-speaking children yielded totally different outcomes. Identification of the common syllable presented little difficulty and was close to perfect in children both pre- and post-literacy (Duncan, Colé, Seymour & Magnan, 2006).

The conclusion from these observations is that the availability of explicit representations of large units such as the syllable is dependent on the *spoken* language of the learner. In some languages, such as French and other Romance languages, syllables are clearly defined and bounded entities which are already established as objects of explicit awareness at the outset of learning to read. A consequence is that the syllable is a useful unit for learning to read the complex (multisyllabic) words which predominate in speech and writing and will be the salient organisational structure during Phases 2 and 3. In other languages, such as English, this is not the case and learning will involve the discovery of units which are buried in the orthographic structure. As already noted, these could be onset and rime structures in Phase 2, and morpheme structures in Phase 3.

UNITARY AND DUAL FOUNDATION MODELS

The implication of the preceding discussion is that the manner in which single word recognition develops is likely to differ between languages depending on features of the phonology as well as the orthography. These variations can be accommodated within the phase structure outlined in Table 1.2 in terms of effects on:

1. The rate of learning, the time required to complete a developmental phase
2. The mode of learning, the cognitive systems or strategies which are implemented
3. The linguistic structures which are emphasised (achieve metalinguistic status)

In other words, it is possible to envisage a family of acquisition models which share the same basic phase structure while differing in details of implementation. This possibility can be illustrated by considering two extreme cases, to be referred to as *unitary* and *dual* foundation models. These extremes are defined by reference to the classification of languages proposed by Seymour et al. (2003) (see Table 1.1). In this scheme, the possession of syllables which have a simple structure and precise and clear definition is a positive feature which facilitates reading acquisition, as is the presence of a straightforward orthography in which there is a reliable bidirectional correspondence between single letter graphemes and phonemes. Complex or poorly defined syllables and variable and inconsistent grapheme-phoneme relationships are negative features which impede acquisition and modify the course of development.

Model 1: Unitary Foundation

Model 1 is intended to be descriptive of word recognition development in languages which have a simple and clear syllable structure combined with a shallow (transparent) orthography. In Table 1.1, Finnish is identified as a language which best meets this specification. The model is also expected to be relevant for other languages which have similar characteristics, such as Greek, Italian or Spanish. A schematic representation is provided in Figure 1.1.

The model is described as a *unitary foundation* because Phase 1 (foundation literacy) involves the development of a single alphabetic decoding procedure as the basis for the formation of orthographic and morphographic levels. The development of single word recognition in a system of this kind can be glossed in the following terms:

Phase 0 – 1: Pre-literacy. There should be implicit phonological awareness, especially of larger units, such as rimes and syllables. Explicit awareness of the syllable is expected to be present. Pre-alphabetic visual word recognition might be observed, but only where the letters are not known and interest in written words (names of self, family, etc) is encouraged.

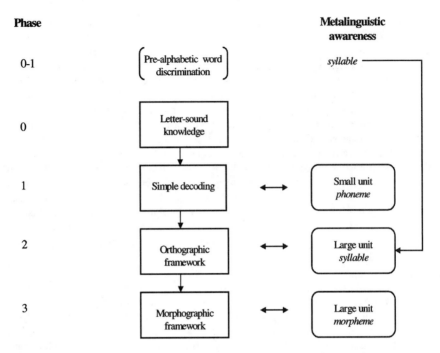

FIGURE 1.1   Schematic representation of unitary foundation model of reading
acquisition.

Phase 0: Letter-sound knowledge. Learning to discriminate and label the letters of
the alphabet by their predominant sounds or names is the essential first step.
When this is achieved depends on educational and cultural factors, particularly
when the letters are (formally or informally) taught and how this learning is
scheduled (e.g., early intensive teaching of the whole alphabet, as in the 'syn-
thetic phonics' method, or a more gradual approach extending over weeks or
months). This phase is probably *not* affected by linguistic factors (phonological complexity, orthographic depth).

Phase 1: Foundation literacy. The foundation process is the sequential decoding
procedure described earlier. This is also probably dependent on educational
approaches, since instruction is required to establish a systematic left-to-right
procedure for serial conversion of letters to sounds and blending of the outcome. This might involve discrete letter sounding or the 'gliding' procedure
used in some educational systems (e.g., Finnish). The decoding procedure creates a demand for the emergence of explicit phonemic awareness, shown by
capacity to perform phoneme manipulation tasks, such as deletion or common
unit identification.

Phase 2: Orthographic literacy. This is viewed as the development of a coordinated system for representation of syllabic forms which is built around the onset, peak and coda structures of the language. Positional constraints are accommodated, if, for example, a phoneme has differing orthographic realisations in the onset and coda positions (as happens for /dz/ in English) and consonant clusters may be unitised. Alternative spellings (one-to-many phoneme-grapheme mappings) and any contextual effects (e.g., influence of consonant on vowel, or vice versa) are incorporated. The outcome is an internalised model of the orthographic representation of the range of possible syllables which reflects statistical properties such as syllable frequency and onset and peak frequency. Obviously, this learning is relatively simple when the set of possible syllables is quite small and there is a predominance of CV structures and perhaps only a limited range of legitimate consonant clusters. Explicit phonological awareness may extend to onset and coda clusters. Explicit awareness of syllables, which is critical for this phase, is likely to be already available but may be enhanced as a concomitant of orthographic development.

Phase 3: Morphographic literacy. In this final phase a system for representation of complex (multisyllabic) words is formed. This can be viewed as primarily a matter of developing *fluency* in the identification and pronunciation of long and complex words. This requires that syllables should be concatenated to form the words of the vocabulary. Such learning might incorporate constraints on the positions occupied by particular syllables. In addition, the learning may take account of morphological structure, including positional constraints regarding word stems, compounds, and affixes serving different functions. Thus, Phase 3 could be viewed as having a lexigraphic and morphographic basis. This is expected to create a demand for the formation of explicit (metalinguistic) representations of words and morphemes and improved capacity to perform explicit morphological awareness tasks.

The important characteristic of this model is that the initial stage of learning (Phases 1 and 2) is expected to be quite rapid and uncomplicated. This follows from the straightforward nature of the decoding procedure and the limited inventory of clearly structured syllables. The difficulties are likely to arise at Phase 3 (morphographic literacy) where reading will remain sequential and dysfluent unless a lexically and morphologically based system can be formed.

Model 2: Dual Foundation

The second model is descriptive of learning to read in languages which have a complex and poorly defined syllabic structure combined with a variable and inconsistent system of grapheme-phoneme correspondences. The model is referred to as a *dual foundation* because it is proposed that there is a difference in the mode of learning reflected in the implementation of a distinct word-form (logographic or lexigraphic)

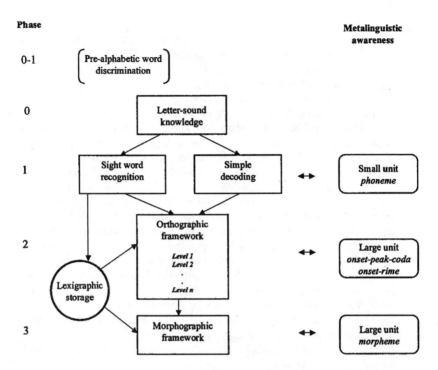

FIGURE 1.2   Schematic representation of dual foundation model of reading acquisition.

process from Phase 1 onwards. In addition to English, the model is applicable to other Germanic languages which have a complex orthography, such as Danish. A schematic representation is provided in Figure 1.2.

The progression through the learning phases is expected to take the following form:

Phase 0 – 1: Pre-literacy. As in Model 1, pre-alphabetic visual word recognition might be observed in children who learn to recognise words in the absence of a knowledge of the letters. Children will be capable of demonstrating implicit awareness of larger linguistic units, such as syllables or rimes, but will lack explicit awareness of these and other units.

Phase 0: Letter-sound knowledge. This phase is also the same as for Model 1. Letter learning will occur at a time and at a rate determined by educational factors (when and how the letters are formally or informally taught). One issue is whether there is a level of maturity which is necessary before children can learn the letters effectively and with fluency (in terms of speed of labelling).

Phase 1: Foundation literacy. Model 2 differs from Model 1 in postulating *two* letter-dependent foundation processes which are initially operationally distinct. One of these is the *alphabetic* decoding procedure for the sequential conversion of letters to phonemes and the blending of the outcome. As in Model 1, the implementation of this procedure, together with knowledge of the letter-sounds, will create a demand for the emergence of explicit representations of phonemes, leading to capacity to perform explicit phoneme manipulation tasks. The second is the word-based procedure which is referred to as "sight word" learning (Ehri, 1992, 1997) or as a *logographic* (or lexigraphic) process (Seymour, 1997). The assumption is that this procedure will be implemented in circumstances where the proportion of words occurring in beginning reading materials which violate the principle of transparency exceeds a threshold of tolerance. Educational factors may also be important. The use of global methods by which children are taught to recognise whole words on flash cards or in texts will encourage the development of this word-based procedure. As already noted, the procedure is assumed to operate in a global way, not in the sense of word shapes or profiles, but rather by the use of letters as identifying features, albeit with a preference for end letters and incorporation of grapheme-phoneme mappings. A consequence of the use of phonological mapping is that words with a transparent structure may be easier to learn than words containing complex features or irregularities. A further assumption is that the letter arrays are entered into a memory store (referred to as the *lexigraphic store* in Figure 1.2). These representations are the basis for abstraction of orthographic principles and for attempts at word spelling.

Phase 2: Orthographic literacy. As in Model 1, this phase involves the abstraction of principles underlying the orthographic representation of monosyllables. The difference is that the process is greatly more complex because the existence of large numbers of legitimate onset clusters (pr, bl, tr, spr, etc) as well as coda clusters (lt, nk, pt, etc) allow for a very large set of possible syllabic forms. Further complexity is added by the need to use multi-letter structures (complex graphemes) to represent some consonants (sh, th, etc) and many vowels (ee, ay, augh, igh, etc). Over and above these factors are the complexities introduced by the variabilities in grapheme-phoneme and phoneme-grapheme mapping which are linked to contextual influences, historical influences, and lexical identities. Construction of an internal model of the spelling of English monosyllables is therefore likely to involve an extended period of learning (cf the simulations of this process by connectionist models (Seidenberg & McClelland, 1989)). According to some views (e.g., Seymour, 1990) this can be seen as a cumulative learning process in which a simple 'core' structure, built around a C-V-C frame, is established first and is then progressively elaborated to incorporate complex onset structures, complex coda structures, unstressed second syllables, complex vowel spellings, as well as lexically specific variants. There may be a hierarchy affecting the rate at which different types of complex feature can be absorbed, therefore, as well

as effects of word frequency, neighbourhood density, and spelling consistency. The capacity to build a complex orthographic knowledge base is held
to be dependent on progress at the earlier foundation phase. One hypothesis is that the development of the sequential decoding mechanism yields the
basis for a phonologically defined onset-peak-coda structure for the orthographic lexicon, and that the lexigraphic store of partial or complete word-
forms contains the exemplars which are needed to abstract general principles.
In English, where a significant proportion of the vocabulary consists of monosyllables and bisyllables with first syllable stress, the existence of contextual
constraints of the coda on the vowel favours the adoption of an onset-rime or
onset-superrime organisation for the lexicon (Duncan, Seymour & Bolik, in
press). If so, it is anticipated that orthographic development will create
demands for the formation of explicit representations of the onset, peak and
coda, and the rime and superrime (Duncan, Seymour & Hill, 2000).

Phase 3: Morphographic literacy. Phase 3 involves the construction of representations of complex, multisyllabic words, as in Model 1. Because the syllable
is an ambiguous and poorly defined structure for English and comparable
languages, it is unlikely that this level involves coordination of syllabic segments. For monomorphs, a lexical basis involving an onset + remainder structure, is more likely. For morphologically complex forms, containing word
stems, compounds, and prefixes or inflectional or derivational suffixes, an
organisation based on free and bound morphemes is suggested. In the model,
the stock of word-forms assembled over time in the Lexigraphic Store contains exemplars of the written forms of morphologically complex words
which are analysed and compared during the process of forming an abstract
representation of the morphography (the system for representing morphological segments). This development is expected to create a demand for the
explicit representation of morphemes. It follows that capacity to perform
explicit morphological awareness tasks, such as the analogy procedure used
by Bryant, Nunes & Bindman (1997), will emerge at this time.

The characteristic feature of Model 2 is that the early phases of acquisition are
complex and require additional learning time. Phase 0 (letter-sound knowledge) is
not affected but Phases 1 and 2 both involve much longer learning processes than
are required for Model 1. In addition, the cognitive structure of the reading system
is different, since a lexical recognition system is implemented at Phase 1 and an
accumulating store of orthographic word-forms is maintained as a source of exemplars in forming the abstract representations of the orthography and morphography.

Intermediate Models

Models 1 and 2 are intended to represent the acquisition of single word recognition
under conditions which fall at opposed extremes according the scheme proposed
by Seymour et al. (2003). In general, Model 1 is optimal for the rapid acquisition of

accurate reading. In Model 2, learning from Phase 1 onwards appears substantially more complex, and is expected to proceed at a slow rate. Other languages referenced in Table 1.1 are expected to produce intermediate outcomes depending on: (1) the degree to which syllables are complex, or ambiguous in boundary, or are poorly articulated in spoken language; and (2) the extent of the departure from the principle of transparency, and (3) the extent to which lexical and morphological features are represented in the orthography.

EMPIRICAL OBSERVATIONS

The above analysis indicates that the development of single word reading might be expected to occur at different rates and in different modes, depending on the combined effects of language, orthography and teaching methods. Verification of this proposition requires a comprehensive comparative study of basic literacy acquisition in a range of languages and cultures. No such study has as yet been undertaken. However, existing bi- and trilateral comparisons support the conclusion that acquisition occurs more slowly in English than in German (Wimmer & Goswami, 1994; Frith, Wimmer & Landerl, 1998) or Welsh (Spencer & Hanley, 2003) or Greek (Goswami, Porpodas & Wheelright, 1997) or French and Spanish (Goswami, Gombert & de Barrera, 1998).

Seymour et al. (2003) compared English with a larger set of European languages (see Table 1.1) using tasks based on the foundation literacy model with children who were close to the end of their first year in primary school. The assessment included a word reading task based on vocabularies of common words typically encountered in children's beginning reading materials. Items were presented in vertical lists for reading aloud and measures of accuracy, speed (time/item) and error type were obtained. Figure 1.3 summarises the accuracy scores for word (and nonword) reading by the various language groups. Single word reading was accurate (> 95 per cent correct) and fluent (1.6 sec/item) in the majority of European orthographies, but significantly poorer in Portuguese, French and Danish (approx 75 per cent correct), and far lower in English (34 per cent in Primary 1, 76 per cent in Primary 2). These are the orthographies which are classed as deep in Table 1.1 suggesting that acquisition of a sight vocabulary of familiar words is indeed delayed by orthographic depth.

A limitation of this study is that reading was assessed at a single time point, making it difficult to estimate the *rate of acquisition*. Seymour et al. (2003) analysed the regression of word reading accuracy against Reading Age and found that a Reading Age above 7 years was needed before word identification in English matched the levels achieved in the majority of languages before the end of the first school year. This implies that the establishment of an effective sight vocabulary needs more than 2 years of learning in English as against less than 1 year in other languages. Subsequently, a further investigation has been implemented, using a longitudinal design and computer presentation of individual words and nonwords, with reaction timing as well as accuracy measurement. This study is still in progress. However, preliminary results confirm that two or more years of learning are required to establish a sight vocabulary and basic decoding procedure in English. The study confirms a

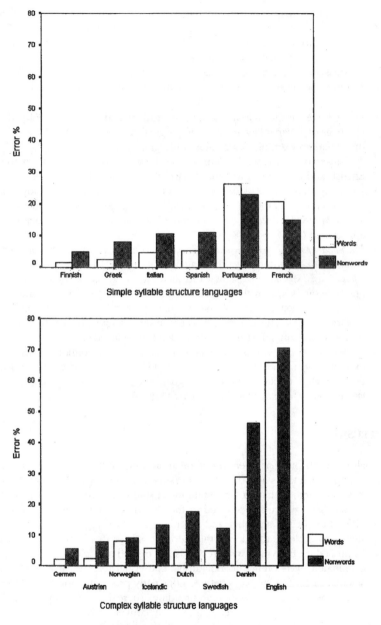

FIGURE 1.3   Error rates (percent) for familiar word and simple nonword reading by Grade 1 children in English and other European languages of varying orthographic depth and syllabic structure (from Seymour et al., 2003).

much higher rate of acquisition in languages such as Finnish and Greek, where all children reach a ceiling level of performance before the end of the first school year. Other languages, for example Icelandic and Portuguese, give evidence of acquisition rates which are intermediate between these extremes.

There are several conclusions which can be put forward on the basis of the results from the Seymour et al. (2003) study and the current longitudinal research.

- *Individual variability.* Children learning to read in a deep orthography display much greater variability in rates of progress and extent of sight vocabulary than children learning in a shallow orthography. Seymour et al. (2003) found that this variability extended almost over the whole of the range for readers of English and Danish but was much narrower in other orthographies.
- *Dependency on letter-sound knowledge.* Results from the new longitudinal study indicate that, in all orthographies, English included, progress in word reading and in simple nonword decoding occurs only after letter-sound knowledge exceeds a threshold (80%).
- *Parallel development of word recognition and decoding.* The growth of sight word reading parallels the growth of decoding, again in all of the languages studied.
- *Effect of complexity.* Rate of sight word learning in English is affected by ortho-graphic complexity, with the gain being faster for words with a transparent spelling (one letter – one phoneme) than for words containing complexities of various types. This effect also occurs in other languages but the magnitude of the complexity effect decreases as depth is reduced.
- *Syllabic and phonemic awareness.* Children in all alphabetic orthographies display explicit phonemic awareness as decoding skill develops. Explicit syllabic aware-ness is high at the outset in some languages (e.g., the Romance languages) but low in some Germanic languages (e.g., English).

CONCLUSIONS

The goal of this chapter has been to outline an account of the development of sight word reading which takes account of the possible continuities and discontinuities in this process. It is argued that the important initial step is the creation of a specialised *symbol processing channel* which is dedicated to the recognition, labelling and interpreta-tion of the letters of the alphabet and the numerals. Development of visual word recognition is possible in advance of this step but only in the form of a *pictographic* or *iconographic* procedure by which written words are treated as a class of visual objects and discriminated by reference to non-alphabetic visual features. It is likely that a developmental discontinuity exists between this early procedure and the later emer-gence of alphabetic word recognition and reading. Thereafter, it is supposed that the development of alphabetic word recognition may conveniently be discussed by ref-erence to a series of overlapping phases. These phases are characterised by the nature of the orthographic knowledge which is acquired and by the linguistic units which are emphasised as objects of explicit awareness. The development of single word reading in all alphabetic orthographies is held to be analysable into a common sequence of four phases, involving: Letter-sound learning (formation of the symbol processing channel); foundation decoding and word recognition; orthographic literacy; and morphographic literacy. However, there are important differences between languages respecting the *rate* at which these phases are traversed as well as the structure of the reading process, particularly the degree to which specifically lexical word recognition and storage may be implicated, and the extent to which the syllable can serve as a convenient unit of decoding.

REFERENCES

Byrne, B., & Fielding-Barnsley, R. (1989) Phonemic awareness and letter knowledge in the child's acquisition of the alphabetic principle. *Journal of Educational Psychology, 81,* 313–321.

Coltheart, M., Patterson, K., & Marshall, J.C. (1980) *Deep Dyslexia.* London: Routledge & Kegan Paul.

Duncan, L. G., Colé, P., Seymour, P. H. K., & Magnan, A. (2006) Differing sequences of metaphonological development in French and English. *Journal of Child Language, 33,* 369–399.

Duncan, L. G. & Seymour, P. H. K. (2000). Phonemes and rhyme in the development of reading and metaphonology: The Dundee longitudinal study. In: N.A. Badian (Ed.) *Prediction and Prevention of Reading Failure.* Parkton, Maryland: The York Press. (pp 275–297).

Duncan, L. G., Seymour, P. H. K., & Bolik, F. (in press) Rimes and superrimes: An exploration of children's bisyllabic ryming and reading skills. *British Journal of Psychology.*

Duncan, L. G., Seymour, P. H. K., & Hill, S. (1997). How important are rhyme and analogy in beginning reading? *Cognition, 63,* 171–208.

Duncan, L. G., Seymour, P. H. K., & Hill, S. (2000). A small to large unit progression in metaphonological awareness and reading? *The Quarterly Journal of Experimental Psychology (Section A), 53,* 1081–1104.

Ehri, L. C. (1992). Reconceptualizing the development of sight word reading and its relationship to recoding. In P. Gough, L. C. Ehri, & R. Treiman (Eds.), *Reading acquisition.* Hillsdale, NJ: Erlbaum. (pp. 107–143).

Ehri, L. C. (1997). Learning to read and learning to spell are one and the same, almost. In C.A. Perfetti, L. Rieben, & M. Fayol (Eds.), *Learning to spell: Research, theory, and practice across languages.* Hillsdale, NJ: Erlbaum. (pp. 237–269).

Fraisse, P. (1967) Latency of different verbal responses to the same stimulus. *Quarterly Journal of Experimental Psychology, 19,* 353–355.

Frith, U. (1985). Beneath the surface of developmental dyslexia. In K.E. Patterson, J.C. Marshall, & M. Coltheart (Eds.), *Surface Dyslexia: Neuropsychological and cognitive studies of phonological reading.* Hillsdale, NJ: Erlbaum. (pp. 301–330).

Frith, U. (1997) Brain, mind and behaviour in dyslexia. In C.Hulme & M.J.Snowling (Eds.), *Dyslexia: Biology, Cognition and Intervention.* London: Whurr. (pp. 1–19).

Frith, U., Wimmer, H., & Landerl, K. (1998) Differences in phonological recoding in German- and English-speaking children. *Journal of the Society for the Scientific Study of Reading, 2,* 31–54.

Gombert, J. E. (1992). *Metalinguistic development.* London: Harvester Wheatsheaf.

Goswami, U., Gombert, J. E., & de Barrera, L. F. (1998) Children's orthographic representations and linguistic transparency: Nonsense word reading in English, French and Spanish. *Applied Psycholinguistics, 19,* 19–52.

Goswami, U., Porpodas, C., & Wheelwright, S. (1997). Children's orthographic representations in English and Greek. *European Journal of Psychology of Education, 12,* 273–292.

Gough, P. B., & Hillinger, M. L. (1980). Learning to read: An unnatural act. *Bulletin of the Orton Society, 30,* 180–196.

Liberman, I. Y., Shankweiler, D., Fischer, F. W., & Carter, B. (1974) Explicit syllable and phoneme segmentation in the young child. *Journal of Experimental Child Psychology, 18,* 201–212.

Marsh, G., Friedman, M., Welch, V., & Desberg, P. (1981) A cognitive-developmental theory of reading acquisition. In G. E.MacKinnon & T. G.Waller (Eds.), *Reading Research: Advances in Theory and Practice, Vol 3.* New York: Academic Press. (pp. 199–221).

Mattingly, I. G. (1972) Reading, the linguistic process, and linguistic awareness. In J. F. Kavanagh & I. G. Mattingly (Eds.), *Language by Ear and by Eye: The Relationship between Speech and Reading.* Cambridge, Mass.: MIT Press. (pp. 133–147).

Morton, J. (1989) An information processing account of reading acquisition. In A. M. Galaburda (Ed.), *From Reading to Neurons.* Cambridge, MA.: MIT Press. (pp 43–66)

Nunes, T., Bryant, P., & Bindman, M. (1997) Morphological spelling strategies: Developmental stages and processes. *Developmental Psychology, 33,* 637–649.

Seidenberg, M. S & McClelland, J. L. (1989) A distributed developmental model of word recognition and naming. *Psychological Review, 96,* 523–568.

Seymour, P. H. K. (1979) *Human Visual Cognition: A Study in Experimental Cognitive Psychology.* West Drayton: Collier Macmillan.

Seymour, P. H. K. (1973) A model for reading, naming and comparison *British Journal of Psychology, 64,* 34–49.

Seymour, P. H. K. (1990). Developmental dyslexia. In M.W. Eysenck (Ed.), *Cognitive Psychology: An International Review.* Chichester: Wiley. (pp. 135–196).

Seymour, P. H. K. (1997). Foundations of orthographic development. In C. A. Perfetti, L. Rieben and M. Fayol (Eds.) *Learning to spell.* Hillsdale, NJ: Erlbaum. (pp. 319–337).

Seymour, P. H. K. (1999). Cognitive architecture of early reading. In I. Lundberg, F.E. Tønnessen, & I. Austad (Eds.), *Dyslexia: Advances in theory and practice.* Dordrecht: Kluwer. (pp. 59–73).

Seymour, P. H. K. (2005) Early reading development in European orthographies. In M. Snowling & C. Hulme (Eds.), *The Science of Reading: A Handbook.* Oxford: Blackwell. (pp. 296–315)

Seymour, P. H. K. (2006) Theoretical framework for beginning reading in different orthographies. In M. Joshi & P.Aaron (Eds.), *Handbook of Orthography and Literacy.* Mahwah, N.J.: Lawrence Erlbaum Associates. (pp. 441–462)

Seymour, P. H. K., Aro, M., & Erskine, J. M. (2003) Foundation literacy acquisition in European orthographies. *British Journal of Psychology, 94,* 143–174.

Seymour, P. H. K. & Duncan, L. G. (2001) Learning to read in English. *Psychology: The Journal of the Hellenic Psychological Society, 8,* 281–299.

Seymour, P. H. K., & Elder, L. (1986). Beginning reading without phonology. *Cognitive Neuropsychology, 3,* 1–36.

Spencer, L. H., & Hanley, J. R. (2003) Effects of orthographic transparency on reading and phoneme awareness in children learning to read in Wales. *British Journal of Psychology, 94,* 1–28.

Stuart, M. & Coltheart, M. (1988) Does reading develop in a sequence of stages? *Cognition, 30,* 139–181.

Turkeltaub, P. E., Gareau, L., Flower, D. L., Zeffiro, T. A., & Eden, G. F. (2003) Development of neural mechanisms for reading. *Nature Neuroscience, 6,*

Treiman, R., Mullennix, J., Bijeljac-Babic, R., & Richmond-Welty, E. D. (1995). The special role of rimes in the description, use, and acquisition of English orthography. *Journal of Experimental Psychology: General, 124,* 107–136.

Treiman, R. & Zukowski, A. (1991) Levels of phonological awareness. In S. A. Brady & D.P.Shankweiler (Eds.), *Phonological Processes in Literacy: A Tribute to Isabelle Y Liberman.* Hillsdale, N.J.: Erlbaum. (pp. 67–83).

Wimmer, H. & Goswami, U. (1994) The influence of orthographic consistency on reading development: Word recognition in English and German children. *Cognition, 51,* 91–103.

CHAPTER TWO

The Visual Skill "Reading"

Tatjana A. Nazir
Institut des Sciences Cognitives–CNRS and Université Lyon 1, France

Anke Huckauf
Bauhaus University, Weimar, Germany

Skilled readers develop a singular form of visual expertise that allows them to process print with remarkable efficiency. Within a fraction of a second, they can extract the critical information needed to identify a word of more than 15 to 20 characters (Erdmann & Dodge, 1898). Although it was long assumed that this skill relied on sophisticated guessing strategies, most researchers in the word-recognition field acknowledge today that this capacity is perceptual in nature (see reviews by Carr, 1986). Top-down feedback from lexical to perceptual stages (e.g., Jacobs & Grainger, 1992; McClelland & Rumelhart, 1981) and functional/structural reorganization of the visual system have been proposed as potential explanations (Cohen & Dehaene, 2004; McCandliss, Cohen, & Dehaene, 2003; see also Caramazza & Hillis, 1990; Cohen, Dehaene, Naccache, Lehéricy, Dehaene-Lambertz, Hénaff, & Michel, 2000; Warrington & Shallice, 1980). However, as the perceptual side of reading has generally been considered to belong to the field of vision research—as opposed to the domain of language (e.g., Frost, 1998)—little effort was made until recently to elaborate on these perceptual processes. Yet, as we will demonstrate, despite their nonlinguistic nature, these processes are essential to skilled reading.

We first develop arguments that support the view that "visual knowledge" about words matters for word recognition. In contrast to a recently developed view in the literature, according to which rapid visual word recognition results from our ability to compute abstract word representations (Cohen & Dehaene, 2004; McCandliss et al.,

2003), we defend the position that rapid recognition of visual words rather relies on the development of word-specific visual pattern memories. We then list a number of empirical results from healthy readers as well as from neurological patients that support these assumptions, and show that skilled visual word recognition breaks down when a reader can no longer access these visual pattern memories.

"LEXICAL KNOWLEDGE" AND "VISUAL KNOWLEDGE" IN WORD RECOGNITION

The phenomenon that ultimately convinced researchers in reading that knowledge about words modifies the way we perceive print was the so-called word superiority effect. Skilled readers identify letters better when they appear in a word than when they appear in a chain of random letters—even when guessing strategies are neutralized (Reicher, 1969). Thus, it is easier to tell apart the letter *k* from the letter *d* when the letter is presented in the word *work* than when it is presented in a meaningless context such as *orwk*. To account for this phenomenon, it was proposed that during stimulus encoding perceptual processes are modulated by "top down" feedback from hierarchically superior word-processing stages where acquired knowledge about words is stored (McClelland & Rumelhart, 1981). Thus, because the word *work*, but not the chain *orwk*, has an entry in the mental lexicon, processing of letters of words, but not of letters in meaningless chains, profits from lexical top-down influences and such letters are effectively better perceived.

Yet, although lexical factors certainly affect visual word recognition, the following example demonstrates that these factors do not by themselves account for the ease with which we perceive print. The left panel in Figure 2.1 plots the proportion of correct identification of words and orthographically legal pseudowords during rapid visual displays (data from Benboutayab, 2004). For both types of stimuli, performance varies systematically with fixation location and the best performance is achieved when the eyes were fixating regions near the center of the chain. Note that although the shapes of the two curves are fairly similar, performance for words is about twice as high as performance for pseudowords. This superiority of words over pseudowords comes from the mentioned influence of lexical knowledge on the processing of orthographic stimuli.

The right panel of Figure 2.1 plots performance for the same set of items when displayed vertically. The resulting graphs are remarkably similar to the one in the left panel. What differs between the two experimental conditions, however, is that to achieve comparable performance, display duration for vertically presented items had to be increased by a factor of ten!

This simple set of data shows two important things. First, lexical knowledge contributes in the same way to word recognition whether the word is presented in the visually familiar horizontal format or in the less familiar vertical format. Second, beyond these lexical factors, word recognition is dramatically affected by visual familiarity with words, because large differences in presentation duration are required to equalize performance in the two display conditions. Why do we need so much more time to read words in visually unusual formats?

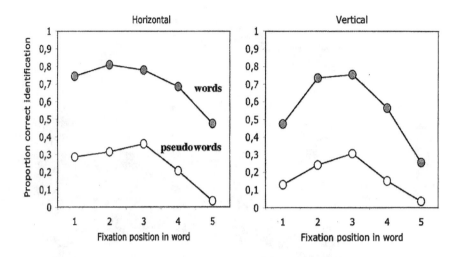

FIGURE 2.1 Proportion of correctly identified words (grey symbols) and pseudo-words (white symbols) for horizontally (left) and vertically (right) displayed stimuli. Stimuli were presented such that the eyes were fixating the first, or the second, or the third etc. letter in the chain. Display duration was limited to 17 ms for horizontal and 170 ms for vertical stimuli, and was followed by a pattern mask. Data are plotted as a function of fixation location in the stimulus (from Benboutayab, 2004).

THE VISUAL WORD FORM AREA: A KEY ELEMENT FOR RAPID WORD RECOGNITION?

In recent years, several brain-imaging studies have called attention to a small zone in the left fusiform gyrus that is systematically active during processing of printed words (e.g., Beauregard, Chertkow, Bub, Murtha, Dixon, & Evans, 1997; Cohen, et al., 2000; Cohen, Lehericy, Chochon, Lemer, Rivaud, & Dehaene, 2002; McCandliss, et al., 2003; Nobre, Allison, & McCarthy, 1994; Polk & Farah, 2002). Figure 2.2 schematically indicates this zone on a three-dimensional representation of the left hemisphere.

The increased interest in this particular zone comes from the fact that damage to regions including this zone produces a peripheral reading deficit called "word blindness" or "letter-by-letter dyslexia." Word blindness can occur in the absence of any other visual or language deficits (Dejerine, 1892; see Black & Behrman, 1994; Cohen, et al., 2000 for reviews). Patients who suffer from this deficit can typically write to dictation and can pronounce words spelled to them—testifying intact lexical knowledge—yet, they seem unable to "see" words. To recognize printed words they regress to a letter-by-letter identification strategy typically observed with beginning readers (Aghababian & Nazir, 2000). Reading latencies, therefore, increase dramatically as words become longer (e.g., Behrman, Plaut, & Nelson, 1998).

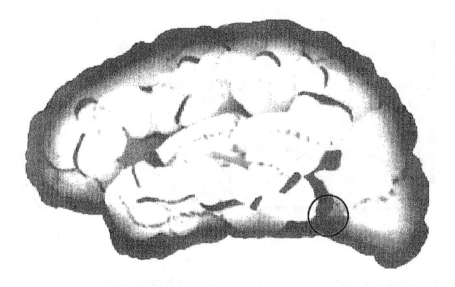

FIGURE 2.2   The visual word form area (VWFA), indicated by the circle, in the fusiform gyrus of the left hemisphere.

When first described by Dejerine (1892), word blindness was seen as the result of a disruption of fibers that lead from visual areas of both hemispheres to the left angular gyrus and to language-related cortical structures in more anterior parts of the left hemisphere. However, more investigators now believe that the critical region in the left fusiform gyrus, an area commonly referred to as the "Visual Word Form area" (VWFA), is not passively carrying information. Rather, the VWFA is held to be critically involved in the elaboration of abstract representations of word forms, which serve lexical access (Cohen et al., 2000; McCandliss et al., 2003; Polk & Farah, 2002; Posner & Raichle, 1994).

Arguments in favor of the existence of such a level of coding come from everyday experiences that provide the (false) impression that we can rapidly identify words regardless of letter size, case, and font, or of the retinal location where the word is displayed. Thus, the word TABLE appears to remain the word *table* whether it is written in lower or upper case, and independently of where it is presented in the visual field (limits of acuity put aside). As brain imaging studies further demonstrate, hemodynamic changes in the VWFA occur irrespective of letter-case (e.g., for *table* as well as for *tAbLe*; Dehaene, Naccache, Cohen, Bihan, Mangin, Poline, & Riviere, 2001; Polk and Farah, 2002), or of the location of the orthographic stimulus in the visual field (e.g., Cohen et al., 2000); thus, this cortical region indeed seems apt to house such a hypothetical mechanism. For some researchers, part of the mystery that underlies rapid visual word recognition therefore resides in this computation of abstract representations (see Cohen and Dehaene, 2004; McCandliss et al. 2003).

Note, however, that identifying vertically presented words requires display durations ten times longer than those required for horizontally presented words, demonstrating that the hypothesized computation of invariant representations is differentially taxing on familiar and unfamiliar visual formats. Yet, if visual word format matters, reading-related learning must occur *before* the VWFA, that is, at processing levels where information about the physical form of words has not yet been abstracted away.

LEARNING-RELATED CHANGES IN THE REPRESENTATION OF VISUAL STIMULI: WORDS "POP OUT"

One intriguing observation with orthographic stimuli is that random letter strings appear visually "messy," whereas words look "neat" (see Figure 2.3). As vertically displayed words look similarly messy, the mental lexicon disqualifies once more as single source of this difference.

Research in vision has shown that basic visual features such as color, orientation, curvature, etc. can be detected as easily in the context of other stimuli (distractors) as they are when presented alone. This phenomenon is frequently referred to as "pop-out." By contrast, the ability to detect complex stimuli that involve combinations of basic features is typically affected by the number of surrounding distractors. Reaction time in a visual search task therefore systematically rises as the number of distractors augments.

These qualitatively different types of visual search have been used to argue that vision involves the interplay of two distinct systems: a preattentive system that operates in parallel and registers the presence of basic features within a retinotopic map in early visual cortices, and an attentive system that operates serially and applies to complex stimuli, which are represented as combinations of basic features in higher cortices (Treisman, 1988). Interestingly, however, several studies have shown that visual training changes the nature of these processes such that even complex stimuli can acquire "pop-out" quality once they are familiar.

In Figure 2.4a we show an example of such a qualitative change taken from a study by Wang, Cavanagh, and Green (1994; cited in Gilbert Sigman, & Crist, 2001). The figure shows that the combination of the same basic features into a complex shape does or does not pop-out from its background depending on the visual familiarity of the shapes. Hence, it is easy to detect the target in the upper panel of the figure because the digit "5" is a familiar stimulus. The same target ceases to pop-out, however, when the display is rotated by 90 degrees such that the stimuli lose visual familiarity.

These training-related changes in pop-out properties have been taken to suggest that stimuli, which prior to training are represented as combinations of basic features in higher cortices, shift their representation down toward retinotopically organized cortices, which, by this virtue, become responsive to complex shapes (Gilbert, et al. 2001; Sigman & Gilbert, 2000). Recent brain imaging data showing a large-scale reorganization of brain activity in the visual pathway following training seem to corroborate this assumption. Hence, analyses of hemodynamic changes associated with trained shapes (e.g., a T rotated at different angles) revealed a

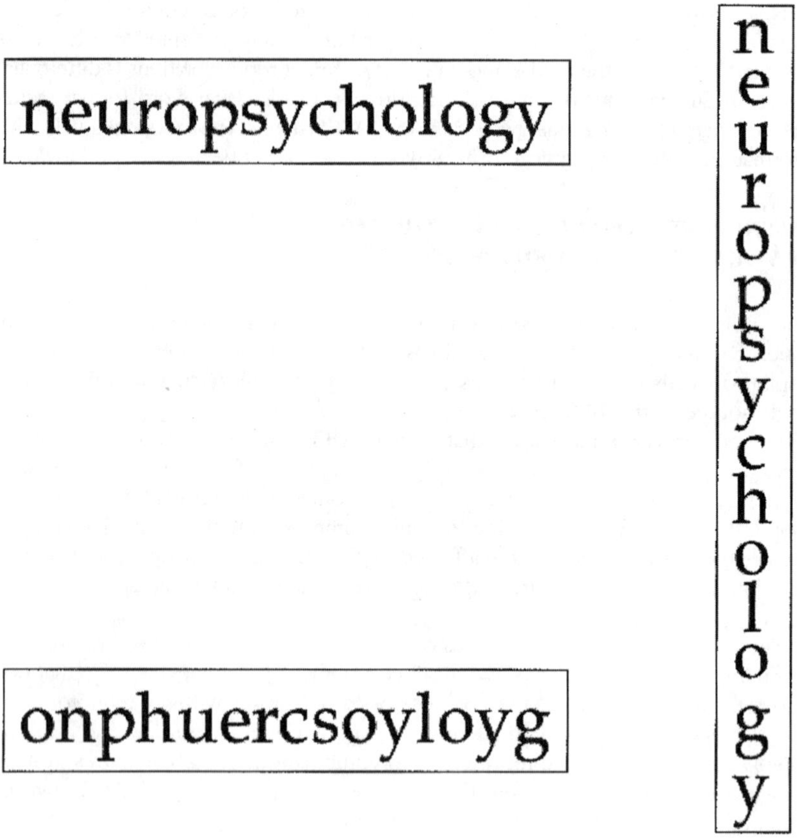

FIGURE 2.3   Horizontally displayed words look visually neat, whereas nonwords and vertically displayed words look visually messy.

systematic increase of activity in the retinotopic cortex and a decrease of activation in the lateral occipital cortex and the dorsal attentional network (posterior parietal and supplementary motor areas) when compared with untrained shapes. Along with this reorganization, activation in the retinotopic cortex became increasingly correlated with participants' performance (Sigman, Pan, Yang, Stern, Silbersweig, & Gilbert, 2005). According to Gilbert and colleagues, the rapid and efficient recognition of frequently encountered visual patterns results from the formation of multiple representations of the same stimulus over the (trained) retinotopically mapped region (Gilbert et al., 2001; Sigman & Gilbert, 2001; Sigman et al., 2005).

Interestingly, Figure 2.4b seems to suggest that this kind of perceptual learning may also develop for recognition of visual words. Thus, whereas the familiar word *chair*

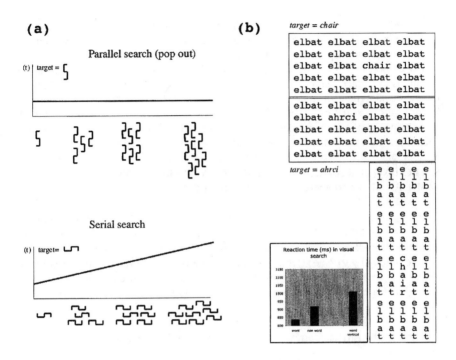

FIGURE 2.4 (a) The familiar shape of the digit "5" pops out from its background independently of the number of surrounding distractors. Search time for these items is typically constant and low. When rotated by 90 degrees the pop-out quality disappears. The increment in reaction time (t) for each additional distractor is taken as indicator for parallel (little or no increment) or serial search (linear increment).

(b) Like for the digit, familiar words seem to acquire pop out quality. The word (chair) is easier to find in the top panel than the nonword (ahrci) in the bottom pannel. The pop out quality for words disappears, however, when the stimuli are presented vertically. Search time for the target in the three conditions is given in the inset.

pops-out from the homogeneous background of random letter sequences, the less familiar nonword *ahrci* does so to a lesser extent. More importantly, like for the digit "5", the word *chair* ceases to pop-out when the stimulus configuration is presented in the visually less familiar vertical display. If visual pop-out is indeed the result of a reorganization of stimulus representations, this observation suggests that reading-related learning may already develop at retinotopically mapped cortical areas where information about the physical shape of the stimulus is still maintained.

The reason why visual word recognition is fast and easy may therefore relate not so much to the ability of elaborating *abstract* word representations (Cohen & Dehaene, 2004; McCandliss et al. 2003), but rather to the development of retinotopically organized, *stimulus-specific* pattern memories that we acquire through extensive training in recognizing print (Nazir, 2000; Nazir et al., 2004). Hence, although literate adults read texts despite disparity in print, script, font, size, or retinal location, the perceptual operation that underlies *skillful* visual word recognition may not adapt to large variations in surface features. Rather, rapid visual word recognition may rely instead on the development of multiple representations of the same visual word pattern at lower levels of visual processing. Combined with lexical knowledge, it is this "visual knowledge" that makes reading such an impressive skill. Empirical evidence that speaks for these speculations is discussed in the following section.

SEARCHING FOR A DOUBLE DISSOCIATION IN PROCESSING VISUALLY FAMILIAR AND UNFAMILIAR CHAINS OF LETTERS

If training changes the way visual shapes are represented in the visual pathway (Sigman et al., 2005), distinct brain lesions may differently affect processing of familiar and unfamiliar chains of letters. Hence, as lesions in occipitotemporal regions seem to disable the ability to "see" (familiar) words while preserving the ability to read in a letter-by letter fashion, other types of brain damage may cause deficits in processing unfamiliar chains while preserving the ability to recognize visually familiar chains of letters.

The Role of the Parietal Cortex

A cortical region known to be involved in mediating the previously discussed conjunction or "binding" of basic features during perception of complex shapes is the right parietal cortex (e.g., Corbetta, Shulman, Miezin, Petersen, & Posner 1995; Nobre, Coull, Walsh, & Frith, 2003; Shafritz, Gore, & Marois, 2002). Accordingly, transcranial magnetic stimulation (TMS) applied over the parietal visual cortex while participants are performing a conjunction (serial) or a "pop-out" (parallel) visual search task has been shown to impair the first but not the latter task (Ashbridge, Walsh, & Cowey, 1997; see also Ellison, Schindler, Pattison, & Milner, 2004). Lesions to these cortical regions are also correlated with a variety of visuospatial deficits. Hence, neurological patients that suffer from parietal lesions can be impaired in their ability to perceive more than one object at a time (a deficit referred to as simultagnosia). They also show difficulties in telling the spatial relation of objects (e.g., whether a visually presented object is to the right of, above or below, etc. another object), or in binding basic features such as color, form, or the size of objects.

Friedman-Hill, Robertson and Treisman (1995), for instance, reported the data of a patient with bilateral parietal-occipital lesions, who miscombined colors and shapes of objects even under free viewing conditions. The ability of this patient to judge the location of one visual shape relative to another shape was also at chance level. Curiously, however, parietal lesions do not seem to dramatically affect reading skill, though patients with these lesions should have problems in perceiving the correct spatial order of letters in words. Note, however, that if representation of complex stimuli changes with training and recognition process shifts from serial to parallel operation for familiar shapes, the following pattern of reading behavior is expected: Previously healthy skilled readers that suffer from parietal lesions should read normally when tested with (visually) familiar words. However, they should dramatically fail when confronted with visually unfamiliar combinations of letters such as nonwords or words displayed in unusual visual formats. This is exactly what is observed.

Simultagnosia and Reading

Baylis, Driver, Baylis, & Rafal (1994) were the first to provide a detailed analysis of visual word recognition in such a patient. They showed that their patient could read isolated letters and words almost perfectly but had difficulty identifying the constituent letters of the words. This behavior testifies to the ability of this patient to bypass prior analysis at the letter level and to directly process the word as single visual unit. A subsequent study by Hall, Humphreys & Cooper (2001) with another patient displaying the same syndrome further specified that, although this patient was able to read words, he was impaired in reading unfamiliar combinations of letters. Hence, the patient correctly identified 69 out of 90 words but only read 2 of 90 nonwords (see also Coslett & Saffran, 1991; Sieroff, Pollatsek & Posner, 1988 for related observations). Although this deficit could be attributed to lexical factors, Hall et al. (2001) also showed that alternating letter case in words (e.g., tAbLe) disrupted their patient's reading performance. The patient was also better at identifying lowercase than uppercase words. Yet, common abbreviations were better identified in the familiar uppercase format. Familiarity with visual aspects of words thus mattered to the performance of the patient.

By analyzing reading performance in another patient with bilateral parietal-occipital lesions, we were able to further complete this picture (Nazir, Benboutayab & Michel, submitted). Like for the other two patients, word recognition skill in our patient was comparable to normal when words were presented in the familiar horizontal format. However, when words were displayed vertically, as in Figure 2.3, her performance dropped to near zero, even under unlimited viewing conditions. Our patient also showed severe difficulties in identifying nonwords regardless of display format and presentation duration. In other words, she performed poorly with all items that were unfamiliar to her, either because of their unusual visual format or because the items were novel (i.e., nonwords).

Thus, manipulation of surface features such as the visual format of words has a detrimental effect on word recognition in patients with parietal lesions. Although these patients are able to access representations for previously "trained" visual words, they are unable to process unfamiliar stimuli for which no such representations exist. To identify unfamiliar letter sequence, they are compelled to assemble individual letters, which—given the visuospatial deficit—is likely to fail. With these behavioral features, patients with parietal lesions thus provide the sought-after counterpart of word blindness, where letter-by-letter reading is preserved but access to previously acquired visual word representations is not possible. This double dissociation seems to support the notion that partly distinct brain regions are involved in processing familiar and unfamiliar combinations of letters.

Effects of Visual Familiarity in Healthy Readers

Qualitative differences in the way visually familiar and unfamiliar orthographic stimuli are processed are evident even in healthy skilled readers. Word length, for instance, has little effect on perception of horizontally displayed words, suggesting that familiar chains of letters may be processed as single unit. By contrast, solid length effects are evident for vertically displayed words or for horizontally displayed pseudowords, indicating that the stimuli are read letter by letter (e.g., Young & Ellis, 1985). Coherent with this pattern of reading behavior, beginning readers who are not yet sufficiently "trained" in recognizing words show strong effects of word length even with horizontal displays (Aghababian & Nazir 2000).

All together, the results described so far suggest that training to see visual words induces a qualitative change in the way we perceive them. Skilled readers seem to develop rather precise visual pattern memories of familiar words, which helps rapid recognition. The reading behavior of patients with parietal lesions, and observations that early lesions to the dorsal processing stream prevent children from acquiring normal reading skills (Gillen & Dutton, 2003), further indicate that feedback from regions in the parietal cortex is needed for the consolidation of these memories. Once acquired, however, processing is less dependent on this feedback and parietal lesions are less likely to harm the perception of already acquired visual word patterns.

DIFFERENTIAL EFFECTS OF READING-RELATED TRAINING ACROSS THE VISUAL FIELD

The claim that rapid visual word recognition can be achieved by developing multiple representations of the same (trained) stimulus across a visuotopic map is also strengthened by correlations between pattern of reading eye movements and word recognition accuracy at different locations in the visual field.

Statistics about where the eyes land in words during natural reading show a very stable and reproducible profile. In texts that use spaces between words, like Roman script, the landing site of the eyes in words describes a skewed distribution, with a maximum slightly before the center of a word (e.g., McConkie, Kerr, Reddix, & Zola, 1988; Rayner, 1979). Despite the fact that ongoing linguistic processing modulates reading eye movements, the location where the eyes initially land in words is mainly determined by low-level visuomotor factors. The apparent preference of the eye to land slightly before the center of words is essentially a consequence of rapidly moving the eye through a given stimulus configuration, guided by coarse visual information such as spaces between words (e.g., Rayner, Fischer, & Pollatzek, & 1998; Kajii, Nazir, & Osaka, 2001; O'Regan, 1990; Rayner, 1998; Vitu, O'Regan, Inhoff, & Topolski, 1995). Inasmuch as most words are fixated only once during natural reading (Rayner and Polatsek, 1989), the landing site distribution is a good estimate of the relative frequency with which skilled readers have seen ("trained") words at different location in their visual field. If the efficiency with which we recognize visual words depends on the amount of training, word recognition accuracy should thus vary with location in the visual field according to this landing distribution (Nazir et al., 2000; 2004).

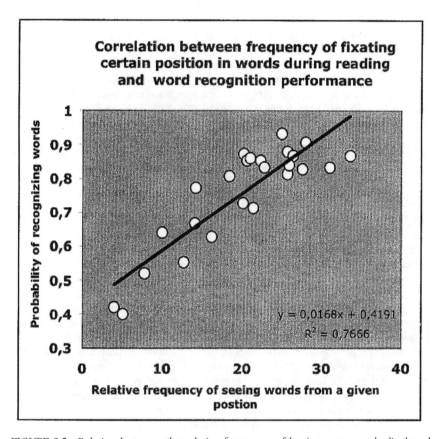

FIGURE 2.5 Relation between the relative frequency of having seen words displayed at a certain location in the visual field (estimated from the landing site distribution during reading), and the probability of recognizing a word when briefly displayed at that specific location in the visual field.

Figure 2.5 plots the relation between the relative frequency of having seen words displayed at a certain location in the visual field (as estimated from the landing site distribution during reading; data from Vitu, O'Regan & Mittau, 1990) and the probability of recognizing a word when briefly displayed at that specific location in the visual field (data from Nazir, 1993). The figure shows that when the probability of landing at a certain location in a word is low (e.g., at the end of long words), the probability of recognizing the word from that location is also low. By contrast, when the probability of landing at a certain location in a word is high (e.g., in the first third of words), the probability of recognizing the word from that location is also high. If visual training matters to word recognition, this is exactly what would be expected.

The notion that reading-related perceptual learning is restricted to the trained regions on the retina is also supported by another curious phenomenon connected to the previously mentioned word-length effect: Word length has no effect on the performance of skilled readers as long as words are displayed on retinal regions that are useful in reading (cf., the perceptual span in reading; see Figure 2.6). However, word-length effects reappear when words are presented beyond this perceptual span (Nazir, 2000; Nazir et al., 2004). The rather peculiar conclusion from these observations is, thus, that familiar visual words acquire pop-out properties only within those regions in the visual field that are useful for reading. As we show below, such a link between perceptual reading span and performance is also observed when cerebral language lateralization is considered.

THE EFFECT OF CEREBRAL LANGUAGE LATERALIZATION ON VISUAL WORD RECOGNITION

In European languages that use the Roman orthography, visual words are generally better perceived in the right than in the left visual field (for a recent review see Chiarello, Lui, & Shears, 2001). Under given display conditions, the probability of recognizing a briefly displayed word can be more than twice as high in the right as in the left visual field (e.g., Bouma, 1973). Visual field asymmetries in recognizing printed words have long been interpreted as reflecting functional differences between the two cerebral hemispheres (e.g. Bradshaw & Nettleton, 1983). As each visual field projects to the visual cortex of the contralateral hemisphere, asymmetries in the perception of laterally displayed stimuli are generally attributed to the cost of information transfer from the stimulus-receiving hemisphere to the hemisphere that is "specialized" for processing that particular stimulus. Given the general dominance of the left hemisphere for language (Broca, 1861; Wenicke, 1874), word stimuli that are sent straight to the left hemisphere are believed to profit from more efficient processing than are those sent initially to the right hemisphere, because the latter must follow a longer pathway to reach the appropriate hemisphere.

Yet, because attentional reading habits and linguistic factors also contribute to visual field differences (Nazir et al., 2004), the real impact of cortical language representation on visual word processing is generally difficult to demonstrate. Although these confounding factors could potentially be disentangled by comparing, for example, visual field effects in readers of scripts that are read in opposite directions (e.g., English or French vs. Hebrew or Arabic), such comparisons are difficult because the morphological structure of the concerned European and Semitic languages is fundamentally different. As a consequence, in contrast to English, distinct visual field asymmetries can be obtained in Hebrew depending on the word material that serves as stimuli (Deutsch & Rayner, 1999; Nazir et al., 2004). When a large set of Hebrew words is used to counterbalance these linguistic effects, no visual field asymmetry is observed (Nazir & Lavidor, submitted).

The variation in visual field effects within and across writing systems has left many researchers unconvinced that language lateralization is essential to visual word recognition. Attentional factors and reading related visual training were considered sufficient

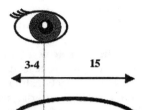

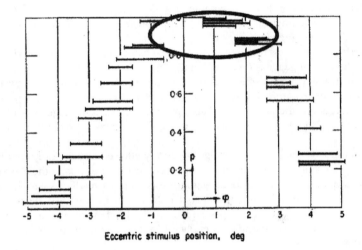

The region from which useful information is extracted from print during a fixation is asymmetric towards the direction of reading.

Eccentric stimulus position, deg

FIGURE 2.6 The perceptual span in reading. The region from which useful informa-tion is extracted from print during a fixation includes an area of approximately 3–4 letters in the visual field to 15 letters in the right visual field (Rayner & Polatesek, 1989). Within this perceputal span word length does not affect recognition performance.
Beyond the perceptual span, however, performace drops as words become longer. Data are displayed as a function of retinal eccentricity and plotted separately for words of different lengths (lengths of lines indicates word length). Negative values gives scores in the left visual field, positive values in the right visual field. Zero corresponds to fix-ation location. (Data from Bouma, 1973).

to explain all the observed phenomena (Nazir, 2000, Nazir et al., 2004). Yet, recent data suggest that this position is incorrect.

To circumvent problems related to attentional factors and languages, we inves-tigated the influence of cortical language representation on visual word processing by contrasting visual field effects of healthy native readers of English with typical and atypical language lateralization (Nazir & Lavidor, submitted). Atypical language lateralization in healthy individuals can be considered as a mirror organization of the more common left-hemisphere dominance, and is not associated with abnormal cognitive behavior (Knecht and colleagues (2000; 2001; 2003). Noninvasive brain imaging techniques such as functional transcranial Doppler sonography (Knecht et al. 2000), or, in our case, EEG recordings (electroencephalogram), of participants performing a verb generation task (Rowan, Liegeois, Vargha-Khadem, Gadian, Connelly, & Baldeweg, 2004) allow identification of which of the two hemispheres is dominant for language. When EEG recordings are used, a sustained slow cortical negativity is typically observed over the language-dominant hemisphere, that is, over the left hemisphere for individuals with typical dominance, and over the right hemisphere for individuals with atypical dominance.

Given that linguistic factors and reading-related habits apply similarly to readers of the same language—regardless of cortical language lateralization—variations in performance across the right and left visual half-fields can be attributed more directly to the way language is organized in the brain. Accordingly, our results allowed assertion that visual field effects in word recognition clearly differed between the two groups of readers (see also Brysbaert, 1994). For readers with typical language lateralization, the well-established right visual field advantage was observed. For readers with atypical language lateralization, the reversed pattern was found, albeit less pronounced. Hence, with script and language characteristics kept constant, hemispheric dominance for language clearly affected visual word recognition.

Interestingly, however, the reversal of visual field effects in these two groups of participants was only evident within the perceptual reading span, that is, up to 6 degrees in the right visual field, but only within the first 2–3 degrees in the left visual field. This relationship seems to imply that beyond visual training, reading-related perceptual learning is amplified by the way language is lateralized in the brain.

CONCLUSION

The cultural invention of "reading" is a visual skill that we acquire early in life and that we practice on a daily basis for many years thereafter. Although reading is the process of determining the pronunciation of words and the construction of meaning from written text, it is first and foremost a visual activity. This chapter broadly outlined some factors that are characteristic of this visual skill and proposed a set of hypotheses about how it is acquired and about what its neural support could be.

Contrary to the view that has been develop recently in the literature, the arguments that we developed in this chapter suggest that the reason reading is so fast and easy is not so much related to our ability to elaborate abstract word representations (e.g., McCandliss et al., 2003; Cohen & Dehaene, 2004). Rather, skilled reading seems to rely on stimulus-specific pattern memories that develop through extensive training with print in early levels of visual processing (Nazir, 2000; Nazir et al., 2004). Our examples show that by depriving a reader use of these visual pattern memories—e.g., by asking the reader to read pseudowords or vertically displayed words, or by presenting words outside of the perceptual reading span—reading performance falls back to pre-training levels. Consequently, word recognition becomes slow and switches to a qualitatively different letter-by-letter mode, which is evidenced by the presence of word-length effects. By comparing characteristics of reading deficits that can occur after occipitotemporal or parietal-occipital lesions, we further suggested that rapid visual word recognition and the slower letter-by-letter reading mode are supported by distinct mechanisms that implicate the VWFA in the left fusiform gyrus as well as the parietal cortex. Together with the observation that reading-related perceptual learning is amplified by the way language is lateralized in the brain, the data discussed here reveal the highly interactive nature of a largely distributed cortical network that supports skillful visual word recognition. Future work should add to this picture by establishing dynamic characteristics of this network and by providing information about how and when different sub-functions develop during the acquisition of reading.

ACKNOWLEDGMENTS

We deeply thank our mentor Dieter Heller for the many prolific discussions we have had throughout the years since we started thinking about reading and visual word recognition.

REFERENCES

Aghababian, V., & Nazir, T. A. (2000). Developing normal reading skills: Aspects of the visual processes underlying word recognition. *Journal of Experimental Child Psychology, 76*, 123–150.

Ashbridge, E., Walsh, V., and Cowey, A. (1997). Temporal aspects of visual search studied by transcranial magnetic stimulation. *Neuropsychologia 35*, 1121–1131.

Baylis, G., Driver, J., Baylis, L. & Rafal, R. (1994). Reading of letters and words in a patient with Balint's syndrome. *Neuropsychologia, 32*, 1273–1286.

Beauregard, M., Chertkow, H., Bub, D., Murtha, S., Dixon, R., Evans, A. (1997). The neural substrate of concrete, abstract, and emotional word lexica; a positron emission tomography study. *Journal of Cognitive Neuroscience, 9*, 441–61.

Benboutayab, N. (2004). Interactions des facteurs visuals et lexicaux au cours de la reconnaissance des mots ecrits: L'effet de la position du regard. (Unpublished doctoral thesis, University of Lyon2).

Black & Behrman, M. (1994).

Behrmann, M., Plaut, D. C., and Nelson, J. (1998). A literature review and new data supporting an interactive account of letter-by-letter reading. *Cognitive Neuropsychology, 15*, 7–51.

Bouma, H. (1973). Visual interference in the parafoveal recognition of initial and final letters of words. *Vision Research*, 13, 767–782.

Bradshaw, J. L. & Nettleton, N. C. (1983). *Human cerebral asymmetry*. Englewood Cliffs, NJ: Prentice-Hall.

Broca, P. (1861) Remarques sur le siége de la faculté du langage articulé: Suivies d'une observation d'aphemie. *Bulletin de la Sociéte Anatomique de Paris, 6*, 330–357.

Brysbaert, M. (1994). Interhemispheric transfer and the processing of foveally presented stimuli. *Behavioral Brain Research, 64*, 151–161.

Carr, T. H. (1986). Perceiving visual language. In: K.R. Boff, L. Kaufman and J.P. Thomas (Eds.) *Handbook of Perception and Human Performance, Vol II*, pp. 29:1– 29:92. New York: Wiley.

Caramazza, A., & Hillis, A. E. (1990). Levels of representation, co-ordinate frames, and unilateral neglect. *Cognitive Neuropsychology, 7*, 391–445.

Chiarello, C., Liu, S., & Shears, C. (2001). Does global context modulate cerebral asymmetries? A review and new evidence on word imageability effects. *Brain and Language, 79*(3), 360–78.

Cohen, L. & Dehaene, S. (2004). Specialization within the ventral stream: the case for the visual word form area. *Neuroimage, 22*(1), 466–76.

Cohen, L., Dehaene, S., Naccache, L., Lehéricy, S., Dehaene-Lambertz, G., Hénaff, M.A., & Michel, F. (2000). The visual word form area: Spatial and temporal characterization of an initial stage of reading in normal subjects and posterior split-brain patients. *Brain, 123*, 291–307.

Cohen, L., Lehericy, S., Chochon, F., Lemer, C., Rivaud, S., Dehaene, S. (2002). Language-specific tuning of visual cortex? Functional properties of the Visual Word Form Area. *Brain, 125*(Pt5), 1054–69.

Corbetta M, Shulman GL, Miezin FM, & Petersen SE. (1995). Superior parietal cortex activation during spatial attention shifts and visual feature conjunction. *Science, 270*(5237), 802–5.

Coslett, H.B., & Saffran, E. (1991). Simultagnosia: To see but not two see. *Brain, 114*, 1523–1545.

Dehaene, S, Naccache, L, Cohen, L, Bihan, D. L, Mangin, J. F, Poline, J. B, Riviere, D. (2001). Cerebral mechanisms of word masking and unconscious repetition priming. *Nature Neuroscience, 4*(7), 752–8.

Déjerine, J. (1892). Contributions à l'étude anatomopathologique et clinique des différentes variétés de cécité verbale. *Mémoires de la Société Biologique, 44*, 61–90.

Deutsch, A., & Rayner, K. (1999). Initial fixation location effects in reading Hebrew words. *Language and Cognitive Processes, 14*(4): 393–421.

Ellison, A., Schindler, I., Pattison, L. L., & Milner, A. D. (2004). An exploration of the role of the superior temporal gyrus in visual search and spatial perception using TMS. *Brain, 127*(Pt 10), 2307–2315.

Erdmann, B. & Dodge, R. (1898). *Psychologische Untersuchungen über das Lesen auf experimentaller Grundlage.* Halle: Niemeyer.

Friedman-Hill, S.R., Robertson, L.C., and Treisman, A. (1995). Parietal contributions to visual feature binding, evidence from a patient with bilateral lessions. *Science, 269*, 853–855.

Frost, R. (1998). Toward a strong phonological theory of visual word recognition: true issues and false trails. *Psychological Bulletin, 123*(1), 71–99.

Gilbert, C.D., Sigman, M., & Crist, R.E. (2001). The neural basis of perceptual learning. *Neuron, 31*(5), 681–97.

Gillen, J. A., and Dutton, G. N., (2003). Balint's syndrome in a 10-year-old male. *Developmental Med Child Neurology, 45*(5), 349–52.

Hall, D. A., Humphreys, G. W., & Cooper, C. G. (2001). Neuropsychological evidence for case-specific reading: Multi-letter units in visual word recognition. *The Quarterly Journal of Experimental Psychology, 54*(2), 439–467.

Holmes, G., & Horrax, G. (1919). Disturbances of spatial orientation and visual attention, with loss of stereoscopic vision. *Archives of Neurology and Psychiatry, Chicago, 1*, 385–407.

Jacobs, A. M., & Grainger, J. (1992). Testing a semistochastic variant of the interactive activation model in different word recognition experiments. *Journal of Experimental Psychology: Human Perception and Performance, 18*(4), 1174–88.

Kajii, N., Nazir, T. A., & Osaka, N. (2001). Eye movement control in reading unspaced text: The case of the Japanese script. *Vision Research, 41*, 2503–2510.

Knecht, S., Drager, B., Deppe, M., Bobe, L., Lohmann, H., Floel, A., Ringelstein, E. B., & Henningsen, H. (2000). Handedness and hemispheric language dominance in healthy humans. *Brain, 123*, 2512–2518.

Knecht, S., Drager, B., Floel, A., Lohmann, H., Breitenstein, C., Deppe, M., Henningsen, H., & Ringelstein, E. B. (2001). Behavioural relevance of atypical language lateralization in healthy subjects. *Brain, 124,* 1657–1665.

Knecht, S., Jansen, A., Frank, A., van Randenborgh, J., Sommer, J., Kanowski, M., & Heinze, H. J. (2003). How atypical is atypical language dominance? *Neuroimage. 18,* 917–927.

McCandliss, B., Cohen, L., & Dehaene, D. (2003) The visual word form area: expertise for reading in the fusiform gyrus. *Trends in Cognitive Sciences, 7*(7), 293–299.

McClelland, J. L., & Rumelhart, D. E. (1981). An interactive activation model of context effects in letter perception: Part I. An account of basic findings. *Psychological Review, 88,* 375–407.

McConkie, G. W., Kerr, P. W., Reddix, M. D., & Zola, D. (1988). Eye movement control during reading: I. The location of initial eye fixations on words. *Vision Research, 28*(10), 1107–18.

Nazir, T. A. (1993). On the relation between the optimal and the preferred viewing position in words during reading. In G. Ydewalle & J. van Rensbergen (Eds.), *Perception & Cognition: Advances in eye movement research* (pp. 349–361). Amsterdam: North-Holand.

Nazir, T. A. (2000). Traces of print along the visual pathway. In A. Kennedy., R. Radach, D. Heller & J. Pynte (Eds), *Reading as a perceptual process* (pp. 3–23). North-Holland.

Nazir, T.A., Benboutayab, N., Decoppet, N., Deutsch, A., & Frost, R. (2004). Reading Habits, Perceptual Learning, and Recognition of Printed Words. *Brain & Language.*

Nazir, T. A., & Lavidor, M. (submitted). A biological advantage in reading from left-to-right.

Nazir, T. A., Benboutayab, N. & Michel (submitted). When visual word recognition succeeds for horizontal displays but fails for vertical displays: Neuropsychological evidence in favor of visual pattern memories for orthographic stimuli.

Nobre, A.C., Allison, T., McCarthy, G. (1994). Word recognition in the human inferior temporal lobe. *Nature, 372,* 260–263.

Nobre, A. C., Coull, J. T., Walsh, V., & Frith, C. D. (2003). Brain activations during visual search: contributions of search efficiency versus feature binding. *Neuroimage.* 2003 Jan;*18*(1):91–103.

O'Regan, J. K. (1990). Eye movements and reading. In E. Kowler (Ed.), *Eye movements and their role in visual and cognitive processes* (pp. 395–453). Amsterdam: Elsevier.

Polk, T. A., & Farah, M. J. (2002). Functional MRI evidence for an abstract, not perceptual, word-form area. *Journal of Experimental Psychology: General, 131*(1), 65–72.

Posner, M. I., & Raichle, M. E. (1994). *Images of Mind.* New York: Scientific American Library.

Rowan, A., Liegeois, F., Vargha-Khadem, F., Gadian, D., Connelly, A., & Baldeweg, T. Cortical lateralization during verb generation: a combined ERP and fMRI study. *Neuroimage, 22*(2), 665–75.

Rayner, K. (1979). Eye guidance in reading: Fixation locations within words. *Perception, 8,* 21–30.

Rayner, K. (1998). Eye movements in reading and information processing: 20 years of research. *Psychological Bulletin, 124,* 372–422.

Rayner, K. & Pollatsek, A. (1989). *The psychology of Reading.* Englewood Cliffs, NJ: Prentice-Hall, Inc.

Rayner, K., Fischer, M. H., & Pollatsek, A. (1998). Unspaced text interferes with both word identification and eye movement control. *Vision Research, 38*(8), 1129–44.

Reicher, G. M. (1969). Perceptual recognition as a function of meaningfulness of stimulus material. *Journal of Experimental Psychology, 81,* 275–280.

Shafritz, K. M., Gore, J. C., & Marois, R. (2002). The role of the parietal cortex in visual feature binding. *Proceedings of the National Academy of Science, 99*(16), 10917–22.

Sieroff, E., Pollatsek, A. & Posner, M. I. (1988). Recognition of visual letter strings following injury to the posterior visual spatial attention system. *Cognitive Neuropsychology, 5,* 427–449.

Sigman, M., Pan, H., Yang, Y., Stern, E., Silbersweig, D., & Gilbert, C. D. (2005). Top-down reorganization of activity in the visual pathway after learning a shape identification task. *Neuron, 46*(5), 823–35.

Sigman, M., & Gilbert C.D., (2000). Learning to find a shape. *Nature Neuroscience, 3*(3), 264–269.

Treisman, A., (1988). Features and objects: The Fourteenth Bartlett Memorial Lecture. Quarterly Journal of Experimental Psychology, 1988, 40A, (2) 201–237.

Vitu, F., O'Regan, J. K., Mittau, M. (1990). Optimal landing position in reading isolated words and continuous text. *Perception & Psychophysics, 47*(6), 583–600.

Vitu, F., O'Regan, J. K., Inhoff, A. W., Topolski, R. (1995). Mindless reading: Eye-movement characteristics are similar in scanning letter strings and reading texts. *Perception & Psychophysics, 57,* 352–364.

Wang Q, Cavanagh P, Green, M. (1994). Familiarity and pop-out in visual search. *Perception & Psychophysics, 56*(5) 495–500.

Warrington, E. K., Shallice, T. (1980). Word-form dyslexia. *Brain, 103,* 99–112.

Wernicke, C. (1874). *Der aphasische Symptomkomplex.* Breslau, Poland: M. Cohn and Weigert.

Young, A. W., & Ellis, A. W. (1985). Different methods of lexical access for words presented in the left and right visual hemifields. *Brain and Language, 24*(2), 326–358.

CHAPTER THREE

The Development of Visual Expertise for Words: The Contribution of Electrophysiology

Urs Maurer and Bruce D. McCandliss
Weill Medical College of Cornell University

Skilled readers are able to process written text at a remarkable speed that surpasses the rate of typical speech. A significant part of this fluent processing of connected writing involves computations applied to individual words. Individual words are processed in order to activate corresponding information about word meaning and pronunciation in the reader's mental lexicon. The current chapter in this book on single word processes focuses on the contribution of electrophysiology for understanding single word processes, especially processes associated with accessing the visual forms of written words. Although some processes applied to single words in isolation have been demonstrated to interact with other processes related to text (for review see Balota, 1994), investigations of mental processes at the single word level represent a critical component process within reading, and also provide scientifically pragmatic paradigms for examining sub-processes involved, from processing the visual forms of words to accessing linguistic representations of phonology and semantics.

The process of rapidly processing visual word forms to access linguistic representations may be understood as a form of perceptual expertise (Gauthier & Nelson, 2001) that develops with reading experience (McCandliss, Cohen, & Dehaene, 2003). Aspects of this fast perceptual process for visual words that is inherent in our ability to rapidly process text have been isolated by several cognitive paradigms (reviewed in this book, chapter 2), and such processes have been localized to a network of brain regions (also reviewed in this book, chapter 17). This chapter investigates the contribution of electrophysiology to understand the neural basis of this skill, as well as its development. Specifically, we examine early perceptual responses related to visual words as well as responses to speech sounds that may be critical to the foundation of reading skills, and have been implicated in both typical and atypical development of reading ability.

BEHAVIORAL EVIDENCE FOR RAPID PERCEPTUAL PROCESSING OF VISUAL WORDS

Naturally, when focusing on fast visual perceptual expertise for reading, issues of time-course of perception of visual words become critical. Eye-tracking studies of reading provide insights into the time-course of information processing for visual words, and have shown that readers typically fixate a word for a short period of time (typically between about 200 and 300 ms) before moving to fixate the next (Rayner, 1998). During this brief fixation, information about the currently fixated word, such as its lexical frequency, influences the amount of time the eye remains on that word, thus providing a lower limit for the estimation of the 'eye-mind' lag in lexical access, suggesting that some information regarding the word being viewed is accessed within the first 200 milliseconds (Reichle, Rayner, & Pollatsek, 2003). Such research, examining single word processing in the context of connected text, converges nicely with a large body of cognitive research conducted using eye tracking, naming, and lexical decision tasks applied in paradigms that present single words in isolation. For example, converging evidence from studies of brief, masked presentation of visual words suggests that the rapid perceptual processes we apply to letter strings are facilitated by common patterns of combining letters into word forms – the word superiority effect (Reicher, 1969) demonstrates that subjects are more accurate in detecting brief exposures to letters presented within words than letters presented alone or within random consonant strings. Such perceptual facilitation even occurs for letters embedded in pronounceable nonwords (pseudoword superiority effect, for a recent study see Grainger, Bouttevin, Truc, Bastien, & Ziegler, 2003). Such studies provide additional information into the nature of processes that occur within early perceptual processes applied to visual words. While these behavioral studies allow inference about fast cognitive processes during reading, such evidence is open to questions about the time-course of processing, as they potentially reflect post-perceptual strategies. Electrophysiology research provides direct means of examining early components of visual word perception through the analysis of electrical signals of brain activity recorded on the human scalp.

A BRIEF INTRODUCTION TO EVENT-RELATED POTENTIALS IN ELECTROPHYSIOLOGY

Basic Concepts

The electroencephalogram (EEG) is the recording of fluctuating voltage differences between electrodes placed on the scalp, and is measured with millisecond precision. The event-related potential (ERP) represents the electrophysiological response in the EEG that is time- and phase-locked to a particular event. An ERP is extracted by averaging many time-locked EEG epochs, thereby suppressing the background activity in the EEG that is unrelated to the particular event.

Traditionally, ERPs are depicted as waveforms at particular electrodes, and the peaks and troughs in the waveforms are thought to reflect components, which are typically labeled according to their polarity and timing. For example, components may be labeled as P1, N1, N170, P300, N400, with the letter depicting whether the component was a positive or negative deviation from baseline, and the component number representing the timing, either in cardinal order (as in P1, N1, P2, N2) or the millisecond latency of the peak (e.g., P300: a positive-going component peaking at about 300 ms after stimulus onset). Additional labels, such as "visual" or "occipital", are often added to the component name, because polarity and timing can vary with stimulus modality and electrode site.

To account for varying head sizes and head forms in interindividual comparisons, electrodes are placed in relation to landmarks (inion, nasion, left and right preauricular points) that can be found on each head. By dividing the distance between these landmarks into equidistant parts of 10% each, one of the commonly used electrode placement system - the 10-10 system - creates a grid on the scalp to place the electrodes (Chatrian, Lettich, & Nelson, 1985). The labels of the grid points (e.g., Oz, P1, C2, F3, Fpz) indicate their anterior-posterior locations on the scalp (Fp: frontopolar, F: frontal, C: central, P: parietal, O: occipital) and their relations to the midline (z: central, odd numbers: left; even numbers: right) with increasing numbers indicating increasing excentricity.

ERP Mapping Approach

In traditional ERP analyses, topographic effects such as laterality are often limited by examination of a few channels on the scalp, but modern EEG systems allow recordings from many channels (commonly as many as 128) providing additional topographic information. One approach to topographic analysis of multi-channel ERP data, termed a "mapping" approach, has been developed that looks at the data primarily as a sequence of topographic ERP maps changing in topography and global strength over time (Lehmann & Skrandies, 1980). Within this approach, analysis methods have been developed that take full advantage of the additional topographic information while preserving the high time-resolution benefits of ERP data (e.g., Brandeis & Lehmann, 1986; Lehmann & Skrandies, 1980; Michel et al., 2004; Pascual-Marqui, Michel, & Lehmann, 1995).

ERP map strength can be described by Global Field Power (GFP; Lehmann & Skrandies, 1980), which is computed as the root mean square of the values at each electrode in an average-referenced map. ERP map topography can be described by map features, such as the locations of the positive and negative maxima (Brandeis & Lehmann, 1986) or the locations of the positive and negative centroids (centers of gravity; Brandeis, Vitacco, & Steinhausen, 1994).

The use of topographic information for ERP analysis is important, because it can resolve ambiguities that result from the fact that amplitude differences between two conditions recorded at a single electrode can result from identical topographies which are stronger in one condition compared to the other or they can result from different topographies which may or may not differ in global strength. This distinction is important because topographic information allows a characterization of the underlying neural processes: different topographies are produced by different neural networks, and identical topographies are likely to reflect the same neural networks.

In an additional step, ERP topographies can be used to estimate location and orientation of the underlying cortical sources, provided that a number of assumptions can be validly adopted. Assumptions are necessary to mathematically solve "the inverse problem" which captures the fact that one can model the scalp topography given a set of neural sources of known location, orientation, and strength, but given a known scalp topography, many potential combinations of number, location, orientation, and strength of neural sources are equally plausible as solutions. Thus, different assumptions about the sources of electrical activity and its propagation to the scalp, as implemented in different source estimation models, have an influence on the nature of the results (for a recent review see Michel 2004).

Topographic 3D Centroid Analysis

The large number of electrodes used in modern EEG systems results in a vast amount of topographic information. Selecting only a subset of these channels for analysis can lead to results that are biased by the pre-selection of the channels. The use of map centroids offers an un-biased means for topographic ERP analysis (see Figure 3.1). The positive and negative 3D centroids are the centers of gravity of the positive and negative fields in 3D space (e.g., Talairach coordinate system, Talairach & Tournoux, 1988) and are computed as the voltage-weighted locations of all electrodes showing positive or negative values, respectively. Accordingly, an ERP map consisting of 129 electrodes can be reduced to 2 centroids, each defined by 3 values representing the x-, y-, and z-coordinates of the 3D space. Subsequent statistical analyses can be computed for the x-, y-, and z-coordinates of the centroids resulting in topographic differences in 3 spatial dimensions "left-right", "posterior-anterior", and "inferior-superior".

Importantly, although the centroids are located within the head space - which is typical for centers of gravity of scalp measures, they are by no means estimations of the underlying sources. The advantage of the centroid measure vs. source estimation is that the centroids are features of the measured topography, whereas source estimations depend on additional assumptions that may or may not apply.

OVERVIEW OF ELECTROPHYSIOLOGY OF VISUAL WORD PROCESSING

Visual word processing has been extensively investigated with ERP measurements, and various aspects of psychological processes involved in reading have been linked to several different ERP components. Perhaps the most studied language component in response to visual words is the N400, a component linked to semantic processes. The N400 component is a negative deflection which is significantly enhanced when a word is presented as semantically anomalous within a sentence (Friederici, Gunter, Hahne, & Mauth, 2004; Kutas & Federmeier, 2000). Studies on

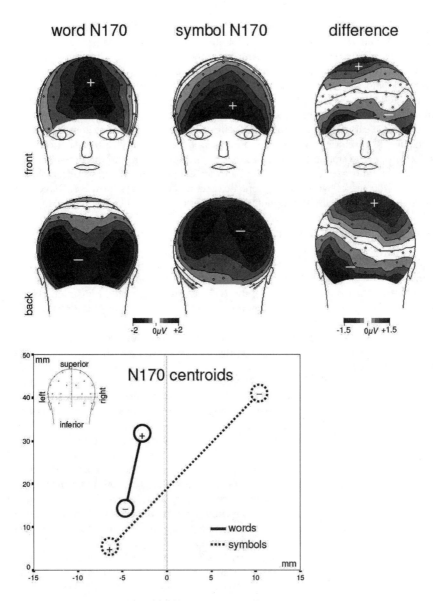

FIGURE 3.1 ERP maps and centroids: The different distribution of the positive (indicated by a "+") and negative (indicated by a "−") fields in the N170 between words and symbols is illustrated in maps seen from the front and from the back (upper figure, left and middle).

syntactic violations in sentence processing have revealed a rather different component, the P600. Differences in topography of the N400 and P600 suggest that distinct processes are involved in processing semantic and syntactic violations, even in cases when manipulations of syntactic expectations produce ERP responses to syntactic violations within 400 ms (Friederici et al., 2004). N400-like effects have also been used to investigate phonological processes in visual word tasks (Rugg, 1984), although some aspects of phonological processing may occur between about 200 and 350 ms, earlier than semantic N400 effects (Bentin, Mouchetant-Rostaing, Giard, Echallier, & Pernier, 1999). For the purposes of the current chapter, each of these effects appear to implicate processes that occur much later than the time-course of specialized word perception, which other cognitive research suggests occurs within the first 200 ms of word perception. Reading-related effects, however, have also been reported in earlier components, especially in the N170 component.

PERCEPTUAL EXPERTISE N170 EFFECTS

The visual N170 (or N1) component of the ERP peaks between 150 and 200 ms and shows a topography with posterior negativity and anterior positivity. Although elicited by visual stimuli in general, the N170 is strongly elicited by certain classes of visual stimuli, such as faces (Bentin et al., 1999; Rossion, Joyce, Cottrell, & Tarr, 2003), compared to control stimuli.

The psychological principles that lead to a larger N170 for one stimulus category compared to another may lie in perceptual expertise with the stimulus category at hand. Increased N170 responses were elicited in bird-experts looking at birds (Tanaka & Curran, 2001), and in car-experts looking at cars (Gauthier, Curran, Curby, & Collins, 2003). An increase of the N170 could even be induced by expertise-training with novel objects (e.g., "greebles", Rossion, Gauthier, Goffaux, Tarr, & Crommelinck, 2002). These results suggest that extensive visual experience with an object category leads to fast, specialized processing within the first 200 ms.

This perceptual expertise framework for evaluating N170 effects may also account for increased N170 responses that skilled readers show for visual words. A robust reading-related N170 specialization in electric fields (as well as a similar component in magnetic fields of magnetoencephalography) is found for contrasts between categories of stimulus classes including words versus other low-level visual control stimuli such as strings of meaningless symbols, forms, shapes, or dots (Bentin et al., 1999; Brem et al., 2005; Eulitz et al., 2000; Maurer, Brandeis, & McCandliss, 2005a; Maurer, Brem, Bucher, & Brandeis, 2005b; Schendan, Ganis, & Kutas, 1998; Tarkiainen, Helenius, Hansen, Cornelissen, & Salmelin, 1999; Zhang, Begleiter, Porjesz, & Litke, 1997). Such overall reading-related N170 specialization appears to be automatic, as it is also detected in tasks that do not require the words to be read (Bentin et al., 1999; Brem et al., 2005; Eulitz et al., 2000; Maurer et al., 2005a; Maurer et al., 2005b; Schendan et al., 2005b; Tarkiainen et al., 1999).

Examination of the pattern of stimuli that elicit an N170 response provides support for a form of similarity gradient in these implicit tasks, such that the more the stimuli resemble letter-strings, the larger their N170 component, as found e.g., in a larger N170 for word-like pseudofonts compared to control stimuli (Eulitz et al., 2000; Schendan et al., 1998; Tarkiainen et al., 1999). On the other hand, words, pseudowords, and even consonant strings have been shown to produce similar N170 responses, which differed from that elicited by symbol strings and other visual forms (Bentin et al., 1999; Maurer et al., 2005b).

Although specialization for words appears to be one example out of a broader class of perceptual expertise stimuli that affect the N170, there is also evidence that visual words represent a special case of perceptual expertise, as N170 responses to words are typically left-lateralized (for review see Maurer et al., 2005a).

LEFT-LATERALIZATION OF THE N170

Several studies have shown that overall reading-related N170 specialization is left-lateralized (Bentin et al., 1999; Maurer et al., 2005ab; Maurer et al., 2005ab; Tarkiainen et al., 1999), with larger amplitudes over the left hemisphere for words than for low-level visual control stimuli. This left-lateralized N170 topography elicited by visual words stands in contrast to N170 responses for other forms of perceptual expertise related to faces or objects of expertise, which are typically bilateral or right-lateralized (Rossion et al., 2003; Tanaka & Curran, 2001). The degree of left-lateralization in the N170, however, varies across studies and seems to depend on additional factors, which are not yet fully understood. In pursuit of a suitable explanation we propose below factors that may help explain this variability.

Source localization estimates for the N170 elicited by words found left-lateralized sources in inferior occipitotemporal cortex (Maurer et al., 2005b; Michel et al., 2001; Rossion et al., 2003). This is in agreement with intracranial recordings finding a negative component around 200 ms in basal occipitotemporal cortex (Nobre, Allison, & McCarthy, 1998) and with source localization of the word-specific M170, the N170 analogue recorded with MEG (Tarkiainen et al., 1999).

The characteristic trend towards a left-lateralized N170 topography for words might be linked to similarly left-lateralized hemodynamic activation during visual word tasks. Functional neuroimaging studies reported reading-related activation in many areas of the extrastriate visual cortex, especially in the left hemisphere (Petersen, Fox, Posner, Mintun, & Raichle, 1988; Price, Wise, & Frackowiak, 1996; Tagamets, Novick, Chalmers, & Friedman, 2000). In particular, an area in the left fusiform gyrus, located in the inferior part of the occipito-temporal cortex, may constitute a Visual Word Form Area, because it shows sensitivity for visual word forms at a highly abstract level (for a review see McCandliss et al., 2003).

Similar sensitivity for abstract properties of visual words may also already occur during the N170 component.

SENSITIVITY OF THE N170 FOR HIGHER LANGUAGE FUNCTIONS

Several studies have also examined the nature of cognitive processing indexed by the N170 word effect by investigating additional stimulus category contrasts. Comparing consonant strings with pseudowords or words serves to control letter expertise while contrasting information on the structure of a word form. One set of results demonstrated that consonant strings have larger N170 amplitudes than words (Compton, Grossenbacher, Posner, & Tucker, 1991; McCandliss, Posner, & Givon, 1997), and orthographically irregular pseudowords were in between (McCandliss et al., 1997). Such results provide support for the notion that perceptual expertise for words indexed by the N170 reflects not just expertise for letter recognition, but also expertise associated with recognition of familiar patterns of letters within visual word forms. Other studies, however, failed to show N170 sensitivity to the contrast between words and pseudowords (Bentin et al., 1999; Wydell, Vuorinen, Helenius, & Salmelin, 2003), and differences between consonant strings and words were found only during explicit lexical and semantic tasks, not during implicit reading (Bentin et al., 1999).

In contrast to such studies that make inferences based on comparisons of different stimulus categories (i.e. words, pseudowords, consonant string), studies that compared different levels of word frequency provide more consistent results regarding the role of lexical information in modulating the N170. Low frequency words typically elicit larger N170 amplitudes than high frequency words in lexical or semantic decision tasks (Assadollahi & Pulvermuller, 2003; Hauk & Pulvermuller, 2004; Neville, Mills, & Lawson, 1992; Sereno, Brewer, & O'Donnell, 2003; Sereno, Rayner, & Posner, 1998, but see also Proverbio, Vecchi, & Zani, 2004), providing evidence of perceptual expertise at the level of accessing specific words. Thus, different approaches to the question of whether N170 responses are sensitive to specific word representations, such as categorical distinctions between words and pseudowords vs. within category parametric manipulations of word frequency provide contrasting answers, and raise new potential questions regarding the nature of processing applied to pseudowords.

As these studies based their analyses mostly on a few channels, an ERP mapping approach, which takes full advantage of the topographic information available, may be able to better characterize the processes involved and to resolve some ambiguities.

N170 ERP MAPPING STUDIES IN GERMAN AND ENGLISH

Reading-related N170 specialization was investigated in two separate studies with the same paradigm in Zurich, Switzerland (Maurer et al., 2005b), and subsequently at the Sackler Institute in New York (Maurer et al., 2005a).

In both studies, literate adult subjects looked at blocks of serially presented stimuli that contained runs of either words, pseudowords, symbol strings, or pictures. For each class of stimuli the subjects remained motionless in response to the majority of stimuli, but pressed a button whenever they detected an occasional immediate stimulus repetition. This 'one-back' paradigm allowed ERPs to be calculated for each word on its initial presentation without any reaction on the part of the subject, and behavioral responses to be collected on occasional repeated stimuli, thus ensuring that subjects engaged in the task. Moreover, as repeated words could be detected even without reading, this implicit reading task could potentially be applied with illiterate children, thus allowing the investigation of changes due to learning to read.

In the Zurich study, German-speaking adults viewed German stimuli, and EEG was recorded from 43 electrodes. Data were analyzed with an ERP mapping strategy, i.e. differences in N170 maps were measured according to global strength (GFP) and topography (3D centroids).

Statistical t-maps showed that among ERP responses to stimuli that required no manual response, larger N170 amplitudes were found for words than symbols particularly over left occipitotemporal electrodes consistent with earlier studies analyzing waveforms at selected channels (Bentin et al., 1999). The mapping analyses showed that GFP was stronger for words than for symbols and that N170 topography differed between words and symbols, implicating different neural networks involved in word and symbol processing within the first 200 milliseconds. The most prominent topographic feature that differed between word and symbol maps was found in the distribution of the centroids along the inferior-superior z coordinate axis. These centroid differences reflected that the negative fields over the posterior part of the scalp were most pronounced at inferior sites for words and at superior sites for symbols, whereas over the anterior part the positive fields were most pronounced at inferior sites for symbols and at superior sites for words. The centroid differences also reflected that the largest negative differences occurred at left inferior occipito-temporal electrodes at the edge of the electrode montage.

For the word-pseudoword contrast, however, there were no N170 differences in response to German words and pseudowords, suggesting that reading-related N170 specialization generalized from words to pseudowords, and thus may reflect perceptual expertise for letters or well-ordered letter strings.

For the pseudoword-symbol contrast, prominent topographic differences in the centroid distribution were similar to thosefor the word-symbol contrast. In addition, the centroids were more left-lateralized for pseudowords than for symbols. This reflected that the negative fields of the N170 were more left-lateralized for pseudowords than for symbols, which was also apparent in the word-symbol comparison where it reached significance in the last two thirds of the N170.

The topographic analysis of the Zurich study extended earlier studies by showing that reading-related N170 specialization is characterized not only by more left-lateralized fields but by more inferior negative fields over the posterior part of the head and more superior positive fields over the anterior part of the head. This suggests that the differences arose because different neural networks were activated in an early phase of word processing compared to symbol processing, rather than the same network being more strongly activated.

In the New York study we investigated whether the effects from the Zurich study could be replicated with the same paradigm (after adaptations for language) in a sample of English speaking participants (Maurer et al., 2005a). An additional aim of the study was to apply a high-density EEG recording system, because this system samples more densely and extends the coverage on the scalp to more inferior locations than traditional EEG systems do. The traditional 10-20 electrode placement system covers only regions as much inferior as the Oz and Fpz electrodes, thus – roughly speaking – electrodes are only placed around the area right above the ears. For signals that presumably originate in inferior brain regions, a more inferior sampling may provide a better characterization of the resulting scalp topography. For this reason the 10-20 system has been extended to more inferior regions in some studies (e.g., Bentin et al., 1999; Maurer et al., 2005b). However, high-density recordings sample from sites that are located even more inferior than those in these previous studies (Luu & Ferree, 2000). As the maximal effect in the Zurich study was found at the edge of the montage at posterior inferior channels, more inferior sampling may provide better characterization of the effects.

The central contrast for the replication study was the most robust contrast of words versus unfamiliar symbol strings in the N170. The statistical t-maps in the New York study showed that words elicited larger N170 amplitudes than symbols at left inferior occipitotemporal electrodes similar to the Zurich results. The mapping analyses revealed that GFP was not larger for words than for symbols, but as in the Zurich study the N170 topographies differed between words and symbols, confirming that specialized neural networks are active within the first 200 ms of word presentation. These topographic differences showed very similar characteristics to the results of the Zurich study with a different centroid distribution along the inferior-superior z coordinate axis between word and symbol responses, suggesting that similar neural networks are specialized for reading across languages.

In addition, a topographic effect was also found in the left-right axis, suggesting a larger involvement of the left hemisphere in word processing and the right hemisphere in symbol processing. A similar difference in left-lateralization was also present in the Zurich data, where it reached significance in the last two thirds of the N170.

These results suggested that overall reading-related N170 specialization can be detected across different languages and EEG systems and that the maximal effect is inferior to the coverage of traditional EEG montages. Because the topographic effects were consistent while the GFP effects varied across studies, it can be inferred that similar neural networks are activated across languages, whereas the relative strength of the engagement of these networks may depend on additional factors. Finally, contrasts between results in German and English may provide additional insights into how differences in these writing systems may lead to different forms of perceptual expertise for reading.

One difference that emerged between the English and German studies involved the responses to pseudowords. While the Zurich study revealed comparable N170 effects for words and pseudowords, in English, N170 topographic effects for pseudowords were not identical to words. Words and pseudowords, when compared to symbol strings, both demonstrated similar topographic effects in the inferior-superior z-axis in both English and German, yet words were more strongly left-lateralized than pseudowords in English.

These findings may suggest that inferior-superior topographic effects may be indexing some form of processing which is constant across these two languages, but that the left-lateralized topographic effect reflects a form of processing that is more language-specific. We suggest that the inferior-superior N170 modulation indicates visual expertise for letters or well-ordered letter strings, and may reflect more general visual perceptual expertise effects that are also found with stimuli outside of reading.

That pseudowords elicit a left-hemisphere modulation of the N170 in German, but not in English, may reflect differences between these writing systems that impact the processing of novel visual word forms. In fact, a prominent difference between the two languages involves the degree of consistency with which letters map onto word sounds. As a result, pseudowords are more ambiguous for English speakers to pronounce than for German speakers. Thus the left-lateralized subtype of perceptual expertise may specifically relate to processes involved in mapping letters onto word sounds. The lack of such a left-lateralization for English pseudowords may suggest that such processes are less automatic in English (Zevin & Balota, 2000), and are engaged to a lesser degree while detecting pseudoword repetitions, because repetition detection does not require explicit pronunciation of the stimuli.

Although direct comparisons of these studies with English and German subjects may be limited by the use of different words, pseudowords, and EEG systems, the results suggest that left-lateralization may be related to spelling-to-sound mapping, which leads to formulation of a more general hypothesis about learning to read and left-lateralized specialization of the N170 word effect — the phonological mapping hypothesis.

THE PHONOLOGICAL MAPPING HYPOTHESIS

Converging evidence from electrophysiological and hemodynamic studies suggests that left-lateralized activation is a characteristic of visual word processing in the brain. As the left hemisphere has long been known to be dominantly involved in speech perception and speech production, one straightforward hypothesis is that during reading acquisition the left-lateralized characteristic of the visual language system is induced by the pre-existing left-lateralization of the auditory language system.

More specifically, the left-lateralization might be driven by a particular aspect of auditory language processing, namely phonological processing, which leads to the phonological mapping hypothesis (McCandliss & Noble, 2003). The essence of this hypothesis is that given that phonological processes are typically left-lateralized (Price, Moore, Humphreys, & Wise, 1997; Rumsey et al., 1997), specialized processing of visual words in visual brain areas also becomes left-lateralized.

The results of the Zurich and the New York ERP mapping studies suggest that the phonological mapping hypothesis also accounts for fast reading-related expertise in the N170 component. Accordingly, the characteristic left-hemispheric modulation of the N170 may be specifically related to the influence of grapheme-phoneme conversion established during learning to read. This left-hemispheric modulation may add up to the inferior-superior modulation thought to reflect visual expertise for letters or well-ordered letter strings, and which may also develop during learning to read. This inferior-superior modulation of the N170 might be more generally related to visual discrimination learning and thus might be less language-specific. However, it cannot be ruled out that this modulation could nonetheless be shaped by grapheme-phoneme conversion or other language-specific aspects during learning to read.

In its simplest form the phonological mapping hypothesis for the left-lateralized N170 component has several implications for reading-related N170 specialization:

1. The left-lateralization of the N170 responses to visual words should be more pronounced in scripts using grapheme-phoneme conversion rules, but less pronounced in logographic scripts which are based on lexical morphemes. Furthermore, the phonological mapping hypothesis is specific to the left-lateralized modulation of the N170, thus the inferior-superior N170 modulation should not be influenced by scripts that differ in their phonological properties.
2. Reading-related N170 specialization, with inferior-superior and left-lateralized modulations, should develop in children when they learn to read, as well as in laboratory experiments that simulate this process.
3. Reading-related N170 specialization in dyslexic readers should show a smaller degree of left-lateralization, because of the phonological core deficit that has been associated with dyslexia, although such disorders could also affect the inferior-superior modulation.
4. Early phonological ability should predict the degree of N170 specialization with reading acquisition, especially with respect to its left-lateralization. Remediation of the phonological core deficit through intervention should specifically increase left-lateralization of the N170 specialization.

We consider the implications of these facets of the phonological mapping hypothesis in a broader consideration of the literature on reading-related N170 specialization.

N170 SPECIALIZATION IN SCRIPTS OF DIFFERENT LANGUAGE SYSTEMS

Comparisons between fundamentally different writing systems may allow conclusions about processes involved during early visual word processing. For example a study with Koreans who were educated in both Chinese characters and written English, reported a left-lateralized N170 for both English words and Korean words, but a bilateral N170 for Chinese characters and pictures (Kim, Yoon, & Park, 2004). Both English and Korean writing systems map characters onto phonemes, whereas Chinese uses a logographic script, in which graphic symbols represent lexical morphemes. Thus, left-lateralization in the N170 was confined to language systems that use spelling-to-sound mapping that can be described at the grapheme-phoneme level, which suggests that the left-lateralization, developed during reading acquisition, is mediated by phonological processing related to grapheme-phoneme conversion.

Such cross-cultural and cross-linguistic differences, although confounded by many challenges of between-group, between-lab, and between-culture factors, nonetheless provide support for the phonological mapping hypothesis for the left-lateralization of the N170.

One such confound in cross-linguistic studies is the possibility of a difference in lateralization between first and second languages. For example, Proverbio et al. (2002)

reported N170 responses for bilinguals that suggested a left-lateralization for the first language (Slovenian), but not for the second language (Italian; Proverbio et al., 2002), a result which was also found in Italian-English interpreters (Proverbio et al., 2004), suggesting that reading skill for languages acquired later in life may be organized somewhat differently than for languages acquired early in life. Contrasts between first and second languages, however, may be complicated by differences in perceptual expertise across the two languages, and thus further studies are needed to clarify whether this lateralization effect is related to differences in spelling-to-sound mapping between first and second languages, differences in the strength of specialization, or whether it represents an additional factor driving left-lateralized N170 specialization.

LEARNING TO READ AND DEVELOPMENT OF N170 SPECIALIZATION

The predictions of the phonological mapping hypothesis on reading acquisition can be tested with developmental studies in children learning to read, as well as within laboratory experiments with adults in which aspects of reading acquisition are simulated.

The most direct evidence for specialization due to learning to read can be obtained by studying the same children before and after the start of reading acquisition. Within the context of the Zurich study, described above, children's N170 responses to words and symbol strings were recorded before and after learning to read. EEG was recorded from pre-literate children in kindergarten, in the same paradigm as described above, as they detected occasional immediate repetitions of words, and pseudowords, (a task which they could perform even without reading skills), as well as immediate repetitions of symbols and pictures. As reported above, adult readers in this paradigm had shown a large difference in the N170 between words and symbol strings, with a bilateral occipito-temporal topography, which was slightly stronger on the left. In contrast, the kindergarten children did not show a reliable difference in the N170 elicited by words and symbols (Maurer et al., 2005b). This result demonstrates that reading-related N170 specialization develops between kindergarten and adulthood. It also suggests that rudimentary levels of visual familiarity with print and letter knowledge are not sufficient to produce the typical reading-related N170 response, as the children could tell whether a stimulus string consisted of letters or other symbols, and could name about half of the letters in the alphabet. A further analysis which examined subsets of children with high and low letter knowledge confirmed that the children with low letter knowledge did not show a N170 specialization at all, but revealed that the children with high letter knowledge showed a weak specialization. The topography of this difference, however, was right-lateralized and strikingly different from the adult N170 effect, which suggested that the children's difference indicated a precursor to the mature fast specialization in adults. This precursor in non-reading children is presumably due to their letter knowledge or visual familiarity with print (Maurer et al., 2005b).

The absence of reading-related N170 specialization in pre-literate Swiss kindergartners, and especially the lack of a left-lateralized N170 modulation, lends some support to the phonological mapping hypothesis, which suggests that N170 responses develop as a result of increased mapping from letters to sounds. In addition, these same children have recently participated in the same paradigm during the middle of the 2nd grade, after they had mastered initial reading training. "The longitudinal data revealed that by 2nd grade a prominent N170 specialization had developed in each child (Maurer et al., 2006), and that the topography of this specialization had become more left-lateralized with learning to read in agreement with the phonological mapping hypothesis (Maurer et al., submitted)."

One cross-sectional developmental study also provides a similar developmental account of N170 specialization. Posner and McCandliss (2000) reported a study looking at four-, seven-, and ten-year-old children, using a contrast between words and consonant strings previously reported to demonstrate visual N170 effects in adults (Compton et al., 1991; McCandliss et al., 1997), modified to ensure that the words used were familiar to both the 7- and 10-year-olds in the study. Using an implicit reading task, they reported that no N170 specialization for words over consonant strings emerged with initial learning to read (between age 4 and 7), but showed that 10-year olds began to demonstrate some evidence of differential N170 responses to words versus consonant strings (Posner & McCandliss, 2000). These results suggest that familiarity with words alone is unlikely to account for such N170 expertise effects, as the 7-year-olds demonstrate familiarity but no N170 effect, and suggest instead that such effects may arise gradually over development of extensive expertise with fluent visual word recognition, a process that is emerging in 10-year-olds.

Developmental studies with children provide crucial data on learning to read that is ecologically valid, and provide insights into the nature of the processes that create the adult specialization, yet such studies raise questions about whether observed changes are specifically linked to learning-based increases in reading expertise or to maturation processes that play out over this same age range. Developmental studies can be usefully complemented by training studies with skilled adult readers to address these very issues. McCandliss and colleagues (McCandliss et al., 1997) introduced a novel way of investigating the impact of visual familiarity and lexical status of visual stimuli, by holding the exact stimulus set constant across a series of repeated testing sessions, but manipulating subjects' experience with a subset of the stimuli. With repeated measures this study investigated potential changes in the N170 induced over the course of 5 weeks as students spent 50 hours learning to read 60 words of a 120-word artificial pseudoword-language called "Keki" (the other 60 were reserved for testing purposes only). All pseudowords were comprised of familiar Roman letters, yet followed a visual word form structure generated by an algorithm that was designed to deviate from English in subtle but identifiable ways (e.g., all words ended in a vowel). N170 responses to several classes of stimuli were collected over the course of the five week learning experiment, and overall results demonstrated a significant effect of stimulus class, such that consonant strings elicited larger N170 responses than words, and responses to the Keki pseudowords fell in between. The central finding from the training study was that fifty hours of training, which increased both the visual familiarity and the associated meanings for the trained Keki words, did not change the stimulus-class effects on the N170 (i.e., no training-by-stimulus-type interaction was present for the N170 component). Even after training, the N170 for trained and untrained Keki words were not significantly different, and responses to the entire class of Keki items were still significantly more negative than for words, and significantly less negative than for consonant strings. In contrast, a component subsequent to the N170 demonstrated a significant and systematic training effect for the trained Keki items in relation to the other stimuli, from approximately 280 to 360 ms, revealing the sensitivity of the electrophysiological technique to training effects. From these results, the authors concluded that the N170 likely reflects orthographic structure, as robust differences persisted across the three classes of stimuli (well structured, English words slightly atypically structured Keki words, and strongly atypically structured consonant strings even though letter familiarity was held constant across stimuli, and lexical familiarity was manipulated over 50 hours to no effect. Furthermore, they suggested that, since the N170 was unresponsive to 50 hours of studying the novel structure of Keki word forms relative to consonant strings, such processes may change very slowly over time. Considering this pattern of results in the context of the phonological mapping hypothesis draws focus to the fact that the Keki words could be decoded via grapheme-phoneme associations related to reading English both before training and throughout training, and thus a lack of N170 training-related changes for the specifically trained Keki items might be predicted. In order to address this implication, future research in training studies should employ novel graphical features that lie outside the ability to generalize based on already existing grapheme-phoneme decoding abilities, and to directly contrast training methods that encourage learning via associations between graphic features and phonemes versus training that encourages associations between entire visual characters and auditory words.

N170 SPECIALIZATION IN DYSLEXIA

The phonological mapping hypothesis of the left-lateralized N170 expertise effect has important implications for dyslexia because it provides a developmental pathway account for how well-documented core phonological deficits present in early childhood and other precursors of dyslexia (for a review see Shaywitz, 2004) impact the developing neural mechanisms underlying fluent visual word recognition. Furthermore, individual differences in phonological mapping ability may also relate to the degree of reading-related N170 specialization in dyslexic children and adults, especially with respect to its left-lateralization.

Evidence for reduced reading-related N170 specialization in dyslexia has come from magnetoencephalographic studies. Helenius and colleagues (1999) presented words and symbol strings to dyslexic adults who attended to the stimuli and were prepared to report them if prompted. In normally reading adults, sources in the inferior occipito-temporal cortex, predominately in the left hemisphere, differed between words and symbols around 150-ms (Tarkiainen et al., 1999). In dyslexic subjects, however, such word-specific sources were undetectable in the same time range (Helenius et al., 1999). This pattern of results is corroborated by another MEG study which found that words and pseudowords activate sources in the left occipito-temporal cortex in normal readers between 100 and 200 ms, but less so in dyslexic readers (Salmelin, Service, Kiesila, Uutela, & Salonen, 1996). Such results are at least consistent with the phonological mapping hypothesis, in that they present further evidence on the link between adult expertise in reading and the left-lateralized N170, and are consistent with the notion that phonological core deficit in dyslexia may impact the process of progressively increasing left-lateralized recruitment of visual regions that are the hallmark of reading-related expertise in the form of the N170. However, such developmental claims about the late emergence of left-later-alized N170 responses for skilled readers, and not dyslexics, require developmental data. Interestingly, two studies that directly compared dyslexic children to age-matched controls did not find group differences in visual word processing in the N170 time range (Brandeis et al., 1994; Simos, Breier, Fletcher, Bergman, & Papanicolaou, 2000). This contrast between the adult and child literature may suggest that differences between normal and dyslexic reading develop only late during childhood and become manifest in adulthood only with the emergence of visual expertise in skilled adult readers.

Future developmental work on the cognitive and neural basis of the N170 effect in dyslexia will need to include longitudinal designs that examine early manifestations of phonological deficits, and relate such deficits directly to the emergence of behavioral and neurophysiological indexes of perceptual expertise in reading. Such developmental work on early phonological deficits may also be enhanced by the inclusion of electrophysiological measures of phonological processes, as behavioral assays of phonological deficits may reflect not only deficiencies in phonological processing, but also deficiencies in other processes such as executive attention functions (for a review see Noble, McCandliss, & Farah, submitted). Such electrophysiological studies of phonological processing have tried to directly measure brain processes related to the phonological core deficit, thus aiming to improve prediction of dyslexia.

One candidate for a neurophysiological measure of phonological processing deficits in dyslexia is the mismatch negativity (MMN), a component of the auditory ERP. The MMN is regarded as a measure of the auditory memory or the central sound representation (Naatanen, Tervaniemi, Sussman, Paavilainen, & Winkler, 2001). MMN responses are also elicited by deviant phonemes and thus may represent a measure for phoneme representations in the brain (Naatanen, 2001). The MMN is also very suited to be used with children, as it measures automatic discrimination, i.e. the participants are given a distracting task, such as reading a book or watching a silent video. The MMN is also regarded as developmentally stable as it has been elicited in young children and even in infants (Cheour, Leppanen, & Kraus, 2000), although in children it can change its topography under certain conditions (Maurer, Bucher, Brem, & Brandeis, 2003a).

Currently, several longitudinal studies with children from families with risk for dyslexia are being conducted that have obtained MMN measures before the start of reading acquisition.

In the Zurich study (described above) that looked at development of reading-related N170 specialization in children before and after learning to read, a subgroup of children came from families with one or more parents demonstrating symptoms of dyslexia. The kindergarten children were tested with two auditory oddball paradigms containing tone stimuli (standard: 1000Hz, deviants: 1030 Hz, 1060 Hz) and phoneme stimuli (standard: ba, deviants: da, ta). Between approximately 300 and 700 ms the children showed a frontally negative mismatch response to the deviant stimulus compared to the standard. This late-MMN differed between children at risk and control children (Maurer, Bucher, Brem, & Brandeis, 2003b). Children at risk for dyslexia demonstrated an attenuated late-MMN response following deviant tone stimuli, and demonstrated an atypical topography of the late-MMN in response to deviant phoneme stimuli. This topographic difference following deviant phonemes was potentially informative, as the control children showed one major positive pole, which was strongly left-lateralized, indicating left-lateralized mismatch processing, whereas the children at risk showed two positive poles of the MMN, indicating bilateral mismatch processing.

These results suggest deviant automatic phoneme perception in children at risk for dyslexia. The attenuated MMN to tones may suggest that the deviant phoneme processing is related to a more low-level auditory processing deficit. Pending longitudinal results may reveal whether such effects are early predictive markers of specific dyslexia-risk for these individual children, or merely markers of familial risk. Moreover, such longitudinal designs provide the framework to test whether these measures of speech perception can predict the degree of reading-related N170 specialization and its left-hemispheric modulation.

Evidence for predictive values of ERP measures of early speech perception for later reading ability comes from studies that have followed children from early perception of speech through development of early reading skills. The Jyvaskyla longitudinal study in Finland, is following the development of children at familial risk for dyslexia in contrast to typically developing children. Testing, including ERP recordings, started in the first days after birth, and will continue intermittently until the 3rd grade. The ERP data, assessing basic speech processing and automatic mismatch response to speech stimuli, showed that the at-risk infants already differed from the control group during their first days and months of infancy (Lyytinen et al., 2004; Lyytinen et al., 2004). Comparison of the ERP data from the first days of life with later language development showed correlations with receptive language skills and verbal memory (Guttorm et al., 2005). Preliminary data also indicates correlations with initial reading and spelling skills (Lyytinen et al., 2004). The results from this longitudinal study are generally consistent with earlier reports that ERP responses to speech sounds recorded within hours after birth are strongly correlated with reading ability at 8 years of age (Molfese, 2000). In this study, some selected indexes derived from the ERP results collected in infancy were able to support discrimination among children into three different groups of reading and IQ impairments with an overall accuracy of 81%.

Such longitudinal studies provide evidence for the role of early speech processing in later language development and reading acquisition. These studies, however, did not investigate reading-related N170 specialization and thus do not allow for a test of the phonological mapping hypothesis with regard to the role of phonological processing for specialized visual word recognition. Based on our review of current findings, such developmental studies would need to include children beyond age seven to characterize the rise of perceptual expertise and N170 responses to visual words.

CONCLUSIONS

Behavioral studies have indicated that word-specific information is processed within the first 200-ms of stimulus presentation. Such fast visual word processing ability in skilled adults may rely on left-lateralized visual expertise effects linked to the N170 component. Converging evidence shows larger N170 amplitudes, especially over the left hemisphere, for words compared to visual control stimuli such as symbol strings, but results regarding specialization among different types of letter strings and the degree of the left-lateralization of the word N170 suggest large variation due to additional factors involved. An ERP mapping approach that takes advantage of modern multi-channel EEG recordings in participants with different language backgrounds suggested two overlapping processes in the N170, leading to the formulation of the phonological mapping hypothesis for the development of reading-related N170 specialization. A left-lateralized modulation may develop under the influence of grapheme-phoneme conversion during learning to read and reflects the involvement of spelling-to-sound mapping during visual word processing. Furthermore, a more domain-general inferior-superior modulation may develop through visual discrimination learning during reading acquisition. This hypothesis frames a set of specific predictions regarding reading-related N170 specialization in language systems using different scripts, in learning to read, and in dyslexia, that can be tested in specific studies. Results that allow such tests are just emerging and seem to support the predictions of the phonological mapping hypothesis for N170 specialization. Emerging and future results that directly examine the developmental and learning changes that link phonological processes to the emergence of expertise in fluent visual word recognition via development and training studies will provide more direct evidence that bear on such predictions, and will likely provide further neural-circuitry-level insights into the developmental and learning pathways that give rise to fluent visual word recognition.

REFERENCES

Assadollahi, R., & Pulvermuller, F. (2003). Early influences of word length and frequency: a group study using MEG. *Neuroreport, 14*(8), 1183–1187.

Balota, D. A. (1994). Visual word recognition: the journey from features to meaning. In M. A. Gernsbacher (Ed.), *Handbook of Psycholinguistics* (pp. 303–358). New York: Academic Press.

Bentin, S., Mouchetant-Rostaing, Y., Giard, M. H., Echallier, J. F., & Pernier, J. (1999). ERP manifestations of processing printed words at different psycholinguistic levels: time course and scalp distribution. *J Cogn Neurosci, 11*(3), 235–260.

Brandeis, D., & Lehmann, D. (1986). Event-related potentials of the brain and cognitive processes: approaches and applications. *Neuropsychologia, 24*(1), 151–168.

Brandeis, D., Vitacco, D., & Steinhausen, H. C. (1994). Mapping brain electric micro-states in dyslexic children during reading. *Acta Paedopsychiatr, 56*(3), 239–247.

Brem, S., Lang-Dullenkopf, A., Maurer, U., Halder, P., Bucher, K., & Brandeis, D. (2005). Neurophysiological signs of rapidly emerging visual expertise for symbol strings. *Neuroreport, 16*(1), 45–48.

Chatrian, G. E., Lettich, E., & Nelson, P. L. (1985). Ten percent electrode system for topographic studies of spontaneous and evoked EEG activity. *Am J EEG Technol, 25*, 83–92.

Cheour, M., Leppanen, P. H., & Kraus, N. (2000). Mismatch negativity (MMN) as a tool for investigating auditory discrimination and sensory memory in infants and children. *Clin Neurophysiol, 111*(1), 4–16.

Compton, P. E., Grossenbacher, P., Posner, M. I., & Tucker, D. M. (1991). A cognitive-anatomical approach to attention in lexical access. *J Cogn Neurosci, 3*(4), 304–312.

Eulitz, C., Eulitz, H., Maess, B., Cohen, R., Pantev, C., & Elbert, T. (2000). Magnetic brain activity evoked and induced by visually presented words and nonverbal stimuli. *Psychophysiology, 37*(4), 447–455.

Friederici, A. D., Gunter, T. C., Hahne, A., & Mauth, K. (2004). The relative timing of syntactic and semantic processes in sentence comprehension. *Neuroreport, 15*(1), 165–169.

Gauthier, I., Curran, T., Curby, K. M., & Collins, D. (2003). Perceptual interference supports a non-modular account of face processing. *Nat Neurosci, 6*(4), 428–432.

Gauthier, I., & Nelson, C. A. (2001). The development of face expertise. *Curr Opin Neurobiol, 11*(2), 219–224.

Grainger, J., Bouttevin, S., Truc, C., Bastien, M., & Ziegler, J. (2003). Word superiority, pseudoword superiority, and learning to read: a comparison of dyslexic and normal readers. *Brain Lang, 87*(3), 432–440.

Guttorm, T. K., Leppanen, P. H., Poikkeus, A. M., Eklund, K. M., Lyytinen, P., & Lyytinen, H. (2005). Brain event-related potentials (ERPs) measured at birth predict later language development in children with and without familial risk for dyslexia. *Cortex, 41*(3), 291–303.

Hauk, O., & Pulvermuller, F. (2004). Effects of word length and frequency on the human event-related potential. *Clin Neurophysiol, 115*(5), 1090–1103.

Helenius, P., Tarkiainen, A., Cornelissen, P., Hansen, P. C., & Salmelin, R. (1999). Dissociation of normal feature analysis and deficient processing of letter-strings in dyslexic adults. *Cereb Cortex, 9*(5), 476–483.

Kim, K. H., Yoon, H. W., & Park, H. W. (2004). Spatiotemporal brain activation pattern during word/picture perception by native Koreans. *Neuroreport, 15*(7), 1099–1103.

Kutas, M., & Federmeier, K. D. (2000). Electrophysiology reveals semantic memory use in language comprehension. *Trends Cogn Sci, 4*(12), 463–470.

Lehmann, D., & Skrandies, W. (1980). Reference-free identification of components of checkerboard-evoked multichannel potential fields. *Electroencephalogr Clin Neurophysiol, 48*(6), 609–621.

Luu, P., & Ferree, T. (2000). *Determination of the Geodesic Sensor Nets' Average Electrode Positions and their 10–10 International Equivalents.* Eugene, Oregon: Electrical Geodesics, Inc.

Lyytinen, H., Ahonen, T., Eklund, K., Guttorm, T., Kulju, P., Laakso, M. L., Leiwo, M., Leppanen, P., Lyytinen, P., Poikkeus, A. M., Richardson, U., Torppa, M., & Viholainen, H. (2004). Early development of children at familial risk for dyslexia—follow-up from birth to school age. *Dyslexia, 10*(3), 146–178.

Lyytinen, H., Aro, M., Eklund, K., Erskine, J., Guttorm, T., Laakso, M. L., Leppanen, P. H., Lyytinen, P., Poikkeus, A. M., & Torppa, M. (2004). The development of children at familial risk for dyslexia: birth to early school age. *Ann Dyslexia, 54*(2), 184–220.

Maurer, U., Brandeis, D., & McCandliss, B. D. (2005a). Fast, visual specialization for reading in English revealed by the topography of the N170 ERP response. *Behav Brain Func, 1*(1), 13.

Maurer, U., Brem, S., Bucher, K., & Brandeis, D. (2005b). Emerging neurophysiological specialization for letter strings. *J Cogn Neurosci, 17*(10), 1532–1552.

Maurer, U., Brem, S., Kranz, F., Bucher, K., Benz, R., Halder, P., Steinhausen, H.-C., & Brandeis, D. (2006). Coarse neural tuning for print peaks when chidren learn to read. *Neuroimage, 33*(2), 749–758.

Maurer, U.,S. Bucher, K., Kranz, F., Benz, Steinhausen, H.-C., & Brandeis, D. (submitted). Impaired visual tuning of fast print-processing in dyslexic children learning to read.

Maurer, U., Bucher, K., Brem, S., & Brandeis, D. (2003a). Development of the automatic mismatch response: from frontal positivity in kindergarten children to the mismatch negativity. *Clin Neurophysiol, 114*(5), 808–817.

Maurer, U., Bucher, K., Brem, S., & Brandeis, D. (2003b). Altered responses to tone and phoneme mismatch in kindergartners at familial dyslexia risk. *Neuroreport, 14*(17), 2245–2250.

McCandliss, B. D., Cohen, L., & Dehaene, S. (2003). The visual word form area: expertise for reading in the fusiform gyrus. *Trends Cogn Sci, 7*(7), 293–299.

McCandliss, B. D., & Noble, K. G. (2003). The development of reading impairment: a cognitive neuroscience model. *Ment Retard Dev Disabil Res Rev, 9*(3), 196–204.

McCandliss, B. D., Posner, M. I., & Givon, T. (1997). Brain plasticity in learning visual words. *Cogn Psychol, 33*(1), 88–110.

Michel, C. M., Murray, M. M., Lantz, G., Gonzalez, S., Spinelli, L., & Grave de Peralta, R. (2004). EEG source imaging. *Clin Neurophysiol, 115*(10), 2195–2222.

Michel, C. M., Thut, G., Morand, S., Khateb, A., Pegna, A. J., Grave de Peralta, R., Gonzalez, S., Seeck, M., & Landis, T. (2001). Electric source imaging of human brain functions. *Brain Res Brain Res Rev, 36*(2–3), 108–118.

Molfese, D. L. (2000). Predicting dyslexia at 8 years of age using neonatal brain responses. *Brain Lang, 72*(3), 238–245.

Naatanen, R. (2001). The perception of speech sounds by the human brain as reflected by the mismatch negativity (MMN) and its magnetic equivalent (MMNm). *Psychophysiology, 38*(1), 1–21.

Naatanen, R., Tervaniemi, M., Sussman, E., Paavilainen, P., & Winkler, I. (2001). "Primitive intelligence" in the auditory cortex. *Trends Neurosci, 24*(5), 283–288.

Neville, H. J., Mills, D. L., & Lawson, D. S. (1992). Fractionating language: Different neural subsystems with different sensitive periods. *Cereb Cortex, 2*, 244–258.

Noble, K. G., McCandliss, B. D., & Farah, M. J. (submitted). Socioeconomic background predicts individual differences in neurocognitive abilities.

Nobre, A. C., Allison, T., & McCarthy, G. (1998). Modulation of human extrastriate visual processing by selective attention to colours and words. *Brain, 121 (Pt 7)*, 1357–1368.

Pascual-Marqui, R. D., Michel, C. M., & Lehmann, D. (1995). Segmentation of brain electrical activity into microstates: model estimation and validation. *IEEE Trans Biomed Eng, 42*(7), 658–665.

Petersen, S. E., Fox, P. T., Posner, M. I., Mintun, M., & Raichle, M. E. (1988). Positron emission tomographic studies of the cortical anatomy of single- word processing. *Nature, 331*(6157), 585–589.

Posner, M., & McCandliss, B. D. (2000). Brain circuitry during reading. In R. Klein & P. McMullen (Eds.), *Converging methods for understanding reading and dyslexia* (pp. 305–337). Cambridge: MIT Press.

Price, C. J., Moore, C. J., Humphreys, G. W., & Wise, R. J. S. (1997). Segregating semantic from phonological processes during reading. *J Cogn Neurosci, 9*(6), 727–733.

Price, C. J., Wise, R. J., & Frackowiak, R. S. (1996). Demonstrating the implicit processing of visually presented words and pseudowords. *Cereb Cortex, 6*(1), 62–70.

Proverbio, A. M., Cok, B., & Zani, A. (2002). Electrophysiological measures of language processing in bilinguals. *J Cogn Neurosci, 14*(7), 994–1017.

Proverbio, A. M., Vecchi, L., & Zani, A. (2004). From orthography to phonetics: ERP measures of grapheme-to-phoneme conversion mechanisms in reading. *J Cogn Neurosci, 16*(2), 301–317.

Rayner, K. (1998). Eye movements in reading and information processing: 20 years of research. *Psychol Bull, 124*(3), 372–422.

Reicher, G. M. (1969). Perceptual recognition as a function of meaningfulness of stimulus material. *J Exp Psychol, 81*(2), 275–280.

Reichle, E. D., Rayner, K., & Pollatsek, A. (2003). The E-Z reader model of eye-movement control in reading: comparisons to other models. *Behav Brain Sci, 26*(4), 445–476; discussion 477–526.

Rossion, B., Gauthier, I., Goffaux, V., Tarr, M. J., & Crommelinck, M. (2002). Expertise training with novel objects leads to left-lateralized facelike electrophysiological responses. *Psychol Sci, 13*(3), 250–257.

Rossion, B., Joyce, C. A., Cottrell, G. W., & Tarr, M. J. (2003). Early lateralization and orientation tuning for face, word, and object processing in the visual cortex. *Neuroimage.*

Rugg, M. D. (1984). Event-related potentials and the phonological processing of words and non-words. *Neuropsychologia, 22*(4), 435–443.

Rumsey, J. M., Horwitz, B., Donohue, B. C., Nace, K., Maisog, J. M., & Andreason, P. (1997). Phonological and orthographic components of word recognition. A PET-rCBF study. *Brain, 120 (Pt 5)*, 739–759.

Salmelin, R., Service, E., Kiesila, P., Uutela, K., & Salonen, O. (1996). Impaired visual word processing in dyslexia revealed with magnetoencephalography. *Ann Neurol, 40*(2), 157–162.

Schendan, H. E., Ganis, G., & Kutas, M. (1998). Neurophysiological evidence for visual perceptual categorization of words and faces within 150 ms. *Psychophysiology, 35*(3), 240–251.

Sereno, S. C., Brewer, C. C., & O'Donnell, P. J. (2003). Context effects in word recognition: evidence for early interactive processing. *Psychol Sci, 14*(4), 328–333.

Sereno, S. C., Rayner, K., & Posner, M. I. (1998). Establishing a time-line of word recognition: evidence from eye movements and event-related potentials. *Neuroreport, 9*(10), 2195–2200.

Shaywitz, S. E. (2004). *Overcoming dyslexia: a new and complete science-based program for overcoming reading problems at any level.*New York: Alfred A. Knopf.

Simos, P. G., Breier, J. I., Fletcher, J. M., Bergman, E., & Papanicolaou, A. C. (2000). Cerebral mechanisms involved in word reading in dyslexic children: a magnetic source imaging approach. *Cereb Cortex, 10*(8), 809–816.

Tagamets, M. A., Novick, J. M., Chalmers, M. L., & Friedman, R. B. (2000). A parametric approach to orthographic processing in the brain: an fMRI study. *J Cogn Neurosci, 12*(2), 281–297.

Talairach, J., & Tournoux, P. (1988). *Co-planar Stereotaxic Atlas of the Human Brain.*Stuttgart: Thieme.

Tanaka, J. W., & Curran, T. (2001). A neural basis for expert object recognition. *Psychol Sci, 12*(1), 43–47.

Tarkiainen, A., Helenius, P., Hansen, P. C., Cornelissen, P. L., & Salmelin, R. (1999). Dynamics of letter string perception in the human occipitotemporal cortex. *Brain, 122*(Pt 11), 2119–2132.

Wydell, T. N., Vuorinen, T., Helenius, P., & Salmelin, R. (2003). Neural correlates of letter-string length and lexicality during reading in a regular orthography. *J Cogn Neurosci, 15*(7), 1052–1062.

Zevin, J. D., & Balota, D. A. (2000). Priming and attentional control of lexical and sublexical pathways during naming. *J Exp Psychol Learn Mem Cogn, 26*(1), 121–135.

Zhang, X. L., Begleiter, H., Porjesz, B., & Litke, A. (1997). Visual object priming differs from visual word priming: an ERP study. *Electroencephalogr Clin Neurophysiol, 102*(3), 200–215.

CHAPTER FOUR

Phonological Representations for Reading Acquisition Across Languages

Usha Goswami
University of Cambridge

Phonological awareness refers to the child's ability to detect and manipulate component sounds in words, and is the key predictor of how well a child will learn to read and write their language (e.g., Bradley & Bryant, 1983; Lundberg, Olofsson & Wall, 1980; Schneider, Roth & Ennemoser, 2000). Phonological awareness is usually assumed to develop via the implicit and then increasingly explicit organisation of the phonological representations that underpin spoken language use. The worlds' languages differ greatly in their phonological complexity, varying for example in syllable structure and the number of vowels and consonant phonemes in the phonological repertoire. Nevertheless, despite these differences, children in all languages so far studied appear to follow a similar developmental pathway in terms of phonological awareness. Children first become aware of relatively "large" phonological units in words, such as syllables, onset-vowel units (e.g., morae) or rimes (vowel-coda units). If they learn to read an alphabetic orthography, they then become aware of smaller units of sound (phonemes) corresponding to graphemes (letters or letter clusters). As there are a variety of ways in which the alphabetic orthographies of the world represent the sound patterns of the worlds' languages, there are differences in the rate and ease of developing such "small unit" knowledge. Nevertheless, these differences can be analysed systematically. Here I present an analysis based on the "psycholinguistic grain size" theoretical framework for single word recognition that I have developed with Johannes Ziegler (e.g., Goswami, Ziegler, Dalton & Schneider, 2001, 2003;

Word		BARGAIN	
Syllable	BAR		GAIN
Onset-Rime	B /a/		G /eN/
Phoneme	B /a/		G /e/ N

FIGURE 4.1

Ziegler & Goswami, 2005). This framework also enables me to highlight gaps in the current research literature.

The syllable is thought to be the primary linguistic processing unit for the majority of the worlds' languages. It is distinguished by a number of auditory cues including rhythm and stress. The intonation patterns of infant-directed speech or "Motherese" serve to emphasize these cues, which are thought to aid early word extraction from the speech stream. Within the syllable, the most prominent phonological segments in European languages are the onset and the rime. The onset comprises the sounds or phonemes before the vowel in any syllable, and the rime is the vowel and any sounds (phonemes) that follow (see Figure 4.1). For example, there are 3 syllables in "popsicle", 2 syllables in "window", and one syllable in "soap". To derive onset-rime units from syllables, the syllable must be divided at the vowel. The onset-rime units in "pop" are P – OP, in "window" they are W-IN and D-O. The linguistic term "rime" signifies the fact that a multi-syllabic word has many rimes. Although "mountain" rhymes with "fountain", it does not rhyme with "captain". Nevertheless, the rime of the final syllable is the same.

Many of the language games, linguistic routines and nursery rhymes of early childhood in European languages act to emphasise phonology by increasing the salience of syllables, onsets and rimes. In English, for example, popular nursery rhymes have strong rhythms that emphasise syllabification (think of Humpty Dumpty), and many contrast rhyming words in ways that distinguish the onset from the rime (e.g., 'Twinkle Twinkle Little Star' rhymes 'star' with 'are', and 'Incy Wincy Spider' rhymes 'spout' with 'out'). These language games of childhood probably have an important developmental function with respect to the emergence of accurate and fine-grained phonological representations for words.

THE ORIGINS OF PHONOLOGICAL REPRESENTATION

Early Language Acquisition: Holistic Representations?

Phonological representations develop as the infant learns to comprehend and produce language. It has long been argued that the phonological representations used for language comprehension and production by the pre-literate infant and child differ qualitatively from the phonological representations used by literate adults (e.g., Ferguson & Farwell, 1975; Charles-Luce & Luce, 1990; Walley, 1993). For example, because young children's primary goal in language acquisition is to recognise and produce whole words, it has been argued that they represent the phonology of words in a holistic manner. It was assumed that children represent early words in terms of holistic properties, such as acoustic shape and prosodic structure, rather than in terms of particular phonetic contrasts. Certainly, when asked to make similarity judgements about words, young children seem to focus on global phonological similarity rather than on segmental structure (segmental structure means shared phonemes, as linguists traditionally call phonemes segments, see Treiman & Breaux, 1982). Nevertheless, pre-literate children can match words in terms of shared phonological structure as well. For example, Carroll and Snowling (2001) gave 3- and 4-year-old children a rhyme matching task in which distractors were matched for global phonological similarity to the target (e.g., *house*: mouse, horse; *bell*: shell, ball). They reported that approximately 30% of the 3-year-olds, 60% of the young 4-year-olds, and 76% of the 4.5-year-olds scored above chance in matching rimes, even though many of the distracters (e.g., horse) were as phonologically similar to the targets (e.g., house) as the correct rime choices (e.g., mouse).

Against the global representations view, it is well known that infants can discriminate the acoustic elements that yield phones from birth onwards (e.g., Eimas, Siqueland, Jusczyk, & Vigorito, 1971). By the end of the first year, infants have honed in on the phonetic distinctions that are critical for the language environment in which they live (e.g., Werker & Tees, 1984). Detailed case studies of phonetic inventories show that by age 3, children with large lexicons have large inventories of individual features, syllable shapes and stress placements (Stoel-Gammon, 1998). The performance of young children can also be highly task dependent. For example, in a study by Swingley and Aslin (2002), infants aged 1;2 and 1;3 were shown pairs of pictures of familiar items while either the correct referent (e.g., 'ball'), or a close mispronunciation (e.g., 'gall'), was presented acoustically. Swingley and Aslin found that the infants spent significantly more time fixating the correct picture for the correctly-pronounced target words, and therefore argued that infants encode words in fine phonetic detail. Nevertheless, of course, phones and phonemes are not the same thing. The ability to distinguish the phonetic features that make /ba/ different from /ga/ is not the same as the ability to categorize the shared sound in "pit", "lap", and "spoon" as the phoneme /p/ (see also Swingley & Aslin, 2000).

Grain Size in Early Phonological Representation

Even if very early phonological representations may be holistic, the speed of lexical acquisition suggests that more phonological detail is soon required in order for the comprehension and production of words to be efficient. Between the ages of 1 and 6 years, children acquire thousands of words. According to some estimates, the average 6-year-old knows 14,000 words (Dollaghan, 1994), whereas the average 1-year-old knows between 100–200. Dollaghan (1994) went on to index by hand the phonemic similarity between monosyllables thought to be known by 1- to 3-year-olds. She found a relatively high degree of phonologically similar entries. If most of the words in the early lexicon are highly similar phonologically, then holistic recognition strategies would be rather ineffective. More recently, Coady and Aslin (2003) used a number of different measures to show that once vocabulary size is taken into account, childrens' lexicons contain more phonologically similar entries than those of adults – their "phonological neighbourhoods" are more dense.

There is increasing interest in the role of phonological neighborhoods in lexical development (e.g., Coady & Aslin, 2003; Garlock, Walley & Metsala, 2001; Storkel, 2001). Phonological neighbours are words that sound similar to each other. The number of phonological neighbours of a given (target) word are usually estimated on the basis of phonemic similarity. The classical speech processing definition of a phonological neighbourhood is the set of words generated by the addition, deletion or substitution of one phoneme to the target (e.g., Landauer & Streeter, 1973; Luce & Pisoni, 1998). For example, the neighbours of the target cop include crop, cap, top and cot. When many words resemble the target, the neighbourhood is said to be dense. When few words resemble the target, the neighbourhood is said to be sparse. Neighbourhood density is highly correlated with phonotactic probability (Vitevitch, Luce, Pisoni & Auer, 1999). Phonotactic probability is the frequency with which phonological segments and sequences of phonological segments occur in words in the English language (Jusczyk, Luce & Charles-Luce, 1994). Unsurprisingly, words with many neighbours tend to be comprised of segments and sequences of segments that are frequent in occurrence.

An alternative view to the holistic one is that early word learning favours words with more frequent sounds and sound combinations (e.g., Menn, 1978; Lindblom, 1992). This view suggests that children should preferentially acquire words from dense neighbourhoods, because these neighbourhoods by definition contain the more frequent sound combinations in the language (they contain words with high phonotactic probability). As these words are acquired first, processing of these words is then facilitated via frequent use. A different view is that acquisition could favour words that are more easily discriminated from other words (e.g., Schwartz, 1988). By this view, children should preferentially acquire the words that fill in the "gaps" in the acoustic space comprising the lexicon, that is, words from sparse neighbourhoods. The former view, that words from dense neighbourhoods have an advantage in acquisition, is best supported by the evidence. For example, Storkel (2001) reported that young children who were taught nonword labels for unfamiliar objects were more likely to acquire novel words from dense neighbourhoods. The focus on phonological frequency and phonological similarity in lexical acquisition has interesting theoretical implications for the development of phonological awareness. If children preferentially acquire similar-sounding words, absolute vocabulary size and the rate of acquisition would be important factors in the development of phonological awareness.

Epilinguistic Development: The Role of Phonological Similarity

One view of the early development of phonological awareness is that it is implicit in nature or "epilinguistic" (see Gombert, 1992). Gombert's claim was that early phonological awareness arises from organisational processes internal to the lexicon that are not yet available for conscious or "metalinguistic" inspection. Hence "epilinguistic" awareness would enable a child to identify and recognise similarities between phonological representations but not to manipulate those representations (e.g., by adding or deleting sounds). One plausible way in which phonological representations could be internally organised is in terms of their phonological similarity. Neighbourhood similarity characteristics are essentially structural regularities present in the lexicon of spoken word forms, and these may form the basis of incidental learning about phonology in the same way that statistical regularities present in sequences of syllables (phonotactic and transitional probabilities) are thought to form the basis of word segmentation and learning (e.g., Saffran, Newport, Aslin, Tunick & Barrueco, 1997). However, in order to use phonological neighbourhood density as a developmental metric, it may be necessary to redefine phonological "neighbours". The classical speech processing definition based on sharing all phonemes except one may not be appropriate. In her 1994 analysis, Dollaghan found that the one-phoneme different criterion of phonological similarity used for adults led to many intuitively dissatisfying exclusions when she was calculating childrens' phonological neighbourhoods (Dollaghan, 1994). For example, the criterion excluded many rhyme neighbours, even though rhyme is an important phonological similarity relation for young children. Clock and sock would not count as phonological neighbours of each other by the one-phoneme-different criterion.

Dollaghan's intuition that a one-phoneme different neighbourhood metric is unsuited to work with children is supported by a recent empirical paper by De Cara and Goswami (2002). We presented an alternative analysis of the distribution of phonological similarity relations among monosyllabic spoken words in English, based on the assumption that the mental lexicon has psycholinguistic structure. Rather than calculating neighbourhoods on the basis of the addition, substitution or deletion of a single phoneme, we calculated neighbourhoods on the basis of the addition, substitution or deletion of a single onset, nucleus or coda (following the hierarchical syllable structure shown in Figure 1). Statistical analyses of the nature of phonological neighbourhoods in terms of the resulting Rime Neighbours (e.g., hat/spat), Consonant Neighbours (e.g., hat/hurt), and Lead Neighbours (e.g., hat/hatch) were reported for all monosyllabic English words in the CELEX corpus (4086 words; Baayen, Piepenbrock, & van Rijn, 1993), and for a number of smaller English lexicons controlled for age of acquisition. These analyses showed that most phonological neighbours in English are Rime Neighbours (e.g., hat / spat). If phonological neighbourhood similarity characteristics form the basis of incidental learning about phonology, then languages with a phonological similarity structure that emphasises the rime should lead to early phonological awareness of syllables, onsets and rimes.

This analysis makes a simple prediction: the lexicons of languages in which onset-rime awareness emerges prior to literacy (e.g., German, Dutch, English, French) should exhibit greater phonological similarity at the rime than at the onset-vowel level when neighbourhood analyses are carried out. Languages in which a post-vowel segmentation of the syllable is preferred (e.g., Korean, Japanese) should not. In Ziegler and Goswami (2005), we carried out analyses of the percentage of rime neighbours, onset-vowel (body) neighbours, and consonant neighbours for English, German, French, and Dutch monosyllables to test this prediction. The English, German and Dutch analyses were based on the monosyllabic words in the CELEX database (Baayen, Piepenbrock, & van Rijn, 1993), the French analyses were based on the monosyllabic words in BRULEX (Content, Mousty & Radeau, 1990). The analyses showed that rime neighbours indeed predominate in English, French, Dutch, and German phonology. In all of these languages, the percentage of rime neighbours in the monosyllabic lexicon is between 40–50%. Hence the early development of phonological awareness in these languages, which is at the "large unit" level of syllable, onset and rime, may depend in part on the organisational structure of phonological similarity neighbourhoods within the lexicon.

Certainly, there is growing evidence that childrens' performance in phonological awareness tasks is influenced by phonological neighbourhood characteristics. In studies of English-speaking children, phonological neighbourhood density appears to enhance performance in phonological tasks. Children are better at making rime judgements about words from dense phonological neighbourhoods when factors like spoken frequency and age of acquisition are controlled (De Cara & Goswami, 2003). They are also better at remembering words and nonwords that contain rimes from words in dense phonological neighbourhoods than at remembering words and nonwords that contain rimes from words in sparse phonological neighbourhoods (Thomson, Richardson & Goswami, in press). At the phoneme level, Metsala (1999) found that 3- and 4-year-old children could blend spoken phonemes to yield words from dense neighbourhoods more easily than to yield words from sparse neigh-bourhoods. Thus there is at least some evidence that early phonological awareness arises from organisational processes internal to the lexicon, such as organisation in terms of phonological similarity neighbourhoods. Further data gathered within this framework across languages would be very welcome.

THE DEVELOPMENT OF PHONOLOGICAL AWARENESS

As noted earlier, phonological awareness refers to the child's ability to detect and manipulate component sounds in words, and is the key predictor of literacy acquisi-tion across languages. For European languages, the development of phonological awareness appears to follow a similar pattern. Prior to learning to read or to receiving specialised training, children appear to be aware of "large" units of phonology within words: syllables, onsets and rimes. As they learn to read an alphabetic script, or if intensive tuition is provided, children become aware of smaller units of sound at the abstract level of phonemes. While awareness of larger units of phonology in words is thought to be epilinguistic in origin, in terms of arising from representa-tional processes that are not at first available to conscious inspection, awareness of phonemes is thought to be metalinguistic. The development of phoneme awareness (awareness of "small units") is dependent on the child achieving explicit or con-scious control over the linguistic structures used for producing and comprehending speech. This metalinguistic control has been described by Gombert (1992) as devel-oping in response to external factors, such as direct teaching about phonemes or the acquisition of literacy. Learning to read and spell is in fact the most common way of achieving phoneme awareness, as phonemes are abstractions from the speech stream rather than consistent acoustic entities (phones are the consistent entities, as described earlier). Illiterate adults never become aware of phonemes, in spite of having well-developed language skills (Morais, Cary, Alegria & Bertelson, 1979).

PHONOLOGICAL AWARENESS PRIOR TO SCHOOLING: IDENTIFYING AND RECOGNISING SIMILARITIES IN PHONOLOGY

Studies of phonological awareness have used a wide range of methods to explore phonological skills in the preschool years. For example, children as young as 3 years can be asked to correct speech errors made by a hand puppet ("sie" for "pie"), to complete nursery rhymes ("Jack and Jill went up the –" [hill]), or to select the odd word out of a group of three rhyming words (oddity detection: pin, win, sit, see Chaney, 1992; Bradley & Bryant, 1983; Bryant, Bradley, MaClean & Crosland, 1989; Ho & Bryant, 1997). Young children perform at above-chance levels on such tasks. For example, Bryant et al. (1989) found that 3-year-olds scored on average 48% correct in the rhyme oddity task (chance = 33%). Bradley and Bryant (1983) found that 4-year-olds were 57% correct at detecting sound oddity when words differed in alliteration (onset detection, e.g., sun, sock, rag), and 75% correct at detecting sound oddity when words differed in rhyme (cot, hat, pot). Chaney (1992) reported that 88% of her 43 3-year-olds could correct the puppet who mispronounced words. This was essentially an onset detection task ("pie" mispronounced as "sie", demonstrating that when single phonemes are onsets, children can be aware of phoneme-sized units even prior to schooling). Bryant et al. (1989) reported that only one of the 64 3-year-olds in their study knew none of the 5 nursery rhymes being tested. On average, the children knew about half of the nursery rhymes (they were scored 1 for partially completing the rhymes and 2 for fully completing them, making a total possible score of 10, the mean score for the group was 4.5).

Similar results have been reported for preschoolers in other European languages. However, as schooling typically begins later in such languages, these children are usually older when they are tested in nursery school. For example, Wimmer, Landerl and Schneider (1994) gave 138 German preschoolers aged 6 years the oddity task, comparing rhyme and alliteration (onset oddity). The children scored 44% correct in the onset task and 73% correct in the rhyme task. In Greek, Porpodas (1999) studied Greek children who had just entered school (7 year olds), giving them the oddity task. Overall performance (presented added across onset and rime) was 89% correct. For Norwegian, a study of 128 preschoolers by Hoien, Lundberg, Stanovich and Bjaalid (1995) measured rhyme awareness using a matching task. The children, who were aged on average 6 years 11 months, were asked to select a match from a choice of 3 pictures to rhyme with a target picture. Performance by the group averaged 91% correct. Hence phonological awareness prior to schooling is well-developed at the larger grain sizes of onset and rime.

PHONOLOGICAL AWARENESS WITH SCHOOLING: MANIPULATING UNITS OF PHONOLOGY

As soon as schooling begins, awareness of phonemes can develop rapidly. However, the rate of development tends to vary with the orthography that children are learning to read. This is demonstrated most clearly when children learning to read different languages are given the same phonological awareness tasks. If task difficulty is equated across languages, differences in achievement between languages are more likely to be due to linguistic differences (at least, if words of equivalent phonological structure are being compared, and children are matched for vocabulary and developmental level). The task that has been used most frequently in different languages to measure phoneme awareness is the counting task. In this task, children are given counters to use to represent the number of phonemes in words. For example, "cat" would require 3 counters and "skip" would require 4 counters. A word like "soap", which has 4 letters but 3 phonemes, would require 3 counters for a correct response.

Table 1 shows performance in phoneme counting tasks by first grade children in a variety of different languages using an alphabetic orthography. Whereas phoneme awareness is virtually at ceiling in this simple task for languages like Greek, Turkish and Italian, it is not close to ceiling in languages like English and French. According to psycholinguistic grain size theory, these differences in the rate of acquiring phoneme awareness reflect orthographic consistency (see Ziegler & Goswami, 2005). In languages with a 1:1 correspondence between letter and sound for reading, like Greek and Turkish, one letter always corresponds to only one phoneme. Hence learning about phonemes via learning to read is a relatively straightforward task – there is only one mapping to learn. In languages like English and French, there is a one-to-many correspondence between letters and phonemes. Most letters correspond to more than one phoneme, and some letters correspond to lots of phonemes (for example, the vowel A in English corresponds to at least 5 different phonemes, as in sat, last, saw, cake, again). Hence learning about phonemes via learning to read is not a straightforward task – the mappings keep changing. Accordingly, it takes English and French children much longer than Greek and Turkish children to develop competent phoneme awareness skills.

Many other tasks requiring the manipulation of phonology show a similar cross-language pattern. For example, Landerl, Wimmer and Frith (1997) asked English and German 8- and 11-year-olds to carry out a "Spoonerism" task using familiar words like "sun" and "moon". Spoonerisms are named after the Reverend Spooner of New College, Oxford, who apparently mixed up the onsets of different words in an amusing manner (as in "You have hissed all my mystery lectures"). Children given the words "sun" and "moon" in a Spoonerism task should respond "mun" and "soon". The English 8-year-olds tested by Landerl et al. solved 35% of the Spoonerisms successfully, while the German 8-year-olds solved 57%. Success levels rose to 60% for the English 11-year-olds, and 68% for the German 11-year-olds. The gap in the rate at which phoneme awareness skills develop for children learning consistent versus inconsistent orthographies is still present at age 8, although it is clearly disappearing by age 11. German and English are a particularly good pair of languages to compare developmentally, as they have a similar orthography and phonology (both are alphabetic, and the languages stem from the same Germanic root). Yet they have dramatic differences in spelling-to-sound consistency. For example, the words "ball", "park" and "hand" are the same in both languages (in German they are Ball, Park and Hand). However, whereas the vowel "a" has 3 different pronunciations in the 3 English words, it has exactly the same pronunciation in the 3 German words. This is the most likely source of the developmental variation in the rate of acquiring phoneme awareness by language. German readers are receiving consistent orthographic feedback in terms of letter-phoneme correspondences, whereas English readers are not.

PHONOLOGICAL AWARENESS AT DIFFERENT
GRAIN SIZES IN NON-EUROPEAN LANGUAGES

Not all of the worlds' languages use an alphabetic code and hence not all of the worlds' languages require phonemic awareness for efficient phonological recoding in word recognition. Furthermore, not all of the worlds' languages emphasise an onset-rime segmentation of the syllable. Japanese is known to follow a moraic organisation, in which the vowel in consonant-vowel (CV) syllables is attached to the onset phoneme. Although in general morae correspond to CV syllables, some syllables include special sounds that constitute separate morae (e.g., certain nasals, geminates, long vowels and "dual" vowels, see Tamaoka & Terao, 2004). These special sounds can create two morae when there is only one syllable. To make a parallel to English, for English any syllable ending in a nasal is still a single syllable (e.g., words like <u>sing</u> and <u>jam</u> are monosyllabic, just like CV words like <u>sea</u> and <u>go</u>). In Japanese, syllables ending in nasals have two morae. Another example is the Japanese loan word for the English trisyllable 'calendar', /kareNdaR/. This word has five morae (/ka re N da R/. The Kana characters used to write Japanese correspond to morae. When English names sucl as "CLINTON" are spoken in Japanese, a mora is required for each phoneme in a cluster (e.g., the onset cluster CL is represented by two morae). It has been claimed that Korean divides syllables into onset-vowel and coda units, designated "body-coda" units (Yoon, Bolger, Kwon, & Perfetti, 2002). Chinese, however, follows an onset-rime syllable division. The basic syllable structure of Chinese is CV, apart from rare codas such as /n/ and /ng/ (e.g., Siok & Fletcher, 2001). There are only about 22 onsets and 37 rimes in Chinese phonology. Hence phonological representations prior to literacy in Chinese should show onset-rime structure, whereas phonological representations prior to literacy in Korean and Japanese should not.

Large Units

Unfortunately, there are rather few studies of phonological development in Japanese and Korean with which to test this prediction (at least, that are available to English speaking readers). Yoon, Bolger, Kwon, & Perfetti (2002) presented

English and Korean students with identical pairs of spoken syllables and asked them to make similarity judgments. English students rated the syllables as more similar if they shared the rime, whereas Korean students rated the same syllables as more similar if they shared the onset-vowel unit. Inagaki, Hatano and Otake (2000) investigated whether pre-school Japanese children would show a preference for moraic or syllabic representation by asking them to segment stimuli incorporating the special sounds. All the practice trials were composed of words sharing the same number of syllables and morae (e.g., kani [crab], 2 syllables and 2 morae). The experimental trials incorporated stimuli using the special sounds. The data essentially revealed a shift from a mixture of syllabic and moraic segmentation in the preschoolers, to moraic segmentation as children learned to read Japanese Kana.

In contrast, studies in Chinese demonstrate onset-rime representation in preschoolers. For example, Ho and Bryant (1997) devised a rhyme oddity task which they gave to 100 Chinese 3-year-olds in Hong Kong. The target word in the oddity task rhymed with and shared the same tone as the correct choice, but had a different rhyme and tone from the incorrect choice. The group of children scored on average 68% correct in this task. Siok and Fletcher (2001) gave Chinese children from Mainland China who were in first grade (6-year-olds) both onset and rhyme versions of the oddity task. The group scored on average 44% correct for the onset version and 54% correct for the rhyme version. Interestingly, Siok and Fletcher (2001) also gave their Chinese children the same oddity tasks using English words. They found no difference in the ability to make oddity judgements: success with Chinese items was on average 51%, and with English items 47%. This suggests that the children had developed an awareness of onsets and rimes as abstract linguistic units. In a separate tone awareness oddity task, the children scored 65% correct. Tone is an important phonological cue in Chinese, as it is a suprasegmental feature that changes the pitch of the syllable. Clearly, in Chinese-speaking children awareness of both syllable structure and tone is well-developed by the first year of schooling.

Small Units

Studies of older children who are learning to read logographic scripts suggests that phoneme awareness does not develop automatically. This is exactly what would be expected if orthographic learning plays a key role in development. Neither Chinese Kanji nor Japanese Kana represent phonology at the phoneme level, hence children learning these orthographies would not be expected to develop awareness of phonemes. However, for Chinese there are two instructional systems for teaching children about characters that operate at the onset/rime level. These are called Pinyin (Mainland China), and Zhu-Yin-Fu-Hao (Taiwan, hereafter Zhuyin). Pinyin uses the Western alphabet to represent the component sounds in syllables, while Zhuyin uses simple characters. In fact, both orthographic systems are simultaneously onset-rime and phonemic systems. In Zhuyin, the characters represent either onsets or rimes. In Pinyin, they represent phonemes. However, because the syllable structure of Chinese is CV apart from rare codas such as /n/ and /ng/, the onset and the rime correspond to single phonemes for the majority of syllables in Chinese (e.g., Siok & Fletcher, 2001). Hence the two instructional systems essentially operate at the same phonological level: that of onset-rime, which for most syllables is equivalent to phoneme segmentation.

Both Pinyin and Zhuyin are taught for about the first 10 weeks of schooling, before children are introduced to the traditional Chinese characters. However, many Chinese-speaking children grow up in Hong Kong, which does not use either instructional system. In Hong Kong, the Chinese characters are learned by rote, very slowly. This difference between Mainland China, Taiwan and Hong Kong allows a natural experiment. If learning an orthographic system that represents phonemes is required for the development of phonemic awareness, then Chinese children growing up in Taiwan and Mainland China should develop phonemic awareness by learning Pinyin or Zhuyin. Chinese children growing up in Hong Kong should not develop phoneme awareness skills. Although there are rather few developmental studies examining this prediction, selected phoneme awareness tasks have been given to Chinese children in the 3 countries at around age 8 (see Huang & Hanley, 1994; Siok & Fletcher, 2001). The 8-year-olds in Mainland China scored on average 82% correct on a phoneme isolation task (Siok & Fletcher, 2001). The children from Taiwan scored 84% correct on a phoneme deletion task (Huang & Hanley, 1994). The children from Hong Kong, however, scored only 27% correct on the same phoneme deletion task (Huang & Hanley, 1994). English children in the same study scored around 80% correct on a similar phoneme deletion task (Huang & Hanley, 1994). Although the tasks used in these studies varied slightly across languages, the poor performance of the Chinese children learning to read Chinese in Hong Kong is striking. This comparison of 8-year-old Chinese children suggests that learning to read an orthographic system that represents phoneme-level information is necessary for phoneme awareness to develop. Because of the structure of Chinese syllables, Pinyin and Zhuyin represent such orthographic systems.

What Is the Role of Letter Learning?

Studies carried out in languages with non-alphabetic scripts are also interesting with respect to the development of phonological representation for another reason. It has occasionally been argued that children do not have any phonological awareness until they learn about letters. Researchers such as Castles and Coltheart (e.g., Castles & Coltheart, 2004) question the idea that phonological awareness is a non-reading precursor to reading that develops naturally as part of language acquisition. For these authors, the studies showing phonological awareness prior to reading are flawed, because the children participating in these studies always know some alphabetic letters (for example, the children participating in Schneider et al. [2000] knew on average 4–5 letters). Castles and Coltheart (2004) pointed out that no study in a European language has measured phonological awareness in children who do not "have any reading or spelling skills whatsoever, including knowledge of letter-sound correspondences". It is of course difficult to find such children in European countries, where environmental print is endemic in the culture and where even 2-year-olds can usually write their names. However, in Chinese-speaking countries this is not the case. Environmental print is not alphabetic. Preschoolers who can write their names write logographs. Hence demonstrations of rhyme awareness in Chinese 3-year-olds (e.g., Ho & Bryant's 1997 study showing 68% correct performance in a rhyme oddity task) is particularly strong evidence for the view that early phonological awareness emerges from language acquisition processes.

THE SOURCES OF PHONOLOGICAL AWARENESS: AUDITORY PROCESSING

As noted earlier, the primary linguistic processing unit for the majority of the worlds' languages is thought to be the syllable. Syllables are distinguished by a number of auditory cues, with speech rhythm and prosody (rhythmic patterning) being particularly important. Infant-directed speech emphasises rhythmic cues, and is characterised in particular by higher pitch, greater pitch and volume variability, and the use of a small set of highly distinctive melodic contours (e.g., Fernald, Taeschner, Dunn, Papousek, de Boysson-Bardies & Fukui, 1989). In all languages the acoustic features of pitch, loudness, speed and silence are combined to produce speech rhythm. However, marked differences in speech rhythm can be found between languages. English has a clear underlying rhythm which is often called stress-timed (or isochronous). Isochronicity is based on stressing syllables that occur at roughly regular intervals in the stream of spoken utterances. For English, stress is not consistently assigned to one syllable in a multi-syllable utterance (although the dominant syllable stress pattern is strong-weak). In contrast, languages using syllable-timed rhythms, such as French and Hungarian, assign syllables equal weight. Stress is consistently placed on one syllable, the final syllable (last full vowel) in French and the first syllable in Hungarian.

This view of linguistic processing is relatively recent. Traditionally, theories of speech perception held that the phoneme was the primary linguistic unit. Classic models of speech perception assumed that the initial analysis of the speech wave-form necessarily yielded a sequence of ordered phonetic segments. This explains the early focus in infant language acquisition on the discrimination of phonetic segments. As noted above, it was soon established that infants can discriminate the acoustic elements that yield phones from birth onwards (e.g., Eimas et al., 1971). This requires the perception of auditory cues such as voice onset time and place of articulation.

Clearly, therefore, there are many auditory cues that are important for establishing well-specified phonological representations as the language system develops. There are cues that are important for a fine-grained analysis of the speech stream into its phonetic elements, and there are cues that are important for a more global analysis centred on the syllable and the rhythmic structure of utterances. Both types of cues have been investigated with respect to phonological awareness and literacy. Early investigations focused on cues thought to be important for perceiving phonemes, such as rapid changes in frequency and the perception of temporal order. More recently, there has been a shift to a focus on supra-segmental cues, such as those contributing to rhythm and stress. It is the latter cues that appear to show the strongest links with individual differences in phonological representational quality.

Auditory Processing of Cues Related to Phoneme Perception

The view that individual differences in auditory perception might be linked to progress in reading was pioneered by Tallal and her colleagues (e.g., Tallal, 1980; Tallal, Miller & Fitch, 1993). Working from a phoneme perspective, they argued that dyslexic children have particular difficulties in processing transient or rapidly changing acoustic events. They suggested that the ability "accurately to perceive stimulus elements at rapid rates of presentation" is fundamental to setting up the phonological system, as "speech occurs at roughly 80 ms per phoneme" (Tallal & Piercy, 1973a, p. 396-7). The original data gathered by Tallal and her colleagues was with dysphasic (Specific Language Impairment or SLI) children rather than with dyslexic children. These language-impaired children were found to have difficulties in distinguishing brief (75 ms) high versus low tones when the stimuli were presented closely spaced in time. The same children were not impaired when the inter-stimulus intervals (ISIs) were longer (greater than 150 ms or 305 ms, depending on the study) or when the tones were longer (250 ms instead of 75 ms, see Tallal & Piercy, 1973a, b; Tallal & Piercy, 1974). Tallal and Piercy thus argued that impaired perception was "attributable solely to the brief duration of the discriminable components" (Tallal & Piercy, 1975, p. 69).

Similar perceptual deficits were then observed in 8 out of 20 dyslexic children (Tallal, 1980). These children were given only brief high and low tones (75 ms duration) separated in time by between 8 – 428 ms. A subgroup of the dyslexics made more errors than control children when the ISI was 305 ms or less. Theoretically, it was argued that dyslexic children might suffer from a "primary perceptual deficit that affects the rate at which they can process perceptual information" (Tallal, 1980, p. 193). It was argued that this deficit would affect literacy, because the ability to process "brief, rapidly successive acoustic cues within the tens of milliseconds [is] needed for optimal phoneme representation", and segmenting words into "sharply represented, discrete phonemes is critical" for learning letter-sound associations (Tallal, 2003). This theory has proved very appealing, because it proposed a simple link between an auditory processing deficit and a reading deficit, a link that depended on phonological representation. However, its reliance on representation at the phoneme level does not fit easily with the growing cross-language database, which suggests that phonemic representation is a consequence rather than a precursor of reading.

Furthermore, the notion that dyslexic children suffer from a deficit in detecting rapidly presented or rapidly changing auditory cues has been increasingly criticised (McArthur & Bishop, 2002; Mody, 2003; Rosen, 2003; for recent reviews). Tallal's initial findings, which all depended on the same group of 12 language impaired children, have been difficult to replicate, and studies that have found differences in her classic same-different judgement task have suffered from experimental designs employing non-adaptive procedures. This means that the number of trials administered around critical threshold regions have typically been small (De Weirdt, 1988; Reed, 1989; Heiervang, Stevenson & Hugdahl, 2002). Other studies have been beset by ceiling effects in control groups (Reed, 1989; De Martino, Espesser, Rey & Habib,

2001). Studdert-Kennedy and Mody (1995; see also Studdert-Kennedy, 2002) have reviewed task-related problems in interpreting existing data for Tallal's rapid processing deficit hypothesis, and they concluded that evidence for non-speech auditory processing deficits is extremely weak. Some studies that have found non-speech difficulties in dyslexic children report that difficulties extend to stimuli presented at long ISIs (e.g., Share, Jorm, MacLean & Matthews, 2002). Most seriously, group differences that are found in non-speech tasks frequently fail to account for independent variance in reading and spelling (Farmer & Klein, 1993; Heiervang, Stevenson & Hughdahl, 2002).

Auditory Processing of Cues Related to Rhythm Perception

Although cross-language studies have converged on the view that phoneme representation develops from letter learning, they have also converged on another conclusion. As discussed earlier, cross-language studies suggest that phonological representations prior to learning to read develop at the syllable and onset-rime (or body-coda) level, that is, at a grain size larger than the phoneme. Individual differences in identifying and recognising phonological similarities at these levels are predictive of reading (e.g., Bradley & Bryant, 1983; Lundberg, Olofsson & Wall, 1980; Hoien, Lundberg, Stanovich and Bjaalid, 1995; Schneider, Roth & Ennemoser, 2000). Hence if an important source of individual differences in phonological awareness is individual differences in auditory processing, we need to measure auditory cues that contribute to syllable and onset-rime representation.

The importance of rhythm and prosody for early language acquisition has already been mentioned. Rhythm is a complex acoustic percept. The auditory cues that are important for rhythm perception include the duration of sounds, their intensity, the depth of amplitude modulation, rise time (the rate of change of the amplitude modulation) and changes in fundamental frequency (pitch changes). Rise time is a particularly interesting cue, because rise time cues syllable isochronicity in all languages, irrespective of their rhythm type. For example, both English and Japanese adults produce syllables rhythmically by timing their speech output in terms of when maximal rise time occurs, even though Japanese is a mora-timed language whereas English is stress-timed (see Hoequist, 1983; also Bregman, 1993; Scott, 1998). Rise time is an aspect of syllable production and is thus expected to be universal (see Hoequist, 1983, who discusses this in terms of "perceptual centres"). Thus rise time could be one cue to speech rhythm that is universally important across languages for phonological representation, whether the languages follow an onset-rime division of the syllable or not.

Rise time is a supra-segmental cue that partially describes the structure of the amplitude envelope. The amplitude envelope is the pattern of amplitude modulation associated with speaking a particular word or phrase. For syllabic processing, temporal segmentation of the continuous acoustic signal is facilitated by particular patterns of amplitude modulation of that signal. An important cue to the syllable is the rate of change of the amplitude envelope at onset, that is, the rise time of the syllable. Rise time carries information about the vowel in any syllable (the vowel is the syllabic nucleus) and periodicity in speech is related to the onsets of the vowels in stressed syllables (Cutler & Mehler, 1993). It has been suggested that the "phonological grammar" of a particular language is built upon the characteristic rhythms of the language at the time scale of syllables (Port, 2003). The amplitude envelope is also important for speech intelligibility (Shannon, Zeng, Kamath, Wygonski & Ekelid, 1995). Perceptually, the onset of the envelope appears to be more important than what follows.

Recently, we have been exploring the role of rise time in phonological representation in children across languages. Our studies of rise time perception have focused on dyslexic children, because dyslexic children have well-documented problems in phonological awareness across languages. We have tried to find out whether dyslexic children have particular problems in perceiving rise time, and whether the severity of any difficulties that they might have are linked to the quality of their phonological representations. Our hypothesis was that individual differences in rise time sensitivity might make an important contribution to phonological representation, and eventually, literacy. The effect of a deficit in rise time perception is expected to affect setting up the phonological system from infancy onwards. To date, we have found that dyslexic children are significantly less sensitive to changes in rise time when compared to typically-developing children (Goswami, Thomson, Richardson, Stainthorp, Hughes, Rosen & Scott, 2002; Richardson, Thomson, Scott & Goswami, 2004). In all of our studies, individual differences in rise time perception have been strongly predictive of phonological awareness abilities, even when factors such as age, verbal and non-verbal I.Q. and vocabulary have been accounted for. For example, in our first study 25% of unique variance in reading and spelling was explained by rise time perception, even after age, vocabulary and non-verbal I.Q. had been controlled (Goswami et al., 2002, study 1). In our second study up to 22% of unique variance in phonological awareness was explained by rise time perception, even after age, vocabulary and verbal and non-verbal I.Q. had been controlled (Richardson et al., 2004). We have also studied precocious readers, who usually have exceptional phonological skills. These children appear to be significantly more sensitive to rise time changes than typically-developing controls (Goswami et al., 2002, study 2). A relative insensitivity to rise time cues in developmental dyslexia is also found in French children (Muneaux, Ziegler, Truc, Thomson & Goswami, 2004) and Hungarian children (Csépe, Surányi, Richardson, Thomson & Goswami, in preparation). This is intriguing, as French and Hungarian are syllable-timed languages, whereas English is a stress-timed language (i.e., the languages represent different rhythm types). Nevertheless, the same relationships between phonological awareness and rise time sensitivity have been found. This suggests that the acoustic cue of rise time plays an important role in the development of phonological representation, and consequently the acquisition of literacy, across languages.

Nevertheless, it is important to stress that rise time is not the only important rhythmic cue. We are also finding that duration perception is impaired in poor readers of English (Corriveau & Goswami, 2005; Richardson et al., 2004; see also Richardson et al. 2003 for a study of Finnish dyslexic children). In our studies to date, perception of the other rhythmic cues of intensity and pitch have generally been unimpaired. Interestingly, however, this is not the case for Swedish. In Swedish, intensity perception as well as rise time and duration perception plays a role in the development of phonological representations (Miller Guron & Goswami, 2005). Thus it is quite possible that the importance of different rhythmic cues to the development of phonological representation may differ depending on the language being studied. Clearly, an analysis of the relative importance of different acoustic cues to speech rhythm across languages would be very useful. Although I am aware of no such analysis, it could be used to inform studies attempting to relate acoustic processing in children to the development of phonological representations prior to literacy. Certainly, existing studies suggest that the scope of enquiry should be widened to acoustic cues that carry supra-segmental rather than purely segmental (phonemic) import.

CONCLUSION

Phonological representations are thought to develop from being fairly holistic in infancy to having segmental structure as language develops and as literacy is acquired. Across languages, experiments suggest that the phonological system is structured with respect to grain size prior to reading. In pre-readers, the grain size represented is relatively large, with children representing syllables, onsets, rimes or morae. Those children who then learn to read an alphabetic script (or a representational system like Zhuyin) develop phoneme awareness fairly rapidly once direct instruction commences. The rate of acquiring phoneme awareness varies systematically with the consistency of the orthography being acquired. Children learning to read alphabetic orthographies with a 1:1 mapping between letter and phoneme, and whose languages have a simple syllabic structure with a fairly limited phoneme repertoire, are most advantaged. Children learning to read alphabetic orthographies with a many:1 mapping between letter and phoneme, and whose languages have a complex syllabic structure with an extended phoneme repertoire usually take longer to acquire phoneme awareness. Individual differences within an orthography in the quality of the phonological representations developed seem to depend on auditory processing skills, particularly at the supra-segmental level.

REFERENCES

Baayen, R. H., Piepenbrock, R. & H. van Rijn, 1993. *The CELEX Lexical Database (CD-ROM)*, University of Pennsylvania, Philadelphia, PA: Linguistic Data Consortium.

Bradley, L. & P. E. Bryant. 1983. Categorizing sounds and learning to read – a causal connection. *Nature, 301*, 419–421.

Bregman, A. S. 1993. Auditory scene analysis: hearing in complex environments. In S. McAdams and E. Bigand (Eds.), *Thinking in sound: the cognitive psychology of human audition* (pp. 10–36). Oxford: Oxford University Press.

Bryant, P. E., Bradley, L., MacLean, M. & Crossland, J. 1989. Nursery rhymes, phonological skills and reading. *Journal of Child Language, 16*, 407–428.

Carroll, J. M., & Snowling, M. J. 2001. The effects of global similarity between stimuli on children's judgment of rime and alliteration. *Applied Psycholinguistics, 22*, 327–342.

Castles, A. & Coltheart, M. 2004. Is there a causal link from phonological awareness to success in learning to read? *Cognition, 91*, 77–111.

Chaney, C. 1992. Language Development, Metalinguistic Skills, and Print Awareness in 3-year-old Children. *Applied Psycholinguistics, 13*, 485–514.

Charles-Luce, J. & Luce, P. A. 1990. Similarity in Neighbourhoods of Words in Young Children's Lexicons. *Journal of Child Language, 17*, 205–215.

Coady, J. A. & Aslin, R. N. 2003. Phonological neighbourhoods in the developing lexicon. *Journal of Child Language, 30*, 441–469.

Content, A., Mousty, P., & Radeau, M. 1990. Brulex. Une base de données lexicales informatisée pour le français écrit et parlé. *Année Psychologique, 90*, 551–566.

Corriveau, K. & Goswami, U. 2005. *Rhythm Processing, Phonological Awareness, and Reading in Specific Language Impairment.* Poster presented at the Biennial Meeting of the Society for Research in Child Development, Atlanta, 7–10 April 2005.

Cossu, G., Shankweiler, D., Liberman, I. Y., Katz, L., & Tola, G. 1988. Awareness of phonological segments and reading ability in Italian children. *Applied Psycholinguistics, 9*, 1–16.

Csépe, V., Surányi, Z., Richardson, U., Thomson, J.M., & Goswami, U. (in preparation). *Sensitivity to Rhythmic Parameters in Dyslexic Children: A Comparison of Hungarian and English.*

Cutler, A. & Mehler, J. 1993. The periodicity bias. *Journal of Phonetics, 21*, 103–108.

De Cara, B., & Goswami, U. 2002. Statistical Analysis of Similarity Relations among Spoken Words: Evidence for the Special Status of Rimes in English. *Behavioural Research Methods and Instrumentation, 34*, 416–423.

De Cara, B., & Goswami, U. 2003. Phonological neighbourhood density effects in a rhyme awareness task in 5-year-old children. *Journal of Child Language, 30*, 695–710.

De Martino, S., Espesser, R., Rey, V., & Habib, M. 2001. The 'temporal processing deficit' hypothesis in dyslexia: New experimental evidence. *Brain and Cognition, 46*, 104–108.

Demont, E. & Gombert, J. E. 1996. Phonological Awareness as a Predictor of Recoding Skills and Syntactic Awareness as a Predictor of Comprehension Skills. *British Journal of Educational Psychology, 66*, 315–332.

De Weirdt, W. 1988. Speech Perception and frequency discrimination in good and poor readers. *Applied Psycholinguistics, 9*, 163–183.

Dollaghan, C. A. 1994. Children's phonological neighbourhoods: Half empty or half full? *Journal of Child Language, 21*, 237–271.

Durgunoglu, A. Y. & Oney, B. 1999. A Cross-linguistic Comparison of Phonological Awareness and Word Recognition. *Reading and Writing: An Interdisciplinary Journal, 11*, 281–299.

Eimas, P. D., Siqueland, E. R., Jusczyk, P. W. & Vigorito, J. 1971. Speech perception in infants. *Science, 171*, 303–306.

Farmer, M. E. & Klein, R. M. 1993. Auditory and visual temporal processing in dyslexic and normal readers: Temporal information processing in the nervous system: Special reference to dyslexia and dysphasia. *Annals of the New York Academy of Sciences, 68*, 339–341.

Ferguson, C. & Farwell, C. 1975. Words and sounds in early language acquisition. *Language, 51*, 419–439.

Fernald, A., Taeschner, T., Dunn, J., Papousek, M., de Boysson-Bardies, B. & Fukui, I. 1989. A cross-language study of prosodic modifications in mothers' and fathers' speech to preverbal infants. *Journal of Child Language, 16*, 477–501.

Garlock, V. M., Walley, A. C. & Metsala, J. L. 2001. Age-of-Acquisition, Word frequency and Neighbourhood Density Effects on Spoken Word Recognition by Children and Adults. *Journal of Memory and Language, 45*, 468–492.

Gombert, J. E. 1992. *Metalinguistic Development.* Hemel Hempstead, Herts: Havester Wheatsheaf.

Goswami, U., Ziegler, J., Dalton, L. & Schneider, W. 2001. Pseudohomophone effects and phonological recoding procedures in reading development in English and German. *Journal of Memory and Language, 45*, 648–664.

Goswami, U., Ziegler, J., Dalton, L. & Schneider, W. 2003. Nonword reading across orthographies: How flexible is the choice of reading units? *Applied Psycholinguistics, 24*, 235–248.

Goswami, U., Thomson, J., Richardson, U., Stainthorp, R., Hughes, D, Rosen, S. & Scott, S.K. 2002. Amplitude envelope onsets and developmental dyslexia: A new hypothesis. *Proceedings of the National Academy of Sciences, 99*, 10911–10916.

Harris, M., & Giannoulis, V. (1999). Learning to read and spell in Greek: The importance of letter knowledge and morphological awareness. In M. Harris & G. Hatano (Eds.), *Learning to Read and Write: A Cross-Linguistic Perspective* (pp. 51–70). Cambridge: Cambridge University Press.

Heiervang,E., Stevenson, J. & Hugdahl, K. 2002. Auditory processing in children with dyslexia. *Journal of Child Psychology and Psychiatry, 43*, 931–938.

Ho, C. S.-H., Bryant, P. 1997. Phonological skills are important in learning to read Chinese. *Developmental Psychology, 33*, 946–951.

Hoequist, C. 1983. The Perceptual Center and Rhythm Categories. *Language and Special, 26*, 367–376.

Hoien, T., Lundberg, I., Stanovich, K. E. & Bjaalid, I.-K. 1995. Components of Phonological Awareness. *Reading and Writing: An Interdisciplinary Journal, 7*, 171–188.

Huang, H. S. & Hanley, J. R. 1994. Phonological Awareness and Visual Skills in learning to Read Chinese and English. *Cognition, 54*, 73–98.

Inagaki K., Hatano, G. & Otake, T. 2000. The effect of Kana literacy acquisition on the speech segmentation unit used by Japanese young children. *Journal of Experimental Child Psychology, 75*, 70–91.

Jusczyk, P. W., Luce, P. A. & Charles-Luce, J. 1994. Infants' sensitivity to phonotactic patterns in the native language. *Journal of Memory and Language, 33*, 630–645.

Landauer, T. K. & Streeter, L. A. 1973. Structural differences between common and rare words: Failure of equivalence assumptions for theories of word recognition. *Journal of Verbal Learning and Verbal Behaviour, 12*, 119–131.

Landerl, K., Wimmer, H. & Frith, U. 1997. The impact of orthographic consistency on dyslexia: A German-English comparison. *Cognition, 63*, 315–334.

Lindblom, B. 1992. Phonological Units as Adaptive Emergents of Lexical Development. In Ferguson, C. A., Menn, L. & Stoel-Gammon, C. (Eds.), *Phonological Development: Models, Research, Implications*. Timonium, MD: York Press.

Luce, P. A. & Pisoni, D. B. 1998. Recognizing Spoken Words: The Neighborhood Activation Model. *Ear and Hearing, 19*, 1–36.

Lundberg, I., Olofsson, A. & Wall, S. 1980. Reading and spelling skills in the first school years predicted from phonemic awareness skills in kindergarten. *Scandinavian Journal of Psychology, 21*, 159–173.

McArthur, G. M. & Bishop, D. V. M. 2002. Event-related potentials reflect individual differences in age-invariant auditory skills. *Neuroreport, 13*, 1–4.

Menn, L. 1978. Phonological units in beginning speech. In Bell, A. & Hooper, J. B. (Eds.), *Syllables and segments*. Amsterdam: North-Holland Publishing Co.

Metsala, J. L. 1999. Young Children's Phonological Awareness and Nonword Repetition as a Function of Vocabulary Development. *Journal of Educational Psychology, 91*, 3–19.

Miller Guron, L., & Goswami, U. (2005). *Rhythm detection, phonological awareness and word reading in Swedish monolingual and bilingual children*. Poster presented at the Biennial Meeting of the Society for Research in Child Development, Atlanta, 7–10 April 2005.

Mody, M. 2003. Phonological basis in reading disability: A review and analysis of the evidence. *Reading and Writing: An Interdisciplinary Journal, 16*, 21–39.

Mody, M. 2003. Rapid auditory processing deficits in dyslexia: a commentary on two differing views. *Journal of Phonetics, 31*, 529–539.

Muneaux, M., Ziegler, J. C., Truc, C., Thomson, J. & Goswami, U. 2004. Deficits in beat perception and dyslexia: Evidence from French. *Neuroreport, 15*, 1–5.

Porpodas, C. D. 1999. Patterns of phonological and memory processing in beginning readers and spellers of Greek. *Journal of Learning Disabilities, 32*, 406–416.

Port, R. F. 2003. Meter and speech. *Journal of Phonetics, 31*, 599–611.

Reed, M. 1989. Speech perception and the discrimination of brief auditory cues in reading disabled children. *Journal of Experimental Child Psychology, 48*, 270–292.

Richardson, U., Leppänen, P. H. T., Leiwo, M. & Lyytinen, H. 2003. Speech perception of infants with high familial risk for dyslexia differ at the age of 6 months. *Developmental neuropsychology, 23*, 385–397.

Richardson, U., Thomson, J., Scott, S. K. & Goswami, U. 2004. Auditory Processing Skills and Phonological Representation in Dyslexic Children. *Dyslexia, 10*, 215–233.

Rosen, S. 2003. Auditory processing in dyslexia and specific language impairment: Is there a deficit? What is its nature? Does it explain anything? *Journal of Phonetics, 31*, 509–527.

Saffran, J. R., Newport, E. L., Aslin, R. N., Tunick, R. A. & Barrueco, S. 1997. Incidental language learning: Listening (and learning) out of the corner of your ear. *Psychological Science, 8*, 101–105.

Schneider, W., Roth, E. & Ennemoser, M. 2000. Training phonological skills and letter knowledge in children at risk for dyslexia: a comparison of three kindergarten intervention programs. *Journal of Educational Psychology, 92*, 284–295.

Schwartz, R.G. 1988. Phonological factors in early lexical acquisition. In M.D. Smith & J. Locke (Eds.). *The emergent lexicon: the child's development of a linguistic vocabulary.* New York: Academic Press.

Scott, S. K. 1998. The point of P-centres. *Psychological Research, 61*, 4–11.

Shannon, R.V., Zeng, F.-G., Kamath, V., Wygonski, J. & Ekelid, M. 1995. Speech Recognition with Primarily Temporal Cues. *Science, 270*, 303–304.

Share, D. L., Jorm, A. F., Maclean, R. & Matthews, R. 2002. Temporal Processing and Reading Disability. *Reading and Writing: An Interdisciplinary Journal, 15*, 151–178.

Siok, W. T. & Fletcher, P. 2001. The Role of Phonological Awareness and Visual-Orthographic Skills in Chinese Reading Acquisition. *Developmental Psychology, 37*, 886–899.

Stoel-Gammon, C. 1998. Sounds and words in early language acquisition: The relationship between lexical and phonological development. In R. Paul (Ed.), *Exploring the Speech-Language Connection* (pp. 25–52). Baltimore: Paul H. Brookes Publishing Co.

Storkel, H. L. 2001. Learning New Words: Phonotactic Probability in Language Development. *Journal of Speech and Language and Hearing Research, 44*, 1321–1337.

Studdert-Kennedy, M. & Mody, M. 1995. Auditory temporal perception deficits in the reading impaired: A critical review of the evidence. Psychonomic *Bulletin and Review, 2*, 508–514.

Studdert-Kennedy, M. 2002. Mirror neurons, vocal imitation and the evolution of particulate speech. In M. Stamenov & V. Gallese (Eds.), *Mirror Neurons and the Evolution of Brain and Language* (pp. 207–227). Amsterdam/Philadelphia: John Benjamins.

Swingley, D. & Aslin, R.N. 2000. Spoken word recognition and lexical representation in very young children. *Cognition, 76*, 147–166.

Swingley, D. & Aslin, R. N. 2002. Lexical neighborhoods and word-form representations of 14-month-olds. *Psychological Science, 13*, 480–484.

Tallal, P. & Piercy, M. 1973a. Defects of Non-Verbal Auditory Perception in Children with Developmental Aphasia. *Nature, 241*, 468–469.

Tallal, P. & Piercy, M. 1973b. Developmental Aphasia: Impaired Rate of Non-Verbal Processing as a Function of Sensory Modality. *Neuropsychologia, 11*, 389–398.

Tallal, P. & Piercy, M. 1974. Developmental Aphasia: Rate of Auditory Processing and Selective Impairment of Consonant Perception. *Neuropsychologia, 12*, 83–93.

Tallal, P. & Piercy, M. 1975. Developmental Aphasia: The Perception of Brief Vowels and Extended Stop Consonants. *Neuropsychologia, 13*, 69–74.

Tallal, P. 1980. Auditory temporal perception, phonics and reading disabilities in children. *Brain and Language, 9*, 182–198.

Tallal, P. & Fitch, R. 1993. Hormones and Cerebral Organization: Implications for the Development and Transmission of Language and Learning Disabilities. In A.M. Galaburda (Ed.), *Dyslexia and Development: Neurobiological Aspects of Extraordinary Brains*. Boston: Harvard University Press.

Tallal, P. 2003. Language Learning Disabilities: Integrating Reseach Approaches. *Current Directions in Psychological Science, 12*, 206–211.

Tamaoka, K. & Terao, Y. 2004. Mora or syllable? Which unit do Japanese use in naming visually presented stimuli? *Applied Psycholinguistics, 25*, 1–27.

Thomson, J., Richardson, U. & Goswami, U. (2005). The role of phonological similarity neighbourhoods in children's short-term memory: Comparing typically-developing children with children with dyslexia. *Memory and Cognition, 33*, 7, 1210–1219.

Treiman, R. & Breaux, A. M. 1982. Common phoneme and overall similarity relations among spoken syllabes: their use by children and adults. *Journal of Psycholinguistic Research, 11*, 581–610.

Tunmer, W. E. & Nesdale, A. R. 1985. Phonemic segmentation skill and beginning reading. *Journal of Educational Psychology, 77*, 417–427.

Vitevitch, M. S., Luce, P. A., Pisoni, D. B. & Auer, E. T. 1999. Phonotactics, neighborhood activation, and lexical access for spoken words. *Brain and Language, 68*, 306–311.

Walley, A. 1993. The role of vocabulary development in children's spoken word recognition and segmentation ability. *Developmental Review, 13*, 286–350.

Werker, J. F. & Tees, R. C. 1984. Cross-language speech perception: Evidence for perceptual reorganisation during the first year of life. *Infant Behaviour and Development, 7*, 46–63.

Wimmer, H., Landerl, K., Linortner, R. & Hummer, P. 1991. The relationship of phonemic awareness to reading acquisition: More consequence than precondition but still important. *Cognition, 40*, 219–249.

Wimmer, H., Landerl, K. & Schneider, W. 1994. The role of rhyme awareness of learning to read a regular orthography. *British Journal of Developmental Psychology, 12*, 469–484.

Yoon, H. K., Bolger, D. J., Kwon, O.-S. & Perfetti, C. A. 2002. Subsyllabic units in reading: A difference between Korean and English. In L. Verhoeven, C. Elbro & P. Reitsma (Eds.), *Precursors of Functional Literacy* (pp. 139–163). Amsterdam: John Benjamins.

Ziegler, J. C. & Goswami, U. 2005. Reading Acquisition, Developmental Dyslexia, and Skilled Reading Across Languages: A Psycholinguistic Grain Size Theory. *Psychological Bulletin, 131*, 3–29.

The Role of Morphology in Visual Word Recognition: Graded Semantic Influences Due to Competing Senses and Semantic Richness of the Stem

Laurie Beth Feldman
The University at Albany, State University of New York
Haskins Laboratories

Dana M. Basnight-Brown
The University at Albany, State University of New York
Haskins Laboratories

We describe several measures of whole word and morpheme frequency, markers to distinguish between holistic and more analytic processing, options of the dual route account for word recognition. Then we introduce a relatively new measure, the ratio of noun to verb stem frequency (e.g., TO HELP, THE HELP). This measure captures the competition between the noun and verb senses of the stem. We show that in addition to surface frequency of the whole word and frequency based on type or token counts on the stem, the noun-to-verb ratio provides a reliable measure of processing speed in a lexical decision task. We also examine the role of semantic richness of the stem. Verbs with regular and irregular past tense forms tend to differ along several dimensions of semantic richness, including number of associates. However, until recently, debates about whether regular and irregular verbs are recognized by analytic and holistic mechanisms respectively the same mechanism have failed to take semantic differences into account. We describe how, when richness is matched, the magnitudes of morphological facilitation in a cross modal primed lexical decision task for verbs with regular and irregular past tense forms differed by only a few milliseconds. Results failed to provide support for two independent processing routes. Noun-to-verb ratio and semantic richness are variables of special interest because they reflect properties of words that produce systematically graded effects in the lexical decision task, that dual route models of morphological processing fail to anticipate effects.

Language is structured at multiple levels. Sentences are composed of words, words are composed of meaningful constituents called *morphemes*, and morphemes are composed of letters or phonemes. In the domain of single word recognition, investigations into both phonological and morphological aspects of constituent structure have had to address similar issues, and the phonological and morphological models that have been proposed are analogous in many respects. In an alphabetic writing system, orthographic units correspond to phonological units, yet often there are ambiguities. There are one to many mappings between written units (graphemes) and phonology so that there can be many phonemic interpretations for a single grapheme. Compare for example the pronunciation of OW in ROW, COW, GOWN, OWN, and FOWL. Complementarily, there are many mappings from phonology back to form. For example note the many ways to write the sound that is common to EIGHT, GREAT, MATE, STRAIGHT and WAIT. With a few notable exceptions (e.g., Stone, Vanhoy, & Van Orden, 1997), models within the phonological domain of word recognition typically focus on the relation of written to spoken form rather than from spoken to written form. A common assumption is that there is an analytic processing option for words that are compositional and a second more holistic process for words that are irregular (e.g., Coltheart, Curtis, Atkins, & Haller, 1993; Coltheart, Rastle, Perry, Langdon, & Ziegler, 2001). The presence of a single letter whose mapping to a spoken form is not consistent with the most common mapping classifies a word as "irregular." In the dual route framework, neither the consequences of multiple atypical grapheme-phoneme mappings within a word nor complexities in the mapping from pronunciation back to written form are of interest.

Parallels arise at the level of morphemes, where units tend to have a typical meaning as well as a typical form (written and spoken) but there can be multiple mappings between written units and meaning. To elaborate, there are two basic classes of morphemes. Some function as affixes (either prefixes or suffixes) and others function as stems. Ambiguous mappings can reflect several functions for one morphemic affix (either inflectional or derivational) or several meanings for one morphemic stem. Compare the role of the affix "S" in HE LANDS, FOREIGN LANDS, LAND'S or of "ING" in WAS RUNNING or HIS RUNNING. In these examples, one affix can serve more than one function. Analogously, in the mapping from meaning back to form, there are many ways to form a noun from a verb as exemplified by the various affixes that form the nouns DEVELOPMENT, TERMINATION, DIVISION, CONSTITUENT, COLLECTIVE as well as LANDING. Ambiguity caused by one to many mappings from the stem to potential derived forms has not been a dominant focus of investigation in the domain of visual word recognition, however. Ambiguity also arises with respect to the meaning of the stem or root morpheme itself. Consider the many related meanings (senses) of the morpheme MARK listed in

Wordnet (Beckwith, Fellbaum, Gross, Miller, 1991; Fellbaum, 1998; Miller, 1990). These include: GRADE, SYMBOL, TARGET, VISIBLE INDICATION, IMPRESSION, STIGMA, UNIT OF MONEY, FOOL, SIGN, INDICATION OF DAMAGE, GOAL. Even when an affix is appended, the relevant sense of the stem cannot always be resolved by examining the whole word in isolation. For example MARKED could refer to GRADE, STIGMA, SIGN or several other senses. Traditional models of word recognition do not encompass semantic properties of the stem and generally ignore the affix.

DUAL ROUTE MODELS

Dual route models of word recognition within the morphological domain are analogous to the phonological models in that they include an analytic process for words that are compositional and a second more holistic option. Here, it is the relation of form to meaning that is either regular or irregular insofar as it can be described by a rule or not. If it cannot, recognition requires the secondary non-analytic backup option. Words are semantically transparent if the meaning of the whole word can be computed from that of its constituents. Words are opaque if the meaning of the whole cannot be computed from that of its components. Some complex word forms (e.g., ALLOWANCE) are opaque with respect to the meaning of the stem (e.g., ALLOW). Purportedly, recognition of these words requires the non-analytic processing option whereas recognition of transparent forms (e.g., ALLOWABLE) would not. In this example, the origins of irregularity are semantic and depend on whether the meaning of the whole word can be predicted from the meaning of its constituent morphemes. However, irregularity also can manifest itself with respect to the predictability of form. In the case of morphologically related word pairs such as RUN-RAN the past tense is not fully predictable is as contrasted with more typical past tense formations such as WALK-WALKED (Berent, Pinker, & Shimron, 2002; Pinker, 1991).

Stated generally, for morphological as well as phonological structure, traditional models define regularity in terms of a one-to one mapping between form and meaning or between written and spoken form. Even a single irregular mapping within a word invalidates the analytic route and forces non-analytic processing. Models that posit two processing options often are termed *parallel route* accounts, as typically the routes are characterized as functioning independently rather than cooperatively. For any given instance of recognition, only one process is responsible. The successful route may depend on surface frequency of the target, on the semantic contribution (transparency) of its stem to the meaning of the whole word (e.g., Feldman & Soltano, 1999), on whether the related prime is formed by inflection or by derivation (e.g., Raveh, 2000) as well as by the productivity of the affix (e.g., Laudanna & Burani, 1995) or stem (e.g., Feldman & Pastizzo, 2003).

In primed variants of the lexical decision task ("Is it a word?"), targets are preceded by a prime word. Changes in decision latencies when the prime word is morphologically related (e.g., WALKED-WALK), relative to unrelated (e.g., BELIEVED-WALK), define morphological facilitation. In the dual route framework, differences in the magnitude of facilitation are revealing about the route for recognition. Typically, the magnitude of facilitation is reduced when the morphologically related prime is high in frequency relative to when it is low. Accordingly, low but not higher frequency primes are recognized in terms of the analytic recognition option resulting in greater facilitation (Meunier & Segui, 1999). Similarly within this framework, attenuated facilitation for irregular (RAN) as contrasted with regular (WALKED) inflected relatives of the target indicates that regular forms are recognized in an analytic manner, while irregulars, are processed more holistically (e.g., Sonnenstuhl, Eisenbeiss, & Clahsen, 1999). Finally, semantically transparent relatives of the target (ALLOWABLE-ALLOW) produce more reliable facilitation than do opaque (ALLOWANCE-ALLOW) relatives (e.g., Feldman & Soltano, 1999). The dual route interpretation of the outcome is that transparent forms are decomposed into stem and affix and benefit from repeated access to the stem, whereas opaque forms are processed as wholes. Facilitation can arise between semantically transparent words because the base morpheme is activated in prime and in target or between whole words because they are semantically related (Marslen-Wilson, Tyler, Waksler & Older, 1994). For words that are not decomposable because they are not transparent, facilitation can arise only when whole forms are semantically related.

The dual route account can accomodate differences in the magnitude of facilitation can be accounted for only by "averaging" over trials. If some trials entail an analytic option and others use a holistic processing option then the average facilitation will be less than if all trials use the analytic option. Otherwise, there is no provision for systematic differences among morphologically related pairs with respect to the magnitude of facilitation that corresponds to variation in the degree of (meaning or form) similarity. Either the stem is activated by the prime and by the target or it is not. Further, an etymological criterion rarely contributes to the definition of morphological relatedness (Marslen-Wilson, et al., 1994). Normally, morphological relatedness is defined in terms of semantic similarity between pairs of words that are similar in form (e.g., DEPARTURE – DEPART but not DEPARTMENT - DEPART) (Marslen-Wilson et al., 1994). Importantly, because semantic effects necessarily signal whole word as contrasted with analytic processing, this class of models fails to predict effects that reflect semantic properties of the stem. For homographic stems like MUG (with senses related to MUGGING FOR THE CAMERA and A VICIOUS MUGGER as well as COFFEE MUGS) that are identical in orthographic form but are not morphologically related, semantic effects must arise between whole words.

Interference between affixed homographic stems (MUGGING-MUGGER) that differs from an effect of shared form (e.g., BITTEN-BITTER) provides evidence for semantic influences on *stem* processing. For example, in a lexical decision task, whether words are presented simultaneously or sequentially, facilitation can arise when word pairs are true morphological relatives, but inhibition can occur when word pairs are homographic or simply orthographically similar (Badecker & Allen, 2002; Laudanna, Badecker, & Caramazza, 1989; Orsolini & Marslen-Wilson, 1997). Inhibition between stems that share form but differ semantically and morphologically (e.g., BITTEN-BITTER), but not between words that are orthographically similar but fail to share a stem (e.g., BUTTER-BITTER), suggests that stems must be differentiated in the lexicon in order that they can compete (Badecker & Allen, 2002). However, all attempts to replicate inhibition between homographic stems have not succeeded (Carreiras, Perdomo, & Meseguer, 2005). Moreover, the original researchers have reported that the effect may arise for verb but not for noun stem targets (Laudanna, Voghere & Gazzellini, 2002). Analogous to the logic for homographic stems, other aspects of a stem's semantic richness (viz., multiple senses of the stem) should not affect the morphologically analytic processing option of the dual route account if the exclusive locus of semantic effects is the whole word.

SINGLE ROUTE MODELS BASED ON GRADED REGULARITY

An alternative approach to recognition posits distributed rather than localized patterns for each word and emphasizes the mapping between form (both orthographic and phonological) and meaning (Harm & Seidenberg, (2004); Plaut, McClelland, & Seidenberg, 1996; Seidenberg & McClelland, 1989). The underlying design principles include sensitivity to the statistical regularity of mappings between orthographic, phonological, and semantic codes and a cooperative division of labor between components. Harm and Seidenberg (2004) implemented such a model that incorporated mappings from both orthography to semantics (OS, analogous to the non-analytic route) and from orthography to phonology to semantics (OPS, analogous to the analytic route). In contrast to the more traditional class of models where activation does or does not occur, in these models distributed representations of meaning are partially activated by input from both routes in the course of recognizing a word. Moreover, the routes are not independent as the properties of each route depend on the other. Crucially there is a division of labor between the processing options; there is no dominant route and no back up option. Central to the framework is that ambiguity in the mapping of letters to phonemes is treated in a graded rather than an all-or-none manner. The emphasis is not on the presence or absence of regularity but rather on the degree of regularity among sequences of letters and their pronunciation in the word as a whole (Seidenberg & McClelland, 1989, 1990). For example, the phonological interpretation of the letters string -EAL is statistically more regular than that of –EAD as all words ending in EAL share a rhyme whereas only a portion of the EAD words do (e.g., BREAD, TREAD). Experimental evidence that controls for surface frequency, suggests that words such as BEAD are slower to recognize than words such as BEAT because the EAD sequence is not always pronounced in the same manner. It is in this way that the model accommodates graded effects of phonological ambiguity.

In the domain of morphology, a similar approach to word recognition is emerging. Researchers focus on the degree of regularity in the mapping of form to meaning implied by the presence of a shared sequence of letters and similar meaning. In essence, they focus on the degree of statistical regularity among sequences of letters and the meanings of the whole words that include that sequence. (Plaut & Gonnerman, 2000; Rueckl, Mikolinski, Raveh, Miner & Mars, 1997). Accordingly, a more common and therefore stronger mapping between form and meaning allows for the more rapid activation of a word's meaning and faster responses in word recognition tasks. Here, there are no rules for decomposition; processing is guided by statistical regularity that emerges over many patterns or words. In contrast to traditional accounts that are based on decomposition of complex word forms into their morphological constituents and rules that apply to some words but must be supplemented by a second, non-decompositional mechanism for others, here there is a single mechanism. Crucially, graded effects are anticipated based on partial activation and on the strength of the mapping between form and meaning.

In a priming task for example, where targets repeat across prime types and prime processing time is adequate for semantic analysis, primes related by derivation to the target such as WALKER-WALK produce attenuated facilitation relative to primes related by inflection to the same target such as WALKED-WALK (Feldman & Raveh, 2003; Raveh, 2000). This arises because derivations tend to be less similar in meaning to their stem morpheme than are inflections. Likewise, irregular inflections like RUN-RAN are less similar in form to their stem morpheme than are regulars like WALKED-WALK, therefore they produce magnitudes of facilitation that are reduced relative to regulars (Feldman, Rueckl, Pastizzo, Diliberto & Vellutino, 2002; Rueckl & Gallantucci, 2005; Rueckl et al., 1997). In single route accounts based on the statistical regularity and the strength of the mapping between form and meaning, degree of prime-target overlap with respect to meaning and to form can influence the magnitude of facilitation.

GRADED DIFFERENCES ACROSS WORD TYPES

Differences due to the systematicity of form-meaning mappings have been observed across words. *Morphological family size* captures one way that the mappings between form and meaning can vary. Family size is based on the number of different derived and compound words that share a base morpheme (Schreuder & Baayen, 1997). For example, MARKER, REMARK, MARKUP, as well as BOOKMARK and TRADEMARK are members of the MARK morphological family. When many words are formed from the same stem, they share a large morphological family and the mapping is strong. When fewer words are formed from a stem the mapping is weaker. There is evidence that both the strength of the correspondence between form and meaning measured over the whole morphological family as well as the orthographic and semantic similarity between a particular prime and its target can influence the magnitude of facilitation. All else being equal, words with large morphological families are recognized faster than those with small families (de Jong, Feldman, Schreuder, Pastizzo & Baayen, 2002; de Jong, Schreuder & Baayen, 2000). However, some word forms within a morphological family are semantically less well specified or ambiguous and this can influence the magnitude of morphological facilitation as well (Feldman & Pastizzo, 2004).

The *noun to verb ratio* of the stem refers to the frequency with which a stem functions as a noun and as a verb. Words vary with respect to word class ambiguity of the stem morpheme (e.g., TO HELP, THE HELP) which relates to its number of Wordnet senses (Beckwith, Fellbaum, Gross, Miller, 1991; Fellbaum, 1998; Miller, 1990). The verb reading allows senses such as GIVE AID, BE OF USE, IMPROVE, SERVE, AVAIL as contrasted with the noun senses of AID, SERVICE, ASSISTANT. In addition, words vary with respect to semantic measures based on the number of semantic associates. Their interconnections or connectivity also play a role (Nelson, McEvoy & Schreiber, 1998). For example, HELP has high connectivity as it has 23 associates, including ME, AID, HURT, TROUBLE, and DANGER. The influence of these and of other measures of semantic richness of the stem on single word recognition latencies has been documented (for an overview see Baayen, Feldman & Schreuder, 2005). Note that all are graded variables, compatible with variation in the strength of mappings between form and meaning. Of particular interest is that stems of regular and irregular verbs tend to differ on a host of semantic (as well as form) measures. Semantic differences between regular and irregular verbs have been observed in three Germanic languages including English, and their influence on performance has been documented in a variety of word recognition tasks (Baayen & del Prado Martín, 2005; Tabak, Schreuder & Baayen, 2005).

The role of semantically graded variables in morphological processing provides the focus of the remaining, more experimental, portion of this chapter. In the next section we describe some of the experimental effects of surface frequency, various measures of morpheme frequency and morphological family size. We then summarize some new evidence of an inhibitory relation between alternative (i.e., noun vs. verb) readings of morphologically ambiguous stems, delineate how that measure complements the more traditional measures of surface and base morpheme frequency, and describe how it poses a challenge to an account whereby effects of meaning arise only at the whole word level. We then verify this inhibitory morphological effect under several experimental conditions (intended to bias one of the two readings). To anticipate, because performance in the lexical decision task can be predicted from the (natural log) *ratio* of noun to verb stem frequency when effects of *total* stem frequency have been accounted for, the implication is that there is a semantically based organization among inflected words formed from a stem. Here, bivalent word class of the stem is treated as a manipulation on the number and distribution of senses. Any differences between nouns and verbs with respect to thematic roles for their arguments are beyond the present scope. Instead, we focus on semantics while acknowledging that semantic and syntactic properties are interrelated.

Finally, in the last section of the chapter, we use a variant of the priming task to demonstrate effects of a target's richness of meaning. To anticipate, we demonstrate that semantic differences among targets provide an alternative interpretation for some of the differences between regularly and irregularly inflected verb forms that arise in a priming task. Throughout the chapter, the unifying theme is graded semantic effects that fail to support an account of morphological processing based on two competing mechanisms, one of which is analytic and operates at the sublexical level and a second of which is holistic and operates at a whole word (lexical and semantic) level.

MEASURE OF FREQUENCY: WHOLE WORD AND STEM

One of the most robust findings in the word recognition literature is that frequency influences the efficiency with which units are processed. Units can be defined with respect to whole words or their morphemic constituents and processing can be defined with respect to a variety of experimental tasks of which lexical decision and naming aloud are foremost. Many experimental studies have focused on whole word frequency in print and have demonstrated that, in the lexical decision task, decision latencies decrease as frequency of a particular word form increases (e.g., Balota & Chumbly, 1984; Forster & Chambers, 1973).

The primary tools used to evaluate componential and whole word contributions to word recognition are based on the frequency of various units. Effects of whole word surface frequency are interpreted to reflect processing at the level of the whole word (lexical processing), while effects of total stem frequency (frequency of stem and inflectional forms) typically provide a window into sublexical processing by relying on the breakdown of words into their morphemic components (Bertram, et al., 2000). As described above, whole word and analytic processes have been viewed as alternative and even competing processes where regular words (e.g., RUNNING) can be recognized by either option, but irregular words (e.g., RAN) must be recognized as wholes (Bergman, Hudson & Eling, 1988; Caramazza, Laudanna & Romani, 1988; Laudanna & Burani, 1995; Schreuder & Baayen, 1995; Schreuder, Burani & Baayen, 2003; Wurm & Aycock, 2003). In this dual-route framework, the emphasis is on units of varying size (word vs. morpheme) where, to reiterate, effects of meaning are assumed to arise at the whole word level (e.g., Rastle, Davis & New, 2004).

In the morphological domain of word recognition, there are several measures of morpheme frequency that have been documented, all of which index the strength of the correspondence between a sequence of letters (or phonemes) and meaning based on the number or on the frequency of the words that share a particular morpheme (morphological relatives). Not surprisingly, measures tend to be intercorrelated, although some are *token based* in that they consider the frequency of the various related forms while others are *type based* in that they consider only the number of different related forms. For example, the words MARKER, MARKUP, BOOKMARK, POSTMARK and REMARK as well as the words MARKS, MARKED and MARKING all contain the (relatively frequent) base morpheme MARK. Latencies in the lexical decision task typically reflect not only the frequency of a particular target word (surface frequency) such as MARKUP, but also the influence of other existing words (e.g., MARKER) formed from the same base morpheme or stem (see Table 5.1).

One measure of morphological frequency is *stem morpheme frequency*, defined as the total frequency of the stem and all its inflectional forms (e.g., LAND, LANDS, LANDED, and LANDING). When words have similar surface frequencies, but differ with respect to the frequency of their base morpheme (cumulative or stem frequency), decision latencies decrease as base frequency increases (Taft, 1979). For example, the inflected words SIZED and RAKED each have surface frequencies of 4 but base frequencies that are very different, 154 (SIZE, SIZES, SIZED, SIZING) and 15 (RAKE, RAKES, RAKED, RAKING), respectively. In an unprimed lexical decision task, Taft (1979) used words of this type (surface frequency was matched, but the base frequency was either high or low) to examine whether base frequency was important in word recognition. The results revealed that words with higher base frequency were recognized significantly faster than those with a lower base frequency. However, in the same study, Taft (1979) conducted an additional experiment that

TABLE 5.1
Frequency Measures for Mark

Form	Surface Frequency	Lemma Frequency	Lemma Total
Mark (verb)	296		
Marks	65		
Marked	420		
Marking	98		
	Σ 879	879	
Mark (noun)	533		
Marks	452		
	Σ 985	985	1864
Marking	39		
Markings	43		
	Σ 82	82	82
Bookmark	5	5	
Marker	37	67	
Markup	N/A	N/A	
Postmark	4	6	
Remark (noun)	341	700	
Remark (verb)	108	552	
Remarkable	678	678	
Trademark	14	20	

examined inflected forms matched on base frequency but not on surface frequency (e.g., THINGS and WORLDS). Results indicated that inflected words with high surface frequency were recognized faster than those with low surface frequency, suggesting that this frequency measure also is important in the word recognition process. Evidently, both dimensions of frequency can play a role in word recognition in English (Taft, 1979). Where there is less consensus is whether the measures are mutually exclusive such that evidence of one can be interpreted as evidence that the other plays no role.

The relevance of surface and base morpheme frequency is not uniform over word types, however. A study by Baayen, Dijkstra, and Schreuder (1997) reported that response latencies to singular words in Dutch that appear more commonly in a plural form are determined by the stem (or base) frequency of words inflected from the base morpheme, whereas latencies to the plural form of those same words are generally determined by surface frequency. For Dutch nouns whose plural is very frequent (SCISSORS, EYES), decision latencies reflect the frequency of the plural form, while decision latencies for lower frequency plural nouns (NEEDLES, EARS) typically reflect stem frequency. In the original studies, the authors concluded that when plural nouns are lower in frequency than their singulars, they are processed in terms of their base morpheme but when plural nouns are higher in frequency than their singulars, they are processed as an unanalyzed form. Similar results have been observed in English and in French (New, Brysbaert, Segui, Ferrand & Rastle, 2001). To reiterate, the underlying assumption is that whole typically and stem morpheme processing work competitively rather than cooperatively and that at any one time only one measure of frequency is responsible for recognition.

A second morphological measure is *family size* (Schreuder & Baayen, 1997), a type-based measure that captures the number of different derived and compound words formed from a base morpheme. Some words like MARK have very large morphological families. In the case of MARK, there are 44 members if we include compounds as well as base morpheme and affix combinations. Other words have much smaller morphological families. For example, the family of CRY includes only 2 members, CRIER and OUTCRY.

A third and related morphological measure is *cumulative family frequency* (Schreuder & Baayen 1997), a token-based measure that refers to the summed frequency of all the different polymorphemic words that share a base morpheme. For example, the summed frequency of MARKER (37), REMARK (341), MARKUP (0), as well as BOOKMARK (5) and the other family members ·omprise the cumulative family frequency of MARK (see Table 5.1).

When surface frequency is controlled, decision latencies for single words are faster for targets composed of a base morpheme that recurs in many words and therefore has a large morphological family size as compared with targets whose base morpheme forms relatively few words (de Jong et al., 2000; de Jong et al., 2002). A facilitatory effect of family size on latencies in an unprimed lexical decision task has been documented in a range of languages (Baayen et al., 1997; Bertram, Baayen, & Schreuder, 2000; Ford, Marslen-Wilson, & Davis, 2003; Moscoso del Prado Martín, 2003; Moscoso del Prado Martín, Bertram, Häikiö Schreuder, & Baayen, in press). Similarly, when word targets appear in isolation in a word recognition task, high token frequency based on the summed frequency of all word tokens derived from the stem can influence decision latencies (Colé, Beauvillain & Segui, 1989).

It is common practice among researchers to manipulate morpheme-based or word-based frequency and interpret the presence of a significant difference as evidence for either analytic or more holistic processing. More recent results based on regression rather than factorial techniques suggest that, in general, a dichotomous conceptualization of variables may be overly simplistic and that processing options are not independent and mutually exclusive as once envisioned (Baayen, 2004; Moscoso del Prado Martín & Baayen, 2005). With respect to cumulative frequency of family members and family size, two highly related measures, it is very difficult and even "ill-advised" (see Baayen, 2004) to manipulate one while holding the other constant. In fact, a regression-based analysis that combines type based measures including morphological family size and token based measures sensitive to the distribution of token-frequency across derived members of the morphological family has revealed an inhibitory effect of stem frequency that serves as a correction once facilitatory effects of family size have been accounted for (Moscoso del Prado Martín, Kostić & Baayen, 2004, see also Baayen, Tweedie & Schreuder, 2002). Further, regression-based analyses show that significant effects of *both* surface and stem frequency measures often manifest themselves in the *same* experimental contexts. These include both the lexical decision and the naming tasks with both visual and auditory presentations of lower frequency words (Wurm & Baayen, 2005).

Concurrent effects of surface and morpheme frequency are more easily accommodated by a single route account than by independent routs (Plaut & Gonnerman, 2000; Rueckl, Mikolinski, Raveh, Miner & Mars, 1997). Accordingly, the emphasis is on mappings between form and meaning and their systematicity rather than the potential for decomposition of a complex word into stem and affix. Hence, morphological family size and other morpheme-based frequency measures capture the mappings between form and meaning and a stronger mapping allows for faster responses in word recognition tasks. A less systematic mapping, more complex semantics, slows access to meaning.

SEMANTIC PROPERTIES OF THE STEM

The underlying assumption of the traditional dual route account is that the success of a processing route depends on the presence or absence of a predictable complex form and of its decomposability. Recognition of irregular inflections and opaque derivations require an association between stored whole forms that is distinct from the rule-based processing that applies for predictable inflected forms. Essentially, as long as the form is predictable, in that it follows a rule, and its meaning is predictable, in that it can be generated from its components so that it is semantically transparent, the word can be analyzed into its components and recognition latencies should be related to stem frequency.

An inherent problem, however, is that semantic transparency varies not only between words but also across various senses of a word. In fact, many words have multiple senses and some senses of the stem are retained more transparently than others. Thus, transparency can vary across members within a family. The implication is that semantic transparency cannot be treated as present or absent as it is not an all-or-none property. Of the many senses of the morpheme MARK listed in Wordnet (Beckwith, et al., 1991; Fellbaum, 1998; Miller, 1990), for example, a form like MARKING captures the SIGN and the GRADE senses of MARK whereas MARKED could just as readily refer to the IMPRESSION, STIGMA or FOOL senses.

The logic delineated above implies that, to the extent that the meaning of the stem morpheme is transparent in complex prime words, morpheme frequency should be a stronger and more reliable predictor of decision latencies than surface frequency. Conversely, semantic complexity due to the potential for multiple senses may compromise effects of stem frequencies. In addition, there is a second factor that diminishes the potential for analysis of morphological constituents. Bertram, Laine, Baayen, Schreuder, and Hyona (2000) have reported that in Finnish the potential for a single affix to have multiple functions may enhance whole word processing.

In English, an argument can be made that all verb affixes are functionally ambiguous. For example, in MARKS the affix S can be the present tense singular verbal inflection ("HE MARKS") or the nominal marker for plural ("MANY MARKS"); in MARKED the affix ED can be the past participle verbal inflection ("HE HAD MARKED"), past tense ("HE MARKED"), or an adjective ("DILIGENTLY MARKED"). Finally, in MARKING the affix ING can be the present progressive verbal inflection ("HE IS MARKING") or the noun derived from a verb ("MANY MARKINGS"). Consistent with the argument of Bertram and his colleagues, because of affix ambiguity, decision latencies for ING forms should correlate more strongly with measures based on surface frequency than with measures based on the cumulative frequency of the inflected forms generated from a base morpheme.

Items like MARKING pose an interesting problem because not only the stem but also the complete from are ambiguous and have multiple senses. There is evidence that the noun and verb senses of ING forms can compete in the course of word recognition even though the meanings are generally semantically related. Readers have a tendency to interpret all ING affixed stems as verbs as if they follow a rule about the suffix. However, any language-general tendency may be complemented by a pattern of usage for specific ING forms. Accordingly, the relative dominance of noun-based usage and verb-based usage for each ING form becomes critical. Beyond any word-praticular frequency-based processing bias that we can doucument, we asked whether the relation between frequency and recognition latencies can be altered either by experimental context (viz., the presence of many other word forms from the same word class) or by a prime (viz., a funtion word prime that precedes the ING target) the potentially biases one reading over another. If there is a bias due to the relative dominance of the noun-based usage versus the verb-based usage, and if it recurs over various experimental contexts, then it suggests a sensitivity to the relative dominance of senses compatible with one word class over the other, a sensitivity that cannot be altered by a late acting selection mechanism (cf Badecker & Allen, 2002). It it fails to recur, the context can shift the bias.

THE INFLUENCE OF STEM AND WHOLE WORD FREQUENCY ON MORPHOLOGICALLY AMBIGUOUS WORDS

In one study, we asked whether various frequency measures predicted latencies to stem and affix ambiguous ING forms in a visual lexical decision task (Feldman & Pastizzo, 2004). We focused on ING- affixed words that were ambiguous in that the same form permitted both a nominal and a verbal interpretation but ignored any potential differences in patterns of occurrence (whether it appeared more frequently as a noun or more frequently as a verb) for ING forms of nouns and verbs in spoken and written texts (Baayen, Feldman & Schreuder, 2005). Words were selected if the stem could be both a noun and a verb (e.g., TO/THE MARK) and if the ING functioned both as a noun and a verb (WAS/THE MARKING). In all cases both the nominal and verbal readings could be semantically transparent with respect to the base morpheme. We estimated the likelihood of both the nominal and verbal readings (surface frequency) and their total stem frequency (lemma frequencies) based on inflected forms. Counts for nominal and verbal frequency for stems tend to be highly correlated, therefore the natural log (ln) of the ratio of nominal to verbal frequency was our frequency variable of primary interest. In addition, we included the more conventional measures of total stem frequency based on all (inflected and uninflected) forms of the stem, which is the conventional marker for analytic processing, as well as total surface frequency of the noun and verb readings of the stem + ING form. To anticipate, as long as the ln ratio of nominal to verbal lemma frequency is not highly correlated with total stem frequency, it can be entered into a regression equation along with the other frequency measures without introducing excessive error due to increased collinearity. In addition to reporting measures based on correlation, we include a manipulation of experimental context and compare words like LANDING, that are more frequent as nouns than as verbs, and words like HELPING that are more frequent as verbs than as nouns.

In each experiment, non-word targets were created to mimic the structure of the word targets (e.g., SILKING). Targets were classified as noun or verb dominant based on the N/V stem frequency ratio. They appeared with filler words (Exp.1a) that were either mixed with respect to word class (nouns, verbs and adjectives) or only nouns (Exp.1b). Results in the unprimed lexical decision task when fillers included equal numbers of nouns, verbs, and adjectives indicated that latencies were faster overall for verb dominant forms (599 ms) than for noun dominant forms (638 ms). Any interpretation of this outcome should take into account the fact that surface frequencies were higher overall for the verb dominant forms. (Note that total stem frequencies were not uniformly higher for the verb dominant forms however.) Correlational analyses based on item means revealed that decision latencies were negatively correlated with total stem frequency based on the sum of the noun and verb stem frequencies [r (37) = -.39, p < .02]. These frequencies are described as the frequency with which a word stem (such as LAND) occurs as a verb and as a noun. Therefore, a stem such as LAND would have one frequency when it occurs as a noun and a second frequency when it is used as a verb. More interestingly, as the ratio between a word's frequency based on nominal ING and on verbal ING increased, response latencies in the visual lexical decision task also increased [r (37) = .45, p < .005]. That is, words ending in functionally ING whose stems occur predominantly as nouns elicited longer decision latencies than did words whose stems occur predominantly as verbs. The more the stem of an ING form is used as a noun as compared to as a verb, the more slowing it incurred. The correlation was slightly stronger and more significant when we partialled for total frequency of the stem [r (36) = .52, p < .001]. Similarly, when we altered the composition of filler items, the ratio of noun to verb frequency and decision latency [r (37) = .35, p < .03] as well as the total surface frequency [r 37) = -.40, p < .01] were significantly correlated with decision latencies. Again, its explanatory potential strengthened slightly when we partialled for total stem freq [r (36) = .42, p < .01]. Results in the unprimed lexical decision task when fillers included only nouns were almost identical except that latencies were slower overall. Importantly, in neither study was a ratio of (whole word) surface frequencies a significant predictor of decision latencies tobivalent ING forms. Measures based on frequencies and latencies are summarized in Tables 5.2 and 5.3 respectively.

TABLE 5.2
Properties of Verb and Noun Dominant Targets

	Dominance	
	Verb-Dominant Helping	Noun-Dominant Landing
Verb stem	3607	548
Noun stem	403	5535
Total stem	4282	6083
ING verb surface	345	67
ING noun surface	179	92
Ratio lemma N-V (ln)	−2.70	2.38
Ratio surface N-V (ln)	−1.19	0.74

TABLE 5.3
Item Means for Experiments 1 and 2

	Filler Context	
	Mixed (Exp. 1a)	Nouns (Exp. 1b)
Verb dominant	599 (44)	694 (54)
Noun dominant	638 (56)	746 (67)

	Prime (SOA 150 ms)		
	the	was	and
Verb dominant	661 (52)	661 (58)	654 (56)
Noun dominant	681 (25)	703 (46)	698 (42)

In a second experiment, we asked whether we could bias the reading of an ambiguous morphologically complex form by manipulating its priming context so as to eliminate the inhibitory relation between the noun stem and the verb stem. Primes consisted of the following three function words: THE, WAS, and AND. We hypothesized that the THE prime would bias the word to be processed as a noun, the WAS prime would bias verb processing, and that the AND prime, which is less distinct with respect to the context in which it appears, would serve as a more neutral prime. If all targets are equally influenced by a prime then latencies may change across priming contexts but will fail to show an interaction with stem dominance. In addition we ask whether correlations between latency and frequency ratio arise in prime contexts.

As anticipated based on targets that appeared without primes, results from item analyses indicated that decision latencies for verb dominant forms were faster than those for noun dominant forms in all prime contexts. There was a main effect of noun vs. verb dominance and, although the pattern of means was suggestive, the relation between noun and verb dominant forms failed to interact reliably with prime context (See Table 5.3). Further, there was no significant correlation between decision latencies and ratios based on noun and verb frequency.

In summary, for ING forms whose stems and affixes are functionally ambiguous in that they can be regular inflected verb forms or nouns derived from a verb, total stem frequency of all inflected forms did not reliably predict decision latencies in the lexical decision task. These results replicated in English what has been reported in the Finnish language when nouns and their inflected plural forms were matched on surface frequency, and base frequency was manipulated factorially (Bertram et al., 2000). Most novel, however, was that a measure based on a ratio of noun and verb stem frequencies correlated reliably with unprimed decision latencies. When surface frequency is controlled, words ending in ING whose stems occur more frequently as nouns than as verbs tend to be slower than those where the form functions more frequently as a verb.

Collectively, the implication is that the absence of a correlation between decision latencies and total stem frequency provides a very weak founation on which to claim that ambiguous forms must be represented as whole (Bertram et al. 2000). Here there was structuring among words that share a morphological stem. It seems that the noun senses and the verb senses are differentiated in the mapping of form to meaning or perhaps that the noun senses and the verb senses provide the basis for separate clusters. Moreover if, depending on its frequency, the noun cluster can offset the typical benefit that accrues for frequent verb readings then we have evidence of a competitive organization within the clustering of words formed from the noun and the verb stem. In essence, our failure to detect an effect of total stem frequency appears to reflect a semantic organization among stem forms. It cannot easily be attributed to differences in frequency devoid of semantics. Finally, while stem noun to verb ratio was a good predictor in noun and mixed filler contexts, the presence of a prime, and it did not matter which, was sufficient to offset the effect. The pattern of differences and, absences of the possibility of a mechanism that can bias selection to either a noun or verb reading.

THE PROCESSING OF IRREGULAR AND REGULAR VERB FORMS

The processing of irregular verbs has been an area of extensive debate in the study of morphological processing (Plunkett & Juola, 1999; Rumelhart & McClelland, 1986). As noted above, some researchers have interpreted differences between regular and irregular forms as support for a dual route architecture with two competing mechanisms (e.g., Frost et al., 2000). Others have argued that all verbs are processed by a single mechanism that is highly sensitive to statistical properties of form and meanin (Rueckl & Galantucci, 2005; Rueckl et al., 1997).

One conventional method to evaluate morphological processing in general and the decompositional status of inflected forms in particular is to compare the differences in primed target decision latencies after morphologically related as compared to unrelated primes (e.g., Sonnenstuhl et al., 1999; Stanners, Neiser, Hernon, & Hall, 1979;

Stolz & Feldman, 1995). When regular and irregular morphological relatives produce similar patterns of facilitation to the target in a lexical decision task it is difficult to argue that regular and irregular morphological relatives differ with respect to
the role of decomposition to the stem or analytic processing. When regular and
irregular morphological relatives differ with respect to the magnitude of morphological facilitation or when regular but not irregular primes produce facilitation,
however, the pattern is consistent with two processing mechanisms. Significant
morphological facilitation due to repetition of the verbal pattern has been documented in Hebrew for verbs with regular roots but not for verbs with weak roots
(Frost, Deutsch, & Forster, 2000; Velan, Frost, Deutsch, & Plaut, 2005) that cannot
be decomposed. Likewise in German cross-modal facilitation due to repetition of a
stem arises for regular but not irregular verb forms (Sonnenstuhl et al., 1999). In
English, cross modal as well as masked facilitation have been documented for
WALKED-WALK but not for DUG-DIG type pairs (Allen & Badecker, 1999; 2002;
Badecker & Allen, 2002; Marslen-Wilson, Hare & Older, 1995). Patterns of facilitation that vary with irregularity have been reported in Italian (Orsolini & Marslen-
Wilson, 1997) and in French (Meunier & Marslen-Wilson, 2005) as well. Similarly,
other tasks reveal differences consistent with a dual route architecture. Judgments
about irregular, but not regular, inflected forms by native speakers of Hebrew are
sensitive to orthographic similarity with other lexical entries that are stored as whole
forms in the lexicon (Berent, Pinker, & Shimron, 1999, 2002).

One popular variant of the priming methodology for measuring the impact of
morphologically related primes on their targets is Forster and Davis' (1984) forward
masked priming variant of the lexical decision task (e.g., Forster & Azuma, 2000;
Masson & Isaak, 1999; Tsapkini, Kehayia, & Jarema, 1999). In this procedure, a
mask of hash marks (#####) appears for 500 milliseconds (ms) after which a prime
appears for a duration that ranges between 40 and 60 ms after which the target
appears. Primes appear in lowercase letters. Targets appear in uppercase letters
immediately after the prime. The change in letter case together with superposition
of the target on the prime serves to backward mask the prime. On most trials, all
participants report no awareness of the prime so that it is unlikely that priming
effects are confounded with conscious processes (Forster, 1999). The advantage for
morphologically related pairs relative to orthographic controls purportedly reflects
activation of morphologically decomposed lexical entries (for a review, see Deutsch,
Frost & Forster, 1998).

COMPARISONS OF IRREGULAR AND REGULAR VERB FORMS
WHEN MEASURES OF FORM SEMANTIC RICHNESS ARE CONTROLLED

Pastizzo and Feldman (2002) compared morphological facilitation for regular and
two types of irregular past tense inflected forms in English. They matched target
types for frequency and number of orthographic neighbors and paired each target
with orthographically similar and morphologically related primes matched with
respect to length and number of overlapping letters with the target. Among irregular inflected forms, they contrasted items such as *fell* that overlap more with their

uninflected stem (e.g., *fall*) than do items such as *taught* with their uninflected stem *teach*. In that study, forward masked priming results with native speakers revealed that recognition of HATCH type items was slower and more prone to error when compared with either type of irregular past tense formations (Pastizzo & Feldman, 2002). Worthy of note was that post hoc analyses revealed baseline differences between verb types (HATCH, FALL, TEACH) that correlated with measures of semantic richness. Nonetheless, relative to a baseline matched for letter overlap, morphologically related primes significantly reduced response latencies for *hatched-HATCH* type items as well as *fell-FALL* type pairs, whereas *taught-TEACH* type irregular items (with less letter overlap) failed to reveal facilitation.

Differences in degree of form similarity between regular and irregular past tense-presence tense pairs are well studied, whereas semantic differences are not. Two recent studies report that regulars and irregulars may differ semantically as well. Ramscar (2002) manipulated sentence context and showed that when participants encounter a nonsense verb such as FRINK or SPRINK in a context compatible with drinking, they tend to respond with an irregular past tense form (FRANK or SPRANK) more often than they do in a WINK or BLINK context where FRINKED or SPRINKED are more typical. The author argued that irregular past tense formations are not independent of semantics. This finding is consistent with corpus based evidence (Baayen & Moscoso del Prado Martín, 2005) showing that irregular forms tend to have richer and more extensive clusterings with associated words than do regular forms. An examination of lexical statistics reveals that not only do irregular verbs tend to have more associates than do regular verbs but that many more of those semantic neighbors are morphologically related. In addition, effects of semantic richness covary with regularity in unprimed visual lexical decision and naming latencies (Baayen and Moscoso del Prado Martín, 2005).

Recently we have ascertained that effects of semantic richness arise in the lexical decision task as well. When primes are auditory and targets are visual, we asked whether regular and irregular verb forms are processed differently when dimensions of semantic richness are controlled. In our cross-modal study, two types of irregular verb target words and two types of regular verb target words were preceded by either a related prime or an unrelated prime that was matched to the related prime word on frequency, length, and initial phoneme. Irregular verb forms included nested forms (*grown*-GROW) as well as irregular change forms (*run*-RAN). Regular verbs varied with respect to their resonance level (Nelson et al., 1998). This is a measure of semantic richness based on the number of semantic associates and the associations among them. Because regular and irregular verbs tend to differ on a host of semantic dimensions, (Baayen & Moscoso del Prado Martín, 2005) we asked whether some of the differences in facilitation attributed to regularity in primed lexical decision could reflect semantic differences among verbs. Therefore, we manipulated semantic richness so that some regular verbs had a higher resonance (*kissed*-KISS) than did others (*cooked*-COOK). We presented verb targets (KISS, COOK) after morphologically related and unrelated primes. Nonwords were also matched in form to the critical items, such that they appeared as nested (*drown*-DROW), irregular (*clan*-CLUN), or regular (*elated*-ELAT) word-nonword pairs.

The results revealed that decision latencies to all four verb types were significantly faster when preceded by a related prime word than by an unrelated one. Data from the irregular verbs showed that nested primes (*grown*-GROW) produced significantly more facilitation (+63 ms) than did irregular change (*ran*-RUN) verbs (+37 ms). In essence, among irregular verb forms, greater letter overlap resulted in larger magnitudes of facilitation. Regular low and high resonance verb primes produced nearly equivalent magnitudes of facilitation (+55 ms and +54 ms, respectively). At the same time, however, the baselines of the regular verbs did vary significantly with semantic resonance (576 ms for regular low resonance versus 556 ms for regular high resonance) suggesting that the increased semantic richness of the high resonance verbs affected recognition but not facilitation. Crucially, when facilitation was computed across both types of irregular verbs (+50 ms) and both types of regular verbs (+54.5 ms) when targets were matched for semantic richness and frequency, the magnitudes of morphological facilitation did not differ as a function of regularity. Stated simply, when semantic variables (e.g., resonance strength) were controlled for, differences in the magnitudes of facilitation between irregular and regular verb forms failed to arise and both produced significant facilitation. There was no evidence that verb types are processed in a dissimilar manner depending on regularity. This finding fails to support a dual route account based on the potential for decomposition due to the presence of a shared morpheme for regular but not for irregular verb forms. Rather, it points to the role of semantic richness of the target and to differences in baseline recognition latencies in any interpretation of the interaction of regularity by morphological facilitation. Finally, manipulations of regularity do not produce differences in the magnitude of morphological facilitation when form similarity of semantic properties of the stem have been accounted for.

CONCLUSION

We have examined graded effects of a word's meaning and have pointed out how they pose a problem for dual route models of word recognition that have been developed in the domain of morphological processing. In addition to surface frequency of the whole word and frequency based on type or token counts on the stem, we have demonstrated the potential of the ratio of noun to verb stem frequency (e.g., THE HELP divided by TO HELP) as a reliable measure of processing speed in a lexical decision task. As the distinction between noun and verb frequency of the stem is intimately tied into semantics and word senses, these findings challenge an account of processing where analytic processes are governed by form and semantic effects arise only at the level of the whole word. Further, we have demonstrated that when comparisons between regular and irregular verbs take into account differences in form and the semantic richness of the stem, the magnitudes of morphological facilitation in a cross modal primed lexical decision task are equivalent and provide no support for two independent processing routes.

ACKNOWLEDGMENTS

The research reported here was partially supported by funds from the National Institute of Child Health and Development Grant HD-01994. Data were collected at the State University of New York, Albany, NY. We would like to thank P. J. de Barros for helpful comments.

REFERENCES

Allen, M., & W. Badecker. (1999). Stem homograph inhibition and stem allomorphy: Representing and processing inflected forms in a multi-level lexical system. *Journal of Memory and Language, 41,* 105–123.

Allen, M., & W. Badecker. (2002). Inflectional regularity: Probing the nature of lexical representation in a cross-modal priming task. *Journal of Memory and Language, 46,* 705–722.

Allen, M., & W. Badecker. (2002). Stem-homographs and lemma level representations. *Brain and Language, 81,* 79–88.

Balota D. A., & Chumbley J. I. (1984). Are lexical decisions a good measure of lexical access? The role of word frequency in the neglected decision stage. *Journal of Experimental Psychology: Human Perception, and Performance, 10,* 340–57.

Baayen, R. H. (2004). Statistics in psycholinguistics: a critique of our current gold standards. In G Libben and K. Nault (Eds.). *Mental Lexicon Working Papers, 1.* (pp. 1–47).

Baayen, R. H., Dijkstra, T., & Schreuder, R. (1997). Morphological influences on the recognition of monosyllabic monomorphemic words. *Journal of Memory and Language, 37,* 94–117.

Baayen, R. H., Feldman, L. B., & Schreuder, R. (2005). Morphological influences on the recognition of monosyllabic monomorphemic words. Ms submitted for publication.

Baayen, R. H. &, F. Moscoso del Prado Martín (2005). Semantic density and past-tense formation in three Germanic languages. *Language. 81,* 1–27.

Baayen, R.H., Piepenbrock, R., & Gulikers, L. (1995). The CELEX lexical database (CD-ROM). Philadelphia: Linguistic Data Consortium, University of Pennsylvania.

Baayen, R. H., Tweedie, F. J. & Schreuder, R. (2002). The subjects as a simple random effect fallacy: Subject variability and morphological family effects in the mental lexicon, *Brain and Language 81,* 55–65.

Badecker, W., & M. Allen. (2002). Morphological parsing and the perception of lexical identity: A masked priming study of stem-homographs. *Journal of Memory and Language, 47,* 125–144.

Beckwith, R., Fellbaum, C., Gross, D., & Miller, G. (1991). WordNet: A lexical database organized on psycholinguistic principles. In: Zernik, U. (Ed.), *Lexical Acquisition: Exploiting on-line Resources to Build a Lexicon.* (pp. 211–232). Hillsdale, NJ: Lawrence Erlbaum Associates.

Berent, I., Pinker, S., & Shimron, J. (1999). Default nominal inflection in Hebrew: evidence for mental variables. *Cognition, 72,* 1–44.

Berent, I., Pinker, S., & Shimron, J. (2002). The nature of regularity and irregularity: Evidence from Hebrew nominal inflection. *Journal of Psycholinguistic Research, 31,* 459–502

Bergman, M. W., Hudson, P. T. W., & Eling, P. A. T. M. (1988). How simple complex words can be: Morphological processing and word representations. *Quarterly Journal of Experimental Psychology, 40A,* 41–72.

Bertram, R., Baayen, R. H., & Schreuder, R. (2000). The balance of storage and computation in morphological processing: the role of word formation type, affixal homonymy, and productivity. *Journal of Experimental Psychology: Learning, Memory, and Cognition, 26,* 419–511.

Bertram, R., Laine, M., Baayen, R. H., Schreuder, R., & Hyona, J. (2000). Affixal homonymy triggers full-form storage, even with inflected words, even in a morphologically rich language. *Cognition, 74,* 13–25.

Caramazza, A., Laudanna, A., & Romani, C. (1988). Lexical access and inflectional morphology. *Cognition, 28*, 297–332.

Coltheart, M., Curtis, B., Atkins, P., & Haller, M. (1993). Models of reading aloud: dual-route and parallel-distributed processing approaches. *Psychological Review, 100*, 589–608.

Coltheart, M., Rastle, K. Perry, C., Langdon, R., & Ziegler, J. (2001) DRC: A dual route cascaded model of visual word recognition and reading aloud. *Psychological Review, 108*, 204–256

Cole, P., Beauvillain, C., & Segui, J. (1989). On the representation and processing of prefixed and suffixed derived words: A differential frequency effect. *Journal of Memory and Language, 28*, 1–13.

de Jong, N. H., Feldman, L. B., Schreuder, R., Pastizzo, M. J. & Baayen, R. H. (2002). The processing and representation of Dutch and English compounds: Peripheral morphological, and central orthographic effects. *Brain and Language, 81*. 555–567. Doi: 10.1006/brln.2001.2547.

de Jong, N. H., Schreuder, R., & Baayen, R. H. (2000). The morphological family size effect and morphology. *Language and Cognitive Processes, 15*, 329–365.

Deutsch, A., Frost, R., & Forster, K.I. (1998). Verbs and Nouns Are Organized and Accessed Differently in the Mental Lexicon: Evidence from Hebrew. *Journal of Experimental Psychology: Learning, Memory, and Cognition, 24*, 1238–1255.

Feldman, L. B., & Pastizzo, M. J. (2004, November). Frequency measures as indices of morphological processing. Paper presented at the Psychonomic Society, Minneapolis. MN.

Feldman, L. B. & Pastizzo, M. J. (2003). Morphological facilitation: The role of semantic transparency and family size. In R. H. Baayen and R. Schreuder (Eds.). *Morphological Structure in Language Processing*. Berlin, Germany: Mouton de Gruyter.

Feldman, L. B., & Raveh, M. (2003). When degree of semantic similarity influences morphological processing: cross language and cross task comparisons. In J. Shimron (ed.) *Language Processing and Language Acquisition in Languages with Root-Based Morphology*. (pp. 187–200). Amsterdam, The Netherlands: John Benjamins.

Feldman, L. B., Rueckl, J., Pastizzo, M. Diliberto, K., & Vellutino, F. (2002). Morphological analysis in beginning readers as revealed by the fragment completion task. *Psychological Bulletin and Review, 77*, 529–535.

Feldman, L. B., & Soltano, E.G. (1999). Morphological priming: The role of prime duration, semantic transparency, and affix position. *Brain and Language, 68*, 33–39.

Fellbaum, C. E. (1998). WordNet: An electronic database. Cambridge, MA: The MIT Press.

Ford, M., Marslen-Wilson, W. D., & Davis, M. H. (2003). Morphology and frequency: contrasting methodologies. In Baayen, R. H. and Schreuder R. (Eds.), *Morphological Structure in Language Processing*. Mouton de Gruyter, Berlin. pp. 89–124.

Forster, K. I., & Chambers, S. M. (1973). Lexical access and naming time. *Journal of Verbal Learning and Verbal Behavior, 12*, 627–635.

Forster, K.I. (1999). The microgenesis of priming effects in lexical access. *Brain and Language, 68*, 5–15.

Forster, K. I., & Azuma, T. (2000). Masked priming for prefixed words with bound stems: Does *submit* prime *permit? Language and Cognitive Processes, 15*, 539–561.

Forster, K.I., & Davis, C. (1984). Repetition priming and frequency attenuation in lexical access. *Journal of Experimental Psychology: Learning, Memory, and Cognition, 10*, 680–698.

Frost, R., Deutsch, A., & Forster, K.I. (2000). Decomposing Morphologically Complex Words in a Nonlinear Morphology. *Journal of Experimental Psychology: Learning, Memory, and Cognition, 26*, 751–765.

Harm, M. W., & Seidenberg, M. S. (2004). Computing the meanings of words in reading: Cooperative division of labor between visual and phonological processes. *Psychological Review, 111*, 662–720.

Laudanna, A., & Burani, C. (1995). Distributional properties of derivational affixes: Implications for processing. In L.B. Feldman (Ed.), *Morphological aspects of language processing* (pp. 345–364). Hilldale, NJ: Erlbaum.

Laudanna, A., Badecker, W., & Caramazza, A. (1989). Priming homographic stems. *Journal of Memory and Language, 28,* 531–546.

Laudanna, A., Voghera, M., & Gazzellini, S. (2002). Lexical representations of written nouns and verbs in Italian. *Brain and Language, 81,* 250–263.

Landauer, T.K., Foltz, P.W., & Laham, D. (1998). Introduction to latent semantic analysis. *Discourse Processes, 25,* pp. 259–284. http://lsa.colorado.edu/.

Marslen-Wilson, W., Tyler, L., Waksler, R., & Older, L. (1994). Morphology and meaning in the English mental lexicon. *Psychological Review, 101,* 3–33.

Masson, M.E.J. & Isaak, M.I. (1999). Masked priming of words and nonwords in a naming task: Further evidence for a nonlexical basis for priming. *Memory and Cognition, 27,* 399–412.

Meunier, F., & Marslen-Wilson, W. (2005). Regularity and irregularity in French verbal inflection. *Language and Cognitive Processes, 20,* 169–206.

Meunier, F., & Segui, J. (1999). Morphological priming effect: The role of surface frequency. *Brain and Language, 68,* 54–60.

Miller, G. A. (1990). Wordnet: An on-line lexical database. *International Journal of Lexicography, 3,* 235–312.

Moscoso del Prado Martín, F., Kostíc, A., & Baayen, R.H. (2004) Putting the bits together: An information theoretical perspective on morphological processing. *Cognition, 94,* 1–18.

Moscoso del Prado Martín, F., Bertram, R., Häikiö, T., Schreuder, R., & Baayen, R. H. (2004). Morphologically family size in a morphologically rich language: the case of Finnish compared to Dutch and Hebrew. *Journal of Experimental Psychology: Learning, Memory, and Cognition. 30,* 1271–1278.

Nelson, D. L., McEvoy, C. L., & Schreiber, T. A. (1998). The University of South Florida word association, rhyme, and word fragment norms. http://www.usf.edu/FreeAssociation/ .

New, B., Brysbaert, M., Segui, J., Ferrand, L., & Rastle, K. (2004). The processing of singular and plural nouns in French and English. *Journal of Memory and Language, 51,* 568–585.

Orsolini, M., & Marslen-Wilson, W. (1997). Univerals in morphological representation: Evidence form Italian. *Language and Cognitive Processes, 12,* 1–47.

Pastizzo, M.J., & Feldman, L.B. (2002). Discrepancies between orthographic and unrelated baselines in masked priming undermine a decompositional account of morphological facilitation. *Journal of Experimental Psychology: Learning, Memory, and Cognition, 28,* 244–249.

Pinker, S. (1991). Rules of language. *Science, 253,* 530–536.

Plaut, D. C., McClelland, J. C., & Seidenberg, M. S. (1996). Reading exception words and pseudowords: Are two routes really necessary? In Bairaktaris and Levy (Eds.), *Connectionist Models of Memory and Language* (pp. 145–159). London, England: UCL Press Limited.

Plaut, D. C., & Gonnerman, L. M. (2000). Are non-semantic morphological effects incompatible with a distributed connectionist approach to lexical processing? *Language and Cognitive Processes, 15,* 445–485.

Plunkett, K., & Juola, P. (1999). A connectionist model of English past tense and plural morphology. *Cognitive Science, 23,* 463–490.

Ramscar, M. (2002). The role of meaning in inflection: Why the past tense does not require a rule. *Cognition, 45,* 45–94.

Rastle, K., Davis, M.H., & New, B. (2004). The broth in my brother's brothel: Morpho-orthographic segmentation in visual word recognition. *Psychonomic Bulletin and Review,* 11, 1090–1098.

Raveh, M. (2002). The contribution of frequency and semantic similarity to morphological processing. *Brain and Language, 312–325.* Doi:10.1006/ brln.2001.2527.

Rueckl· J., & Galantucci, B. (2005). The locus and time course of long-term morphological priming. *Language and Cognitive Processes, 20,* 115–138.

Rueckl, J., Mikolinski, Raveh, Miner, & Mars (1997). Morphological priming, fragment completion, and connectionist networks. *Journal of Memory and Language, 36,* 382–405.

Rumelhart, D., & McClelland, J. (1986). On learning the past tense of English verbs: implicit rules or parallel distributed processing? In J. McClelland, D. Rumelhart and the PDP Research Group (Eds.), *Parallel distributed processing: Explorations in the microstructure of cognition.* Cambridge, MA: MIT Press.

Schreuder, R., & Baayen, R. H. (1995). Modeling morphological processing. In L.B. Feldman (Ed.), *Morphological aspects of language processing* (pp. 131–154). Hilldale, NJ: Erlbaum.

Schreuder, R., & Baayen, R. H. (1997). How complex simplex words can be. *Journal of Memory and Language, 37,* 118–139.

Schreuder, R., Burani, C., & Baayen, R.H. (2001).Parsing and semantic opacity in morphological processing. In E. Assink and D. Sandra (Eds.), *Reading complex words.* (pp. 159–189). Dordrecht: Kluwer.

Seidenberg, M. S., & McClelland, J. L. (1990). More words but still no lexicon: Reply to Besner et al. *Psychological Review, 97,* 447–452.

Sonnenstuhl, I., Eisenbeiss, S., & Clahsen, H. (1999). Morphological priming in the German mental lexicon. *Cognition, 72,* 203–236.

Stanners, R.F. Neiser, J.J., Hernon, W.P. & Hall, R. (1979). Memory representation for morphologically related words. *Journal of Verbal Learning and Verbal Behavior, 18,* 399–412.

Stolz, J. A., & Feldman, L. B. (1995). The role of orthographic and semantic transparency of the base morpheme in morphological processing. In L.B. Feldman (Ed.), *Morphological aspects of language processing* (pp. 109–129). Hillsdale, NJ: Lawrence Erlbaum Ass.

Stone, G. O., Vanhoy, M., & Van Orden, G.C. (1997). Perception is a two-way street: Feedforward and feedback phonology in visual word recognition. *Journal of Memory and Language, 36,* 337–359.

Strain, E. & Herdman, C. (1999) Imageability effects in word naming: An individual differences analysis. *Canadian Journal of Experimental Psychology, 53,* 347–359.

Tabak, W., Schreuder, R. & Baayen, R.H. (2005). Lexical statistics and lexical processing: semantic density, information complexity, sex, and irregularity in Dutch. in M. Reis and S. Kepser (Eds.), *Linguistic Evidence Mouton,* 529–555.

Taft, M. (1979). Recognition of affixed words and the word frequency effect. *Memory and Cognition, 7* 263–272.

Taft, M. (2004). Morphological decomposition and the reverse base frequency effect. *Quarterly Journal of Experimental Psychology, 57A,* 745–765.

Tsapkini, K., Kehayia, E., & Jarema, G. (1999). Does Phonological Change Play a Role in the Recognition of Derived Forms Across Modalities? *Brain and Language 68,* 318–323.

Velan, H., Frost, R., Deutsch, A., & Plaut, D. C. (2005). The processing of root morphemes in Hebrew: Contrasting localist and distributed accounts. *Language and Cognitive Processes, 20,* 169–206.

Wurm, L., & Aycock, J. (2003). Recognition of spoken prefixed words: The early role of conditional root uniqueness points. In R. H. Baayen and R. Schreuder (Eds.) *Morphological structure in language processing* (pp. 259–286). Berlin: Mouton de Guyter.

Wurm, L., & Baayen, R. H. (2005). Surface frequency effects below threshold: Comparing types, tasks and modalities. Ms submitted for publication.

CHAPTER SIX

Learning Words in Zekkish: Implications for Understanding Lexical Representation

Lesley Hart
Yale University Child Study Center

Charles Perfetti
University of Pittsburgh

Reading skill has, as its core, single words. When we consider phonology, we talk about the sounds of a language and their combination into words. When we consider orthography, we talk about the spelling of single words and the overall language structure that dictates spelling rules for single words. When we consider semantics, we talk about qualities of a word's meaning that give it its place in the lexicon. Even when we consider comprehension, we discuss the feeding of word-level, lexical information into a system that can build and maintain a representation of text that is being read.

To be sure, there are many other processes that contribute to skilled reading comprehension. These processes have been shown to be stronger in skilled readers than in less skilled readers. Researchers have associated keen inference-making abilities (Long, Oppy, & Seely, 1997; Oakhill, Cain, & Yuill, 1998; St. George, Mannes, & Hoffman, 1997), large verbal working memory spans (Cohen, Netley, & Clarke, 1984; Oakhill, Cain, & Yuill, 1998), good attention and motivation (Jonkman, Licht, Bakker, & van den Broek-Sandmann, 1992; O'Neill & Douglas, 1991; Whyte, 1994), and strong metacognitive skills (Cornoldi, 1990; Oakhill, 1994; Vauras, Kinnunen, & Kuusela, 1994) with skilled text comprehension. However, each of these contributory skills can actually be associated with broader domains of functioning than reading, and even, in many cases, than language processing. Understanding that skills such as working memory and attention apply to more than reading does not make their contribution to reading any less important, but it does imply their status as moderating, rather than mediating, associates of reading skill. Further, it illustrates the necessity of identifying reading-specific processes that can account for reading disabilities in the absence of more general language or processing problems. For example, while preschool children with Specific Language Impairments (SLI) often have reading difficulties as they get older (Bishop & Adams, 1990; Catts, Fey, Tomblin & Zhand, 2002; Scarborough, 1990; Snowling, Bishop, & Stothard, 2000), and while reading can certainly be delayed along with other general processing delays, many children with SLI go on to have reading skills in the normal range, and not all children with reading disabilities have other pro-cessing delays. And coming full circle, understanding deficits specific to reading impairments can suggest how those same mechanisms are used for skilled reading.

Two of the strongest and most replicated findings in the reading literature are that children (and adults) with reading disabilities have deficits in word decoding, often in the absence of any other reading-specific or general deficits (Felton & Wood, 1992; Osmon, Braun, & Plambeck, 2005), and that lexical skill (orthographic, phonological, and semantic) covaries with reading comprehension skill (Gernsbacher, 1990; Perfetti, 1985; Stanovich, West, & Cunningham, 1991). These associations can be found across writing systems, particularly those with deeper orthographies, when better decoding skills are necessary to navigate less reliable spelling-sound mappings. For example, decoding and lexical skills have been asso-ciated with reading comprehension in Chinese, Japanese, and Arabic (Ho, 2003; Paradis, 1989; and Abu-Rabia 2003, respectively; also see overviews by Aaron & Joshi, 1989; Perfetti & Bolger, 2004). Shallower orthographies like Greek and German, with more reliable mappings of spelling to sound, do not show these asso-ciations (Nikolopoulos, Goulandris, & Snowling, 2003; Wimmer, 1996, respectively), presumably because the decoding system is required to utilize fewer rules to sys-tematize the mappings (e.g., i before e, except after c…). The associations between decoding skill and reading comprehension can also be found across languages; decoding skill in a first language (L1) predicts decoding skill – and comprehension skill – in a second language (L2; Oren & Breznitz, 2005; Wade-Woolley, 1999). Decoding skill and comprehension skill are related even after early elementary school, when decoding is more automatized than when children are learning to read (Miller-Shaul, 2005; Vellutino & Scanlon, 1988).

Because words serve as an important base for reading skill, it is crucial to iden-tify the qualities of a word that affect its utility in the lexicon. Some of these qual-ities come from the language structure itself – consistency of letter to sound mappings (grapheme-phoneme correspondence, or GPC), frequency with which phonemes occur together (e.g., bigram frequency), and the extent to which words share qualities with other words (neighborhood effects), for example. Some of these qualities come from the language use of both the individual and the population as a whole. Written word usage within a population determines the frequency with which each word is encountered; the reading experience of each individual modifies the written frequency of each word into a personal frequency set of word encounters.

In this chapter we will discuss the Lexical Quality Hypothesis (Perfetti & Hart, 2001, 2002), a framework for understanding how lexical quality is built, the characteristics of language experience that can produce higher or lower lexical quality lexical representations, and how higher quality lexical representations can support better text comprehension. We will discuss, in detail, three types of words that are lower in lexical quality and their implications for word and text processing – homographs, ambiguous words, and homophones.

We will then focus on studies that use homophones to examine the lexical quality differences in more-skilled and less-skilled comprehenders. We will report findings by Gernsbacher (Gernsbacher, 1990; Gernsbacher & Faust, 1991; Gernsbacher, Varner, & Faust, 1990) that less-skilled comprehenders have a different pattern of responses to homophones versus non-homophones. We will then report three of our studies replicating, extending, and suggesting a causal link for Gernsbacher's original results.

THE LEXICAL QUALITY HYPOTHESIS

We (Perfetti & Hart, 2001, 2002) have attempted to illustrate the qualities of lexical representations that allow them to support efficient comprehension in the Lexical Quality Hypothesis. Lexical representations are the word entries in the lexicon, or mental dictionary. Words are acquired and added to the mental dictionary as they are learned through spoken or written language. Their meanings are fleshed out and their places in the lexicon are fortified by hearing, using, and reading the words multiple times in a variety of contexts. Their strength and stability in the lexicon define their lexical quality.

The Lexical Quality Hypothesis is built on modifications of two theories of Perfetti (1985, 1992). In *Reading Ability* (1985), Perfetti outlined Verbal Efficiency Theory. High quality lexical representations have been built from good phonological and semantic information, usually fortified by multiple word encounters, which further strengthens the phonological and semantic information. The strong lexical representations can be quickly re-activated when they are read, which makes the lexical information available to comprehension processes. In The Representation Problem in Reading Acquisition (1992), Perfetti revised the definition of high-quality lexical representations to include two new concepts. Lexical representations need to be specific; they need to associate a single orthographic representation (spelling) with a single lexical item. For example, the specificity of "bank" is low because the single orthographic representation is associated with the lexical entries meaning "river edge" and "financial institution." Lexical representations also need to be built and accessed with redundant information. That is, sound information from speech and from print need to be associated with the same lexical entry. For example, "sow" receives information from speech that is only partially redundant for each of two lexical entries. The two pronunciations, meaning "female pig" and "plant crops," each support the same spelling but two different lexical representations. Both of these lexical representations have low redundancy.

The Lexical Quality Hypothesis (Perfetti & Hart, 2001, 2002) describes lexical entries as having three constituents: orthography, phonology, and semantics; all three are necessary for a coherent lexical entry. Lexical entries are described as being coherent when the three constituents are synchronous. When the orthographic, phonological, and semantic information associated with a word are activated simultaneously, the impression is that the lexical item is being activated from three sources. Repeated encounters of the triads of orthographic, phonological, and semantic information increase their coherence as a unitary lexical entry. The greater the coherence, the higher the likelihood that the particular combination of lexical constituents will activate one and only one triad, or lexical entry. That is, a coherent lexical representation allows the reader to pull from the lexicon the exact word that is printed, instead of bits of the word that may be associated with other words as well.

The Lexical Quality Hypothesis also includes an assertion that fast activation of high quality lexical representations is required to support efficient comprehension. Only words efficiently and effortlessly activated are able to free processing resources for building a text representation and comprehending the resulting structure. Thus, factors involved in building high quality lexical representations are a likely site of impairment in readers with reading disabilities, and possibly more specific to reading processes than factors such as verbal working memory span or motivation. Again, words serve as a basis for understanding skilled and impaired reading processes not just at the lexical level but also in smaller units at the sublexical level and in larger units at the level of structure building and text comprehension.

HOMOPHONES, HOMOGRAPHS, AND AMBIGUOUS WORDS

Several naturally occurring patterns in most language systems afford researchers a clever and sneaky way to quantify the process of lexical access, which occurs on the order of milliseconds. One way to measure lexical quality (and the resulting lexical access) is to occasionally intentionally degrade the process of lexical access by sneaking words of low specificity and/or redundancy into experiments and comparing performance with these words to words of higher lexical quality. Scientists can then capitalize on these sneaked-in words by devising experiments with parameters designed to elucidate particular qualities of the activation process. That is, the specifics of the experiment will determine the consequences of the lower lexical quality.

Homographs

Homographs are words that have a single orthographic representation, but two phonological representations and two semantic values (See Figure 6.1 for representations of orthographic, phonological, and semantic connections in homograph representations). For example, *bass* can be pronounced with a short a sound to mean a fish, or with a long a sound to mean a musical instrument. This is not a specific representation. When the orthographic pattern is presented, there is not a single

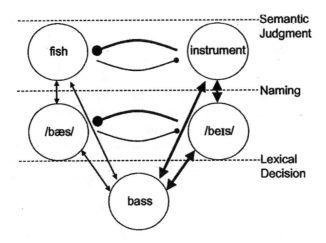

FIGURE 6.1   Connections among orthographic, phonological, and semantic components of homographs.

unique triad that is activated; instead there is a rise in activation for two lexical items. The coherence of the representation dictates the speed and rise of the activation. A fisherman is likely to have a coherent representation for the fish meaning, and a less coherent, less efficiently activated representation for the instrument meaning, because he is likely to have encountered the orthographic pattern more often when it is associated with the long-a phonology and the fish meaning. The more coherent representation is called dominant, and the less coherent representation is called subordinate. A musician is likely to have the opposite pattern of dominance. The result in both cases is that the activation of one lexical entry competes with the activation of the other lexical entry, leading to a period of lexical indecision. In the case of homographs, the context in which the word appears is necessary to disambiguate the meaning, dampening the activation of one homograph lexical entry and raising the activation of the other entry, although the relative coherence of the entries from word experience (Gorfein, Viviandi, & Leddo, 1982) can provide a useful clue.

Homograph Naming.   Tasks that require the naming of homographs usually show a slowed response time for homographs compared to control words. This is a reflection of the competition between the phonological representations that are activated from the orthography. Gottlob, Goldinger, Stone & Van Orden (1999) found that response times were slowed regardless of whether the word meaning was dominant or subordinate. Pronunciations from orthographies that are more frequent improve reaction times. The more dominant meaning is often the one that has an irregular orthography; that is the word which is most often encountered is the one that is pronounced with a phonology that is less often associated with that orthography. For example, on average, the lexical entry for a musical instrument is dominant for the "bass" orthography, but the long-a pronunciation is less often associated with an *a* in a consonant-vowel-consonant(s) (CVCC) word. This increases reaction time, illustrating again that naming occurs at a lower level than semantic judgment (Kawamoto & Zemblidge, 1992).[1]

Homograph Semantic Judgments.   Tasks that require semantic categorization of homographs can show fairly normal response times for the dominant meaning, and dramatically slowed response times for the subordinate meaning, because the much higher activation of the dominant meaning must be overcome before the ambiguity is resolved. For example, making the decision that "affect" and "influence" are related in meaning is easier than making the decision that "affect" and "emotion" are related in meaning. The difference is that the first pronunciation, with the accent on the second syllable, is much more frequently encountered than the second pronunciation.[2]

Including homographs in experiments can elucidate the role of inhibitory connections such as those between dominant and subordinate meanings, of statistical likelihood of pronunciation and meaning, and of personal experience with each meaning.

Ambiguous Words

Ambiguous words have a single orthographic representation and a single phonological representation, but two semantic values (See Figure 6.2). For example, the word "spring"can mean a metal coil or the season between winter and summer. Again, this is not a specific lexical representation. When the orthography and phonology are activated, there is a rise in activation for the lexical items of both meanings. With ambiguous words there is no phonological competition; however, the context and the extent of bias in the context in which the word appears (Vu, Kellas Petersen & Metcalf, 2003), word-specific qualities such as word structure (Almeida & Libben, 2005), and the relative frequency of use of each of the meanings (Collins, 2002) remains necessary for choosing among multiple activated lexical entries.[3]

---

[1]While irregular pronunciations increase reaction time, there is also a top-down effect of meaning dominance; Kawamoto & Zemblidge (1992) found a similar response time to the naming of dominant and subordinate homographs, which can be construed as an interaction of pronunciation and meaning frequencies.

[2]The easily recognizable pronunciation difference is the shift in the accented syllable. This shift changes the pronunciation of the vowels as well. They are pronounced as the short vowel sound when the syllable is accented, and as a schwa when it is not.

[3]This is actually an oversimplified representation of ambiguous words, because many ambiguous words have more than two meanings competing for dominance. For example, "jam" can mean jelly, blockage, predicament, crush, or stop working. Some of the definitions share semantic qualities, however. It is also the case that homographs and homophones can have more than two meanings associated with them. This quality of multiple meanings is not dealt with in this paper.

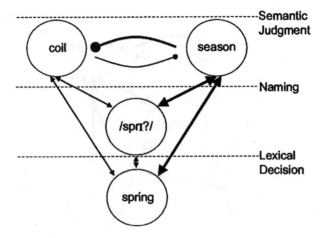

FIGURE 6.2   Connections among orthographic, phonological, and semantic components of ambiguous words.

Ambiguous Word Naming.   Naming of ambiguous words sometimes produces no increase in response time, because word production does not require disambiguation of meanings before a response can be made (Rodd, Gaskell, & Marslen-Wilson, 2002). In fact, some experiments actually show an advantage for ambiguous words, because the activation of both meanings feeds back to the phonology, while control words have positive feedback from only one meaning (Balota, Ferrara, & Connor, 1991).

Ambiguous Word Semantic Judgments.   Unlike naming tasks, categorization tasks involving ambiguous words often show an increase in reaction time for the subordinate meaning. This is because no decision can be made until one meaning has been settled on, and inhibitory connections between the meanings lengthen the time it takes a single meaning to reach some activation threshold. There is some debate as to the power of biasing contexts to speed the response time for subordinate meanings. For example, can reading "bank" in a sentence like "There were crocodiles sunning themselves on the bank" improve response times to the river meaning of bank more than sentences like "We took a picture of the bank," for which either meaning of "bank" can be appropriate? Martin, Vu, Kellas & Metcalf (1999) claim that strongly biasing context can override word meaning biases from frequency, whereas weakly biasing context cannot. Binder & Rayner disagree with the power of strongly biasing context; they find that strongly biasing context does not have enough strength to increase the activation rate of lower frequency word meanings.

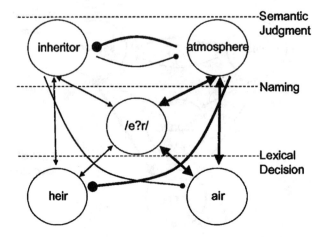

FIGURE 6.3   Connections among orthographic, phonological, and semantic components of homophones.

Homophones

Homophones have two orthographic representations, one phonological representation, and one semantic value for each orthographic pattern (See Figure 6.3). For example, "heir" and "air" have the same phonological representation (/eyr/), but the first orthographic pattern means "one who inherits" whereas the second means "atmosphere." Homophones threaten lexical quality because there is competition between the two meanings as well as between the two orthographic patterns. "Air" is the more frequently encountered word (except perhaps for an estate lawyer) so it is more quickly and efficiently activated than "heir" because of the strong connections that have been built for "air." Unlike homographs and ambiguous words, sentence or text context is not necessary for disambiguation; the orthography can do that all by itself.

Context can influence the speed and efficiency of activation of the appropriate meaning by pre-activating the semantic constituent appropriate for the context. Context can thus improve the speed and efficiency of activation of both dominant and subordinate homophone meanings (Perfetti & Hart, 2001).

HOMOPHONES AND READING SKILL

Differences in response time patterns between reading disabled readers and fluent readers can indicate processes contributing to the reading difficulties of the impaired group (Gernsbacher & Faust, 1991; Gernsbacher, Varner & Faust, 1990; Perfetti & Hart, 2001, 2002).

Suppression

Gernsbacher (Gernsbacher, 1990; Gernsbacher & Faust, 1991; Gernsbacher, Varner, & Faust, 1990) has studied the dual activation of homophone lexical entries and the subsequent meaning disambiguation. She presented more-skilled and less-skilled text comprehenders with sentences in which the final word was a homophone. The sentence context was designed to be non-biasing. Some examples are "He examined his sole" and "She took the yolk." Sentences were presented one word at a time, followed by a probe word. On critical trials the probe word was related to the alternate version of the homophone. The probe word followed the final word by approximately 450 ms or 1350 ms; a time differential known as the stimulus onset asynchrony (SOA). Compared to sentences in which the final word was not a homophone, all participants showed slower reaction times to homophones at 450 ms SOA. This is evidence that lexical entries for both homophones had been activated, and that disambiguation had not yet taken place. By 1350 ms SOA, more skilled comprehenders showed similar reaction times for homophones and controls, while less skilled comprehenders continued to show longer reaction times for homophones. Gernsbacher's conclusion was that less-skilled comprehenders have a less efficient suppression mechanism, which resulted in less-skilled comprehenders' inability to effectively dampen activation for the lexical entry of the inappropriate homophone. An inefficient suppression mechanism results in more words remaining active, producing an over-complex text structure with irrelevant and sometimes even misleading information, and, consequently, less efficient comprehension.

Disambiguation

We (Perfetti & Hart, 2001, 2002) replicated and extended these results. First, homophones and control words were presented in isolation so that sentence contexts could not unintentionally bias a reader toward one homophone over the other. Second, the 450 ms SOA was retained but both earlier (150 ms) and later (2000 ms) SOAs were added. Further, we examined high frequency and low frequency words separately, because frequency is also a manipulation of lexical quality. We replicated Gernsbacher's results at 450 ms. Both more-skilled and less-skilled comprehenders showed homophone interference. At 150 ms, only more skilled comprehenders showed homophone interference (the opposite result of Gernsbacher's 1350 ms SOA). At 2000 ms, no comprehenders showed homophone interference.

The conclusion we drew from this study was that more skilled comprehenders simply activated both homophone entries and settled on the correct activation, dampening the other one, more efficiently and quickly than less skilled comprehenders. In other words, the activation function was simply shifted earlier for the more skilled comprehenders. This explanation not only supports the lexical quality hypothesis, but is also parsimonious in that it does not require the invoking of an additional suppression mechanism. In addition, the more skilled comprehenders showed this effect only for low-frequency words while the less skilled comprehenders showed this effect only for high frequency words. Less-skilled comprehenders, who also tend to be less frequent readers, have a lower relative frequency for all words. What is a high frequency homophone for a more skilled comprehender is likely a low frequency word for a less skilled comprehender. What is a low frequency word for a low skilled comprehender might not be in less skilled comprehenders' vocabularies at all.

Manipulating Lexical Quality

Two aspects of our homophone experiment led us to an individualized training design. First, in the prior experiment, the same stimulus set was used for all participants. It is likely that each participant would have had some percentage of words that were simply unknown to them. This has implications not only for increasing error variance, but also for changing homophone dynamics. A high frequency homophone for which its lower frequency mate is unknown has no homophone interference at all and acts as a control. Exactly which words are unknown to each participant was not tested and cannot be inferred from responses, because even when guessing, participants had a 50% chance of giving the correct answer. Second, less-skilled comprehenders will have more unknown words than more skilled comprehenders, an assertion made from the patterns of responses for high and low frequency words in the previous experiment. What we felt we needed was a control of relative frequency, individualized by participant.

We interviewed sixteen more skilled and ten less skilled text comprehenders. We asked them to spell homophones (spoken aloud to them) two different ways, and to provide the definition for each spelling. We then asked them to rate each homophone according to their familiarity with the words. From this information we developed a stimulus set for each individual subject consisting of twelve homophone pairs for which one was rated as very familiar, and the other was rated as known but very unfamiliar. Creating these stimulus sets effectively removed the differences between groups in relative frequency. It also ensured that all words were known to participants, so homophone dynamics were maintained.

Participants were tested using Gernsbacher's experimental design. They were then trained on the meanings of half the low-frequency homophones in three 45 minute game-like sessions. Then they repeated the testing. Prior to training, all participants showed homophone interference for low frequency homophones at 150 ms SOA that was gone by 450 ms SOA. Equating personal frequency also equated the performance of the skill groups. After training participants still showed homophone interference, but for the high frequency homophones. Some simple training reversed the relative frequency pattern of the homophone pairs. From this experiment it is clear that there are a number of risks to lexical quality: homophony, written frequency, relative homophone frequency, and personal word frequency. Comprehension skill does not appear to be a risk except for its association with lower personal word frequencies.

Improving Lexical Quality

Our experiment manipulating lexical quality using some simple learning procedures did not completely control for all likely sources of differences between comprehension groups. Familiarity as a proxy for personal frequency is only as good as the participants' perceptions and reporting. In addition, knowledge of English spelling patterns, reading strategies, and other variables that apply to words in general can affect performance. To control for the effects of these variables as much as possible we developed a training experiment using an artificial orthography called Zekkish.

The purpose of the Zekkish experiment was to control the effects of English reading experience in order to examine the development of homophone effects, specifically homophone interference and recovery from interference in a semantic task. An artificial orthography allows reading experience to be tightly controlled. The artificial orthography was as different from English as possible so that participants would not apply their knowledge of English to the reading of Zekkish. Using an artificial orthography also gave us complete control over other word effects such as frequency, word length, and frequency of semantic values of the Zekkish words.

Participants and Screening Sample.   Over the course of several semesters we have built a database of scores on reading tests from nearly 800 undergraduate Intro Psych students at the University of Pittsburgh. These students took a variety of reading tasks which assessed their levels of orthographic, phonological, and text comprehension skill, the size of their vocabulary, and the extent of their English reading experience. The scores from each test were standardized, and from these z-scores we calculated a composite variable measuring reading skill. The resultant variable is normally distributed. The 45 subjects that participated in the current experiment were drawn from across the distribution of reading scores, and there was no significant difference between the reading skills of these 45 students and the remainder of the group (F (1, 795) = 1.84, p > 1).[4]

Artificial Orthography Training.   A distinct advantage of using an artificial orthography is the ability to take a great deal of artistic license in setting up a cover story for the language. In this experiment, participants were told that they were to be Earth Ambassadors to the Planet Zek, and that they needed to speak enough Zekkish to interact with the Zek Ambassadors to Earth. The three ambassadors served as incentive (participants got attached to their favorite Zeks), and as stimuli. They were the actors in the scenes that provided the semantic values for each

---

[4]Participants were also divided into more- and less-skilled comprehenders and more- and less-skilled decoders based on these tests. Data on the Zekkish tasks have also been analyzed using this two by two design, and the results will be reported elsewhere.

FIGURE 6.4   Zek characters (Teb, Dek, and Gep), and sample vocabulary concepts.

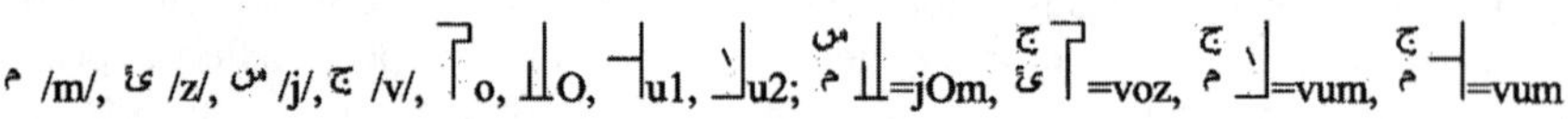

ᵉ /m/, ⁱˢ /z/, ᵒᵘ /j/, ᶜ /v/, ⌐o, 𝖫o, ⌐u1, 𝖫u2; ᵒ 𝖫=jOm, ᶜ ⌐=voz, ᶜ 𝖫=vum, ᵉ ⌐=vum

FIGURE 6.5   Examples of Zekkish letters and words.

Note: o = short o, and O = long o.

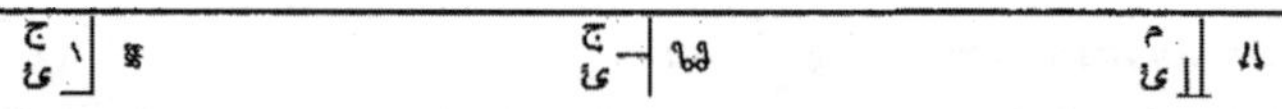

ᶜ ⌐ 𝟕	ᶜ ⌐ ʬ	ᵉ 𝖫 ⅄
Vuz, Teb.	Vuz, Dek.	Moze, Gep.
Flying plane, Teb.	Painting portrait, Dek.	Snorkeling shark, Gep.

FIGURE 6.6   Examples of Zekkish sentences.

Zekkish word, and they were the stimulus probes in the subsequent testing phases. The three Zeks are shown in Figure 6.4, along with three sample concepts

The orthography itself was fairly simple. All words were of CVC format, with two consonants stacked on top of each other to the left of a vowel. Words were read clockwise from the top consonant. Homophones were created by having two vowels make the same sound. Frequency was differentiated by having half of the words presented three times as often as the other half. Letters and sample words are shown in Figure 6.5, and sample sentences are shown in Figure 6.6.

Sentences were written with the concept word (subject/direct object) followed by the name of a Zek to set up the experimental task based on Gernsbacher & Faust's (1991) semantic judgment task and Perfetti & Hart's extensions of this task. Note that the homophones involve two different Zeks doing two different things. This characteristic provides homophone interference (e.g., Who performs the action?)

Development of Homophone Interference.   Participants were trained to decode words, retrieve word meanings, and read simple Zekkish sentences, over approximately 20 hours. The goal of training was not only to prepare for testing sessions, but also to watch the unfolding of homophone interference.

As homophones were encountered at low frequency and high frequency, and as the lexical quality of each lexical representation was increased with repeated trials, the high frequency lexical representation caused more and more interference during the activation of the low frequency homophone. The buildup of interference occurred because the lexical quality of the lexical entry for the high frequency homophone was strengthened faster than that of the low frequency lexical entry given the 1:3 low frequency to high frequency presentation ratio. Further, the functional frequency difference of the words changed, even though the absolute frequency difference remained 1:3. In other words, when both words were of fairly low lexical quality (e.g., 2 trials: 6 trials), there was less reliable interference than when both lexical entries were of relatively higher frequencies (e.g. 20 trials : 60 trials).

Another bonus of the Zekkish training paradigm is that once participants began learning the meanings of the words, two responses were necessary, the first for naming the word and the second for providing the meaning of the word. Thus Zekkish allows us to test the pattern of response times at two of the three choice points shown in Figure 6.3. Recall that homophone naming has the advantage of a facilitative effect from semantic-phonological feedback which improves naming of homophones relative to nonhomophone controls. Homophone semantic judgments are subject to inhibitory connections between semantic values which slow response times, especially for low frequency homophones.

All participants reached the appropriate accuracy criteria for letter-sound learning and pseudoword decoding, so by the time they began to learn the vocabulary, they were already fairly accurate decoders for all words and the decoding results reflect this (See Figure 6.7). In this graph and the graphs to follow, homophone accuracy has been subtracted from control accuracy, and control response time has been subtracted from homophone response time. Higher numbers indicate greater interference. By the time semantic values of the words were introduced, there was little homophone interference left when participants were decoding. Meaning results, however, clearly show an effect of interference secondary to inhibitory connections between the semantic constituents (See Figure 6.8). Here, low frequency is a liability. By their second experience with the vocabulary words, the lexical quality difference between low frequency and high frequency words already caused much slower and less accurate responses to low frequency homophones compared to their controls.

When they are first confronted with word meanings, in groups of 12 words at a time, participants already show a facilitative effect of homophony on naming of low frequency words, and an inhibitory effect of homophony on recalling meanings of all homophones, with the effect increasing rapidly for low frequency homophones. In the next stage of the experiment, participants were confronted with all 48 words at once. Accuracy continued to increase for decoding responses because this task did not change. Accuracy decreased and response times slowed at first for meaning responses because of the increased load of differentiating 48 word meanings instead of 12. Here again there is a marked increase in homophone interference for

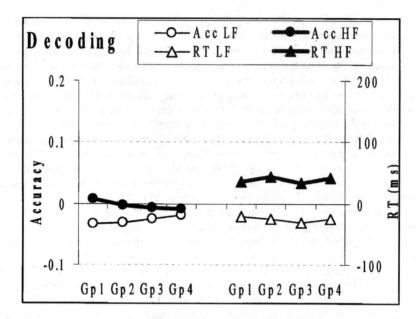

FIGURE 6.7   Homophone interference for word decoding during vocabulary learning.

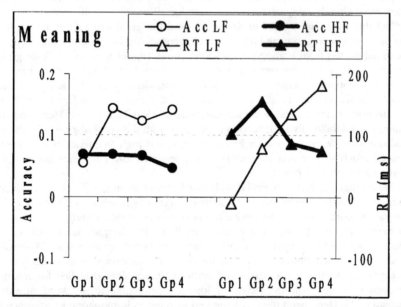

FIGURE 6.8   Homophone interference during early vocabulary learning.

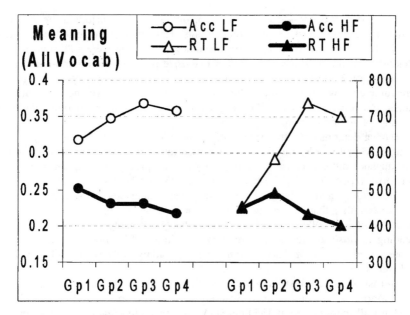

FIGURE 6.9 Homophone interference during early vocabulary learning with a heavy learning load: 48 vocabulary words.

low frequency homophones. There is a decrease in homophone interference for high frequency homophones as well, as the relative lexical quality between low frequency words and high frequency word changes over time. The development of homophone and frequency effects is clear both in accuracy and in response time (See Figure 6.9).

These data provide a clear example of how word frequency increases the coherence and efficiency of activation of lexical items, i.e. how reading experience builds lexical quality. The lexical quality of high frequency words increases to the point that their activation is protected from being unduly affected by interference from low frequency competitors. Homophone interference decreases with experience. The lexical quality of low frequency words is incremented (because performance on control words improves), but not nearly as quickly as for high frequency words. Consequently, the inhibitory influence the high frequency competitors have on the lexical activation of low-frequency homophones increases over time.

This pattern of facilitation and inhibition continued over the next session, when participants were learning the grammar of Zekkish, and after the first testing session, when participants were gaining additional experience with Zekkish in order to make the processes of reading and activating meaning, if not automatic, then highly efficient. One particularly high-performing subject, bored and with nowhere to improve, having hit nearly 100% accuracy and an asymptote on response time by the end of the first experience session, complained "I can't even read the words without automatically getting the meaning anymore."

Participants were tested on a variety of different tasks, including the standard semantic judgment task, at two time points. First, they were tested when they reached a minimum criterion of 85% accuracy while they were still novices with Zekkish. Second, they were tested after extensive practice reading and relating the meanings of Zekkish sentences. At the "novice" testing session, participants had encountered low frequency and high frequency words an average of 20 and 60 times, and at the "experienced" testing session, they had encountered the words an average of 40 and 120 times.

Having demonstrated the process of building lexical quality through experience with individual words, and the ways in which interactions between words of varying qualities differ because of homophony and frequency characteristics, we now turn to a replication of Gernsbacher and Faust's (1991) study of skilled and less skilled readers, and Perfetti & Hart's subsequent extensions of the experiment. In this case, rather than having two participant groups, one of more-skilled readers and one of less-skilled readers, we assert that participants with little experience reading Zekkish are less-skilled readers of Zekkish. With practice, they become more-skilled readers of Zekkish, thus making reading ability essentially a within-subjects variable.

Gernsbacher & Faust demonstrated that manipulating the SOA between a homophone and a probe word resulted in homophone interference at 450 ms SOA for all readers and at 1350 ms SOA for less-skilled readers. Skilled readers had resolved the dual homophone activation by 1350 ms, and no longer showed longer response times to homophones than to controls. Perfetti & Hart showed that extending the SOA revealed a difference in time course for skilled and less skilled readers, but that no suppression mechanism needed to be invoked to explain the pattern of results. Skilled readers had homophone interference by 150 ms SOA that disappeared by 1350 ms SOA. Less-skilled readers had homophone interference by 450 ms SOA that disappeared by 2000 ms SOA. Both studies defined their reading groups based on reading comprehension, which suggests that reading comprehension depends at least in part on lexical quality.

Replicating this experiment in Zekkish allows us to test the hypothesis that the reading skill difference that was measured by these researchers is based on reading experience. It can be posited that the less skilled readers in these semantic judgment experiments had spent less time reading than the skilled readers, resulting in a lower functional frequency for them, for all words. If this is a plausible explanation then the Zekkish experiments should show a shift in the activation/deactivation curve from the "novice" testing session to the "expert" testing session as the readers increase their relative frequencies with all the words, mimicking the shifts between less-skilled and skilled readers in Perfetti & Hart's experiment.

Figure 6.10 shows the results of the "Novice" testing session, when participants had learned the Zekkish language, but only to a minimum criterion of 85% correct. These participants could also be called inexperienced readers, or slow and effortful readers, or, we claim, less-skilled or poor readers. In this figure and the one to

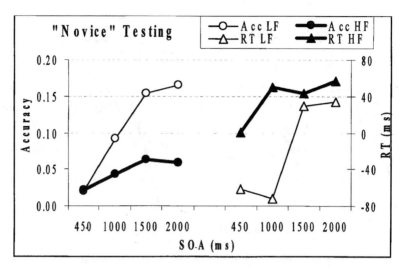

FIGURE 6.10   Homophone interference (and facilitation) effects early in training, while participants were still "novices" with the language.

follow, we have plotted the difference between homophone and control performance to indicate the degree of homophone interference. For accuracy, homophones were subtracted from controls. For reaction time, controls were subtracted from homophones. This produced a difference score for which more homophone interference is related to higher difference scores.

When these readers were less-skilled, with enough time to decode the word, they were more accurate for controls than for homophones. We chose to increase the first SOA from the Gernsbacher experiments because these readers were much less skilled than typical less-skilled college students reading English. Even with this longer SOA most of the participants claimed they had barely seen the word in 450 ms, much less read it. Their accuracy performance shows that they had not yet activated their Zekkish lexical representations by 450 ms. By 1000 ms, however, their accuracy scores indicate that some interference was present – but only for low frequency words. This is much like the pattern we found in our original experiment; readers were more accurate to controls than to homophones and high frequency words than to low frequency words. And as SOA increased, the frequency difference between homophones and controls increased.

Reaction time at the novice testing session tells a different story. Homophone interference first occurs at the second SOA, occurs earlier for high frequency words than for low frequency words, like the less-skilled comprehenders in our original experiment. However, unlike our previous experiment, these readers are actually showing a homophone *advantage* at the earliest two SOAs for low-frequency words. Homophone advantage is typical of experiments in which a response can be made based only on

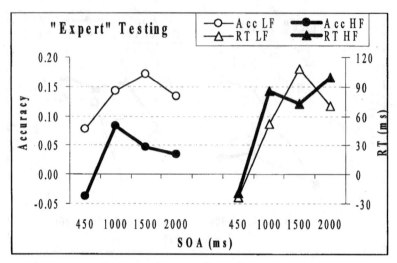

FIGURE 6.11   Homophone interference effects after multiple training sessions, when participants were "experts" with the language.

orthography and/or phonology, such as lexical decision and naming tasks.[5] This suggests that at the earlier SOAs readers may actually be using the phonological information, but only reaching semantic activation for high frequency words. For low frequency words, they do not activate the complete lexical item, for either homophones or controls, so the more supported, stronger phonological activation of the homophones results in a faster response to homophones than to controls.

So with the "novice" testing session, we replicated the findings of our original experiment, except that we included an SOA short enough to show some pre-activation homophone advantage for low frequency words.

The "expert" testing session (See Figure 6.11) was designed to model the performance of more-skilled English readers, because between the novice and expert testing sessions, participants gained a great deal of experience decoding words and accessing their meanings. As a result, the activation curve shifts, with activation occurring earlier and homophone advantage disappearing. The accuracy data show the frequency difference by the first SOA, and it continues throughout.[6]

The reaction time data also shows a shift in the activation curve. The homophone advantage is gone, and there are true indications of homophone interference by the

_____

[5]This is not to say that experiment participants never use semantic information in lexical decision and naming tasks, nor that back-propogation from semantics to orthography cannot take place. Sometimes it does, resulting in interference, but the typical pattern of responses shows either no homophone-control difference (usually high frequency words) or a homophone advantage (usually low frequency words).

[6]Note that the differences are much more significant at the expert testing session. This is due to a dramatic decrease in performance variability.

second SOA. New data patterns also arise. There is no evidence of a recovery from interference, and interference occurs for both high frequency and low frequency homophones.

There are two likely reasons that interference does appear until the second SOA. The first reason is simply that we did not choose the optimal SOAs to accurately capture the entire activation/deactivation curve. While we're calling our participants experts by the second testing session, and while they are much more fluent in Zekkish than at the novice testing session, there is still a world of difference between our expert Zekkish readers and the typical college reader of English – regardless of English reading skill. Our participants show a pattern typical of an intermediate stage; some expertise, but not true automaticity. We hypothesize that with more training the pattern of results would become more and more like that of the more-skilled readers in our previous experiments. It is also possible, however, that beyond two seconds to view the Zekkish word some qualitative aspects of the process might change. For example, the time to read each word would become irrelevant and the time to search long term memory for the Zek linked to the word would become more important.

SUMMARY

In this chapter we have asserted that lexical quality is the basis for efficient word reading skill, and efficient word reading skill, in turn, is at the heart of good reading comprehension. We have discussed ways to test this assertion by sneaking words of lower lexical quality into experiments (homophones, homographs, ambiguous words), and the pattern of results that come from these experiments. We have discussed a series of our own experiments based on one by Gernsbacher & Faust (1991), and made the following claims based on the results of these experiments.

- By adequately covering the range of activation/deactivation of word meanings with the appropriate SOAs, we can elicit responses that occur prior to activation, during activation, and after activation.
- By varying reading skill and word frequency, we can demonstrate shifts in this activation curve. We claim that both reading skill and word frequency are manipulations of experience with words.
- By assuring that experiment participants know word meanings of both members of homophone pairs, performance of skilled and less skilled readers can be equated.
- By training participants on the lower frequency member of a homophone pair, we can reverse the pattern of interference such that the trained word becomes the higher frequency word.

In short, it appears that lexical quality can be enhanced or threatened by a number of different factors that are associated with word experience. Word frequency, as well as shared orthography, phonology, and meaning, affect lexical quality from the structure of a language's lexicon. Reading experience, including specific training, can affect individuals' lexical quality. Regardless of the origin, better lexical quality is associated with reading at multiple levels, from decoding to fluency to comprehension.

REFERENCES

Aaron, P. G., & Joshi, R. M. (1989). *Reading and writing disorders in different orthographic systems*. New York, NY: Kluwer Academic/Plenum Publishers.

Abu-Rabia, S. (1997). Reading in Arabic orthography: The effect of vowels and content on reading accuracy of poor and skilled native Arabic readers in reading paragraphs, sentences, and isolated words. *Journal of Psycholinguistic Research, 26*, 465–482.

Almeida, R., & Libben, G. (2005). Changing morphological structures: The effect of sentence context on the interpretation of structurally ambiguous English trimorphemic words. *Language and Cognitive Processes, 20*, 373–394.

Balota, D. A., Ferraro, F. R., & Connor, L. T. (1991). On the early influence of meaning in word recognition: A review of the literature. In P. J. Schwanenflugel [Ed.], *The psychology of word meanings*. Hillsdale, NJ: Lawrence Erlbaum Associates, Inc.

Binder, K. S., & Rayner, K. (1998). Contextual strength does not modulate the subordinate bias effect: Evidence from eye fixations and self-paced reading. *Psychonomic Bulletin and Review, 5*, 271–276.

Bishop, D. V., & Adams, C. A. (1990). A prospective study of the relationship between specific language impairment, phonological disorders and reading retardation. *Journal of Child Psychology and Psychiatry, 31*, 1027–1050.

Catts, H. W., Fey, M. E., Tomblin, J. B, & Zhang, X. (2002). A longitudinal investigation of reading outcomes in children with language impairments. *Journal of Speech, Language, and Hearing Research, 45*, 1142–1157.

Cohen, R. L., Netley, C., & Clarke, M. A. (1984). On the generality of the short-term memory/reading ability relationship. *Journal of Learning Disabilities, 17*, 218–221.

Collins, M. (2002). Interhemispheric communication via direct communications for alternative meanings of ambiguous words. *Brain and Language, 80*, 77–96.

Cornoldi, C. (1990). Metacognitive control processes and memory deficits in poor comprehenders. *Learning Disability Quarterly, 13*, 245–255.

Felton, R. H., & Wood, F. B. (1992). A reading level match study of nonword reading skills in poor readers with varying IQ. *Journal of Learning Disabilities, 25*, 318–326.

Gernsbacher, M. A. (1991). Cognitive processes and mechanisms in language comprehension: The structure building framework. In G. H. Bower (Ed.). *The psychology of learning and motivation: Advances in research and theory, Vol. 27*. San Diego, CA: Academic Press, Inc.

Gernsbacher, M.A. (1990). *Language Comprehension as Structure Building*. Hillsdale, NJ: Lawrence Erlbaum Asociates.

Gernsbacher, M.A., & Faust, M. (1991). The mechanism of suppression: A component of general comprehension skill. *Journal of Experimental Psychology: Learning, Memory, and Cognition, 17*, 245–262.

Gernsbacher, M.A., Varner, K.R., & Faust, M. (1990). Investigating differences in general comprehension skill. *Journal of Experimental Psychology: Learning, Memory, and Cognition, 16*, 430–445.

Gorfein, D. S., Viviani, J. M., & Leddo, J. (1982). Norms as a tool for the study of homography. *Memory & Cognition, 10*, 503–509.

Gottlob, L. R., Goldinger, S. D., Stone, G. O., & Van Orden, G. C. (1999). Reading homographs: Orthographic, phonologic, and semantic dynamics. *Journal of Experimental Psychology: Human Perception and Performance, 25*, 561–574.

Ho, C. S. (2003). Reading acquisition and developmental dyslexia in Chinese: A cognitive perspective. In N. Goulandris (Ed). *Dyslexia in different languages: Cross-linguistic comparisons.* Philadelphia, PA: Whurr Publishers, Ltd.

Jonkman, I., Licht, R., Bakker, D. J., & van den Broek-Sandmann, T. M. (1992). Shifting of attention in subtyped dyslexic children: An event-related potential study. *Developmental Neuropsychology, 8,* 243–259.

Kawamoto, A. H., & Zemblidge, J. H. (1992). Pronunciation of homographs. *Journal of Memory and Language, 31,* 349–374.

Long, D. L., Oppy, B. J., & Seely, M. R. (1997). Individual differences in readers' sentence and text-level representations. *Journal of Memory and Language, 36,* 129–145.

Martin, C., Vu, H., Kellas, G., & Metcalf, K. (1999). Strength of discourse context as a determinant of the subordinate bias effect. The Quarterly *Journal of Experimental Psychology, 52A,* 813–839.

Miller-Shaul, S. (2005). The characteristics of young and adult dyslexics readers on reading and reading related tasks as compared to normal readers. *Dyslexia: An International Journal of Research and Practice, 11,* 132–151.

Nikolopoulos, D., Goulandris, N., & Snowling, M. J. (2003). Developmental dyslexia in Greek. In N. Goulandris (Ed). *Dyslexia in different languages: Cross-linguistic comparisons.* Philadelphia, PA: Whurr Publishers, Ltd.

Oakhill, J. (1994). Individual differences in children's text comprehension. In M. A. Gernsbacher, (Ed). *Handbook of Psycholinguistics,* San Diego, CA: Academic Press, Inc.

Oakhill, J., Cain, K., & Yuill, N. (1998). *Individual differences in children's comprehension skill: Toward an integrated model.* Mahwah, NJ: Lawrence Erlbaum Associates.

O'Neill, M. E., & Douglas, V. I. (1991). Study strategies and story recall in attention deficit disorder and reading disability. *Journal of Abnormal Child Psychology, 19,* 671–692.

Oren, R., & Breznitz, Z. (2005). Reading processes in L1 and L2 among dyslexic as compared to regular bilingual readers: Behavioral and electrophysiological evidence. *Journal of Neurolinguistics, 18,* 127–151.

Osmon, D. C., Braun, M. M., & Plambeck, E. A. (2005). Processing abilities associated with phonologic and orthographic skills in adult learning disability. *Journal of Clinical and Experimental Neuropsychology, 27,* 2005, 544–554.

Paradis, M. (1989). Linguistic parameters in the diagnosis of dyslexia in Japanese and Chinese. In P. G. Aaron, & R. M. Joshi, (Eds), *Reading and writing disorders in different orthographic systems.* New York, NY: Kluwer Academic/Plenum Publishers.

Perfetti, C. A. (1985). *Reading ability.* New York, NY: Oxford University Press.

Perfetti, C. A. (1992). The representation problem in reading acquisition. In P. B. Gough, L. C. Ehri, & R. Treiman, (Eds), *Reading acquisition.* Hillsdale, NJ: Lawrence Erlbaum Associates, Inc.

Perfetti, C. A., & Bolger, D. J. (2004). The brain might read that way. *Scientific Studies of Reading, 8,* 293–304.

Perfetti, C. A., & Hart, L. (2001). The lexical basis of comprehension skill. In D. S. Gorfein, (Ed), *On the consequences of meaning selection: Perspectives on resolving lexical ambiguity.* Washington, DC: American Psychological Association.

Perfetti, C.A., & Hart, L. (2002). The lexical quality hypothesis. In L. Verhoeven. C. Elbro, & P. Reitsma (Eds.), *Precursors of Functional Literacy* Amsterdam/Philadelphia: John Benjamins.

Perfetti, C. A., Wlotko, E. W., & Hart, L. A. (2005). Word Learning and Individual Differences in Word Learning Reflected in Event-Related Potentials. *Journal of Experimental Psychology: Learning, Memory, and Cognition, 31,* 1281–1292.

Rodd, J., Gaskell, M., & Marslen-Wilson, W. (2004). Modelling the effects of semantic ambiguity in word recognition. *Cognitive Science, 28,* 89–104.

Scarborough, H. S. (1990). Very early language deficits in dyslexic children. *Child Development, 61*, 1728–1743.

Snowling, M. J., Bishop, D. V. M., & Stothard, S. E. (2000). Is preschool language impairment a risk factor for dyslexia in adolescence? *Journal of Child Psychology and Psychiatry, 41*, 587–600.

St. George, M., Mannes, S., & Hoffman, J. E. (1997). Individual differences in inference generation: An ERP analysis. *Journal of Cognitive Neuroscience, 9*, 776–787.

Stanovich, K. E., West, R. F., & Cunningham, A. E. (1991). Beyond phonological processes: Print exposure and orthographic processing. In S. A. Brady & D. P. Shankweiler, (Eds), *Phonological processes in literacy: A tribute to Isabelle Y. Liberman*. Hillsdale, NJ: Lawrence Erlbaum Associates, Inc.

Vauras, M., Kinnunen, R., & Kuusela, L. (1994). Development of text-processing skills in high-, average-, and low-achieving primary school children. Journal of Reading Behavior, 26, 361–389.

Vellutino, F. R., & Scanlon, D. M. (1988). Phonological coding, phonological awareness, and reading ability: Evidence from a longitudinal and experimental study. In K. E. Stanovich, (Ed), *Children's reading and the development of phonological awareness*. Detroit, MI: Wayne State University Press.

Vu, H., Kellas, G., Petersen, E., & Metcalf, K. (2003). Situation-evoking stimuli, domain of reference, and the incremental interpretation of lexical ambiguity. *Memory and Cognition, 31*, 1302–1315.

Wade-Woolley, L. (1999). First language influences on second language word reading: All roads lead to Rome. *Language Learning, 49*, 447–471.

Whyte, J. (1994). Attentional processes and dyslexia. *Cognitive Neuropsychology, 11*, 99–116.

Wimmer, H. (1996). The early manifestation of developmental dyslexia: Evidence from German children. *Reading and Writing, 8*, 171–188.

CHAPTER SEVEN

Cross-Code Consistency in a Functional Architecture for Word Recognition

Jonathan Grainger
Centre National dela Recherche Scientifique, University of Provence

Johannes C. Ziegler
Centre National dela Recherche Scientifique, University of Provence

Understanding how literate adults can read single words has been one of the major objectives of cognitive psychology since the very inception of this science (Huey, 1908). The process of silent word reading (reading for meaning) minimally requires two types of codes: orthography (knowledge about letter identities and letter position) and semantics (knowledge about the meanings of words). The process of reading aloud minimally requires an orthographic code and a phonological/articulatory code in order to generate a pronunciation. Although no more than two critical codes are necessarily required for each task, it has become increasingly clear that all three codes (orthography, phonology, and semantics) are involved in both silent reading and reading aloud. The empirical evidence to be reviewed in the present chapter suggests that these different codes interact in the on-going reading process and conjointly influence observable performance. This has led to the development of a generic architecture for word recognition (see Figure 7.1) that emphasizes the critical role of such cross-code interactions. It is the precise nature of the interactions between orthographic, phonological, and semantic codes during the perception of printed words that forms the focus of the present chapter.

Behavioral data have accumulated over the last thirty years, allowing a better understanding of how each type of information (orthographic, phonological, semantic) is processed during skilled reading, and how the mechanisms necessary for skilled performance develop during reading acquisition (Harm & Seidenberg, 1999).

129

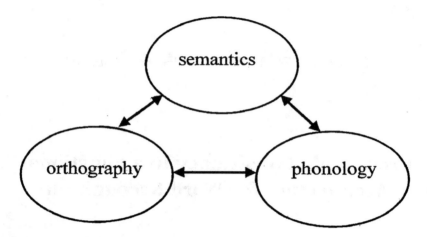

FIGURE 7.1   A generic architecture for word recognition based on the triangle model of Seidenberg and McClelland (1989).

These data have been obtained by experimental psychologists using a variety of behavioral techniques involving mostly single word presentation. In a typical experiment, participants are asked to read aloud as rapidly and as accurately as possible (word naming task), or to indicate with a button press whether the word belongs to a particular semantic category (semantic categorization task), or to decide whether the string of letters they see form a word they know (lexical decision task). In some studies, the word stimulus is degraded by pattern masking and reduced stimulus exposures, and participants just have to say what word they saw (perceptual identification task). Finally, data about the processing of critical words presented in a sentence context can be obtained using eye movement recordings (Rayner, 1998). It is mostly results obtained with these techniques testing skilled adult readers that have provided critical constraints in the development of a functional architecture for word recognition. We focus on these particular data in the present chapter.

However, there are three other key sources of data that also help constrain possible architectures for word recognition, and which are therefore implicitly taken into consideration in the theoretical contribution to this chapter. These sources of data are provided by research on reading acquisition, by research on atypical word recognition (developmental and acquired language disorders), and brain imaging research. We will briefly summarize recent research in these three areas before returning to the main thrust of the present chapter.

Research on reading acquisition has clearly shown the importance of phonology in learning to read. Indeed, the first steps in becoming literate require the acquisition of a system for mapping distinctive visual symbols (letters) onto units of sound (phonemes). This mapping process is called <u>phonological recoding</u> (see Ziegler & Goswami, 2005). Mastery of this process allows the children to access the thousands of words that are present in their spoken lexicons prior to reading, and also to recode words that they have heard but never seen before. Phonological recoding works well as a self-teaching device, because the relationship between symbol and sound is systematic in most languages (e.g., the symbol 'D' is always pronounced /d/ at the beginning of a word). In contrast, mapping visual symbols directly onto units of meaning, as would be required by some sort of visual or "logographic" learning, is difficult because the relationship between symbol and meaning is mostly arbitrary.

Because learning to read requires children to associate letters to sounds, problems in representing and using units of sound will almost always lead to impaired reading (developmental dyslexia). Indeed, research has shown that the majority of children with dyslexia have problems in the representation and use of phonological information. They perform more poorly than their peers in tasks, such as verbal short term memory, rapid automatized naming, phonological awareness, or phonological decoding (for review, see Snowling, 2000). Most intervention programs are based on improving phonological processes and the link between letters and sounds (Tallal, 2003). Nevertheless, reading is a complex task, and it seems clear that visual or attentional problems might also lead to reading problems. For example, some developmental dyslexics complain that small letters appear to blur and move around when they are trying to read, which has led some authors to suggest that abnormalities of the magnocellular component of the visual system might be responsible for some forms of developmental dyslexia (Stein & Walsh, 1997). Even if these visual subtypes of dyslexia exist, it is probably fair to say that they are less common than phonological types of dyslexia (see Ramus et al., 2003).

Developmental dyslexia must be distinguished from acquired dyslexia, which results from a neural insult to a fully developed system. For more than one century, the study of brain damaged patients has been a rich source of information for specifying the architecture of the reading system and its localization in the brain. The most well studied acquired dyslexias are phonological and surface dyslexia. Phonological dyslexia is a condition in which after brain damage a previously skilled reader has a selective deficit in reading nonwords aloud (e.g., Funnell, 1983). Surface dyslexia is a condition in which after brain damage a previously skilled reader has a selective deficit in reading irregular words aloud (e.g., McCarthy & Warrington, 1986). This double dissociation has provided the major motivation for postulating the existence of two independent routes to reading aloud, one lexical orthographic route and one nonlexical phonological route. This architecture was implemented in the well-known dual route model of reading aloud (see Coltheart, Rastle, Perry, Langdon & Ziegler, 2001). The modelling work to be presented in the present chapter has drawn inspiration from different theoretical sources, including dual-route theory.

Recent advances in brain imaging technology with higher levels of spatial resolution (e.g., fMRI, MEG) have allowed researchers to map the component processes of single word reading in the brains of literate adults with increasing degrees of accuracy (e.g., Cohen, Dehaene, Naccache, Lehericy, Dehaene-Lambertz, Henaff, & Michel, 2000; Dehaene, Le Clec'H, Poline, Le Bihan, & Cohen, 2002; McCandliss, Cohen, & Dehaene, 2003; Nobre, Allison, & McCarthy, 1994). Although there is a lively ongoing debate as to just how localized such component processes might be in the brain (see e.g., Price & Devlin, 2003), the evidence at present is in favor of preferential processing of specific types of code by specific brain regions. Thus orthographic processing has been replicably located (using both fMRI and MEG) in a small part of left fusiform gyrus dubbed the "visual word form area" (VWFA). Well-structured pseudowords typically produce stronger fMRI responses than random consonant strings in this region (Cohen et al., 2002; Dehaene et al., 2002). Furthermore, recent research using magnetoencephalography (MEG) has estimated that the VWFA becomes significantly active after about 200 ms post-stimulus onset (Pammer et al., 2004).

More diverse regions have been associated with phonological processing associated with printed words, probably because there are diverse forms of phonological coding (i.e., phonology involved in silent reading vs. phonology involved in reading aloud). Several fMRI studies have found greater activation of the left IFG during pseudoword reading as opposed to word reading, and interpreted this as evidence for sublexical conversion of orthographic information into a phonological output code (e.g., Fiebach, Friederici, Müller, & von Cramon, 2002; Fiez & Petersen, 1998; Hagoort et al., 1999; Pugh et al., 1996). Cohen, Jobert, Le Bihan, and Dehane (2004, see also Booth, Burman, Meyer, Gitelman, Parrish & Mesulman, 2002) found that a part of lateral inferior temporal cortex was always strongly activated by both visually and auditorily presented words. Finally, brain imaging research with developmental dyslexics suggests that the core deficit is an underactivation of the left temporo-parietal cortex, a region responsible for the fine-grain analysis of phonology and the mapping of letters onto sounds (Paulesu et al., 2001). Recent intervention studies have also shown that behavioral remediation ameliorates these dysfunctional neural mechanisms in children with dyslexia (e.g., Temple et al., 2003).

Thus studies using imaging techniques with high spatial resolution (fMRI, MEG) are beginning to help define further architectural constraints for a model of word recognition (how the different component processes might be interconnected in neural hardware). On the other hand, brain imaging techniques with high temporal resolution (EEG, MEG) are important for specifying the time-course of these different component processes. Event-related potentials (ERPs) reflect the electrical activity generated by the brain as measured at the surface of the head, and are sensitive to both the physical characteristics of stimuli and their psychological dimensions such as word frequency, concreteness, etc. ERPs are obtained by averaging over large number of trials such that random electrical activity (as seen in the electroencephalogram or EEG) is cancelled out, leaving mostly stimulus-generated activity that provides a fine-grained temporal measure of on-going stimulus processing. ERPs measured at the surface of the scalp can help determine when a specific type of code (e.g., individual letters, letter clusters, phonemes) is operational relative to another type of code (Grainger & Holcomb, 2007). Recent work using this technique has helped uncover a cascade of ERP components triggered on presentation of a printed word stimulus that start as early as 90 ms post-word-onset and continue through to as late as 600 ms (Holcomb & Grainger, 2006). Each of these components is thought to reflect a specific type of processing along the pathway that leads from visual feature analysis to meaning.

All the above-mentioned sources of empirical data on visual word recognition have helped develop and refine various theoretical accounts of the information processing performed by the brain during reading. In the present chapter we will focus on one particular theoretical approach, often referred to as connectionist or neural-network modeling, as a promising means to understanding the interactions between orthographic, phonological, and semantic codes that are inferred from the empirical data. Connectionist models, such as McClelland and Rumelhart's (1981) interactive-activation model, and Seidenberg and McClelland's (1989) triangle model (Figure 7.1), were developed in the context of the more general goal to describe psychological phenomena using more "brain-like" mechanisms. The currency of connectionist networks is a neuron-like information processing device that takes numerical values (activation) from different sources as input, and outputs numerical values to multiple destinations after summing and transforming the input using some specific algebraic function. Typically, all processing units function identically in such networks, and it is the pattern of connection weights linking different processing units that determines how the whole system will "react" to a given input. In such models, the processing of complex objects such as a printed word involves the activation of many such simple processing units at different levels. In localist versions of connectionst models (e.g., McClelland & Rumelhart, 1981), complex objects can be represented by a single processing unit that preferentially responds to a given set of activation inputs from other levels of processing. In distributed versions of connectionist models (e.g., Seidenberg & McClelland, 1989), complex representations involve the co-activation of a relatively large number of processing units at the same level (see Grainger & Jacobs, 1998, for a discussion of localist versus distributed representations).

Figure 7.1 describes a minimalist architecture for word recognition that highlights the interactive nature of processing, which is central to the theoretical contribution of the present chapter. Orthographic representations communicate bi-directionally with both phonological and semantic representations as activation is propagated through the network of processing units following presentation of a printed word stimulus. However, behavioral evidence and the results of recent brain imaging research (summarized above) all point to a system for visual word recognition that is organized hierarchically in increasingly abstract levels of representation. In the following section we present an initial attempt at adding more hierarchical structure to the generic framework of Figure 7.1.

VISUAL WORD RECOGNITION AND CROSS-CODE CONSISTENCY

Within the generic architecture for word recognition described above, cross-code consistency plays an important role for efficient functioning and stable learning. The notion of cross-code consistency refers to the level of compatibility or coherence of all co-activated representations across the three types of code: orthographic, phonological, and semantic. At a more general level of theorizing, consistency refers to the conditional probabilities that describe the mapping of items in one set (i.e., one level of representation or one type of code) onto items in another set, measured over a certain number of occurrences of these items. For a given set of occurrences of item i in set A, the consistency of the mapping of that item onto a given item in set B is measured by the conditional probability of that mapping relative to the complete set of mappings of A(i) onto B. Thus, for example, a given item A(i) maps onto several items in set B (i, j, k), with the different mappings (A(i) => B(i), A(i) => B(j), A(i) => B(k)) being associated with different contexts for the occurrence of A(i). The conditional probability of one specific mapping (e.g., A(i) => B(i)) is given by the frequency of that mapping divided by the sum of the frequencies of the complete set of mappings of A(i) onto B. This conditional probability measures how well the presence of A(i) predicts the occurrence of B(i) relative to B(j) and B(k), for example. Conditional probabilities can be measured in both directions (A => B, B => A) with different values associated with each direction. Often the terms feedforward and feedback consistency are used to refer to these two directions. Note also that conditional probabilities provide a means of quantifying the more general notion of one-to-many relations.

Conditional probabilities are implemented in connectionist networks, such as the triangle model described above, in terms of the distribution of weights linking two sets (A, B) of units (orthographic and phonological, for example). The conditional probability of a given mapping from unit A(i) to unit B(j) can affect performance in connectionist models, either by determining the weight strength between these two units as a function of the learning algorithm that is used (backpropagation for Seidenberg & McClelland's, 1989, model), and/or via competitive mechanisms across units in the same set (i.e., within-level inhibition).

In the first possibility, conditional probabilities affect the learning process such that mappings with lower conditional probabilities are harder to establish than mappings with higher conditional probabilities. The way conditional probabilities can affect learning in connectionist networks has been most forcefully illustrated using the concept of resonance in recurrent networks with bi-directional activation flow (cf. Kawamoto 1993; Stone & Van Orden, 1994; Van Orden & Goldinger, 1994). In a recurrent network, cross-code consistency both in feedforward and feedback directions guarantees stable and fast learning. Consistent symmetrical relations are reflected in stable attractor states in such models. Stable attractors imply state dynamics that reach a stable-state quickly, requiring fewer cycles of interactive activation. Inconsistent relations are multistable. By definition, multistable relations exist if the same stimulus word systematically produces more than one response. Multistable relations are more slowly resolved than the consistent, symmetrical, relations of stable attractors (Tuller, Case, Ding, & Kelso, 1994; Van Orden, 2002; Van Orden, Jansen op de Haar, & Bosman, 1997; Ziegler, Van Orden, & Jacobs, 1997).

Conditional probabilities can also affect performance in connectionist networks via lateral inhibition operating across co-activated representations at the same level. Here, conditional probabilities reflect the relative activation levels of all representations that are compatible with a given input, but incompatible with each other. It is this explanatory mechanism, implemented in interactive-activation models (e.g., McClelland & Rumelhart, 1981) that will form the theoretical focus of the present work.

In terms of model architecture, in our own work (e.g., Grainger & Ferrand, 1994; Jacobs, Rey, Ziegler, & Grainger, 1998; Ziegler, Muneaux, & Grainger, 2003), we

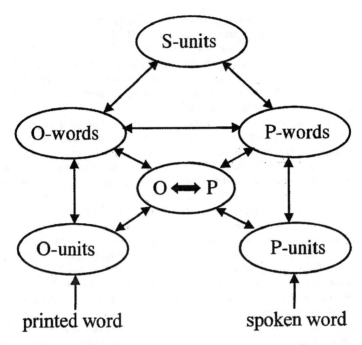

FIGURE 7.2 Architecture of a bimodal interactive activation model of word recognition in which a sublexical/lexical division is imposed on orthographic (O) and phonological (P) representations.

have added a sublexical/lexical distinction to the framework described in Figure 7.1. Thus, orthographic and phonological codes are separated into two distinct processing pools corresponding to whole-word representations and representations that correspond to orthographic and phonological sequences smaller than the whole-word. Sublexical representations refer to the latter type, which will typically be letter and phoneme-sized representations in localist models (Coltheart et al., 2001; McClelland & Rumelhart, 1981). Lexical representations refer to whole-word orthographic and whole-word phonological representations that provide the major gateway to higher-level semantic information. This particular architecture is presented in Figure 7.2. In the following sections, this framework will guide our discussion of consistency effects in word recognition.

The bi-modal interactive-activation model was initially designed to account for rapid, automatic involvement of phonological information during visual word recognition (see Frost, 1998, for a review). Critical evidence in favor of rapid, automatic phonological activation has been provided using the masked priming paradigm. In this paradigm, pattern-masked prime stimuli are briefly presented prior to target word presentation. Typical results show that prime stimuli that are phonologically related to target words (e.g., mayd-MADE) facilitate responding compared to orthographically related control primes (e.g., mard-MADE). These phonological priming effects have been observed with very brief prime exposure durations (Ferrand & Grainger, 1992; 1993; 1994; Frost, Ahissar, Gotesman, & Tayeb, 2003; Lukatela & Turvey, 1994; Perfetti & Bell, 1991; Ziegler, Ferrand, Jacobs, Rey, & Grainger, 2000). According to the time-course analyses provided by Ferrand and Grainger (1993) and Ziegler et al. (2000), phonological code activation lags about 20-30 ms behind orthographic code activation.

In the bi-modal interactive activation architecture described in Figure 7.2, a printed word stimulus activates a sublexical orthographic code (O-units) that is likely to include information about letter identities and their relative positions (e.g., Grainger & Whitney, 2004). This early orthographic code then sends activation onto the central interface between orthography and phonology (OP) that allows sublexical orthographic representations to be mapped onto their corresponding phonological representations, and vice versa. Thus a printed word stimulus rapidly activates a set of sublexical phonological representations (which we assume will include phoneme-sized units) that can influence the course of visual word recognition via their interaction with sublexical orthographic representations, or via the activation of whole-word phonological representations. It is this central interface between orthography and phonology that provides the mechanism by which words that are phonologically similar to the stimulus (its phonological neighbors) can influence the process of visual word recognition.

Figure 7.2 shows a processing architecture that is compatible with many different types of processing algorithms, both connectionist and symbolic, and modular or interactive. Within the specific framework we have adopted, information processing is described by the basic processing assumptions of interactive-activation (McClelland & Rumelhart, 1981): 1) processing is cascaded; 2) processing is interactive; and 3) mutual compatibility determines the type of information exchange (positive, negative, or neutral) between two processing units. All three characteristics determine how cross-code consistency affects processing in an interactive-activation model. We will attempt to demonstrate how this theoretical framework provides a parsimonious account of the currently available empirical evidence.

In the present chapter, we examine the utility of a single theoretical construct, cross-code consistency, for explaining well-known phenomena in the field of word recognition. During single word reading, the spread of activation across orthography, phonology and semantics generates a large set of co-activated representations. We will assume that all co-activated representations can affect the global state of coherence (resonance) in an interactive-activation framework as a function of the consistency of the mappings that connect them. The set of representations that are activated on presentation of a given target word will include the orthographic, phonological, and semantic representations of the target word itself, and also representations for words that are orthographically and phonologically similar to the target word (its orthographic and phonological neighbors). In the following sections, we will simplify matters by isolating specific mappings as a function of the type of code that is predominantly involved (sublexical or lexical; orthographic, phonological, or semantic).

SUBLEXICAL MAPPINGS BETWEEN ORTHOGRAPHY AND PHONOLOGY

Beware of heard, a dreadful word
That looks like beard and sounds like bird
And dead: it's said like bed, not bead;
For goodness sake, don't call it deed.

As nicely illustrated in the above lines, spelling-to-sound inconsistency hurts. Inconsistency can either occur at the level of pronunciations when a given ortho-graphic pattern (e.g., -eard) is pronounced differently in different words (e.g., "beard" vs. "heard") or at the level of spelling when a given phonological pattern can be spelled differently in different words (e.g., "bird" versus "word"). Glushko (1979) was the first to demonstrate that inconsistent words take longer to name than consistent words of similar frequency. He focused on the spelling-to-sound consis-tency of word bodies, the <u>body</u> being everything that is left after removing the ini-tial consonant(s) in a monosyllabic word. Accordingly, a word like "pint" is inconsistent because most of the English words that end in "-int" rhyme with "mint", "lint", "tint" or "print". In fact, Glushko (1979) compared two groups of words that were both <u>regular</u> according to grapheme-phoneme correspondence rules but dif-fered in consistency. For example, the pronunciation of a "regular inconsistent" word, such as "wave" can be correctly determined by rule. However, "wave" is nev-ertheless inconsistent because the –ave body is pronounced differently in "have". Glushko's finding of a consistency effect was extremely important because it showed that the pronunciation of a word is influenced by the knowledge of other, similarly spelled words.

Subsequent research replicated the existence of consistency effects in naming and demonstrated that the size of the consistency effect depended on the ratio of friends to enemies (Jared, 1997; 2002; Jared, McRae, & Seidenberg, 1990). Note that for a word like "mint", "hint" and "lint" are "friends" while "pint" is an "enemy". "Mint" is more consistent than "pin " because it has a higher ratio of friends to ene-mies (for statistical analyses, see Ziegler, Stone & Jacobs, 1997). This friend to enemy ratio is the conditional probability of the sublexical mapping of the ortho-graphic string "int" onto its different sublexical phonological realizations. Although it was initially believed that consistency effects could only be seen in low-frequency words (i.e., the famous consistency by frequency interaction), subsequent research also demonstrated that consistency can affect the naming of high-frequency words provided that the friend/enemy ratio of the high-frequency words was similar to that of low frequency words (Jared, 1997).

Within the framework presented in Figure 7.2, the above described consistency effects reflect the parallel mapping of a single sublexical orthographic form (letter or letter cluster) onto several sublexical phonological forms (phonemes or phoneme clusters) that then compete following the principle of within-level lateral inhibition. This is illustrated in Figure 7.3 for the letter string "ave" that has two dis-tinct pronunciations as in the words "have" and "save", for example. Given that reading aloud requires the computation of a phonological/articulatory code, it is not

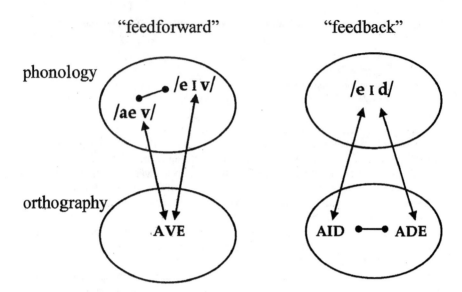

FIGURE 7.3   Illustration of inconsistent sublexical mappings from orthography to phonology (left-hand panel), often referred to as *feedforward inconsistency*, and inconsistent sublexical mappings from phonology to orthography (right-hand panel) or *feedback inconsistency*.

surprising that this type of sublexical consistency effect is particularly strong in the naming task. Such effects are generally absent or much smaller in the lexical decision task (Coltheart, Besner, Jonasson, & Davelaar, 1979; Waters & Seidenberg, 1985, but see Gibbs & Van Orden, 1998).

Early research on the consistency effect in reading typically manipulated consistency only between spelling and phonology, but not between phonology and spelling. The exclusive focus on "one-way consistency effects" was probably due to the fact that, in traditional information processing models, information only flows downstream, as from spelling to phonology (with visually presented words). As noted in the introduction, interactive-activation and resonance models predicted effects in the opposite direction as well. Stone, Vanhoy and Van Orden (1997) challenged the "one-way-consistency" perspective. They demonstrated that performance in a visual lexical decision task was not only influenced by inconsistency of the spelling-to-sound mapping (pint versus mint) but also by inconsistency of the sound-to-spelling mapping. The latter kind of inconsistency was called feedback inconsistency. For example, the word heap is feedback inconsistent because heap's pronunciation rime /_ip/ has more than one conventional spelling (compare _eap as in heap versus _eep as in deep). Indeed, Stone et al showed that feedback inconsistent words, such as heap, produced slower correct "yes" responses in lexical decision than feedback consistent words, that is, words with phonological rimes that could only be spelled one way (e.g., /uk/ as in "duck" or "luck"). As illustrated in Figure 7.3, an interactive-activation account of sublexical consistency effects actually predicts that "feedback consistency" should affect performance in tasks where orthography is important, and more so than "feedforward inconsistency." Tasks where phonology is important (word naming, for example) should, on the other hand, reveal stronger effects of "feedforward consistency," when the stimuli are presented visually.

Subsequent to the original report, the pattern of feedforward and feedback consistency effects was replicated in French (Ziegler, Montant, & Jacobs, 1997). However, soon after this publication, the existence of feedback consistency effects was called into question by Peereman, Content and Bonin (1998). They failed to replicate the effect and claimed that an otherwise successful replication of Ziegler et al. (1997) was actually an effect of subjective (rated) familiarity, not feedback consistency. A problem with this logic, in our view, is that rated familiarity is a performance variable, a dependent variable, like response time or error rate. A lexical decision experiment asks a participant to categorize letter strings on the basis of familiarity. Familiar letter strings are called "words"; unfamiliar letter strings are called "nonwords," and correct "word" response times estimate the ease with which the familiarity judgment is made. In fact, these performance variables should converge. But even so, the existence of feedback consistency effects has now been replicated in two independent studies, which both controlled their material for subjective rated familiarity (Perry, 2003; Lacruz & Folk, 2004).

An important extension of the cross-code consistency hypothesis was discovered when examining its predictions relative to auditory word recognition. The cross-code hypothesis predicted that phonology feeds back to orthography even when words are presented auditorily. Therefore, performance in auditory tasks should be affected when a word's phonology contains inconsistent sound-spelling relations. This prediction was confirmed in an auditory lexical decision task in French (Ziegler & Ferrand, 1998). Indeed, these authors found that auditory lexical decisions to words whose rimes could be spelled in multiple ways were slower than to words whose rimes could be spelled only one way. This finding has been replicated in Portuguese (Ventura, Morais, Pattamadilok and Kolinsky, 2004) and English (Miller & Swick, 2003). Subsequent research has also demonstrated that the consistency effect in auditory word recognition was not due to subtle phonological or phonetic differences between consistent and inconsistent items (Ziegler, Ferrand, & Montant, 2004). The symmetry between visual and auditory word recognition is important theoretically. It supplies a strong theoretical motivation that a synthesis may be possible between separate theories of visual and auditory word recognition (see Ziegler & Goswami, 2005).

LEXICAL MAPPINGS BETWEEN ORTHOGRAPHY AND PHONOLOGY

For languages that use alphabetic orthographies, ambiguity in spelling-to-sound and sound-to-spelling at the level of whole-word representations exists in the form of heterographic homophones and heterphonic homographs. Heterographic homophones are words that are pronounced identically but have different spellings associated with different meanings (e.g., MADE-MAID). Heterophonic homographs are words that are spelled the same way but have different pronunciations associated with different meanings (e.g., BOW, pronounced /bo/ or /bau/). English has few such heterophonic homographs, hence much of the work in English (and French) examining orthography-phonology consistency effects at the whole-word level has focused on heterographic homophones. In this case, the main direction of inconsistency is from phonology to orthography. In this section, we will summarize work showing that heterographic homophones are harder to recognize as printed words than unambiguous control words.

Interference effects on the low-frequency member of heterographic homophone pairs (e.g., MAID as a homophone of MADE) were first reported by Rubenstein, Lewis, and Rubenstein (1971). In a lexical decision task, correct positive responses to these stimuli were significantly slowed compared to non-homophone controls. Coltheart, Davelaar, Jonasson, and Besner (1977) failed to replicate this result using stimuli that were better controlled for word frequency. However, the absence of a homophone effect in the Coltheart et al. study was shown to be due to the presence of pseudohomophones (nonwords that can be pronounced like a real word, e.g., ROZE) as stimuli eliciting negative lexical decision responses (Davelaar, Coltheart, Besner, & Jonasson, 1978). In the absence of such pseudohomophone stimuli, the low-frequency members of a heterographic homophone pair produced longer response times (RTs) than non-homophone control words. Davelaar et al. concluded that their participants abandoned use of an "optional phonological encoding strategy" in the presence of pseudohomophone stimuli, hence the absence of a homophone disadvantage in this situation.

Pexman, Lupker, and Jared (2001), replicated the homophone disadvantage observed by Davelaar et al. (1978) in a lexical decision task with regular nonwords. However, these authors failed to replicate the absence of a homophone disadvantage when all the nonwords are pseudohomophones (it should be noted that Davelaar et al. had tested different homophone stimuli in the different nonword contexts). Indeed, the homophone disadvantage even increased in this situation compared to the regular nonword condition, with effects appearing for both the high and the low-frequency members of the homophone pair (see also Gibbs & Van Orden, 1998). With regular nonwords, Pexman et al. (2001) found that homophone interference effects are only reliable for the low-frequency member of polarized homophone pairs (i.e., when there is a notable difference in frequency of occurrence in the two words, such as maid-made, with maid having a much lower frequency of occurrence than made).

Homophone disadvantages have also been reported in a perceptual identification task (Hawkins, Reicher, Rogers, & Peterson, 1976), a semantic categorization task (Jared & Seidenberg, 1991; Van Orden, 1987), and a letter search task (Ziegler, Van Orden, & Jacobs, 1997). Hawkins et al. reported that participants performed worse with homophone than non-homophone stimuli in the Reicher-Wheeler task (Reicher, 1969; Wheeler, 1970). Participants had to choose which of two orthographically similar words (e.g., WORD-WORK) had been presented in degraded conditions (i.e., short stimulus duration and pattern masking). Participants were often at chance level performance when the choice had to be made between two homophones (e.g., SENT-CENT). In a semantic categorization task, Van Orden (1987) reported that participants made significantly more false positive errors when the homophone mate of the target word was a member of the pre-specified category (e.g., is ROWS a FLOWER?), compared to orthographic controls (is ROBS a FLOWER?). In the letter search task, Ziegler et al. (1997) reported that with low-frequency homophone stimuli, participants made more false positive errors in the target absent condition (e.g., A in LEEK) when the target letter was present in the homophone mate of the test word (A in LEAK). Also, more false negative errors were made in the target present condition, when the target letter did not figure in the homophone mate of the test word (e.g., A in SEAM is not present in SEEM). Finally, a homophone disadvantage has been reported in studies measuring eye-movements during reading (Folk, 1999), and several eye-movement studies have shown that replacing a word with its homophone mate disrupts the reading process less than when a non-homophonic orthographically similar word is inserted instead (see Jared, Rayner, & Levy, 1999, for a review).

The homophone disadvantage observed in these different tasks is subject to certain restrictions. Hawkins et al. (1976) reported that increasing the percentage of homophone stimuli removed the homophone disadvantage in the Reicher-Wheeler task. This suggests that, on becoming aware of the presence of homophone pairs, participants could modify their response strategy, placing more reliance on orthographic information when matching available information from the stimulus to the two possible responses (see Verstaen, Humphreys, Olson, & d'Ydewalle, 1995, for a similar result using a backward masking paradigm). In the letter search task, the homophone disadvantage is strongest for the low-frequency printed forms of homophones (Ziegler et al., 1997), as is generally the case for the homophone disadvantage in lexical decision (Pexman et al., 2001), and semantic categorization (Jared & Seidenberg, 1991). Finally, it has been shown that the homophone disadvantage in semantic categorization is significantly larger when homophone pairs have high orthographic similarity (Coltheart, Patterson, and Leahy, 1994; Jared & Seidenberg, 1991; Van Orden, 1987).

Ferrand and Grainger (2003) investigated the possibility that some of the divergences in prior reports of homophone interference effects might be due to uncontrolled influences of high-frequency orthographically similar stimuli (i.e., high-frequency orthographic neighbors, for example, maid-said) known to affect visual word recognition (Grainger, 1990; Grainger, O'Regan, Jacobs, & Segui, 1989). When holding neighborhood density constant at zero (i.e., words had no orthographic neighbors), Ferrand and Grainger (2003) found robust homophone interference effects in French for heterographic homophones with orthographically dissimilar mates (e.g., AUTEL-HOTEL (altar-hotel)) in comparison with non-homophone stimuli. RTs to these homophone stimuli in both the lexical decision and progressive demasking tasks (an on-line perceptual identification task, see Grainger & Segui, 1990) were longer than RTs to words with no high frequency neighbors. This was one of the first demonstrations of a "pure" homophone disadvantage that was unlikely to be contaminated by uncontrolled effects of orthographic neighborhood.

In the same study, it was shown that non-homophonic words with high frequency orthographic neighbors were responded to more slowly and less accurately than non-homophonic words with no high frequency neighbors. This neighborhood frequency effect, as observed in prior studies (e.g., Grainger et al., 1989; Grainger, 1990; Grainger & Jacobs, 1996) is an important comparison point for the homophone disadvantage effect. This is particularly true for the situation tested by Ferrand and Grainger (2003) where target words in the high frequency neighbor condition had only a single high frequency orthographic neighbor. In this situation, a direct comparison could be made between competition arising from these unique high frequency neighbors and competition generated by the unique high frequency homophone mate of homophone target words. In Ferrand and Grainger's study, these manipulations produced roughly equivalent effects on behavioral responses.

In terms of cross-code consistency in an interactive-activation model of word recognition, these robust effects of homophone interference reflect the incompatibility between whole-word phonological representations and whole-word orthographic representations. That is, although a single phonological representation is activated by MAID or MADE, competition arises because this phonological representation is compatible with more than one orthographic representation (see Pexman et al., 2001, for a similar interpretation). The competition is all the greater when a low-frequency orthographic form must be recognized in face of competition from a high-frequency homophone mate. This reflects the relative frequency of each of the phonology-orthography mappings that are associated with a given heterographic homophone. Thus the high frequency member has automatically a higher conditional probability than its lower frequency mate for that specific mapping of a given phonological form onto orthographic forms.

In terms of processing dynamics, the presentation of a low-frequency homophone (e.g., MAID) causes activation in the whole-word phonological representation/meid/which then generates activation in the high-frequency whole-word orthographic form (MADE) that is incompatible with the stimulus (see Figure 7.4). Thus, there is an initial feedforward flow of information from orthography to phonology followed by feedback from phonology to orthography that results in competition, and the observed cost in processing such heterographic homophones.

Finally, in studies of single word reading, homophone interference effects have been primarily reported with the lexical decision task. The effects have also been found in the word naming task, but the effects observed in this task are much smaller than those obtained in the lexical decision task (Edwards, Pexman, & Hudson, 2004). This is likely due to the fact that lexical decision responses to printed words are primarily based on activity in whole-word orthographic representations, whereas naming responses must partly involve phonological/articulatory representations. When standard lexical decision procedure is replaced with a phonological lexical decision (say "yes" when the printed stimulus sounds like a word), then homophone interference effects disappear (Pexman, Lupker, & Reggin, 2002). Therefore, as predicted by the model, when responses are generated on the basis of activity in phonological representations (as opposed to orthographic representations), heterographic homophones no longer show inhibition.

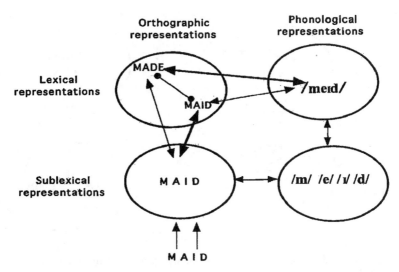

FIGURE 7.4 Processing an example heterographic homophone (MAID) in a bimodal interactive-activation model of visual word recognition (the architecture has been simplified by removing the central O ⇔ P interface).

MAPPINGS BETWEEN FORM AND MEANING

Researchers have been interested in semantic ambiguity ever since the resurge of work on visual word recognition in the 1970s (Rubenstein, Garfield, & Millikan, 1970). Although the early results in this area are just about as ambiguous as the stimuli they tested, a consensus has emerged in recent years as to exactly when and how semantic ambiguity does affect the process of printed word perception. Ambiguous words are words with several clearly distinct meanings. For example the word BANK in English has one meaning clearly defined in terms of a place where money is kept, and clearly distinct from an alternative meaning defined in terms of a sloping edge. It is important to distinguish words with multiple meanings (homonyms) from words with multiple related senses (polysemous words), since the level of ambiguity is clearly not the same in these two situations. Rodd, Gaskell, and Marslen-Wilson (2002) drew a distinction between what they called accidental ambiguity in the case of homonyms such as "bank" or "bark" and systematic ambiguity in the case of polysemous words such as "twist".

Homonyms will provide the first interesting test-case for effects of form-meaning consistency. In these words, a single orthographic / phonological form maps onto multiple meaning representations (see Figure 7.5). Several studies have now successfully replicated the early finding of Rubenstein et al. that ambiguous words are easier to respond to in a lexical decision task (e.g., Borowsky & Masson, 1996; Gottlob, Goldinger, Stone, & Van Orden, 1999; Hino & Lupker, 1996; Hino, Lupker, & Pexman, 2002; Jastrzembski, 1981; Kellas, Ferraro, & Simpson,1988; Millis & Button, 1989).

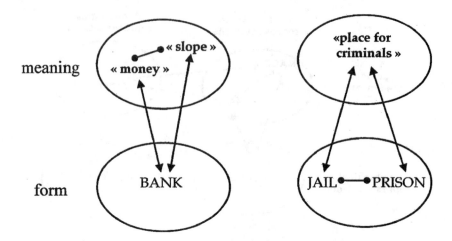

FIGURE 7.5   Cross-code inconsistency in the mapping of form to meaning (left panel) and meaning to form (right panel).

Balota, Ferraro, and Connor (1991) offered an explanation for this ambiguity advantage in lexical decision in terms of the extra feedback from semantics to orthography generated in the case of words with multiple meanings. In the same line of reasoning, Hino and Lupker (1996) argued that an ambiguity advantage is found in lexical decision because responses in this task are predominantly generated on the basis of orthographic representations. On the other hand, in a task where responses are based primarily on semantic representations, then an ambiguity DISadvantage should be observed. This is indeed what Hino, Lupker, and Pexman (2002) found. Thus the effects of semantic ambiguity nicely illustrate how the effects of cross-code consistency vary across different tasks, depending on the type of code that is predominantly used to generate a response in these tasks.

The part of the lexical network that captures these effects of semantic ambiguity is shown in the left-hand panel of Figure 7.5. The figure shows how an ambiguous word, or homonym such as "bank", leads to competition across two co-activated semantic representations. This captures the ambiguity disadvantage found in tasks where performance is predominantly determined by activity in semantic representations. On the other hand, the feedback from co-activated semantic representations to the same form representation can generate facilitatory effects of semantic ambiguity when response-generation is predominantly determined by activation in form representations.

A similar advantage for semantically ambiguous words has also been reported with cross-language homographs in bilingual subjects. The word "coin", for example, has two distinct meanings in French and English. Dijkstra, Grainger, and van Heuven (1999) found facilitatory effects of such cross-language semantic ambiguity in both a lexical decision task and a word identification task. Cross-language homographs were easier to respond to than matched non-ambiguous words, and this advantage was quite stable across the two tasks used. It is interesting to note that in the same experiments, cross-language phonological overlap had an inhibitory influence. Thus, words like "cow" and "kou" (which means "cold" in Dutch, and is pronounced similarly to "cow") are cross-language heterographic homophones, and show the same kind of inhibitory influence as within-language homophones (see preceding section). These effects of cross-language cross-code consistency can be accommodated by a model of bilingual word recognition that assumes that words of both languages are processed by the same network, and participate in the competitive and cooperative dynamics of the system in the same manner as words of the same language (Grainger & Dijkstra, 1992).

Furthermore, as would be expected on the basis of the account of ambiguity effects shown in Figure 7.5, polysemous words do not behave the same way as ambiguous words (e.g., Rodd et al., 2002). While it is clear that the two meanings of the word "bank" are completely incompatible with each other (hence the inhibitory connections in the model), the different senses of a polysemous word such as "twist" are clearly not completely incompatible with each other. One would therefore expect to observe a processing advantage for polysemous words compared to ambiguous words, which is what Rodd et al. (2002) observed.

On the other side of the coin to semantic ambiguity effects lie synonymy effects, another interesting test-case for form-meaning consistency effects. When a given meaning can be expressed in different ways (different forms), then synonymy arises (e.g., jail, prison). In this case a single meaning maps onto multiple forms, and this should therefore generate increased competition across form representations receiving feedback from the same semantic representations (see Figure 7.5). This pattern of results has been reported in several studies. Pecher (2001) and Hino et al. (2002) found that words with frequent synonyms were harder to respond to in lexical decision and naming. On the other hand, Hino et al. (2002) showed that no such synonymy effect was apparent in a semantic judgment task, as predicted by the above account. As can be seen in the right-hand panel of Figure 7.5, synonymy generates competition across form (orthographic and/or phonological) representations that are compatible with a common semantic representation. One could ask, however, why a facilitatory effect is not observed in a semantic task, in analogy to the facilitation observed with ambiguous words (e.g., bank) in the lexical decision task. One possible answer concerns the number of processing steps necessary to generate the effect. The facilitatory effect for ambiguous words arises after two processing steps (form-to-meaning-to-form), whereas a facilitatory effect for synonyms in a semantic task would require three processing steps (form-to-meaning-to-form-to-meaning).

NEIGHBORHOOD EFFECTS AS CONSISTENCY EFFECTS

"You can tell a word by the company it keeps"

Since the seminal work of Coltheart and colleagues (1977), the influence of a word's orthographic neighborhood on how we perceive printed words has attracted considerable attention from experimental psychologists. The number of orthographic neighbors of a given word is defined as the number of other words of the same length that share all but one letter in the same position (e.g., <u>work</u> and <u>ford</u> are neighbors of <u>word</u>). Andrews (1989, 1992) demonstrated that words with many such orthographic neighbors were responded to more rapidly, in both the lexical decision and word naming tasks, than words with few neighbors (see also, Forster & Shen, 1996; Sears, Hino, & Lupker, 1995). This facilitatory effect of neighborhood density interacted with word frequency such that only words with relatively low printed frequencies showed the facilitation.

One central debate has concerned the role played by the relative frequencies of the target word and its orthographic neighbors. Grainger and colleagues (e.g., Grainger et al., 1989; Grainger, 1990; Grainger & Jacobs, 1996) reported that low-frequency words that have a high-frequency orthographic neighbor are actually harder to recognize than low-frequency words with only low-frequency neighbors. This inhibitory effect runs counter to the more typical facilitatory effect of neighborhood density, mentioned above. The interactive-activation model (McClelland & Rumelhart, 1981) predicts such inhibitory effects of orthographic neighborhood (co-activated word representations inhibit each other, and this inhibition is a function of the activation levels of word units). This led Grainger and Jacobs (1996) to account for facilitatory effects of neighborhood density in terms of processes specific to the tasks (lexical decision and naming) with which these effects are observed. In line with this reasoning, Grainger and Jacobs found inhibitory effects of neighborhood density in a perceptual identification task where such mechanisms could not be operational (see also Carreiras, Perea, & Grainger, 1997). Thus, one simple explanation for the diverging patterns of results reported on neighborhood density effects on visual word recognition is that words with more neighbors generate more activation, and this can facilitate or inhibit a behavioral response depending on whether the extra activation is useful or not for generating that response. In the present section, we will examine to what extent cross-code consistency can account for at least part of the influence of variables defined in terms of a word's orthographic or phonological neighborhood.

As we have just noted, there is still much controversy surrounding the precise mechanisms that are responsible for effects of orthographic neighborhood density in visual word recognition (Andrews, 1997; Grainger & Jacobs, 1996; Mathey & Zagar, 2000; Ziegler & Perry, 1998). This is possibly because orthographic neighborhood density correlates highly with other variables that can influence visual word recognition, such as the frequency of sublexical orthographic units such as rimes (Ziegler & Perry, 1998), or phonological variables such as phonological neighborhood density (Grainger, Muneaux, Farioli, & Ziegler, 2005; Yates, Locker, & Simpson, 2004). Concerning the latter variable, much prior work has shown that increasing phonological neighborhood density systematically gives rise to inhibitory effects in spoken word recognition. Words with many phonological neighbors are harder to recognize in noise, they take longer to respond to in auditory lexical decision, and they produce longer shadowing latencies than words with few phonological neighbors (e.g., Cluff & Luce, 1990; Goldinger, Luce, & Pisoni, 1989; Luce & Pisoni, 1998; Vitevitch, Luce, Pisoni, & Auer, 1999).

Most accounts of neighborhood effects to date have been unimodal in nature, either in terms of orthographic influences or in terms of phonological influences on target word recognition. In one of the first studies to break with this tradition, Ziegler, Muneaux, and Grainger (2003) investigated effects of orthographic neighborhood density in spoken word recognition. Increasing the number of orthographic neighbors was found to facilitate the processing of auditorily presented words. Ziegler et al. (2003) offered an account of this effect expressed within the framework of the bi-modal interactive–activation model. On presentation of an auditory target word, activation of phonological representations automatically generates activation in corresponding orthographic representations. Ziegler et al. argued that it is the level of consistency across these co-activated phonological and orthographic representations that underlies the facilitatory effects of orthographic neighborhood density in auditory word recognition.

Two recent studies have examined whether phonological neighborhood density affects visual word recognition (Grainger et al., 2005; Yates et al., 2004). In two lexical decision experiments with visually presented words and nonwords, Yates et al. found that increasing the number of phonological neighbors of word stimuli, while holding number of orthographic neighbors constant, caused a decrease in response times. Grainger et al. (2005) manipulated the number of phonological and orthographic neighbors of visually presented target words in three word recognition experiments. In all three experiments, effects of phonological neighborhood density interacted with effects of orthographic neighborhood density. However, as can be seen in Figure 7.6, the precise form of the interaction differed across tasks. In Experiments 1 and 2 (lexical decision), a cross-over interaction was observed, such that effects of phonological neighborhood density were inhibitory in words with few orthographic neighbors and facilitatory in words with relatively large numbers of orthographic neighbors. In Experiment 2, this cross-over interaction was exaggerated by presenting pseudohomophone stimuli among the nonwords in the lexical decision task. In the word identification task of Experiment 3 (progressive demasking), the form of the interaction was modified, reflecting the fact that phonological neighborhood density no longer affected performance to words with many orthographic neighbors, but continued to inhibit processing of words with few orthographic neighbors. The precise form of these interactions is show in Figure 7.6 along with the auditory lexical decision results obtained by Ziegler et al. (2003).

Grainger et al. (2005) argued that the main factor driving the pattern of phonological neighborhood effects observed in their study was the level of compatibility across co-activated orthographic and phonological representations during the word recognition process. In applying the concept of cross-code consistency to explaining the results of this study, we argued that when number of orthographic neighbors is maintained at a low value, then increasing the number of phonological neighbors will generate an increase in the level of inconsistency across simultaneously activated orthographic and phonological representations. On the other hand, when number of orthographic neighbors is held constant at a high value, then increasing the number of phonological neighbors will decrease the level of inconsistency. This is hypothesized to be the central mechanism generating the interaction

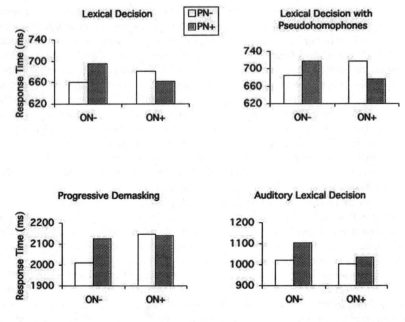

FIGURE 7.6   Summary of the pattern of RTs observed in the lexical decision (upper panel) and progressive demasking (lower left panel) experiments of Grainger et al. (2005).

between orthographic and phonological neighborhood density observed in that study. In order to capture the pattern of results obtained in the word identification (progressive demasking) task of Experiment 3, we argued that a lexical inhibition mechanism acted in combination with the cross-code consistency mechanism in order to modulate the cross-over interaction observed in the lexical decision task. The progressive demasking task requires unique word identification, and therefore cannot be performed using some measure of global lexical activity (as is likely to be the case for lexical decision; Grainger & Jacobs, 1996). This implies that inhibitory effects of neighborhood density should dominate in this task, compared to the lexical decision task, as is generally observed with manipulations of orthographic neighborhood (Grainger & Jacobs, 1996; Carreiras, Perea, & Grainger, 1997). Assuming that increasing the number of phonological neighbors will have a similar impact on the level of lexical inhibition received by the target word representation, this mechanism predicted an inhibitory effect of phonological neighborhood density in the progressive demasking task. In combination with cross-code consistency, words with small numbers of orthographic neighbors will suffer inhibition from both mechanisms as number of phonological neighbors is increased. However, when target words have large numbers of orthographic neighbors, then the effects of lateral inhibition and cross-code consistency cancel each other out.

This interpretation of how phonological neighborhood influences visual word recognition is in line with the explanation offered by Ziegler et al. (2003) for effects of orthographic neighborhood in auditory word recognition. Since auditory lexical decision always shows inhibitory effects of phonological neighborhood density (e.g., Luce & Pisoni, 1998; Vitevitch & Luce, 1999), we expect lexical inhibition to combine with cross-code consistency in much the same way as the progressive demasking experiment of the Grainger et al. study. Inhibitory effects of phonological neighborhood density should be observed in words with few orthographic neighbors, since both mechanisms operate in the same direction. On the other hand, the phonological neighborhood effects should diminish in words with large numbers of orthographic neighbors, since the two mechanisms generate opposing effects. This is exactly what was found by Ziegler et al. (2003), as can be seen in the lower right-hand panel of Figure 7.6. The major difference between the progressive demasking results of Grainger et al. and the lexical decision results of Ziegler et al. concerns the main effect of orthographic neighborhood density, which is inhibitory in the former and facilitatory in the latter. This suggests that in applying the mechanisms of cross-code consistency and lexical inhibition to capture effects of orthographic neighborhood density, cross-code consistency dominates in auditory lexical decision (as argued by Ziegler et al., 2003), whereas lexical inhibition dominates in visual word identification. This seems reasonable given that orthographic neighborhood density is a "cross-modality" manipulation with auditory stimuli, and a "within-modality" manipulation for visually presented stimuli.

Finally, effects of neighborhood density could also reflect variations in the consistency in the mapping of form to meaning, as discussed in the preceding section. In a cascaded activation model, the multiple whole-word representations activated by a given set of letters will send activation onto their corresponding semantic representations, the majority of which will be incompatible with the target word. Holcomb, Grainger, and O'Rourke (2002) found that orthographic neighborhood density had a significant influence on the amplitude of the N400 component of event-related potentials (ERPs), a negative-going waveform that typically peaks at around 400 ms post-stimulus onset (for printed words). In the Holcomb et al. (2002) study, words with many neighbors generated larger N400 amplitudes than words with few neighbors. Since modulations of N400 amplitude are generally interpreted as reflecting processing differences during semantic integration (Holcomb, 1993), Holcomb et al. interpreted the increased amplitude of this component for words with large numbers of orthographic neighbors as reflecting an increased difficulty in settling on a unique form-meaning association. This increase in noise at the form-meaning interface could affect behavioral responses very differently as a function of the type of response required. Interestingly, this account predicts that neighborhood effects should be observed in semantic categorization tasks, and this is indeed the case (Carreiras et al., 1997; Forster & Hector, 2002; Pecher, Zeelenberg, & Wagenmakers, 2005). Most important is that the direction of effects of orthographic neighborhood in semantic categorization tasks depends on whether or not the orthographic neighbors are in the same response category as the target word or not (Pecher et al., 2005), as predicted by a cascaded activation account of these effects (Carreiras et al., 1997).

Concluding this section on neighborhood effects in single word reading, it appears that multiple mappings from orthography to phonology, from orthography to semantics, and also within orthography (lexical-sublexical mappings) are all potential sources of the neighborhood effects reported in experiments. Indeed, it appears from the present analysis that effects of similarity neighborhoods are best considered as a special case of the more general phenomenon of cross-code consistency. Just like the effects of ambiguity discussed in sections 3-5, similarity leads to co-activation which leads to competition, the effects of which will depend on the type of code used for response read-out.

CONCLUSIONS

In the present chapter, we have attempted to demonstrate how the theoretical construct of cross-code consistency can provide a coherent and parsimonious account of a very large set of empirical observations in the field of word recognition. Cross-code consistency is best defined in the context of interactive, dynamic models of word recognition, such as the interactive-activation model (McClelland & Rumelhart, 1981). These models implement a bidirectional flow of activation. Interactivity allows activation to evolve over time, even if the external input to the system remains constant. Thus, over time, the network's pattern of activation across orthographic phonological and semantic units migrates towards a stable state. Cross-code consistency is the major force in that process. Because consistency is at the heart of the processes underlying stable word recognition, it is easy to see why consistency not only can account for existing, sometimes controversial effects (neighborhood effects in visual word recognition, e.g., Grainger et al., 2005) but can also predict new phenomena, such as orthographic neighborhood effects in spoken word recognition (Ziegler et al., 2003).

In this chapter, we summarized empirical research in two of the most central areas of recent visual word recognition research: effects of ambiguity and effects of similarity neighborhoods. We showed how the concept of cross-code consistency can explain why effects of ambiguity vary as a function of a) the level of ambiguity under study (sublexical, lexical); b) the type of representation that is ambiguous (orthographic, phonological, semantic); c) the direction of the ambiguity; and d) the type of task performed by participants. In each specific case of ambiguity that we examined, a simple interactive-activation model with orthographic, phonological, and semantic representations provided a coherent and parsimonious account of the available data. In our account, the effects of ambiguity arise when a representation at a given level that is compatible with more than one representation at another level (i.e., one-to-many relation). Such one-to-many mappings will lead to a processing cost due to competition among simultaneously activated representations at a given level. This is one of the consequences of cross-code consistency in an interactive-activation model. In our analysis of the effects of similarity neighborhoods in visual word recognition, we showed how an extension of this concept provides a means of accommodating recently observed interactions in effects of orthographic and phonological neighborhood. Therefore, the notion of cross-code consistency has provided a unified account of two key phenomena, effects of ambiguity and effects of similarity neighborhoods, that have traditionally been examined in isolation.

Finally, it is important to note that cross-code consistency might operate at different time scales (see Rueckl, 2002). At the faster time scale, cross-code consistency affects the flow of activation within the network, possibly at a rate at which individual words are read. Processes of on-line competition between lexical candidates operate at this time scale. At the slower time scale, however, cross-code consistency might affect learning, that is, the pattern of connectivity within the network. This slower process adjusts the weights to attune the network to the structure of the task or the environment. More research is now needed to investigate consistency effects across modalities and different times scales, and in words of greater complexity. Polysyllabic and polymorphemic words are increasingly the focus of empirical research (e.g., Frost, Grainger, & Rastle, 2005), and it will be important to integrate these findings within a general account of consistency effects in word recognition. It is empirical and theoretical research along these lines that will help develop our understanding of the complex process that allows young children to associate printed letters with meaning in their efforts to master the art of literacy. It should also shed light on the stumbling blocks that prevent certain children from attaining this important goal.

ACKNOWLEDGMENTS

We thank Elena Grigorenko, Debra Jared, Penny Pexman, and Guy Van Orden for helpful comments on an earlier version of this work. This chapter was written while the first author was visiting research Professor at Tufts University, supported by NIH grants HD25889 and HD043251. Correspondence to Jonathan Grainger, Laboratoire de Psychologie Cognitive, Université de Provence, 3 pl. Victor Hugo, 13331 Marseille, France (grainger@up.univ-mrs.fr).

REFERENCES

Andrews, S. (1989). Frequency and Neighborhood Effects on Lexical Access - Activation or Search. *Journal of Experimental Psychology-Learning Memory and Cognition, 15*(5), 802–814.

Andrews, S. (1992). Frequency and Neighborhood Effects on Lexical Access - Lexical Similarity or Orthographic Redundancy. *Journal of Experimental Psychology-Learning Memory and Cognition, 18*(2), 234–254.

Andrews, S. (1997). The effect of orthographic similarity on lexical retrieval: Resolving neighborhood conflicts. *Psychonomic Bulletin & Review, 4*(4), 439–461.

Balota, D. A., & Ferraro, F. R. (1993). A dissociation of frequency and regularity effects in pronunciation performance across young-adults, older adults, and individuals with senile dementia of the Alzheimer-type. *Journal of Memory and Language, 32*(5), 573–592.

Balota, D.A., Ferraro, F.R. & Connor, L.T. (1991). On the early influence of word meaning in word recognition: A review of the literature. In P.J. Shwanenflugel (Ed.) *The psychology of word meanings* (pp. 187–222). Hillsdale, NJ: Erlbaum.

Borowsky, R., & Masson, M. E. J. (1996). Semantic ambiguity effects in word identification. *Journal of Experimental Psychology-Learning Memory and Cognition, 22*(1), 63–85.

Booth, J.R., Burman, D.D., Meyer, J.R., Gitelman, D.R., Parrish, T.B, & Mesulman, M.M. (2002). Functional anatomy of intra- and cross-modal lexical tasks. *NeuroImage, 16*, 7–22.

Carreiras, M., Perea, M., & Grainger, J. (1997). Effects of the orthographic neighborhood in visual word recognition: Cross-task comparisons. *Journal of Experimental Psychology: Learning, Memory, & Cognition, 23*(4), 857–871.

Cluff, M. S., & Luce, P. A. (1990). Similarity neighborhoods of spoken two-syllable words: retroactive effects on multiple activation. *J Exp Psychol Hum Percept Perform, 16*(3), 551–563.

Cohen, L., Dehaene, S., Naccache, L., Lehericy, S., Dehaene-Lambertz, G., Henaff, M. & Michel, F. (2000). The visual word form area: Spatial and temporal characterization of an initial stage of reading in normal subjects and posterior split-brain patients. *Brain, 123,* 291–307.

Cohen, L., Jobert, A., Le Bihan, D. & Dehaene, S. (2004). Distinct unimodal and multimodal regions for word processing in the left temporal cortex. *Neuroimage, 23,* 1256–1270.

Coltheart, M., Besner, D., Jonasson, J. T., & Davelaar, E. (1979). Phonological encoding in the lexical decision task. *Quarterly Journal of Experimental Psychology, 31,* 489–507.

Coltheart, M., Davelaar, E., Jonasson, J. T., & Besner, D. (1977). Access to the internal lexicon. In S. Dornic (Ed.), *Attention and Performance VI* (pp. 535–555). London: Academic Press.

Coltheart, M., Rastle, K., Perry, C., Langdon, R., & Ziegler, J. C. (2001). DRC: A dual route cascaded model of visual word recognition and reading aloud. *Psychological Review, 108*(1), 204–256.

Coltheart, V., Patterson, K., & Leahy, J. (1994). When a Rows Is a Rose - Phonological Effects in Written Word Comprehension. *Quarterly Journal of Experimental Psychology Section a-Human Experimental Psychology, 47*(4), 917–955.

Cornelissen, P., Tarkiainen, A., Helenius, P., & Salmelin, R. (2003). Cortical effects of shifting letter position in letter strings of varying length. *Journal of Cognitive Neuroscience, 15,* 731–746.

Davelaar, E., Coltheart, M., Besner, D., & Jonasson, J. T. (1978). Phonological recoding and lexical access. *Memory and Cognition, 6,* 391–402.

Dehaene, S., Le Clec'H, G., Poline, J.B., Le Bihan, D., & Cohen, L. (2002). The visual word form area: A prelexical representation of visual words in the fusiform gyrus. *NeuroReport, 13,* 321–325.

Dijkstra, T., Grainger, J., & van Heuven, W. J. B. (1999). Recognition of cognates and interlingual homographs: The neglected role of phonology. *Journal of Memory and Language, 41*(4), 496–518.

Edwards, J., Pexman, P., & Hudson, C. (2004). Exploring the dynamics of the visual word recognition system: Homophone effects in LDT and naming. *Language and Cognitive Processes, 19*(4), 503–532.

Ferrand, L. & Grainger, J. (1992). Phonology and orthography in visual word recognition: Evidence from masked nonword printing. *Quarterly Journal of Experimental Psychology, 45A,* 353–372.

Ferrand, L., & Grainger, J. (1993). The time course of orthographic and phonological code activation in the early phases of visual word recognition. *Bulletin of the Psychonomic Society, 31*(2), 119–122.

Ferrand, L., & Grainger, J. (1994). Effects of orthography are independent of phonology in masked form priming. *Quarterly Journal of Experimental Psychology: Human Experimental Psychology, 47A*(2), 365–382.

Ferrand, L. & Grainger, J. (2003). Homophonic interference effects in visual word recognition. *Quarterly Journal of Experimental Psychology, 56A,* 403–419.

Fiebach, C.J., Friederici, A.D., Müller, K., & von Cramon, D.Y (2002). fMRI evidence for dual routes to the mental lexicon in visual word recognition. *Journal of Cognitive Neuroscience, 14,* 11–23.

Fiez, J.A., & Petersen, S.E. (1998). Neuroimaging studies of word reading. *Proceedings of the National Academy of Sciences, USA, 95,* 914–921.

Folk, J.R. (1999). Phonological codes are used to access the lexicon during silent reading. *Journal of Experimental Psychology:Learning Memory and Cognition, 25*(4), 892–906.

Forster, K. I., & Hector, J. (2002). Cascaded versus noncascaded models of lexical and semantic processing: the turple effect. *Mem Cognit, 30*(7), 1106–1117.

Forster, K. I., & Shen, D. (1996). No enemies in the neighborhood: Absence of inhibitory neighborhood effects in lexical decision and semantic categorization. *Journal of Experimental Psychology: Learning, Memory, & Cognition, 22*(3), 696–713.

Frost, R. (1998). Toward a strong phonological theory of visual word recognition: True issues and false trails. *Psychological Bulletin, 123*(1), 71–99.

Frost, R., Ahissar, M., Gotesman, R., & Tayeb, S. (2003). Are phonological effects fragile? The effect of luminance and exposure duration on form priming and phonological priming. *Journal of Memory & Language, 48*(2), 346–378.

Frost, R., Grainger, J., & Rastle, K. (2005). Current issues in morphological processing: An introduction. *Language and Cognitive Processes, 20*, 1–5.

Funnell, E. (1983). Phonological processing in reading: New evidence from acquired dyslexia. *British Journal of Psychology, 74*, 159–180.

Gibbs, P., & Van Orden, G. C. (1998). Pathway selection's utility for control of word recognition. *Journal of Experimental Psychology: Human Perception & Performance, 24*(4), 1162–1187.

Glushko, R. J. (1979). The organization and activation of orthographic knowledge in reading aloud. *Journal of Experimental Psychology: Human Perception & Performance, 5*(4), 674–691.

Goldinger, S. D., Luce, P. A., & Pisoni, D. B. (1989). Priming lexical neighbors of spoken words: Effects of competition and inhibition. *Journal of Memory & Language, 28*(5), 501–518.

Gottlob, L. R., Goldinger, S. D., Stone, G. O., & Van Orden, G. C. (1999). Reading homographs: Orthographic, phonologic, and semantic dynamics. *Journal of Experimental Psychology: Human Perception & Performance, 25*(2), 561–574.

Grainger, J. (1990). Word frequency and neighborhood frequency effects in lexical decision and naming. *Journal of Memory & Language, 29*(2), 228–244.

Grainger, J. (2000). From print to meaning via words? In A. Kennedy, R. Radach, D. Heller, & J. Pynte (Eds). *Reading as a perceptual process.* Oxford: Elsevier.

Grainger, J. & Dijkstra, T. (1992). On the representation and use of language information in bilinguals. In R.J. Harris (Ed.) *Cognitive processing in bilinguals.* Amsterdam: North Holland.

Grainger, J., & Ferrand, L. (1994). Phonology and orthography in visual word recognition: Effects of masked homophone primes. *Journal of Memory & Language, 33*(2), 218–233.

Grainger, J. & Holcomb, P.J. (2007). Neural constraints on a functional architecture for word recognition. In M. Kringelbach et al. (Eds.), *The Neural Basis of Reading.* Oxford: Oxford University Press.

Grainger, J., & Jacobs, A. M. (1996). Orthographic processing in visual word recognition: A multiple read-out model. *Psychological Review, 103*(3), 518–565.

Grainger, J. & Jacobs, A.M. (1998). On localist connectionism and psychological science. In J. Grainger & A.M. Jacobs (Eds.), *Localist connectionist approaches to human cognition.* Mawhah, NJ.: Erlbaum.

Grainger, J., Muneaux, M., Farioli, F., & Ziegler, J. C. (2005). Effects of phonological and orthographic neighbourhood density interact in visual word recognition. *Quarterly Journal of Experimental Psychology, 58A*, 981–998.

Grainger, J., Oregan, J. K., Jacobs, A. M., & Segui, J. (1989). On the Role of Competing Word Units in Visual Word Recognition - the Neighborhood Frequency Effect. *Perception & Psychophysics, 45*(3), 189–195.

Grainger, J. & Van Heuven, W. (2003). Modeling Letter Position Coding in Printed Word Perception. In P. Bonin (Ed.), *The Mental lexicon.* New York : Nova Science Publishers (pp. 1–24).

Grainger, J., & Whitney, C. (2004). Does the huamn mnid raed wrods as a wlohe? *Trends in Cognitive Sciences, 8*(2), 58–59.

Hagoort, P., Indefrey, P., Brown, C., Herzog, H., Steinmetz, H., & Steiz, R.J. (1999). The neural circuitry involved in the reading of German words and pseudowords: A PET study. *Journal of Cognitive Neuroscience, 11,* 383–398.

Hawkins, H. L., Reicher, G. M., Rogers, M., & Peterson, L. (1976). Flexible coding in word recognition. *J Exp Psychol Hum Percept Perform, 2*(3), 380–385.

Harm, M. W., & Seidenberg, M. S. (1999). Phonology, reading acquisition, and dyslexia: Insights from connectionist models. *Psychological Review, 106*(3), 491–528.

Hino, Y. & Lupker, S.J. (1996). Effects of polysemy in lexical decision and naming: An alternative to lexical access accounts. *J Exp Psychol Hum Percept Perform, 22,* 1331–1356.

Hino, Y., Lupker, S. J., & Pexman, P. M. (2002). Ambiguity and synonymy effects in lexical decision, naming, and semantic categorization tasks: Interactions between orthography, phonology, and semantics. *Journal of Experimental Psychology-Learning Memory and Cognition, 28*(4), 686–713.

Holcomb, P.J. (1993). Semantic priming and stimulus degradation: Implications for the role of the N400 in language processing. *Psychophysiology. 30,* 47–61.

Holcomb, P.J. & Grainger, J. (2006). *On the time-course of visual word recognition: An ERP investigation using masked repetition priming. Journal of Cognitive Neuroscience, 18,* 1631–1643.

Holcomb, P. J., Grainger, J., & O'Rourke, T. (2002). An electrophysiological study of the effects of orthographic neighborhood size on printed word perception. *J Cogn Neurosci, 14*(6), 938–950.

Huey, E.B. (1908). *The psychology and pedagogy of reading.* Macmillan: London.

Jacobs, A. M., Rey, A., Ziegler, J. C., & Grainger, J. (1998). MROM-p: An interactive activation, multiple readout model of orthographic and phonological processes in visual word recognition. In J. Grainger & A. M. Jacobs (Eds.), *Localist connectionist approaches to human cognition* (pp. 147–188). Mahwah, NJ: Lawrence Erlbaum Associates.

Jared, D. (1997). Spelling-sound consistency affects the naming of high-frequency words. *Journal of Memory and Language, 36*(4), 505–529.

Jared, D. (2002). Spelling-sound consistency and regularity effects in word naming. *Journal of Memory & Language, 46,* 723–750.

Jared, D., McRae, K., & Seidenberg, M. S. (1990). The basis of consistency effects in word naming. *Journal of Memory & Language, 29*(6), 687–715.

Jared, D., & Seidenberg, M. S. (1991). Does word identification proceed from spelling to sound to meaning. *Journal of Experimental Psychology-General, 120*(4), 358–394.

Jared, D., Rayner, K., & Levy, B.A. (1999). The role of phonology in the activation of word meanings during reading: Evidence from proofreading and eye movements. *Journal of Experimental Psychology-General, 128*(3), 219–264.

Jastrzembski, J. E. (1981). Multiple Meanings, Number of Related Meanings, Frequency of Occurrence, and the Lexicon. *Cognitive Psychology, 13*(2), 278–305.

Kawamoto, A. H. (1993). Nonlinear dynamics in the resolution of lexical ambiguity: A parallel distributed processing account. *Journal of Memory & Language, 32*(4), 474–516.

Kellas, G., Ferraro, F.R., & Simpson, G.B. (1988). Lexical ambiguity and the timecourse of attentional allocation in word recognition. *J Exp Psychol Hum Percept Perform, 14,* 601–609.

Lacruz, I. & Folk, J.R. (2004). Feedforward and feedback consistency effects for high- and low-frequency words in lexical decision and naming. *Quarterly Journal of Experimental Psychology, 57A,* 1261–1284.

Luce, P. A., & Pisoni, D. B. (1998). Recognizing spoken words: the neighborhood activation model. *Ear Hear, 19,* 1–36.

Lukatela, G., & Turvey, M.T. (1994). Visual access is initially phonological: 2. Evidence from phonological priming by homophones, and pseudohomophones. *Journal of Experimental Psychology: General, 123,* 331–353.

Mathey, S., & Zagar, D. (2000). The neighborhood distribution effect in visual word recognition: words with single and twin neighbors. *J Exp Psychol Hum Percept Perform, 26*(1), 184–205.

McCandliss, B.D., Cohen, L. & Dehaene, S. (2003). The visual word form area: expertise for reading in the fusiform gyrus. *Trends in Cognitive Sciences, 7*, 293–299.

McCarthy, R., & Warrington, E. K. (1986). Phonological reading: Phenomena and paradoxes. *Cortex, 22*, 359–380.

McClelland, J. L., & Rumelhart, D. E. (1981). An Interactive Activation Model of Context Effects in Letter Perception .1. An Account of Basic Findings. *Psychological Review, 88*(5), 375–407.

Miller, K. M., & Swick, D. (2003). Orthography influences the perception of speech in alexic patients. *J Cogn Neurosci, 15*(7), 981–990.

Millis, M. L., & Button, S. B. (1989). The effect of polysemy on lexical decision time: now you see it, now you don't. *Mem Cognit, 17*(2), 141–147.

Nobre, A.C., Allison, T. & McCarthy, G. (1994). Word recognition in the human inferior temporal lobe. *Nature, 372*, 260–263.

Paulesu, E., Démonet, J.-F., Fazio, F., McCrory, E., Chanoine, V., Brunswick, N., Cappa, S. F., Cossu, G., Habib, M., Frith, C. D., & Frith, U. (2001). Dyslexia - cultural diversity and biological unity. *Science, 291*, 2165–2167.

Pammer, K., Hansen, P.C., Kringelbach, M.L., Holliday, I., Barnes, G., Hillebrand, A., Singh, K.D., & Cornelissen, P.L. (2004). Visual word recognition: the first half second. *NeuroImage, 22*, 1819–1825.

Pecher, D. (2001). Perception is a two-way junction: feedback semantics in word recognition. *Psychon Bull Rev, 8*(3), 545–551.

Pecher, D., Zeelenberg, R., & Wagenmakers, E. J. (2005). Enemies and friends in the neighborhood: orthographic similarity effects in semantic categorization. *J Exp Psychol Learn Mem Cogn, 31*(1), 121–128.

Perfetti, C. A., & Bell, L. (1991). Phonemic activation during the first 40 ms of word identification: Evidence from backward masking and priming. *Journal of Memory & Language, 30*(4), 473–485.

Perry, C. (2003). A phoneme-grapheme feedback consistency effect. *Psychonomic Bulletin & Review, 10*(2), 392–397.

Pexman, P. M., Lupker, S. J., & Hino, Y. (2002). The impact of feedback semantics in visual word recognition: Number-of-features effects in lexical decision and naming tasks. *Psychonomic Bulletin & Review, 9*(3), 542–549.

Pexman, P. M., Lupker, S. J., & Jared, D. (2001). Homophone effects in lexical decision. *Journal of Experimental Psychology-Learning Memory and Cognition, 27*(1), 139–156.

Pexman, P. M., Lupker, S. J., & Reggin, L. D. (2002). Phonological effects in visual word recognition: Investigating the impact of feedback activation. *Journal of Experimental Psychology-Learning Memory and Cognition, 28*(3), 572–584.

Price, C. J. & Devlin, J. T. (2003). The myth of the visual word form area. *Neuroimage, 19*(3), 473–481.

Pugh, K.R., Shaywitz, B.A., Shaywitz, S.E., Constable, R.T., Skudlarski, P., Fulbright, R.K., Bronen, R.A., Shankweiler, D.P., Katz, L., Fletcher, J.M., & Gore, J.C. (1996). Cerebral organization of component processes in reading. *Brain, 119*, 1221–1238.

Ramus, F., Rosen, S., Dakin, S. C., Day, B. L., Castellote, J. M., White, S., et al. (2003). Theories of developmental dyslexia: insights from a multiple case study of dyslexic adults. *Brain, 126*, 841–865.

Rayner, K. (1998). Eye movements in reading and information processing: 20 years of research. *Psychological Bulletin, 124*(3), 372–422.

Reicher, G. M. (1969). Perceptual recognition as a function of meaninfulness of stimulus material. *J Exp Psychol, 81*(2), 275–280.

Rodd, J., Gaskell, G., & Marslen-Wilson, W. (2002). Making sense of semantic ambiguity: Semantic competition in lexical access. *Journal of Memory and Language, 46,* 245–266.

Rubenstein, H., Lewis, S.S., & Rubenstein, M.A. (1971). Evidence for phonemic recoding in visual word recognition. *Journal of Verbal Learning and Verbal Behavior, 10,* 645–657.

Rueckl, J. G. (2002). The dynamics of visual word recognition. *Ecological Psychology, 14*(1–2), 5–19.

Sears, C.R., Hino, Y., & Lupker, S.J. (1995). Neighborhood size and neighborhood frequency effects in word recognition. *Journal of Experimental Psychology: Human Perception and Performance, 21,* 876–900.

Sears, C. R., Lupker, S. J., & Hino, Y. (1999). Orthographic neighborhood effects in perceptual identification and semantic categorization tasks: a test of the multiple read-out model. *Percept Psychophys, 61*(8), 1537–1554.

Seidenberg, M. S., & McClelland, J. L. (1989). A distributed, developmental model of word recognition and naming. *Psychological Review, 96*(4), 523–568.

Snowling, M. (2000). *Dyslexia.* Oxford: Blackwell.

Stein, J., & Walsh, V. (1997). To see but not to read: The magnocellular theory of dyslexia. *Trends in Neurosciences, 20*(4), 147–152.

Stone, G. O., & Van Orden, G. C. (1994). Building a resonance framework for word recognition using design and system principles. *Journal of Experimental Psychology: Human Perception & Performance, 20*(6), 1248–1268.

Stone, G. O., Vanhoy, M., & Van Orden, G. C. (1997). Perception is a two-way street: Feedforward and feedback phonology in visual word recognition. *Journal of Memory & Language, 36*(3), 337–359.

Tallal, P. (2003). Language learning disabilities: Integrating research approaches. *Current Directions in Psychological Science, 12*(6), 206–211.

Temple, E., Deutsch, G. K., Poldrack, R. A., Miller, S. L., Tallal, P., Merzenich, M. M., et al. (2003). Neural deficits in children with dyslexia ameliorated by behavioral remediation: Evidence from functional MRI. *Proceedings of the National Academy of Sciences of the United States of America, 100*(5), 2860–2865.

Tuller, B., Case, P., Ding, M., & Kelso, J. A. (1994). The nonlinear dynamics of speech categorization. *J Exp Psychol Hum Percept Perform, 20*(1), 3–16.

Van Orden, G. C. (1987). A ROWS is a ROSE: Spelling, sound, and reading. *Memory & Cognition, 15*(3), 181–198.

Van Orden, G. C. (2002). Nonlinear dynamics and psycholinguistics. *Ecological Psychology, 14*(1–2), 1–4.

Van Orden, G. C., & Goldinger, S. D. (1994). Interdependence of form and function in cognitive systems explains perception of printed words. *Journal of Experimental Psychology: Human Perception & Performance, 20*(6), 1269–1291.

Van Orden, G. C., Jansen op de Haar, M. A., & Bosman, A. M. T. (1997). Complex dynamic systems also predict dissociations, but they do not reduce to autonomous components. *Cognitive Neuropsychology, 14*(1), 131–165.

Van Orden, G. C., Pennington, B. F., & Stone, G. O. (1990). Word identification in reading and the promise of subsymbolic psycholinguistics. *Psychological Review, 97*(4), 488–522.

Ventura, P., Morais, J., Pattamadilok, C., & Kolinsky, R. (2004). The locus of the orthographic consistency effect in auditory word recognition. *Language and Cognitive Processes, 19*(1), 57–95.

Verstaen, A., Humphreys, G.W., Olson, A., & d'Ydewalle, G. (1995). Are phonemic effects in backward masking evidence for automatic prelexical phonemic activation in visual word recognition? *Journal of Memory and Language, 34,* 335–356.

Vitevitch, M. S., & Luce, P. A. (1998). When words compete: Levels of processing in perception of spoken words. *Psychological Science, 9*(4), 325–329.

Vitevitch, M. S., Luce, P. A., Pisoni, D. B., & Auer, E. T. (1999). Phonotactics, neighborhood activation, and lexical access for spoken words. *Brain & Language. Special Issue: Mental lexicon, 68*(1–2), 306–311.

Waters, G. S., & Seidenberg, M. S. (1985). Spelling-sound effects in reading: Time course and decision criteria. *Memory & Cognition, 13*(6), 557–572.

Wheeler, D. D. (1970). Processes in word recognition. *Cognitive Psychology, 1*, 59–85.

Yates, M., Locker, L., Jr., & Simpson, G. B. (2004). The influence of phonological neighborhood on visual word perception. *Psychon Bull Rev, 11*(3), 452–457.

Ziegler, J. C., Ferrand, L., Jacobs, A. M., Rey, A., & Grainger, J. (2000). Visual and phonological codes in letter and word recognition: Evidence from incremental priming. *Quarterly Journal of Experimental Psychology: Human Experimental Psychology, 53A*(3), 671–692.

Ziegler, J. C., Ferrand, L., & Montant, M. (2004). Visual phonology: The effects of orthographic consistency on different auditory word recognition tasks. *Memory & Cognition, 32*(5), 732–741.

Ziegler, J. C., & Goswami, U. (2005). Reading acquisition, developmental dyslexia, and skilled reading across languages: a psycholinguistic grain size theory. *Psychol Bull, 131*(1), 3–29.

Ziegler, J. C., Montant, M., & Jacobs, A. M. (1997). The feedback consistency effect in lexical decision and naming. *Journal of Memory & Language, 37*(4), 533–554.

Ziegler, J. C., Muneaux, M., & Grainger, J. (2003). Neighborhood effects in auditory word recognition: Phonological competition and orthographic facilitation. *Journal of Memory and Language, 48*(4), 779–793.

Ziegler, J. C., & Perry, C. (1998). No more problems in Coltheart's neighborhood: Resolving neighborhood conflicts in the lexical decision task. *Cognition, 68*(2), B53–B62.

Ziegler, J. C., Rey, A., & Jacobs, A. M. (1998). Simulating individual word identification thresholds and errors in the fragmentation task. *Memory & Cognition, 26*(3), 490–501.

Ziegler, J. C., Stone, G. O., & Jacobs, A. M. (1997). What is the pronunciation for -ough and the spelling for u/? A database for computing feedforward and feedback consistency in English. *Behavior Research Methods, Instruments & Computers, 29*(4), 600–618.

Ziegler, J. C., Van Orden, G. C., & Jacobs, A. M. (1997). Phonology can help or hurt the perception of print. *Journal of Experimental Psychology: Human Perception & Performance, 23*(3), 845–860.

CHAPTER EIGHT

Feedback-Consistency Effects in Single-Word Reading

Brett Kessler and Rebecca Treiman
Washington University in St. Louis

John Mullennix
University of Pittsburgh at Johnstown

The goal of this chapter is to examine one of the most intriguing claims that has been made during the past decade of research in single-word reading—the idea that feedback consistency influences fluent adults' performance. It has been reported in several studies (Lacruz & Folk, 2004; Perry, 2003; Stone, Vanhoy, & Van Orden, 1997; Ziegler, Montant, & Jacobs, 1997) that adults are slowed when reading a word like *hurl* because other words that *hurl* rhymes with, such as *girl* and *pearl*, have different spellings of the same rhyme. This effect is surprising, because inconsistency in the sound-to-letter direction, something that might logically make writing difficult, would seem to play no necessary role in reading, which involves mapping letters to sounds. We begin this chapter by reviewing the literature on the feedback consistency effect, pointing out some methodological problems in several of the studies that have argued for its existence. We then report new analyses designed to determine whether feedback consistency has a reliable effect on the speed with which people read individual words.

PRIOR RESEARCH

The speed with which readers can process individual written words has long been a focus of research in literacy and lexical processing (Balota, 1994). Such data can

159

be crucial for the development and verification of models of reading. For example, it is well known that words that a reader has seen with great frequency are processed faster than other words. For this, among other reasons, the DRC (dual-route cascaded) model of Coltheart, Rastle, Perry, Langdon, and Ziegler (2001) includes a lexical route that can retrieve high-frequency words from the mental lexicon quicker than one can access a word via letter-to-sound rules. Likewise, connectionist models such as those of Plaut, McClelland, Seidenberg, and Patterson (1996) are trained most thoroughly on high-frequency words, thereby building up particularly strong connections for them. Such findings support the popular idea that fluent readers process some words as wholes: so-called sight words.

It is also commonly agreed that reading involves phonological processing as well, at least for words of lesser frequency. In phonographic orthographies such as that of English, individual written words are built up from units that represent the sounds of the spoken words. One productive line of research has looked at how various aspects of these phonographic representations affect processing. Several studies have reported that words containing ambiguous letter-to-sound mappings are processed more slowly than other words (e.g., Balota, Cortese, Sergent-Marshall, Spieler, & Yap, 2004; Glushko, 1979; Lacruz & Folk, 2004; Treiman, Mullennix, Bijeljac-Babic, & Richmond-Welty, 1995). All other things being equal, a word like *stead* will be processed more slowly than a word like *shell*, because analogous words in English suggest two different pronunciations for the former: the corrects/st ɛd/[1] (cf. *head*) and the incorrect /stid/ (cf. *bead*). In contrast, all words that end in *ell* are pronounced to rhyme with *shell*. Again, all models of reading need to take such facts into account. In DRC, for example, words with the most typical letter-to-sound correspondences, as in *shell*, can be processed by the moderately efficient phonological assembly route, while words that have letters with unusual sound correspondences can be retrieved only by the lexical route, which can be fairly slow for low-frequency words like *stead*. On a more practical level, this *consistency effect* indicates that phonological decoding is involved even in the skilled reading of college students, the subjects of most adult reading research, and may therefore encourage reading teachers to acknowledge the usefulness of phonics-based reading instruction.

Although the consistency effect has been supported by much research, it is not unchallenged, nor have all the details of its effects been settled, such as whether it applies to high-frequency words (Jared, 1997, 2002), or exactly how consistency is to be measured (Massaro & Jesse, 2005). For example, some researchers treat consistency as a binary measure: If the letters that spell the rhyme of the word have different pronunciations in different words, then the word is inconsistent and will be processed more slowly than other words, ceteris paribus (Glushko, 1979). Other researchers treat consistency as a continuous measure that may be computed over different parts of the word, not just the rhyme: Consistency is the proportion of all words with the same letters that also have the same pronunciation, and different degrees of inconsistency may slow readers by different amounts (Treiman et al.,

---

[1]Phonetic transcriptions follow the conventions of the International Phonetic Association (2005).

1995). But however consistency is defined, consistency theory has intuitive appeal. If it is accepted that readers do any phonological decoding at all, then it makes sense that words like *stead*, which could theoretically be read two different ways, would cause them to slow down or stumble.

In 1997, Stone et al. announced a much less intuitive consistency effect: that of feedback consistency. In their main experiment, a lexical decision task, they presented subjects with a series of 100 strings of letters and asked them to quickly judge whether each string was a word or a nonword. All the real words were monosyllabic and of fairly low frequency and had rhyme letters, that is, the letters from the vowel to the end of the word, that were completely consistent in the spelling-to-sound direction. However, half of the words, such as *heap*, were inconsistent in the reverse, or feedback, direction: the sounds /ip/ can also be spelled as in *deep*. The other half of the words, like *probe*, contained rhyme pronunciations that can only be spelled one way; these were called feedback consistent words. Stone et al. (1997) found that it took, on average, 774 ms to correctly identify the feedback consistent stimuli as words, while the feedback inconsistent words took 33 ms longer to identify as words. The error rate was also higher on the feedback inconsistent words compared to the feedback consistent words: 9.8% as opposed to 3.9%.

The idea that sound-to-spelling consistency should affect reading is surprising because there does not seem to be any practical reason for people to consult the spelling of rhyming words as part of the task of deciding whether *heap* is a word. However, the results of the experiment made sense in the context of Stone and Van Orden's (1994) theory of *recurrent networks* in word perception. In a recurrent network, the flow of activation is inherently bidirectional. When, in the course of reading, the activation of letter units in one's perceptual input results in the activation of sound units in one's mental lexical networks, those sound units, in turn, automatically activate letter units, just as if those sound units had been activated by sensory input. When reading a word like *probe*, the letters activate the sounds /prob/, which in turn activate the letters *probe*, an internally consistent state of affairs that allows the network to quickly settle on a decision. In contrast, reading *heap* activates the sounds /hip/, which in turn activate, in addition to *heap*, the conflicting spelling *heep*. This conflicting information creates an unstable feedback loop, which requires more time to settle into a state that represents a confident decision.

Thus the possibly counterintuitive results of Stone et al.'s (1997) experiment could be taken as evidence in favor of recurrent networks, a rather exciting theoretical development. In the context of Stone et al.'s recurrent network theory of reading, the traditional consistency of the letter-to-sound mappings was now considered *feedforward* consistency, and the new role played by consistency of the mapping in the reverse direction, from sounds to letters, was called *feedback* consistency. Other researchers have adopted this terminology regardless of their theoretical perspective, and several have joined the search for feedback consistency effects in the lexical decision task, with varying degrees of success. Perry (2003) and Lacruz and Folk (2004) reported a feedback consistency effect in English lexical decision, but Massaro and Jesse (2005) reported there was none. Balota et al. (2004) reported mixed results: Effects were not significant by items but only by subjects, and only for slower participants. In French, a language that shares with English the fact that sounds may be spelled inconsistently across words, Ziegler et al. (1997) reported a feedback consistency effect in lexical decision, but those results were contradicted by Peereman, Content, and Bonin (1998); and see further Ziegler and Van Orden (2000) for a counterrebuttal.

Several factors may account for the conflicting results in lexical decision tasks, some of which will be addressed below. One important issue is that of covariables. So many different factors affect lexical processing that it is very difficult to tease them apart or to design a factorial experiment that perfectly balances lexical stimuli on all factors besides feedback consistency (Cutler, 1981; Massaro & Jesse, 2005). For example, Peereman et al. (1998) noted that Stone et al.'s (1997) attempts to balance words by their frequency appeared to be faulty because the latter used frequency estimates based on a corpus of inadequate size. More subtly, it is possible that only certain types of words may evoke feedback effects. It is often believed, for example, that phonological factors like feedback consistency would not affect the processing of high-frequency words (though see Lacruz and Folk, 2004, for a demurral).

Another important issue is how feedback consistency is defined and measured. As mentioned above, some researchers have treated consistency as a binary property. As applied to feedback consistency, this means that a sound either has a consistent spelling or it does not. One may immediately object that, by that definition, every word of English is feedback inconsistent, because every word has at least one sound that can be spelled more than one way (all vowel sounds, for example, are inconsistent). This objection has generally been rendered irrelevant by the fact that most research has only looked at one-syllable words and has assumed that the rhymes of words are processed as units (e.g., Balota et al., 2004; Lacruz & Folk, 2004; Peereman et al., 1998; Stone et al., 1997; Ziegler et al., 1997); many rhymes have consistent spellings in both English and French. This assumption of a prominent role for the rhyme is venerable in reading research (e.g., Glushko, 1979) and has much empirical and theoretical support (summarized by Treiman & Kessler, 1995), but it is far from obvious that feedback consistency effects should manifest themselves at the level of the rhyme and nowhere else. Perry (2003) looked at the feedback consistency of vowels, which was made possible by the fact that he adopted a graded definition of consistency: Vowels can be more or less consistent. It is conceivable that readers are sensitive to only certain types of feedback consistency and that incompatible findings may be due to the fact that experimenters are measuring somewhat different things.

A third issue that calls into question the lexical decision results is that of ecological validity. The lexical decision task has a long and respectable history, but it is difficult to know what it reveals. It is far from clear that lexical decision per se ever occurs in the course of natural reading. As Henderson (1989, p. 358) noted, the task "obliged the reader to journey exactly as far as the portals of the lexicon, to ring the bell and, if someone answered, to run home without further ado to report this happy domestic circumstance." Certainly lexical access occurs, and sometimes it fails. But we do not fully understand what happens when we ask someone to explicitly judge whether lexical access is possible for a given stimulus. Different people could approach this artificial task in different ways, and the approaches could be influenced by subtle differences in participant samples or in experiment administration. It is not inconceivable that subjects who weigh accuracy over speed may choose to assess the lexicality of *heap* by decoding its pronunciation to /hip/, checking whether /hip/ means something, then asking themselves how to spell /hip/, to see if the results match the spelling they were originally presented with. Such a suspicion is supported by Balota et al.'s (2004) finding that feedback consistency effects in the lexical decision task were reliable only for participants whose average word response latencies were slower than the median. If inconsistency in the sound-to-letter direction slows the task of deciding whether /hip/ is spelled *heap*, that is interesting enough in its own right. But if the participant has more or less explicitly generated a spelling subtask, sound-to-letter consistency has become a feedforward factor, and the experiment arguably is not addressing the key theoretical issue of whether feedback is an automatic component of the normal reading process.

Naming studies are much less subject to charges of the lack of ecological validity. In these studies, participants are shown a word and asked to read it aloud as quickly and accurately as possible, and the experimenter records how long it takes the participant to begin saying the word. While the exact conditions of a naming experiment are, as in most experiments, rather artificial, it is also clear that the task much more closely approximates the natural process of reading, which is often done orally, quickly, and with concern for accuracy. In particular, the naming task omits the mysterious and potentially misleading judgment component of the lexical decision task. For this reason, the naming task has been the second major avenue for researching feedback consistency effects.

In their experiment on French word naming, Ziegler et al. (1997) reported a feedback consistency effect. It took participants, on average, 8 additional milliseconds to pronounce feedback inconsistent words as compared to feedback consistent ones, and they made 2.7% more errors. But these numbers were much smaller than those obtained from their own lexical decision experiment, which involved a 33-ms difference and an 8.7% increase in error rate. Most importantly, the significance levels from the naming experiment were not reassuring. The difference in response time was significant when computed by subjects but not by items, and the difference in error rate was not significant either way, using a cutoff of .05. When Massaro and Jesse (2005) obtained similar results in English, they, more conservatively, reported a lack of evidence for feedback consistency. Peereman et al. (1998) also reported no significant feedback consistency effect on either response time or error rates in French. On the other hand, Lacruz and Folk (2004) reported success in English, and Balota et al. (2004) reported that feedback consistency of both the onset and the rhyme affected naming response times in all their analyses, with very strong significance. Intriguingly, their results were more robust for naming than for lexical decision, the opposite of the pattern reported by Ziegler et al.

The lack of agreement in results across the naming studies may be due to many of the same problems that afflict lexical decision studies of feedback consistency.

Lexical covariables are just as likely to mask or imitate feedback consistency in the naming task, and there are many different ways of conceptualizing and measuring consistency. In addition, naming studies have a serious handicap that lexical decision studies do not have. The differences in response time between feedback consistent and inconsistent words are small, with values of around 10 ms or less commonly reported. At such small time scales, the physics of speech production becomes a major player. For two words that have the same lexical access time—which is essentially the datum that one wishes to measure—it can take different amounts of time to plan and realize their articulation. Moreover, even after the articulation begins, it may take different amounts of time for the vocal tract to emit sufficient acoustic energy for a measuring device to register sound above background levels. In experiments using standard devices such as voice keys, these differences often are an order of magnitude larger than the purported difference between consistent and inconsistent words (Kessler, Treiman, & Mullennix, 2002).

Such a problem would be considered nothing more than an annoying source of noise, were it not for its quasi-systematicity. On the one hand, the variability is too irregular to control with simple mathematical adjustments. An experiment can get completely different patterns of errors due to differences in the sensitivity of the microphone, the distance between the speaker's mouth and the microphone, the threshold setting on the voice key, and how loud the speaker speaks. On the other hand, there is just enough systematicity to be troubling. On average, a loud response will appear to have been uttered sooner than a soft response, because the word will more quickly reach a threshold of acoustic amplitude. Or a response uttered at a faster tempo will generally appear, falsely, to have been uttered before a response uttered at a slower tempo, even if the response actually began at the same time, because at a faster tempo the speaker will generally get through any subthreshold initial portion of the word more quickly. Naturally, the experimenter does not want to confound soft amplitude or slow tempo with slow response time, since these phenomena may have quite different explanations in terms of the functioning of a cognitive network.

Most perniciously, response time measurements are correlated with the phonetic segments that occur at or near the beginning of a word, for both articulatory and acoustic reasons. For example, words beginning /tɑ/, /sɑ/, /si/, and /stɑ/ may all have systematically different response times associated with them. Unfortunately, the details are difficult to predict in a natural experimental setting, even to the extent of their relative order: /stɑ/ may be associated with unusually fast response times or unusually slow response times, depending on such factors as the measurement technology (Sakuma, Fushimi, & Tatsumi, 1997) and how loud the participant is speaking. The particular danger lies in the fact that the identity of the same phonemes that contribute to systematic measurement bias is an essential part of the computation of the feedback consistency measurement. That is, there is a quasi-systematic relationship between feedback consistency and response time measurements that has nothing to do with the cognitive process under investigation. This bias, naturally, is most troublesome in a study that investigates the feedback consistency of the onset (prevocalic) consonants or of the word's head (onset plus vowel), because phonemes at the beginning of the word have the strongest effect. But problems can arise even if the study looks only at the consistency of the rhyme of one-syllable words (the vowel plus coda, i.e., the following consonants), because there are many words that begin with a vowel, and vowels can influence response time measurement bias even when preceded by onset consonants (Kessler et al., 2002).

Most studies of feedback consistency that measure naming response time have taken some notice of these measurement biases and have attempted to work around them in some way. Ziegler et al. (1997) added a delayed-naming task. After the participants had gone through the normal trials, pronouncing the words as quickly as possible, they went through a second round where they were given time to mentally prepare before being asked to pronounce each word. Because feedback consistency did not significantly affect response time measurements in the delayed condition, the authors concluded that the feedback effects measured in the normal trials must reflect the time taken for mental preparation, that is, settling of the mental lexical networks. But Massaro and Jesse (2005) got the opposite results from using the delayed-naming task. They found that feedback consistency affected response time just as strongly in delayed trials as in normal, immediate trials, and concluded that measured feedback effects must therefore be due at least in part to processes that follow the act of reading. Of course, while such demonstrations are suggestive, they have some shortcomings. For example, in repeated measures designs, participants may behave systematically differently on delayed trials, whether because of fatigue or familiarity with the materials. Also, delayed trials may subtract out some articulatory contributions to response time in addition to the cognitive processing time they are intended to target, because speakers may, for example, position their articulators to pronounce the first phoneme while anticipating the cue to speak.

Massaro and Jesse (2005) used several other controls in addition to the delayed-naming task. Instead of relying on voice keys, they studied digitally produced waveforms to determine the onset of speech. They also adopted the technique of Kawamoto, Kello, Jones, and Bame (1998), whereby the participant is asked to drone a neutral vowel, /ə/, up to the point where the response is uttered. When the word in question begins with an obstruent, measuring the end of the drone vowel can be a more accurate estimate of the beginning of the word than an attempt to detect the sound of the consonant itself. These methods greatly reduce bias due to acoustic factors. However, bias due to articulatory factors necessarily remains, even under perfect measurement conditions. Some initial sounds will measure systematically differently because they take longer to articulate. These differences are real but regrettable, because it can be difficult to tell whether a slow response is due to articulatory factors or to feedback inconsistency. Massaro and Jesse attempted to compensate for remaining phonetic biases by balancing their experimental stimuli by manner of articulation of the initial consonant and by using words that do not vary by number of initial consonants.

Massaro and Jesse (2005) addressed phonetic bias problems with unusual and exemplary thoroughness. However, not all of their techniques can easily be adopted in all experiments. In particular, megastudies, which have been gaining in popularity, are not easily analyzed in these ways. Lexical megastudies are experiments that use thousands of words as stimuli, often thoroughly covering appreciable subsets of a language's vocabulary. Seidenberg and Waters (1989), Kessler et al. (2002), and Balota et al. (2004) describe experiments where participants read virtually all common, simple, one-syllable words of English and their response times for each word were recorded. Such studies are typically analyzed using regression analyses rather than factorial ANOVAs, freeing the experimenter from having to equate lexical stimuli across conditions on the many covariables that can affect performance. Megastudies have several other advantages as well (see Balota et al., 2004, for a thorough discussion), not least of which is a great potential for reusing data for other purposes than they were originally collected for. But they require the researcher to revisit the question of how to address phonetic bias, because the manual analysis of waveforms may be prohibitively expensive or may not be available at all when retrospectively analyzing megastudy datasets for which only voice key measurements are available.

Several researchers (Balota et al., 2004; Spieler & Balota, 1997; Treiman et al., 1995) addressed the problem of phonetic bias in megastudy regression analyses by introducing several variables to stand for the articulatory features of the first phoneme of the word, indicating, for example, whether it is a bilabial sound, or a fricative, or voiced. When this technique was introduced in 1995, 10 binary variables probably seemed more than enough to account for known voice key biases. Nowadays, however, it is better understood that the biases extend beyond the first phoneme of the word. More importantly, the contributions of different features to voice key bias are simply not additive (Kessler et al., 2002). This point is crucial because of the logic of investigating feedback consistency via linear regression. If one claims that an analysis shows that feedback consistency makes a significant contribution to predicting response time that cannot be attributed to other variables, that is tantamount to saying that all effects caused by the covariables, including the phonetic features, have been adequately accounted for by the additive, linear, model of the regression. If that claim is not credible, then the claim of feedback consistency effects is not credible.

Because there is no well-established way to decompose into linear components the phonetic bias contributions of all the different heads that can begin simple monosyllabic words in English, one might think instead to treat the different heads as levels of a category variable. Within the context of an ordinary linear regression, the categorical variable could be represented by dummy variables. Unfortunately, there are over 600 different heads, and therefore over 600 dummy variables. Such a huge number of variables can prove intractable, quite apart from whether one believes one could trust the results generated with such a huge model.

A RETROSPECTIVE ANALYSIS OF FEEDBACK CONSISTENCY EFFECTS IN NAMING

In this section we introduce a new way of addressing whether there are true feedback consistency effects in word naming. In order to deal with the issues identified in the previous section, we have experimented with a hybrid solution to the problem of running a regression analysis while controlling for phonetic heads. In the first step, an ordinary regression is run, using response time in a reading task as the dependent variable and, as independent variables, a variety of quantitative measures that may have an effect on response time. This step omits the feedback consistency measures that are the real target of the research, as well as the categorical variables, the heads of the words. The goal of this first step is to fit a model that accounts for as much of the variation in response time as we possibly can, before we get to the target variable and the less tractable heads.

As a second step, we apply the fitted linear model to all the words in the same study, to find the difference between the observed response time and the time predicted by the model. If the first step was reasonably accurate, these residuals will comprise a mixture of random variation and the effects of variables we have not yet considered.

In the last step, we see whether these residuals can be accounted for by the feedback consistency measures. We see whether the two numbers correlate in a monotonically ascending or descending order, a more liberal test than seeing whether they stand in a straight-line relation, as a standard regression would do. At the same time, we test for significance using permutation tests that only rearrange data between words that have the same phonetic heads. That way, the p value will disregard any variability that is due to the phonetic heads. This procedure therefore completely eliminates all known sources of phonetic bias, whether articulatory or acoustic in origin.

Materials

Data were analyzed (Table 8.1) from four previous megastudies that used voice keys to measure response time of U. S. and Canadian college students in naming tasks: Kessler et al. (2002) , henceforth KTM; Seidenberg and Waters (1989), SW; Spieler and Balota (1997; Balota et al., 2004), SB; and the English Lexicon Project (Balota et al., 2005), ELP. For the purpose of comparability, analyses here are limited to data available for all four studies: response times averaged across all participants for each of 2,326 simple, one-syllable words. Error rates were also analyzed, although the data are not completely commensurable across studies. In KTM and SW, errors were coded by the experimenter, whereas in SB and ELP, errors were noted only if reported by the participants themselves immediately after naming the word in question.

Table 1 shows the dependent variables that were collected for each word for use as covariables in the regression step. Most of these variables were chosen because previous studies had indicated that they may have an effect on response time, and most of them have been taken into account in careful studies of feedback consistency. A few others were included because we suspected that they may affect response time and correlate with feedback consistency, so failing to include them could lead to spurious effects. For example, spelling–sound correspondences that have low feedback consistency, such as the *gn* /n/ of *gnat*, will usually have spellings that are less frequent in text: More words have onset *n* than *gn*. It is reasonable to surmise that readers may hesitate when they encounter less common letter groups like *gn*, but such behavior would not constitute evidence for recurrent networks. In

TABLE 8.1

Significant Contributions to Response
Time and Error Rates in Step 1 Regressions

Variable	Response Time[a]				Error Rate[b]			
	KTM	SW	SB	ELP	KTM	SW	SB	ELP
Whole word[c]								
Frequency[d]	_***	_**	_***	_***	_***	_**	_*	_***
Familiarity[e]	_***	_*	_**	_***	_***		_***	_***
Imageability[f]			_***		_**			_**
Bigrams[g]	_***	_*						
Neighborhood[h]			_***					
Syllable parts[i]								
Letters[j]								
Onset	+*		_**					
Head								
Vowel								
Rhyme	+**	+*		+**	_***			
Coda					+***			
Phonemes[k]								
Onset	+*	+*	+***	+*			+***	
Coda		_**	_*	_*				
Written frequency[l]								
Onset	_*		_**					
Head								+*
Vowel					_***	_***	_***	_***
Rhyme	_**	_*	_*	_*		_**		_**
Coda	+**					_*		_*
Spoken frequency[m]								
Onset	+*							
Head	_**						_***	
Vowel	+***	+**	+**	+***	+**	+***	+***	+***
Rhyme			+*	+*				
Coda						+***		+**
Feedforward consistency[n]								
Onset	_***	_***	_***	_***	_*		_***	
Head		_***		_*				
Vowel					_***	_*	_***	_***
Rhyme	_*		_***	_**	_***	_**	_***	_***
Coda						_***		

(*Continued*)

TABLE 8.1
(*Continued*)

Variable	Response Time[a] KTM	SW	SB	ELP	Error Rate[b] KTM	SW	SB	ELP
Feedback consistency°								
Onset	—	—	—	—			—*	
Head	—	—	—	—				—**
Vowel	—	—	—	—	+***	+*	+***	+***
Rhyme	—	—	—	—				
Coda	—	—	—	—		+**		+*
R²	.32	.26	.39	.34	.16	.05	.14	.17

Note. Each column gives the result of a separate simultaneous linear multiple regression; total variance accounted for is in the last row. Signs tell effect of increased level of variable on response time and error rate and are shown only when two-tailed significance is less than .05.
[a]Time elapsed between presentation of word and tripping of voice key after response was initiated.
[b]Percentage of mispronounced responses, excluding those with outlying response times or failures to respond.
[c]Measures computed over the entire word.
[d]Corpus frequency in Zeno, Ivenz, Millard, and Duvvuri (1995), log transformed.
[e]Scaled 1 (*least familiar*) to 7; most ratings are from Nusbaum, Pisoni, & Davis (1984). Values for some words not covered by that study were supplied from a small experiment at Wayne State University.
[f]Cortese and Fugett (2004).
[g]Average text frequency of the two-letter sequences in the spelling (Solso & Juel, 1980), square-root transformed.
[h]Coltheart's N: Number of words in full collegiate lexicon that differ by substituting one letter (Coltheart, Davelaar, Jonasson, & Besner, 1977); square-root transformed.
[i]Measures computed for each phonological parse of the syllable: Onset is all consonants before the vowel, coda is all consonants after the vowel, head is onset plus vowel, rhyme is vowel plus coda.
[j]Number of letters in syllable part.
[k]Number of phonemes in syllable part (constant 1 for vowel).
[l]Sum of the natural log of the frequencies (per Zeno et al.) of all words in the Kessler and Treiman (2001) list that have the same spelling of this syllable part, regardless of pronunciation; square-root transformed.
[m]Counting words as in footnote (m), the sum of all words in the list that have the same pronunciation of this syllable part, regardless of spelling.
[n]Counting words as in footnote (m), the count of words whose syllable part is spelled the same and has the same pronunciation, divided by the count of all words whose syllable part is spelled the same.
[o]Counting words as in footnote (m), the count of words whose onset and so on, is pronounced the same and has the same spelling, divided by the count of all words whose onset, and so on, is pronounced the same. Not used in Step 1 regressions on response times.

the absence of the written frequency variables, some of the effect due to spelling frequency could be spuriously attributed to feedback consistency.

For the last step, the correlation, we collected also feedback consistency measures using measures analogous to the feedforward measures. The phonetic head was also determined for each word.

Procedure

For each of the four studies, ordinary least squares linear regressions were run using response time as the dependent variable and, as independent variables, the measures listed in Table 8.1. Residuals were extracted for each word, giving one residual per study per word. Correlations were run between each of the four sets of residual measurements and each of the five ways of computing feedback consistency (onset, head, vowel, rhyme, and coda). The correlation measure consisted of multiplying the residual and the consistency measure for each word, then summing those products across all words. This measure was chosen because the sum of products is minimized as the pairs of numbers approach inverse rank order. That is, if the words were to be ordered by increasing residual value, such a measure would be at a minimum if the corresponding consistency measures were in decreasing order. Therefore, significance of the correlation measure was determined by randomly rearranging the associations between residual and consistency 10,000 times and counting how many times the rearranged measure was less than or equal to the observed measure. This tested the hypothesis that increased consistency is associated with decreased (faster) response time. To factor out any effect of phonetic heads from the significance measure, the random rearrangements only took place between words that have the same phonetic head.

To test the effect of feedback consistency on error rates in each of the four studies, all predictor variables, including the feedback consistency measures, were entered into a simultaneous regression. Because there is no reason to expect that phonetic factors will correlate with error rates, no steps were taken to block by phonetic head.

Results and Discussion

The columns labeled *Response Time* in Table 8.1 show which variables accounted for significant variance in response time in the regression analyses of Step 1. Significance levels vary among the four different studies, but studies generally agree in the direction of any effect. Note that a plus sign in the table indicates greater response time, that is, slower reading. Some of the results are unsurprising. For example, the more frequent and familiar a word is, or the more common the spelling of its rhyme, the faster one can read the word. Other results are perhaps less expected. For example, the more common vowel phonemes are associated with slower response times. Of course, this part of the analysis ignores feedback consistency and the phonetic heads of the words, and so these specific results should not be taken as definitive. More important is the result of the correlation, which happens after the regression step and so is not shown in Table 8.1. Of the

20 analyses of response time (4 studies with 5 ways of computing feedback consistency), only one showed an effect in the predicted direction: The SB data showed increased feedback consistency in the onset as being associated with faster response times ($p = .04$). The finding of one significant test out of 20 is what one would expect by chance at a significance threshold of .05.

Our regression analyses of error rates are presented in the right half of Table 8.1. Recall that for error rates, we considered it safe to treat feedback consistency directly in the simultaneous regressions, because there was no reason to expect phonetic voice key biases to interfere with the measurements. The results for error rates do not tell any unified story—sporadic effects in both directions can be seen in the table—but it is not completely clear what effects would be predicted for feedback consistency in the first place. On the one hand, anything that perturbs the equilibrium of networks enough to increase response time might be expected to also lead to increased errors. By this reasoning, we would expect feedback consistency to lead to reduced error rates (minus signs in the table), but the only reliably replicated effect appears to be that vowel feedback consistency is associated with increased error rates. On the other hand, the argumentation behind feedback consistency experiments depends crucially on the assumption that the reader has decoded the correct pronunciation in the initial, feedforward, steps. Why, then, should an error emerge? The only type of error that would specifically be predicted on the basis of recurrent networks would be the result of feedback from the feedback. Upon seeing the word *rose* and decoding it to the correct /roz/, the network might generate, among other respellings, *rows*. In turn, feedback from the feedback spelling *rows* could generate the error pronunciation /rɑʊz/, rhyming with *cows*. It would be intriguing if people do indeed read *rose* as /rɑʊz/. Unfortunately, none of the actual mispronunciations generated in the megastudies have been made available, so it is impossible to evaluate this implication of recurrence theory.

CONCLUSION

The results of our experiment in factoring out phonetic bias were not encouraging for the hypothesis that feedback inconsistency slows readers' performance in word-naming tasks. This conclusion does not appear out of step with past research. Some of the strongest results supporting a feedback effect on naming have either not controlled for phonetic biases at all (e.g., Lacruz & Folk, 2004) or have done so in a way that is arguably inadequate (e.g., the binary feature variables in Balota et al., 2004). Other results are more tepid (e.g., Ziegler et al., 1997) or agree with us in being negative (e.g., Massaro & Jesse, 2005; Peereman et al., 1998). Further, our study took into account additional predictor variables that may have been confounded with feedback properties in several prior studies, such as the frequency of the letter group that spells the unit whose feedback consistency is being measured. All in all, there are strong grounds for being skeptical of the idea that there is a proven feedback consistency effect in naming.

Does that mean that no effect will ever be demonstrated? Current research protocols make such an undertaking almost hopelessly difficult. Any effect of feedback on the speech stream is surely so small that it is difficult to pick out amidst all the other complicated and noisy variables in the system. Possibly progress on this research front will come from the adoption of methodologies that do not attempt to measure speech onset. Another tack could be to see whether feedback effects are more characteristic of less experienced readers. One could study children, or teach adult subjects an artificial symbol system with the crucial properties of English- or French-like orthographies. This latter approach would have the additional advantage of letting the experimenter disentangle feedback consistency measures from the many other factors that facilitate or inhibit the fluent reading of single words.

We would be as intrigued as anyone to eventually see convincing proof that reading activates the same sound-encoding processes that were developed for use in writing. However, our appraisal of the current state of knowledge, along with our reanalyses of several megastudies using our new, stronger, controls on phonetic voice key biases, leads us to conclude that there is no reason to require models of oral reading to predict feedback consistency effects, whether by making networks recurrent or by other means.

ACKNOWLEDGMENTS

Brett Kessler and Rebecca Treiman, Department of Psychology, Washington University in St. Louis. John Mullennix, Department of Psychology, University of Pittsburgh at Johnstown.

This work was supported in part by grant BCS-0130763 from the National Science Foundation. We thank David Balota, Howard Nusbaum, Mark Seidenberg, and Melvin Yap for making their data files available to us.

Correspondence concerning this article should be addressed to Brett Kessler, Department of Psychology, Washington University in St. Louis, Campus Box 1125, One Brookings Dr., St. Louis MO 63130-4899. E-mail: bkessler@wustl.edu

REFERENCES

Balota, D. A. (1994). Visual word recognition: The journey from features to meaning. In M. A. Gernsbacher (Ed.), *Handbook of psycholinguistics* (pp. 303–348). San Diego, CA: Academic Press.

Balota, D. A., et al. (2005). *English Lexicon Project web site*. Retrieved April 1, 2005, from the Washington University in St. Louis web site, http://elexicon.wustl.edu

Balota, D. A., Cortese, M. J., Sergent-Marshall, S. D., Spieler, D. H., & Yap, M. J. (2004). Visual word recognition of single-syllable words. *Journal of Experimental Psychology: General, 133,* 283–316.

Coltheart, M., Davelaar, E., Jonasson, J. T., & Besner, D. (1977). Access to the internal lexicon. In S. Dornič (Ed.), *Attention and performance VI* (pp. 535–555). Hillsdale, NJ: Erlbaum.

Coltheart, M., Rastle, K., Perry, C., Langdon, R., & Ziegler, J. (2001). DRC: A dual route cascaded model of visual word recognition and reading aloud. *Psychological Review, 108,* 204–256.

Cortese, M. J., & Fugett, A. (2004). Imageability ratings for 3,000 monosyllabic words. *Behavior Methods and Research, Instrumentation, & Computers, 36,* 384–387.

Cutler, A. (1981). Making up materials is a confounded nuisance: or, Will we be able to run any psycholinguistic experiments at all in 1990? *Cognition, 10,* 65–70.

Glushko, R. J. (1979). The organization and activation of orthographic knowledge in reading aloud. *Journal of Experimental Psychology: Human Perception and Performance, 5,* 674–691.

Henderson, L. (1989). On mental representation of morphology and its diagnosis by measures of visual access speed. In W. Marslen-Wilson (Ed.), *Lexical representation and process* (pp. 357–391). Cambridge, MA: MIT Press.

International Phonetic Association (2005). *The International Phonetic Association.* Retrieved April 26, 2005, from http://www.arts.gla.ac.uk/ipa

Jared, D. (1997). Spelling–sound consistency affects the naming of high-frequency words. *Journal of Memory and Language, 36,* 505–529.

Jared, D. (2002). Spelling–sound consistency and regularity effects in word naming. *Journal of Memory and Language, 46,* 723–750.

Kawamoto, A. H., Kello, C. T., Jones, R., & Bame, K. (1998). Initial phoneme versus whole-word criterion to initiate pronunciation: Evidence based on response latency and initial phoneme duration. *Journal of Experimental Psychology: Learning, Memory, and Cognition, 24,* 862–885.

Kessler, B., & Treiman, R. (2001). Relationships between sounds and letters in English monosyllables. *Journal of Memory and Language, 44,* 592–617.

Kessler, B., Treiman, R., & Mullennix, J. (2002). Phonetic biases in voice key response time measurements. *Journal of Memory and Language, 44,* 592–617.

Lacruz, I., & Folk, J. R. (2004). Feedforward and feedback consistency effects for high- and low-frequency words in lexical decision and naming. *The Quarterly Journal of Experimental Psychology, 57A,* 1261–1284.

Massaro, D. W., & Jesse, A. (2005). The magic of reading: Too many influences for quick and easy explanations. In T. Trabasso, J. Sabatini, D. W. Massaro, & R. C. Calfee (Eds.), *From orthography to pedagogy: Essays in honor of Richard L. Venezky* (pp. 37–61). Mahwah, NJ: Erlbaum.

Nusbaum, H. C., Pisoni, D. B., & Davis, C. K. (1984). *Sizing up the Hoosier mental lexicon: Measuring the familiarity of 20,000 words* (Research on Speech Perception Progress Report, 10). Bloomington: Indiana University.

Peereman, R., Content, A., & Bonin, P. (1998). Is perception a two-way street? The case of feedback consistency in visual word recognition. *Journal of Memory and Language, 39,* 151–174.

Perry, C. (2003). A phoneme–grapheme feedback consistency effect. *Psychonomic Bulletin & Review, 10,* 392–397.

Plaut, D. C., McClelland, J. L., Seidenberg, M. S., & Patterson, K. (1996). Understanding normal and impaired word reading: Computational principles in quasi-regular domains. *Psychological Review, 103,* 56–115.

Sakuma, N., Fushimi, T., & Tatsumi, I. (1997). Onseiha no shisatsu ni yoru kana no ondokusenji no sokutei: Ondokusenji wa gotôon no chôonhô ni yori ôkiku kotonaru. [Naming latency measurements of kana based on inspection of voice waveforms: Naming latency varies greatly depending on the manner of articulation of the initial phoneme.] *Shinkeishinrigaku, 13,* 126–136.

Seidenberg, M. S., & Waters, G. S. (1989, November). *Reading words aloud: A mega study* [Abstract]. *Bulletin of the Psychonomic Society, 27,* 489.

Solso, R. L., & Juel, C. L. (1980). Positional frequency and versatility of bigrams for two-through nine-letter English words. *Behavior Research Methods & Instrumentation, 12,* 297–343.

Spieler, D. H., & Balota, D. A. (1997). Bringing computational models of word naming down to the item level. *Psychological Science, 8,* 411–416.

Stone, G. O., & Van Orden, G. C. (1994). Building a resonance framework for word recognition using design and system principles. *Journal of Experimental Psychology: Human Perception & Performance, 20,* 1248–1268.

Stone, G. O., Vanhoy, M., & Van Orden, G. C. (1997). Perception is a two-way street: Feedforward and feedback phonology in visual word recognition. *Journal of Memory and Language, 36,* 337–359.

Treiman, R., & Kessler, B. (1995). In defense of an onset–rhyme syllable structure for English. *Language and Speech, 38,* 127–142.

Treiman, R., Mullennix, J., Bijeljac-Babic, R., & Richmond-Welty, E. D. (1995). The special role of rimes in the description, use, and acquisition of English orthography. *Journal of Experimental Psychology: General, 124,* 107–136.

Zeno, S. M., Ivenz, S. H., Millard, R. T., & Duvvuri, R. (1995). *The educator's word frequency guide* [Electronic data file]. Brewster, NY: Touchstone Applied Science Associates.

Ziegler, J. C., Montant, M., & Jacobs, A. M. (1997). The feedback consistency effect in lexical decision and naming. *Journal of Memory and Language, 37,* 533–554.

Ziegler, J. C., & Van Orden, G. C. (2000). Feedback consistency effects. *Behavioral & Brain Sciences, 23,* 351–352.

CHAPTER NINE

Three Perspectives on Spelling Development

Tatiana Cury Pollo
Rebecca Treiman
Brett Kessler
Washington University in St. Louis

Learning how to read and write can be one of the biggest challenges in children's lives. One of the most important components of writing at the single-word level is spelling. Although interest in spelling development has increased in recent years, the study of spelling has still not attracted as much attention as the study of reading (Caravolas, Hulme, & Snowling, 2001; Treiman, 1998). Studies of spelling development are important not only because of the pedagogical interest in understanding how children acquire this major facet of literacy, but also because children's early spellings provide information about their initial knowledge of the graphic and phonological characteristics of writing that could not be obtained in other ways.

Rather than exhaustively review the literature on the topic, we present in this chapter three current approaches to the study of early spelling development in alphabetic writing systems: the *phonological, constructivist,* and *statistical-learning* perspectives. We devote special attention to studies that have examined spelling development crosslinguistically, because such studies are crucial for differentiating universal properties of spelling development from those that are adaptations to specific features of the child's language or target writing system.

THE PHONOLOGICAL PERSPECTIVE

The phonological perspective holds that children's biggest challenge when learning to spell in alphabetic writing systems is understanding the idea that letters represent phonemes (e.g., Liberman, Shankweiler, Fischer, & Carter, 1974). Children also need to possess alphabetic knowledge, or knowledge of specific sound-to-letter correspondences, but gaining the ability to analyze spoken language into strings of phonemes is a bigger hurdle, in this perspective, than learning specific links between phonemes and letters.

The phonological perspective describes the development of children's spelling skills in terms of their increasing ability to map sounds of words to phonetically appropriate letters, a process often called *encoding* (Ehri, 1992; Gough & Hillinger, 1980). Theorists such as Ehri (1991; 1992; 1998), Frith (1985), Henderson and colleagues (Beers, Beers, & Grant, 1977; Henderson, 1985), and Gentry (1982) represent the phonological perspective. These theorists have proposed phase and stage models of spelling development that differ slightly from each other but follow a similar pattern: Children move from an initial stage in which spellings are nonphonological to a later stage in which spellings are phonologically adequate.

As children pass through different phases or stages, they rely predominantly on different types of knowledge. In common to the different theories is a focus on young children's attempts to represent the sounds of words in their spellings. In what follows, we will outline two representative theories: the stage theory proposed by Gentry, who proposed his model based on a case study of a child who began to spell without instruction (Bissex, 1980), and the phase theory proposed by Ehri.

These theorists believe that children's spellings are initially random strings of letters that have no relationship to the sounds in the words. For example, children may spell *quick* as HS^1 (Ehri, 1991); the letters H and S bear no relationship to the sounds in the word *quick*. This is what Ehri called the *prealphabetic* phase and Gentry called the *precommunicative* stage.

As children learn about letter names and sounds, they start to understand that letters symbolize sounds. Children then represent a few of the sounds in words with phonologically appropriate letters. Gentry (1982) cites an example of a 5-year-old child who, trying to get attention from his mother, spelled *RUDF* for *Are you deaf?* (Bissex, 1980, p. 3). These types of spellings are called *partial alphabetic* or *semiphonetic*. At this point in development, many of children's initial sound representations are based on a letter name strategy (e.g., R for *are* and U for *you*).

Many studies have shown that knowledge of letter names plays a particularly important role in young children's early spelling (e.g., Treiman & Kessler, 2003). Letter names are frequent within words (Pollo, Kessler, & Treiman, 2005), and children may spell a letter name with its corresponding letter: the so-called *letter name strategy* (Treiman, 1993; 1994). Thus children may spell *car* as *CR* or *tell* as *TL*, using the consonants R and L to spell all of the sounds in the names of those letters. Because the name of a vowel letter is also typically one of the sounds it spells in English, evidence for the use of vowel letter names is more indirect. For example, Treiman (1993) showed the importance of vowel names when she observed that children more often wrote vowel letters when spelling a vowel sound that was the

---

[1]Children's spellings are written in uppercase. Phonemes are represented using the conventions of the International Phonetic Association (1999).

same as a letter name. Effects of letter name knowledge on reading and spelling have been documented not only in English but also in languages such as Hebrew (Levin, Patel, Margalit, & Barad, 2002) and Portuguese (Abreu & Cardoso-Martins, 1998; Cardoso-Martins, Resende, & Rodrigues, 2002; Martins & Silva, 2001).

The next phase or stage is when children produce spellings that more completely represent the phonological forms of words. This is called the *full alphabetic* phase or *phonetic* stage. Children may be able to spell correctly many words such as *CAR* or provide phonologically plausible spellings such as *KAR*. In this stage, all or most of the phonemes of the words are represented in children's spelling.

Consistent with the phonological perspective, many researchers have demonstrated that children's early spellings are in large part attempts to represent the sounds in words (e.g., Read, 1975, 1986; Treiman, 1993). Those researchers reported that, when children do not know how to spell certain sounds, they sometimes invent their own spellings for those sounds. These early phonological attempts are called *invented spellings*.

The pioneering work on invented spellings was done by Read (1975; 1986). Read's observations of early spellings questioned the traditional view that children learn to spell by memorizing each word individually and shifted attention to the creative aspects of young children's spellings. Children's spelling mistakes show that they are aware of phonetic distinctions that adults no longer notice, perhaps because of all their exposure to correct spellings. Children may spell words that start with *tr* with *ch* instead—spelling *truck* as *CHRAC* or *troubles* as *CHRIBLS*. At first, these mistakes look bizarre, but they have a perfectly good phonological explanation: Before /r/, the phoneme /t/ is phonetically similar to the initial sound of *chat*. A similar pattern occurs with /d/ before /r/, which children may spell with a *j* or *g*.

As illustrated above, children in the phonetic stage are thought to assign letters to sounds with no regard to the conventions of orthography. As children start to learn more about conventional spellings and spelling patterns that occur in words, they are said to enter a *transitional* stage (Gentry, 1982). Finally, children attain the *correct* stage (Gentry) or *consolidated alphabetic* phase (Ehri, 1998). At this point in development, children are competent readers and spellers.

It is difficult to overstate the importance of the phonological perspective in the study of spelling development. The major strength of this perspective lies in the idea that children have linguistic knowledge that they use in their invented spellings. This perspective is strongly opposed to the earlier idea that learning to spell is purely a matter of rote memorization, an idea that had gained currency because of the belief that English spelling is so complex and irregular that it could not be learned any other way. Work following this phonological perspective pioneered the idea that children's early misspellings reflect their knowledge about the sound properties of words.

Studies within the phonological framework have led to theories of spelling development that are able to explain a broad range of phenomena, stimulating research and guiding educators. Another positive aspect of this approach is that researchers have used not only naturalistic data (e.g., Gentry, 1982) but also experimental data (e.g., Ehri & Wilce, 1985; Read, 1975). This combination allows researchers to bring together the ecological validity of naturalistic observations and the quantitative rigor of experiments.

Because most of the work within the phonological perspective has targeted the English language, the question arises as to the generalizabilility of its models to children learning to spell in other languages. Wimmer and Hummer (1990), for example, have suggested that children learning to read and spell in more regular writing systems such as German skip the earliest phases and move straight into the full alphabetic phase. But other researchers have found evidence for prephonetic and phonetic phases of development in languages in which sound-to-letter encodings are more regular than in English. For example, Cardoso-Martins and colleagues found evidence that children learning to read and spell in Portuguese follow a similar pattern of development as that proposed by Ehri (Abreu & Cardoso-Martins, 1998; Cardoso-Martins, 2005).

One feature of writing systems that receives special attention in the phonological perspective is the regularity of the relations between the phonemes and the letters. Many studies in the phonological perspective have shown this to be an important factor in literacy acquisition (e.g., Aro & Wimmer, 2003; Defior, Martos, & Cary, 2002; Seymour, Aro, & Erskine, 2003). Children learning languages that are regular read better, faster, and commit fewer mistakes than children learning to read in languages like English that are more irregular. Although large-scale crosslinguistic studies are not as common in spelling research, similar kinds of differences have been observed. Several findings suggest that the rate of spelling development is slower for English than for more regular writing systems such as Czech (Caravolas & Bruck, 1993) and German (Wimmer & Landerl, 1997). The differences found between spelling development in English and other languages are attributed to differences between spelling-to-sound regularities among those writing systems (see Caravolas, 2004, for a review), but for the most part these differences have not been systematically quantified. In fact, few researchers have comprehensively investigated the spelling–sound relationships of languages other than English; among the exceptions are Ziegler, Jacobs, and Stone (1996) and Lange and Content (1999), both investigating French. There is a need for reliable and comprehensive information about other orthographic systems and, in addition, about other language characteristics that could be relevant to children who are learning to spell.

The most significant drawback of research in the phonological perspective is that it tends to give short shrift to nonphonological aspects of learning to spell in the earliest phases. Researchers in this tradition grant that many young children possess certain literacy-related skills, including knowledge about letters' shapes and names. Indeed, the fact that young children in the prealphabetic phase (or precommunicative stage) of spelling development often use real letters as opposed to other symbols when asked to spell suggests that children have some knowledge about the writing system. However, researchers who subscribe to the phonological perspective have not usually studied how such knowledge is deployed in spelling. For example, these researchers have not tested the assumption that children's random-letter spellings are indeed random. Productions that appear to be random letter strings from a phonological perspective may consist of letters from a young child's name (Treiman, Kessler, & Bourassa, 2001) or may reflect certain characteristics of the writing system to which the children have been exposed, such as the relative frequencies of different letters. Studies show that U. S. children as young as kindergarten (about 5 to 6 years old) show some sensitivity to graphic patterns and permissible letter sequences in spelling. For example, English-speaking children have some understanding that certain letter sequences like *ck* or *rr* rarely occur at the beginnings of words. Evidence for this early sensitivity comes from naturally produced spellings (Treiman, 1993) as well as from experimental studies in which children rated nonwords like *baff* as more wordlike than nonwords like *bbaf* (Cassar & Treiman, 1997). The same pattern of results is found for other languages. For example, Pacton, Perruchet, Fayol, and Cleeremans (2001) showed that French-speaking children in Grade 1 (about 6 years old) are sensitive to which letters can be doubled. Such results suggest that early spelling involve more than phonology. In our view, nonphonological knowledge is important from early in the course of spelling development and is not restricted to later phases.

THE CONSTRUCTIVIST PERSPECTIVE

A second theoretical perspective in the study of spelling development may be called the constructivist perspective. This perspective is well represented in many non-English-speaking countries, including those using French (e.g., Besse, 1996), Italian (e.g., Pontecorvo, 1985; Pontecorvo & Zuchermaglio, 1988), Portuguese (e.g., Martins & Silva, 2001; Silva & Alves-Martins, 2002; Rego, 1999), and Spanish (e.g., Ferreiro & Teberosky, 1982). In the United States, it falls under the rubric of emergent literacy research (e.g., Sulzby, 1985). Researchers in this tradition prefer to use the term *writing* rather than *spelling* because they wish to embrace what "preschoolers know about general features of writing, not just what they know about the orthographic conventions of particular scripts" (Tolchinsky & Teberosky, 1998, p. 2).

Researchers in the constructivist tradition have been influenced by the work of Piaget. Piaget created a method of clinical observation to understand how children view the world and postulated a general developmental stage theory that was later applied to a variety of specific behaviors, including children's literacy skills. Ferreiro was particularly influential in extending the Piagetian framework to literacy development. Her work was based mostly on observations of Spanish-speaking children. Ferreiro and colleagues (Ferreiro, 1990; Ferreiro & Teberosky, 1982; Vernon & Ferreiro, 1999) focused on children's early conceptions about written language, proposing that children know a good deal about writing even before they grasp the alphabetic principle. This knowledge includes beliefs about written language and how words should be written.

Ferreiro and colleagues (e.g., Ferreiro & Teberosky, 1982) described three broad stages in the evolution of writing, in the course of which children adopt and abandon different hypotheses about written language until they understand the alphabetic principle. At first, in what Ferreiro called the *presyllabic* stage, children do not understand that the function of writing is to represent sounds of the language. Even at this point, though, children hold hypotheses about written language. One of these is the principle of *minimum quantity*, whereby children think that a text needs to have several letters. For example, children are more likely to accept the sequence *BDC* as a word than *BD*, even though they probably saw neither of those exact letter sequences before. According to Ferreiro, this minimum is fixed for a given child and is typically either three or four letters; it is independent of the minimum number of letters per word in the child's language. In the same stage, children also believe that the letters in a word must be different from each other—what Ferreiro called the *variation* hypothesis. For example, children prefer the string of letters *BDC* over *BBB*. Children are unlikely to have seen either sequence, a fact that advocates of the constructivist perspective take to mean that children generate rather abstract ideas on their own. Moreover, Ferreiro and colleagues suggested that children's preference for variation is independent of the frequency of doubled letters in the writing systems to which they are exposed (Ferreiro, Pontecorvo, & Zucchermaglio, 1996).

Although children at this first stage may be very good at discriminating writing from drawing (Tolchinsky-Landsmann & Levin, 1985), they are inclined to represent words in terms of their semantic attributes. They may believe that variation in the written forms of object's names reflects variation of the properties of the objects. For example, in a study of Italian preschoolers, Stella and Biancardi (1990) showed that children tended to use longer spellings to represent bigger objects. In this study, children spelled *coccinella* 'ladybug' and *farfalla* 'butterfly' with fewer letters than they used for *orso* 'bear' and *mucca* 'cow'. Also, children used more letters to spell *palle* 'straws' than *palla* 'straw', even though both words have the same number of phonemes. In these cases, children appeared to match the number of letters in the spellings to semantic properties of the objects, namely their size or quantity.

As children learn more about print, they observe that the physical characteristics of objects rarely match the physical features of written words. According to Ferreiro and colleagues, children now hypothesize that the individual letters they see in print stand for syllables. This hypothesis results in *syllabic* spellings, in which children write one symbol per syllable. For example, children may spell the Spanish dissyllabic words *palo* 'stick' and *sapo* 'frog' as *AO* (Ferreiro & Teberosky, 1982). Reports of syllabic spellings among preschool children are frequent not only in Spanish but also in other Romance languages such as Portuguese. For example, Nunes Carraher and Rego (1984) cited a Portuguese-speaking child who spelled *urubu* 'vulture' as *UUU*, and Rego (1999) described spellings such as *OA* for *bota* 'boot' and *AE* for *café* 'coffee'. In Italian, there are reports of spellings such as *IAEA* for *primavera* 'spring' (Pontecorvo, 1996).

The syllabic stage is a crucial intermediary stage in Ferreiro's theory of spelling development, because it is taken to be the child's first attempt to represent in print the sounds of language. As children gain more experience with print, they observe that the number of letters in written words usually exceeds the number of syllables in the corresponding spoken words. This causes children to move from the syllabic stage to the alphabetic stage, when they understand that letters stand for smaller sounds than syllables, namely, phonemes.

A strength of constructivist theories is their acknowledgment that young children in literate societies learn a good deal about writing before they understand that it represents language at the level of phonemes, or indeed before they understand that it represents language at all. In Romance-speaking countries, Ferreiro's theory is by far the predominant paradigm for explaining young children's spelling acquisition, to such an extent that early literacy instruction is generally approached as an effort to guide children out of the presyllabic stage of spelling and into the syllabic and later stages (Silva & Alves-Martins, 2002). However, despite its widespread popularity and acceptance, Ferreiro's theory has some limitations.

It has been surprisingly difficult to formulate rigorous empirical criteria for determining whether a child is in the syllabic stage. If children are asked to spell a list of words, some matches between the number of syllables in words' spoken forms and the numbers of letters in children's spellings would be expected to occur by chance. Procedures are needed to determine whether the number of matches exceeds the number that would occur by chance, and these have not been offered by advocates of syllabic theories.

Another limitation is that there is a lack of evidence for the syllabic stage—the most distinctive stage in Ferreiro's theory—in certain languages. Kamii, Long, Manning, and Manning (1990), for example, did not find evidence for a syllabic stage among English-speaking children. Instead, they reported children representing words with only consonants—what the authors called a *consonantal* stage. Advocates of the syllabic hypothesis have proposed that the apparent discrepancy between English and Romance languages reflect differences between the languages. Kamii et al. pointed to the unclearness of many of the unstressed vowels in English polysyllables as a reason for the predominant use of consonants by English-speaking children. Ferreiro (1990) argued that syllabic spellings are rare or absent among English-speaking preschoolers because English has more one-syllable words than other languages such as Spanish. In any case, an expansion of the theory is necessary to account for the data of English-speaking children.

A last weakness of Ferreiro's theory of literacy development is that the original theory does not account for literacy development after children reach the alphabetic stage. As discussed earlier, many studies have shown that spelling development is not complete after children reach the alphabetic stage. Nonphonological knowledge plays an important role in mastering the complexities of the spelling system.

STATISTICAL-LEARNING PERSPECTIVE

The statistical-learning perspective agrees with the constructivist idea that young children in literate societies formulate and deploy hypotheses about the nature of writing before they understand that letters represents phonemes. In children's earliest spellings, where classical phonological theorists see random strings of letters, statistical-learning theorists agree with constructivists in finding meaningful patterns. However, while constructivism tends to emphasize constructions emerging spontaneously from the mind of the child, the statistical-learning perspective emphasizes that children's writing reflects the characteristics of the input to which they have been exposed, as filtered through their perceptual and learning mechanisms.

Statistics, in this context, refers to frequencies. A statistical pattern or regularity is said to exist when a set of events or objects co-occur more often than expected by chance. Considerable evidence shows that people, including young children and infants, implicitly learn statistical regularities (Zacks & Hasher, 2002). Saffran and colleagues (Saffran, Aslin, & Newport, 1996; Aslin, Saffran, & Newport, 1999), for example, have shown that statistical relationships between sounds in speech help infants, young children, and adults to segment words. The applicability of the statistical learning perspective to spelling is suggested by the fact that in most literate societies, children often see words on street signs, in books and magazines, and so on. Children's early spellings may reflect the knowledge that they have gained by exposure to such material. A statistical perspective seeks to minimize the number of stipulations that must be made, by showing how theories of language learning and of learning in general can account for the learning of spelling.

An important implication of the statistical-learning perspective is that the same basic mechanism underlies spelling acquisition throughout development. This contrasts with the idea that children move through stages whose operative principles are divorced from those of previous stages. In a statistical perspective, one expects children to learn a variety of information simultaneously: A child may, for example, learn some principles of graphotactics quite early, such as the proper placement of capital letters, and other patterns later; this contrasts with the phonological perspective that all important graphotactic learning occurs in the final stage of spelling development. Another implication of the statistical-learning perspective is that children's early strategies may be strongly informed by unique properties of their language and the writing system they are learning. Thus, we may expect quite different productions from speakers of different languages, even before they generate phonetically plausible spellings.

The connectionist framework provides a simple but powerful model of how people might learn statistical regularities. Connectionist models attempt to explain cognition in terms of networks of simple units. Pattern learning involves modifying the connections between the units in response to exposure to a substantial number of examples (Seidenberg, 1997). Recent studies of reading and spelling emphasize that connectionist learning mechanisms pick up subtle regularities in the input, arguably providing a better explanation of skilled reading and reading development than previous models that focus on all-or-none rules. For example, Hutzler, Ziegler, Perry, Wimmer, and Zorzi (2004) argued that connectionist models are able to explain an advantage of learning to read in regular versus irregular languages. Although more research using a connectionist framework has been done on reading than on spelling, connectionist models have recently been developed to account for data on normal and impaired spelling (e.g., Houghton & Zorzi, 2003). Such models require further development before they simulate human spelling in all respects. But with their emphasis on learners' sensitivity to the properties of the input, they provide an important foundation for the statistical-learning perspective being proposed here.

Consistent with the statistical-learning framework, studies have shown that the letter patterns that children and adults see in their daily experiences with printed words influence their reading and spelling. One pattern that exerts an important influence on children early in life is their own first name. Young children see the spelling of their own name quite often and find it quite interesting, and this appears to play a central role in early literacy development. For example, studies have shown that young children identify the letters from their own first name more accurately than other letters. This has been demonstrated in languages as distinct as English (Treiman & Broderick, 1998), Hebrew (Levin & Aram, 2004), and Portuguese (Treiman, Kessler, & Pollo, 2006). Other studies, as mentioned previously, have shown that U.S. kindergartners tend to overuse letters of their own names when trying to spell other words (Treiman et al., 2001). Children's overuse of letters from their own name reflects the disproportionate frequency with which they encounter those letters.

As children are exposed to a greater number of printed words, the effects of exposure to their own names may be proportionately reduced: Children start to be influenced more by the general patterns of the writing system. Supporting this view are studies that have shown that when children (about 6 years old) make intrusion errors—inserting letters that are not phonologically appropriate—they are more likely to use letters that are frequent in their reading materials (Treiman et al., 2001).

If statistical properties of printed words influence children's spelling very early in spelling development, then certain phenomena that have been described by researchers in the constructivist perspective may find a more parsimonious explanation under the statistical-learning framework. This perspective can also help to explain some of the observed differences and similarities among children who speak different languages, because the children will have been exposed to different linguistic and orthographic input. Indeed, we consider quantitative crosslinguistic studies to be crucial in understanding literacy acquisition. In what follows, we will discuss a crosslinguistic study conducted in our lab (Pollo, Kessler, & Treiman, 2005) that illustrates how the statistical-learning framework can help explain early differences in children's spelling.

As mentioned previously, several differences have been reported between spellings produced by English speakers and those produced by speakers of Romance languages. Pollo et al. (2005) addressed two of those differences by investigating early acquisition of spelling in Portuguese and English. The first difference is in the postulated syllabic stage of spelling development. As described earlier in this chapter, young spellers of Romance languages have been reported to spell one symbol per syllable, while children learning English are rarely reported as spelling words in a syllabic manner. A second difference involves the acquisition of consonants and vowels. While Romance speakers often omit consonants, producing all-vowel spellings (e.g., Ferreiro & Teberosky, 1982), vowel omissions represent a large part of spelling mistakes among English-speaking children (Kamii et al., 1990; Read, 1986; Treiman, 1993; Varnhagen, Boechler, & Steffler, 1999). Pollo et al. tested the hypothesis that such differences in spellings reflect children's propensity to use letter names in spelling, as discussed earlier. Languages can vary to a great extent in how many letter names are found in words (e.g., Cardoso-Martins et al., 2002) and in the relative frequency with which the different letters are represented. Asymmetries between languages in letter name systems and in vocabularies could lead to different patterns in the spellings of young children.

In order to quantify some of the differences in language statistics that could lead children's spelling to differ in English and Portuguese, Pollo et al. (2005) counted how frequently letter names occurred within words in texts that young children would be likely to see. The analyses showed that Portuguese words have many more vowel letter names than English. Words like *bola* /bɔa/—in which both vowel phonemes are the names of letters—are very common in Portuguese, whereas words like the English translation *ball* /bɔl/—in which the vowel is not the name of a letter—are more typical of English. Consonant letter names are much less commonly found within words than are vowels in either language. Pollo et al. also showed that the ratio of vowels to consonants is twice as high in Portuguese as in English, as exemplified again by the words for 'ball'. Thus, Portuguese-speaking children should encounter vowel letters and vowel letter names proportionately much more often than English-speaking children.

To verify the hypothesis that children are affected by these properties of the writing systems, Pollo et al. (2005) asked five-year-old Portuguese and English speakers to spell words that were matched except for whether the word contained one letter name (like *bunny*, which ends in the name of the letter *e*) or two (like *pony*, which contains the names of *o* and *e*); all the letter names were those of vowels. In both languages, the words with more letter names were spelled with more vowels and elicited more spellings that were phonologically plausible, showing that both groups of children often applied the strategy of spelling sounds with the letters whose names comprise those sounds.

There were also notable differences between the two groups of children. Portuguese-speaking children used more vowels than English-speaking children, even though the stimuli for both languages had equal numbers of vowels. These differences can be explained by the aforementioned statistical differences between the two writing systems. Because Portuguese speakers see more vowel letters in texts, they may write more vowel letters in their spellings. More importantly, because Portuguese speakers hear more vowel letter names in words, they may be more encouraged to use letter name spelling strategies when spelling vowel sounds than are young speakers of English.

The data of Pollo et al. (2005) also support an alternative explanation for syllabic spellings. Spellings such as *AO* for Spanish *sapo* are often adduced as syllabic spellings, because the child wrote two letters for a word with two syllables. However, this example is typical in that the letters that were written correspond to the only two letter names heard in the words. Our results support the alternative hypothesis that these spellings reflect children's use of letter names (Cardoso-Martins & Batista, 2003; Treiman & Kessler, 2003). It was demonstrated that vowel letter names are extremely frequent in Portuguese words and that words with vowel letter names are spelled with more vowel letters. The confluence of these two facts could explain why all-vowel spellings are reported in Romance languages. Putatively syllabic spellings could be a result of children's attempt to spell by letter names, which is a more parsimonious explanation than stipulating the presence of a syllabic stage of development.

The Pollo et al. (2005) study demonstrated that differences among languages in their systems of letter names and the prevalence of letter names in their vocabularies are one source of crosslinguistic differences in early spelling development. However, together with researchers in the phonological tradition, we believe that the regularity of the mappings between phonemes and letters is also important. We maintain that differences among languages in their sound-to-letter links must be quantified more precisely than has been done in the past. Previous classifications of writing systems have often been made impressionistically, for example, by asking researchers who are speakers of different languages to categorize their languages into one of several levels of regularity (Seymour et al., 2003). Kessler and Treiman (2001) studied the sound-to-spelling relationships in the monosyllabic words of English in a more quantitative way, finding that English is not as irregular as is often assumed. Although many phonemes have more than one possible spelling, consideration of context can increase the predictability of sound-to-spelling translation. That is, regularity is higher when context is taken into account. Studies have shown that children benefit from the contextual regularities that English provides, using probabilistic patterns that are based on the statistics of the language (Hayes, Treiman, & Kessler, 2006).

In summary, the statistical-learning perspective holds that children can take advantage of statistical regularities of printed words in the language early in their development. These regularities give children information about graphical as well as phonological patterns of the language that is reflected even in their very early spellings. We believe that statistics of the languages may explain apparent differences between spellings of children in different languages.

CONCLUSIONS

In this chapter we have described several approaches for studying spelling development. The phonological perspective holds that the key insight in literacy development is the understanding that letters represent the sounds in spoken words. For a child who has not yet grasped the alphabetic principle, spellings are basically random strings of letters (e.g., Ehri, 1998; Frith, 1985; Gentry, 1982). This perspective is predominant in English-speaking countries. A second theoretical approach is what we call the constructivist perspective. This perspective acknowledges that young children in literate societies know something about writing before they understand that letters represent phonemes. However, some of the key ideas of the constructivist perspective, such as the syllabic stage theory, have not been defined precisely enough to enable rigorous experimental verification. This perspective is well represented in many Romance-speaking countries, and advocates have not clearly explained why the spelling development of English speakers does not appear to follow the same patterns.

In the last part of the chapter we presented a third perspective, which we call the statistical-learning perspective on spelling development. It holds that statistical properties of printed words and spoken languages influence children's spellings early in development. This perspective encourages crosslinguistic studies because they are important for determining how specific properties of a language can make it easier or harder for children to read and spell. An important start has been made in the phonological perspective with crosslinguistic comparisons of sound-to-letter regularity. However, the statistical-learning perspective suggests that additional features of language may influence children in their literacy development. Thus, it is vital to analyze other aspects of languages that have been neglected in previous studies. We summarized work showing the importance of letter names and letter patterns in young children's spelling development and showing how differences in spelling performance can be explained by those characteristics of the writing systems. We hope that this chapter will encourage further work along these lines.

ACKNOWLEDGMENT

This work was supported in part by Award 0130763 from the National Science Foundation.

REFERENCES

Abreu, M. D. de, & Cardoso-Martins, C. (1998). Alphabetic access route in beginning reading acquisition in Portuguese: The role of letter-name knowledge. *Reading and Writing: An Interdisciplinary Journal, 10*, 85–104.

Aro, M., & Wimmer, H. (2003). Learning to read: English in comparison to six more regular orthographies. *Applied Psycholinguistics, 24*, 621–635.

Aslin, R. N., Saffran, J. R., & Newport, E. L. (1999). Statistical learning in linguistic and nonlinguistic domains. In B. MacWhinney (Ed.), *The emergence of language* (pp. 359–380). Mahwah, NJ: Erlbaum.

Beers, J. W., Beers, C. S., & Grant, K. (1977). The logic behind children's spelling. *Elementary School Journal, 77*, 238–242.

Besse, J. (1996). An approach to writing in kindergarten. In C. Pontecorvo, M. Orsolini, B. Burge, & L. Resnick (Eds.), *Children's early text construction* (pp. 127–144). Mahwah, NJ: Erlbaum.

Bissex, G. L. (1980). *Gnys at wrk.* Cambridge, MA: Harvard University Press.

Caravolas, M. (2004) Spelling development in alphabetic writing systems: A cross-linguistic perspective. *European Psychologist, 9*, 3–14.

Caravolas, M., & Bruck, M. (1993). The effect of oral and written language input on children's phonological awareness: A cross-linguistic study. *Journal of Experimental Child Psychology, 55*, 1–30.

Caravolas, M., Hulme, C., & Snowling, M. J. (2001). The foundations of spelling ability: Evidence from a 3-year longitudinal study. *Journal of Memory and Language, 45*, 751–774.

Cardoso-Martins, C. (2005). Beginning reading acquisition in Brazilian Portuguese In R. M. Joshi & P. G. Aaron (Eds.), *Handbook of orthography and literacy* (pp. 171–188). Mahwah, NJ: Erlbaum.

Cardoso-Martins, C., & Batista, A. C. E. (2003, April). *The role of letter name knowledge in learning to connect print to speech: Evidence from Brazilian Portuguese-speaking children.* Paper presented at the meeting of the Society for Research in Child Development, Tampa, FL.

Cardoso-Martins, C., Resende, S. M., & Rodrigues, L. A. (2002). Letter name knowledge and the ability to learn to read by processing letter-phoneme relations in words: Evidence from Brazilian Portuguese-speaking children. *Reading and Writing: An Interdisciplinary Journal, 15*, 409–432.

Cassar, M., & Treiman, R. (1997). The beginnings of orthographic knowledge: Children's knowledge of double letters in words. *Journal of Educational Psychology, 89*, 631–644.

Defior, S., Martos, F., & Cary, L. (2002). Differences in reading acquisition development in shallow orthographies: Portuguese and Spanish. *Applied Psycholinguistics, 23*, 135–148.

Ehri, L. C. (1991). The development of reading and spelling in children: An overview. In M. Snowling & M. Thomson (Eds.), *Dyslexia: Integrating theory and practice* (pp. 63–94). London: British Dyslexia Association.

Ehri, L. C. (1992). Reconceptualizing the development of sight word reading and its relationship to recoding. In P. B. Gough, L. C. Ehri, & R. Treiman (Eds.), *Reading acquisition* (pp. 107–143). Hillsdale, NJ: Erlbaum.

Ehri, L. C. (1998). Grapheme–phoneme knowledge is essential for learning to read words in English. In J. L. Metsala & L. C. Ehri (Eds.), *Word recognition in beginning literacy* (pp. 3–40). Mahwah, NJ: Erlbaum.

Ehri, L. C., & Wilce, L. S. (1985). Movement into reading: Is the first stage of printed word learning visual or phonetic? *Reading Research Quarterly, 20*, 163–179.

Ferreiro, E. (1990). Literacy development: Psychogenesis. In Y. Goodman (Ed.), *How children construct literacy: Piagetian perspectives* (pp. 12–25). Newark, DE: International Reading Association.

Ferreiro, E., Pontecorvo, C., & Zucchermaglio, C. (1996). *Pizza* or *piza?* How children interpret the doubling of letters in writing. In C. Pontecorvo, M. Orsolini, B. Burge, & L. Resnick (Eds.), *Children's early text construction* (pp. 145–163). Mahwah, NJ: Erlbaum.

Ferreiro, E., & Teberosky, A. (1982). *Literacy before schooling*. New York: Heinemann.

Frith, U. (1985). Beneath the surface of developmental dyslexia. In K. E. Patterson, J. C. Marshall, & M. Coltheart (Eds.), *Surface dyslexia: Neuropsychological and cognitive studies of phonological reading* (pp. 301–330). London: Erlbaum.

Gentry, J. R. (1982). An analysis of developmental spelling in *GNYS AT WRK. Reading Teacher, 36*, 192–200.

Gough, P. B., & Hillinger, M. L. (1980). Learning to read: An unnatural act. *Bulletin of the Orton Society, 30*, 179–196.

Hayes, H., Treiman, R. & Kessler, B. (2006). Children use vowels to help them spell consonants. *Journal of Experimental Child Psychology, 94*, 27–42.

Henderson, E. (1985). *Teaching spelling*. Boston: Houghton Mifflin.

Houghton, G., & Zorzi, M. (2003). Normal and impaired spelling in a connectionist dual-route architecture. *Cognitive Neuropsychology, 20*, 115–162.

Hutzler, F., Ziegler, J. C., Perry, C., Wimmer, H., & Zorzi, M. (2004). Do current connectionist learning models account for reading development in different languages? *Cognition, 91*, 273–296.

International Phonetic Association (1999). *Handbook of the International Phonetic Association: A guide to the use of the International Phonetic Alphabet*. Cambridge, England: Cambridge University Press.

Kamii, C., Long, R., Manning, M., & Manning, G. (1990). Spelling in kindergarten: A constructivist analysis comparing Spanish-speaking and English-speaking children. *Journal of Research in Childhood Education, 4*, 91–97.

Kessler, B., & Treiman, R. (2001). Relationships between sounds and letters in English monosyllables. *Journal of Memory and Language, 44*, 592–617.

Lange, M., & Content, A. (1999, June). *The grapho-phonological system of written French: Statistical analysis and empirical validation*. Paper presented at the 37th Annual Meeting of the Association for Computational Linguistics, College Park, MD.

Levin, I., & Aram, D. (2004). Children's names contribute to early literacy: A linguistic and a social perspective. In D. Ravid & H. Bat-Zeev Shyldkrot (Eds.), *Perspectives on language and language development* (pp. 219–239). Dordrecht, The Netherlands: Kluwer.

Levin, I., Patel, S., Margalit, T., & Barad, N. (2002). Letter names: Effect on letter saying, spelling, and word recognition in Hebrew. *Applied Psycholinguistics, 23*, 269–300.

Liberman, I. Y., Shankweiler, D., Fischer, F. W., & Carter, B. (1974). Explicit syllable and phoneme segmentation in the young child. *Journal of Experimental Child Psychology, 18*, 201–212.

Martins, M. A., & Silva, C. (2001). Letter names, phonological awareness and the phonetization of writing. *European Journal of Psychology of Education, 4*, 605–617.

Nunes Carraher, T. & Rego, L. R. B. (1984). Desenvolvimento cognitivo e alfabetização. [Cognitive developmental and literacy] *Revista Brasileira de Estudos Pedagógicos, 63*, 38–55.

Pacton, S., Perruchet, P., Fayol, M., & Cleeremans, A. (2001). Implicit learning out of the lab: The case of orthographic regularities. *Journal of Experimental Psychology: General, 130*, 401–426.

Pollo, T. C., Kessler, B., & Treiman, R. (2005). Vowels, syllables, and letter names: Differences between young children's spelling in English and Portuguese. *Journal of Experimental Child Psychology, 92*, 161–181.

Pontecorvo, C. (1985). Figure, parole, numeri: Un problema di simbolizzazione [Pictures, words, numbers: A problem of symbolization]. *Età Evolutiva, 22*, 5–33.

Pontecorvo, C. (1996). Introduction. In C. Pontecorvo, M. Orsolini, B. Burge, & L. Resnick (Eds.), *Children's early text construction* (pp. 345–357). Mahwah, NJ: Erlbaum.

Pontecorvo, C., & Zucchermaglio, C. (1988). Modes of differentiation in children's writing construction. *European Journal of Psychology of Education, 3*, 371–384.

Read, C. (1975). *Children's categorization of speech sounds in English.* (NCTE Research Report No. 17). Urbana, IL: National Council of Teachers of English.

Read, C. (1986). *Children's creative spelling.* London: Routledge & Kegan Paul.

Rego, L. R. B. (1999). Phonological awareness, syntactic awareness and learning to read and spell in Brazilian Portuguese. In M. Harris & G. Hatano (Eds.), *Learning to read and write: A cross-linguistic perspective* (pp. 71–88). Cambridge, England: Cambridge University Press.

Saffran, J. R., Aslin, R. N., & Newport, E. L. (1996). Statistical learning by 8-month-old infants. *Science, 274*, 1926–1928.

Seidenberg, M. S. (1997). Language acquisition and use: Learning and applying probabilistic constraints. *Science, 275*, 1599–1603.

Seymour, P. H. K., Aro, M., & Erskine, J. M. (2003). Foundation literacy acquisition in European languages. *British Journal of Psychology, 94*, 143–175.

Silva, C., & Alves-Martins, M. (2002). Phonological skills and writing of pre-syllabic children. *Reading Research Quarterly, 37*, 466–483.

Stella, G., & Biancardi, A. (1990). Accesso alla lingua scritta e sistema verbale: Una integrazione complessa. [Oral language and the beginning of writing: A complex integration] *Età Evolutiva, 35*, 38–49.

Sulzby, E. (1985). Kindergartners as writers and readers. In M. Farr (Ed.), *Advances in writing research, Volume 1. Children's early writing development* (pp 127–199). Norwood, NJ: Ablex.

Tolchinsky, L., & Teberosky, A. (1998). The development of word segmentation and writing in two scripts. *Cognitive Development, 13*, 1–24.

Tolchinsky-Landsmann, L., & Levin, I. (1985). Writing in preschoolers: An age-related analysis. *Applied Psycholinguistics, 6*, 319–339.

Treiman, R. (1993). *Beginning to spell: A study of first-grade children.* New York: Oxford University Press.

Treiman, R. (1994). Use of consonant letter names in beginning spelling. *Developmental Psychology, 30*, 567–580.

Treiman, R. (1998). Why spelling? The benefits of incorporating spelling into beginning reading instruction. In J. L. Metsala & L. C. Ehri (Eds.), *Word recognition in beginning literacy* (pp. 289–313). Mahwah, NJ: Erlbaum.

Treiman, R., & Kessler, B. (2003). The role of letter names in the acquisition of literacy. In R. Kail (Ed.), *Advances in Child Development and Behavior, Vol. 31* (pp. 105–135). San Diego: Academic Press.

Treiman, R., Kessler, B., & Bourassa, D. (2001). Children's own names influence their spelling. *Applied Psycholinguistics, 22*, 555–570.

Treiman, R., Kessler, B., & Pollo, T. C. (2006). Learning about the letter name subset of the vocabulary: Evidence from U.S. and Brazilian preschoolers. *Applied Psycholinguistics, 27,* 211–227.

Varnhagen, C. K., Boechler, P. M., & Steffler, D. J. (1999). Phonological and orthographic influences on children's vowel spelling. *Scientific Studies of Reading, 4,* 363–379.

Vernon, S. A., & Ferreiro, E. (1999). Writing development: A neglected variable in the consideration of phonological awareness. *Harvard Educational Review, 69,* 395–414.

Wimmer, H., & Hummer, P. (1990). How German speaking first graders read and spell: Doubts on the importance of the logographic stage. *Applied Psycholinguistics, 11,* 349–368.

Wimmer, H., & Landerl, K. (1997). How learning to spell German differs from learning to spell English. In C. Perfetti, L. Rieben, & M. Fayol (Eds.), *Learning to spell: Research, theory, and practice across languages* (pp. 81–96).

Zacks, R. T., & Hasher, L. (2002). Frequency processing: A twenty-five year perspective. In P. Sedlmeier (Ed.), *Frequency processing and cognition* (pp. 21–36). London: University Press.

Ziegler, J. C., Jacobs, A. M., & Stone, G. O. (1996). Statistical analysis of the bidirectional inconsistency of spelling and sound in French. *Behavior Research Methods, Instruments, & Computers, 28,* 504–515.

Comprehension of Single Words: The Role of Semantics in Word Identification and Reading Disability

Janice M. Keenan & Rebecca S. Betjemann
University of Denver

The word "comprehension" is commonly applied to processing sentences and texts, i.e., verbal units larger than a single word. So, the reader might wonder what a chapter on comprehension is doing in a book titled, **Single Word Reading**. There are two reasons.

One reason is to show the contribution of semantic processes to word identification, and to counter the relative neglect of semantics in understanding word decoding. Often single word reading is characterized as the process of mapping the orthography onto the phonology of the word, and little attention is given to the role semantics may play in this process. It is assumed that if reading is assessed with lists of unrelated words, then the semantic component is irrelevant because the words have been removed from context. In this chapter, we will examine evidence that counters this view of semantics as a separate functional component that can be easily removed from the evaluation of decoding skill. While the contribution of semantics will vary depending on both one's familiarity with the referent of the word and on the context in which it occurs, it does appear to be a contributor in the constraint satisfaction process that constitutes word identification.

The fact that semantics is a significant contributor to word identification leads to the other reason for this chapter, and that is to explore whether deficits in semantics may be contributing to word decoding problems in children with reading disability. Reading disability is typically associated with deficits in phonological and/or orthographic representations, not semantic representations. In fact, semantic representations are sometimes thought to be their strength because disabled readers tend to compensate for their deficits in phonological representations by relying more on semantic context than normal readers to assist in word identification (Nation & Snowling, 1998a; Stanovich, 1980). But if the only thing wrong with disabled readers' processing is in the mappings between orthographic and phonological representations, then we might expect that when such mappings are not involved, in other words when they are listening rather than reading, that they should not show deficits. It is typical, however, to find that children with reading problems tend to also do poorly on listening comprehension (Betjemann, Keenan, & Olson, 2003; Catts, Hogan, & Fey, 2003; Mann, Liberman, & Shankweiler, 1980; Mann, Shankweiler, & Smith, 1984). In our own work examining over 400 children, many of whom have reading problems, we find that listening and reading comprehension measures correlate $r = .68$. This suggests that many disabled readers have additional deficits, and in this chapter we explore whether deficits might exist in their semantic representations of single words.

MODELS OF SINGLE WORD IDENTIFICATION—IS SEMANTICS A PLAYER?

The function of an orthography is to convey meaning. Thus, it would seem that the architecture of word identification should incorporate influences of meaning. Yet, for a long time, models of word identification in the English language relegated meaning to the end of the word identification process; it was the prize one obtained as a result of successfully mapping the graphemes onto the sounds of the language.

Early models of word recognition assumed that the process of identifying a word is completely independent of the process of retrieving a word's meaning (e.g., Forster, 1976). Much like finding the definition of a word in the dictionary only after having mapped the spelling onto the dictionary entries, so too in these models, only after the correct lexical entry was identified was the semantic information available.

In the highly influential dual route model of word recognition (Coltheart, 1978), the focus again was on mapping the orthography onto the phonology. This could be done using either the nonlexical assembled route, wherein the mapping was based on regularities within the language, or by directly accessing a lexical representation via the whole-word orthographic route. Again, semantics was activated only when the lexical entry was accessed.

Connectionist models of word recognition eschewed the notions of lexical access and the existence of lexical entries (Seidenberg, 1990), but early models gave the same short shrift to semantics by leaving semantics out entirely. Seidenberg and McClelland's (1989) model of word recognition had only orthographic and phonological units. This was likely more for practical reasons than theoretical reasons, the practical reason being that it is tough to specify semantic units. In connectionist models of word identification the units are specified by the modeler and the model learns the connections between the units. Specifying the units is relatively easy to do for orthographic representations – single letters, bigrams, trigrams – and for phonological representations – phonetic features. It is less obvious for semantic representations what

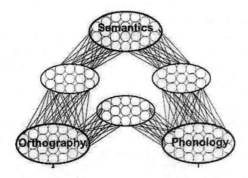

FIGURE 10.1   Connectionist Model of Word Identification from Plaut (1998).

the units should be. Attempts to explicitly identify semantic features result in what has been described by O'Reilly & Munakata (2000, p. 334) as "cartoon" semantics because these features fail to capture the full meanings of the terms. Identification of semantic features will likely be more successful using computers given vast amounts of linguistic inputs and mathematical decomposition to discover the units (Landauer, Foltz & Laham, 1998) rather than having researchers explicitly generate them.

Despite being cartoon-like, when the semantic feature set developed by Plaut and Shallice (1993) was added to the Seidenberg & McClelland model, as depicted in Figure 10.1, not only was the model better able to pronounce nonwords and perform the lexical decision task, a principle reason for adding semantics, but it also provided a better account of exception word learning (Plaut, McClelland, Seidenberg, & Patterson, 1996). Also, because the inclusion of semantics allows activation to spread to cohorts based not only on phonological and orthographic similarity, but also on semantic similarity, it provided an account of surface dyslexia, an acquired dyslexia that spares regular word reading but results in deficits in reading exception words. Basically, by having the system acquire its word representations based on semantics and then deleting or lesioning the semantic connections, the system produced errors similar to a surface dyslexic's. The main outcome of adding semantics to the model, therefore, is that the phonological pathways learn to partially depend on semantics. Plaut et al. (1996) showed that these semantic pathways fill voids in phonological-orthographic processing in individuals with impaired orthographic-phonological mappings, such as those found in readers with dyslexia.

The fact that semantics can fill voids in phonological-orthographic processing when an individual suffers damage to the network raises an interesting possibility for semantics in intact organisms. Namely, semantics may play a role, or more of a role, when the orthography leaves voids in the phonological-orthographic mappings. So for example, in orthographies that are logographies, the weighting would be much more on semantics; it is important to note, however, that despite the frequent characterization of logographies as having symbols that only represent morphemes, there is not a complete void of the orthographic-phonological route in these orthographies, but rather a difference in weighting (Perfetti, 2003). Most importantly for present purposes, it raises the possibility that semantics may alleviate the need for phonological pathways alone to master all the words in languages, like English, where the mappings between orthography and phonology are often inconsistent.

The idea that the architecture of the word recognition system may vary across languages as the result of the consistency of orthographic mappings onto the spoken language was recently suggested by Ziegler & Goswami (2005) as part of their Psycholinguistic Grain Size Theory. Grain sizes refer to units in connectionist models that emerge as the result of pressure to distinguish one input from another. For example, in distinguishing the sound of *cat* from *hat*, the system would develop separate representations for the initial sounds (referred to as the *onsets*), the /c/ and the /h/, and for the remainder of the syllable (referred to as the *rime*), /at/. Examples along the dimension of phonological grain size would be: the word, the syllable, the onset/rime, and the phonemes. Grain sizes do not emerge at a given point in development across the whole lexicon, but rather emerge as a function of experience with words and are word- and neighborhood-specific.

Inconsistent orthographies are those in which the grain sizes that develop for distinguishing words in the oral language do not map readily onto the grain sizes of the orthography. In English, the smallest grains that develop for oral language are the syllable and onset/rimes; but because the orthography is an alphabet, the beginning reader needs to develop smaller grain sizes in the oral language, namely phonemes, to map onto the letters. The development of mappings for reading is further complicated by the fact that in English, these mappings at the letter-to-phoneme level are often inconsistent, thereby requiring readers to also develop larger grain size units than just single letters in their orthographic representations to achieve consistencies in mapping onto the sounds of the language. Thus, the beginning reader is faced with both developing smaller grains in their phonological representations and larger grains in their orthographic representations. This development of multiple grain sizes is an efficient and necessary response to orthographies with inconsistent mappings. Children with reading disability can be thought of as having difficulty in this development; that is, in addition to their well established difficulty in developing smaller grains in the oral language (Snowling, 2000), it is likely that they may also have difficulty in developing the larger grains in the orthography.

Semantics appears to play a role in the development of at least some of these larger orthographic grain sizes. Suffix morphemes, like *tion*, violate small grain size mappings, but they are consistent at a larger grain size. Furthermore, this larger grain size maps nicely on to semantics; *tion* conveys information that the word refers to a thing or condition as opposed to an action or a quality. Another situation where the orthographic-phonological mappings are inconsistent at smaller grain sizes, but consistent at larger grain sizes, is where spellings are specifically designed to preserve semantics. For example, spelling *vineyard* with an *e* preserves the larger semantic grain, *vine*, at the cost of having the pronunciation yield inconsistent small grain size mappings between phonological-orthographic units. In sum, languages like English that have many inconsistent mappings at small grain sizes may be shown to be more consistent when larger orthographic grain sizes and semantics are taken into account (cf. Treiman & Kessler, 2005). Thus, we may find that semantics and larger grain sizes play more of a role in identifying words in inconsistent orthographies, like English, than in more consistent orthographies.

DOES SEMANTICS PLAY A ROLE IN WORD IDENTIFICATION WHEN THERE IS NO CONTEXT?

One reason that semantics may have been ignored in models of word identification is the difficulty of specifying more than just a handful of semantic features. But another reason was likely the assumption that semantics only plays a role when words occur in context. It has long been known that context facilitates visual word identification (Tulving & Gold, 1963). Most models implement this finding by having the context words constrain the set of possible meanings, and in the case of homographs, constrain the pronunciation. These top-down semantic constraints supplement the orthographic constraints so that the constraint-satisfaction process of word identification can more quickly settle on a particular word.

But what happens when there is no context? Does removing a word from context remove the role of semantics in word identification? In other words, are semantic effects only generated from top-down processing? In Plaut, et al.'s (1996) model, semantic effects are also generated bottom-up from the activation of orthographic and phonological units and their connections to semantic units. However, judging from the way in which word reading skills are typically assessed, by having children read lists of unrelated words aloud, and the way that results of such tests are interpreted – as reflecting skills in mapping graphemes only onto the sounds of the language – it appears that there is a tendency to assume that when one removes words from context, one removes the semantic component. We first consider whether this is a reasonable assumption to make, and then present evidence to show that semantics play a role in word identification even when the word occurs in isolation.

Arguments for Semantic Involvement in Single Word Reading

We know from the reading acquisition literature that semantic representations activated by the phonology play a role initially because they can actually interfere with the acquisition of mappings of the orthography onto the phonology. Byrne & Shea (1979) presented both anecdotal and experimental evidence to show this. In the anecdotal evidence, they described a 4-year-old child, named Tom, who was shown and read the word "Tomato" on a label, and shown that his name was contained within that word. Even though Tom could read and print his own name, he could not comprehend that another word could contain it as an element, and asserted that the label must say "Tom tomato." This suggests that the semantics kept the phonological code from being able to be broken into components by the orthography. If meaning can be such a forceful obstacle to a child learning how to break down the phonological form into its components, it seems unlikely that it would be banished to the sidelines once the orthographic-phonological code is learned, especially since the whole reason for mapping the orthography onto the phonology in the first place is to access the word's meaning.

Another reason for thinking that semantic representations may play a role in word identification is that there are several lines of research showing that highly associated representations get activated, even when they are not required by the task. They get activated simply because of the strength of their connection to the activated representation. For example, in a visual lexical decision task, where the task is to say whether or not a string of letters constitutes a word, there is no reason to activate semantics because the judgment can be based either on the orthography (does this string look like a familiar word?) or the mapping of the orthography onto the phonology (does this string sound like a familiar word?). Nonetheless, semantics play a role in these judgments (Meyer & Schvaneveldt, 1971); significantly faster responses occur when the preceding word is semantically related (NURSE-DOCTOR) than when it is not related (BUTTER-DOCTOR).

Similarly, tasks involving spoken word recognition often show effects of orthography, even though the orthography is irrelevant to the task. For example, in rhyme judgment tasks involving auditory presentation, words are judged more readily when they have the same spelling (PIE-DIE) than when they do not (PIE-RYE) (Seidenberg & Tanenhaus, 1979). Again, it appears that when there are well-established associations between lexical units, activating one, in this case the phonological representation of a word, automatically activates others, even when they are not required by the task.

We have tried to make the case why it would be reasonable that mapping the orthography onto the phonology in word identification would simultaneously activate its semantic representation, as in Plautt, et al.'s (1996) model of word identification. We turn now to examine the evidence.

Evidence for Semantic Involvement in Word Identification

If context is the only impetus for semantic representations to play a role in word identification, then it would seem that only appropriate meanings of an ambiguous word, such as *straw*, would ever be activated when a word occurs in context. However, many studies have shown that the inappropriate, as well as the appropriate, meanings of ambiguous words are activated briefly (Onifer & Swinney, 1981; Seidenberg et al., 1982; Swinney, 1979; Tanenhaus, et al., 1979). This is an important finding because if meanings incompatible with a context are activated, it shows that it is not just the context that is activating the meanings. Rather, the word itself must be activating the meaning. Thus, semantics must be part of word identification independent of sentence context.

Demonstrations of the effects of semantic variables on single word recognition have examined concreteness, imagability, and meaningfulness. Concrete words (e.g., *dog*) are more easily read or identified than abstract words (e.g., *joy*). Although this finding can sometimes be due to confounding factors, such as word frequency and familiarity of letter strings, even when these factors are controlled, the effect still occurs (Schwanenflugel, Harnishfeger, & Stowe, 1988). Similarly, within concrete words, high-imagability words are responded to more quickly in a lexical decision task than low-imagability words (Strain, Patterson, & Seidenberg, 1995, 2002; Tyler, Voice, & Moss, 2000). Another semantic factor, meaningfulness, has been investigated by examining the effect of the number of meanings a word possesses. Words having many dictionary meanings (high meaningfulness) can be responded to faster in a lexical decision task than words with fewer meanings (Jastrzembski, 1981), and ambiguous words that have two distinct meanings, such as *straw*, can be named faster (Balota & Ferraro, 1993) and responded to faster in a lexical decision task (Kellas, Ferraro, & Simpson, 1988) than nonambiguous words. Also, the number of associates a word has predicts the identification of a word in a lexical decision task above and beyond other related variables such as frequency and length (Chumbley & Balota, 1984).

Many of these findings of semantic effects have been known since the 1980s. Yet models of word identification did not change to include semantics in the identification process; rather, semantics was thought to have its influence only *after* orthographic-phonological processing, what came to be called *post-access*, which meant after the lexical entry was identified. A number of more recent findings, however, show that the influence of semantics is earlier; that is, it is a player, along with orthographic and phonological units, in the constraint satisfaction process constituting word identification. One of these findings is that the imagability effect, wherein high-imagability words are responded to more quickly than low-imagability words, occurs only for words that have many similar neighbors (Tyler, Voice, & Moss, 2000), or what are known as cohort competitors in Plaut et al.'s (1996) model. This interaction suggests that semantics is indeed affecting the word identification process itself because if the locus of the effect were post-access, then it would affect all words equally, regardless of their cohort size.

A related finding comes from studies showing that what gets activated is not only the target word's meaning, but also meanings of visually similar words, as would be expected from Plaut, et al.'s (1996) model. In the first study to demonstrate this, Forster and Hector (2002) had participants categorize letter strings (animal vs. nonanimal), where some of the nonanimals were nonwords. Participants were slower to reject nonwords like *turple*, that has the visually similar neighbor, *turtle*, that is an animal than they were to reject nonwords that had visually similar neighbors that were not animals, such as *tabric*, which is similar to *fabric*. In order to explain why there is more competition between *turtle* and *turple* than there is between *tabric* and *fabric*, one must assume activation of semantic representations. Forster and Hector suggested that the semantic information activated need not be the full semantic representation for the word, but would at least be a semantic field relevant to membership in the animal category. Rodd (2004) noted that one explanation of this finding is that *turple* may activate the meaning of *turtle* because it has no meaning of its own. So, she redid the study having all the items be words. Again, it took longer to reject words like *leotard* whose visually similar neighbor, *leopard*, is an animal than words with equally similar visual neighbors (*cellar*, *collar*) but which are not animals.

Finally, support for early semantic involvement comes from evidence that the semantics of a word can be activated even without correct identification of the word. Case studies of children with developmental dyslexia have reported them making semantic substitutions occasionally when reading single words (Johnston, 1983; Siegel, 1985; Temple, 1988). The words substituted were not visually similar to the actual word presented, but were semantically related, for example, *down → up, chair → table, seven → eight.* In some instances, the errors were first visual, and then semantic, such as *sleep → lamb (via sheep).* Since the words were presented as single words in a list, there was no context that could give the readers a clue to the meaning of the word. Thus, some semantics must be activated from the visual presentation of the word even before the correct phonology of the word is identified.

These findings of semantic effects on single word identification suggest that semantic information becomes available before words are uniquely identified and influences the discrimination between competing lexical neighbors in the constraint satisfaction process that constitutes word identification. One of the interesting implications of this is that deficits in single word reading may therefore reflect not just deficits in phonological representations and the mappings of orthography onto those phonological representations. If semantic representations also contribute to word recognition, then they may serve to either compensate for deficits in the orthographic or phonological mappings or they may themselves be the source of word reading problems. We turn now to briefly consider some evidence from our laboratory designed to examine this issue.

DO READING DISABLED CHILDREN HAVE DEFICITS IN SEMANTIC REPRESENTATIONS?

The question of whether disabled readers have difficulties with semantic representations may seem odd in light of the finding that they tend to compensate for their deficits in orthographic-phonological representations by relying more on semantic context than normal readers in identifying words in context (Nation & Snowling, 1998a; Stanovich, 1980). There is a tendency to assume that if semantics can help compensate for other deficient representations, then the semantic system itself is not impaired. Of course, this assumption does not follow logically. Just because a mother can care for her sick children does not mean that she herself may not also be sick; so too, just because semantics can help word identification does not mean that it too is not impaired.

In examining the question of whether impairments in semantics underlie reading problems, we will first show that our poor readers, like those examined by other researchers, rely more on context than more skilled readers. We then go on to show that this reliance on context does not mean that their semantic representations are a strength. Quite the contrary. They have poorer vocabulary, they show less use of the larger orthographic grain sizes that might be associated with semantics, and they appear to be deficient in semantic priming. Before we present the details of these results, we will give a brief description of the project that provided the resources for this research.

The Colorado Learning Disabilities Research Center

The CLDRC is one of a small number of NIH-funded centers in the United States dedicated specifically to understanding learning disabilities (DeFries et al., 1997). It is housed at the Institute for Behavioral Genetics at the University of Colorado in Boulder, but a number of investigators of the various component projects are, like us, at other universities. The focus of the research is to better understand both the cognitive mechanisms of reading and the genetic etiology of learning problems such as reading disability and attention deficit disorder. We test monozygotic and dizygotic twins, between the ages of 8 and 18, at least one of whom has had a school history of reading difficulty. In addition, we test control twins matched to the reading disabled (RD) probands on age and demographics but neither of whom have a history of reading difficulty. Participants are recruited from school districts across the broad Denver metropolitan area. The twins undergo a range of tests of reading and cognitive skills related to reading over two full days of testing. Our particular component is concerned with assessing listening and reading comprehension skills. While most of our assessments involve discourse processing, we also have some assessments of single word processing. It is that data which we now consider.

It should be noted that the children we refer to as RD in our data were recruited based on school records, but were classified as reading disabled based on their performance on our measures of their skills. Specifically, we compute a word decoding z-score for each child that is a composite of scores on the Peabody Individual Achievement Test (PIAT) Word Recognition subtest (Dunn & Markwardt, 1970) and the Timed Word Recognition Test (Olson, Forsberg, Wise, & Rack, 1994), standardized against the control population and adjusted for age and age-squared. Because word reading skill is normally distributed, any cutoff value for defining RD is arbitrary; we are interested in the most disabled children, so those we refer to as RD have a decoding score below a z-score of -1.5, or the bottom 6.67% of the sampled Colorado population.

Context Effects

To examine context effects on word identification, our participants first read a set of 8 words as part of a larger list of unrelated words on their first day of testing. On their second day of testing, on average around a month later, they read passages from the Qualitative Reading Inventory (QRI) (Leslie & Caldwell, 2001) that contain those target words in context. We evaluated their ability to decode the words by scoring their readings as either automatic, identified but not automatic, or not identified. To be rated as automatic, the identification had to be made correctly without pausing at the word or sounding out the word, whereas words rated as identified were eventually read correctly but were not automatic. Automatic words are scored as a 1, identified words as a 2, and not identified as a 3 (i.e., errors and omissions); thus, the scores can be regarded as more like error scores because the higher the number, the poorer the word identification.

TABLE 10.1

Mean Word Identification Scores as a Function of Context
for Reading- Disabled and Normal Skill Children
(1 = Automatic, 2 = Identified, But Not Automatic, 3 = Not Identified)

Context Condition	Reading Disabled (N = 76)		Normal Skill (N = 287)	
	Mean	(SD)	Mean	(SD)
Out of context	2.09	(.47)	1.37	(.38)
In context	1.72	(.49)	1.18	(.26)

Table 10.1 shows that everyone does better with context, ($M_{\text{Out of Context}}$ = 1.52, $M_{\text{In Context}}$ = 1.29); semantics indeed helps word identification. Perhaps because poor readers identify significantly fewer words than nondisabled readers, we find, like others (Nation & Snowling, 1998a; Stanovich, 1980), that they also show more advantage of reading in context; that is, the interaction between reading skill and context is significant.

Because our study involves extensive testing of comprehension skills, we were able to also examine the use of context by children who have specific deficits in comprehension. As Oakhill and colleagues (e.g., Oakhill, Cain, & Bryant, 2003) have shown, there are children who have adequate word reading skills, but who have specific deficits in understanding what they read. In order to have a sufficient number of such children in our analyses, we defined comprehension deficit (CD) as children who were in the lowest 25% on a Listening Comprehension Composite Score, but whose word decoding score was well above the cutoff for RD; this 25% cutoff has been used in other studies of CD (Fletcher, et al., 1994; Stanovich & Siegel, 1994). In order to compare comprehension deficit (CD) children to reading disabled (RD) children, we did an age-matched analysis (mean = 10.5 years old) on word identification scores in and out of context. The results are presented in Table 10.2. The first column shows that this subset of the RD children exhibit basically the same pattern as the larger group of RD children shown in Table 10.1. Interestingly, the second column of Table 10.2 also looks like the second column of Table 10.1. We had thought that perhaps children who have comprehension problems would be so poor at getting the gist of the discourse that they might not show any bene-fit from context. But just like the larger group of nondisabled children, they too show a benefit of context, though again not as large as the RD children: the inter-action of comprehension skill and context is significant.

In both Tables 10.1 and 10.2 it is apparent that the poor readers' average word identification score *in context* is considerably lower than the *out of context* score of nondisabled readers. This suggests that sentence context is insufficient to "guess" the words and that in addition to decoding problems, word knowledge differences likely underlie differences between RD and No RD children. We turn now to examine what some of those word knowledge differences are.

TABLE 10.2

Mean Word Identification Scores as a Function of Context
for Age-Matched Reading-Disabled and Comprehension Deficit
Children (1 = Automatic, 2 = Identified, But Not Automatic, 3 = Not Identified)

Context Condition	Reading Disabled (N = 21)		Comprehension Deficit. (N = 21)	
	Mean	(SD)	Mean	(SD)
Out of Context	2.05	(.44)	1.32	(.27)
In Context	1.65	(.54)	1.16	(.27)

Vocabulary

One difference is knowledge of word meanings as tested by vocabulary tests. It is common to find that less skilled readers have less knowledge of word meanings than do skilled readers (Dixon, LeFevre, & Twilled, 1988; Hannon & Daneman, 2001; Sternberg & Powell, 1983), and the same holds for our sample. The RD children's mean scaled score from the WISC-III Vocabulary Subtest is significantly lower (9.34) than that of the No RD children (12.22). Similarly, on the Similarities test of the WISC-III, where children must generate a category name to say how two objects are alike, the RD children perform significantly worse (10.53) than the No RD children (13.28). These vocabulary differences translate into comprehension differences, with vocabulary correlating $r = .65$ with reading comprehension and $r = .60$ with listening comprehension.

Grain Size Differences

In their Psycholinguistic Grain Size theory, Ziegler & Goswami (2005) note that in languages having fairly consistent mappings of the orthography onto the phonology, children's ability to read nonwords is equivalent to their ability to read words, whereas in languages with inconsistent mappings, words are read more accurately than nonwords. Ziegler & Goswami state that in inconsistent alphabets, a mix of larger and smaller phonological and orthographic grain sizes is required for successful decoding. Of course, the largest grain size of all is the whole word, and children struggling with mastering orthographic-phonological mappings may show an advantage of words over nonwords because of such whole word mappings. In this case, vocabulary knowledge allows children to guess partially decoded irregular words; thus, accuracy on words should be highly related to vocabulary. However, it is not just whole word knowledge that gives words their advantage over nonwords; if it was, you would expect to see the word-nonword difference in consistent orthographies as well.

TABLE 10.3

Mean Percent Accuracy on Words and Nonwords in Visual and Auditory Lexical
Decision Tasks (LDT) for Reading-Disabled and Normal Skill Children

	Word Accuracy	(SD)	Nonword Accuracy	(SD)
Visual LDT				
Reading disabled	83	(.16)	66	(.19)
Normal skill	92	(.09)	84	(.13)
Auditory LDT				
Reading Disabled	82	(.15)	82	(.15)
Normal Skill	91	(.11)	89	(.10)

What is needed to successfully read both words and nonwords in English are
not only smaller grains in the phonological representations, i.e., phonemes to use
in mapping onto graphemes, but also orthographic grain sizes that are larger than
individual letters (but smaller than the whole word) because many orthographic-
phonological mappings that are inconsistent at the phoneme-grapheme level are
found to be consistent when larger orthographic units are used. To the extent that
less skilled readers have failed to develop these larger grain sizes, such as *tion*, and
are struggling to apply erroneous letter-phoneme mappings, they should struggle
more on nonwords, where vocabulary cannot bootstrap the process, than on words.
We evaluated this hypothesis by examining the accuracy with which children in our
study were able to correctly classify letter strings as words or nonwords, that is,
accuracy on a lexical decision task (LDT).

One advantage of using the LDT to evaluate word-nonword decoding differences, rather than have children read words and nonwords aloud, is that we can
then examine their performance doing the task both when the letter strings are
visual and when they are auditory, whereas reading is obviously restricted to a
visual presentation. The modality comparison is important because it allows us to
determine whether the same advantage for words over nonwords occurs in the
auditory domain as in the visual domain. If it does, then the word-nonword difference likely reflects simply vocabulary knowledge. If, however, the word-
nonword difference reflects skill in using larger grain sizes in the orthographic-
phonological mappings, as we have been suggesting, then when the stimuli are
auditory and such mappings are not involved, there should be no differences in
accuracy of identification between words and nonwords.

The top rows of Table 10.3 present the word and nonword accuracies on the
Visual LDT for RD and No RD children. For both groups of children, accuracy is
significantly greater for words than nonwords. This finding replicates the advantage
of decoding words over nonwords that has been reported by others for the English
language when children read, but our replication uses a very different paradigm;
we thus both replicate and extend this finding. As would be expected, we found
that RD children are less accurate than nondisabled readers. Also, the word-nonword difference is greater for RD children; that is, the interaction of word/nonword

with reading skill is significant. This interaction may be due to nondisabled readers' accuracy being close to ceiling, but it also fits with the notion that RD children may have less skill in using larger grain sizes in the orthographic-phonological mappings.

The bottom rows of Table 10.3 present the word and nonword accuracies on the Auditory LDT. The most striking finding is that the interaction of word/nonwords with reading skill, which was significant for the Visual LDT, does not occur for the Auditory LDT. Both groups show no advantage when identifying words versus identifying nonwords when they are presented auditorily. When both modalities are combined in one analysis, the three-way interaction between modality, word/nonwords, and reading skill is significant. This is an important finding. It shows that the interaction in the Visual LDT does not represent a tendency for RD children to be biased to classify all stimuli as words; they only show such a bias in the visual domain. It supports the psycholinguistic grain size theory that decoding difficulties arise not only from a lack of small grains, i.e., phonemes, but also from a lack of larger grain sizes in orthographic representations because the word-nonword difference in accuracy only occurs in the domain for which they have inadequate mappings. Also in accord with the grain size theory, we found that vocabulary bootstraps the decoding process because accuracy on both words and nonwords in each domain was found to be significantly related to vocabulary.

Our results are consistent with the view that RD children may be deficient not only in small grains in phonological representations, but also larger grain sizes in orthographic representations. This is likely due both to deficits in cognitive mechanisms as well as less exposure to visual words because if reading is difficult, there is a tendency to avoid it. If RD children are less likely to use larger orthographic grain sizes, and if it is these larger grain sizes that map onto semantics, then it is possible that we may find that they also have deficits in activating semantic representations. We turn now to some data that speak to this hypothesis.

Semantic Priming

It is important to evaluate activation of semantic representations not only for their contributions to the comprehension of single words but also because they are the basis for the comprehension of texts. Discourse comprehension is a process of activating word meanings and integrating those meanings into a coherent representation. A good comprehender is one whose semantic representations can automatically drive the construction of this representation using passive resonance between concepts (Myers & O'Brien, 1998) as opposed to effortful conscious thinking about what each concept means and how it is related to the previous ones.

Priming is a way to evaluate this automatic activation of words by related words. Priming is evaluated by determining if the time to process a target word is shorter following a related prime word than following an unrelated prime word. The notion is that processing the prime will preactivate the target when the prime is related to it; thus, with the target already preactivated by the prime, less processing is required when the target is presented to bring it to full activation.

TABLE 10.4

Auditory Lexical Decision Times, Facilitation, and Baseline Adjusted Proportions
of Facilitation as a Function of Priming Condition for Children with Reading-
Disability (RD) and Chronological-Age Matched Controls

Prime Condition	Reaction Time		Facilitation		Proportion Facilitation	
	RD	Controls	RD	Controls	RD	Controls
Unrelated (YIELD-BOAT)	1,274	1,197	—	—	—	—
Semantic (SHIP-BOAT)	1,249	1,146	24$^{n.s.}$	50*	.015	.03
Phonological (GOAT-BOAT)	1,195	1,112	79**	85**	.059	.066
Combined (FLOAT-BOAT)	1,198	1,089	76**	108**	.056	.083

Reaction time and facilitation are reported in milliseconds.
** $p < .01$
* $p < .05$

We have been evaluating priming in an auditory lexical decision paradigm in order to determine if children with RD have deficits in either their phonological representations or their semantic representations. Deficits in phonological representations are commonly thought to be the source of reading problems (Snowling, 2000); thus, RD children may show deficits in phonological priming. On the other hand, if the deficit in RD is not in the phonological representations themselves, but in the mappings onto the orthography, then they may not show any deficits in phonological priming when the task is auditory. Because children with RD show deficits in listening comprehension as well as reading comprehension, we were also interested in determining whether they would show any deficits in activating semantic representations. If so, then this could help explain their listening and reading comprehension problems, because when representations are slower to become activated, comprehension is more labored. It could also provide further reasons for their difficulties in word decoding.

There were four types of primes: Unrelated, Semantic, Phonological, and Combined. The Combined primes combined phonological and semantic priming in one prime word, e.g., FLOAT - BOAT. Table 10.4 shows examples of what the prime in each condition was for the target word, *boat*. The Semantic primes were half associates and half synonyms, and the semantic relationship in the combined primes was also half associates and half synonyms. Each child heard the target word only once in a given priming condition; but across participants, each target appeared in all priming conditions an equal number of times. Children made lexical decisions to both the primes and the targets.

Table 10.4 presents the data for 42 RD children and their chronological-age-matched controls (M_{age} = 10.9). We present the target response times, the priming facilitation (computed by subtracting the mean response time for the prime condition from the Unrelated condition), and the baseline-adjusted facilitation. The latter is necessary because as can be seen in Table 10.4, even though the task does not involve reading, RD children responded more slowly than the controls; comparing facilitation amounts across children with such different baselines is not recommended (Chapman, Chapman, Curran, & Miller, 1994; Nation & Snowling, 1998), so we adjusted for baseline differences by computing the facilitation as *(Unrelated − Prime)/Unrelated.*

Although we thought that RD children might show deficits in phonological priming, they do not; they show significant phonological priming and as much as the controls. Where the RD children appear to have a deficit is in semantic priming. RD children do not show significant Semantic priming, but the Controls do. The Combined condition functions as a replication of the Semantic alone condition in the sense that if no priming occurs in the Semantic condition, then the Combined condition should also show no semantic priming; in other words, the amount of facilitation from the Combined primes in this case should be equivalent to that from just the Phonological primes. Indeed, the amount of priming that RD children show in the Combined condition is no greater than that in the Phonological condition. Thus, they show a semantic deficit in both the Semantic and Combined conditions. In contrast, the Control children show facilitation from the Combined primes that is greater than that from either the Phonological or Semantic prime condition by itself.

In neither the Semantic nor the Combined conditions do the RD children show a benefit from having just processed a semantically related prime. This suggests that RD entails a deficit in activating semantic representations. The deficit may simply reflect slowness with accessing semantic representations, or the slowness may stem from a deficit in the semantic representations themselves. Regardless, it appears that for RD children, semantics does not get activated in time to influence the decision arrived at by the phonological representation settling on a solution.

Our findings of semantic priming deficits, but not phonological priming deficits, are quite similar to those reported by Nation and Snowling (1998b). They studied children who were defined as having comprehension problems, but not word reading problems. They found that less skilled comprehenders scored lower than controls on a synonym judgment task (Do BOAT and SHIP mean the same thing?) but not on a rhyme judgment task (Do BOAT and GOAT rhyme?). They were also slower to generate semantic category members, but not slower at generating rhymes. Our results extend the Nation and Snowling findings in two ways. First, we show that semantic deficits occur not just in children who have comprehension problems, but also in children who have word decoding problems. Second, our results show that these semantic deficits are not just due to differences in *explicit* knowledge between disabled and nondisabled children. Although Nation and Snowling's tasks tapped explicit knowledge of phonology and semantics, our priming task did not require any explicit knowledge of semantic relationships; it tapped only implicit knowledge and yet we still found semantic deficits.

Our demonstration that semantic deficits underlie word reading problems, in addition to comprehension problems, provides an important link between word identification processes and comprehension. It is a link that Nation and Snowling (1998b) also helped forge when they found that their comprehension deficit children showed significant deficits in reading exception words, even though their nonword reading was comparable to controls. Because exception words violate grapheme-phoneme correspondence rules, they are exactly the kinds of words whose identification would be more likely to engage semantics. Thus, this finding, together with our findings, raise the possibility that many comprehension problems may stem from word-level semantic deficits.

A detailed discussion of how word-level semantic deficits may form the foundation for comprehension problems is beyond the scope of this chapter, so we simply give an example to illustrate the point. Because word-level semantic representations drive the construction of discourse representations using passive resonance between concepts (Myers & O'Brien, 1998), weak semantic representations can require additional cognitive computations that would not be required with richer representations. To illustrate, consider the phrases: *He began to inspect the car's engine. The pistons....* These will cohere if a reader's representation of *engine* includes the information that pistons are part of the car engine, but will require a computationally complex inference to connect the two clauses if the representation does not include such information. In short, good semantic representations can eliminate the need for more resource-demanding higher-level comprehension processes, and weak semantic representations may exacerbate problems in a system that may already be dealing with other resource-demanding activities, such as decoding in a child with RD. As a result we might expect, as Leach, Scarborough, & Rescorla (2003) report, that many late-emerging comprehension problems are associated with poor word-level skills.

CONCLUSION

The triangle model depicted in Figure 10.1 shows semantics to be an equal player to orthographic and phonological representations in the identification of single words. This inclusion of semantics is not unique to connectionist models; even the most recent formulation of the dual route model has a semantic component (Coltheart, et al., 2001). But despite such depictions, semantics has been the neglected side of the triangle. It is often ignored in explanations of single word reading and is typically only invoked to explain word identification when words occur in context, or to explain special phenomena such as surface dyslexia.

In this chapter we have tried to counter this neglect by making a case for the involvement of semantics in single word identification both from a theoretical perspective and from empirical evidence. We contend that, at least in the English language, the case for semantic involvement is compelling.

Because semantics appears to be a significant contributor to the identification of single words even when they occur out of context, researchers need to look to semantics in their explanations of word reading problems. We hope that the research we summarized from our lab showing semantic deficits in children with RD will stimulate others to investigate semantic processing in children with reading problems. We also hope that it will give further support to those researchers investigating morphological training in the remediation of reading problems (e.g., Adams, 1990; Elbro & Arnbak, 1996; Henry, 1993), although it remains to be seen whether explicit training is necessary or whether morphological awareness develops with reading experience.

While each side of the word identification triangle in Figure 10.1 may get different weighting depending on specific word, context, and reader characteristics, we think it is important that semantics be regarded as being just as important a contributor to word identification as it is depicted to be in the triangle model (c.f., Reichle & Perfetti, 2003). We believe that more emphasis on semantics in word identification will serve to improve not only our understanding of reading, but also our understanding of reading disability and its remediation.

ACKNOWLEDGMENTS

This research was supported by a grant from NIH HD27802 to the Colorado Learning Disabilities Research Center, with a subcontract for the comprehension project to J.M. Keenan at the University of Denver. We are grateful to Dick Olson and Bruce Pennington for comments on the manuscript, and to all the participants and their families who participated in our research.

Correspondence concerning this article should be sent to Janice M. Keenan, Department of Psychology, University of Denver, 2155 S. Race, Denver, Colorado 80208. E-mail: jkeenan@du.edu.

REFERENCES

Adams, M. (1990). Beginning to read: Thinking and learning about print. Cambridge, MA: The MIT Press.

Balota, D. A., & Ferraro, F. R. (1993). A dissociation of frequency and regularity effects in pronunciation performance across young adults, older adults, and individuals with senile dementia of the Alzheimer type. *Journal of Memory & Language, 32*, 573–592.

Betjemann, R. S., Keenan, J. M., & Olson, R. K. (2003). Listening comprehension in children with reading disability. *Poster presented at the meeting of the Society for the Scientific Study of Reading.*

Byrne, B., & Shea, P. (1979). Semantic and phonetic memory codes in beginning readers. *Memory & Cognition, 7*(5), 333–338.

Catts, H. W., Hogan, T. P., & Fey, M. E. (2003). Subgrouping poor readers on the basis of individual differences in reading-related abilities. *Journal of Learning Disabilities, 36*(2), 151–164.

Chapman, L. J., Chapman, J. P., Curran, T. E., & Miller, M. B. (1994). Do children and the elderly show heightened semantic priming? How to answer the question. *Developmental Review, 14*(2), 159–185.

Chumbley, J. I., & Balota, D. A. (1984). A word's meaning affects the decision in lexical decision. *Memory & Cognition, 12*, 590–606.

Coltheart, M. (1978). Lexical access in simple reading tasks. In G. Underwood (Ed.), *Strategies of information processing.* (pp. 151 – 216). London: Academic.

Coltheart, M., Rastle, K., Perry, C., Langdon, R., & Ziegler, J. (2001). A dual-route cascaded model of visualwordrecogntion andreadingaloud. *Psychological Review, 108,* 204 – 256.

Defries, J. C., Filipek, P. A., Fulker, D. W., Olson, R. K., Pennington, B. F., Smith, S. D. et al. (1997). Colorado Learning Disabilities Research Center. *Learning Disabilities, 8,* 7–19.

Dixon, P., LeFevre, J.-A., & Twilley, L. C. (1988). Word knowledge and working memory as predictors of reading skill. *Journal of Educational Psychology, 80,* 465–472.

Dunn, L. M., & Markwardt, F. C. (1970). *Examiner's Manual: Peabody Individual Achievement Test.* Circle Pines, MN: American Guidance Service.

Elbro, C., & Arnbak, E. (1996). The role of morpheme recognition and morphological aware-ness in dyslexia. *Annals of Dyslexia, 46,* 209–240.

Fletcher, J.M., Shaywitz, S.E., Shankweiler, D.P., Katz, L., Liberman, I.Y., Stuebing, K.K., Francis, D.J., Fowler, A.E., And Shaywitz, B.A. (1994) Cognitive profiles of reading disability: Comparisons of discrepancy and low achievement definitions. Journal of Educational Psychology, 86, 6–23.

Forster, K. (1976). Accessing the mental lexicon. In R. J. Wales & E. Walker (Eds.), *New approaches to language mechanisms.* (pp. 257 – 287). Amsterdam: North Holland.

Forster, K., & Hector, J. (2002). Cascaded versus noncascaded models of lexical and semantic processing the turple effect. *Memory & Cognition, 30,* 1106–1116.

Hannon, B., & Daneman, M. (2001). A new tool for measuring and understanding individual differences in the component processes of reading comprehension. *Journal of Educational Psychology, 93,* 103–128.

Henry, M. K. (1993). Morphological structure: Latin and Greek roots and affixes as upper grade code strategies. *Reading & Writing, 5,* 227–241.

Jastrzembski, J. E. (1981). Multiple meanings, number of related meanings, frequency of occur-rence, and the lexicon. *Cognitive Psychology, 13,* 278–305.

Johnston, R. S. (1983). Developmental deep dyslexia? *Cortex, 19,* 133–139.

Kellas, G., Ferraro, F. R., & Simpson, G. B. (1988). Lexical ambiguity and the timecourse of attentional allocation in word recognition. *Journal of Experimental Psychology: Human Perception & Performance, 14,* 601–609.

Landauer, T. K., Foltz, P. W., & Laham, D. (1998). An introduction to latent semantic analysis. *Discourse Processes, 25,* 259–284.

Leslie, L., & Caldwell, J. (2001). *Qualitative Reading Inventory - 3.* New York: Addison Wesley Longman, Inc.

Leach, J. M., Scarborough, H.S., Rescorla, L. (2003). Late-emerging reading disabilities. *Journal of Educational Psychology, 95(2),* 211–224.

Mann, V. A., Liberman, I. Y., & Shankweiler, D. (1980). Children's memory for sentences and word strings in relation to reading ability. *Memory & Cognition, 8(4),* 329–335.

Mann, V. A., Shankweiler, D., & Smith, S. T. (1984). The association between comprehension of spoken sentences and early reading ability: The role of phonetic representation. *Journal of Child Language, 11(3),* 627–643.

Meyer, D. E., & Schvaneveldt, R. W. (1971). Facilitation in recognizing words: Evidence of a dependence upon retrieval operations. *Journal of Experimental Psychology, 90,* 227–234.

Myers, J. L., & O'Brien, E. J. (1998). Accessing the discourse representation during reading. *Discourse Processes, 26,* 131–157.

Nation, K., & Snowling, M. J. (1998a). Individual differences in contextual facilitation: Evidence from dyslexia and poor reading comprehension. *Child Development, 69(4),* 996–1011.

Nation, K., & Snowling, M.J. (1998b). Semantic processing and the development of word-recognition skills: Evidence from children with reading comprehension difficulties. *Journal of Memory and Language, 39,* 85–101.

Nation, K., & Snowling, M.J. (1999). Developmental differences in sensitivity to semantic relations among good and poor comprehenders: Evidence from semantic priming. *Cognition, 70,* B1–13.

Oakhill, J., Cain, K.E., & Bryant, P.E. (2003). The dissociation of word reading and text comprehension: Evidence from component skills. *Language and Cognitive Processes, 18,* 443– 468.

Olson, R. K., Forsberg, H., Wise, B., & Rack, J. (1994). Measurement of word recognition, orthographic, and phonological skills. In G. R. Lyon (Ed), *Frames of Reference for the Assessment of Learning Disabilities: New Views on Measurement Issues* (pp. 243–277). Baltimore: Paul H. Brookes Publishing Co.

Onifer, W., & Swinney, D. A. (1981). Accessing lexical ambiguities during sentence comprehension: Effects of frequency of meaning and contextual bias. *Memory & Cognition, 9,* 225–236.

O'Reilly, R. C., & Munakata, Y. (2000). *Computational explorations in cognitive neuroscience: Understanding the mind by simulating the brain.* Cambridge, MA: MIT Press.

Perfetti, C. A. (2003). The universal grammar of reading. *Scientific Studies of Reading, 7,* 3–24.

Plaut, D. C. (1998). A connectionist approach to word reading and acquired dyslexia: Extension to sequential processing. *Cognitive Science, 23 ,* 543–568.

Plaut, D. C., & Shallice, T. (1993). Deep dyslexia: A case study of connectionist neuropsychology. *Cognitive Neuropsychology, 10,* 377–500.

Plaut, D. C., McClelland, J. L., Seidenberg, M. S., & Patterson, K. E. (1996). Understanding normal and impaired word reading: Computational principles in quasi-regular domains. *Psychological Review, 103*(1), 56–115.

Reichle, E. D., & Perfetti, C. A. (2003). Morphology in word identification: A word-experience model that accounts for morpheme frequency effects. *Scientific Studies of Reading, 7,* 219–237.

Rodd, J. M. (2004). When do leotards get their spots? Semantic activation of lexical neighbors in visual word recognition. *Psychonomic Bulletin & Review, 11,* 434–439.

Schwanenflugel, P. J., Harnishfeger, K. K., & Stowe, R. W. (1988). Context availability and lexical decisions for abstract and concrete words. *Journal of Memory & Language, 27,* 499–520.

Seidenberg, M. S. (1990). Lexical access: Another theoretical soupstone? in D. A. Balota, G. B. Flores d.Arcais, & K. Rayner (Eds), *Comprehension Processes in Reading* (pp. 33–71). Hillsdale, NJ: Erlbaum.

Seidenberg, M. S., & McClelland, J. L. (1989). A distributed, developmental model of word recognition and naming. *Psychological Review, 96*(4), 523–568.

Seidenberg, M. S., & Tanenhaus, M. K. (1979). Orthographic effects on rhyme monitoring. *Journal of Experimental Psychology: Human Learning & Memory, 5,* 546–554.

Seidenberg, M. S., Tanenhaus, M. K., Leiman, J. M., & Bienkowski, M. (1982). Automatic access of the meanings of ambiguous words in context: Some limitations of knowledge-based processing. *Cognitive Psychology, 14,* 489–537.

Siegel, L. S. (1985). Deep dyslexia in childhood? *Brain & Language, 26,* 16–27.

Snowling, M.J. (2000). *Dyslexia,* 2nd Edition. Oxford: Blackwell.

Stanovich, K. E. (1980). Toward an interactive-compensatory model of individual differences in the development of reading fluency. *Reading Research Quarterly, 16,* 32–71.

Stanovich, K. E., & Siegel, L.S. (1994) The phenotypic performance profile of reading-disabled children: A regression-based test of the phonological-core variable-difference model. *Journal of Educational Psychology, 86,* 24–53.

Sternberg, R. J., & Powell, J. S. (1983). Comprehending verbal comprehension. *American Psychologist, 38,* 878–893.

Strain, E., Patterson, K., & Seidenberg, M. S. (1995). Semantic effects in single-word naming. *Journal of Experimental Psychology: Learning, Memory, & Cognition, 21,* 1140–1154.

Strain, E., Patterson, K., & Seidenberg, M. S. (2002). Theories of word naming interact with spelling—sound consistency. *Journal of Experimental Psychology: Learning, Memory, & Cognition, 28*, 207–214.

Swinney, D. A. (1979). Lexical access during sentence comprehension: (Re)consideration of context effects. *Journal of Verbal Learning & Verbal Behavior, 18*, 645–659.

Taft, M., & Forster, K. I. (1976). Lexical storage and retrieval of polymorphemic and polysyllabic words. *Journal of Verbal Learning & Verbal Behavior, 15*, 607–620.

Tanenhaus, M. K., Leiman, J. M., & Seidenberg, M. S. (1979). Evidence for multiple stages in the processing of ambiguous words in syntactic contexts. *Journal of Verbal Learning & Verbal Behavior, 18*, 427–440.

Temple, C. M. (1988). Red is read but eye is blue: A case study of developmental dyslexia and follow-up report. *Brain & Language, 34*, 13–37.

Treiman, R., & Kessler, B. (2005). Writing systems and spelling development. In M. Snowling & C. Hulme (Eds.), *The Science of Reading: A Handbook*. Oxford, UK:Blackwell.

Tulving, E., & Gold, C. (1963). Stimulus information and contextual information as determinants of tachistoscopic recognition of words. *Journal of Experimental Psychology, 66*, 319–327.

Tyler, L. K., Voice, J. K., & Moss, H. E. (2000). The interaction of meaning and sound in spoken word recognition. *Psychonomic Bulletin & Review, 7*(2), 320–326.

Ziegler, J. C. & Goswami, U. C. (2005). Reading Acquisition, Developmental Dyslexia and Skilled Reading across Languages: A Psycholinguistic Grain Size Theory. *Psychological Bulletin*.

CHAPTER ELEVEN

Single-Word Reading: Perspectives From Magnetic Source Imaging

Panagiotis G. Simos
University of Crete, Greece
Rebecca Billingsley-Marshall
Shirin Sarkari
Andrew C. Papanicolaou
Vivian L. Smith Center for Neurologic Research, Department of Neurosurgery,
University of Texas, Health Science Center-Houston

Several methods of investigation have been used to identify the cerebral mechanisms for reading single words. Lesion studies have been used at least since Dejerine (1892) to determine the brain regions necessary for successful reading. Deficits that become apparent following brain damage necessarily imply that part of the lesioned area was critical to successful reading performance, either by hosting neurophysiological processes that support particular component operations involved in reading, or disrupting connections between such brain regions. Cortical stimulation studies in individuals undergoing awake craniotomies have also provided important insights regarding the location of brain areas that serve as components of the brain mechanism for single-word reading. In addition, transcranial magnetic stimulation (TMS) has been used by researchers to identify critical areas for reading by temporarily inhibiting the activity in specific cortical sites. While these techniques rely on the study of deficits caused by either transient or permanent interference with the brain mechanisms for reading, functional brain imaging methods attempt to reveal the outline of the said mechanisms simply by recording "echos" of the healthy, working brain, in the form of various types of electromagnetic signals, while the person engages in reading tasks. From these studies it has become apparent that single-word reading requires a highly integrated network of closely interconnected brain areas, the majority of which reside in the left cerebral hemisphere. This network or "mechanism" presumably includes separate circuits, each composed of distinct neurophysiological processes that take place in one or more brain regions. A recently proposed model (see for instance Pugh, Mencl, Jenner, Lee, Katz, Frost, Shaywitz, & Shaywitz, 2001) postulates three brain circuits, two of which reside in posterior brain regions while the third comprises anterior brain areas. Of the two posterior circuits, one resides mainly in temporoparietal cortices (roughly corresponding to Wernicke's area) and the angular gyrus, and is mainly involved in phonological analysis and in establishing associations between word-like stimuli and phonological representations. The second posterior circuit includes higher-order visual association areas in both lateral and ventral occipito-temporal cortices and appears to be primarily involved in the visual analysis of print according to graphemic conventions. The third, anterior circuit involves ventrolateral prefrontal and premotor cortices (in the vicinity of Broca's area). It appears to be involved in articulatory recoding during both oral and silent reading.

Here we briefly review these four approaches to the study of brain function (see Table 11.1), and then explore in greater depth functional brain imaging studies of the reading mechanism. We focus on the contributions of magnetic source imaging (MSI), and include new research on individual variability inherent in brain activity at posterior cortical sites during single-word reading.

LESION STUDIES

Lesion studies have identified several regions of the left hemisphere that are important for reading. Dejerine's (1892) original post-mortem studies showed that a patient with damage to the left angular gyrus had both reading and writing deficits. A second patient of Dejerine's (1892) who had reading but no writing deficits had damage in the left occipital lobe. Since those observations, lesion studies have indicated other important areas involved in the reading mechanism. Acquired surface dyslexia, in which individuals show greater difficulty in reading irregular words as compared to their ability in reading pseudowords and regular words, has been correlated with lesions of the left superior temporal gyrus, the left middle temporal gyrus, and left parieto-temporal cortex (Black & Behrmann, 1994). Acquired phonological or deep dyslexia, in which individuals show greater difficulty in reading pseudowords than real words, has been associated with lesions involving the left posterior temporal gyrus, the medial and inferior frontal gyrus, the angular gyrus, and the inferior parietal lobe (supramarginal gyrus) (Black & Behrmann, 1994). Pure alexia, also termed letter-by-letter reading or alexia without agraphia, has been associated with lesions of inferior occipital-temporal cortex, including the posterior portion of the fusiform gyrus (Rapcsak & Beeson, 2004). Individuals with pure alexia retain their ability to spell words correctly but show great difficulty reading words they write.

The behavior of individuals with various types of reading deficits and lesions has led to the development of cognitive models of reading focusing primarily on lexical versus sub-lexical skills, and the relations between orthography, phonology, and

TABLE 11.1

Common and Distinct Features of Conventional
Approaches to Study Brain Function

Permits Study of:	Healthy Brain	Multiple Cortical Sites in Each Person	Areas Indispensable for a Particular Function	Regional Connectivity Patterns	The Relative Timing of Regional Cortical Engagement
Lesion studies			+		
Electrocortical stimulation mapping	+[1]		+		+[2]
TMS	+	+	+[3]		+
Functional brain imaging techniques	+	+		+[4]	+[5]

[1]Restricted spatial scope by clinical considerations.
[2]But rarely examined due to time limitations.
[3]Complete inactivation of underlying cortical regions may not be possible for many applications to prevent side effects.
[4]Indirectly through complex statistical analyses (in PET, fMRI, and MEG), and by studying the relative timing of regional activity (MEG only).
[5] MEG only.

semantics. According to dual-route cognitive models of reading, orthographic representations are converted to phonological representations at either a sublexical (from individual letters or graphemic segments to phonemes or subword-level phonological representations) or lexical (whole-word) level. These models postulate that, in some instances, semantic representations may be accessed directly from lexical representations, and in others after the phonological representation is formed or accessed (Coltheart et al., 1993; Plaut et al., 1996). Individuals with acquired surface dyslexia who are better at reading pseudowords than real words, and those with pure alexia who can write but not read words they have just written, are thought to have a processing deficit at the lexical level. Individuals with acquired phonological dyslexia who have difficulty reading pseudowords, on the other hand, are thought to have a deficit in sub-lexical processing (Price et al., 2003).

A limitation of lesion studies in defining the brain mechanism for single-word reading is that the region identified as associated with a given reading deficit is not usually the only lesioned area in a patient. Large lesions and multi-infarcts are more common than discrete lesions that map onto or reveal discrete types of reading deficits. Often patients have more than one clinical deficit, making correlations between brain damage and behavior even more challenging. The analysis of overlapping lesions in multiple patients with similar deficits shows likely targets for areas necessary for mediating particular functions (Damasio and Damasio, 1989; Dronkers, Wilkins, Van Valin, Redfern, & Jaeger, 2004), but potential individual variability in those regions essential for a given function prevents general conclusions (Steinmetz & Seitz, 1991). Moreover, a deficit in reading ability may be due to the anatomical disconnection between areas of the brain, not to damage to a specific region (Paulesu et al., 1996).

ELECTROCORTICAL STIMULATION

Intra-operative cortical stimulation has been used to determine the effect of transient interference with local neurophysiological function through direct electrical stimulation of cortical regions exposed during neurosurgery. In their pioneering studies of electrocortical stimulation of language-specific sites, Ojemann and colleagues observed areas in the temporal lobe that, upon stimulation, interrupted reading specifically (Ojemann, Creutzfeldt, Lettich, & Haglund, 1988). Early electrocortical stimulation studies, however, were not directed specifically at understanding the brain mechanism for single-word reading; rather, their primary goal was to delineate receptive and expressive language-specific sites. Ojemann and colleagues found over the course of numerous operations substantial individual variations in neuronal populations in the perisylvian region that appeared to mediate specific language functions, including reading (see Ojemann, 2003, for review).

In a series of 54 patients who together underwent a total of 76 cortical stimulation mapping studies, Roux et al. (2004) identified multiple sites where electrical interference caused deficits in the ability to read aloud connected text (sentences). Stimulation in the dominant supramarginal gyrus and posterior superior temporal gyri resulted in reading errors (paralexias), whereas stimulation in pre- and post-central gyri interfered with articulation. Other sites that showed significant interference with reading, albeit less frequently, were the dominant inferior and middle frontal gyri, the angular gyrus, and the posterior aspect of the dominant middle temporal gyrus; but considerable individual variability of the exact location of stimulation sites resulting in reading interference was also observed.

Intra- and extra-operative stimulation mapping has been used in conjunction with functional brain imaging to determine language- and reading-specific sites in patients undergoing epilepsy surgery (Simos et al., 1999, 2000a; FitzGerald et al., 1997; Rutten et al., 2002). Simos et al. (1999) compared MSI-derived activation sites, associated with reading single words, with the sites of effective intra-operative electrical stimulation in posterior temporal and inferior parietal regions that were documented by surgeons photographically. In extra-operatively stimulated cases, Simos et al. (1999) evaluated the concordance of MSI-derived activity sources by overlaying them on high-resolution MR images acquired after grid placement. In all 13 of their cases, intra- or extra-operative stimulation sites found to elicit reading errors overlapped with dipolar sources of the MSI-derived reading maps within the temporal and parietal lobes. A subsequent electrocortical stimulation study by Simos et al. (2000a) provided direct evidence supporting the role of the dorsal system in sublexical phonological analysis, in which electrical interference with a small portion of the posterior superior temporal gyrus consistently impaired the patients' ability to decode pseudowords, sparing the ability to read real words which did not require phonological decoding.

There are important limitations to electrocortical stimulation. First, only individuals having surgery for other medical reasons (e.g., epilepsy, tumors) undergo awake craniotomies during which stimulation is appropriate. These disease processes are likely to affect brain organization especially when they appear early in development (see for instance Papanicolaou et al., 2001; Pataraia et al., 2004). Moreover, the extent of the cortical area that can be examined with invasive electrical stimulation techniques either intra- or extra-operatively, is very limited and strictly determined by clinical considerations.

TRANSCRANIAL MAGNETIC STIMULATION

Transcranial magnetic stimulation (TMS), in contrast to cortical stimulation, can be performed on neurologically intact (or normal) individuals. TMS targets discrete regions of cortex and temporarily inihibits their function. In some cases, depending on the type of magnetic stimulation delivered, an excitatory effect has been observed (Jahanshahi & Rothwell, 2000; Wassermann, 2002). To date, most published TMS studies involving reading have involved the occipital and frontal lobes (Epstein et al., 1999; Leff, Scott, Rothwell, & Wise, 2001; Lavidor and Walsh, 2003; Mottaghy, Gangitano, Krause, & Pascual-Leone, 2003; Meister et al., 2003; Liederman et al., 2003). Stimulation of the posterior aspect of Brodmann area (BA) 37, part of the inferior temporal lobe, during word and pseudoword reading has also been reported, with no resulting disruption or slowing of reading ability (Stewart, Meyer, Frith, & Rothwell, 2001). TMS applications to the study of reading, however, are difficult to undertake because, in order to stimulate most regions of the temporal lobe, the technique requires rapid repetitive stimulation over an area that contains muscles (e.g., the temporalis muscle), causing painful contractions. Therefore, current TMS applications to the study of reading, particularly for functions supported by temporal neocortex, are limited at this time (see also Epstein, Woodard, Stringer et al., 2000). Functional brain imaging techniques, on the other hand, do not share these limitations and are therefore capable of providing a more complete picture of the cerebral mechanism of complex linguistic functions such as reading.

FUNCTIONAL BRAIN IMAGING

Three primary functional brain imaging methods used to study reading vary in how brain function is measured and in the spatial and temporal resolution they afford (Papanicolaou, 1998): 1) position emission tomography (PET); 2) functional magnetic resonance imaging (fMRI); and 3) magnetoencephalography (MEG) or magnetic source imaging (MSI). Surface electrophysiological methods (electroencephalography-EEG-and event-related potentials-ERPs) are also used to measure brain function. We do not discuss these latter methods because their capability for imaging brain anatomy is not as developed as the other primary modalities (see Bentin, 1993 for a review).

We previously have proposed several criteria for establishing the utility of a functional neuroimaging method for the study of language and reading function (Billingsley, Simos, and Papanicolaou, 2004). These are specificity, reliability, external validity, spatial and temporal resolution, and pragmatic utility. In short, an imaging technique should demonstrate task- and function-specific profiles; show reliable profiles across subjects and within subjects over time; be validated against invasive functional brain mapping methods, including electrocortical stimulation; have sufficient spatial and temporal resolution for distinguishing the distinct activity of different brain regions in real time during the performance of specific tasks; and be practically and logistically feasible to use within reasonable time limits in both child and adult populations.

The rationale behind functional brain imaging is straightforward (for a recent review see Papanicolaou, Pugh, Simos, & Mencl, 2004). When a person engages in a cognitive operation like thinking, remembering, reading, or otherwise using language, changes occur in the brain. Oxygen is consumed, which can be reflected metabolically by glucose utilization or shifts in regional blood flow (hemodynamic changes). These changes are the basis for PET and fMRI. Similarly, when a person engages in a cognitive task (such as deciding whether a letter string is a word or not), regional increases in neuronal signaling take place. The increased neurophysiological activity within specific populations of neurons entails increased extra- and intracellular flow of electrical current (ions) in active brain regions. These electrical changes can be recorded at the surface of the head in the form of EEG, ERP, and MEG signals. The latter measures minute changes in magnetic flux associated with intracellular electrical currents. MSI refers to the techniques used to extract information about where and when the brain produced the changes in the magnetic signals. A structural MRI scan is usually obtained and the patterns of brain activation are superimposed on this MRI to identify specific areas where changes are taking place. While MEG and fMRI do not involve radiation, and therefore can be used with children, PET involves the use of a radioactive isotope that is ingested in order to measure changes in brain function. Exposure to small amounts of radioactivity precludes participation of children, unless they can directly benefit from PET due to a neurological or other medical condition. The radioactivity also limits the number of times an adult can participate in studies involving PET.

At present no single imaging technique fulfills each aspect of the criteria we have proposed (see Billingsley et al., 2004 for review). Of the three techniques, PET has the poorest spatial and temporal resolution. MSI and fMRI have excellent spatial resolution at the neocortical level; fMRI, but not MSI, has excellent subcortical spatial resolution. The regional changes in brain physiology recorded by both PET and fMRI take place *after* the neurophysiological activity actually involved in the execution of a particular cognitive function has taken place, so that the temporal resolution of these methods is weak. MSI, on the other hand, affords measurement of neurophysiological activity in real time and provides information on the actual time course of neuronal events. MSI can be used to determine not only which cortical areas participate in reading, but also *how* these areas might interact with each other in real time to enable this function. This feature may prove particularly important in future studies of the brain mechanism that supports single-word reading, in view of the many inconsistencies apparent in the functional brain imaging literature regarding the precise role of discrete brain areas within this mechanism (see below). In addition, the capacity of MSI to provide accurate and detailed maps of language-specific cortex has been validated in the context of large clinical studies against invasive cortical mapping techniques (Breier et al., 1999a, 2001; Papanicolaou et al., 2004; Simos et al., 1999, 2000a).

SUMMARY OF FUNCTIONAL MRI, PET, AND MSI STUDIES OF SINGLE-WORD READI1NG

A meta-analysis of 11 PET studies of single-word reading reported by Turkeltaub et al. (2002) revealed several brain regions that were found to show increased regional metabolic rates with some consistency across studies during reading aloud of single words. Common regions of activity were bilateral motor and superior temporal cortex, premotor and supplementary motor cortex, left fusiform gyrus, and bilateral cerebellum. A follow-up fMRI study in which participants were required to read aloud single words revealed similar peaks of activation as the PET meta-analysis, with several additional areas showing significant activity, including left inferior frontal gyrus and bilateral middle temporal cortex (Turkeltaub et al., 2002).

   Four of these regions have attracted a lot of attention in recent studies, the fusiform gyrus (i.e., occipitotemporal cortex in the ventral portion of Brodmann's area 37), the posterior portion of the middle temporal gyrus (BA 21) which could include two distinct regions one located ventrally near the border with BA 37, and one located more dorsally in the vicinity of the superior temporal sulcus), the angular gyrus (BA 39), and the posterior portion of the superior temporal gyrus (BA 22). There is general consensus among researchers that in the majority of right handed readers without history of learning disability or brain damage, the brain mechanism for single word reading relies primarily upon these areas in the left hemisphere. The selection of these areas for the discussion that follows is supported by the well-documented fact that acquired deficits in single-word reading are typically associated with lesions that encompass one or more of these regions (e.g., Damasio and Damasio, 1983).

   On the basis of recent fMRI data showing increased hemodynamic activity in the left posterior fusiform gyrus in response to letter strings that comply with the phonotactic rules of the English language (words and pseudowords) relative to stimuli that do not comply with these rules (unpronounceable letters strings), it was proposed that this region hosts neurophysiological processes specific to the processing of word forms (Cohen et al., 2000, 2002). While other brain regions may show a similar pattern of hemodynamic responses (see review by Jobard, Crivello, & Tzurio-Mazoyer, 2003), this notion receives strong support by lesion studies indicating that pure alexia with agraphia can result from damage to left ventral occipitotemporal cortices (Rapcsak & Beeson, 2004; Warrington & Shallice, 1980). Although a role for this region in graphemic processing, likely involving stored visual-word information, is not disputed, it remains to be seen if ventral occipitotemporal cortex is the only brain region that directly supports such processes. Also awaiting closer examination is the possibility (see for instance Damasio & Damasio, 1983), that large occipitotemporal lesions produce alexia by disrupting white matter pathways that run between the visual cortex and temporal regions which may be specialized for word-level orthographic processing (see below).

The second area implicated in single-word reading is the posterior portion of the middle temporal gyrus. Previous MEG (Halgren et al., 2002) and fMRI studies (Booth et al., 2002; Gaillard et al., 2001) have reported increased activity in this region during performance of a variety of tasks, including detection of semantically incongruous sentence endings, semantic comparisons, sentence reading and passage comprehension. Distinct cortical patches within this region were shown to be indispensable to oral reading of sentences in a significant proportion of patients undergoing electrocortical stimulation mapping (Roux et al., 2004). As in the case of the fusiform gyrus, however, hemodynamic data are inconclusive regarding the task-specific pattern of activation observed in this region. Most likely candidate operations, which neuronal populations located within this area may be involved in, include access to visual or phonological word forms (Hagoort, Indefrey, Brown et al., 1999; Fiebach, Friederici, Muller, & von Cramon, 2002; Hart et al., 2000) and semantic processing (Pugh et al., 1996; Mummery et al., 1998; Kuperberg et al., 2000).

The third area that has been linked to single word reading is the angular gyrus. This area has been implicated in memory for word form, or lexical processing, by lesion studies of individuals with pure alexia (Price, 2000; Friedman et al., 1993) and by fMRI and PET studies (Joubert et al., 2004; Hart, Kraut, Kremen, Soher, & Gordon, 2000; Howard et al., 1992; Price et al., 1994; Menard et al., 1996). Primary dysfunction of the left angular gyrus or impaired functional connectivity of this region with the other component areas of the posterior reading circuits has been hypothesized as a key precipitating factor in developmental dyslexia (Horwitz, Rumsey, & Donohue, 1998; Shaywitz et al., 1998; Eden & Zeffiro, 1998; Rumsey et al., 1999). Interestingly this area did not emerge as a reliable focus of hemodynamic activity in Turkletaub et al.'s (2002) meta-analysis nor by Fiez and Petersen's (1998) earlier meta-analysis involving many of the same studies. This discrepancy has been hypothesized to be due to the putative role of the angular gyrus in mediating access to semantic content that may be unnecessary for the simple recognition and pronunciation of high frequency words (Turkeltaub et al., 2002). However, this possibility cannot account for Joubert et al.'s (2004) finding of angular gyrus activation for high-frequency words and pseudowords but not for low-frequency words, each compared with a baseline condition of viewing and pronouncing strings of consonants. A simpler explanation for the discordance between functional brain imaging studies is that the majority of positive findings implicating the angular gyrus in reading were based on multiple task and group comparisons which are more likely to detect small changes in hemodynamic signals buried in the global patterns of task-specific activation. Further, it is possible (and this is supported by MSI data) that stimulus evoked neurophysiological activation in the angular gyrus is very transient, giving rise to very small increases in regional metabolic demands. This pattern of activity would produce a very small electromagnetic BOLD signal which may not be consistently detected with customary statistical thresholds used in most fMRI studies.

Activation peaks in the fourth area discussed in this section, namely the superior temporal gyrus, are consistently noted in PET and fMRI studies during single-word reading tasks (Pugh et al., 1996; Fiebach, Friederici, Müller, & von Cramon, 2002; Binder et al., 2003; Joseph, Noble, & Eden, 2001). Reading of unfamiliar letter strings (pseudowords and low-frequency words) is sometimes found to produce increased activity in this region relative to reading high-frequency words (Joubert et al., 2004; Fiez et al., 1999; Herbster et al., 1997). Moreover, reduced activity in the left posterior superior temporal gyrus, as detected by fMRI, PET, and MSI, is associated with poor performance on tasks requiring assembled phonology (i.e., sublexical processing) in impaired readers (Shaywitz et al., 1998, 2004; Simos et al., 2000b,c, 2002a). There is broad consensus among researchers that neurophysiological activity in this region is involved in the phonological analysis of print, i.e. in establishing the correspondence between print and sound. Incidentally, a similar pattern of activity is typically observed among skilled readers in the inferior frontal cortex but this activity takes place very late during single word processing—500–600 ms or more—to be considered an indispensable component of the brain mechanism involved in word recognition per se (Salmelin et al., 1996; Simos et al., 2001; 2005).

Like fMRI and PET, MSI has been employed successfully in the area of reading development, reading disability, and intervention. Studies that meet all the criteria for scientific merit outlined at the beginning of this section provide a highly consistent but rather basic view into the brain mechanism that supports reading. Regions that show increased levels of activation consistently, both within and across individuals include the following: the primary visual cortex, ventral and lateral temporo-occipital areas (association visual cortex), the posterior portion of the superior temporal gyrus extending posteriorly into the supramarginal gyrus (Wernicke's area), the posterior portion of the middle temporal gyrus, and the inferior frontal gyrus (Broca's area) (Salmelin et al., 1996; Tarkiainen et al., 1999; Helenius, Salmelin, Service, & Connolly, 1998; Simos et al., 2001, 2005; Papanicolaou et al., 2003). Neuromagnetic activity emanating from the angular gyrus is observed with much less consistency across studies and subjects in agreement with PET and fMRI results mentioned previously. In addition to the static activation maps provided by hemodynamic data, MSI provides spatiotemporal maps of neurophysiological activity associated with the presentation of a particular type of stimulus (e.g., a word or pseudoword) to answer the question of whether detectable activity is present or not in a particular brain region for a given subject and stimulus type. Detectable magnetic activity (usually measured every 4 ms after stimulus onset) can be quantified in terms of the strength of the recorded magnetic flux at each point in time, the estimated amplitude of intracellular electrical current in each region, and the duration of that current during stimulus processing. With the exception of primary visual cortex (and association cortices in young readers), where activation has been observed bilaterally for printed stimuli presented in the center of the visual field, activity in all other areas is stronger in the left hemisphere in the majority of fluent readers, who have never experienced difficulties in learning to read, regardless of age.

Findings from each of the neuroimaging methods converge in suggesting that tasks involving different aspects of reading are associated with increased activation in ventral occipito-temporal (or basal) regions, the posterior portion of the superior and middle temporal gyri extending into inferior parietal areas (supramarginal and angular gyri), and the inferior frontal lobe areas, primarily in the left hemisphere (Eden & Zeffiro, 1998; Papanicolaou et al., 2003; Rumsey et al., 1997; Shaywitz et al., 2000). There are inconsistencies involving the precise involvement of particular areas (Poeppel, 1996); but it is apparent that a set of areas is common across methods, activated to a different degree depending upon the modality and the reading task.

Approaches to addressing the problem of inconsistent results across functional imaging studies of reading have typically relied on data from a single source, namely the spatial profile of brain areas that show increased levels of activity during reading tasks, obtained using a particular functional imaging technique (e.g., Pugh et al., 1996; Price et al., 1996; Rumsey et al., 1997; Mechelli, Gorno-Tempini, & Price, 2003). Typically, functional activation maps are presented as group averages, which may obscure individual differences. Alternative examples of addressing these issues are presented below. These include the study of individual differences in the precise spatial extent and temporal course of activation, and direct tests of the manner in which different brain areas may operate together during reading tasks, depending on the type of word encountered. As described above, equally important is the combined use of invasive and non-invasive methods in order to ensure that active regions are indispensable (and not redundant) components of the reading mechanism (Simos et al., 1999, 2000a).

MSI ANALYSIS OF INDIVIDUAL DIFFERENCES

The presence of individual differences in the outline of the brain mechanisms that support various linguistic functions has received very little attention in neurolinguistics. On the other hand, it is a well-recognized phenomenon with serious implications for neurosurgical planning (Roux et al., 2003). Both lesion and electrocortical stimulation studies have documented often dramatic differences in the location of cortical regions that appear to be associated with the same type of linguistic deficit (e.g., Ojemann et al., 1988). These findings are often accounted for as reflecting deviations from the "typical" form of brain organization triggered by brain damage or pathology, given that these studies were conducted on patients with some form of neurological disease (e.g., stroke, epilepsy, or tumors). However, careful inspection of the results of functional brain imaging studies suggests the presence of considerable variability in the precise location of activated cortical patches during performance of the same language task (Seghier et al., 2004; Xiong et al., 2000).

A potential source of inter-subject differences in activation profiles is anatomical variability: individual differences in sulcal and gyral patterns and in the borders of cytoarchitectonic areas (Steinmetz, Fürst, & Freund, 1990, Thompson, Schwartz, Lin, Khan, & Toga, 1996). As a result the precise location of distinct cortical patches, that host specific neurophysiological processes in stereotaxic coordinates, may differ from person to person. Another potential source of individual variability may be differences in the location of activated cortical patches with respect to a particular anatomical landmark, such as a gyrus or sulcus. In view of these findings it is important to assess potential individual differences in the location of cortical regions that show elevated levels of neurophysiological activity. Moreover, it is important to establish in these studies that individual differences reflect stable features of the brain mechanism specialized for a particular function. To achieve that multiple measurements are required from each participant performing the same task (to establish reproducibility) as well as slightly different tasks that presumably involve the same function (to establish generalizability).

In a recently completed MSI study we attempted to establish the intra-subject reproducibility of spatiotemporal activation maps associated with word recognition in experienced readers. Word recognition was operationalized as the phenomenon that takes place when someone is attempting to determine whether a letter string is a (correctly spelled) real word in a lexical decision task. Pseudowords (none of which sounded like a real word) served as distractors (foils) with a relative probability of 50%. Stimuli were presented for 700 ms (in order to delay visual offset responses that could contaminate the event-related magnetic response) at the relatively fast rate (for a functional imaging study) of 1 word every 2 seconds. Under these conditions it is assumed that participants are less likely to employ a "decoding" strategy (i.e., to access an assembled phonological representation of each stimulus to facilitate lexical access). If, on the other hand, subjects engaged a decoding strategy, we predicted that activity in the posterior portion of the left superior temporal gyrus would take place relatively early, probably immediately following activity in visual association cortices.

Participants were 17 healthy, right-handed adults, native English speakers, without history of learning disability. Having set up conditions that would enable the identification of relatively invariable features of brain activation maps, the ultimate goal of the study was to examine the degree of inter-subject variability in time-dependent regional activity, which could bias group results, often reported in the literature. MEG recordings were made with a whole-head neuromagnetometer (Magnes 3600, 4-D Neuroimaging, Inc., San Diego, CA) consisting of 248 axial gradiometer coils. To establish the reliability of spatiotemporal activation maps each subject's data were split into eight consecutive "split-data sets" with a sufficient number of single-trial event-related fields (ERFs) in each data set to ensure adequate signal-to-noise ratio. ERFs associated with word and pseudoword stimuli were averaged separately, and only word-related data will be reported here. The intracranial generators of the observed ERFs (henceforth referred to as "activity sources") were modeled as single equivalent current dipoles and fitted at successive 4-ms intervals. Each activity source, accounting for the surface distribution of magnetic flux at each 4-ms time window, identified the geometric center of the cortical patch producing the dipolar magnetic flux distribution at that time point. The derived activation maps consisted of strings of temporally contiguous activity sources that were typically localized in the same anatomical region.

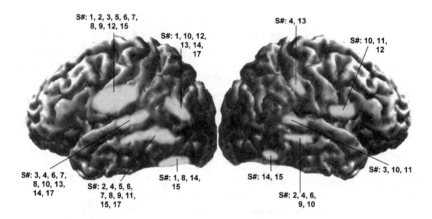

FIGURE 11.1 Brain regions in which activation was observed in the left and right hemispheres of each participant (indicated by subject #s, $N = 17$) in response to the word stimuli (targets) during the lexical decision task.

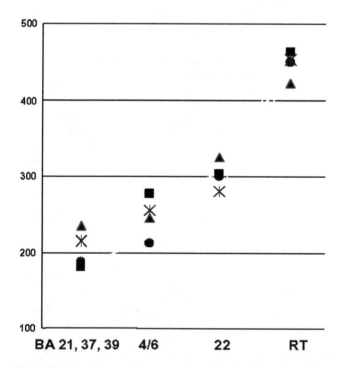

FIGURE 11.2 Temporal progression of neurophysiological activity associated with performance of the lexical decision task. Different symbols indicate onset latency estimates obtained for each of the eight consecutively acquired data sets in response to word stimuli.

Identification of patches of cortex that showed reliable neurophysiological activity across all eight data sets was performed blindly with the aid of a clustering algorithm (for details see Papanicolaou et al., 2004). This method resulted in a limited set of well-delineated active regions for each participant and hemisphere, which were then co-registered on the participants' own high resolution MRI scan.

Visual inspection of the resulting activation profiles showed that activity sources were consistently found in the following brain regions. All participants showed activation in motor and premotor cortex (BA 4 and 6, in either the left or the right hemisphere, or both), and in the posterior portion of the superior temporal gyrus (BA 22) in the left hemisphere. There was considerable individual variability in the precise location of the remaining activity sources which were noted predominantly in the left hemisphere. Eleven participants showed activity sources in the posterior portion of the middle temporal gyrus (BA 21), four in ventral occipitotemporal cortex (ventral BA 37), and six in lateral occipitotemporal cortices (lateral BA 37) and the angular gyrus (BA 39 [some participants displayed sources in more than one posterior temporal or inferior parietal location, as shown in Figure 11.1]). In all cases, there was a clear temporal progression of activation from BA 37/39/21 to BA 4/6 and finally to BA 22. As shown in Figure 2, the train of regional activity took place, on average, over 450 ms after stimulus onset culminating in the participant's behavioral response, which occurred between 530 and 580 ms across the eight consecutively acquired data sets.

These data suggest that there may be important individual differences in the spatial extent of brain activation during word reading tasks. Such individual differences may in part account for discrepancies in activation observed in parietal-occipital and temporal-occipital areas across different brain imaging studies during the performance of single-word reading tasks, as described above (e.g., Joubert et al., 2004; Turkletaub et al., 2002; Horwitz et al., 1998). Our findings also demonstrate a systematic temporal sequence of regional activity where, as predicted, activity in BA 22 took place later than activity in motor/premotor cortices. Although, it is still possible that activity in BA 22 was in fact critically involved in the word recognition process, we believe the data are more consistent with a secondary role of this region, and perhaps also of the phonological decoding operation, in this task, in skilled readers.

The nature of the lexical decision task we used did not permit conclusions on the nature of the component process(es) that take(s) place in posterior temporal and inferior parietal cortices (where significant individual variability was noted). Preliminary data were subsequently obtained from two of the participants (Subjects 1 & 2) who were tested on a word-likeness decision task: they were presented with non-words which either contained consonant combinations that are encountered in the same position in English (e.g. fi/k) or not (e.g., fi/v). The results revealed spatiotemporal activation maps that were very similar to the ones obtained during performance of the lexical decision task (see Figure 3, which displays combined data for the two subjects). The most interesting finding was that the same posterior temporal region was active in each subject at the same latency as before: Subject 1 showed activity sources in the same patch of the ventral portion of BA 37 (in the posterior portion of the fusiform gyrus between 140 and 180 ms after stimulus onset),

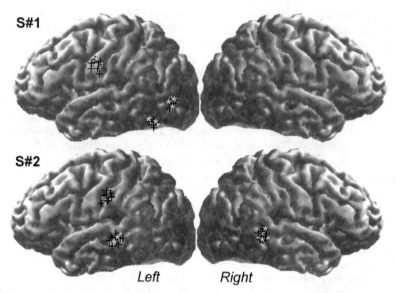

FIGURE 11.3   Location of clusters of magnetic activity sources obtained during performance of a lexical decision task *(word stimuli; stars)* and a word-likeness decision task *(orthographically plausible pseudowords; crosses)*.

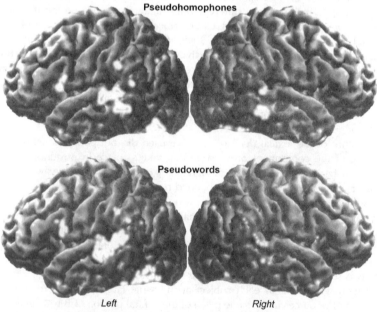

FIGURE 11.4   Profiles of brain activity preceding pronunciation of two types of print: pseudowords *(like yote)* and pseudohomophones *(like burth)*.

while Subject 2 had activity sources in the posterior portion of BA 21 in the vicinity of the superior temporal sulcus (between 280 and 350 ms—incidentally the mean reaction times for Subject 2 were 160 ms longer than the mean RTs for Subject 1). These sources were noted consistently in 12 different data sets obtained on three testing sessions separated by one week.

Taken together these group and individual data further support the notion that there are significant individual differences in at least some components of the brain mechanism involved in lexical and sublexical processing. Perception of pseudo-words that were either orthographically consistent or inconsistent with English words in the word likeness task resulted in highly reliable activity in either the posterior portion of BA 37 (fusiform gyrus and lateral occipitotemporal cortex–S#1) or the posterior portion of BA 21 (superior temporal sulcus–S#2). The preliminary nature of the data does not allow examination of any subtler differences between the two types of stimuli across studies (words versus orthographically plausible pseudowords) at present. It would be interesting to examine if a dissociation might surface between different measures of neurophysiological activity, whereby pseu-dowords are associated with increased duration of activity (indicating prolonged search among several orthographically similar sublexical units) and words produce increased strength of instantaneous activity (indicating recruitment of a greater population of neurons upon accessing a stored visual-lexical representation).

We next attempted to determine whether these individual differences may be related to the manner in which the pseudowords are processed, that is, as assembled or addressed phonology (Simos et al., 2002b). According to dual-process models of reading, the brain mechanism for reading words that require assembled phonology (i.e., involving sublexical processing), in experienced readers, is different from the mechanism for reading words that do not. If distinct regions exist for addressed phonology (i.e., requiring whole-word processing), they may be involved in lexical access, which, according to dual route models, mediate pronunciation of irregular, or exception, words. We measured reaction time of pronunciation in order to determine whether individual differences previously observed in posterior temporal and inferior parietal regions would be associated with the onset latency and speed of processing particular word types. The second question we addressed is whether reading mean-ingful and meaningless words (pseudowords) is mediated by different brain structures.

To address these question, we obtained MSI-derived brain activation profiles dur-ing reading of three types of print: exception words (relying more on addressed phonology and having meaning), pseudohomophones (requiring assembled phonol-ogy and also having meaning), and pseudowords (requiring assembled phonology but having no meaning). The prediction was that activity in posterior temporal and inferior parietal regions known to be involved in reading would differentiate process-ing of a) meaningful and meaningless items and b) letter strings that require assem-bled phonology and those that do not.

The spatiotemporal activation profiles associated with reading aloud each of the three different types of print displayed a number of common features: First, the regular progression of activation from occipital to ventral occipito-temporal areas within the first 150–200 ms after stimulus onset; second, the subsequent "spread" of activation to postero-lateral temporal regions; and third, the strong left hemisphere predominance in the degree of activation in both ventral occipito-temporal and postero-lateral temporal regions. While all subjects showed activity in the posterior portion of the left superior temporal gyrus (BA 22) in all three conditions, a prominent feature of the activation profile associated with reading aloud both exception words and pseudohomophones involved the posterior middle temporal gyrus (BA 21) and mesial temporal regions (in 14/16 participants). However, reading aloud pseudowords involved very sparse activity in these regions. Thus, as described above based on previous MSI studies, BA 21 shows reduced neurophysiological activity as well as reduced regional cerebral blood flow during pseudoword as compared to real word reading (see also Hagoort et al., 1999). Moreover, it appears that the left BA 21 plays a special role in exception word reading. The significant correlation between onset of activity in the left BA 21 and naming latency of exception words indicated that the earlier the engagement of this area, following word presentation, the faster the pronunciation of the printed stimuli. The fact that activity in BA 21 did not predict pronunciation speed for pseudo-homophones (or pseudowords) suggests that engagement of this area may be a byproduct of phonological access achieved through the assembled route for non-words that sound like real words. Involvement of BA 21 in lexical/semantic analysis is suggested by several independent sources of evidence, including hemodynamic functional imaging investigations (Hart et al., 2000; Mummery et al., 1998; Kuperberg et al., 2000) and lesion studies (Damasio & Damasio, 1989).

But what may the role of the left BA 22 in single word reading given that it is associated with both hemodynamic and neuromagnetic activity during performance of a variety of reading tasks (reading aloud and silent reading) and stimuli (words, pseudowords)? In MSI studies of oral reading, activity in this region takes place relatively early during stimulus processing (between 250–500 ms after stimulus onset), prior to activity in inferior frontal cortex. While the degree and duration of activity in this region may be higher for pseudowords than for real words (Wydell et al., 2003), correlational data provide further support for the notion that this activity is more closely involved in the pronunciation of unfamiliar letter strings. It has been noted that the onset latency of neuromagnetic activity in BA 22 accounts for a significant amount of the variability in reading latencies of pseudowords and pseudohomophones (Simos et al., 2002b) No such relation was found for real words with irregular orthographies. These findings were corroborated directly by the results of an electrocortical stimulation study (Simos et al., 2000a), demonstrating that transient inactivation of cortex in the left BA 22 disrupted the ability to pronounce pseudowords, but did not affect reading aloud of irregular words.

Taken together, our data demonstrate that, at least in experienced readers, the posterior portion of BA 22, although routinely activated during reading aloud of all types of pronounceable letter strings, is not an indispensable or specialized component of the mechanism for reading aloud words that do not contain common print-to-sound correspondences. An alternative mechanism that could support access to phonological representations for pronouncing real words may involve engagement of the middle temporal gyrus.

CONCLUSIONS

According to a popular theory of word recognition, access to word-like representations of printed stimuli relies heavily upon a ventral circuit, consisting primarily of ventral temporo-occipital regions and the posterior portion of the middle temporal gyrus, when the stimulus is familiar and task demands are appropriate (Pugh et al., 2001). Notably, activity in ventral association areas takes place early during reading (Breier et al., 1998, 1999; Simos et al., 2001). Conversely, the mechanism that supports reading relies more heavily upon a dorsal system (consisting of Wernicke's area and the angular gyrus) and an anterior (frontal) component (Broca's area), when the stimulus is novel or low frequency (Pugh et al., 2001). This functional differentiation within the brain mechanism for reading corresponds to some extent to the two routes of classical dual route theory (Coltheart, Curtis, Atkins, & Haller, 1993). The two posterior systems (temporoparietal and occipitotemporal) appear to parallel the two systems proposed by Logan (Logan, 1997) as critical for the development of skilled, automatic reading. One system involves word analysis, operates on individual units of words such as phonemes, requires attentional resources and processes relatively slowly. It is reasonable to propose that this system involves the temporo-parietal region.

Perhaps of even greater importance to skilled reading is the second system proposed by Logan, a system that operates on the whole word (word form), an obligatory system that does not require attention and one which processes very rapidly. This system has historical roots that were also described by Dejerine (Dejerine 1892), a system located in another posterior brain region, the occipito-temporal area. There is continuing dispute regarding the identify of the brain regions that serve as the anatomical components of this system. On the basis of lesion data and the relative sequence of activity within the brain mechanism for single-word reading, BA 37 (primarily its ventral aspect but possibly extending into the lateral surface of the occipito-temporal junction) and BA 21 (again in the vicinity of the occipito-temporal junction) appear as likely candidates. The MSI studies reported here suggest, first, that there is significant yet systematic inter-subject variability in reading both words and pseudowords. Spatial normalization and averaging techniques used in most group studies may therefore mask important individual differences. Individual variability may bias group results which in turn may account for discrepancies reported for activity in temporal and parietal areas between studies using similar methodologies. Our data suggest that individual variability associated with reading real words and pseudowords may depend both on whether the word has inherent meaning for the reader and whether the word is recognized by way of addressed or assembled phonology.

Therefore, to be successful in addressing issues related to the general outline of the brain mechanism for reading recounted above, future studies should closely assess individual profiles of activity in a variety of reading tasks, examine multiple measures of regional brain activity (preferably assessing both the strength and duration of activity), and establish patterns of correlations between various parameters of brain activation and behavioral performance. The ultimate goal of future research should be to describe how different activated brain areas may operate together during reading tasks, and the degree and type of contribution of each area to reading performance.

ACKNOWLEDGMENTS

The work described in this manuscript was supported by NICHD Grant HD38346 to Dr. Papanicolaou and NSF Grant REC-9979968 to Drs. Fletcher and Papanicolaou.

REFERENCES

Bentin, S. (1989). Electrophysiological studies of visual word perception, lexical organization, and semantic processing: a tutorial review. *Language and Speech, 32,* 205–220.

Billingsley-Marshall, R. L., Simos, P. G., & Papanicolaou, A. C. (2004). Reliability and validity of functional neuroimaging techniques for identifying language-critical areas in children and adults. *Developmental Neuropsychology, 26,* 541–563.

Binder, J. R., McKiernan, K. A., Parsons, M. E., Westbury, C. F., Possing, E. T., Kaufman, J. N., et al. (2003). Neural correlates of lexical access during visual word recognition. *Journal of Cognitive Neuroscience, 15,* 372–393.

Booth, J. R., Burman, D. D., Meyer, J. R., Gitelman, D. R., Parrish, T. B., & Mesulam, M. M. (2003). Modality independence of word comprehension. *Human Brain Mapping, 16,* 251–261.

Breier, J. I., Simos, P. G., Papanicolaou, A. C., Zouridakis, G., Wilmore, L. J., Wheless, J. W., et al. (1999). Language dominance determined by magnetic source imaging: A comparison with the Wada Procedure. *Neurology, 22,* 938–945.

Breier, J. I., Simos, P. G., Wheless, J. W., Constantinou, J. E. C., & Papanicolaou, A. C. (2001). Hemispheric language dominance in children determined by magnetic source imaging. *Journal of Child Neurology, 16,* 124–130.

Cohen, L., Dehaene, S., Naccache, L., Lehericy, S., Dehaene-Lambertz, G., Henaff, M. A., et al. (2000). The visual word form area: spatial and temporal characterization of an initial stage of reading in normal subjects and posterior split-brain patients. *Brain, 123,* 291–307.

Cohen, L., Lehericy, S., Chochon, F., Lemer, C., Rivaud, S., Dehaene, S. (2002). Language-specific tuning of visual cortex? Functional properties of the visual word form area. *Brain, 125,* 1054–1069.

Coltheart, M., Curtis, B., Atkins, P., & Haller, M. (1993). Models of reading aloud: dual-route and parallel-distributed-processing approaches. *Psychological Review, 100,* 589–608.

Damasio H. & Damasio, A. (1983). The anatomic basis of pure alexia. *Neurology, 33,* 1573–1583.

Damasio, H. & Damasio, A. (1989). *Lesion Analysis in Neuropsychology.* New York: Oxford University Press.

Dejerine, J. (1892). Sur un cas de ceci verbale avec agraphie, suivi d'autopsie. *Comptes Rendus Hebdomadaires des Séances moirés Society of Biologie, 9th Séries, 3,* 197–201.

Dronkers, N. F., Wilkins, D. P., Van Valin, R. D., Jr, Redfern, B. B., & Jaeger, J. J. (2004). Lesion analysis of the brain areas involved in language comprehension. *Cognition, 92,* 145–177.

Eden, G. F. & Zeffiro, T. A. (1998). Neural systems affected in developmental dyslexia revealed by functional neuroimaging. *Neuron, 21,* 279–282.

Epstein, C. M., Meador, K. J., Loring, D. W., Wright, R. J., Weissman, J. D., Sheppard, S., et al. (1999). Localization and characterization of speech arrest during transcranial magnetic stimulation. *Clinical Neurophysiology, 110,* 1073–1079.

Epstein, C. M., Woodard, J. L., Stringer, A. Y., Bakay, R. A., Henry, T. R., Pennell, P. B., et al. (2000). Repetitive transcranial magnetic stimulation does not replicate the Wada test. *Neurology, 55,* 1025–1027.

Fiebach, C. J., Friederici, A. D., Muller, K., & von Cramon, D. Y. (2002). fMRI evidence for dual routes to the mental lexicon in visual word recognition. *Journal of Cognitive Neuroscience, 14,* 11–23.

Fiez, J. A., Balota, D. A., Raichle, M. E., & Petersen, S. E. (1999). Effects of lexicality, frequency, and spelling-to-sound consistency on the functional neuroanatomy of reading. *Neuron, 24,* 205–218.

Fiez, J. A. & Petersen, S. E. (1998). Neuroimaging studies of word reading. *Proceedings of the National Academy of Science, 95,* 914–921.

FitzGerald, D. B., Cosgrove, G. R., Ronner, S., Jiang, H., Buchbinder, B. R., Belliveau, J. W., et al. (1997). Location of language in the cortex: a comparison between functional MR imaging and electrocortical stimulation. *American Journal of Neuroradiology, 18,* 1529–1539.

Friedman, R. B., Beeman, M., Lott, S. N., Link, K., Grafman, J., & Robinson, S. (1993). Modality-specific phonological alexia. *Cognitive Neuropsychology, 10,* 549–568.

Gaillard, W. D., Pugliese, M., Grandin, C. B., Braniecki, S. H., Kondapaneni, P., Hunter, K., et al. (2001). Cortical localization of reading in normal children: an fMRI language study. *Neurology, 57,* 47–54.

Hagoort, P., Indefrey, P., Brown, C., Herzog, H., Steinmetz, H., & Seitz, R. J. (1999). The neural circuitry involved in the reading of German words and pseudowords: A PET study. *Journal of Cognitive Neuroscience, 11,* 383–398.

Halgren, E., Dhond, R. P., Christensen, N., Van Petten, C., Marinkovic, K., Lewine, J. D., et al. (2002). N400-like magnetoencephalography responses modulated by semantic context, word frequency, and lexical class in sentences. *NeuroImage, 17,* 1101–1116.

Hart, J., Jr, Kraut, M. A., Kremen, S., Soher, B., & Gordon, B. (2000). Neural substrates of orthographic lexical access as demonstrated by functional brain imaging. *Neuropsychiatry and Neuropsychology Behavioral Neurology, 13,* 1–7.

Helenius, P., Salmelin, R., Service, E., & Connolly, J. F. (1998). Distinct time courses of word and context comprehension in the left temporal cortex. *Brain, 121,* 1133–1142.

Herbster, A. N., Mintum, M. A., Nebes, R. D., & Becker, J. T. (1997). Regional cerebral blood flow during word and nonword reading. *Human Brain Mapping, 5,* 84–92.

Horwitz, B., Rumsey, J. M., & Donohue, B. C. (1998). Functional connectivity of the angular gyrus in normal reading and dyslexia. *Proceedings of the National Academy of Science, USA, 95,* 8939–8944.

Howard, D., Patterson, K., Wise, R., Brown, W. D., Friston, K., Weiller, C., et al. (1992). The cortical localization of the lexicons. Positron emission tomography evidence. *Brain, 115,* 1769–1782.

Jahanshahi, M. & Rothwell, J. (2000). Transcranial magnetic stimulation studies of cognition: an emerging field. *Experimental Brain Research, 131,* 1–9.

Jobard, G., Crivello, F., & Tzourio-Mazoyer, N. (2003). Evaluation of the dual route theory of reading: a metanalysis of 35 neuroimaging studies. *NeuroImage, 20,* 693–712.

Joseph, J., Noble, K., & Eden, G. (2001). The neurobiological basis of reading. *Journal of Learning Disabilities, 34,* 566–579.

Joubert, S., Beauregard, M., Walter, N., Bourgouin, P., Beaudoin, G., Leroux, J. M., et al. (2004). Neural correlates of lexical and sublexical processes in reading. *Brain and Language, 89,* 9–20.

Kuperberg, G. R., McGuire, P. K., Bullmore, E. T., Brammer, M. J., Rabe-Hesketh, S., Wright, I. C., et al. (2000). Common and distinct neural substrates for pragmatic, semantic, and syntactic processing of spoken sentences: An fMRI study. *Journal of Cognitive Neuroscience, 12,* 321–341.

Lavidor, M., & Walsh, V. (2003). A magnetic stimulation examination of orthographic neighborhood effects in visual word recognition. *Journal of Cognitive Neuroscience, 15,* 354–363.

Leff, A. P., Scott, S. K., Rothwell, J. C., & Wise, R. J. (2001). The planning and guiding of reading saccades: a repetitive transcranial magnetic stimulation study. *Cerebral Cortex, 11,* 918–923.

Liederman, J., McGraw Fisher, J., Schulz, M., Maxwell, C., Theoret, H., & Pascual-Leone, A. (2003). The role of motion direction selective extrastriate regions in reading: a transcranial magnetic stimulation study. *Brain and Language, 85,* 140–155.

Logan, G. (1997). Automaticity and reading: perspectives from the instance theory of automatization. *Reading and Writing Quarterly: Overcoming Learning Disabilities, 13,* 123–146.

Mechelli, A., Gorno-Tempini, M. L., & Price, C. J. (2003). Neuroimaging studies of word and pseudoword reading: consistencies, inconsistencies, and limitations. *Journal of Cognitive Neuroscience, 15,* 260–271.

Meister, I. G., Boroojerdi, B., Foltys, H., Sparing, R., Huber, W., & Topper, R. (2003). Motor cortex hand area and speech: implications for the development of language. *Neuropsychologia, 41,* 401–406.

Menard, M. T., Kosslyn, S. M., Thompson, W. L., Alpert, N. M., & Rauch, S. L. Encoding words and pictures: a positron emission tomography study. *Neuropsychologia, 34,* 185–194.

Mottaghy, F. M., Gangitano, M., Krause, B. J., & Pascual-Leone, A. (2003). Chronometry of pariet al and prefrontal activations in verbal working memory revealed by transcranial magnetic stimulation. *NeuroImage, 18,* 565–575.

Mummery, C. J., Patterson, K., Hodges, J. R., & Price, C. J. (1998). Functional neuroanatomy of the semantic system: divisible by what? *Journal of Cognitive Neuroscience, 10,* 766–777.

Ojemann. G. A. (2003). The neurobiology of language and verbal memory: observations from awake neurosurgery. *International Journal of Psychophysiology, 48,* 141–146.

Ojemann, G. A., Creutzfeldt, O., Lettich, E., & Haglund, M. M. (1988). Neuronal activity in human lateral temporal cortex related to short-term verbal memory, naming and reading. *Brain, 111,* 1383–1403.

Papanicolaou, A. C., Pugh, K. C., Simos, P. G., & Mencl, W. E. (2004). Functional brain imaging: An introduction to concepts and applications. In P. McCardle and V. Chhabra (Eds) *The Voice of Evidence: Bringing Research to Classroom Educators.*

Papanicolaou, A. C., Simos, P. G., Breier, J. I., Fletcher, J. M., Foorman, B. R., Francis, D., et al. (2003). Brain mechanisms for reading in children with and without dyslexia: a review of studies of normal development and plasticity. *Developmental Neuropsychology, 24,* 593–612.

Papanicolaou, A. C., Simos, P. G., Breier, J. I., Wheless, J. W., Mancias, P., Baumgartner, J. E., et al. (2001). Brain plasticity for sensory and linguistic functions: A functional imaging study using MEG with children and young adults. *Journal of Child Neurology, 16,* 241–252.

Papanicolaou, A. C., Simos, P. G., Castillo, E. M., Breier, J. I., Sarkari, S., Pataraia, E., et al. (2004). Magnetocephalography: a noninvasive alternative to the Wada procedure. *Journal of Neurosurgery, 100,* 867–876.

Pataraia, E., Simos, P. G., Castillo, E. M., Billingsley-Marshall, R. L., McGregor, A. L., Breier, J. I., et al. (2004). Reorganization of language-specific cortex in patients with lesions or mesial temporal epilepsy. *Neurology, 63,* 1825–1832.

Paulesu, E., Frith, U., Snowling, M., Gallagher, A., Morton, J., Frackowiak, R. S., et al. (1996). Is developmental dyslexia a disconnection syndrome? Evidence from PET scanning. *Brain, 119,* 143–157.

Plaut, D., McClelland, J., Seidenberg, M., & Patterson, K. (1996). Understanding normal and impaired word reading: computational principles in quasi-regular domains. *Psychological Review, 103,* 56–115.

Poeppel, D. (1996). A critical review of PET studies of phonological processing. *Brain and Language, 55,* 317–351.

Price, C. J. (2000). The anatomy of language: contributions from functional neuroimaging. *Journal of Anatomy, 197,* 335–359.

Price, C. J., Gorno-Tempini, M. L., Graham, K. S., Biggio, N., Mechelli, A., Patterson, K., et al. (2003). Normal and pathological reading: converging data from lesion and imaging studies. *Neuroimage, 20,* S30–41.

Price, C. J., Wise, R. J., Watson, J. D., Patterson, K., Howard, D., & Frackowiak, R. S. (1994). Brain activity during reading. The effects of exposure duration and task. *Brain, 117,* 1255–1269.

Pugh, K. R., Mencl, W. E., Jenner, A. R., Katz, L., Frost, S. J., Lee, J. R., et al. (2001). Neurobiological studies of reading and reading disability. *Journal of Communication Disorders, 34,* 479–492.

Pugh, K. R., Shaywitz, B. A., Shaywitz, S. E., Constable, R. T., Skudlarski, P., Fulbright, R. K., et al. (1996). Cerebral organization of component processes in reading. *Brain, 119,* 1221–1238.

Rapcsak, S. Z. & Beeson, P. M. (2004). The role of left posterior inferior temporal cortex in spelling. *Neurology, 62,* 2221–2229.

Roux, F. E., Boulanouar, K., Lotterie, J. A., Mejdoubi, M., LeSage, J. P., & Berry, I. (2003). Language functional magnetic resonance imaging in preoperative assessment of language areas: correlation with direct cortical stimulation. *Neurosurgery, 52,* 1335–1345.

Roux, F. E., Lubrano, V., Lauwers-Cances, V., Tremoulet, M., Mascott, C. R., & Demonet, J. F. (2004). Intra-operative mapping of cortical areas involved in reading in mono- and bilingual patients. *Brain, 127,* 1796–1810.

Rumsey, J. M., Horwitz, B., Donohue, B. C., Nace, K. L., Maisog, J. M., & Andreason, P. (1999). A functional lesion in developmental dyslexia: left angular gyral blood flow predicts severity. *Brain and Language, 70,* 187–204.

Rutten, G. J., Ramsey, N. F., van Rijen, P. C., Noordmans, H. J., & van Veelen, C. W. (2002). Development of a functional magnetic resonance imaging protocol for intraoperative localization of critical temporoparietal language areas. *Annals of Neurology, 51,* 350–360.

Salmelin, R., Service, E., Kiesila, P., Uutela, K., & Salonen, O. (1996). Impaired visual word processing in dyslexia revealed with magnetoencephalography. *Annals of Neurology, 40,* 157–162.

Seghier, M. L., Lazeyras, F., Pegna, A. J., Annoni, J. M., Zimine, I., Mayer, E., et al. (2004). Variability of fMRI activation during a phonological and semantic language task in healthy subjects. *Human Brain Mapping, 23,* 140–155.

Shaywitz, B. A., Shaywitz, S. E., Blachman, B. A., Pugh, K. R., Fulbright, R. K., Skudlarski, P., et al. (2004). Development of left occipitotemporal systems for skilled reading in children after a phonologically- based intervention. *Biological Psychiatry, 55,* 926–933.

Shaywitz, S. E., Shaywitz, B. A., Pugh, K. R., Fulbright, R. K., Constable, R. T., Mencl, W. E., et al. (1998). Functional disruption in the organization of the brain for reading in dyslexia. *Proceedings of the National Academy of Science USA, 95,* 2636–2641.

Simos, P. G., Breier, J. I., Fletcher, J. M., Bergman, E., & Papanicolaou, A. C. (2000c). Cerebral mechanisms involved in word reading in dyslexic children: A Magnetic Source Imaging approach. *Cerebral Cortex, 10,* 809–816.

Simos, P. G., Breier, J. I., Fletcher, J. M., Foorman, B. R., Castillo, E. M., & Papanicolaou, A. C. (2002b). Brain mechanisms for reading words and pseudowords: An integrated approach. *Cerebral Cortex, 12,* 297–305.

Simos, P. G., Breier, J. I., Fletcher, J. M., Foorman, B. R., Mouzaki, A., & Papanicolaou, A. C. (2001). Age-related changes in regional brain activation during phonological decoding and printed word recognition. *Developmental Neuropsychology, 19,* 191–210.

Simos, P. G., Breier, J. I., Wheless, J. W., Maggio, W. W., Fletcher, J. M., Castillo, E. M., et al. (2000a). Brain mechanisms for reading: the role of the superior temporal gyrus in word and pseudoword naming. *Neuroreport, 11,* 2443–2447.

Simos, P. G., Fletcher, J. M., Bergman, E., Breier, J. I., Foorman, B. R., Castillo, E. M., et al. (2002a). Dyslexia-specific brain activation profile become normal following successful remedial training. *Neurology, 58,* 1203–1213.

Simos, P. G., Fletcher, J. M., Sarkari, S., Billingsley-Marshall, R. L., Francis, D. J., Castillo, E. M., et al. (2005). Early development of neurophysiological processes involved in normal reading and reading disability. *Neuropsychology, 19,* 787–798.

Simos, P. G., Papanicolaou, A. C., Breier, J. I., Fletcher, J. M., Foorman, B. R., Bergman, E., et al. (2000b). Brain activation profiles in dyslexic children during nonword reading: A magnetic source imaging study. *Neuroscience Letters, 290,* 61–65.

Simos, P. G., Papanicolaou, A. C., Breier, J. I., Wheless, J. W., Constantinou, J. E., Gormley, W. B., et al. (1999). Localization of language-specific cortex by using magnetic source imaging and electrical stimulation mapping. *Journal of Neurosurgery, 91,* 787–796.

Steinmetz, H., Fürst, G., & Freund, H. J. (1990). Variation of perisylvian and calcarine anatomic landmarks within stereotaxic proportional coordinates. *American Journal of Neuroradiology, 11,* 1123–1130.

Steinmetz, H. & Seitz, R. J. (1991). Functional anatomy of language processing: neuroimaging and the problem of individual variability. *Neuropsychologia, 29,* 1149–1161.

Stewart, L., Meyer, B., Frith, U., & Rothwell, J. (2001). Left posterior BA37 is involved in object recognition: a TMS study. *Neuropsychologia, 39,* 1–6.

Tarkiainen, A., Helenius, P., Hansen, P. C., Cornelissen, P. L., & Salmelin, R. (1999). Dynamics of letter string perception in the human occipitotemporal cortex. *Brain, 122,* 2119–2132.

Thompson, P. M., Schwartz, C., Lin, R. T., Khan, A. A., & Toga, A. W. (1996). Three-dimensional statistical analysis of sulcal variability in the human brain. *Journal of Neuroscience, 16,* 4261–4274.

Turkeltaub, P. E., Eden, G. F., Jones, K. M., & Zeffiro, T. A. (2002). Meta-analysis of the functional neuroanatomy of single-word reading: method and validation. *Neuroimage, 16,* 765–780.

Warrington, E. K. & Shallice, T. (1980). Word-form dyslexia. *Brain, 103,* 99–112.

Wassermann, E. M. (2002). Variation in the response to transcranial magnetic brain stimulation in the general population. *Clinical Neurophysiology, 113,* 1165–1171.

Wydell, T. N., Vuorinen, T., Helenius, P., & Salmelin, R. (2003). Neural correlates of letter-string length and lexicality during reading in a regular orthography. *Journal of Cognitive Neuroscience, 15,* 1052–1062.

Xiong, J., Rao, S., Jerabek, P., Zamarippa, F., Woldorff, M., Lancaster, J., et al. (2000). Intersubject variability in cortical activations during a complex language task. *NeuroImage, 12,* 326–339.

CHAPTER TWELVE

Genetic and Environmental Influences on Word-Reading Skills

Richard K. Olson
University of Colorado, Boulder

Deficits in reading isolated words accurately and fluently are highly correlated with word-reading deficits in context. These deficits constrain the comprehension of text (Perfetti, 1985; Shankweiler, 1989), and they are often considered to be the hallmark of developmental dyslexia. In 1982, investigators in the Colorado Learning Disabilities Research Center (CLDRC) initiated a study of identical and fraternal twins to advance our understanding of the genetic and environmental etiology of reading disabilities, including isolated word reading and related skills. In 1999, the CLDRC joined an international collaboration with investigators in Australia (Brian Byrne) and Scandinavia (Stefan Samuelsson) on a longitudinal twin study of individual differences in preliteracy and early literacy development beginning in preschool. In this chapter I will provide an overview of some of the methods, major results, and future directions for these two ongoing research programs. I want to emphasize that research in the CLDRC has been and continues to be a highly collaborative effort across our different laboratories. I serve as the Center Director in the Institute for Behavioral Genetics at the University of Colorado. The current co-principle investigators in the CLDRC include, Brian Byrne (University of New England), Janice Keenan and Bruce Pennington (University of Denver), Shelley Smith (University of Nebraska), and John DeFvies, Sally Wadsworth and Erik Willcutt and Barbava Wise (University of Colorado).

The chapter is divided into 4 main sections. The first section presents the background for our measures of component word-reading and language skills that are being studied in a large school-age twin sample. The second section presents the methods and major results of our behavior-genetic analyses with this sample that reveal average genetic, shared environment, and non-shared environmental influences on extreme group deficits in the different skills, and on the degree to which genetic and environmental influences on these group deficits are shared between the skills. The third section of the chapter summarizes results from our studies of genetic and environmental influences on individual differences across the entire normal range of word reading ability, including preliminary results from our international longitudinal study of twins in preschool through the second grade. The last section of the chapter reviews preliminary evidence that genetic and environmental influences on reading comprehension and higher-level language skills are partly independent from those that influence individual differences in word reading.

MEASURES OF WORD READING AND RELATED SKILLS

When we began our studies of word reading and related skills in twins, there was increasing evidence from non-genetic research for two partly independent component processes in word identification. This evidence came both from the study of individual differences among normal readers (Baron, 1979), and among children with reading disabilities (Boder, 1973; Mitterer, 1982). The basic idea was that word reading in English involved a *phonological decoding* component that supported sounding out and blending the most common grapheme-phoneme correspondences, and a second *orthographic coding* component skill that supported the rapid recognition of whole-word spelling patterns for exception words such as "said" and "yacht", as well as for regular words that could be read "automatically" as whole words after repeated exposure (Laberge & Samuels, 1974). Baron identified individual differences among children with normal levels of reading ability in their relative strength for these two skills, while Boder and Mitterer described subtypes of children with word-reading difficulties that were uniquely deficient in either phonological decoding or exception word reading. Similar distinctions were concurrently being made between phonological and surface forms of acquired dyslexia.

To explore these component word-reading processes in our research with twins, we developed two computer-based measures of phonological decoding, one involving the timed oral reading of isolated nonwords (e.g., storch, tegwop, framble), the other requiring subjects to silently select on the computer one of three letter strings (e.g., coam-baim-goam) that would sound like a common English word (e.g., coam = comb), as quickly as possible. The second component word-reading skill, orthographic coding, was also assessed in two different tasks on the computer: The first "orthographic choice" task had subjects quickly select one of two phonologically identical letter strings that spelled a common word (i.e., rain rane) (Olson, Kliegl, Davidson, & Foltz, 1985). In a second "homophone-choice" task, a spoken sentence such as "Which is a fruit?" was presented and subjects selected the correct homophone (i.e., pair pear) as quickly as possible (see Olson, Forsberg, Wise, & Rack, 1994, for a full description of the measures). Factor analyses confirmed that the "homophone choice" and "orthographic choice" measures loaded on a separate factor from one that included the two phonological decoding measures, though the factors were significantly correlated in oblique rotation (Olson, Forsberg, & Wise,

1994). In many of our analyses we have combined the orthographic-choice and homophone-choice z scores to form an orthographic coding composite score or latent trait, and the oral and silent phonological decoding measures' z scores to form a phonological decoding composite or latent trait.

Early evidence from Liberman et al. (1977) suggested that phonological-decoding deficits in reading were largely due to a language deficit in the awareness of individual phonemes in speech that are important for learning the relations between letter patterns and sound. Therefore we developed two measures of *phoneme awareness* that involved the isolation and manipulation of phonemes in oral language. One was a "Pig Latin" game that required moving the initial consonant to the end of each spoken target word and adding the /ay/ sound. The other was a measure of "phoneme deletion" based on earlier research by Bruce (1964). This task required the deletion of an initial, medial, or final phoneme in a spoken word or nonword, and pronunciation of the result within a six second time limit.

The causal link between deficits in phoneme awareness, phonological decoding and word reading has been supported in two ways. One is that when older children with reading disability are matched on raw scores with younger children without reading disability on standard measures of word recognition, most of the older children with reading disability perform significantly worse on measures of phoneme awareness and phonological decoding (Conors & Olson, 1990; Hulslander & Olson, submitted; Olson, 1985; Rack, Snowing, & Olson, 1992; Snowling, 1981). In our most recent analysis of these group deficits in phoneme awareness and phonological decoding, Hulslander and Olson found that the older group with word-reading disabilities was about .6 to .7 standard deviations below that of the reading-level-matched younger group of normally developing readers. In other words, both phoneme awareness and phonological decoding in the older group with word-reading disabilities were significantly lower than expected from their absolute level of word-reading ability.

The second line of evidence for the influence of phonological processing deficits on word-reading disabilities has come from training studies. Preschool training in phonological awareness alone has a significant but small effect on early reading development (Lundberg, Frost, & Peterson, 1988). Combined training in phonological awareness and phonological decoding has stronger benefits for the development of early word-reading skills (National Reading Pannel, 2000). However, the benefits from explicit phonological training may be limited for fluent word reading and comprehension in the later grades, compared to accurate reading practice in text (Wise, Ring, & Olson, 2000).

Orthographic coding deficits are also apparent in children with word-reading disabilities when compared to chronological age-matched normal children, but the origin and specific causal role of orthographic coding deficits in word-reading disabilities is less clear. The word reading-level-match comparisons that show phonological processing deficits do not typically show similar deficits in our measures of orthographic coding, where poor readers' performance has been similar to that of the younger normal group matched on word recognition (Olson, 1985; Olson et al., 1989). Some researchers have speculated that poor performance in reading exception words and in orthographic coding tasks is due to deficits in visual processes for whole-word recognition (Boder, 1973; Talcott et al. 2002). However, there have been no replicated findings of a specific link between orthographic coding and visual processing deficits. Other researchers have suggested that environmental constraints on print exposure may be the primary cause of orthographic coding deficits (Manis et al., 1996). There has also been some suggestion that speed in naming of numbers and letters is specifically linked to the amalgamation of the whole-word representations that are needed in exception word reading and orthographic coding tasks (Wolf & Bowers, 1999), so we have included measures of rapid picture-, color-, letter-, and number-naming in our test battery for the twins.

There are many other measures included in the full twin test battery that is administered in four CLDRC laboratories across two testing days. Two of these are measures of isolated word recognition, including the Peabody Individual Achievement Test (PIAT) for word recognition (Dunn & Markwardt, 1970), and an experimental time-limited measure with words presented on the computer (Olson et al., 1989). Z scores for these two highly correlated measures are combined in our behavior genetic analyses to form a highly reliable composite score or latent trait for isolated word recognition. In the concluding section of the chapter I will describe several additional measures in the twin test battery when reviewing new behavior genetic evidence linking word reading, higher-level language skills, and reading comprehension.

BEHAVIOR-GENETIC ANALYSES OF GROUP DEFICITS IN WORD READING AND RELATED SKILLS

Identical and fraternal twins reared together can be uniquely informative about the relative influence of genetic, shared family environment, and non-shared environment influences on average behavior in the sampled population. The key difference between identical or monozygotic (MZ, one egg) and dizygotic (DZ, two egg) twins is of course their different genetic similarities: MZ twins are genetically identical, while the DZ twins share half of their segregating genes on average (Plomin, DeFries, McClearn, & McGuffin, 2000). Therefore, greater average similarity in behavior within MZ twin pairs provides evidence for genetic influence. If genetic influence were complete, with no influence from shared or non-shared environment, MZ twins would be identical in behavior, while DZ twins would be "half similar" on average, because they share half their segregating genes on average. Most readers of this chapter are probably familiar with the statistical method of correlation for estimating average similarity for individual differences within groups of MZ and DZ twin pairs. The hypothetical identical behavior for MZ pairs would be indicated by a perfect correlation of 1, while the average "half similar" situation for DZ pairs would be indicated by a correlation of .5. Thus, total genetic influence on the twins' individual differences can be approximately estimated by doubling the difference between the MZ and DZ correlations. I will return to this correlation-based approach when considering the evidence for genetic and environmental influences on individual differences in reading across the normal range. A different type of analysis is more appropriate for assessing the etiology of extreme deviant scores that I will turn to next.

Earlier studies of genetic influence on "dyslexia" used categorical definitions of the disorder and compared the proportions of MZ and DZ twin pairs who were "concordant" for sharing the categorical disorder (for review see Pennington and Olson, 2005). However, it is clear that reading ability in the population is normally distributed (Rogers, 1983), and a continuous analysis of twin-pair similarity is more appropriate for assessing genetic and environmental influences on deviant group membership. DeFries and Fulker (1985) recognized that if affected twins (referred to as "probands" in behavior-genetic studies) were identified below a cut point in the low tail of the normal distribution for reading or any other behavior, the average genetic and environmental influences on the proband group's membership in the low tail could be estimated from a comparison of average MZ and DZ cotwin regression toward the normal population mean. For example, if genes were entirely responsible for group membership in the low tail of the distribution, both members of MZ twin pairs would be probands, while average cotwin regression for DZ pairs with one or more probands would be half way to the population mean, because DZ twins share half their genes on average. Of course complex behaviors like reading are not under complete genetic control, and there are likely to be significant environmental influences as well. The influence of non-shared environment, including measurement error that is almost always present for complex behavior, can be estimated from average MZ cotwin regression to the population mean: Since MZ twins share all their genes, any difference within MZ pairs must logically be due to environmental influences that they do not share. Shared environment influences, defined simply as environmental influences that make twins more similar, are indicated if the difference between average MZ and DZ cotwin regression to the population mean is less than expected from the difference in their genetic similarity. For an extreme example, if MZ and DZ cotwins *both* regressed on average only 10% of the distance to the population mean, in spite of their different average genetic similarity, that would indicate that 10% of the group deficit was due to non-shared environment, 90% of the group deficit was due to shared environment, and there was no genetic influence.

The DeFries and Fulker (1985) basic regression procedure (now commonly referred to as the "DF" model) has become widely used for estimating the genetic and environmental etiology of deviant group membership for normally distributed behavior. The DF model can also be used to assess the shared etiological basis for two different correlated skills by the selection of probands on one skill, say orthographic coding, and analysis of cotwin regression on a second skill, say phoneme awareness. Thus, we can assess the degree to which deficits in two skills are due to the same genes or environmental factors. A second useful extension of the basic DF model involves the assessment of genetic and environmental influences on a skill, say word recognition, depending on some other characteristic, such as gender or IQ.

The Twin Sample for DF Analyses in the CLDRC

Staff of the CLDRC identify twins with at least one member of each pair having a broadly defined school history of reading disabilities based on school records from 27 Colorado school districts. The twins are then invited for extensive laboratory testing over two days on weekends at the University of Colorado and at the University of Denver. To date (6/13/05), 928 such twin pairs from age 8 to 18 have been tested. In addition, a normal control group of 711 twin pairs with no school history of reading disability (though some did have reading difficulties when tested in the laboratory) have also been tested. This normal-range group is used to establish the normal population mean and variance for DF analyses, and for behavior genetic analyses of individual differences across the normal range.

To be included in the proband group for the DF analyses described in this chapter, the twins must have a school history of reading disability, English as their first language, no neurological signs such as seizures, and normal school attendance. For most analyses, the twins' minimum IQ score had to be at least 85 on the Wechsler (1974) verbal or performance scales.

It should be emphasized that requiring English as a first language excludes many Hispanic children in Colorado who are struggling in reading because of this important environmental factor, and our estimates of genetic and environmental influence can not be extended to this population. In addition, African American children are underrepresented in our sample, partly due to the school districts that have agreed to participate in our study, and partly due to a lower parental response to letters from the schools requesting their twins' participation in our studies. Again, our estimates of genetic and environmental influence can not be extended to this population, and they are not at all informative about the reasons for any minority group differences in reading compared to the general population in Colorado. I will consider some of these sampling issues again in the concluding section of the paper.

Univariate Genetic and Environmental Estimates for Group Deficits

It was apparent in our earliest analyses that group deficits in printed word recognition, phonological decoding, and phoneme awareness had significant genetic etiologies, although the genetic influence on orthographic coding was not significant in that small sample (Olson et al., 1989). The lack of significant genetic influence for orthographic coding seemed to support the idea that deficits in this skill were largely due to the environment, but we have since learned that this initial null result was due to the small sample size. Gayan and Olson (2001) employed DF analyses of data from a much larger sample of identical and same-sex fraternal twins wherein probands were separately selected for deficits below −1.5 SD from the normal mean in word recognition, phonological decoding, phoneme awareness, or orthographic coding. The results for genetic (h^2_g), shared environment (c^2_g), and non-shared environment (e^2_g) influences on deviant group membership are presented in Table 12.1.

The effects of genetic influences on group deficits were substantial and significant for all measures, though the balance of genetic and environmental influence seemed to vary somewhat. Genetic influence was lower and shared-environment influence was higher for the group deficit in word recognition, compared to the other variables. Shared environment influences related to differences in print exposure may have a greater impact on measures of word recognition than on underlying component processing skills that constrain the development of word recognition: Genetic influence

TABLE 12.1

Genetic (h^2_g), Shared Environment (c^2_g), and Nonshared Environment (e^2_g) Estimates and Standard Errors (SE) for Group Deficits.

Task	h^2_g (SE)	c^2_g (SE)	e^2_g (SE)
Word recognition	.54 (.08)*	.39 (.09)*	.06 (.03)*
Phonological decoding	.71 (.10)*	.18 (.10)	.12 (.04)*
Phoneme awareness	.72 (.14)*	.15 (.14)	.13 (.06)*
Orthographic coding	.67 (.12)*	.17 (.12)	.16 (.04)*

Note. From "Genetic and Environmental Influences on Orthographic and Phonological Skills in children with Reading Disabilities," by J. Gayan and R.K. Olson, 2001, *Developmental Neuropsychology, 20*, p. Copyright 2001 by. Adapted with permission.
*$p < .05$.

was relatively high and shared environment influence was low and non-significant for phonological decoding, phoneme awareness, and orthographic coding.

Harlaar, Spinath, Dale, and Plomin (2005) have recently published results of their DF analyses for group deficits below the 10th percentile on a composite measure of word reading and nonword reading efficiency (Torgesen, Wagner, & Rashote, 1999) that was administered by telephone to twins in the U.K. near the end of first grade, age 7. The Harlaar et al. estimates of genetic (h^2_g = .60), shared environment (c^2_g = .28), and non-shared environment (e^2_g = .12) influences were quite similar to the estimates for word-reading deficits in our older sample of twins. Thus, it seems that genetic influences on word-reading deficits exert their influence very early in reading development and continue to do so throughout the school years (Gayan & Olson, 2001).

Bivariate Genetic Correlations for Group Deficits

Gayan and Olson (2001) also conducted a number of bivariate DF analyses to assess shared genetic influences between the variables. A most interesting result was that the group-deficit genetic correlation was .67 for the language skill of phoneme awareness (phoneme deletion) and phonological decoding, but only .28 for phoneme awareness and orthographic coding, a significant contrast, and one that is also reflected in the behavior-genetic analyses of individual differences discussed in the next main section of the chapter. Another intriguing result was that the genetic correlation for group deficits in word recognition and phonological decoding was estimated at .99, indicating that virtually the same genes are involved in both of these group deficits. A similar result was obtained in our analyses of individual differences in word reading and phonological decoding discussed in the next section. Other group-deficit genetic correlations included .73 for orthographic coding and phonological decoding, .81 for orthographic coding and word recognition, and .67 for phoneme awareness and word recognition.

Other interesting results from our bivariate DF analyses include that group deficits in rapid naming have significant genetic correlations with deficits in word reading skills, particularly for reading measures that have a speed component (Compton, Davis, DeFries, Gayan, & Olson, 2001; Davis et al., 2001). Also, since a sub-sample of the twins studied in the CLDRC has been selected for a school history of Attention Deficit Hyperactivity Disorder (ADHD), we have been able to conduct bivariate DF analyses with ADHD proband selection and cotwin regression on reading measures. These analyses have revealed significant group-deficit genetic correlations between ADHD and reading that are mostly due to attention deficits rather than the hyperactivity component of ADHD (Willcutt et al., in press). Thus, there is a partly shared genetic etiology for ADHD and reading disability that is largely responsible for their partial phenotypic comorbidity of about 30%.

Genetic and Environmental Etiologies Vary with "Subtypes"

Several of our DF analyses have shown that group deficits in word reading skills tend to be mostly heritable in children with higher IQ scores, while the group deficits in children with lower IQ scores were predominantly due to shared-environment influences (Olson et al., 1999; Wadsworth et al., 2000; Knopik et al., 2002). Consistent with this result, children with lower IQ scores also had significantly fewer books in the home. We have argued that if shared-environment influence is the main source of reading and related deficits in children with below-average IQ, this supports the importance of actively compensating for these environmental effects rather than excluding children from remedial services because they do not meet some arbitrary criteria for a reading-IQ discrepancy (see similar arguments by Lyon et al., 2001).

Castles, Datta, Gayan, & Olson (1999) explored the differential genetic etiology of "surface" and "phonological" dyslexic subtypes, defined by the difference between phonological decoding and accuracy in reading strange and relatively rare exception words such as "yacht." They found that genetic influence accounted for most of the group deficit in the "phonological" subtype, but shared environment accounted for most of the group deficit in the "surface" subtype that had relatively low exception-word reading compared to their phonological decoding. Castles et al. also found that the "surface" subtype had significantly lower print exposure, estimated from recognition of book titles, thus supporting the hypothesis of Manis et al. (1996) that at least some cases of surface dyslexia may be due to lack of print exposure.

Gender has long been a "subtype" of interest in studies of reading disability. We have conducted several DF analyses of gender differences in genetic etiology for reading disability over the years in the CLDRC, and all have found no significant differences. The most recent analyses by CLDRC investigators with a composite measure of word recognition, spelling, and reading comprehension found that h^2_g was .53 for males and .63 for females, a non significant difference (Wadsworth & DeFries, 2005). This does not prove that the specific genetic mechanisms are the same for both sexes, but it appears that they are very similar in their average effect.

There is much continuing interest in various "subtypes," or more properly "dimensions," of individual differences in the classification of reading disabilities which emerge from the partial phenotypic independence of different component reading skills (Bailey, Manis, Pedersen, & Seidenberg, 2004; Griffiths & Snowling, 2002; Manis et al., 1996). We are continuing to explore the genetic and environmental etiologies of individual differences or subtypes among children with disabilities in these skills. Better understanding of their etiologies is needed to improve classification and optimize interventions for different reading disabilities.

Molecular Genetic Analyses of Group Deficits

The highly heritable group deficits in orthographic coding, phonological decoding, and phoneme awareness reported by Gayan and Olson (2001) have made these measures attractive ones for molecular genetic linkage and association analyses (Deffenbacher et al., 2004; Fisher et al., 2002; Franks et al., 2002, Francks et al., 2004; Gayan et al., 2005; Kaplan et al., 2002, Knopik et al., 2002; Meng et al., 2005; Smith et al., 2001; Willcutt et al., 2002). Our continued collection of twin and sibling data on the different skills will support more powerful molecular genetic analyses. These analyses may eventually reveal significant differences in linkage, association, and possibly some alleles with at least some degree of specificity for deficits in different reading-related phenotypes. Recall that group deficits in orthographic coding and phoneme awareness were very highly heritable, but they had a low genetic correlation in the bivariate DF analyses of Gayan and Olson (2001). In a prior linkage analysis on chromosome 6 near the region first identified by Cardon et al. (1994), Gayan et al. (1999) found a highly significant LOD score of 3.10 (LOD is an index of the statistical probability that a gene related to the deficit is in a particular region on a chromosome) for deficits in orthographic coding, but only a marginally significant LOD score of 1.46 for phoneme awareness. Similarly, later bivariate analyses revealed stronger evidence for bivariate linkage between ADHD and orthographic coding (Bivariate LOD = 2.98) than for deficits in phonological coding or a composite reading score (LOD = 1.1 – 1.2). Although these differences in LOD scores are not statistically significant with our current sample size, the consistent pattern suggests that molecular genetic analyses of component reading and language phenotypes may reveal important differences in their specific genetic etiology. As we continue to expand our sample of twins and siblings in the CLDRC, we will be able to conduct more powerful linkage and association analyses for the different measures at different genetic loci, and these analyses may eventually be powerful enough to detect significant differences in the molecular genetic etiology of different reading-related phenotypes that have been suggested by non-significant trends in our own and other studies (c.f., Grigorenko et al., 1997; Grigorenko, Wood, Meyer, & Pauls, 2000).

When looking for different molecular genetic mechanisms for different reading related phenotypes, we should keep in mind that the phenotypes vary widely in their behavior genetic correlations, and significantly different molecular genetic mechanisms are more likely to be found for highly heritable phenotypes with low correlations in bivariate DF analyses, such as the low genetic correlation of .28 that we found for phoneme awareness and orthographic coding. In contrast, we are not likely to find different genes for group deficits in measures such as word recognition and phonological decoding that have a very high genetic correlation. If we do, we should be concerned that the results may be due to Type I error (i.e., declaring a difference when it is actually due to chance).

A more complete discussion of molecular genetic studies is presented in the chapter by Barr (this volume).

GENETIC AND ENVIRONMENTAL INFLUENCES
ON INDIVIDUAL DIFFERENCES

In this section I will discuss results from behavior genetic analyses of individual differences that were conducted with two very different twin samples. The first sample included the school-age twins from 8 to 18 years of age, with and without school history for reading disability, that were included in our DF analyses for group deficits reported in the previous section. The second sample includes twins initially tested in preschool and in follow-up assessments at the end of kindergarten and the first grade.

Individual Differences in Twins 8 to 18 Years of Age

Gayan & Olson (2003) compared the variance-covariance matrices for 880 MZ and DZ twins to estimate genetic and environmental influences on individual differences across the normal range in latent traits for word reading and related skills (see Table 12.2). Heritability for individual differences in the word-reading latent trait was estimated at $h^2 = .85$ with a 95% confidence interval of .69 −.92. A similar result has been found by Harlaar, Spinath, Dale, and Plomin (2005) for a word and nonword reading-efficiency composite score in a large and representative sample of 3,496 7-year-old twin pairs from the U.K. ($h^2 = .73$; $p < .05 = .64$ -.83). The h^2 estimates from these two studies may be too high if there are significant non-additive genetic influences at play, and they may not reflect the strong influence of extreme negative environments for reading development, since families in these extreme environments may be less likely to be participants in twin studies (Olson, 2004). Nevertheless, it is clear that there are substantial genetic influences on individual differences in word reading within normal-range reading environments, just as there are for extreme group deficits in word reading.

Gayan and Olson (2003) also assessed the genetic correlations and independence among IQ and latent variables for word recognition, phoneme awareness, phonological decoding, and orthographic coding. Four of the most theoretically interesting results will be mentioned here. First, a significantly higher genetic correlation for phoneme awareness with phonological decoding ($r_g = .79$) vs. orthographic coding ($r_g = .55$) was observed that mirrored the pattern observed for the group-deficit genetic correlations found by Gayan and Olson (2001). Second, full-scale IQ was included in the hierarchical genetic model to show that although there was shared genetic influence between IQ and reading skills (results for full-scale and verbal IQ were virtually the same), there was substantial genetic variance in the word reading skills and phoneme awareness that was independent from IQ. Interestingly, when phoneme awareness was entered first, it completely accounted

TABLE 12.2

Genetic (h^2), Shared Environment (c^2), and Nonshared Environment (e^2) Estimates
and 95% Confidence Intervals for Individual Differences

Task	h^2	c^2	e^2_g
Word recognition	.85 (.69–.92)	.04 (.00–.19)	.11 (.08–.15)
Phonological decoding	.80 (.62–.88)	.05 (.00–.21)	.15 (.11–.20)
Phoneme awareness	.83 (.62–.94)	.08 (.00–.27)	.09 (.05–.14)
Orthographic coding	.87 (.75–.94)	.01 (.00–.11)	.12 (.06–.20)

From "Genetic and Environmental Influences on Individual Differences in Printed Word
Recognition," by J. Gayan and R. K. Olson, 2003, *Journal of Experimental Child Psychology, 84,*
p. Copyright 2003 by. Reprinted with permission.

for the genetic correlation between the word-reading skills and IQ. Third, we found
that the genetic correlation for individual differences in word reading and phonological decoding was very high (r_g = .97), just as it was for group deficits (Gayan
and Olson, 2001). Fourth, although the genetic correlation between phonological
decoding and orthographic coding was substantial (r_g = .82), there was also significant independent genetic variance for these component word reading skills. This
result again raises the possibility that there may be at least partly different molecular
genetic contributions to these skills, both for group deficits, and for individual
differences across the normal range.

Genetic and Environmental Influences on Prereading and Early Reading Skills

The foregoing evidence for substantial genetic influence on word reading and
related skills in school-age children has led us to explore its influence beginning at
preschool age 4, prior to formal literacy instruction, with follow-up assessments at
the end of kindergarten, first grade, and second grade. Our ongoing international
longitudinal twin study of early reading development includes twins from Australia,
Scandinavia (Norway and Sweden), and Colorado. At present, the combined sample from Australia and the U.S. is large enough to reliably assess genetic and environmental influences at preschool, and to conduct preliminary developmental
genetic analyses of early reading skills at the end of kindergarten and first grade.

The preschool twins are tested separately by different testers in one-hour sessions
over five days, in their homes or in quiet preschool locations. Phenotypic results from
the extensive preschool test battery including 21 different measures were factor analyzed, resulting in factors that we labeled "General Verbal Ability" (including multiple
measures of vocabulary, verbal memory, grammar and morphology), "Phonological
Awareness" (including 6 different measures of static phonological awareness and a
measure of phonological learning), Rapid Naming (of pictures and colors), and "Print
Knowledge" (including measures of letter name and letter sound knowledge, environmental print, and print conventions). The preschool measures are described in
Byrne et al. (2002, 2005) and in Samuelsson et al. (in press).

TABLE 12.3

Genetic (a^2), Shared Environment (c^2), and Nonshared Environment (e^2) Influences on Latent Trait Parameter Estimates

	a^2	c^2	e^2
Variable	Latent Trait	Latent Trait	Latent Trait
General verbal ability	.43 (.30, .58)	.52 (.37, .64)	.06 (.03, .08)
Phonological awareness	.61 (.41, .83)	.30 (.10, .48)	.09 (.05, .14)
Rapid naming	.64 (.40, .81)	.11 (.00, .57)	.25 (.18, .32)
Print knowledge	.23 (.12, .35)	.68 (.56, .77)	.10 (.06, .14)

Note. 95% Confidence intervals in parentheses. All estimates are significantly greater than 0 ($p < .05$), except for Rapid Naming c^2.
From "Environmental and Genetic Influences on Pre-Reading Skills in Australia, Scandinavia, and the U.S.," by S. Samuelsson et al., 2005, *Journal of Educational Psychology*, p. 0 Copyright by adapted with permission.

Samuelsson et al. (2005) used the main variables contributing to each preschool factor to form latent traits for univariate Mx analyses of genetic and environmental influences (Neale, Boker, Xie, & Maes, 2002). Results for the main factor latent traits are presented in Table 12.3. Note that while genes are the primary influence on individual differences in Rapid Naming and Phonological Awareness, Shared Environment is the strongest influence on General Verbal Ability and particularly on Print Knowledge. Samuelsson et al. found that at least part of these strong shared environment influences could be accounted for by parent questionnaire data regarding their teaching of letter names and reading books to their children.

Samuelsson et al. (2005) also conducted several multivariate genetic analyses to determine the degree of shared and independent genetic and environmental influences among the variables. We noted with particular interest that although genetic influence was high for Phonological Awareness and low for Print Knowledge (a significant contrast), their genetic correlation was substantial ($r_g = .68$). Thus, genes that account for a small proportion of the total variance in preschool print knowledge are mostly the same genes that account for the larger amount of genetic variance in phonological awareness. The difference between these two latent traits in total genetic influence may result from differences in the environmental range for each latent trait. Perhaps shared-environment factors account for a larger proportion of the variance in Print Knowledge due to large differences among pre-readers' home and preschool environments for exposure to books and teaching of the alphabet. After relatively uniform exposure to reading instruction in the early grades that is present for most older twins in behavior-genetic research, individual differences in reading ability may become strongly influenced by genes. Before discussing our preliminary analyses of reading at the end of kindergarten, it should also be noted that the genetic correlation between preschool Print Knowledge and Phonological Awareness was significantly less than perfect, and there was significant independent genetic influence on Print Knowledge after controlling for genetic influences shared with the other three latent traits.

TABLE 12.4

Mx Model Fitting Estimates for Kindergarten Latent Traits

Variable	a^2	c^2	e^2
Reading	.70 (.52, .93)[a]	.22 (.00, .40)[a]	.07 (.05, .09)
Spelling	.39 (.18, .63)[a]	.40 (.17, .59)[a]	.20 (.14, .29)
Phonological awareness	.63 (.36, .92)[a]	.28 (.00, .53)	.10 (.05, .16)
Rapid naming	.60 (.33, .82)[a]	.17 (.00, .41)	.23 (.17, .31)

Note. 95% Confidence intervals in parentheses. a component cannot be dropped without significant loss of fit, ($p < .05$) From "Longitudinal Twin Study of Early Literacy Development: Preschool and Kindergatten Phases." By B. Byrne et al., 2005, *Scientific Studies of Reading*, 9, p. Copyright 2005 by. Adapted with permission.

Byrne et al. (2005) conducted our first end-of-kindergarten analysis of latent traits for Reading (word and nonword reading efficiency on the TOWRE), Spelling, Phonological Awareness, and Rapid Naming (now including colors, letters, and numbers). The results are shown in Table 12.4. Of particular note is the substantial genetic influence on Reading that is already present at the end of kindergarten. In contrast, genetic and shared environment influences were almost equal for Spelling. The magnitude of genetic and environmental influences on Phonological Awareness and Rapid Naming were nearly the same as in preschool. However, while these two measures had significant shared genetic influences between preschool and kindergarten, there were also significant new genetic influences in kindergarten. For Rapid Naming, these new genetic influences were tied specifically to the introduction of letter and number naming tasks. For Phonological Awareness, we hypothesized that the new genetic influences (not significant in Byrne et al., 2005, but significant with an expanded sample in Byrne et al., in press) were due to the reciprocal effect from genetic influence in reading on the development of Phonological Awareness in kindergarten.

Among the many interesting results of our developmental genetic analyses from preschool through the end of kindergarten, one is particularly intriguing. Put in quantitative terms, preschool Print Knowledge is less than half as influenced by genes in this sample (.24) compared to kindergarten Reading (.70), yet the genetic correlation between these variables is high, at .79, higher in fact that the genetic correlation between the highly heritable preschool Phonological Awareness latent trait and kindergarten Reading at .54. Thus, although Phonological Awareness is highly heritable at preschool, more so than Print Knowledge, only some of its underlying genetic sources are also at work in determining variability in Reading and Spelling at the end of kindergarten. Moreover, after accounting for genetic effects from preschool Phonological Awareness on reading at the end of kindergarten, there still are additional significant genetic influences on reading from preschool Print Knowledge. In contrast, no additional genetic variance in kindergarten Reading is accounted for by preschool Phonological Awareness after controlling for preschool Print Knowledge. Of course, the pattern may change as we add later school years to the database, or even as the sample size increases, but for the moment this pattern raises interesting issues. One implication, for instance, is that there may be an "amplification" effect at work: Thus, the genetic influence on preschool Print Knowledge and Reading at the end of kindergarten is mostly due to the same genes, but their effect is amplified, or more strongly expressed, on Reading. The nature of the genetic influence on preschool Print Knowledge that is linked to kindergarten Reading remains to be determined, but other investigators who have studied early reading development have noted that preschool children have varied interests in print that do not seem to be completely accounted for by their phonological awareness (Anne Cunningham, personal communication).

We have also conducted preliminary analyses with our limited longitudinal sample combined across Australia and the U.S. (currently 167 MZ pairs and 152 DZ pairs) that has completed testing through the end of first grade. For the composite measure of word and nonword reading efficiency, genetic influence (95% confidence intervals in parentheses) has increased (a^2 = .83 (.59-.88)) and shared environment influence has decreased (c^2 = .01 (.00, .24)) from the levels we observed in kindergarten, although these differences between the end of kindergarten and first grade do not approach significance with this small sample. For spelling, an even stronger shift toward genetic (a^2 = .72 (.46, .90)) and away from shared environment (c^2 = .06 (.00, .30)) influences was observed, compared to kindergarten levels. We hypothesize that shared environment influences are more apparent in kindergarten due to the varied emphasis on reading and spelling in different kindergarten classes, compared to more uniform formal instruction and reading practice in first grade classes. However, it is surprising that school and family environment effects are not more evident in our estimates of shared environment influences among our twins at the end of first grade. I will consider some potential reasons for these low shared environment estimates in the final section.

In summary, analyses of data from our longitudinal twin study have shown that individual differences in preschool print knowledge are largely influenced by shared environment, but by the end of kindergarten, spelling is equally influenced by genetic and shared-environment factors, and word reading skills are predominantly influenced by genes. The dominance of genetic influence appears to further increase for reading and spelling skills tested at the end of first grade, although this increase is not yet statistically significant in the present small sample. We expected that phonological awareness measured in preschool would share its genetic influence with subsequent reading and spelling, and it did. However, we were surprised to find that the modest but significant genetic influence on preschool print knowledge actually accounted for more genetic influence on later word reading and spelling than did preschool phonological awareness, or any of the other preschool measures of rapid naming, verbal memory, vocabulary, and grammar/morphology. Results for reading comprehension might be different.

We also included the Woodcock-Johnson III (Woodcock, McGrew, & Mather, 2001) measure of reading comprehension at the end of first grade. Genetic influence was high (a^2 = .76 (.46, .90)) for this measure as well, and its genetic correlations with word/nonword Reading (r_g = .97) and Spelling (r_g = .95) were also high. Thus, it is not surprising that after controlling for genetic influences on word/nonword Reading, there were no significant genetic influences on this measure of reading comprehension at the end of first grade. Does that mean that word reading skills and reading comprehension will continue to be completely interdependent in the later grades?

The answer is probably not. For one thing, it turns out that the reading comprehension measure we selected for the first grade follow-up testing (Woodcock-Johnson III) has an unusually high correlation of .74 with word reading skills (Keenan, Betjemann, & Roth, 2005). In contrast, standardized and experimental reading comprehension measures that required the integration of longer passages had more modest correlations of .39 − .44 with word reading skills. Also, there is much evidence from cross sectional studies that word reading and reading comprehension skills develop greater independence in the later grades (Curtis, 1980; Leach, Scarborough, & Rescorla, 2003). Therefore, we have proposed an extension of our longitudinal twin study through the 3rd and 4th grades, when some children with adequate word reading skills begin to fail in more complex reading comprehension tasks. We will be interested to learn the etiology of individual differences in different component skills in reading comprehension that are independent from word reading skills. It is possible that these individual differences are primarily due to shared environment (as vocabulary is in preschool), and that the genetic influence on complex reading comprehension is primarily mediated through genetic influences on word recognition. Or, it is possible that genetic influences specific to higher level language and memory skills are also strongly expressed in reading comprehension.

We have begun to explore this question in our school-age sample of twins from 8 to 18 years of age. In addition to the measures of word reading and related skills I have already described for that sample, we recently introduced a number of reading and listening comprehension measures to our test battery. Preliminary analyses in a small twin sample (74 MZ and 122 DZ pairs) have found that heritability estimates (95% confidence limits in parentheses) for individual differences in word reading (a^2 = .67 (.44, .82)), reading comprehension (a^2 = .51 (.24, .74)), and listening comprehension (a^2 = .51 (.24, .74)) were similarly and significantly heritable (Keenan et al., in press). It might seem possible from these results that all the genetic influence on reading comprehension was through word recognition, but that was not the case. Both word recognition and listening comprehension contributed to significant independent genetic influences on reading comprehension, and together they accounted for *all* of the genetic influence on a composite measure of reading comprehension. It remains to be seen if this pattern of results will be maintained as our sample expands, and we look forward to further exploration of influences on reading and listening comprehension related to individual differences and deficits in our measures of vocabulary, memory, world knowledge, rapid naming, etc. If we continue to find independent genetic influences from word reading and listening/reading comprehension in the older twins, it will again raise the possibility of at least partly different molecular genetic pathways for different reading-related phenotypes.

CONCLUSION

I would like to conclude with some reflection on our astonishingly high estimates of genetic influence on individual differences in word-reading skills that emerge by the end of the first year or two of formal schooling, and on the very low estimates for shared environment. It should be noted that while our shared environment estimates in both the older and younger twin samples were below .1, their confidence limits range up to around ~.2. Also, in the very large twin study in the U.K. reported in Harlaar et al. (2005), the shared environment estimate for word/nonword reading efficiency near the end of first grade was significant for both boys and girls (c^2 = .19 for boys, .17 for girls). Still, many readers may think that these estimates of shared environment influence are too low when they think of the varied levels of performance between schools. When discussing our genetic and environmental estimates for individual differences in our older twin sample, I acknowledged that the genetic estimates may be too high and shared environment estimates too low if there are any non-linear genetic influences (dominance or epistasis) at play (see Plomin et al., 2000, for a discussion of these issues). On the other hand, there is ample evidence for assortative mating on reading ability, and this influence would lead to an underestimation of genetic influence and an overestimation of shared environment in models like ours that assume additive genetic influence and no assortative mating. Coventry and Keller (2005) have recently explored these issues with extended family data and have concluded that at least some nonadditive genetic influences are likely for most complex behavior. Thus, they argued that additive genetic models of twin data often significantly overestimate additive genetic influence, but they also allowed that the total genetic influence from both additive and non-additive sources may be only slightly lower than estimates for additive genetic influence in our classical twin design.

A second qualification of our results is that they probably do not reflect the influence of the full environmental range that is relevant for reading ability in the population. We know that there are substantial average differences in literacy levels between the different school districts in Colorado, and between schools within some of the more diverse districts. Some of the district and school differences are associated with the proportion of children who are learning to read in their second language, and these children are not included in our twin sample. Other differences are associated with conditions of poverty and generally poor instruction in poorly organized schools, but few of our twins come from these very poor learning environments because their families generally do not respond to our requests for their participation. Thus, we are assessing genetic and environmental influences within a partly restricted environmental range that likely increases estimates of genetic influence and reduces estimates of shared environment influence, compared to what we might find if the twin sample were completely representative of Colorado twins.

We also know that concerted attempts to improve reading instruction in the schools can lead to substantial increases in literacy levels. There is a clear example of this in Colorado where a high-poverty school district in one of our larger cities substantially raised its reading scores through increased emphasis on literacy and monitoring of student progress, while a neighboring district with similar demographics continued to have low reading scores. There are many such examples throughout the country showing that the school environment matters. In addition, a number of studies with children who fail in normal schools have shown significant gains from intensive intervention (Lyon, Fletcher, Fuchs, & Chhabra, 2006). Some of these successful interventions have been conducted through computer-assisted reading programs by co-investigators in the CLDRC (Wise, Ring, & Olson, 1999, 2000). Clearly, the environment for reading can matter a lot when there are substantial differences in the environment.

Nevertheless, within normal educational environments, it is clear that genetic differences account for the majority of individual differences and group deficits in word reading and related skills. Learning exactly how they account for this variation in interaction with the environment remains a major challenge for research in behavioral genetics, molecular genetics, neuroscience, and education.

ACKNOWLEDGMENTS

Our research in the Colorado Learning Disabilities Research Center has been supported by program project and center grants from NICHD (HD-11681 and HD-27802). Additional support for the Longitudinal Twin Study of Early Reading Development was provided by HD-38526 and several grants from the Australian Research Council.

REFERENCES

Bailey, C. E., Manis, F. R., Pedersen, W. C., & Seidenberg, M. S. (2004). Variation among developmental dyslexics: Evidence from a printed-word-learning task. *Journal of Experimental Child Psychology, 87,* 125–154.

Baron, J. (1979). Orthographic and word specific mechanisms in children's reading of words. *Child Development, 50,* 60–72.

Boder, E. (1973). Developmental Dyslexia: A diagnostic approach based on three typical reading-spelling patterns. *Developmental Medicine and Child Neurology, 15,* 663–687.

Bradley, L., & Bryant, P. E. (1978). Difficulties in auditory organisation as a possible cause of reading backwardness. *Nature, 271,* 746–747.

Bruce, D. J. (1964). The analysis of word sounds by young children. *British Journal of Educational Psychology, 34,* 158–170.

Byrne, B., Delaland, C., Fielding-Barnsley, R., Quain, P., Samuelsson, S., Hoien, T., Corley, R., DeFries, J.C., Wadsworth, S., Willcutt, E., & Olson, R.K. (2002). Longitudinal twin study of early reading development in three countries: Preliminary results. *Annals of Dyslexia, 52,* 49–74.

Byrne, B., Olson, R. K., Samuelsson, S., Wadsworth, S., Corley, R., DeFries, J.C., & Willcutt, E. (in press).Genetic and environmental influences on early literacy. *Journal of Reading Research*

Byrne, B., Wadsworth, S., Corley, R., Samuelsson, S., Quain, P., DeFries, J.C., Willcutt, E., & Olson, R.K. (2005). Longitudinal twin study of early literacy development: Preschool and kindergarten phases. *Scientific Studies of Reading, 9,* 219–235.

Cardon, L. R., Smith, S., Fulker, D., Kimberling, W., Pennington, B. & DeFries, J. (1994). Quantitative trait locus for reading disability on chromosome 6. *Science, 266,* 276–279.

Castles, A., Datta, H., Gayan, J., & Olson, R. K. (1999). Varieties of developmental reading disorder: Genetic and environmental influences. *Journal of Experimental Child Psychology, 72,* 73–94.

Compton, D. L., Davis, C. J., DeFries, J. C., Gayan, J., & Olson, R. K. (2001). Genetic and environmental influences on reading and RAN: An overview of results from the Colorado Twin Study. In M. Wolf (Ed.), *Conference proceedings of the Dyslexia Research Foundation Conference in Extraordinary Brain Series: Time, fluency, and developmental dyslexia (pp. 277–303)*. Baltimore MD: York Press.

Conners, F., and Olson, R. K. (1990). Reading comprehension in dyslexic and normal readers: A component-skills analysis. In D. A. Balota, G. B. Flores d'Arcais, & K. Rayner (Eds.), *Comprehension processes in reading*. Hillsdale, NJ: Erlbaum. pp. 557–579.

Curtis, M. E. (1980). Development of components of reading skill. *Journal of Educational Psychology, 72, 656–669.*

Davis, C. J., Gayán, J., Knopik, V. S., Smith, S. D., Cardon, L. R., Pennington, B. F., Olson, R. K., & DeFries, J. C. (2001a). Etiology of reading difficulties and rapid naming: The Colorado twin study of reading disability. *Behavior Genetics, 31, 625–635.*

Deffenbacher, K. E., Kenyon, J. B., Hoover, D. M., Olson, R. K., Pennington, B. F., DeFries, J. C., & Smith, S. D. (2004). Refinement of the 6P21.3 QTL influencing dyslexia: Linkage and association analyses. *Human Genetics, 115, 128–138.*

DeFries, J. C., & Fulker, D. W. (1985). Multiple regression analysis of twin data. *Behavior Genetics, 15, 467–478.*

Denkla, M. B., & Rudel, R. G. (1976). Rapid "automatized" naming of pictured objects, colors, letters, and numbers by normal children. *Cortex, 10, 186–202.*

Dunn, L. M., & Markwardt, F. C. (1970). *Peabody Individual Achievement Test.* Circle Pines, MN: American Guidance Service.

Fisher, S. E., Francks, C., Marlow, A. J., MacPhie, L., Williams, D. F., Cardon, Lon R., Ishikawa-Brush, Y., Talcott, J. B., Richardson, A. J., Gayan, J., Olson, R. K., Pennington, B. F., Smith, S. D., DeFries, J. C., Stein, J. F., & Monaco, A. P. (2002). Genome-wide scans in independent samples reveal strong convergent evidence for a chromosome 18 quantitative-trait locus influencing developmental dyslexia. *Nature Genetics, 30, 86–91.*

Franks, C., Fisher, S. E., Olson, R. K., Pennington, B. F., Smith, S. D., DeFries, J. C., & Monaco, A. P. (2002). Fine mapping of the chromosome 2p12–16 dyslexia susceptibility locus: Quantitative association analysis and positional candidate genes SEMA4F and OTX1. *Psychiatric Genetics, 12, 35–41.*

Francks, C., Paracchini, S., Smith, S. D., Richardson, A. J., Scerri, T. S., Cardon, L. R., Marlow, A. J., MacPhie, L. I., Walter, J., Pennington, B. F., Fisher, S. E., Olson, R. K., DeFries, J. C., Stein, J. F., & Monaco, A. P. (2004). A 77 kilobase region of chromosome 6p22.2 is associated with dyslexia in families from the United Kingdom and from the United States. *American Journal of Human Genetics, 75, 1046–1058.*

Gayan, J., & Olson, R. K. (2001). Genetic and environmental influences on orthographic and phonological skills in children with reading disabilities. *Developmental Neuropsychology, 20, 483–507.*

Gayan, J., Smith, S. D., Cherny, S. S., Cardon, L. R., Fulker, D. W., Kimberling, W. J., Olson, R. K., Pennington, B., & DeFries, J. C. (1999). Large quantitative trait locus for specific language and reading deficits in chromosome 6p. *American Journal of Human Genetics. 64, 157–164.*

Gayán, J., & Olson, R. K. (2003). Genetic and environmental influences on individual differences in printed word recognition. *Journal of Experimental Child Psychology, 84, 97–123.*

Gayan, J., Willcutt, E. G., Fisher, S. E., Franks, C., Cardon, L. R., Olson, R. K., Pennington, B. F., Smith, S. D., Monaco, A. P., & DeFries, J. C. (2005). Bivariate linkage scan for reading disability and attention-deficit/hyperactivity disorder localizes pleiotropic loci. *Journal for Child Psychology & Psychiatry, 46, 1045–1056.*

Griffiths, Y. M., & Snowling, M. J. (2002). Predictors of exception word and nonword reading in dyslexic children: The severity hypothesis. *Journal of Educational Psychology, 94, 34–43.*

Grigorenko E. L., Wood F. B, Meyer M. S, Hart L. A, Speed W. C, Shuster A, Pauls D. L. 1997. Susceptibility loci for distinct components of developmental dyslexia on chromosomes 6 and 15. *Am J Hum Genet 60(1)*: 27–39.

Grigorenko E. L, Wood F. B, Meyer M. S, Pauls D. L. 2000. Chromosome 6p influences on different dyslexia-related cognitive processes: further confirmation. *Am J Hum Genet 66*: 715–723.

Harlaar, N., Spinath, F. M., Dale, P. S., & Plomin, R. (2005). Genetic influences on early word recognition abilities and disabilities: A study of 7-year-old twins. *Journal of Child Psychology and Psychiatry, 46*, 373 – 384.

Hulslander, J., & Olson, R. K. (submitted).The Influence of Orthographic Skills on Phoneme Awareness Task Performance in Non-Disabled and Disabled Readers

Kaplan, D. E., Gayan, J., Ahn, J., Won, T. W., Pauls, D., Olson, R., DeFries, J. C., Wood, F., Pennington, B., Page, G., Smith, S. D., & Gruen, J. R. (2002). Evidence for linkage and association with reading disability on 6P21.3–22. *American Journal of Human Genetics, 70*, 1287–1298.

Keenan, J. M., Betjemann, R. S., & Roth, L.S. (2005). A comparison of comprehension tests. Presented at the *Seventy- seventh Meeting of the Midwestern Psychological Association*, Chicago, May, 2005.

Keenan, J. M., Betjemann, R., Wadsworth, S. J., DeFries, J. C., & Olson, R. K. (2006). Genetic and environmental influences on reading and listening comprehension. *Journal of in Reading Research, 29*, 75–91.

Keller, M. C., & Coventry, W. L. (2005). Assessing parameter bias in the classical twin design: A comparison of parameter estimates from the extended twin-family and classical twin designs. *Twin Research, 8(3)*.

Knopik, V. S., Smith, S. D., Cardon, L., Pennington, B., Gayan, J., Olson, R. K., & DeFries, J. C. (2002). Differential genetic etiology of reading component processes as a function of IQ. *Behavior Genetics, 32*, 181–198.

LaBerge, D., & Samuels, S. J. (1974). Toward a theory of automatic information processing in reading. *Cognitive Psychology, 6*, 293–323.

Leach, J. M., Scarborough, H. S., Rescorla, L. (2003). Late-emerging reading disabilities. *Journal of Educational Psychology, 95(2)*, 211–224.

Liberman, I. Y., Shankweiler, D., Liberman, Am. M., Fischer, F. W., & Fowler, C. (1977). Phonetic segmentation and recoding in the beginning reader. In A. S. Reber and D. Scarborough (Eds.), *Toward a psychology of reading (pp. 207–225)*. Hillsdale, NJ: Lawrence Erlbaum Associates.

Lundberg, I, Frost, J, and Peterson, O. (1988). Effects of an extensive program for stimulating phonological awareness. *Reading Research Quarterly, 23*, 263–84.

Lyon, G. R., Fletcher, J. M., Fuchs, L. S., & Chhabra, V. (2006). Learning disabilities. In E. Mash and R. Barkley (Eds.), *Treatment of childhood disorders (2nd Ed.)*. New York: Guilford. pp. 512–591.

Lyon, G. R., Fletcher, J. M., Shaywitz, S. E., Shaywitz, B. A., Torgesen, J. K., Wood, F. B., Schulte, A., & Olson, R. K. (2001). Rethinking learning disabilities. In C.E. Finn, A. J. Rotherham, & C. R. Hokanson Jr. (Eds.), *Rethinking special education for a new century (pp. 259–287)*. Progressive Policy Institute and the Thomas B. Fordham Foundation.

Manis, F. R., Seidenberg, M. S., Doi, L. M., McBride-Chang, C., & Peterson, A. (1996). On the bases of two subtypes of developmental dyslexia. *Cognition, 58*, 157–195.

Meng, H., Smith, S. D., Hager, K., Held, M., Page, G. P., Olson, R. K., Pennington, B. F., DeFries, J. C., & Gruen, J. R. (2005). Linkage, Association, and Mutation Analysis with EKN1 and Dyslexia in a Colorado Twin Cohort. *Human Genetics, 18*, 87–90.

Mitterer, J. O. (1982). There are at least two kinds of poor readers: Whole-word poor readers and recoding poor readers. *Canadian Journal of Psychology, 36*, 445–461.

National Institute of Child Health and Development (2000). Report of the National Reading Panel. *Teaching Children to Read: An evidence-based assessment of the scientific research literature and its implications for reading instruction*. (NIH Pub. No. 00–4754). Washington, DC: U.S. Government Printing Office.

Olson, R. K. (1985). Disabled reading processes and cognitive profiles. In D. Gray and J. Kavanagh (Eds.). *Biobehavioral Measures of Dyslexia* pp. 215–244. Parkton, MD: York Press.

Olson, R. K. (2004). SSSR, environment, and genes. *Scientific Studies of Reading, 8(2)*, 111–124.

Olson, R. K., Datta, H., Gayan, J., & DeFries, J. C. (1999). A behavioral-genetic analysis of reading disabilities and component processes. In R. M. Klein & P .A. McMullen (Eds.), *Converging methods for understanding reading and dyslexia (pp. 133–153)*. Cambridge Mass.: MIT Press.

Olson, R. K., Forsberg, H., & Wise, B. (1994). Genes, environment, and the development of orthographic skills. In V. W. Berninger (Ed.), *The varieties of orthographic knowledge I: Theoretical and developmental issues (pp. 27–71)*. Dordrecht, The Netherlands: Kluwer Academic Publishers.

Olson, R., Forsberg, H., Wise, B., & Rack, J. (1994). Measurement of word recognition, orthographic, and phonological skills. In G. R. Lyon (Ed.) *Frames of reference for the assessment of learning disabilities: New views on measurement issues (pp. 243–277)*. Baltimore: Paul H. Brookes Publishing Co.

Olson, R. K., Kliegl, R., Davidson, B. J., & Foltz, G. (1985). Individual and developmental differences in reading disability. In G. E. MacKinnon and T. G. Waller (Eds.), *Reading research: Advances in theory and practice, Vol. 4. (pp. 1–64)*. New York: Academic Press.

Olson, R. K., Wise, B., Conners, F., Rack, J. & Fulker, D. (1989). Specific deficits in component reading and language skills: Genetic and environmental influences. *Journal of Learning Disabilities, 22*, 339–348.

Pennington, B. F., & Olson, R. K. (2005). Genetics of dyslexia. In M. Snowling & C. Hulme, (Eds.), *The science of reading: A handbook (pp. 453–472)*. Oxford: Blackwell.

Perfetti, C.A. (1985). *Reading ability*. New York: Oxford University Press.

Plomin, R., DeFries, J. C., McClearn, G. E., & McGuffin, P. (2000). *Behavioral Genetics*. New York: W.H. Freeman.

Rack, J. P., Snowling, M. J., & Olson, R. K. (1992). The nonword reading deficit in developmental dyslexia: A review. *Reading Research Quarterly, 27*, 28–53.

Rodgers, B. (1983). The identification and prevalence of specific reading retardation. British *Journal of Educational Psychology, 53*, 369–373.

Samuelsson, S., Byrne, B., Quain, P., Corley, R., DeFries, J.C., Wadsworth, S., Willcutt, E., & Olson, R. K. (in press). Environmental and genetic influences on pre-reading skills in Australia, Scandinavia, and the U.S. *Journal of Educational Psychology*.

Shankweiler, D. (1989). How problems of comprehension are related to difficulties in decoding. In D. Shankweiler & I.Y. Liberman (Eds.) *Phonology and Reading Disability: solving the reading puzzle*. Ann Arbor: University of Michigan Press.

Smith, S. D., Kelley, P. M., Askew, J. W., Hoover, D. M., Deffenbacher, K. E., Gayan, J., Brower, A., & Olson, R. K. (2001). Reading disability and chromosome 6p21.3: Evaluation of MOG as a candidate gene. *Journal of Learning Disabilities, 34*, 512–519.

Snowling, M. J. (1981). Phonemic deficits in developmental dyslexia. *Psychological Research, 43*, 219–234.

Stanovich, K. E., Siegel, L. S., & Gottardo, A. (1997). Converging evidence for phonological and surface subtypes of reading disability. *Journal of Educational Psychology, 89*, 114–127.

Talcott, J. B., Witton, C., Hebb, G. S., Stoodley, C. J., Westwood, E. A., France, S. J., et al. (2002). On the relationship between dynamic visual and auditory processing and literacy skills: Results from a large primary-school study. *Dyslexia, 8*, 204–225.

Wadsworth, S. J. & DeFries, J. C. (2005). Genetic etiology of reading difficulties in boys and girls. Twin Research and Human Genetics, *8*(6), 594–601.

Wadsworth, S. J., Olson, R. K., Pennington, B. F., & DeFries, J. C. (2000). Differential genetic etiology of reading disability as a function of IQ. *Journal of Learning Disabilities, 33*, 192–199.

Wechsler, D. (1974). *Examiner's Manual: Wechsler Intelligence Scale for Children – Revised*. New York: The Psychological Corp.

Willcutt, E. G., Pennington, B. F., Olson, R. K., & DeFries, J. C. (in press). Understanding comorbidity: A twin study of reading disability and attention-deficit/hyperactivity disorder. *Neuropsychiatric Genetics.*

Willcutt, E. G., Pennington, B. F., Smith, S. D., Cardon, L. R., Gayan, J., Knopic, V. S., Olson, R. K., & DeFries, J. C. (2002). Quantitative trait locus for reading disability on chromosome 6p is pleiotropic for attention-deficit/hyperactivity disorder. *American Journal of Medical Genetics (Neuropsychiatric Genetics), 114,* 260–268.

Wise, B. W., Ring, J., & Olson, R. K. (1999). Training phonological awareness with and without attention to articulation. *Journal of Experimental Child Psychology, 72,* 271–304.

Wise, B. W., Ring, J., & Olson, R. K. (2000). Individual differences in gains from computer-assisted remedial reading with more emphasis on phonological analysis or accurate reading in context. *Journal of Experimental Child Psychology, 77,* 197–235.

Wolf, M., & Bowers, P. G. (1999). The double-deficit hypothesis for the developmental dyslexias. *Journal of Educational Psychology, 91,* 415–438.

Woodcock, R. W., McGrew, K. S., & Mather, N. (2001). *Woodcock-Johnson Battery - III.* Itaska, IL: Riverside.

CHAPTER THIRTEEN

Molecular Genetics of Reading

Cathy L. Barr
Toronto Western Research Institute

Jillian M. Couto
Toronto Western Research Institute

Specific reading disabilities (RD), also known as developmental dyslexia, is a major educational, social and mental health issue. RD is a specific learning disability, characterized by difficulties with fluent word recognition, and by poor spelling and decoding abilities (Lyon 2003). Three to 6% of otherwise normally developing children demonstrate this developmental neurocognitive disorder, and deficits often persist into adulthood. For many years RD has been known to be familial and evidence from twin studies indicates that RD has a substantial genetic component. Genetic studies have found evidence for linkage, or association, to chromosomes 1p34-p36 (Rabin et al. 1993; Grigorenko et al. 2001; Tzenova et al. 2004), 2p11 (Kaminen et al. 2003), 2p15-16 (Fagerheim et al. 1999; Fisher et al. 2002; Petryshen et al. 2002; Francks et al. 2004), 3p12-q13 (Nopola-Hemmi et al. 2001; Stein et al. 2004), 6p21.3-22 (Smith and Kimberling 1991; Cardon et al. 1994; Grigorenko et al. 1997; Gayan et al. 1999; Kaplan et al. 2002; Grigorenko et al. 2003; Turic et al. 2003; Deffenbacher et al. 2004; Francks et al. 2004; Cope et al. 2005a), 6q11.2-q12 (Petryshen et al. 2001), 7q32 (Kaminen et al. 2003), 11p15.5 (Fisher et al. 2002; Hsiung et al. 2004), 15q (Smith et al. 1983; Smith et al. 1991; Grigorenko et al. 1997; Morris et al. 2000), and 18p11.2 (Fisher et al. 2002; Marlow et al. 2003). There has been unprecedented replication of linkage findings for this complex trait, for the loci on chromosomes 2, 6, and 15, however these have not replicated in all studies. At this point it is not clear if the failure to replicate is due to power, phenotypic (large families, age of the subjects, ascertainment strategy, ethnic composition) or locus heterogeneity. Furthermore, the possibility of false positive results for some of the linkage reports cannot be ruled out, until further confirmatory replication studies. Fine mapping studies have begun and some of these chromosomal regions have been sufficiently narrowed to allow for gene identification. On chromosome 15q21, a chromosomal translocation breakpoint has identified a gene, *EKN1* (*DYX1C1*), which may be the first gene identified contributing to RD (Taipale et al. 2003). At the current time, the evidence for this gene as contributing to RD has not been supported in all samples, and it remains unclear if this is the susceptibility gene on 15q. In the other linked chromosomal regions, fine-mapping studies will undoubtedly lead to gene identification in the next few years. These gene findings will be the first step in understanding the neurobiology underlying this uniquely human, cognitive process.

COMPONENTS OF READING

The process of reading is complex, with a number of component skills necessary for fluent reading and comprehension (Pennington 1997). Early studies of RD focused on deficits in visual systems based on the belief in the significance of letter reversals, however, subsequent research has led to the consensus that the primary deficit in RD is language-based and is evident by difficulties in processing and manipulating speech sounds (Bradley and Bryant 1983; Pratt and Brady 1988). Five processes significantly affect the development of reading skills in the English language: phonology, syntax, working memory, semantics and orthography (Siegel 2003). Current theories of reading acquisition stress that phonological processing (phonology), and it's components, namely phoneme awareness and decoding, are the most significant processes for reading (Siegel 2003). Phoneme awareness is the explicit awareness of the individual speech sounds of a language, tested by auditory-oral methods. Deficits in phoneme awareness are thought to be an early core problem that can be detected in "at risk" children (i.e., have a parent with RD), prior to reading in kindergarten (Lefly and Pennington 2000). Phonological coding is tested by the ability to pronounce letter strings that have never been seen before, and is generally measured by reading pronounceable nonwords or "pseudowords", for example "barp" or "felly". The ability to pronounce pseudowords demonstrates an understanding of the rules governing the translation of written letters into spoken sounds. Without this understanding, children must learn all new words through memorization. These phonological deficits have been found to persist in adults, even after they obtain a normal standard of reading (Felton et al. 1990; Bruck 1992).

Along with recognizing and connecting the sounds of language, the reading processes also requires knowledge of the structural constraints placed on words of a particular language (e.g., English words will never start with dl) (Siegel 2003; Vellutino et al. 2004). This knowledge is used as part of the component process termed orthographic coding – the recognition, and use of patterns of symbols that represent sound, to read words. This skill can be tested using a forced choice task where subjects are given a pair of phonologically identical words from which they have to pick out the correct spelling, e.g.: "joak" and "joke" (Olson et al. 1994).

Some studies suggest that this component of reading can be problematic for children with RD (Vellutino et al. 2004), while others have found otherwise (Siegel 2003). Difficulties in spelling, a skill related to orthographic coding, is often seen in individuals with RD, and involves both orthographic and phonological skills.

In addition to problems with phonological processing, individuals with dyslexia are often impaired in rapid access to and retrieval of the names of visual symbols (Denckla and Rudel 1976). This skill is tested by having the subjects name as rapidly as possible 50 items; colors, shapes, letters or digits, displayed simultaneously on a sheet. A deficit in rapid naming is associated more with single word reading, than with phonological decoding. This skill can be used, along with phonological aware- ness, in differentiating poor readers from normal-achieving readers, and as a pre- dictor of long-term reading difficulties (Wolf and Bowers 1999; Wolf et al. 2002). According to the double-deficit hypothesis, subjects who have difficulties with both phonological awareness and rapid naming are more impaired on measures of sin- gle word identification, non-word reading, and passage comprehension, compared to their counterparts who only have difficulties with one of those processes (Lovett et al. 2000).

Individuals with reading difficulty often have deficits in verbal short-term memory — the ability to hold phonological information in short-term memory (Rugel 1974; Jorm 1979; Stanovich 1982). This ability is tested by having the person recite a string of orally-presented numbers (digit span) or repeat nonsensical words of increasing complexity and length (non-word repetition) (Gathercole et al. 1994; Bishop et al. 1996).

GENETICS OF READING DISABILITIES
AND READING-RELATED PROCESSES

Reading and spelling disabilities have long been noted to be familial (Finucci et al. 1976; Lewitter et al. 1980; Pennington et al. 1991; Schulte-Korne et al. 1996) and evi- dence for a genetic basis has been provided by twin studies (Pennington 1990; DeFries and Gillis 1993; Pennington 1999; Lovett and Baron 2003). Twin studies of RD indicate the heritability to be between 30 and 70% (DeFries et al. 1987; DeFries and Gillis 1993; Wadsworth et al. 2000) and between 62 and 75% for spelling disabilities (Stevenson et al. 1987). The components of reading (e.g., word identifi- cation, phonological awareness, phonological coding, spelling, orthographic coding) have also been shown to be heritable with estimates in the range of 0.45 to 0.62 (Gayan and Olson 1999; Hohnen and Stevenson 1999; Gayan and Olson 2001). Further, multivariate analyses indicate that there are common as well as indepen- dent genetic influences for some of the processes (Gayan and Olson 1999). For example, there is substantial genetic overlap between the etiologies of deficits in single-word reading and those of phonological coding, as well as between deficits in phonological coding and phoneme awareness (Gayan and Olson 1999; Gayan and Olson 2001). Orthographic coding has both shared and independent genetic influences compared to those operating on phonological coding (Gayan and Olson 1999). Reading related processes; rapid naming (Davis et al. 2001), verbal short-term memory (Wadsworth et al. 1995), and general language ability (Hohnen and Stevenson 1999), are also heritable with evidence for shared and independent genetic factors with phonological skills.

GENETIC ASPECTS OF THE OVERLAP BETWEEN RD AND ATTENTION DEFICIT HYPERACTIVITY DISORDER (ADHD)

Many individuals with RD are also diagnosed with attention-deficit hyperactivity disorder (ADHD) with the estimates of the comorbidity ranging between 20–40% (Gilger et al. 1992; Willcutt and Pennington 2000). The genetic relationship between these two disorders is unclear and has, thus far, only been the subject of a few studies (Gilger et al. 1992; Willcutt et al. 2000). In one study using reading-disabled twin pairs, Gilger et al., (1992) examined the possibility of a common genetic etiology for the reported association of ADHD and RD (Gilger et al. 1992). Substantial heritability was evident in their sample for both RD (84% for MZ and 64% for DZ twins) and ADHD (81% for MZ and 29% for DZ twins). Cross-concordance for the combination of RD and ADHD was low (44% and 30% for MZ and DZ twins, respectively), suggesting that a genetically-mediated subtype of RD+ADHD may exist. The most recent twin study suggests that the genetic contribution to the overlap was found to differ for different dimensions of ADHD: 95% of the overlap between inattention and RD was due to the influence of the same genes, while only 21% of the overlap between hyperactivity/impulsivity symptoms and RD was due to common genetic influences (Willcutt et al. 2000).

In summary, RD and the components of reading, as well as associated phenotypes (verbal short-term memory, language ability, symptoms of inattention) are highly heritable. Further, there is overlapping heritability between these phenotypes suggesting that there will be shared and independent genes contributing to these processes and the development of RD. This information from twin studies has been used to determine the most heritable and informative phenotypes and direct the molecular genetic analyses. Initial studies utilized a categorical approach with a cut off of extreme scores for the "affected" status. More recent studies included analyses of the continuous scores of the reading component processes using a quantitative approach. Both approaches have been successful in identifying, and fine mapping, chromosomal regions containing genes contributing to RD and are reviewed below.

MAPPING GENETIC RISK FACTORS

The confirmation from twin studies that RD was heritable as well as being familial, led to the search for the genetic risk factors (Grigorenko 2001; Fisher and DeFries 2002). The first studies used multigenerational families and the available polymorphic markers at that time. These were relatively few and allowed only for the search of a limited number of chromosomal regions. DNA polymorphisms are variations in DNA sequence that exist between individuals, and can be used for identification of susceptibility genes based on their known chromosomal location. The variation among individuals is used to track the inheritance of a specific chromosomal region in families or populations. The types of polymorphic sequences that can be utilized for these studies are changes to a single DNA base pair (bp) known as single nucleotide polymorphisms or SNPs, insertions/deletions of a block of nucleotides or changes to the number of repeat units of blocks of DNA. These can be either repeats of a few nucleotides (microsatellites or simple tandem repeats), larger blocks (variable number of tandem repeats, VNTRs), or even much larger units, all of which change the size of the inherited sequence.

To follow the inheritance of a gene or chromosomal region, each individual is genotyped to determine their alleles, one of several alternative forms of the polymorphism occupying a given position on a chromosome. Each person inherits a combination of two alleles at each position from their parents. These marker alleles can be used to analyze inheritance of either a specific targeted chromosomal region (eg: a gene), or an entire genome (a genome scan). The latter approach investigates the inheritance of the alleles of polymorphic markers spaced at regular intervals across all the chromosomes.

Initial genetic studies of RD used a small number of large multigenerational families. While these types of analyses are very powerful for disorders that are inherited in a clear Mendelian fashion (single disease-causing gene change within a family), for complex traits there are some limitations. First, large, multi-generational pedigrees that are the most informative for genetic studies, and the most likely to come to the attention of a geneticist, may be bilineal with susceptibility genes coming in from both parental sides. Second to trace the pattern of inheritance of the susceptibility genes, the diagnosis of adults in the pedigree must be made. While many of the core deficits remain in adults with RD, compensation can result for many of the skills. Adult ceiling effects can also reduce the variance of the psychometric tests and reduce power for quantitative analyses. Determining a retrospective diagnosis for analysis as a categorical trait can also be problematic. Lastly, if there is a high degree of locus heterogeneity (different susceptibility genes at different chromosomal locations), as is clearly the case for RD, then a limited number of large pedigrees will not be able to detect all of these susceptibility genes. Because of these complexities, some of the more recent studies have utilized a large number of small nuclear families (children and their parents) including dizygotic twins.

Linkage studies test for increased sharing of chromosomal regions in affected family members, indicating the location of susceptibility genes. Since sharing is analyzed in related individuals, these regions are generally quite large and can encompass hundreds of genes. To narrow these regions or to test specific candidate genes, association studies are often used. Association tests for the tendency of two characteristics (phenotypes or marker alleles) to occur together more often than expected by chance. The identification of a true genetic association depends on the presence of linkage disequilibrium. This occurs when a particular marker allele lies very close to the disease susceptibility allele such that these alleles will be inherited together over many generations. The same allele will be detected in affected individuals in many, apparently unrelated, families. Allelic association can be identified by a significantly increased or decreased frequency of alleles in cases compared to ethnically

matched controls. Association can also be identified in nuclear families by deviations from the expected random transmission of a marker allele from parents to
affected children.

The analysis of a combination of alleles across a group of polymorphisms over
a small chromosomal region, or haplotype, can often be used to obtain more information on the ancestry of the chromosome and to increase the power of the association study. Once association is confirmed, the gene or genes in the region are
screened for differences in the DNA sequence to identify the change that would
potentially influence the function of the gene. Generally the exons, regions of the
gene that are transcribed into the mature RNA product, are screened first as it is easier to identify, and predict, changes in the amino acid sequence that are likely to
change the function of the protein, the resulting product of the mature RNA.
Following this, the regions responsible for the controlled expression of the gene are
screened. These regions can be quite far from the gene, making the identification
of DNA changes, as well as a prediction of the change in expression, much more
difficult. Lastly, functional studies are required to determine if the identified DNA
change(s) result in a functional change at the molecular or cellular level.

Linkage studies have indicated the location of at least 8 regions contributing to
RD and studies in three of these regions have used association studies to begin the
process of gene identification. Chromosomal diagrams indicating the regions of the
linkage findings can be found in the two references (Fisher and DeFries 2002;
Grigorenko 2003). The linkage and association studies are reviewed below by chromosome in the chronological order in which they were reported.

Chromosome 15q (DYX1)

The first report of genetic linkage to RD using 9 multi-generational families found
linkage to chromosome 15 in a subset of the families tested (Smith et al. 1983). RD
was defined categorically as reading ability two years below expected reading level
in that study. If there was a discrepancy between test results and a history of RD in
adults in the family, then history was used to determine the affected status of these
individuals. This finding was not initially replicated in other families including an
expanded sample of the original families (Bisgaard et al. 1987; Rabin et al. 1993;
Cardon et al. 1994; Fisher et al. 2002). However, analysis of individual families from
the original sample indicated that one of the families was significantly associated
with the heteromorphisms (Smith et al. 1991). Locus heterogeneity (different chromosomal regions involved in different families) was suggested as an explanation for
these findings. More precise definitions of the phenotype, as well as the availability
of a broader range of genetic markers, allowed subsequent studies to find evidence
for linkage to this region, confirming the original finding (Fulker et al. 1991). In one
study, the phenotype of word identification provided evidence for linkage to this
chromosome in multi-generational families with the most significant LOD score for
the marker D15S413 (Grigorenko et al. 1997). The logarithm of the odds, or LOD
score, is a measure of the likelihood of the genetic linkage between the marker and
disorder, or between two markers. The LOD is expressed as the log (base 10) of

the odds that there is linkage, compared to no evidence for linkage, with the LOD calculated at different genetic distances (recombination fractions) from the marker. An additional study in 7 extended families for the phenotype of spelling disabilities, defined as severe discrepancy between spelling disability and IQ, provided some support for this region with a multipoint LOD score peak of 1.78 at D15S143, for suggestive evidence for linkage (Schulte-Korne et al. 1998; Nothen et al. 1999).

The most recent linkage study using 111 families with 898 family members, targeted for study four regions previously identified with linkage to RD, 2p, 6p, 15q, and 18p (Chapman et al. 2004). Linkage was only observed with markers on chromosome 15q with the maximum single marker analysis result at 3 centimorgan (cM, a unit of genetic distance defined by the number of recombinant chromsomes) from the marker D15S143 in the interval between D15S143 and the marker GATA50C03. This study, in combination with the two previous studies that found evidence using a linkage approach, provide fairly strong support for the region centered on the marker D15S143 (Nothen et al. 1999; Grigorenko et al. 2000).

The chromosome 15q linkage finding was further supported by association studies of markers in this region. Using 8 microsatellites and haplotype analysis of these markers, Morris and colleagues identified a three marker haplotype (D15S994, D15S214, and D15S146) associated with RD in two independent samples of families collected in the United Kingdom (Morris et al. 2000). The marker D15S994 maps within a gene, phospholipase C b 2 (PLCB2), that is a possible candidate based on the previous evidence suggesting the involvement of phospholipid metabolism in RD (MacDonell et al. 2000; Taylor et al. 2000; Taylor et al. 2001). This gene, and the gene for phospholipase A2, group IVB (PLA2G4B), located 1.6 Mb from PLCB2 were investigated as candidate genes for RD using an association study, however, no significant evidence for association was found (Morris et al. 2004).

A more recent association study of 121 nuclear Italian families (probands and parents), replicated an association in this region finding evidence for association with a three-marker haplotype of the markers D15S214, D15S508, and D15S182 (Marino et al. 2004). There was no evidence for association with the marker D15S994 as identified in the UK sample however, the D15S944 marker is located in the region covered by this haplotype of markers, thereby supporting this same region. Because the alleles are not the same as the ones identified in the UK sample, this suggests the possibility of different risk alleles at this locus in the two different populations, or differing linkage disequilibrium between the markers and the risk alleles.

A gene has recently been located in the 15q21 region that is reported as the first gene identified to be contributing to RD (Taipale et al. 2003). This gene was identified because of a chromosomal translocation breakpoint that cosegregates with a father and three children with RD in one Finnish family (Nopola-Hemmi et al. 2000; Taipale et al. 2003). A translocation is the transfer of chromosomal regions between two non-homologous chromosomes that can disrupt the function of the gene, by separating it on two different chromosomes. The breakpoint of the translocation was found to be located within exons 8 and 9 of a gene termed EKN1, or DYX1C1 for dyslexia 1 (Taipale et al. 2003). The function of this gene is currently not known.

Sequence comparison indicates that it codes for a 420 amino acid protein with three tetratricopeptide repeat motifs. These protein motifs are known to function in protein-protein interactions however, this finding gives no other indication of the function of this gene. In general, these motifs are found in a number of genes with very distinct functions, such as chaperones, proteins involved in cell-cycle control, transcription (the production of a RNA molecule from a gene), protein transport, and neurotransmitter release (Blatch and Lassle 1999).

The expression of this gene is fairly ubiquitous, expressed in numerous tissues including heart, brain, placenta, lung, liver, skeletal muscle, kidney, pancreas, spleen, thymus, prostate, testis, ovary, small intestine, colon, and leukocytes (Taipale et al. 2003). Further, the gene is fairly highly conserved across species differing from humans by only six amino acids in orangutans (*Pongo pygmaeus*), two in bonobos (pygmy chimpanzees, *Pan paniscus*), and three in chimpanzees (*Pan troglodytes*) (Taipale et al. 2003). These characteristics of this gene are perhaps not what one would have expected for a gene contributing to a uniquely human cognitive process. But considering that so little is known about the biology of reading, it is not clear what we might expect. Recent progress in the genome project of the chimpanzee indicates that there may be few human specific genes and that remaining differences result from duplications, inactivations, deletions, expression changes, or amino acid changes (Watanabe et al. 2004). The genes that contribute to the process of reading may not themselves be human specific, but may instead allow for the process of reading based on the impact of other genes that influence encephalization, brain metabolism, size, specialization or lateralization.

Further, *EKN1* (*DYX1C1*) is at a fair distance (15 cM) from the markers previously reported to be associated with RD (Turic et al. 2003; Marino et al. 2004) and is not in linkage disequilibrium with D15S994, a marker previously reported as having strong evidence of association to RD (Cope et al. 2005b). Therefore it is surprising that this gene could account for those findings.

To determine if this gene contributes to dyslexia in RD families, other than the family with the translocation, the region of the *EKN1* (*DYX1C1*) gene that codes for the protein sequence was screened in 20 Finnish RD subjects and the identified DNA changes were used in an association study (Taipale et al. 2003). Eight changes in the DNA sequence (variants) were identified, two of which were found to be associated with RD. These two changes were identified as (*i*) a G to A base pair (bp) change located 3 bp before the beginning of the sequence that codes for the *EKN1* protein (-3G/A) and (*ii*) a G to T change at position 1249 in the region coding for the protein (1249G/T) (Taipale et al. 2003). Further, the least common haplotype of these two DNA changes (-3A and 1249T) was found to be associated with RD in the Finnish samples suggesting that the inheritance of either change, or a combination of the two, results in risk to RD. The frequency of this haplotype, 0.13 in subjects, was significantly different from the frequency of 0.05 in controls. Not all of the cases used for the association analyses in that study were unrelated, with some from the same families. The chromosomes were therefore not completely independent, which can increase the sharing of alleles and provide false evidence in favor of association. Therefore the results should be interpreted with caution at this point.

Because of the location of the G to A change 3 bp prior to the initiation of the start codon, it was suggested that this change could potentially influence the efficiency of protein translation. The G to T change at position 1249 results in a premature termination of the protein by 4 amino acids which could also alter the function of the protein.

We investigated the role of this gene, and specifically these two DNA changes in RD. In our sample collected in Toronto, we found no evidence for an association for these two changes or the haplotype (Wigg et al. 2004). However there was a trend for the biased transmission of the alternative allele at –3, the G allele, when the components of reading were analyzed as quantitative traits. Further there was a trend for the biased transmission of the most common haplotype of the –3G/A and 1249G/T polymorphisms (-3G and 1249G). This is opposite to the finding in the Finnish samples where the least common haplotype was associated. An additional study from the UK found evidence for association of the common –G3/1249G haplotype (Scerri et al. 2004), as found in the Toronto sample. Other studies have also not been able to confirm an association with the two specific changes associated in the Finnish sample (Cope et al. 2005b; Marino et al. 2005).

While these results fail to confirm the reported association of the two specific alleles identified in the Finnish sample, our further studies of additional markers in this gene identified an association with alleles in a polymorphism located in intron 4 (Wigg et al. 2004). The intron is the region between exons that is initially transcribed with the exons into messenger RNA. They are later spliced out in the production of mature RNA, that results in protein product.

In total, these findings suggest that the –3G/A and 1249G/T changes in *EKN1* (*DYX1C1*) are unlikely to contribute to the RD phenotype however there may be other changes in this gene that are contributing to risk that have not been identified. An alternative explanation is that the translocation in the *EKN1* gene is affecting the regulation of neighboring genes through a "positional effect". This phenomenon has been documented for a number of chromosomal translocations and is caused by differential expression of a gene brought about by a change in the position of that gene relative to its normal chromosomal environment (Kleinjan and van Heyningen 1998). These effects can influence genes at a large distance from the translocation site, potentially genes closer to the markers previously associated with RD. However, the association observed with markers in *EKN1* (*DYX1C1*), indicate that the causative alleles are in linkage disequilibrium with alleles in *EKN1* (*DYX1C1*) and are therefore likely to be located close to this gene. Given that DNA changes in the coding region (the region that codes for the amino acid sequence) of this gene can be ruled out (Taipale et al. 2003), a search for changes in regulatory regions in *EKN1(DYX1C1)*, as well as investigating neighboring genes as possible susceptibility loci, is warranted.

Chromosome 6p (DYX2)

The most studied chromosomal region in connection to RD has been on chromosome 6p. Linkage to 6p in the region of the human leukocyte antigen (HLA) complex was first observed using multi-generational families and affected sibling pairs from these families (Smith and Kimberling 1991; Smith et al. 1991). The finding of linkage to the HLA region of chromosome 6 was particularly intriguing given the possible association between RD and autoimmune disorders (Geschwind and Behan 1982; Pennington et al. 1987; Urion 1988; Gilger et al. 1992b). This initial linkage finding was further supported by the identification of a quantitative trait locus (QTL) for RD in the same region of the HLA (Cardon et al. 1994) using a sample of 114 sib pairs taken from the 19 multigenerational families that had previously been reported to be linked to chromosome 6, and 46 dizygotic (DZ) twin pairs of whom one was reading disabled. This sample was originally reported as 50 DZ pairs but 4 pairs were found to be monozygotic (Cardon et al. 1995). Criteria for affected status in this study was reading performance at least two years below expected grade level and a family inheritance pattern consistent with autosomal dominant inheritance. The position of the QTL was further narrowed to a 2 centimorgan (cM) region within the region flanked by markers D6S105 and *TNFB*.

The study of Grigorenko and colleagues examined components of reading ability as phenotypes for linkage (Grigorenko et al. 1997). Families were subtyped using two measures each for phonological awareness, phonological decoding, rapid automatized naming, and single-word reading. For each of the four phenotypes, affected status required scoring below the normative 10th percentile on one of the tests, or below the normative 25th percentile on both of the tests. Six extended families were examined. Two of the families had a bilateral history of reading problems suggesting some assortative mating (marriage between people of similar phenotypes). This study reported significant linkage between phoneme awareness and chromosome 6, and single word recognition and chromosome 15. A significant difference between the results for each measure at each genetic location was not observed. This may be because single word reading is not cognitively separate from phonemic awareness, as phonemic awareness is essential for single word reading, and therefore genetic linkage should overlap (Pennington 1997). In a further study by this group, two new families were collected and analyzed using the same approach (Grigorenko et al. 2000). In these two families, single word reading was more significantly linked to the 6p region markers than other reading phenotypes examined.

Additional reports have provided support for the locus influencing reading ability at chromosome 6p (Fisher et al. 1999; Gayan et al. 1999). Fisher et al., (1999) tested 181 sibling pairs (125 independent pairs) from 82 nuclear families for several quantitative measures (word recognition, irregular word reading, and non-word reading). Multipoint analysis supported the interval between D6S422 and D6S291 with a peak around D6S276 and D6S105. The authors concluded that the locus affects both phonological and orthographic skills and is not specific to phonemic awareness as originally identified (Grigorenko et al. 1997).

Gayan et al., 1999, collected a new sample of 126 sib pairs (101 independent pairs) and measured performance for several measures of word recognition and component skills of orthographic coding, phonological decoding, and phoneme awareness using a quantitative approach (Gayan et al. 1999). Significant evidence for linkage was found across a distance of at least 5 cM for deficits in orthographic (LOD=3.10) and phonological skills (LOD= 2.42). The evidence for linkage varied among the phenotypes, and it was suggested that this locus may influence the measures of reading and language performance differentially. The peak linkage region for the two most significant measures, orthographic choice and phoneme deletion was 2 to 3 cM proximal to D6S461 in the region flanked by markers D6S276 and D6S105.

Several studies have failed to replicate the linkage finding on chromosome 6p. These include studies using a large collection of families from Canada with the phenotypic data analyzed as categorically defined deficits in phonological coding (Field and Kaplan 1998) or for four quantitative measures of RD: phonological awareness, phonological coding, spelling, and rapid-automatized-naming (RAN) speed (Petryshen et al. 2000). Two additional studies from Finland, one of a single large pedigree (Nopola-Hemmi et al. 2001) and the other, of 11 families (Kaminen et al. 2003), as well as a recent targeted study of 6p (Chapman et al. 2004) found no evidence for linkage to the region. Some of the studies have used samples larger than used in the original linkage reports therefore it is unlikely that these non-replications are simply an indication of power and other factors are likely to be involved.

Despite these non-replications, the linkage findings for chromosome 6 have been one of the most replicated findings for a complex trait with general agreement for the linked region across studies. Overall the region narrowed using linkage analysis indicates the location of the susceptibility gene to between the markers D6S109 and D6S291 with the strongest agreement from the studies supporting the region flanked by the markers D6S461 and D6S105 (Deffenbacher et al. 2004). However, the linked region was still relatively large and only recently have association studies been employed to focus the search for genes.

Two studies have used microsatellite markers across the region and statistical methods that rely on linkage disequilibrium (Kaplan et al. 2002; Turic et al. 2003). Results from the Turic et al., (2003) study of 22 markers across 18 cM of this region, found the strongest evidence for association using a three marker haplotype of D6S109, D6S422, and D6S1665 (Turic et al. 2003). Association was observed for this haplotype and the phenotypes of single-word reading, spelling, phonological awareness, phonological decoding, orthographic accuracy, and random automatized naming but not with vocabulary or attention-deficit hyperactivity disorder (ADHD).

A study of 104 families and 29 microsatellite markers spanning this region identified the strongest evidence for association for the marker JA04 with the most likely location within 4 cM on either side of this marker (Kaplan et al. 2002). Gruen and colleagues (Londin et al. 2003) followed up their association analysis of microsatellites by using a computer database search to identify expressed sequence tags (ESTs). These are partial or incomplete complimentary DNA (cDNA) sequences prepared from different tissues and deposited in public databases. Complimentary DNA is prepared by using an enzyme, reverse transcriptase, that copies the messenger RNA into DNA. Two million base pairs surrounding the peak of transmission disequilibrium of marker JA04 were screened using this approach, identifying 19 genes and 2 pseudogenes. The expression pattern of each gene was characterized by qualitative reverse transcriptase polymerase chain reaction (RT-PCR) from RNA extracted from 20 different human tissues. The pattern of expression pointed to six genes as the most promising due to increased, or exclusive, expression in the brain. These were vesicular membrane protein P24 (*VMP*), *KIAA0319* (a gene of unknown function), NAD(+)-dependent succinic semialdehyde dehydrogenase (*SSADH* or *ALDH5A1* for aldehyde dehydrogenase 5 family, member A1), *KIAA0386* (*C6orf32 or PL48*), *HT012* (now identified as *THEM2* for thioesterase superfamily membrane 2), and glycosylphosphatidylinositol specific phospholipase D1 (*GPLD1*).

Current evidence indicates that *VMP* is expressed exclusively in the brain and immunohistochemical data indicates that vesicular membrane protein is distributed mainly in dendrites (Cheng et al. 2002). It has been suggested that VMP may have a role in neural organelle transport based on sequence homology in the C-terminus to the microtubule-binding domains of microtubule-associated proteins (MAPs). *SSADH* or *ALD5A1*, encodes an enzyme, succinic semialdehyde dehydrogenase, that is required for 4-aminobutryric acid (GABA) degradation. Deficiency of this enzyme has been associated with variable presentation of neurological deficits including mild retardation in mental, motor and language development, to more severe neurological deficits including hypotonia, ataxia, and seizures (Chambliss et al. 1998). *KIAA0386* functions in a trophoblast differentiation pathway during blastocyst implantation in the uterus. A different isoform is expressed in peripheral white blood cells and circulating myelnoma cells (Morrish et al. 1998). *GPLD1* selectively hydrolyzes inositol phosphate linkage *in vitro*, releasing the protein bound to the plasma membrane via a glycosylphosphatidylinositol anchor into the cytosol. *THEM2* is not well characterized, but is a member of the thioesterase superfamily, and was first described as a hypothalamus-expressed gene (Hu et al. 2000). While the function of the *KIAA0319* gene is not known it is very highly expressed in brain. Additional support for this gene results from the Kaplan and colleagues (2002) study, where the most significant marker of the study, JA04, was located within the *KIAA0319* gene.

Only recently have association studies begun to examine single nucleotide polymorphisms (SNPs) focusing on candidate genes in the 6p region. Smith and colleagues (Deffenbacher et al. 2004), following on the linkage study of Gayan et al., (1999) with an expansion of the sample, first used microsatellites to narrow the linked region in their families to a 3.24 megabase (Mb) region between markers D6S1597 and D6S1571 with a peak between markers and D6S276 and D6S1554. This was followed by further fine-mapping using a dense map of SNPs. They identified 13 markers of the 31 tested with significant p values using one of four quantitative phenotypes or a composite measure of reading performance. These markers clustered over five genes in the region; *VMP, DCDC2, KIAA0319*, tumour necrosis factor (TNF) receptor-associated factor (TRAF) and TNF receptor associated protein (*TTRAP*), and *THEM2*. TTRAP is a member of a superfamily of Mg^{2+}/Mn^{2+}-dependent phosphodiesterases that associates with CD40 and tumour necrosis factor receptor-associated factors (TRAFs). It has been shown to inhibit nuclear factor-*k*B (NF-*k*B), a transcription factor (protein involved in regulating the expression of a gene) known to play a role in synaptic plasticity (Pype et al. 2000). *DCDC2* contains a doublecortin-homology domain that is noteworthy because the gene doublecortin (*DCX*) has been implicated in X-linked lissencephaly and is required for neuronal migration (Gleeson et al. 1998). Association with markers in the *VMP* and *DCDC2* genes were detected with all 5 phenotypes. Haplotypes were significant across these same genes and an additional gene, the *ALDH5A1* gene.

Using three samples of siblings selected to include severely affected probands, two from the UK (Fisher et al. 2002), and the other collected as part of the Colorado Reading Disability Study used in the previous studies above (Kaplan et al. 2002; Deffenbacher et al. 2004), association studies implicated a 77 kilobase pairs (kb) region spanning the gene for *TTRAP*, the first exons of *KIAA0319*, and *THEM2* (Francks et al. 2004). The main risk haplotype identified for the markers rs4504469, rs2038137 and rs2143340, was found at a frequency of 12% in the RD samples and was distinguished by the marker rs2143340. The frequency of the minor allele of this marker was increased in probands that were selected for phenotypic severity, 28% compared to the frequency of the entire sample of probands 15 to 16%. The exons, and predicted promoters of these three genes, as well as the gene for *ALDH5A1*, were screened for DNA changes using 32 probands, however, no DNA changes were identified that would predict a change in function and explain the association results. One coding region SNP (rs4504469) was identified in exon 4 (Ala to Thr) of *KIAA0319*, however the allele frequency was very common (0.47) and therefore unlikely to explain this association, as it was not unique to the risk haplotype identified.

This region containing the genes for *MRS2L* (magnesium homeostatsis factor), *KIAA0319*, *TTRAP* and *THEM2* was confirmed as being the most likely location for the RD susceptibility gene in the most recent study, with the evidence implicating *KIAA0319* specifically as the most likely gene of these four (Cope et al. 2005a). This study used a dense map of markers to cover a 575 kb region of 6p22 and observed 17 of the 137 markers to be associated in a case-control sample with 13 of these in *KIAA0319*. Using stepwise logistic regression analyses, two polymorphisms in the *KIAA0319* gene best explained the results, rs4504469 and rs6935076. The haplotype of these two markers was significantly associated with RD (global P = 0.00001 in the case-control sample and 0.02 in a sample of trios) with under representation of the most common haplotype in the cases. The haplotype of the three markers identified as associated in the Franks 2004 study (rs4504469, rs2038137 and rs2143340) did not identify the same haplotype as associated, however, another haplotype of those same markers, was significantly associated. This haplotype was found more often in controls than in the cases. These results implicate the same region, however, they are not strictly a replication because the same haplotype is not associated.

In summary, association studies have narrowed the region of shared haplotypes to five genes with three of the genes supported in independent studies. The results from the most recent study strongly support one of these genes, *KIAA0319*, as the most likely candidate. All of these genes are brain expressed and based on the essentially nonexistent information currently available on the biology of the reading process, a rationale could be proposed for all of these genes. Further fine mapping and functional studies will undoubtedly lead to the determination of the causative gene on 6p shortly.

Chromosome 1p (DYX8)

The third chromosomal region reported to be linked to RD was located on 1p. Evidence for linkage to chromosome 1 in the region of the Rh protein and the marker D1S165 (1p34-p36) was first reported using nine three-generational families (Rabin et al. 1993). Additional support for this locus was obtained in a study by Grigorenko and colleagues, with the strongest evidence for linkage with the rapid automatized naming phenotype (Grigorenko et al. 2000). Further, using a two-locus model, they found evidence for an interaction of the 1p locus with the 6p region.

An additional study has also confirmed the 1p linkage finding using a sample of 100 Canadian families (Tzenova et al. 2004). Qualitative and quantitative analysis provided evidence for linkage to the same region as identified in the two previous reports with the most significant evidence for linkage over the region spanned by the markers D1S552 and D1S1622. Thus far, there have been no published fine mapping studies for this chromosome.

Chromosome 2p (DYX3)

Two loci have been reported for RD on chromosome 2p. The first locus was reported on 2p15-p16 (Fagerheim et al. 1999) and the second on 2p11 (Kaminen et al. 2003). While these two regions are relatively close and there could in fact be one risk gene on this chromosome, the current data indicates that they are two distinct loci (Peyrard-Janvid et al. 2004). The 2p15-p16 region was first identified during a genome scan of a large Norwegian family in which RD segregated as an autosomal dominant trait (Fagerheim et al. 1999). The findings of this group suggest the most likely placement of the gene is in the 4 cM region between D2S2352 and D2S1337. This locus was further supported in a sample of Canadian families (Petryshen et al. 2002) and by the genome scan of nuclear families discussed under the chromosome 18p section (Fisher et al. 2002). The genome scan on 11 families with 38 affected family members (88 family members in all) from Finland confirmed a locus on chromosome 2p (Kaminen et al. 2003) however the linkage peak was 34 cM from the previous reported linkage peak (Fagerheim et al. 1999).

As a result of these linkage findings, fine mapping has begun in the 2p region. Based on the 119 nuclear families used in the genome scan of nuclear families (Fisher et al. 2002), and a panel of 21 microsatellite markers across 2p12-16, the chromosome 2 region was narrowed to 12 cM (Francks et al. 2002). The most likely location identified in that study was between the markers D2S337 and D2S286. Two markers, D2S2378 and D2S2114 showed evidence of association using a quantitative method for several reading phenotypes, however, these two markers are 25 cM apart and are not in linkage disequilibrium. This suggests that the results from one, or possibly both, of these markers are false positives. Alternatively, if there are two genes on chromosome 2p, they could reflect distinct linkage disequilibrium signals.

Two potential candidates in this region were screened in that study for DNA changes in the exons. These two genes, Semaphorin 4F (*SEMA4F*), which encodes a protein involved in axon growth cone guidance, and *OTX1*, a homeodomain transcription factor involved in forebrain development, were considered candidates based on their reported function and expression patterns. The exons of these two genes were screened for DNA sequence changes using denaturing high performance liquid chromatography (dHPLC); a sensitive method for the detection of DNA changes. However, no variants were found that were predicted to change the amino acid sequence. Using synonymous (silent substitution of a nucleotide that replaces one amino acid with the same amino acid) and intronic DNA changes that were identified during this screen for association analysis did not provide any evidence for association. These results led the authors to conclude that these two genes were unlikely to be contributing to RD.

In the Finnish families linked to this region, fine mapping of the 2p region narrowed the linked region to a 12 Mb chromosomal segment between D2S2116 and D2S2181 (Peyrard-Janvid et al. 2004). Because there was no overlap in this region and the 2p15-16 region, the author's conclude that this locus is a distinct locus from the one discussed above. One specific gene within the 2p11 region, *TACR1*, encoding the G-protein-coupled receptor for tachykinin substance P/neurokinin 1, involved in the modulation of neuronal activity, inflammation and mood, was excluded based on finding no evidence of a shared haplotype within the families examined. The coding region was also screened and no DNA changes were identified that would predict a change in function.

Chromosome 6q (DYX4)

A study of 96 families (877 individuals) reported evidence for linkage to the 6q11.2-q12 region using phonological coding as a categorical trait and quantitative analysis of phonological awareness, coding, spelling and rapid automatized naming speed (Petryshen et al. 2001). The region identified as linked to RD, is 40 cM distal to the 6p locus and is therefore a distinct locus. Thus far, no further targeted studies of this region have been published.

Chromosome 3p (DYX5)

A genome scan in a single large family from Finland identified linkage to the centromeric region of chromosome 3 (3p12-q13) (Nopola-Hemmi et al. 2001). Fine mapping with additional markers in this region identified 19 of 21 affected family members shared the same 20 cM chromosomal haplotype identical by descent between markers D3S3039 and D3S3045. This locus was linked with phonological awareness, rapid naming, and verbal short-term memory.

This region was also identified in a study of speech-sound disorder (SSD), a behavioural disorder characterized by speech-sound production errors associated with deficits in articulation, phonological processing, and cognitive linguistic processes (Stein et al. 2004). SSD is often comorbid with disorders of language, spelling, and RD. Based on the evidence that SSD and RD may share some shared genetic influences, the chromosome 3 centromeric region was investigated in a sample of 77 families with a proband with SSD. The strongest evidence for linkage was identified in the 3p region for measures of phonological memory and for speech-sound production. Tests of word identification and decoding were also significant. Analysis of haplotypes in sib pairs from these families, with evidence for linkage to this region identified a shared region of 4.9 cM bounded by the markers D3S3059 and D3S3045. This region overlaps completely with the linkage region in the Finnish families suggesting that the 3p locus is pleiotropic for SSD and reading component skills, further refining the linked region.

Chromosome 18p (DYX6)

In the only genome scan to use nuclear families, the most significant evidence for linkage was to 18p (Fisher et al. 2002). This study used two sets of RD families, one from the UK and one from the US drawn from the Colorado Reading Disability Twin Study. A subset of both the UK and US families were previously reported to be linked to 6p (Cardon et al. 1994; Fisher et al. 1999; Gayan et al. 1999). In both samples, the most significant single point finding was for markers on chromosome 18p11.2 for the trait of single word reading ability. Measures of orthographic and phonological processing also showed evidence of linkage to this locus. Analysis of a third set of families for this region support linkage to the trait of phoneme awareness. This locus therefore appears to influence a number of reading related processes and may be a general risk factor for RD influencing several reading processes. Another region with evidence for linkage in this sample was the 2p15-p16 region previously identified in the Norwegian family as discussed above, however, there was no evidence reported to linkage to the 1p or 15q regions. Other chromosomal regions with significant results for at least one of the reading component measures were also identified and further fine mapping of these regions is now required.

Chromosome 7q32

As well as the identification of a locus on chromosome 2p11, the genome scan using 11 families from Finland as discussed above, pointed to a new locus on chromosome 7q32 (Kaminen et al. 2003). There was no evidence in this study for linkage to the other chromosomal regions previously identified as linked to RD (15q, 6p, 3p, or 18p).

LINKAGE ANALYSIS FOR READING COMPONENTS

Twin studies of reading components indicate that there will be shared, as well as specific genes contributing to these phenotypes as discussed above. Linkage and association studies have sought to determine the contribution of each of the chromosomal loci to the reading phenotypes using quantitative analysis of reading components. Further, the choice of the correct phenotype for the analysis will improve the power of the analysis and the correct estimation of the location of the gene. Initial linkage findings using reading processes as phenotypes suggested that different loci contributed differently to these reading phenotypes. With additional studies, these distinctions have become less clear, with different studies showing support for different phenotypes to the same chromosomal regions. A number of factors can influence the linkage findings using quantitative measures including ascertainment method, the measures of the phenotype chosen, and frequency and variance of the phenotype in the sample (Pennington 1997). Adult ceiling effects can also reduce the variance of the psychometric tests and reduce power in studies that used adults in the analysis. Allelic heterogeneity may also be a factor — different alleles in the same gene may contribute to different reading processes in different families. At this time it is premature to make conclusions concerning the relationship of these phenotypes to each locus and further studies are warranted. Identification of genes and the identification of the functional DNA variants will undoubtedly help clarify the relationship of each gene to the phenotype.

LINKAGE OVERLAP OF RD AND ATTENTION-DEFICIT HYPERACTIVITY DISORDER (ADHD)

Based on the findings from twin studies for overlap in the heritability for RD and ADHD symptoms, particularly the inattention symptoms, several groups have begun to investigate the genetic relationship of RD and ADHD. Results from the linkage studies of RD, and the genome scans and candidate gene studies of ADHD, have indicated several regions that overlap. Notably, two regions, 6q12-q14 and 15q, previously identified for linkage to RD, were identified in genome scans of sibling pairs affected with ADHD (Bakker et al. 2003; Ogdie et al. 2004). Although not significant, the most promising region identified in the genome scan of 164 Dutch sibling pairs with ADHD (Bakker et al. 2003) was the 15q region overlapping the region identified in the linkage studies for RD as reviewed above. In a separate study, the 6q12-q14 chromosomal region was identified with suggestive evidence for linkage in an initial genome scan of 270 affected sibling pairs with ADHD collected in Southern California (Ogdie et al. 2003). A follow up study of this region with an expanded sample of families (308 sibling pairs) and a dense set of markers (~2 cM grid) across this region provided significant evidence for linkage (Ogdie et al. 2004).

To investigate this relationship more directly, the genome scan results of a subset of this same sample collected at UCLA (233 affected sibling pairs with ADHD), was analyzed for measures of reading ability using quantitative analysis of both a composite score of several reading measures (reading recognition, spelling, and reading comprehension subtests from the PIAT-R) and the reading recognition measure individually (Loo et al. 2004). No significant evidence for linkage of reading measures was identified, however, several regions were found with suggestive evidence for linkage for the composite score. Two of these were previously identified as linked to ADHD in this sample, 16p and 17q, and a third, 10q, was identified in an independent genome scan for ADHD (Bakker et al. 2003). The 2p region previously identified as linked to RD was also identified. These results suggest the possibility that these particular loci may contribute to ADHD and to RD.

A number of genes have been reported to be linked or associated with ADHD over the past few years, The chromosomal location of some of these coincides with the regions linked to RD, suggesting the possibility that these genes are contributing to both phenotypes. Thus far, the genes with the strongest support for association with ADHD include the dopamine transporter (Cook et al. 1995; Gill et al. 1997; Barr et al. 2001), and the dopamine receptors D4 (*DRD4*) (Faraone et al. 2001), and D5 (*DRD5*) (Lowe et al. 2004). Additional genes with multiple studies reporting association include the gene for the snaptosomal-associated protein of 25 kd (*SNAP25*) (Barr et al. 2000; Kustanovich et al. 2001; Brophy et al. 2002; Mill et al. 2002; Mill et al. 2004) as well as the gene for the serotonin receptor 1B (*HTR1B*) (Quist et al. 1999; Hawi et al. 2002; Quist et al. 2003; Li et al. 2005). The *HTR1B* gene is particularly noteworthy as it resides in 6q13, a region reported to be linked to RD (Petryshen et al. 2001) and identified in the genome scan of ADHD (Ogdie et al. 2004)

Two groups have found some evidence for linkage of the RD phenotype to the 11p15 (DYX7) region (Petryshen et al. 1999; Fisher et al. 2002), the location of the DRD4 gene. The first study found linkage to the marker D11S1363, located 3 cM distal to DRD4 (Petryshen et al. 1999). This finding was followed by a study in that sample using 14 microsatellite markers across the region, two in the DRD4 gene (Hsiung et al. 2004). Analysis of the DRD4 gene showed significant evidence for linkage to this gene (MFLOD = 2.68, p=0.001), however, there was no evidence for association with the exon 3, 48 bp repeat polymorphism that had previously been reported to be associated with ADHD. This could suggest that a different allele is associated with RD in the samples, or alternatively, that DRD4 is not the risk gene in this region for RD. The recent genome scan for RD in siblings further support this region with evidence for linkage to D11S1338 located ~9 cM proximal to DRD4 (Fisher et al. 2002).

Interestingly, previous reports of association between ADHD and *DRD4* indicated that the association was stronger for inattention symptoms than with hyperactive/impulsive symptoms (Rowe et al. 1998). An additional study reported a stronger association of this gene with the inattentive subtype than with the hyperactive/impulsive and combined subtypes analyzed together (McCracken et al. 2000). The finding of a stronger relationship to inattention symptoms is further supported by unpublished results from our group where we identified significant evidence for association with parent reported inattention symptoms (p=0.009) but no significant evidence for association to parent hyperactive/impulsive symptoms, however there was a trend for this association (Crosbie et al., in preparation). The previous findings from twin studies indicating genetic overlap between inattention symptoms and RD (Willcutt et al. 2000), suggests the possibility that DRD4 may contribute to both RD and inattention symptoms. This relationship needs to be further explored in families with RD.

One last study targeted the relationship of ADHD in the 6p region linked to RD. In a sample of siblings ascertained with reading difficulties, and previously linked to 6p for reading measures, evidence for linkage to ADHD symptom count was also identified for the 6p region (Willcutt et al. 2002).

These studies, in total, suggest that some of the genes that contribute to RD will be pleiotropic, contributing to ADHD, particularly the inattention symptoms. Further studies of regions and genes identified in ADHD as contributors to RD are therefore warranted.

SUMMARY

In total, these studies strongly support a genetic basis for RD and the components of reading skill (phonological awareness, decoding, single word reading, spelling, orthographic coding), and reading-related processes (verbal short term memory, language). The different chromosomal linkage findings suggest the possibility of at least eight genes contributing to RD, although some of the linkage reports await replication before these regions can be considered definitive locations. Further, some of these regions may be general risk factors for reading ability influencing multiple reading processes, and some may have greater influence on specific aspects of the phenotype. Other loci contributing to these phenotypes will undoubtedly be detected as suggested by other, less significant, positive regions detected from the recent genome scan of nuclear families (Fisher et al. 2002). These loci may become more significant with larger samples and fine mapping. Further, studies of ADHD suggest there may be some shared susceptibility factors as well.

The unprecedented degree of replication for a complex trait, the consistency in the regions of the linkage findings, and the progress in fine mapping for some of the regions is proving to be very promising for gene identification. The cloning of the *EKN1* gene found by a translocation breakpoint in the Finnish family, and the identification of association for markers in this gene may be a major breakthrough in the identification of the chromosome 15q locus. However, this finding is not clearly replicating across samples and further confirmation is required before this gene can be conclusively identified as a gene contributing to RD.

In the 6p region, the current results point to only a few genes, with one gene in particular, *KIAA0319*, being associated in several independent studies. Further confirmation in independent samples is now required to determine if this is the susceptibility gene in this region.

Of course gene identification is only the first step in understanding how these genes work in a developmental framework to contribute to the risk of the development of RD. The interaction of these genes and the mechanism by which they are modulated by environmental factors will take years to unravel.

REFERENCES

Bakker, S. C., van der Meulen, E. M., Buitelaar, J. K., Sandkuijl, L. A., Pauls, D. L., Monsuur, A. J., van 't Slot, R., Minderaa, R. B., Gunning, W. B., Pearson, P. L., & Sinke, R. J. (2003). A whole-genome scan in 164 Dutch sib pairs with attention-deficit/hyperactivity disorder: suggestive evidence for linkage on chromosomes 7p and 15q. *American Journal of Human Genetics, 72,* 1251–1260.
Barr, C. L., Feng, Y., Wigg, K., Bloom, S., Roberts, W., Malone, M., Schachar, R., Tannock, R., & Kennedy, J. L. (2000). Identification of DNA variants in the SNAP-25 gene and linkage study of these polymorphisms and attention-deficit hyperactivity disorder. *Molecular Psychiatry, 5,* 405–409.

Barr, C. L., Xu, C., Kroft, J., Feng, Y., Wigg, K., Zai, G., Tannock, R., Schachar, R., Malone, M., Roberts, W., Nothen, M. M., Grunhage, F., Vandenbergh, D. J., Uhl, G., Sunohara, G., King, N., & Kennedy, J. L. (2001). Haplotype study of three polymorphisms at the dopamine trans-porter locus confirm linkage to attention-deficit/hyperactivity disorder. *Biological Psychiatry, 49,* 333–339.

Bisgaard, M. L., Eiberg, H., Moller, N., Niebuhr, E., & Mohr, J. (1987). Dyslexia and chromosome 15 heteromorphism: negative lod score in a Danish material. *Clinical Genetics, 32,* 118–119.

Bishop, D. V., North, T., & Donlan, C. (1996). Nonword repetition as a behavioural marker for inherited language impairment: evidence from a twin study. *Journal of Child Psychology and Psychiatry, 37,* 391–403.

Blatch, G. L., & Lassle, M. (1999). The tetratricopeptide repeat: a structural motif mediating protein-protein interactions. *Bioessays, 21,* 932–939.

Bradley, L., & Bryant, P. E. (1983). Categorizing sounds and learning to read - a causal connection. *Nature, 301,* 419–421.

Brophy, K., Hawi, Z., Kirley, A., Fitzgerald, M., & Gill, M. (2002). Synaptosomal-associated pro-tein 25 (SNAP-25) and attention deficit hyperactivity disorder (ADHD): evidence of linkage and association in the Irish population. *Molecular Psychiatry, 7,* 913–917

Bruck, M. (1992). Persistence of dyslexics' phonological awareness deficits. *Developmental Psychology, 28,* 874–886.

Cardon, L. R., Smith, S. D., Fulker, D. W., Kimberling, W. J., Pennington, B. F., & DeFries, J. C. (1994). Quantitative trait locus for reading disability on chromosome 6. *Science, 266,* 276–279.

Cardon, L. R., Smith, S. D., Fulker, D. W., Kimberling, W. J., Pennington, B. F., & DeFries, J. C. (1995). Quantitative trait locus for reading disability: correction [letter]. *Science, 268,*1553.

Chambliss, K. L., Hinson, D. D., Trettel, F., Malaspina, P., Novelletto, A., Jakobs, C., & Gibson, K. M. (1998). Two exon-skipping mutations as the molecular basis of succinic semi-aldehyde dehydrogenase deficiency (4-hydroxybutyric aciduria). *American Journal of Human Genetics, 63,* 399–408.

Chapman, N. H., Igo, R. P., Thomson, J. B., Matsushita, M., Brkanac, Z., Holzman, T., Berninger, V. W., Wijsman, E. M., & Raskind, W. H. (2004). Linkage analyses of four regions previously impli-cated in dyslexia: confirmation of a locus on chromosome 15q. *American Journal of Medical Genetics Part B: Neuropsychiatric Genetics, 131,* 67–75.

Cheng, C., Xu, J., Ye, X., Dai, J., Wu, Q., Zeng, L., Wang, L., Zhao, W., Ji, C., Gu, S., Xie, Y., & Mao, Y. (2002). Cloning, expression and characterization of a novel human VMP gene. *Molecular Biology Reports, 29,* 281–286.

Cook, E. H., Jr., Stein, M. A., Krasowski, M., D., Cox, N. J., Olkon, D. M., Kieffer, J. E., & Leventhal, B. L. (1995) Association of attention-deficit disorder and the dopamine trans-porter gene. *American Journal of Human Genetics, 56,* 993–998.

Cope, N., Harold, D., Hill, G., Moskvina, V., Stevenson, J., Holmans, P., Owen, M. J., O'Donovan, M. C., & Williams, J. (2005a) Strong Evidence That KIAA0319 on Chromosome 6p is a susceptibility gene for Developmental Dyslexia. *American Journal of Human Genetics, 76,* 581–591.

Cope, N. A., Hill, G., van den Bree, M., Harold, D., Moskvina, V., Green, E. K., Owen, M. J., Williams, J., O'Donovan, M. C. (2005b). No support for association between dyslexia sus-ceptibility 1 candidate 1 and developmental dyslexia. *Molecular Psychiatry 10,* 237–238.

Davis, C. J., Gayan, J., Knopik, V. S., Smith, S. D., Cardon, L. R., Pennington, B. F., Olson, R. K., & DeFries, J. C. (2001). Etiology of reading difficulties and rapid naming: the Colorado Twin Study of Reading Disability. Behavior Genetics, 31, 625–635.

Deffenbacher, K. E., Kenyon, J. B., Hoover, D. M., Olson, R. K., Pennington, B. F., DeFries, J. C., & Smith, S. D. (2004). Refinement of the 6p21.3 quantitative trait locus influencing dyslexia: linkage and association analyses. *Human Genetics, 115,* 128–138. Epub: 2004 May 11.

DeFries, J. C., Fulker, D. W., LaBuda, M. C. (1987). Evidence for a genetic aetiology in reading disability of twins. *Nature, 329,* 537–539.

DeFries, J. C., &Gillis, J. J. (1993) Genetics of Reading Disability. In R. Plomin & G. E. McClearn (eds), *Nature, Nurture, and Psychology,* pp 121–145. American Psychological Association, Washington, D.C.

Denckla, M. B., & Rudel, R. G. (1976). Rapid "automatized" naming (R.A.N): dyslexia differentiated from other learning disabilities. *Neuropsychologia, 14,* 471–479.

Fagerheim, T., Raeymaekers, P., Tonnessen, F. E, Pedersen, M., Tranebjaerg, L., & Lubs, H. A. (1999). A new gene (DYX3) for dyslexia is located on chromosome 2. *Journal of Medical Genetics, 36,* 664–669.

Faraone, S. V., Doyle, A. E., Mick, E., & Biederman, J. (2001). Meta-analysis of the association between the 7-repeat allele of the dopamine D(4) receptor gene and attention deficit hyperactivity disorder. *American Journal of Psychiatry, 158,* 1052–1057.

Felton, R. H., Naylor, C. E., & Wood, F. B. (1990). Neuropsychological profile of adult dyslexics. *Brain and Language, 39,* 485–497.

Field, L. L., & Kaplan, B. J. (1998). Absence of Linkage of Phonological Coding Dyslexia to Chromosome 6p23- p21.3 in a Large Family Data Set. *American Journal of Human Genetics, 63,* 1448–1456.

Finucci, J. M., Guthrie, J. T., Childs, A. L., Abbey, H., & Childs, B. (1976). The genetics of specific reading disability. *Ann Hum Genet* 40:1–23.

Fisher, S. E., & DeFries, J. C. (2002). Developmental dyslexia: genetic dissection of a complex cognitive trait. *Nature Reviews Neuroscience, 3,* 767–780.

Fisher, S. E., Francks, C., Marlow, A. J., MacPhie, I. L., Newbury, D. F., Cardon, L. R., Ishikawa-Brush, Y., Richardson, A. J., Talcott, J. B., Gayan, J., Olson, R. K., Pennington, B. F., Smith, S. D., DeFries, J. C., Stein, J. F., & Monaco, A. P. (2002). Independent genome-wide scans identify a chromosome 18 quantitative-trait locus influencing dyslexia. *Nature Genetics, 30,* 86–91.

Fisher, S. E., Marlow, A. J., Lamb, J., Maestrini, E., Williams, D. F., Richardson, A. J., Weeks, D. E., Stein, J. F., & Monaco, A. P. (1999). A quantitative-trait locus on chromosome 6p influences different aspects of developmental dyslexia. *American Journal of Human Genetics, 64,* 146–156.

Francks, C., Fisher, S. E., Olson, R. K., Pennington, B. F., Smith, S. D., DeFries, J. C., & Monaco, A. P. (2002). Fine mapping of the chromosome 2p12-16 dyslexia susceptibility locus: quantitative association analysis and positional candidate genes SEMA4F and OTX1. *Psychiatric Genetics, 12,* 35–41.

Francks, C., Paracchini, S., Smith, S. D., Richardson, A. J., Scerri, T. S., Cardon, L. R., Marlow, A. J., MacPhie, I. L., Walter, J., Pennington, B. F., Fisher, S. E., Olson, R. K., DeFries, J. C., Stein, J. F, & Monaco, A. P. (2004). A 77-kilobase region of chromosome 6p22.2 is associated with dyslexia in families from the United Kingdom and from the United States. *American Journal of Human Genetics, 75,* 1046–1058.

Fulker, D. W., Cardon, L. R., DeFries, J. C., Kimberling, W. J., Pennington, B. F., & Smith, S. D. (1991). Multiple regression analysis of sib-pair data on reading to detect quantitative trait loci. *Reading and Writing: An Interdisciplinary Journal, 3,* 299–313.

Gathercole, S. E., Willis, C. S., Baddeley, A. D., & Emslie, H. (1994). The Children's Test of Nonword Repetition: a test of phonological working memory. *Memory, 2,* 103–127.

Gayan, J., & Olson, R. K. (1999). Reading disability: evidence for a genetic etiology. *European Child and Adolescent Psychiatry, 8,* Supplement 3, 52–55.

Gayan, J., & Olson, R. K. (2001). Genetic and environmental influences on orthographic and phonological skills in children with reading disabilities. *Developmental Neuropsychology, 20,* 483–507.

Gayan, J., Smith, S. D., Cherny, S. S., Cardon, L. R., Fulker, D. W., Brower, A. M., Olson, R. K., Pennington, B. F., & DeFries, J. C. (1999). Quantitative-trait locus for specific language and reading deficits on chromosome 6p. *Amercian Journal of Human Genetics, 64,* 157–164.

Geschwind, N., & Behan, P. (1982). Left-handedness: association with immune disease, migraine, and developmental learning disorder. *Proceedings of the National Academy of Science of the United States of America, 79,* 5097–5100.

Gilger, J. W., Pennington, B. F., & DeFries, J. C. (1992a). A twin study of the etiology of comorbidity: attention-deficit hyperactivity disorder and dyslexia. *Journal of the American Academy Child and Adolescent Psychiatry, 31,* 343–348.

Gilger, J. W., Pennington, B. F., Green, P., Smith, S. M., & Smith, S. D. (1992b). Reading disability, immune disorders and non-right-handedness: twin and family studies of their relations. *Neuropsychologia, 30,* 209–227.

Gill, M., Daly, G., Heron, S., Hawi, Z., & Fitzgerald, M. (1997). Confirmation of association between attention deficit hyperactivity disorder and a dopamine transporter polymorphism. *Molecular Psychiatry, 2,* 311–313.

Gleeson, J. G., Allen, K. M., Fox, J. W., Lamperti, E. D., Berkovic, S., Scheffer, I., Cooper, E. C., Dobyns, W. B., Minnerath, S. R., Ross, M. E., & Walsh, C. A. (1998). Doublecortin, a brain-specific gene mutated in human X-linked lissencephaly and double cortex syndrome, encodes a putative signaling protein. *Cell, 92,* 63–72.

Grigorenko, E. L. (2001). Developmental dyslexia: an update on genes, brains, and environments. *Journal of Child Psychology and Psychiatry, 42,* 91–125.

Grigorenko, E. L. (2003). The first candidate gene for dyslexia: Turning the page of a new chapter of research. *Proceedings of the National Academy of Sciences of the United States of America, 100,* 11190–11192.

Grigorenko, E. L., Wood, F. B., Golovyan, L., Meyer, M., Romano, C., & Pauls, D. (2003). Continuing the search for dyslexia genes on 6p. *American Journal of Medical Genetics Part B: Neuropsychiatric Genetics, 118,* 89–98.

Grigorenko, E. L., Wood, F. B., Meyer, M. S., Hart, L. A., Speed, W. C., Shuster, A., & Pauls, D. L. (1997). Susceptibility loci for distinct components of developmental dyslexia on chromosomes 6 and 15. *American Journal of Human Genetics, 60,* 27–39.

Grigorenko, E. L., Wood, F. B., Meyer, M. S., & Pauls, D. L. (2000). Chromosome 6p influences on different dyslexia-related cognitive processes: further confirmation. *American Journal of Human Genetics, 66,* 715–723.

Grigorenko, E. L., Wood, F. B., Meyer, M. S., Pauls, J. E., Hart, L. A., & Pauls, D. L. (2001). Linkage studies suggest a possible locus for developmental dyslexia on chromosome 1p. *American Journal of Medical Genetics, 105,* 120–129.

Hawi, Z., Dring, M., Kirley, A., Foley, D., Kent, L., Craddock, N., Asherson, P., Curran, S., Gould, A., Richards, S., Lawson, D., Pay, H., Turic, D., Langley, K., Owen, M., O'Donovan, M., Thapar, A,, Fitzgerald, M., & Gill, M. (2002). Serotonergic system and attention deficit hyperactivity disorder (ADHD): a potential susceptibility locus at the 5-HT(1B) receptor gene in 273 nuclear families from a multi-centre sample. *Molecular Psychiatry, 7,* 718–725.

Hohnen, B., & Stevenson, J. (1999). The structure of genetic influences on general cognitive, language, phonological, and reading abilities. *Developmental Psychology, 35,* 590–603.

Hsiung, G. Y., Kaplan, B. J., Petryshen, T. L., Lu, S., & Field, L. L. (2004). A dyslexia susceptibility locus (DYX7) linked to dopamine D4 receptor (DRD4) region on chromosome 11p15.5. *American Journal of Medical Genetics, 125B,* 112–9

Hu, R. M., Han, Z. G., Song, H. D., Peng, Y. D., Huang, Q. H., Ren, S. X., Gu, Y. J., et al. (2000) Gene expression profiling in the human hypothalamus-pituitary-adrenal axis and full-length cDNA cloning. *Proceedings of the National Academy of Sciences of the United States of America, 97,* 9543–9548.

Jorm, A. F. (1979). The cognitive and neurological basis of developmental dyslexia: a theoretical framework and review. *Cognition, 7,* 19–33

Kaminen, N., Hannula-Jouppi, K., Kestila, M., Lahermo, P., Muller, K., Kaaranen, M., Myllyluoma, B., Voutilainen, A., Lyytinen, H., Nopola-Hemmi, J., & Kere, J. (2003). A genome scan for developmental dyslexia confirms linkage to chromosome 2p11 and suggests a new locus on 7q32. *Journal of Medical Genetics, 40,* 340–345.

Kaplan, D. E., Gayan, J., Ahn, J., Won, T. W., Pauls, D., Olson, R. K., DeFries, J. C., Wood, F., Pennington, B. F., Page, G. P., Smith, S. D., & Gruen, J. R. (2002). Evidence for linkage and association with reading disability on 6p21.3–22. *American Journal of Human Genetics, 70,* 1287–1298.

Kleinjan, D. J., & van Heyningen, V. (1998). Position effect in human genetic disease. *Human Molecular Genetics, 7,* 1611–1618.

Kustanovich, V., Merriman, B., Crawford, L., Smalley, S., & Nelson, S. (2001). An association study of SNAP-25 alleles shows evidence for biased paternal inheritance in attention defict hyperacitivity disorder. *American Journal of Human Genetics, 69,* 582

Lefly, D. L., & Pennington, B. F. (2000). Reliability and Validity of the Adult Reading History Questionnaire. *Journal of Reading Disabilities, 33,* 286–296.

Lewitter, F. I., DeFries, J. C., & Elston, R. C. (1980). Genetic models of reading disability. *Behavior Genetics, 10,* 9–30.

Li, J., Wang, Y., Zhou, R., Zhang, H., Yang, L., Wang, B., Khan, S., & Faraone, S. V. (2005). Serotonin 5-HT1B receptor gene and attention deficit hyperactivity disorder in Chinese Han subjects. *American Journal of Medical Genetics Part B: Neuropsychiatric Genetics, 132,* 59–63.

Londin, E. R., Meng, H., & Gruen, J. R. (2003). A transcription map of the 6p22.3 reading disability locus identifying candidate genes. *BMC Genomics, 4,* 25.

Loo, S. K., Fisher, S. E., Francks, C., Ogdie, M. N., MacPhie, I. L., Yang, M., McCracken, J. T., McGough, J. J., Nelson, S. F., Monaco, A. P., Smalley, S. L. (2004). Genome-wide scan of reading ability in affected sibling pairs with attention-deficit/hyperactivity disorder: unique and shared genetic effects. *Molecular Psychiatry, 9,* 485–493.

Lovett, M., & Baron, R. W. (2003). Developmental Reading Disorders. In: T. E. Feinberg, MF (ed), *Behavioral Neurology and Neuropsychology, 2nd.* McGraw-Hill, New York, pp 801–819

Lovett, M. W., Steinbach, K. A., & Frijters, J. C. (2000). Remediating the core deficits of developmental reading disability: A double deficit perspective. *Journal of Learning Disabilities, 33,* 334–358.

Lowe, N., Kirley, A., Hawi, Z., Sham, P., Wickham, H., Kratochvil, C. J., Smith, S. D., et al. (2004). Joint Analysis of the DRD5 Marker Concludes Association with Attention-Deficit/Hyperactivity Disorder Confined to the Predominantly Inattentive and Combined Subtypes. *American Journal of Human Genetics, 74,* 348–356.

Lyon, G. R. (2003). Part I, Defining Dyslexia, Comorbidity, Teachers' Knowledge of Language and Reading. *Annals of Dyslexia, 53,* 1–14.

MacDonell, L. E., Skinner, F. K., Ward, P. E., Glen, A. I., Glen, A. C., Macdonald, D. J., Boyle, R. M., & Horrobin, D. F. (2000). Increased levels of cytosolic phospholipase A2 in dyslexics. *Prostaglandins, Leukotrienes, and Essential Fatty Acids, 63,* 37–39.

Marino, C., Giorda, R., Luisa Lorusso, M., Vanzin, L., Salandi, N., Nobile, M., Citterio, A., Beri, S., Crespi, V., Battaglia, M., & Molteni, M. (2005). A family-based association study does not support DYX1C1 on 15q21.3 as a candidate gene in developmental dyslexia. *European Journal of Human Genetics, 13,* 491–499.

Marino, C., Giorda, R., Vanzin, L., Nobile, M., Lorusso, M. L., Baschirotto, C., Riva, L., Molteni, M., & Battaglia, M. (2004). A locus on 15q15-15qter influences dyslexia: further support from a transmission/disequilibrium study in an Italian speaking population. *Journal of Medical Genetics, 41,* 42–46.

Marlow, A. J., Fisher, S. E., Francks, C., MacPhie, I. L., Cherny, S. S., Richardson, A. J., Talcott, J. B., Stein, J. F., Monaco, A. P., Cardon, L. R. (2003). Use of multivariate linkage analysis for dissection of a complex cognitive trait. *American Journal of Human Genetics, 72,* 561–570.

McCracken, J. T., Smalley, S. L., McGough, J. J., Crawford, L., Del'Homme, M., & Cantor, R. M., Liu A, & Nelson, S. F. (2000). Evidence for linkage of a tandem duplication polymorphism upstream of the dopamine D4 receptor gene (DRD4) with attention deficit hyperactivity disorder (ADHD). *Molecular Psychiatry, 5*, 531–536.

Mill, J., Curran, S., Kent, L., Gould, A., Huckett, L., Richards, S., Taylor, E., & Asherson, P. (2002). Association study of a SNAP-25 microsatellite and attention deficit hyperactivity disorder. *American Journal of Medical Genetics, 114*, 269–271.

Mill, J., Richards, S., Knight, J., Curran, S., Taylor, E., & Asherson, P. (2004). Haplotype analysis of SNAP-25 suggests a role in the aetiology of ADHD. *Molecular Psychiatry, 9*, 801–810.

Morris, D. W., Ivanov, D., Robinson, L., Williams, N., Stevenson, J., Owen, M. J., Williams, J., & O'Donovan, M. C. (2004). Association analysis of two candidate phospholipase genes that map to the chromosome 15q15.1–15.3 region associated with reading disability. *American Journal of Medical Genetics Part B: Neuropsychiatric Genetics, 129B*, 97–103.

Morris, D. W., Robinson, L., Turic, D., Duke, M., Webb, V., Milham, C., Hopkin, E., Pound, K., Fernando, S., Easton, M., Hamshere, M., Williams, N., McGuffin, P., Stevenson, J., Krawczak, M., Owen, M. J., O'Donovan, M. C., & Williams, J. (2000). Family-based association mapping provides evidence for a gene for reading disability on chromosome 15q. *Human Molecular Genetics, 9*, 843–848.

Morrish, D. W., Dakour, J., & Li, H. (1998) Functional regulation of human trophoblast differentiation. *Journal of Reproductive Immunology, 39*, 179–195.

Nopola-Hemmi, J., Myllyluomam, B., Haltiam, T., Taipale, M., Ollikainen, V., Ahonen, T., Voutilainen, A., Kere, J., & Widen, E. (2001). A dominant gene for developmental dyslexia on chromosome 3. *Journal of Medical Genetics, 38*, 658–564.

Nopola-Hemmi, J., Taipale, M., Haltia, T., Lehesjoki, A. E., Voutilainen, A., & Kere, J. (2000). Two translocations of chromosome 15q associated with dyslexia. *Journal of Medical Genetics, 37*, 771–775.

Nothen, M. M., Schulte-Korne, G., Grimm, T., Cichon, S., Vogt, I. R., Muller-Myhsok, B., Propping, P., & Remschmidt, H. (1999). Genetic linkage analysis with dyslexia: evidence for linkage of spelling disability to chromosome 15. *European Child and Adolescent Psychiatry, 8*, 56–59.

Ogdie, M. N., Fisher, S. E., Yang, M., Ishii, J., Francks, C., Loo, S. K., Cantor, R. M., McCracken, J. T., McGough, J. J., Smalley, S. L., & Nelson, S. F. (2004). Attention deficit hyperactivity disorder: fine mapping supports linkage to 5p13, 6q12, 16p13, and 17p11. *American Journal of Human Genetics, 75*, 661–668.

Ogdie, M. N., Macphie, I. L., Minassian, S. L., Yang, M., Fisher, S. E., Francks, C., Cantor, R. M., McCracken, J. T., McGough, J. J., Nelson, S. F., Monaco, A. P., & Smalley, S. L. (2003). A genomewide scan for attention-deficit/hyperactivity disorder in an extended sample: suggestive linkage on 17p11. *American Journal of Human Genetics, 72*, 1268–1279.

Olson, R., Forsberg, H., Wise, B., & Rack, J. (1994). Measurement of word recognition, orthographic, and phonological skills. In: G. R. Lyon (ed.), *Frames of Reference for the Assessment of Learning Disabilities* (pp. 243–277). Paul H. Brookes: Baltimore, MD.

Pennington, B. F. (1990). The genetics of dyslexia. *Journal of Child Psychology and Psychiatry, 31*, 193–201.

Pennington, B. F. (1997). Using genetics to dissect cognition. *American Journal of Human Genetics, 60*, 13–16.

Pennington, B. F. (1999). Dyslexia as a neurodevelopmental disorder. In: H. Tager-Flushberg, (ed), *Neurodevelopmental Disorders* (pp. 307–330). MIT Press, Cambridge, MA.

Pennington, B. F., Gilger, J. W., Pauls, D., Smith, S. A., Smith, S. D., & DeFries, J. C. (1991). Evidence for major gene transmission of developmental dyslexia. *JAMA, 266*, 1527–1534.

Pennington, B. F., Smith, S. D., Kimberling, W. J., Green, P. A., & Haith, M. M. (1987). Left-handedness and immune disorders in familial dyslexics. *Archives of Neurology, 44*, 634–639.

Petryshen, T. L., Kaplan, B. J., Hughes, M. L., & Field, L. L. (1999). Linkage and association analysis of GABA receptor, dopamine receptor, and dopamine transporter genes in phonological coding dyslexia. *Molecular Psychiatry, 4,* S85.

Petryshen, T. L., Kaplan, B. J., Hughes, M. L., Tzenova, J., & Field, L. L. (2002). Supportive evidence for the DYX3 dyslexia susceptibility gene in Canadian families. *Journal of Medical Genetics, 39,* 125–126.

Petryshen, T. L., Kaplan, B. J., Liu, M. F., & Field, L. L. (2000). Absence of significant linkage between phonological coding dyslexia and chromosome 6p23–21.3, as determined by use of quantitative-trait methods: confirmation of qualitative analyses. *American Journal of Human Genetics, 66,* 708–714.

Petryshen, T. L., Kaplan, B. J., Liu, M. F., Schmill de French, N., Tobias, R., Hughes, M. L., & Field, L. L. (2001). Evidence for a susceptibility locus on chromosome 6q influencing phonological coding dyslexia. *American Journal of Medical Genetics (Neuropsychiatric Genetics) 105,* 507–517.

Peyrard-Janvid, M., Anthoni, H., Onkamo, P., Lahermo, P., Zucchelli, M., Kaminen, N., Hannula-Jouppi, K., Nopola-Hemmi, J., Voutilainen, A., Lyytinenm, H., & Kerem, J. (2004). Fine mapping of the 2p11 dyslexia locus and exclusion of TACR1 as a candidate gene. *Human Genetics, 114,* 510–516.

Pratt, A. C., & Brady, S. (1988). Relation of phonological awareness to reading disability in children and adults. *Journal of Educational Psychology, 80,* 319–323

Pype, S., Declercq, W., Ibrahimi, A., Michiels, C., Van Rietschoten, J. G., Dewulf, N., de Boer, M., Vandenabeele, P., Huylebroeck, D., Remacle, J. E. (2000). TTRAP, a novel protein that associates with CD40, tumor necrosis factor (TNF) receptor-75 and TNF receptor-associated factors (TRAFs), and that inhibits nuclear factor-kappa B activation. *Journal of Biological Chemistry, 275,* 18586–18593.

Quist, J. F., Barr, C. L., Schachar, R., Roberts, W., Malone, M., Tannock, R., Basile, V. S., Beitchman, J., & Kennedy, J. L. (2003). The serotonin 5-HT1B receptor gene and attention deficit hyperactivity disorder. *Molecular Psychiatry 8,* 98–102.

Quist, J. F., Barr, C. L., Shachar, R., Roberts, W., Malone, M., Tannock, R., Bloom, S., Basile, V. S., Kennedy, J. L. (1999). Evidence for an association of the serotonin 5-HT1B G861C polymorphism with ADHD. *Molecular Psychology, 4,* S93.

Rabin, M., Wen, X. L., Hepburn, M., Lubs, H. A., Feldman, E., & Duara, R. (1993). Suggestive linkage of developmental dyslexia to chromosome 1p34–p36. *Lancet, 342,* 178.

Rowe, D. C., Stever, C., Giedinghagen, L. N., Gard, J. M., Cleveland, H.H., Terris, S. T., Mohr, J. H., Sherman, S., Abramowitz, A., & Waldman, I. D. (1998) Dopamine DRD4 receptor polymorphism and attention deficit hyperactivity disorder. *Molecular Psychiatry, 3,* 419–426.

Rugel, R. P. (1974). WISC subtest scores of disabled readers: a review with respect to Bannatyne's recategorization. *Journal of Learning Disabilities, 7,* 57–64.

Scerri, T. S., Fisher, S. E., Francks, C., MacPhie, I. L., Paracchini, S., Richardson, A. J., Stein, J. F., & Monaco, A. P. (2004). Putative functional alleles of DYX1C1 are not associated with dyslexia susceptibility in a large sample of sibling pairs from the UK. *Journal of Medical Genetics, 41,* 853–857.

Schulte-Korne, G., Deimel, W., Muller, K., Gutenbrunner, C., & Remschmidt, H. (1996). Familial aggregation of spelling disability. *Journal of Child Psychology and Psychiatry, 37,* 817–822.

Schulte-Kornem, G., Grimmm, T., Nothen, M. M., Muller-Myhsok, B., Cichon, S., Vogt, I. R., Propping, P., & Remschmidt, H. (1998). Evidence for linkage of spelling disability to chromosome 15. *American Journal of Human Genetics, 63,*279–282.

Siegel, L. S. (2003). Basic Cognitive Processes and Reading Disabilities. In: H. L., Swanson, K. R. Harris, & S. Graham (eds.), *Handbook of Learning Disabilities* (pp 158–181). Guilford Press: New York.

Smith, S. D., & Kimberling, W. J. (1991). Reading Disabilities. In: B. Pennington (ed.), *Genetic and Neurological Influences*. Kluwer Academic, Boston

Smith, S. D., Kimberling, W. J., & Pennington, B. F. (1991). Screening for multiple genes influencing dyslexia. *Reading and Writing: An Interdisciplinary Journal, 3*, 285–298.

Smith, S. D., Kimberling, W. J., Pennington, B. F., & Lubs, H. A. (1983). Specific reading disability: identification of an inherited form through linkage analysis. *Science, 219*, 1345–1347.

Stanovich, K. E. (1982). Individual differences in the cognitive processes of reading: II. Text-level processes. *Journal of Learning Disabilities, 15*, 549–554.

Stein, C. M., Schick, J. H., Taylor, H. Gerry, Shriberg, L. D., Millard, C., Kundtz-Kluge, A., Russo, K., Minich, N., Hansen, A., Freebairn, L. A., Elston, R. C., Lewis, B. A., & Iyengar, S. K. (2004). Pleiotropic effects of a chromosome 3 locus on speech-sound disorder and reading. *American Journal of Human Genetics, 74*, 283–297. Epub, 2004 Jan 20.

Stevenson, J., Graham, P., Fredman, G., & McLoughlin, V. (1987). A twin study of genetic influences on reading and spelling ability and disability. *Journal of Child Psychology and Psychiatry, 28*, 229–247.

Taipale, M., Kaminen, N., Nopola-Hemmi, J., Haltia, T., Myllyluoma, B., Lyytinen, H., Muller, K., Kaaranen, M., Lindsberg, P. J., Hannula-Jouppi, K., & Kere, J. (2003). A candidate gene for developmental dyslexia encodes a nuclear tetratricopeptide repeat domain protein dynamically regulated in brain. *Proceedings of the National Academy of Science of the United States of America, 100*, 11553–11558.

Taylor, K. E., Higgins, C. J., Calvin, C. M., Hall, J. A., Easton, T., McDaid, A. M., & Richardson, A. J. (2000). Dyslexia in adults is associated with clinical signs of fatty acid deficiency. *Prostaglandins, Leukotriens, and Essential Fatty Acids, 63*, 75–78.

Taylor, K. E., Richardson, A. J., & Stein, J. F. (2001). Could platelet activating factor play a role in developmental dyslexia? *Prostaglandins, Leukotriens, and Essential Fatty Acids, 64*, 173–180.

Turic, D., Robinson, L., Duke, M., Morris, D. W., Webb, V., Hamshere, M., Milham, C., Hopkin, E., Pound, K., Fernando, S., Grierson, A., Easton, M., Williams, N., Van Den Bree, M., Chowdhury, R., Gruen, J., Stevenson, J., Krawczak, M., Owen, M. J., O'Donovan, M. C., & Williams, J. (2003). Linkage disequilibrium mapping provides further evidence of a gene for reading disability on chromosome 6p21.3–22. *Molecular Psychiatry, 8*, 176–185.

Tzenova, J., Kaplan, B. J., Petryshen, T. L., & Field, L. L. (2004). Confirmation of a dyslexia susceptibility locus on chromosome 1p34–p36 in a set of 100 Canadian families. *American Journal of Medical Genetics Part B: Neuropsychiatric Genetics, 127*, 117–124.

Urion, D. K. (1988). Nondextrality and autoimmune disorders among relatives of language-disabled boys. *Annals of Neurology, 24*, 267–269.

Vellutino, F. R., Fletcher, J. M., Snowling, M. J., &Scanlon, D. M. (2004). Specific reading disability (dyslexia): what have we learned in the past four decades? *Journal of Child Psychology and Psychiatry, 45*, 2–40.

Wadsworth, S. J., DeFries, J. C., Fulker, D. W., Olson, R. K., & Pennington, B. F. (1995). Reading performance and verbal short-term memory: a twin study of reciprocal causation. *Intelligence, 20*, 145–167.

Wadsworth SJ, Olson RK, Pennington BF, DeFries JC (2000) Differential genetic etiology of reading disability as a function of IQ. J Learn Disabil 33:192–9.

Watanabe, H., Fujiyama, A., Hattori, M., Taylor, T. D., Toyoda, A., Kuroki, Y., Noguchi, H., et al. (2004). DNA sequence and comparative analysis of chimpanzee chromosome 22. *Nature, 429*, 382–388.

Wigg, K. G., Couto, J. M., Feng, Y., Anderson, B., Cate-Carter, T. D., Macciardi, F., Tannock, R., Lovett, M. W., Humphries, T. W., Barr, C. L. (2004). Support for EKN1 as the susceptibility locus for dyslexia on 15q21. *Molecular Psychiatry, 9*, 1111–1121.

Willcutt, E. G., & Pennington, B. F. (2000) Comorbidity of reading disability and attention-deficit/hyperactivity disorder: differences by gender and subtype. *Journal of Learning Disabilities, 33*,179–191.

Willcutt, E. G., Pennington, B. F., & DeFries, J. C. (2000). Twin study of the etiology of comorbidity between reading disability and attention-deficit/hyperactivity disorder. *American Journal of Medical Genetics, 96,* 293–301.

Willcutt, E. G., Pennington, B. F., Smith, S. D., Cardon, L. R., Gayan, J., Knopik, V. S., Olson, R. K., & DeFries, J. C. (2002). Quantitative trait locus for reading disability on chromosome 6p is pleiotropic for attention-deficit/hyperactivity disorder. *American Journal of Medical Genetics, 114,* 260–268.

Wolf, M., & Bowers, P. G. (1999). The double-deficit hypothesis for the developmental dyslexias. *Journal of Educational Psychology, 91,* 415–438.

Wolf, M., Goldberg, A., Gidney, C., Lovett, M. W., Cirino, P., & Morris, R. D. (2002). The second deficit: An investigation of the independence of phonological and naming-speed deficits in developmental dyslexia. *Reading and Writing: An Interdisciplinary Journal, 15,* 43–72.

CHAPTER FOURTEEN

Four "Nons" of the Brain–Genes Connection

Elena L. Grigorenko
Yale University

Human beings are unique among the planet's species. There is nothing quite like us. Our closest genetic relatives are great apes, but many might argue that we are far removed from them. Grossly speaking, we are different from other apes in our relatively large brain size and distinct brain topology, cranial properties, the presence of a chin, S-shaped spine, distinct dimensions of the pelvis, complete bipedalism, relative limb length, body shape and thorax, skull balanced upright on vertebral column, elongated thumb and shortened fingers, small canine teeth, reduced hair cover, long ontogeny and lifespan, advanced tool-making capabilities, and, most importantly in the context of this chapter, language (Carroll, 2003).

The main objective of the chapter is to discuss various possibilities of direct and indirect connections among genes, the brain, and language-related behaviors in general and single-word processing in particular. The chapter is divided into four parts.

To speak, read, write, rumor, and create, tell, and comprehend words and stories—these, as far as we know, are exclusively human activities, the center of which is language, spoken and written. If humans alone have language, then it must have been important for nature to distinguish us somehow from the rest of the planet's inhabitants and to preserve this change for many generations through evolutionary mechanisms. What biological mechanisms underlie this uniqueness? To provide the reader with a glimpse of the current state of knowledge regarding this question, the first part of the chapter ventures into comparative genomics.

The *second* and *third* parts of the chapter connect to the first part by suggesting that, based on what we know about the psychology of human behavior, genetics of human behavioral traits and developmental disorders (for example, developmental dyslexia—a disorder whose central feature is in the challenged representation of printed single words—see the chapter by Piasta and Wagner), and comparative genomics, it is most likely that the distinction between species of humans and non-humans, even such close human relatives as chimpanzees, is determined by complex traits orchestrated by complex genetic mechanisms. These parts of the chapter briefly present commentaries on the parallels and bridges between mapping complex behavioral traits in the human brain and human genome and contain a number of illustrations and examples from the literature on studies of dyslexia in adults.

The *fourth*, concluding, part of the chapter summarizes the argument and provides illustrations of a variety of genetic mechanisms currently discussed in the field as potentially relevant to the etiology of complex traits in general and single-word reading in particular.

Conceptually, the chapter is built around a single concept: *pleiotropy*. There is growing recognition in the field that this concept, which originated in the field of genetics, appears to be central to linking sciences that attempt to understand biological bases of complex traits. Pleiotropy, from the Greek *pleio,* or many, and *tropos,* manner, assumes "multiple impact," indicating diverse properties of a single agent, or that a single cause might have multiple outcomes. This concept also underscores one of nature's main principles: economy of effort with maximization of outcome. In other words, when possible, nature attempts to create new wholes from already-existing parts by reassembling them and prescribing them new and unique functions. During the last decade or so, a number of discoveries have led researchers to the realization of a number of "nons": relative nonuniqueness of the organization of human biology in the context of evolution, relative nonspecificity of brain areas in the context of their involvement in human behavior, relative nonselectivity of genetic impacts on human behavior, and relative nondifferentiation of human behaviors in the course of development. These four "nons" presented themselves in the empirical research somewhat unexpectedly, almost against all rhyme and reason. It is this unexpectedness and the subtle wisdom of nature in recruiting the same genes, anatomical structures, physiological pathways, and simple behaviors multiple times to establish new superstructures with new functional possibilities that makes us uniquely human. In other words, pleiotropy is not only relevant to ways genes operate on complex behaviors; it appears to embody the generic principle of economical use of available resources in the development and manifestations of complex traits.

SURPRISES OF NONUNIQUENESS

The major tool of evolutionary genetics, the branch of science concerned with genetic bases of human origin, is comparative analysis. These analyses are aimed at pinpointing genetic differences between humans and their "different-degree-relatives" connected through the last common ancestor (Olson & Varki, 2003). Among currently existing species, the primary object of comparison with the human genome is the genome of the common chimpanzee (*Pan troglodytes*). Our common ancestor can be traced to about 6 to 7 million years ago (Ruvolo, 2004).

A whole-genome draft assembly of the entire *Pan troglodytes* genome was made public in 2005 (Chimpanzee Genome Resources, http://www.ncbi.nlm.nih.gov/genome/guide/chimp/), and scientists are now engaged in the effort to fill in the gaps and carry out chimp–human comparative analyses. The draft and the commentaries on the data available up to now tell us that DNA sequences of human and chimpanzee genomes differ by only a small fraction, a few percent (Li & Saunders, 2005). Yet, although this similarity is stunning, given how large both genomes are, the small discrepancies percent-wise result in 35 million nucleotide differences in the sequence itself, 5 million differences in the number of insertions or deletions (indel[1]), and many chromosomal rearrangements (Cheng et al., 2005; Linardopoulou et al., 2005; The Chimpanzee Sequencing and Analysis Consortium, 2005).

To appreciate the magnitude and pattern of these similarities and dissimilarities, consider a study of structural differences between the genomes of *Pan troglodytes* and *Homo sapiens* carried out via a comparative analysis of chimp chromosome 22 (PTR_{22}), the ortholog[2] of human chromosome 21 (HSA_{21})[3] (Watanabe et al., 2004). This analysis resulted in a number of interesting observations.

First, it appears that PTR_{22} and HSA_{21} differ at only ~1.44% of their 33 million aligned nucleotides (basepairs, bp). In other words, the chromosomes of humans and chimpanzees are ~98.5% identical in genome sequence.

Second, in spite of substantial overlap in the sequence, ~80% of the 179 orthologous genes of equal length show discrepancies of at least one amino acid between the two species. In addition, there appear to be three coding sequences that are present in chimpanzees but not in humans, and six sequences that are present in humans but not in chimpanzees. There is a sequence that is active in chimpanzees but not in humans, and there are four sequences that might be active in humans but that are not in chimpanzees. It is also of great interest that the most divergent regions between the two species are those in so-called 5′-untranslated regions of the genes, which typically contain regulatory elements. Thus, there are regions of the human genome that do not appear to be present in other apes, but the number of such regions is surprisingly few.

Third, the two chromosomes differ in about 68,000 rather short (~300bp in size) indels, suggesting that those are a "major source of sequence divergence between humans and chimpanzees" (Mikkelsen, 2004, p. 238). The human genome is "longer" than the chimpanzee's, primarily because of the novel insertions. However, it appears that the difference in length might have resulted predominantly in neutral substitutions and the expansion and shrinkage of repetitive elements over a long period of time.

---

[1]Type of genetic mutation resulting in gain or loss of segments of repetitive DNA. Indels can arise both within and outside coding regions (Taylor, Pontig, & Copley, 2004), but when outside, tend to appear in gene neighborhoods (Frazer et al., 2003).

[2]Genetic material (chromosome, region, gene) in different species that evolved from a common ancestral source.

[3]The trisomy of chromosome 21 in humans leads to Down syndrome, one of the most common causes of mental retardation.

Fourth, there appear to be two loosely defined groups of genes. One group includes genes with known functions and recognizable rodent orthologs; these genes appear to be highly conserved and exhibit little between-species variation (for both primates and nonprimates). The second group encompasses genes that are novel to the primate lineage and of largely unknown function. This observation leads to a question of relative contributions of rapidly changing, novel genes and highly conserved mammalian genes to human evolution.

To summarize, "Humans and chimpanzees are an order of magnitude more different, in terms of genetic changes, than any two humans, but an order of magnitude less different than mice and rats are from each other" (Mikkelsen, 2004, p. 238).

Thus, the genetic overlap between humans and chimps is far and above greater than was expected based on how "incomparable" they are behaviorally. This rather surprising degree of similarity is supported by the analyses of gene expression in both humans and chimpanzees (Enard, Khaitovich, et al., 2002).

Given the similarity of DNA, it is no surprise to see a degree of similarity in proteins. Indeed, when gene expression analyses are conducted, it appears that the majority of expression differences carry little or no functional significance. To add to the investigation a different dimension of gene expression, i.e., expression intensity, Enard and colleagues (Enard, Khaitovich et al., 2002) investigated the amount of RNA expression from Brodmann's area 9 of the left prefrontal lobe and neocortex in humans, chimpanzees, and other apes. The researchers registered an apparent acceleration of gene expression in the human brain. Because genetic upregulation has been observed along the human lineage (Enard & Paabo, 2004), the general finding of upregulation is not surprising. However, later research indicated that these expression differences are at least as much or more pronounced in the livers of humans and chimpanzees than in their brains (Ruvolo, 2004). In other words, although humans are somewhat different from chimpanzees in their proteins and the intensity in which these proteins express, neither dimension of this analysis appears to provide enough evidence that the change in the quality and quantity of proteins in the brain can explain the emergence of language and other higher-order functions in humans as compared with chimpanzees. The current hypotheses entertain the idea of differential ratios of an increase in expression level in a subset of brain-expressed genes as compared with other genes in the lineage leading to humans (e.g., Uddin et al., 2004).

To illustrate some of the points above, consider the following example.

The *FOXP2* gene, located on the long arm of chromosome 7 (7q31), encodes a transcription factor (i.e., a protein that aids in transcription of other genes by binding to a *cis*-regulatory element such as an enhancer or a TATA box and that directly or indirectly affects the initiation of transcription) and, by nature of its function, is expected to control the expression of other genes (e.g., many transcription factors aid RNA polymerase to recognize promoters that regulate translation). This gene was mapped, cloned, and characterized in the process of studying a family with severe speech and language issues and a number of other disturbances (Vargha-Khadem, Watkins, Alcock, Fletcher, & Passingham, 1995). Consequently, it was found that other disruptions in the gene cause similar language-related problems in other patients

(Macdermot et al., 2005). Following the discovery of the gene (Lai, Fisher, Hurst, Vargha-Khadem, & Monaco, 2001), it was identified as "non-unique to humans" and was found in other species. Moreover, the gene is rather preserved evolutionarily; it differs from gorilla and chimpanzee versions by only two amino acid changes in the highly conserved forkhead transcription factor. In addition, there is no evidence that these replacements are functionally important (i.e., change the protein structure), yet they might change the expression pattern and, because it is a transcription factor, influence other genes (Carroll, 2003). Moreover, the amino acid changes and the pattern of nucleotide polymorphism in human *FOXP2* suggest the possibility that the gene has been the target of selection during *recent* (i.e., after the appearance of *Homo sapiens*) human evolution (Enard, Przeworski et al., 2002). To conclude, given what we know about the genetic architecture of complex human traits, it is, of course, highly unlikely that *FOXP2* is solely responsible for the evolution of human language; but since we do not have other candidates, we cannot evaluate *FOXP2*'s relevant contribution. What is quite likely, however, is that *FOXP2* acts pleiotropically and an aspect of its function might be related to language.

Although this discussion only touched on relevant discoveries in the field of comparative genetics, one thing is quite obvious even from this brief overview—there is no super "human" gene that makes us human. Most likely, the distinction between humans and chimpanzees is determined by complex traits orchestrated by complex genetic mechanisms (Carroll, 2003). It is likely, too, that the same gene is involved in a number of different functions (or a given protein is involved in a number of different functions), acting pleiotropically and permitting new human functions through novel combinations of pleiotropic genes.

Understanding these principles is crucial for understanding the biological bases of language and language-related processes, including single-word reading. First, as I hope is clear from the text above, no "language gene" or "dyslexia gene" is going to be found. That our closest evolutionary relatives do not have language and reading in their repertoire of skills most likely does not mean that humans carry genes that are responsible for language (and, correspondingly, whose malfunction is responsible for language disorders) and reading (and, correspondingly, whose malfunction is responsible for dyslexia). The point of this section was to show that it is likely that distinctly human features, including reading, are a result of the emergence of "new" psychological functions using some "old" players (i.e., functions that are orchestrated by human genes whose orthologs exist in chimpanzees). The challenge is to understand how these new functions emerge evolutionarily with the use of primarily "old" genetic material and what modifications are applied to this old genetic material to warrant the emergence of a new complex trait.

This is a great challenge, and researchers in multiple domains of science are attempting to address it. In the context of studying dyslexia, this challenge is translated into understanding the psychological texture of dyslexia (i.e., what psychological processes constituting reading must break for dyslexia to emerge) and figuring out the biological bases of the psychological components of reading.

So, what is known about the underlying biological bases of human complex traits? What generalizations can be made of the currently available broader literature that will be helpful in understanding genetic bases of reading, dyslexia, and reading-related processes such as single-word recognition?

SURPRISES OF NONDIFFERENTIATION

Unlike other species—even such close human relatives as chimpanzees, who have *only* ecosystems surrounding them and who become a part of their environment—humans inhabit not only ecosystems, but cultures as well. One of the many impacts of culture on humans is expressed in the establishment of priorities. It is quite remarkable that across multiple human civilizations and cultures understanding a disorder *before* understanding a typical condition has been a priority. In other words, we have wanted to understand disease before understanding normative development (e.g., we invest more resources into understanding mental retardation than into understanding normative intellectual development). This situation has started to change: The task of tackling typical human behavior and complex traits has become less daunting and more doable, and therefore more exciting, with current technologies and computing. Yet, we know more about atypical than typical development, and a number of developmentalists commit their careers to learning about atypical development to enrich our knowledge of both regular and irregular developmental pathways. However, today, our cultural priorities are changing, and more and more scientists suggest that knowing what is "typical" is extremely important for understanding both human abilities and disabilities (Johnson, 2001).

Historically, partially because of traditions in medical science and partially because of a lack of resources, researchers studying atypical developmental pathways concentrated on particular isolated deficits. Indeed, it has been noted that, as a type of disturbance, neuropsychiatric conditions are characterized by a large amount of heterogeneity, both manifestational and etiological (Manji, Gottesman, & Gould, 2003). Correspondingly, to minimize the heterogeneity of the patient sample and ease the generation of insight into the etiological, the majority of studies in neuropsychiatric genetics were done with somewhat "isolationist" and "reductionist" all-or-nothing approaches. However, the last few years of research in developmental psychopathology have resulted in the realization that developmental impact is much more generalized than on a single function.

There are two sources of relevant knowledge in this context. The first relates to studying developmental disorders of identified genetic origin and cognitive disturbances observed in these disorders (also referred to as genetic developmental syndromes—e.g., Down syndrome, Williams syndrome, Prader-Willi syndrome, Angelman syndrome, Rett syndrome). It has been appreciated for some time that, although the genetic causes of these syndromes are well characterized, there is a great deal of developmental variation both in the magnitude and timing of the genetic impact and in the way this impact is manifested in the phenotype (Scerif & Karmiloff-Smith, 2005). This variability is of great interest because if its sources are understood, relevant medical and therapeutic approaches can be designed and applied to other individuals suffering from a comparable genetic cause whose phenotypic manifestations are more severe than expected based on the contribution of genetic causes per se. The second source relates to phenotypically well-characterized developmental conditions of unknown genetic origin (e.g., developmental dyslexia, speech and language disorders, autism). Here the relevant realization is that the most productive way of studying these complex conditions might be in identifying so-called endophenotypes, typically defined as components of the holistic phenotype of the disorder (Gottesman & Gould, 2003). It is assumed that by dissecting a complex multidimensional phenotype into lower-level componential processes, the field has a better chance of identifying the genetic causes underlying (directly) these components and (indirectly) the phenotype of the disorder of interest. These two positions are considered in more detail in this part of the chapter.

The first position is represented in the model developed by Karmiloff-Smith and her colleagues. According to this model, a disorder can be traced back to a particular genetic factor that is challenged in this disorder. This factor can include one, a number of, or many genes, but is discrete and identifiable in its nature. This genetic factor has a function in typical development and can be characterized by its role and timing in the maturation and functioning of a human organism. For example, if it is a single-gene factor, it is important to know when in development the expression of the gene matters and the importance of the gene protein. To capture the impact of the *abnormally* functioning genetic factor, Karmiloff-Smith and her colleagues use the word "perturbation" (the state of deviation or disruption from a regular status, *Webster's Dictionary*, p. 1447). Implied here is the existence of some "typical" or "normal" course of events either orchestrated by or involving the genetic factor of interest, so that a defect in this factor results in the perturbation of the normal course of events, causing a shift from typical to atypical development. However, this shift occurs under heavy pressure on the biological and social machinery that assured programmed typical development; in response to the impact of the deficient genetic mechanisms, numerous plasticity forces start operating to minimize the perturbation. Thus, the ultimate outcome of the impact of the abnormal genetic factor is a complex interplay of the function and timing of expression of the factor itself, the success with which plasticity forces compensate for the impact, and the remediational efforts available through the environment. In sum, there is no reason to expect identical or even highly homogeneous phenotypic outcomes from genetically identical abnormal factors (e.g., identical risk alleles carried by two different individuals), because these impacts are moderated by the broad developmental context of the individual (i.e., his or her "other" genetic makeup and the environment). In other words, any phenotypic manifestation of a developmental disorder is a systemic output formed by a system of interacting factors. Nothing is "static" in development—everything is influenced by multiple changing factors and is, by definition, fluid and dynamic. One extremely interesting conclusion derivable from this theoretical model is that of molarity versus modularity of impact. Specifically, what follows is that the impact is more modularized if the timing of the gene expression is later in development (Scerif & Karmiloff-Smith, 2005). Correspondingly, if an impact occurs early, the outcome might be more generalized and manifested more broadly.

The second position is represented by Gottesman and colleagues and their many followers (Gottesman & Gould, 2003). These researchers widely use the concept of "endophenotype," initially proposed about 35 years ago by Gottesman and Shields (Gottesman & Shields, 1972) and defined later as "measurable components unseen by the unaided eye along the pathway between disease and distal genotype" (Gottesman & Gould, 2003, p. 636). When this concept was introduced, the intention, according to the authors, was to fill the gap between the holistic manifestation of the disorders and the gene. According to the argument for this concept, there is a strong association between the number of genes affecting specific disorders and the number of relevant endophenotypes. In other words, the fewer the genes involved in the manifestation of a particular disorder, the fewer the componential dimensions (i.e., endophenotypes) required to describe and characterize the phenotype; the more genes involved and the more complex the genetic mechanism is, the more complex the phenotypic manifestations of the phenotype are. From this point of view, the impact of a single gene might be adequately captured by a single dimension of the holistic phenotype, but more dimensions are required to reflect differentially the impact of multiple genes.

In summary, the positions adopt different "starting points" for their research (i.e., bottom-up for Karmiloff-Smith and top-down for Gottesman) and allow a certain degree of uncertainty in their pathways toward "solving for unknowns." The differences in the starting point of these movements allow each to formulate interesting predictions and, correspondingly, to open certain aspects of their approaches for criticism.

Specifically, Karmiloff-Smith and her colleagues (Karmiloff-Smith, Scerif, & Ansari, 2003) argue that an "inspiring and intriguing" interpretation assuming differential impact on the development of specific psychological functions in the presence of profound deficit in others should be toned down by the appreciation of empirical data suggesting that the idea of preservation of an isolated ability at a normal level in the presence of a profound deficit is not absolute, but relative. For example, the authors argue, children with Williams syndrome perform better on verbal than on nonverbal tasks, but this advantage is far from the normative level of performance and only relative to their profound disability. Although many will agree with the qualitative judgment (i.e., verbal functioning is better preserved than is nonverbal functioning), they will disagree that this relativistic evaluation (not as good as in typical children) rules out a possibility of independent or semi-independent genes acting differentially so that brain pathways engaged in verbal and nonverbal functioning develop in such a way that a profound difference in performance is observed. The unevenness of the profiles observed in specific developmental disorders (e.g., highly developed circumscribed interests in selected individuals with autism in the presence of serious maladaptive functioning in a number of other psychological domains, Grigorenko, Klin, & Volkmar, 2003) does not appear to be "explainable" by mechanisms of developmental plasticity-based regrouping in response to a "perturbation." Although challenging the assumption of "absolute" modularity, the developmental perturbation explanation does not account for the substantial "residual" modularity observed in many developmental syndromes.

Similarly, the approach of endophenotypes can also be challenged on specific assumptions. Consider the difficulty of extending the endophenotype-specific genetic background "outside" the framework of a particular condition. For example, one of the most productive approaches to studying schizophrenia within the last few years has been decomposing its holistic phenotype into a number of cognitive endophenotypes, one of which is an executive functioning endophenotype (Egan et al., 2001). When characterized, this phenotype is typically assessed with task performance, which can be administered to typical and atypical individuals and is normally distributed in the general population. The question then is if a particular gene (e.g., *COMT*, see section 4 of this chapter) appears to be associated with this particular phenotype in a sample of individuals with schizophrenia, is it then a finding specific to schizophrenia or to this endophenotype? In other words, are researchers reporting on the genetic basis of typical executive functioning in an atypical sample of individuals with schizophrenia with a restriction of range, or are they reporting on a schizophrenia gene that seems to be modularly involved with this particular cognitive function?

In short, each of the two positions presented above appears to be beneficial for providing theoretical context for further explorations of the links among genes, brains, and behaviors, but neither of them, at this point, can be used to answer the many questions in the field. Broadly speaking, both positions have been influential and productive: The syndromal approach is of great interest in specifying further the phenotypic variation in Rett syndrome with regard to the distribution of the *MECP2* gene mutations within this syndrome. It is also useful for comparing phenotypes across other conditions associated with mental retardation (Couvert et al., 2001), as is the endophenotype approach in dissecting the genetic background of dyslexia (Grigorenko, 2005). And, both positions point to two aspects of nondifferentiation that are important in the context of this chapter: According to the first position, the early perturbative impact challenges the process of differentiation and modularization; according to the second position, an endophenotype spans the full spectrum of a skill and might not differentiate the genetic etiology for affected and unaffected individuals.

This brings us back to the issue of pleiotropy: Although not proving it, both positions raise the possibility of the same genes being involved in multiple psychological functions (e.g., verbal and nonverbal) across the whole spectrum of development!

Finally, given the discussion in the previous section of this chapter, it is important to note that yet another major difference between humans and chimpanzees is in the relatively delayed rate of development and maturation of the human brain. This delayed maturation might provide an opportunity for the environment (from prenatal and early postnatal to prekindergarten environments) to "sculpt inter- and intraregional connections within the cortex, eventually resulting in the highly specialized adult brain" (Johnson, 2001, p. 475). With regard to dyslexia, this "window of opportunity" for environment to interfere might lead, hypothetically, to at least two distinct outcomes. If, as supposed in the first section of this chapter, the biological predisposition for dyslexia emerges from the involvement of multiple genes, then this predisposition will not be passed deterministically from generation to generation in families with dyslexia (i.e., the modes of familial transmission will not follow

Mendelian fashions). This is exactly what has been observed in studies of children of adult individuals with dyslexia (Carroll & Snowling, 2004; Gallagher, Frith, & Snowling, 2000; H. Lyytinen et al., 2004; P. Lyytinen & Lyytinen, 2004; Snowling, Gallagher, & Frith, 2003; van Alphen et al., 2004; Viholainen, Ahonen, Cantell, Lyytinen, & Lyytinen, 2002). Moreover, because reading is an emergent trait whose manifestation appears to be controlled by multiple genes, its slow emergence leaves a lot of room for environmental impact, if the genetic predisposition is detected early and acted on with the necessary environmental interventions. Indeed, there are an ample number of studies indicating that dyslexia, when detected early, can be rather successfully compensated for in adulthood, assuming that the necessary environmental interventions are lengthy and provide scaffolding throughout the life of an individual with dyslexia in spite of many remaining process-based deficits (e.g., Ben-Yehudah, Banai, & Ahissar, 2004; Breznitz & Misra, 2003; Birch & Chase, 2004; Conlon, Sanders, & Zapart, 2004; Hamalainen, Leppanen, Torppa, Muller, & Lyytinen, 2005; McNulty, 2003; Miller-Shaul, 2005; Ramus et al., 2003; Ransby & Swanson, 2003; Sperling, Lu, & Manis, 2004; Wilson & Lesaux, 2001).

So, if it is hypothesized that the manifestation of dyslexia is controlled by multiple genes and the impact of these genes individually and collectively is modifiable by environmental influences, what is known about the intermediate role between the genes and the environment played by the brain? What areas are employed when this highly specialized "reading brain" is envisioned? What is known about the brain engaged in such an exceptionally human activity as reading?

SURPRISES OF NONSPECIFICITY

Within the last few years, a number of exciting publications have examined the links between genes and cognition as moderated by patterns of brain activation. Those include, but are not limited to, the role of polymorphisms in the brain-derived neurotrophic factor (*BDNF*) gene and human memory (Egan et al., 2003; Tsai, Hong, Yu, & Chen, 2004), in the *DRD4* and *DAT* genes for the function of attention (DiMaio, Grizenko, & Joober, 2003), and in the *COMT* gene in executive functioning (Diamond, Briand, Fossella, & Gehlbach, 2004).

It has been suggested that the phenotypes generated from neuroimaging studies represent "more sensitive assays of cognitive functioning than behavioral measures used alone" (Goldberg & Weinberg, 2004, p. 325). However, the first study has yet to be conducted that reliably and validly bridges patterns of brain activation and genetic variability. Given that mapping the brain areas involved in reading and hunting for genes contributing to the manifestation of poor reading are both active and productive avenues, such a study is only a matter of time. However, it does not yet exist and, therefore, such "more sensitive assays" cannot be discussed here.

The general field of neuroscience began the "brain mapping" exercise with the assignment of a function to an area. This early assumption has long since been refuted, as, geographically speaking, the brain is a relatively small organ that hosts an endless variety of psychological functions. Therefore, inevitably, multiple functions get mapped to the same area and multiple areas get mapped to the same function. Once again, here is the pleiotropy principle in action—the economical use of available resources (in this case, brain areas) to form new combinations of excitations and inhibitions supporting new psychological functions (both general and unique to humans). So then, what areas of our brains read and how does the activation pattern originate and get distributed?

Stated generally, a developed, automatized skill of reading in adults is carried out by engaging a left-hemispheric network of brain areas spanning a pathway from occipitotemporal, through temporal, toward frontal lobes (e.g., Fiez & Petersen, 1998; Mechelli, Gorno-Tempini, & Price, 2003; Petersen, Fox, Posner, Mintun, & Raichle, 1988; Price, Wise, & Frackowiak, 1996; Pugh et al., 2001; Snyder, Abdullaev, Posner, & Raichle, 1995; Turkeltaub, Gareau, Flowers, Zeffiro, & Eden, 2003). Per recent reviews (Pugh et al., this volume; Simos et al., this volume), the four areas of particular interest are the fusiform gyrus (i.e., the occipitotemporal cortex in the ventral portion of Brodmann's area 37, BA 37), the posterior portion of the middle temporal gyrus (roughly BA 21, but possibly more specifically, the ventral border with BA 37 and the dorsal border of the superior temporal sulcus), the angular gyrus (BA 39), and the posterior portion of the superior temporal gyrus (BA 22). The process of reading is multifaceted and involves evocation of orthographic, phonologic, and semantic (Fiez, 1997; Poldrack et al., 1999; Pugh et al., 1996; Tagamets, Novick, Chalmers, & Friedman, 2000) representations that, in turn, call for activation of brain networks participating in visual, auditory, and conceptual processing (for a review, see Turkeltaub, Eden, Jones, & Zeffiro, 2002). The dorsal–ventral model of reading acquisition explains the developmental changes in patterns of brain functioning as progressive, behaviorally modulated development of left-hemispheric areas along with progressive disengagement of right-hemispheric areas (Eden et al., 2004; Gaillard, Balsamo, Ibrahim, Sachs, & Xu, 2003; Pugh et al., 2001; Turkeltaub et al., 2003). Important, also, is that the elements of this model have been supported by studies of brain activity in remediated and nonremediated adults (e.g., Eden et al., 2004; Shaywitz et al., 2003).

A few points are important to make here. First, by virtue of the techniques that capture changes occurring in the brain in response to an externally provided cognitive challenge (i.e., a "push the button in response to a stimulus" task), regional increases in the area engagement (i.e., regional signaling) take place, which result in regional changes in currents that can be registered by today's machinery. The issue here is that, by definition, these changes are correlational, not causal, and, correspondingly, the association between these changes and the participant's performance cannot be interpreted within parameters of causal reasoning.

Second, none of the many techniques currently available for brain mapping really meet all the relevant expectations for registering neocortical and subcortical patterns of activities at desired levels of spatial and temporal resolution (Simos, Billingsley-Marshall, Sarkari, & Papanicolaou, this volume).

Third, four genes that are currently considered as gene candidates for dyslexia, *DYX1C1* (Taipale et al., 2003), *KIAA0319* and *DCDC2* (Deffenbacher et al., 2004), and *ROBO1* (Kere, 2005), are expressed in the brain, but specific regional patterns of their expression are not yet known. Correspondingly, it is difficult to say whether there is any correlation between the posterior and anterior circuits of reading and the current candidate genes for dyslexia. It is of interest that all four genes are expressed in the brain and appear to be involved with axon guidance. It is possible that in the near future mouse models will demonstrate whether the expressions of *DYX1C1, KIAA0319, DCDC2*, and *ROBO1* are observed in the areas of the circuitry involved in reading in humans. It is also possible that a careful investigation of various mutations in the four genes and their associations with brain-activation endophenotypes of reading will reveal the specific gene–brain bases of this exclusively human function.

Fourth, although the general tradition is to discuss pathways of reading, each of the above-mentioned areas appears to reflect a particular specialization (as reviewed in Simos et al., this volume). Specifically, it is assumed that the left posterior fusiform gyrus is functionally responsible for processing word forms; the posterior portion of the middle temporal gyrus appears to be accessed for processing visual, phonological, and semantic word forms; the angular gyrus has been associated with processing memory for word forms (i.e., lexical processing); and the superior temporal gyrus is assumed to be involved in phonological analysis of print. Clearly, this specialization does not assume that a given "specialized" area is engaged in a particular function only; quite on the contrary, the angular gyrus, for example, has been associated with a number of other psychological processes in addition to being linked to lexical processing (Hinton, Harrington, Binder, Durgerian, & Rao, 2004). Thus, once again, the rule of pleiotropy is to map multiple functions onto the same region and attribute the same complex psychological function to many regions acting as a network. The surprising aspect of the powerful body of literature on neuroimaging of reading and reading-related componential processes is the multifunctionality and nonspecificity of the brain areas engaged in brain networks.

One of the areas that fully demonstrates the principle of multifunctionality and pleiotropy by engaging with (or by influencing) many relevant psychological functions, including those directly related to reading, is the broadly defined prefrontal cortex (Eden & Zeffiro, 1998; Papanicolaou et al., 2003; Pugh et al., 2001; Rumsey et al., 1999). This section of the chapter began with a discussion of using neuroimaging phenotypes as endophenotypes in studying genetic bases of reading. If the prefrontal cortex is used as an example of localization of a reading-related function, what kind of hypotheses might enhance our attempts to find genes related to dyslexia?

SURPRISES OF NONSELECTIVITY

When preparing to test specific candidate genes for association with dyslexia, it is instrumental to have a mechanism in mind that could form a basis for a specific testable hypothesis. Here the hypothesis of an involvement of a candidate gene is based on the possibility that genetic bases of developmental dyslexia are inclusive of or related to broader deficits, for example poorer working memory (e.g.,

Swanson & Sachse-Lee, 2001) and poorer executive functioning (e.g., Helland & Asbjornsen, 2000). Although there have been no directly relevant publications, it is important in this context to mention innovative work on the genetic bases of individual differences carried out in a number of laboratories.

Two lines of convergent evidence are important to consider. The first line originates from work on the role of the prefrontal cortex in general and its concentration of dopamine in working memory (Goldman-Rakic, Castner, Svensson, Siever, & Williams, 2004) and selective attention (Servan-Schreiber, Carter, Bruno, & Cohen, 1998a, 1998b). The second line of evidence has to do with the fact that the concentration of the dopamine-transporter protein (DAT), which has a high affinity for dopamine and is a critical agent in terminating the synaptic actions of dopamine (i.e., in initiating dopamine uptake to presynaptic nerve terminals), appears to be present at low levels in the cortex, especially in its prefrontal region (Huotari et al., 2002; Lewis et al., 2001; Sesack, Hawrylak, Guido, & Levey, 1998). Correspondingly, inactivation of dopamine in the prefrontal cortex might depend on other catabolic enzymes, including Catechol-*O*-methyltransferase (*COMT*, EC 2.1.1.6, using the nomenclature of the International Union of Biochemistry and Molecular Biology), implicated in extraneuronal dopamine uptake (Chen et al., 2004; Huotari et al., 2002).

COMT[4] is a methylation enzyme involved in the biotransformation of both endogenous (e.g., catechol hormones, including catecholestrogenes, and catechol neurotransmitters, including dopamine, epinephrine, and norepinephrine) and exogenous (e.g., catechol drugs such as anti-Parkinson's disease agent L-dopa and the antihypertensive methyldopa) catechol compounds by methylating their catechol moieties (Weinshilboum et al., 1999). The enzyme occurs in two distinct forms, as a soluble cytosolic protein (S-COMT, 25kDA) and as a membrane-bound protein (MB-COMT, 39 kDA); the enzyme is expressed ubiquitously, although S-COMT's expression is observed at higher levels than is MB-COMT in the majority of tissues, except the brain (Tenhunen et al., 1994). The level of COMT is genetically variable, with a three- to four-fold difference in activity between the extremes of its distribution (Boudikova, Szumlanski, Maidak, & Weinshilboum, 1990), and is characterized by a trimodal (low, intermediate, and high) distribution of the enzyme. The nature of this distribution was initially stated to correspond to the three genotypes in a two-allele system[5] (www.ncbi.nih.gov, Lachman et al., 1996; Lotta et al., 1995), but

---

[4]COMT catalyzes, in the presence of Mg^{2+}, the transfer of the methyl group from the methyl donor S-adenosylmethionine to either the *meta*- or the *para*-hydroxyl moiety of the catechol-nucleus based substrates (i.e., catechols or substituted catechols). For example, COMT converts released dopamine to 3–methoxytyramine and the dopamine metabolite dihydroxyphenylacetic acid to homovanilic acid (Weinshilboum, Otterness, & Szumlanski, 1999).

[5]The ancestral allele in exon 4 at codon 108 of the S-COMT and codon 158 of the MB-COMT (108/158) is G (*rs*4680, average frequency is ~ .50% in the population of Caucasian ancestry), which codes for the amino acid Valine (Val); the substitution of the G allele into the A allele results in the production of the different amino acid, Methionine (Met). The GG homozygous produces the Val–Val phenotype, which is associated with the high distribution of the enzyme; the Met–Met phenotype is associated with the low (by ~60% than Val–Val) enzyme level. The heterozygous phenotype is correspondingly associated with the intermediate

recent evidence indicates that this distribution might be associated with a susceptibility haplotype that includes more than one additively acting allelic system[6] in the gene (Bray et al., 2003; Lee et al., 2005; Palmatier et al., 2004; Shield et al., 2004). It also was noted that there are dramatic ethnic differences (i.e., from monomorphism to high levels of polymorphism) in allele frequencies in these systems across different populations (Ameyaw, Syvanen, Ulmanen, Ofori-Adjei, & McLeod, 2000; Lee et al., 2005; Palmatier, Kang, & Kidd, 1999; Shield et al., 2004; Shifman et al., 2002), although, within a given population, a variable site is rather polymorphic.

Of interest is that different extremes of the enzyme level have been observed in different special samples. For example, it has been reported that COMT activity is *higher* in children with Down syndrome (Gustavson, Floderus, Jagell, Wetterberg, & Ross, 1982; Gustavson, Wetterberg, Backstrom, & Ross, 1973) than in typical individuals, but *lower* in suicide attempters than in control individuals (Lester, 1995).

The gene coding for both forms of the COMT protein is located at 22q11.2 and is characterized by high levels of polymorphism. The gene has six exons and two promoter regions; a proximal promoter (P1) gives rise to the S-COMT mRNA, and a distal promoter (P2) initiates the transcription of the MB-COMT mRNA (Tenhunen et al., 1994).

Currently, the *COMT* gene is a candidate for susceptibility to a number of neuropsychiatric disorders, including velocardiofacial syndrome (e.g., Dunham, Collins, Wadey, & Scambler, 1992), anorexia nervosa (e.g., Frisch et al., 2001), ADHD (e.g., J. Eisenberg et al., 1999; Qian et al., 2003), drug abuse (e.g., Horowitz et al., 2000; T. Li et al., 2004; Vandenbergh, Rodriguez, Miller, Uhl, & Lachman, 1997), alcohol abuse (e.g., Tiihonen et al., 1999; Wang et al., 2001), phobic anxiety (e.g., McGrath et al., 2004), suicide (e.g., Ono, Shirakawa, Nushida, Ueno, & Maeda, 2004), obsessive–compulsive disorder (e.g., Karayiorgou et al., 1997), Parkinson's

---

levels of the enzyme. Correspondingly, the G allele is typically designated by the letter H (for high activity), and the A allele is marked by the letter L (for low activity). The Val Met substitution was shown to affect the thermotropic behavior of COMT, so that the enzyme activity decreases dramatically at physiological temperatures higher than 37°C, although high variation is observed both among various tissues and among individuals. The 108/158 residue has been proposed to be of importance for overall stability of the enzyme (Dawling, Roodi, Mernaugh, Wang, & Parl, 2001), although the biological machinery of the substitution is not yet clearly understood (Cotton, Stoddard, & Parson, 2004; Li et al., 2004; Meyer-Linderberg et al., 2005). The high observed variation in the phenotype suggests the presence of other functional polymorphisms in the gene (Chen et al., 2004).

[6]Specifically, it has been suggested that a single-nucleotide polymorphism (SNP) in P2 (*rs*2097603), the promoter that controls transcription of the MB-COMT, can contribute to the variation in enzyme activity (Palmatier et al., 2004). Moreover, an exon 4 nonsynonymous SNP G? A (*rs*5031015) at codon 52/102 that causes the substitution of Alanine (Ala) into Threonine (Thr) was reported; the Thr52 allozyme does not appear to alter function, although it was found to be associated with increased levels of the S-COMT protein (Shield, Thomae, Eckloff, Wieben, & Weinshilboum, 2004). In addition, nonsynonymous SNP at codon 22/72 (*rs*6267) causing Alanine (Ala) to be substituted with Serine (Ser) was also reported to be associated with reduced COMT enzyme activity (Lee et al., 2005).

disorder (e.g., Wu et al., 2001), response to pain (Zubieta et al., 2003), and schizophrenia (e.g., Kunugi et al., 1997; Shifman et al., 2002). However, for each disorder there are both positive and negative findings (e.g., see Glatt, Faraone, & Tsuang, 2003 for a meta-analysis of the evidence supporting the involvement of the *COMT* gene in the manifestation of schizophrenia). In addition, some conditions (e.g., drug abuse) were reported to be associated with the allele connected to higher levels of enzyme (the H allele), whereas other conditions (e.g., obsessive–compulsive disorder) were associated with the allele related to lower levels of enzyme (the L allele).

Although this brief overview is not comprehensive, it is informative. The intent here is to introduce an illustration of a highly influential and complex genetic system that appears to have pleiotropic and differential impacts on a number of neuropsychiatric conditions. Yet, it is only a peek at the puzzle, because the most relevant discussion of the role of the *COMT* gene has yet to unfold: the evidence implicating *COMT* and its polymorphisms in individual differences in cognition in the general population.

Building on years of neuropsychological research indicating the presence of deficits in cognitive functions engaging the dorsolateral prefrontal cortex in patients with schizophrenia and their relatives, Egan and colleagues (Egan et al., 2001) investigated the connection between the H (for high) and L (for low) alleles of the *COMT* gene, the behavioral indicators on the Wisconsin Card Sorting Test (considered to be a well-established indicator of cognitive executive functioning and working memory), and brain activation patterns during the performance of the N-back task (another working memory task). The results indicated an association between the L allele of the *COMT* gene, a lower number of perseverative errors on the Wisconsin Card Sorting Task, and more efficient physiological response in the prefrontal cortex while engaged in the N-back task. These findings were interpreted in the context of previous neuronal network modeling work suggesting that reduction of dopamine in synapses (e.g., its catalysis by the COMT protein) should result in less efficient processing (Servan-Schreiber, Printz, & Cohen, 1990). Subsequently, the general pattern of results highlighting the selective cognitive advantage of the LL genotype has been replicated by other researchers in samples of individuals with schizophrenia (Bilder et al., 2002; Gallinat et al., 2003; Goldberg et al., 2003; Joober et al., 2002; Rosa et al., 2004; Weickert et al., 2004) and their unaffected relatives (Callicott et al., 2003), as well as samples of typical healthy individuals, both adults (Malhotra et al., 2002) and children (Diamond et al., 2004). When considered together, these studies indicate that the variation in the *COMT* gene accounts for 2% to 41% of variation in cognitive performance on cognitive tasks engaging the prefrontal cortex. Of note here is that this observed cognitive advantage among the LL genotype schizophrenia patients does not seem to result in better prognoses: There are reports that LL patients have significantly higher levels of hostility (Volavka et al., 2004).

The interest in the association between the *COMT* gene variation and variation on psychological traits in the general population has also permeated the field of personality psychology. For example, researchers administered the Perceptual

Aberration scale, the Schizotypical Personality Questionnaire, and the Aggression Questionnaire to a sample of ~350 healthy males whose *COMT* genotypes for H and L alleles were known (Avramopoulos et al., 2002). It was reported that HH individuals presented higher mean scores on all self-reports; significant effects were obtained for multivariate analyses and two out of three scales (with the exception of the Aggression Questionnaire) univariately. In contrast, in a study of novelty seeking and *COMT*, results showed that individuals with the LL genotype score higher on this self-reported trait (Strobel, Lesch, Jatzke, Paetzold, & Brocke, 2003).

In summary, it appears that *COMT* and its functions in the brain demonstrate another example of pleiotropy. The nonspecificity, or stated differently, the scale of *COMT*'s impact, is surprisingly broad. Although it is clear that the field might have not described and quantified all possible impacts of *COMT* on various psychological functions, it is clear that *COMT* is not a gene for "something" (e.g., schizophrenia or executive function). *COMT* is a gene whose protein is incredibly important for the normal functioning of the dopaminergic cycle; changes in the properties of this protein arise from a functional polymorphism (or possibly polymorphisms) in the gene and affect a variety of function in the organism.

COMT is a well-characterized gene with a number of well-known functions; however, it has not been looked at with regard to its potential involvement with dyslexia. The field of dyslexia has four of its own gene candidates, *DYX1C1*, *KIAA0319*, *ROBO1* and *DCDC2* (see discussion above and Barr & Couto, this volume; Olson, this volume). All four genes have been associated with dyslexia and the field is now engaged in determining these genes' pathways and evaluating their relevance to the holistic phenotype of dyslexia and its endophenotypes.

CONCLUSION

In this chapter, a number of topics at the frontier of knowledge regarding the brain–gene mechanism of language in general and a number of language-related processes were discussed. The discussion unfolded in the context of the presentation of the principle of pleiotropy, realized through the four "nons" of human cognition—nonuniqueness, nondifferentiation, nonspecificity, and nonselectivity. Selected transparent examples were provided to illustrate these topics. Specifically, the chapter began with the presentation of the principle of nonspecificity, a discussion of the comparative genetics of humans and chimpanzees in an attempt to understand the context of the development of a hypothetical, evolutionarily established genetic mechanism supporting the development and manifestation of oral and written language in humans. The discussion was extended to include the principle of nondifferentiation through the presentation of two different approaches to investigating genetics of complex traits in humans. Then, the literature on the representation of the pathways of reading in the brain was briefly reviewed and the principle of nonspecificity was discussed. Finally, one of the featured areas of these pathways was examined in more detail to illustrate a gene whose function appears to be quite central to the function of this brain area as a whole. The magnitude of the impact of this gene illustrated the principle of nonselectivity.

The central conceptual point of the discussion was the importance of pleiotropy for understanding the development and manifestation of both typical and atypical (dyslexic) reading and single-word processing in children and adults. The main message of the chapter was that there are probably no exclusive dyslexia genes and no dyslexia brain areas. Similarly, there are probably no exclusive single-word processing genes and brain areas. Many genes and many brain areas contribute to the manifestation of typical reading and, when one or several of these genes or brain areas are challenged, atypical (dyslexic) reading can develop. Dyslexia is extremely heterogeneous etiologically, and pleiotropy at multiple levels of the biological machinery of reading likely explains this.

In concluding the chapter, three comments should be made. First, the concept of pleiotropy points to significant cross-mapping between brains and genes. The idea that patterns of excitation in somewhat isolated brain regions should be mapped on somewhat specific sets of cognitive functioning appears to be too simple to be true. It is unlikely that there will be a specific gene whose role is to contribute to variation on a specific trait in the general population. Yet, this idea rarely penetrates the public perception. The public interprets complex gene discoveries as identification of the gene for a specific function (e.g., the gene *FOXP2* has been referred to as the "language gene"). This desire for "hopeful monsters" is not supported by research. "Despite our enhanced understanding of functional genetic architecture, there remains a tendency to associate the development, function or evolution of a trait with single genes (genes 'for' speech, cancer and so one). The ghost of 'hopeful monsters' still haunts biology and is, unfortunately, a prevalent misconception in the scientific and general press" (Carroll, 2003, p. 856). Most likely, there are going to be no "genes for," but rather, "genes contributing to...." In other words, we should not expect to find the gene for dyslexia, but rather, to find many genes contributing to dyslexia.

Second, although important, structural changes in DNA (e.g., mutations) that introduced diversity might or might not translate to the phenotype of interest. In other words, it is possible that genetic regulation of particular phenotypes is carried out differently, without specific involvement of the original application. One such "epigenetic" phenomenon is methylation. It appears that ~1% of mammalian DNA bases are modified by attaching a methyl group to carbon–5 of the cytosine pyrimidine ring, mostly at CpG dinucleotides (2'-deoxyribo, cytidine–phosphate–guanosine). Recent discoveries about methylation suggest that this process is crucial both for the completion of embryonic development and for maturation after birth (Jones & Takai, 2001). In mammals, methylation of CpG-rich promoters is a mechanism for preventing transcriptional initiation and for silencing the inactive X chromosome and imprinted genes and parasitic DNA (Jones & Takai, 2001). CpG dinucleotides have been reported to be methylated more in brains than in any other tissue and more in human brains than in chimpanzee brains (Enard et al., 2004). Abnormal methylation of the promoters of regulatory genes, although causing gene silencing, has also been shown to be a pathway to cancer development (Jones & Laird, 1999) and various developmental disorders (e.g., Kriaucionis & Bird, 2003). For example, Rett syndrome, an autism-spectrum type of mental retardation in girls, appears to be caused by changes in methylation machinery (Kriaucionis & Bird, 2003). Thus, although structural changes are important to understand, when trying to capture the connection between genes and the brain, it is important to evaluate "other" genetic mechanisms as potential agents of this connection. To my knowledge, there have been no studies of methylation and its relation to genetics of dyslexia or single-word reading processing, although, theoretically, this might be an important mechanism to consider.

Third, it is of interest that highly and broadly expressed genes (i.e., genes that are expressed at high levels of intensity in many tissues) have been reported to have shorter introns and exons and to code for shorter proteins as compared with narrowly expressed genes (i.e., genes that are expressed in selected tissues or at specific periods of development only), whose proteins are longer and more complex (Castillo-Davis, Mekhedov, Hartl, Koonin, & Kondrashov, 2002; Eisenberg & Levanon, 2003; Urrutia & Hurst, 2003). In addition, genes of increased specificity appear to be surrounded by larger intergenic spacers, which might indicate more complex regulation of translation and transcription (Vinogradov, 2004a, 2004b). It is possible that some of these high-specificity genes are involved in the networks discussed in this chapter. However, before we can measure the impact of such genes, we first have to find them in the genome! But we cannot exclude the possibility of evolutionary late genes (e.g., genes that occurred relatively late in human evaluation) responsible for specific proteins. These genes might be of great importance for evolutionarily "late" human-specific functions, such as reading.

Recent discoveries have brought a number of interesting realizations with regard to the connection between the brain and genes. Most of these realizations point to the economy principle used by nature in establishing this connection. It appears that the rule of the game is to recycle everything and to be creative in doing it. This is only a first impression, however, and much needs to be done to confirm or disconfirm it.

Finally, given the high level of activity in research on both brain pathways of reading and genetic foundations of reading, we should expect multiple exciting discoveries in the near future. Let's keep our eyes open!

ACKNOWLEDGMENTS

Preparation of this essay was supported by Grant REC-9979843 from the National Science Foundation and by a grant under the Javits Act Program (Grant No. R206R00001) as administered by the Institute for Educational Sciences, U.S. Department of Education. Grantees undertaking such projects are encouraged to express freely their professional judgment. This article, therefore, does not necessarily represent the position or policies of the NSF, the Institute for Educational Sciences, or the U.S. Department of Education, and no official endorsement should be inferred. The author expresses sincere gratitude to Ms. Robyn Rissman for her editorial assistance. Correspondence should be addressed to Dr. Elena L. Grigorenko, Yale University, PACE Center, 230 S. Frontage Road, New Haven, CT 06519 (or via elena.grigorenko@yale.edu).

REFERENCES

Ameyaw, M. M., Syvanen, A. C., Ulmanen, I., Ofori-Adjei, D., & McLeod, H. L. (2000). Pharmacogenetics of catechol-O-methyltransferase: Frequency of low activity allele in a Ghanaian population. *Human Mutation, 16*, 445–446.

Avramopoulos, D., Stefanis, N. C., Hantoumi, I., Smyrnis, N., Evdokimidis, I., & Stefanis, C. N. (2002). Higher scores of self reported schizotypy in healthy young males carrying the COMT high activity allele. *Molecular Psychiatry, 7*, 706–711.

Ben-Yehudah, G., Banai, K., & Ahissar, M. (2004). Patterns of deficit in auditory temporal processing among dyslexic adults. *Neuroreport: For Rapid Communication of Neuroscience Research, 15*, 627–631.

Bilder, R. M., Volavka, J., Czobor, P., Malhotra, A. K., Kennedy, J. L., Ni, X., et al. (2002). Neurocognitive correlates of the COMT Val(158)Met polymorphism in chronic schizophrenia. *Biological Psychiatry, 52*, 701–707.

Birch, S., & Chase, C. (2004). Visual and language processing deficits in compensated and uncompensated college students with dyslexia. *Journal of Learning Disabilities, 37*, 389–410.

Boudikova, B., Szumlanski, C., Maidak, B., & Weinshilboum, R. (1990). Human liver catechol-O-methyltransferase pharmacogenetics. *Clinical Pharmacology & Therapeutics, 48*, 381–389.

Bray, N. J., Buckland, P. R., Williams, N. M., Williams, H. J., Norton, N., Owen, M. J., et al. (2003). A haplotype implicated in schizophrenia susceptibility is associated with reduced COMT expression in human brain. *American Journal of Human Genetics, 73*, 152–161.

Breznitz, Z., & Misra, M. (2003). Speed of processing of the visual–orthographic and auditory–phonological systems in adult dyslexics: The contribution of "asynchrony" to word recognition deficits. *Brain and Language, 85*, 486–502.

Callicott, J. H., Egan, M. F., Mattay, V. S., Bertolino, A., Bone, A. D., Verchinksi, B., et al. (2003). Abnormal fMRI response of the dorsolateral prefrontal cortex in cognitively intact siblings of patients with schizophrenia. *American Journal of Psychiatry, 170*, 709–719.

Carroll, J. M., & Snowling, M. J. (2004). Language and phonological skills in children at high risk of reading difficulties. *Journal of Child Psychology and Psychiatry, 45*, 631–640.

Carroll, S. B. (2003). Genetics and the making of Homo sapiens. *Nature, 422*(6934), 849–857.

Castillo-Davis, C. I., Mekhedov, S. L., Hartl, D. L., Koonin, E. V., & Kondrashov, F. A. (2002). Selection for short introns in highly expressed genes. *Nature Genetics, 31*, 415–418.

Chen, J., Lipska, B. K., Halim, N., Ma, Q. D., Matsumoto, M., Melhem, S., et al. (2004). Functional analysis of genetic variation in catechol-O-methyltransferase (COMT): Effects on mRNA, protein, and enzyme activity in postmortem human brain. *American Journal of Human Genetics, 75*, 807–821.

Cheng, Z., Ventura, M., She, X., Khaitovich, P., Graves, T., Osoegawa, K., et al. (2005). A genome-wide comparison of recent chimpanzee and human segmental duplications. *Nature, 437*, 88–93.

Conlon, E., Sanders, M., & Zapart, S. (2004). Temporal processing in poor adult readers. *Neuropsychologia, 42*, 142–157.

Cotton, N. J., Stoddard, B., & Parson, W. W. (2004). Oxidative inhibition of human soluble catechol-O-methyltransferase. *Journal of Biological Chemistry, 279*, 23710–23718.

Couvert, P., Bienvenu, T., Aquaviva, C., Poirier, K., Moraine, C., Gendrot, C., Verloes, A., Andres, C., Le Fevre, A. C., Souville, I., Steffann, J., des Portes, V., Ropers, H. H., Yntema, H. G., Fryns, J. P., Briault, S., Chelly, J., Cherif, B. (2001). MECP2 is highly mutated in X-linked mental retardation. *Human Molecular Genetics, 10*, 941–946.

Dawling, S., Roodi, N., Mernaugh, R. L., Wang, X., & Parl, F. F. (2001). Catechol-O-methyltransferase (COMT)-mediated metabolism of catechol estrogens: Comparison of wild-type and variant COMT isoforms. *Cancer Research, 61*, 6716–6722.

Deffenbacher, K. E., Kenyon, J. B., Hoover, D. M., Olson, R. K., Pennington, B. F., DeFries, J. C., Smith, S. D. (2004). Refinement of the 6p21.3 quantitative trait locus influencing dyslexia: linkage and association analyses. *Human Genetics, 115,* 128–138.

Diamond, A., Briand, L., Fossella, J., & Gehlbach, L. (2004). Genetic and neurochemical modulation of prefrontal cognitive functions in children. *American Journal of Psychiatry, 161,* 125–132.

DiMaio, S., Grizenko, N., & Joober, R. (2003). Dopamine genes and attention-deficit hyperactivity disorder: A review. *Journal of Psychiatry & Neuroscience, 28,* 27–38.

Dunham, I., Collins, J., Wadey, R., & Scambler, P. (1992). Possible role for COMT in psychosis associated with velo-cardio-facial syndrome. *Lancet, 340,* 1361–1362.

Eden, G. F., Jones, K. M., Cappell, K., Gareau, L., Wood, F. B., Zeffiro, T. A., et al. (2004). Neural changes following remediation in adult developmental dyslexia. *Neuron, 44,* 411–422.

Eden, G. F., & Zeffiro, T. A. (1998). Neural systems affected in developmental dyslexia revealed by functional neuroimaging. *Neuron, 21,* 279–282.

Egan, M. F., Goldberg, T. E., Kolachana, B. S., Callicott, J. H., Mazzanti, C. M., Straub, R. E., et al. (2001). Effect of COMT Val108/158 Met genotype on frontal lobe function and risk for schizophrenia. *Proceedings of the National Academy of Sciences of the United States of America, 98,* 6917–6922.

Egan, M. F., Kojima, M., Callicott, J. H., Goldberg, T. E., Kolachana, B. S., Bertolino, A., et al. (2003). The BDNF val66met polymorphism affects activity-dependent secretion of BDNF and human memory and hippocampal function. *Cell, 112,* 257–269.

Eisenberg, E., & Levanon, E. Y. (2003). Human housekeeping genes are compact. *Trends in Genetics, 19,* 363–365.

Eisenberg, J., Mei-Tal, G., Steinberg, A., Tartakovsky, E., Zohar, A., Gritsenko, I., et al. (1999). Haplotype relative risk study of catechol-O-methyltransferase (COMT) and attention deficit hyperactivity disorder (ADHD): Association of the high-enzyme activity Val allele with ADHD impulsive–hyperactive phenotype. *American Journal of Medical Genetics, 88,* 497–502.

Enard, W., Fassbender, A., Model, F., Adorjan, P., Paabo, S., & Olek, A. (2004). Differences in DNA methylation patterns between humans and chimpanzees. *Current Biology, 14,* R148–149.

Enard, W., Khaitovich, P., Klose, J., Zollner, S., Heissig, F., Giavalisco, P., et al. (2002). Intra- and interspecific variation in primate gene expression patterns. *296*(340–343).

Enard, W., & Paabo, S. (2004). Comparative primate genomics. *Annual Review of Genomics & Human Genetics, 5,* 351–378.

Enard, W., Przeworski, M., Fisher, S. E., Lai, C. S., Wiebe, V., Kitano, T., et al. (2002). Molecular evolution of FOXP2, a gene involved in speech and language. *Nature, 418,* 869–872.

Fiez, J. A. (1997). Phonology, semantics, and the role of the left inferior prefrontal cortex. *Human Brain Mapping, 5,* 79–83.

Fiez, J. A., & Petersen, S. E. (1998). Neuroimaging studies of word reading. *Proceedings of the National Academy of Sciences of the United States of America, 95,* 914–921.

Frazer, K. A., Chen, X., Hinds, D. A., Pant, P. V., Patil, N., & Cox, D. R. (2003). Genomic DNA insertions and deletions occur frequently between humans and nonhuman primates. *Genome Research, 13,* 341–346.

Frisch, A., Laufer, N., Danziger, Y., Michaelovsky, E., Leor, S., Carel, C., et al. (2001). Association of anorexia nervosa with the high activity allele of the COMT gene: A family-based study in Israeli patients. *Molecular Psychiatry, 6,* 243–245.

Gaillard, W. D., Balsamo, L. M., Ibrahim, Z., Sachs, B. C., & Xu, B. (2003). fMRI identifies regional specialization of neural networks for reading in young children. *Neurology, 60,* 94–100.

Gallagher, A., Frith, U., & Snowling, M. J. (2000). Precursors of literacy delay among children at genetic risk of dyslexia. *Journal of Child Psychology and Psychiatry, 4,* 202–213.

Gallinat, J., Bajbouj, M., Sander, T., Schlattmann, P., Xu, K., Ferro, E. F., et al. (2003). Association of the G1947A COMT (Val(108/158)Met) gene polymorphism with prefrontal P300 during information processing. *Biological Psychiatry, 54*, 40–48.

Glatt, S. J., Faraone, S. V., & Tsuang, M. T. (2003). Association between a functional catechol O-methyltransferase gene polymorphism and schizophrenia: Meta-analysis of case–control and family-based studies. *American Journal of Psychiatry, 160*, 469–476.

Goldberg, T. E., Egan, M. F., Gscheidle, T., Coppola, R., Weickert, T., Kolachana, B. S., et al. (2003). Executive subprocesses in working memory: Relationship to catechol-O-methyltransferase Val158Met genotype and schizophrenia. *Archives of General Psychiatry, 60*, 889–896.

Goldberg, T. E., & Weinberg, D. R. (2004). Genes and the parsing of cognitive processes. *TRENDS in Cognitive Sciences, 8*, 325–335.

Goldman-Rakic, P. S., Castner, S. A., Svensson, T. H., Siever, L. J., & Williams, G. V. (2004). Targeting the dopamine D1 receptor in schizophrenia: Insights for cognitive dysfunction. *Psychopharmacology, 174*, 3–16.

Gottesman, I. I., & Gould, T. D. (2003). The endophenotype concept in psychiatry: Etymology and strategic intentions. *American Journal of Psychiatry, 160*, 636–645.

Gottesman, I. I., & Shields, J. (1972). *Schizophrenia and genetics: A twin study vantage point.* New York: Academic Press.

Grigorenko, E. L. (2005). A conservative meta-analysis of linkage and linkage-association studies of developmental dyslexia. *Scientific Studies of Reading, 9*, 285–316.

Grigorenko, E. L., Klin, A., & Volkmar, F. (2003). Annotation: Hyperlexia: Disability or super-ability? *Journal of Child Psychology & Psychiatry & Allied Disciplines, 44*, 1079–1091.

Gustavson, K. H., Floderus, Y., Jagell, S., Wetterberg, L., & Ross, S. B. (1982). Catechol-o-methyltransferase activity in erythrocytes in Down's syndrome: Family studies. *Clinical Genetics, 22*, 22–24.

Gustavson, K. H., Wetterberg, L., Backstrom, M., & Ross, S. B. (1973). Catechol-O-methyltransferase activity in erythrocytes in Down's syndrome. *Clinical Genetics, 4*, 279–280.

Hamalainen, J., Leppanen, P. H. T., Torppa, M., Muller, K., & Lyytinen, H. (2005). Detection of sound rise time by adults with dyslexia. *Brain and Language, 94*, 32–42.

Helland, T., & Asbjornsen, A. (2000). Executive functions in dyslexia. *Child Neuropsychology, 6*, 37–48.

Hinton, S. C., Harrington, D. L., Binder, J. R., Durgerian, S., & Rao, S. M. (2004). Neural systems supporting timing and chronometric counting: An FMRI study. *Cognitive Brain Research, 21*, 183–192.

Horowitz, R., Kotler, M., Shufman, E., Aharoni, S., Kremer, I., Cohen, H., et al. (2000). Confirmation of an excess of the high enzyme activity COMT val allele in heroin addicts in a family-based haplotype relative risk study. *American Journal of Medical Genetics, 96*, 599–603.

Huotari, M., Santha, M., Lucas, L. R., Karayiorgou, M., Gogos, J. A., & Mannisto, P. T. (2002). Effect of dopamine uptake inhibition on brain catecholamine levels and locomotion in catechol-O-methyltransferase–disrupted mice. *Journal of Pharmacology & Experimental Therapeutics, 303*, 1309–1316.

Johnson, M. H. (2001). Functional brain development in humans. *Nature Reviews Neuroscience, 2*, 475–483.

Jones, P. A., & Laird, P. W. (1999). Cancer epigenetics comes of age. *Nature Genetics, 21*, 163–167.

Jones, P. A., & Takai, D. (2001). The role of DNA methylation in mammalian epigenetics. *Science, 293*, 1068–1070.

Joober, R., Gauthier, J., Lal, S., Bloom, D., Lalonde, P., Rouleau, G., et al. (2002). Catechol-O-methyltransferase Val–108/158–Met gene variants associated with performance on the Wisconsin Card Sorting Test. *Archives of General Psychiatry, 59*, 662–663.

Karayiorgou, M., Altemus, M., Galke, B. L., Goldman, D., Murphy, D. L., Ott, J., et al. (1997). Genotype determining low catechol-O-methyltransferase activity as a risk factor for obsessive–compulsive disorder. *Proceedings of the National Academy of Sciences of the United States of America, 94*, 4572–4575.

Karmiloff-Smith, A., Scerif, G., & Ansari, D. (2003). Double dissociations in developmental disorders? Theoretically misconceived, empirically dubious. *Cortex, 39*, 161–163.

Kriaucionis, S., & Bird, A. (2003). DNA methylation and Rett syndrome. *Human Molecular Genetics, 12*, R221–R227.

Kunugi, H., Vallada, H. P., Sham, P. C., Hoda, F., Arranz, M. J., Li, T., et al. (1997). Catechol-O-methyltransferase polymorphisms and schizophrenia: A transmission disequilibrium study in multiply affected families. *Psychiatric Genetics, 7*, 97–101.

Lachman, H. M., Papolos, D. F., Saito, T., Yu, Y. M., Szumlanski, C. L., & Weinshilboum, R. M. (1996). Human catechol-O-methyltransferase pharmacogenetics: Description of a functional polymorphism and its potential application to neuropsychiatric disorders. *Pharmacogenetics, 6*, 243–250.

Lai, C. S., Fisher, S. E., Hurst, J. A., Vargha-Khadem, F., & Monaco, A. P. (2001). A forkhead-domain gene is mutated in a severe speech and language disorder. *Nature, 431*, 519–523.

Lee, S. G., Joo, Y., Kim, B., Chung, S., Kim, H. L., Lee, I., et al. (2005). Association of Ala72Ser polymorphism with COMT enzyme activity and the risk of schizophrenia in Koreans. *Human Genetics, 116*, 319–328.

Lester, D. (1995). The concentration of neurotransmitter metabolites in the cerebrospinal fluid of suicidal individuals: A meta-analysis. *Pharmacopsychiatry, 28*, 45–50.

Lewis, D. A., Melchitzky, D. S., Sesack, S. R., Whitehead, R. E., Auh, S., & Sampson, A. (2001). Dopamine transporter immunoreactivity in monkey cerebral cortex: Regional, laminar, and ultrastructural localization. *Journal of Comparative Neurology, 432*, 119–136.

Li, W.-H., & Saunders, M. A. (2005). The chimpanzee and us. *Nature, 437*, 50–51.

Li, T., Chen, C. K., Hu, X., Ball, D., Lin, S. K., Chen, W., et al. (2004). Association analysis of the DRD4 and COMT genes in methamphetamine abuse. *American Journal of Medical Genetics (Part B, Neuropsychiatric Genetics), 129*, 120–124.

Li, Y., Yao, J., Chang, M., Nikolic, D., Yu, L., Yager, J. D., et al. (2004). Equine catechol estrogen 4-hydroxyequilenin is a more potent inhibitor of the variant form of catechol-O-methyltransferase. *Chemical Research in Toxicology, 17*, 512–520.

Linardopoulou, E. V., Williams, E. M., Fan, Y., Friedman, C., Young, J. M., & Trask, B. J. (2005). Human subtelomeres are hot spots of interchromosomal recombination and segmental duplication. *Nature, 437*, 94–10.

Lotta, T., Vidgren, J., Tilgmann, C., Ulmanen, I., Melen, K., Julkunen, I., et al. (1995). Kinetics of human soluble and membrane–bound catechol O-methyltransferase: A revised mechanism and description of the thermolabile variant of the enzyme. *Biochemistry, 34*, 4202–4210.

Lyytinen, P., & Lyytinen, H. (2004). Growth and predictive relations of vocabulary and inflectional morphology in children with and without familial risk for dyslexia. *Applied Psycholinguistics, 25*, 397–411.

Macdermot, K. D., Bonora, E., Sykes, N., Coupe, A. M., Lai, C. S., Vernes, S. C., et al. (2005). Identification of FOXP2 truncation as a novel cause of developmental speech and language deficits. *American Journal of Human Genetics, 76*, 1074–1080.

Malhotra, A. K., Kestler, L. J., Mazzanti, C., Bates, J. A., Goldberg, T., & Goldman, D. (2002). A functional polymorphism in the COMT gene and performance on a test of prefrontal cognition. *American Journal of Psychiatry, 159*, 652–654.

Manji, H., Gottesman, I. I., & Gould, T. D. (2003). Signal transduction and genes-to-behaviors pathways in psychiatric diseases. *Science's Stke [Electronic Resource]: Signal Transduction Knowledge Environment, 207*, pe49.

McGrath, M., Kawachi, I., Ascherio, A., Colditz, G. A., Hunter, D. J., & De Vivo, I. (2004). Association between catechol-O-methyltransferase and phobic anxiety. *American Journal of Psychiatry, 161*(703–705).

McNulty, M. A. (2003). Dyslexia and the life course. *Journal of Learning Disabilities, 36*, 363–381.

Mechelli, A., Gorno-Tempini, M. L., & Price, C. J. (2003). Neuroimaging studies of word and pseudoword reading: Consistencies, inconsistencies, and limitations. *Journal of Cognitive Neuroscience, 15*, 260–271.

Meyer-Linderberg, A., Kohn, P. D., Kolachana, B., Kippenhan, S., McInerney-Leo, A., Nussbaum, R., et al. (2005). Midbrain dopamine and prefrontal function in humans: Interaction and modulation by COMT genotype. *Nature Neuroscience, Published online 10 April 2005.*

Mikkelsen, T. S. (2004). What makes us human? *Genome Biology, 238*, 238.

Miller-Shaul, S. (2005). The characteristics of young and adult dyslexics readers on reading and reading related cognitive tasks as compared to normal readers. *Dyslexia: An International Journal of Research and Practice, 11*, 132–151.

Olson, M. V., & Varki, A. (2003). Sequencing the chimpanzee genome: Insights into human evolution and disease. *Nature Reviews Genetics, 4*, 20–28.

Ono, H., Shirakawa, O., Nushida, H., Ueno, Y., & Maeda, K. (2004). Association between catechol-O-methyltransferase functional polymorphism and male suicide completers. *Neuropsychopharmacology, 29*, 1374–1377.

Palmatier, M. A., Kang, A. M., & Kidd, K. K. (1999). Global variation in the frequencies of functionally different catechol-O-methyltransferase alleles. *Biological Psychiatry, 46*, 557–567.

Palmatier, M. A., Pakstis, A. J., Speed, W., Paschou, P., Goldman, D., Odunsi, A., et al. (2004). COMT haplotypes suggest P2 promoter region relevance for schizophrenia. *Molecular Psychiatry, 9*, 1359–4184.

Papanicolaou, A. C., Simos, P. G., Breier, J. I., Fletcher, J. M., Foorman, B. R., Francis, D., et al. (2003). Brain mechanisms for reading in children with and without dyslexia: A review of studies of normal development and plasticity. *Developmental Neuropsychology, 24*, 593–612.

Petersen, S. E., Fox, P. T., Posner, M. I., Mintun, M., & Raichle, M. E. (1988). Positron emission tomographic studies of the cortical anatomy of single-word processing. *Nature, 331*, 585–589.

Poldrack, R. A., Wagner, A. D., Prull, M. W., Desmond, J. E., Glover, G. H., & Gabrieli, J. D. (1999). Functional specialization for semantic and phonological processing in the left inferior prefrontal cortex. *Neuroimage, 10*, 15–35.

Price, C. J., Wise, R. J., & Frackowiak, R. S. (1996). Demonstrating the implicit processing of visually presented words and pseudowords. *Cerebral Cortex, 6*, 62–70.

Pugh, K. R., Mencl, W. E., Jenner, A. R., Katz, L., Frost, S. J., Lee, J. R., et al. (2001). Neurobiological studies of reading and reading disability. *Journal of Communication Disorders, 34*, 479–492.

Pugh, K. R., Shaywitz, B. A., Shaywitz, S. E., Constable, R. T., Skudlarski, P., Fulbright, R. K., et al. (1996). Cerebral organization of component processes in reading. *Brain, 119*, 1221–1238.

Qian, Q., Wang, Y., Zhou, R., Li, J., Wang, B., Glatt, S., et al. (2003). Family-based and case–control association studies of catechol-O-methyltransferase in attention deficit hyperactivity disorder suggest genetic sexual dimorphism. *American Journal of Medical Genetics (Part B, Neuropsychiatric Genetics), 118*, 103–109.

Ramus, F., Rosen, S., Dakin, S. C., Day, B. L., Castellote, J. M., White, S., et al. (2003). Theories of developmental dyslexia: insights from a multiple case study of dyslexic adults. *Brain, 126*, 841–865.

Ransby, M. J., & Swanson, H. L. (2003). Reading comprehension skills of young adults with childhood diagnoses of dyslexia. *Journal of Learning Disabilities, 36*, 538–555.

Rosa, A., Peralta, V., Cuesta, M. J., Zarzuela, A., Serrano, F., Martinez-Larrea, A., et al. (2004). New evidence of association between COMT gene and prefrontal neurocognitive function in healthy individuals from sibling pairs discordant for psychosis. *American Journal of Psychiatry, 161*, 1110–1112.

Rumsey, J. M., Horwitz, B., Donohue, B. C., Nace, K. L., Maisog, J. M., & P., A. (1999). A functional lesion in developmental dyslexia: Left angular gyral blood flow predicts severity. *Brain Language, 70*, 187–204.

Ruvolo, M. (2004). Comparative primate genomics: The year of the chimpanzee. *Current Opinion in Genetics & Development, 14*, 650–656.

Scerif, G., & Karmiloff-Smith, A. (2005). The dawn of cognitive genetics? Crucial developmental caveats. *TRENDS in Cognitive Sciences, 9*, 126–135.

Servan-Schreiber, D., Carter, C. S., Bruno, R. M., & Cohen, J. D. (1998a). Dopamine and the mechanisms of cognition: Part I. A neural network model predicting dopamine effects on selective attention. *Biological Psychiatry, 43*, 713–722.

Servan-Schreiber, D., Carter, C. S., Bruno, R. M., & Cohen, J. D. (1998b). Dopamine and the mechanisms of cognition: Part II. D-amphetamine effects in human subjects performing a selective attention task. *Biological Psychiatry, 43*, 723–729.

Servan-Schreiber, D., Printz, H., & Cohen, J. D. (1990). A network model of catecholamine effects: Gain, signal-to-noise ratio, and behavior. *Science, 249*, 892–895.

Sesack, S. R., Hawrylak, V. A., Guido, M. A., & Levey, A. I. (1998). Cellular and subcellular localization of the dopamine transporter in rat cortex. *Advances in Pharmacology, 42*, 171–174.

Shaywitz, S. E., Shaywitz, B. A., Fulbright, R. K., Skudlarski, P., Mencl, W. E., Constable, R. T., et al. (2003). Neural systems for compensation and persistence: young adult outcome of childhood reading disability. *Biological Psychiatry, 54*, 25–33.

Shield, A. J., Thomae, B. A., Eckloff, B. W., Wieben, E. D., & Weinshilboum, R. M. (2004). Human catechol O-methyltransferase genetic variation: Gene resequencing and functional characterization of variant allozymesb. *Molecular Psychiatry, 9*, 151–160.

Shifman, S., Bronstein, M., Sternfeld, M., Pisante-Shalom, A., Lev-Lehman, E., Weizman, A., et al. (2002). A highly significant association between a COMT haplotype and schizophrenia. *American Journal of Human Genetics, 71*, 1296–1302.

Snowling, M. J., Gallagher, A., & Frith, U. (2003). Family risk of dyslexia is continuous: Individual differences in the precursors of reading skill. *Child Development, 74*, 358–373.

Snyder, A. Z., Abdullaev, Y. G., Posner, M. I., & Raichle, M. E. (1995). Scalp electrical potentials reflect regional cerebral blood flow responses during processing of written words. *Proceedings of the National Academy of Sciences of the United States of America, 92*, 1689–1693.

Sperling, A. J., Lu, Z.-L., & Manis, F. R. (2004). Slower implicit categorical learning in adult poor readers. *Annals of Dyslexia, 54*, 281–303.

Strobel, A., Lesch, K. P., Jatzke, S., Paetzold, F., & Brocke, B. (2003). Further evidence for a modulation of Novelty Seeking by DRD4 exon III, 5–HTTLPR, and COMT val/met variants. *Molecular Psychiatry, 8*, 371–372.

Swanson, H. L., & Sachse-Lee, C. (2001). A subgroup analysis of working memory in children with reading disabilities: Domain-general or domain-specific deficiency? *Journal of Learning Disabilities, 34*(249–264).

Taipale, M., Kaminen, N., Nopola-Hemmi, J., Haltia, T., Myllyluoma, B., Lyytinen, H., Muller, K., Kaaranen, M., Lindsberg, P. J., Hannula-Jouppi, K., Kere, J. (2003). A candidate gene for developmental dyslexia encodes a nuclear tetratricopeptide repeat domain protein dynamically regulated in brain. *Proceedings of the National Academy of Sciences of the United States of America, 100*, 11553–11558.

Tagamets, M. A., Novick, J. M., Chalmers, M. L., & Friedman, R. B. (2000). A parametric approach to orthographic processing in the brain: An fMRI study. *Journal of Cognitive Neuroscience, 12*, 281–297.

Taylor, M. S., Pontig, C. P., & Copley, R. R. (2004). Occurrence and consequences of coding sequence insertions and deletions in mammalian genomes. *Genome Research, 14*, 555–566.

Tenhunen, J., Salminen, M., Lundstrom, K., Kiviluoto, T., Savolainen, R., & Ulmanen, I. (1994). Genomic organization of the human catechol O-methyltransferase gene and its expression from two distinct promoters. *European Journal of Biochemistry, 223*, 1049–1059.

The Chimpanzee Sequencing and Analysis Consortium. (2005). Initial sequence of the chimpanzee genome and comparison with the human genome. *Nature, 437*, 69–87.

Tiihonen, J., Hallikainen, T., Lachman, H., Saito, T., Volavka, J., Kauhanen, J., et al. (1999). Association between the functional variant of the catechol-O-methyltransferase (COMT) gene and type 1 alcoholism. *Molecular Psychiatry, 4*, 286–289.

Tsai, S. J., Hong, C. J., Yu, Y. W., & Chen, T. J. (2004). Association study of a brain-derived neurotrophic factor (BDNF) Val66Met polymorphism and personality trait and intelligence in healthy young females. *Neuropsychobiology, 49*, 13–16.

Turkeltaub, P. E., Eden, G. F., Jones, K. M., & Zeffiro, T. A. (2002). Meta-analysis of the functional neuroanatomy of single-word reading: Method and validation. *Neuroimage, 16*, 765–780.

Turkeltaub, P. E., Gareau, L., Flowers, D. L., Zeffiro, T. A., & Eden, G. F. (2003). Development of neural mechanisms for reading. *Nature Neuroscience, 6*, 767–773.

Uddin, M., Wildman, D. E., Liu, G., Xu, W., Johnson, R. M., Hof, P. R., et al. (2004). Sister grouping of chimpanzees and humans as revealed by genome-wide phylogenetic analysis of brain gene expression profiles. *Proceedings of the National Academy of Sciences of the United States of America, 101*, 2957–2962.

Urrutia, A. O., & Hurst, L. D. (2003). The signature of selection mediated by expression on human genes. *Genome Research, 13*, 2260–2264.

van Alphen, P., de Bree, E., Gerrits, E., de Jong, J., Wilsenach, C., & Wijnen, F. (2004). Early language development in children with a genetic risk of dyslexia. *Dyslexia: An International Journal of Research & Practice, 10*, 265–288.

Vandenbergh, D. J., Rodriguez, L. A., Miller, I. T., Uhl, G. R., & Lachman, H. M. (1997). High-activity catechol-O-methyltransferase allele is more prevalent in polysubstance abusers. *American Journal of Medical Genetics, 74*, 439–442.

Vargha-Khadem, F., Watkins, K., Alcock, K., Fletcher, P., & Passingham, R. (1995). Praxic and nonverbal cognitive deficits in a large family with a genetically transmitted speech and language disorder. *Proceedings of the National Academy of Sciences of the United States of America, 92*, 930–933.

Viholainen, H., Ahonen, T., Cantell, M., Lyytinen, P., & Lyytinen, H. (2002). Development of early motor skills and language in children at risk for familial dyslexia. *Developmental Medicine & Child Neurology, 44*, 761–769.

Vinogradov, A. E. (2004a). Compactness of human housekeeping genes: Selection for economy or genomic design? *Trends in Genetics, 20*, 248–253.

Vinogradov, A. E. (2004b). Evolution of genome size: Multilevel selection, mutation bias or dynamical chaos? *Current Opinion in Genetics & Development, 14*, 620–626.

Volavka, J., Kennedy, J. L., Ni, X., Czobor, P., Nolan, K., Sheitman, B., et al. (2004). COMT158 polymorphism and hostility. *American Journal of Medical Genetics (Part B, Neuropsychiatric Genetics), 127*, 28–29.

Wang, T., Franke, P., Neidt, H., Cichon, S., Knapp, M., Lichtermann, D., et al. (2001). Association study of the low-activity allele of catechol-O-methyltransferase and alcoholism using a family-based approach. *Molecular Psychiatry, 6*, 109–111.

Watanabe, H., Fujiyama, A., Hattori, M., Taylor, T. D., Toyoda, A., Kuroki, Y., et al. (2004). DNA sequence and comparative analysis of chimpanzee chromosome 22. *Nature, 429*, 382–388.

Weickert, T. W., Goldberg, T. E., Mishara, A., Apud, J. A., Kolachana, B. S., Egan, M. F., et al. (2004). Catechol-O-methyltransferase val108/158met genotype predicts working memory response to antipsychotic medications. *Biological Psychiatry, 56,* 677–682.

Weinshilboum, R. M., Otterness, D. M., & Szumlanski, C. L. (1999). Methylation pharmacogenetics: Catechol O-methyltransferase, thiopurine methyltransferase, and histamine N-methyltransferase. *Annual Review of Pharmacology & Toxicology, 39,* 19–52.

Wilson, A. M., & Lesaux, N. K. (2001). Persistence of phonological processing deficits in college students with dyslexia who have age-appropriate reading skills. *Journal of Learning Disabilities, 34,* 394–400.

Wu, R. M., Cheng, C. W., Chen, K. H., Lu, S. L., Shan, D. E., Ho, Y. F., et al. (2001). The COMT L allele modifies the association between MAOB polymorphism and PD in Taiwanese. *Neurology, 56,* 375–382.

Zubieta, J. K., Heitzeg, M. M., Smith, Y. R., Bueller, J. A., Xu, K., Xu, Y., et al. (2003). COMT val158met genotype affects mu-opioid neurotransmitter responses to a pain stressor. *Science, 299,* 1240–1243.

CHAPTER FIFTEEN

Dyslexia: Identification and Classification

Shayne B. Piasta and Richard K. Wagner
Florida State University,
Florida Center for Reading Research

Developmental dyslexia, reading disability, and reading impairment are three interchangeable terms that refer to unexpected poor performance in reading (Wagner, 2005). Expected levels of reading performance can be based on normative data from age-matched peers or based on an individual's oral language or general cognitive ability. The observed poor reading performance is unexpected in the sense of not being explained either by lack of an opportunity to learn (i.e., ineffective instruction) or by other potential causes including severe intellectual deficits, language impairments, or impaired basic sensory capacities such as blindness. Developmental dyslexia is distinguished from acquired dyslexia, with acquired dyslexia referring to impaired reading in formerly normal readers due to brain injury or illness. Our focus in the present chapter will necessarily be limited to developmental as opposed to acquired dyslexia. We begin by considering the role of single-word reading in identifying individuals with dyslexia, and then review attempts to classify individuals with dyslexia into subtypes on the basis of their pattern of performance at single-word reading as a function of the kind of stimuli that are read.

IDENTIFYING INDIVIDUALS WITH DEVELOPMENTAL DYSLEXIA

Fortunately, the context of single-word reading is not a constraining one for considering the topic of identifying individuals with developmental dyslexia. Indeed, we shall argue that for most such individuals, the nexus of their reading problem is in their inability to decode single words with sufficient accuracy and speed.

Introduction to Developmental Dyslexia

"Dyslexia" is one of the most widely known terms that describes an impaired intellectual function. However, the key features of developmental dyslexia are misunderstood by most laypersons (Wagner & Muse, 2006). For example, Oprah Winfrey, host of the popular American television show, featured dyslexia in one recent program. The program contained numerous accounts by self-reported dyslexic members of the audience of seeing words backwards. Indeed, the most popular misconception of dyslexia is that it derives from seeing mirror images of words or letters. Thus, individuals with dyslexia are reported to read 'WAS' as 'SAW,' or to confuse the letters 'b' and 'd.' This misconception even received scientific support in the form of Samuel Orton's theory of mixed cerebral dominance (Hallahan & Mock, 2003).

There is a ready explanation for this popular misconception of dyslexia: Children with developmental dyslexia, who commonly are identified in second or third grade, indeed can be observed to confuse 'WAS' for 'SAW' and 'b' for 'd.' So how is this a misconception? It turns out that these kinds of reversal errors are among the easiest kinds of errors to make, and they are quite common in kindergarten and first-grade classrooms among normally-developing readers. Reading 'WAS' as 'WAS' rather than as 'SAW' requires that the word is read from left to right and not from right to left. But the fact that words in English are to be read from left to right as opposed to right to left is an arbitrary fact of our system of print that must be learned by beginning readers. Other scripts are read from right to left, or even vertically. Confusions between letters such as 'b' and 'd' are explainable in that these letter pairs are both visually confusable (to beginning readers, the letter 'b' can be seen as a stick and a ball whereas the letter 'd' is a ball and a stick) and similar in sound (i.e., both stop consonants). The critical piece of evidence is that second-grade readers with dyslexia make no more reversal errors than do younger normal readers who are matched at the same level of reading (Crowder & Wagner, 1992; Werker, Bryson, & Wassenberg, 1989). What explains the popularity of this mistaken view is that teachers and parents of second-grade readers only see children with reading problems making these errors. Teachers and parents of beginning readers know that such errors are quite common. Overall, the notion of dyslexia as representing a visual-perceptual deficit has not been supported (see reviews in Rayner, 1998; Stanovich, 1982).

Another mistaken idea about dyslexia is that it results from deficient eye-movements. Reading requires highly sophisticated and coordinated eye-movements (Rayner & Poletsek, 1989). When reading, the eyes move across the page a little bit at a time in a series of tiny ballistic movements called saccades. Saccades are ballistic much like the velocity and trajectory of a cannon ball, which is driven by an initial burst of energy. During saccades, the eyes are moving too fast to see letters or words clearly. Nearly all information is acquired during the fixations or brief pauses between saccades.

As you read the words on this page, it seems that you are moving your eyes smoothly across the page. However, this perception is far from reality, as can be observed with a simple experiment. Ask a friend who is an average or better reader to read directly across from you, holding a book low enough so you can observe your friend's eyes across the top of the book. What you will see if you look carefully is that your friend's eyes indeed move across the page in a series of small, but observable jerky movements.

Perform the same experiment on an individual with reading impairment and it will be apparent that the individual's eyes move much more erratically, even moving in the wrong direction at times. Observations like these were viewed as confirmation of the deficient eye-movement account of developmental dyslexia, and led to interventions that trained skill at moving the eyes smoothly to follow a moving target. However, it has turned out that erratic eye-movements are not the cause of dyslexia, but rather a byproduct: The eye-movements of individuals with dyslexia do not move across the page as smoothly as do those of normal readers simply because they are having trouble reading the words. This also explains their greater frequency of backward eye-movements or regressions. Conclusive evidence was provided by careful studies in which normal readers were given material that was as difficult for them to read as is grade-level reading material for individuals with reading impairment, and individuals with reading impairment were given very easy reading material that they could read as well as normal readers could read grade-level material. Under these conditions, the eye-movements of normal readers deteriorated to match the previously reported erratic eye-movements of individuals with reading impairment, and the eye-movements of the individuals with reading impairment now looked normal. Additional confirmation came from the results of eye-movement training studies. Although eye-movement training did result in gains performance on eye-movement tasks outside the context of reading, reading performance did not improve (Crowder & Wagner, 1992).

Current Approaches to Identification

Current approaches to identifying individuals with dyslexia utilize exclusionary criteria in order to operationalize the "unexpectedness" of the disorder: Poor readers whose impairments are primarily due to sensory, motor, or emotional impairments, mental deficiency, economic or cultural disadvantage, or inadequate reading instruction are excluded from consideration (Lyon, Shaywitz, & Shaywitz, 2003). In many states, formal identification for purposes of becoming eligible for special education services requires a discrepancy between aptitude, as measured by intelligence tests or achievement tests outside the realm of reading (e.g., mathematics), and reading skill. Such a discrepancy approach was consistent with how the federal government had defined specific learning disabilities since they were included in the original Education for All Handicapped Children Act (PL 94-142) in 1977 and how this definition was operationalized in the Individuals with Disabilities in Education Act (IDEA), the federal legislation that governs eligibility for special education assistance for individuals with dyslexia or other learning disabilities:

SPECIFIC LEARNING DISABILITY

(A) IN GENERAL —The term "specific learning disability" means a disorder in 1 or more of the basic psychological processes involved in understanding or in using language, spoken or written, which disorder may manifest itself in the imperfect ability to listen, think, speak, read, write, spell, or do mathematical calculations.

(B) DISORDERS INCLUDED —Such term includes such conditions as perceptual disabilities, brain injury, minimal brain dysfunction, dyslexia, and developmental aphasia.

(C) DISORDERS NOT INCLUDED —Such term does not include a learning problem that is primarily the result of visual, hearing, or motor disabilities, of mental retardation, of emotional disturbance, or of environmental, cultural, or economic disadvantage.

CRITERIA FOR DETERMINING THE EXISTENCE
OF A SPECIFIC LEARNING DISABILITY

(A) A team may determine that a child has a specific learning disability if—

(1) The child does not achieve commensurate with his or her age and ability levels in one or more of the areas listed in paragraph (a)(2) of this section, if provided with learning experiences appropriate for the child's age and ability levels; and

(2) The team finds that a child has a severe discrepancy between achievement and intellectual ability in one or more of the following areas:

(i)   Oral expression.
(ii) Listening comprehension.
(iii) Written expression.
(iv) Basic reading skill.
(v)   Reading comprehension.
(vi) Mathematics calculation.
(vii) Mathematics reasoning.

(B) The team may not identify a child as having a specific learning disability if the severe discrepancy between ability and achievement is primarily the result of—

(1) A visual, hearing, or motor impairment;
(2) Mental retardation;
(3) Emotional disturbance; or
(4) Environmental, cultural or economic disadvantage.

However, current research-based definitions omit a discrepancy requirement, largely on the basis of the fact that the most appropriate intervention for beginning readers who are at risk for reading failure does not vary depending of whether or not the child's reading is discrepant from aptitude (Fletcher, Francis, Rourke, Shaywitz, & Shaywitz, 1992; Fletcher, Morris, & Lyon, 2003; Francis, Shaywitz, Stuebing, Shaywitz, & Fletcher, 1996; Lyon et al., 2001, 2003; Shaywitz, Fletcher, Holahan, & Shaywitz, 1992; Shaywitz & Shaywitz, 2003; Siegel, 2003; Stanovich, 1994; Stanovich & Siegel, 1994). Based in part on this literature (see Fletcher et al., 2004 for review), the recent reauthorization of IDEA in 2004 no longer requires such a discrepancy between aptitude and achievement for receiving services:

SPECIFIC LEARNING DISABILITIES

(A)   IN GENERAL — Notwithstanding section 607(b), when determining whether a child has a specific learning disability as defined in section 602, a local educational agency shall not be required to take into consideration whether a child has a severe discrepancy between achievement and intellectual ability in oral expression, listening comprehension, written expression, basic reading skill, reading comprehension, mathematical calculation, or mathematical reasoning.

(B)   ADDITIONAL AUTHORITY — In determining whether a child has a specific learning disability, a local educational agency may use a process that determines if the child responds to scientific, research-based intervention as a part of the evaluation procedures described in paragraphs (2) and (3).

The new regulations allow state education agencies more leeway in how they identify children with learning disabilities, including those with dyslexia, for special education services. The changes are also commensurate with the aims of the No Child Left Behind Act of 2001; the federal regulations specifically state that children who "lack of appropriate instruction in reading, including in the essential components of reading instruction (as defined in section 1208(3) of the Elementary and Secondary Education Act of 1965)" are not eligible for special education services. Thus, the means by which children are identified with dyslexia has been broadened to include response to instruction (RTI) criteria (see subsection B in the regulations above).

RTI represents a more process-oriented approach to the identification of learning disabilities in general. The "unexpectedness" of the disability is still characterized by a discrepancy, but the discrepancy now reflects a comparison of the child's performance and the learning opportunities he or she has had, as opposed to one between the child's aptitude and academic performance. Basically, an RTI approach to identification of dyslexia (or any other learning disability) consists of moving a poorly performing child through a number of progressively more rigorous and intensive stages of assessment and instruction. Fuchs, Mock, Morgan, and Young (2003) outline the steps as follows: (1) students receive quality instruction within their general education classrooms, (2) progress monitoring is utilized to highlight those children who are performing poorly and/or are not showing typical progress in the area of concern (e.g., reading), (3) these non-responders are provided with additional, more intensive instruction (e.g., small group instruction, tutoring, a different reading program), (4) progress monitoring continues, and (5) either steps (3) and (4) are repeated at a more intense level or the child is referred for special education services, depending on the specific RTI model that is implemented. Benefits of the RTI approach include a push for improvements in the quality of general classroom reading instruction, earlier identification and targeted intervention for struggling and disabled readers, reduction of false positives (over-identification) and false negatives (under-identification) in classification, and inclusion of both absolute achievement levels and rate of growth in the definition of dyslexia. Although number of investigations into the validity and utility of RTI have been carried out (e.g., Case, Speece, & Malloy, 2003; Fuchs et al., 2003; Fuchs & Fuchs, 1998; Fuchs, Fuchs, McMaster, & Al Otaiba, 2003), research in this area is ongoing (see e.g., Fuchs, Deshler, & Reschly, 2004).

Dyslexia and Single-Word Reading

Despite the differences in the manner in which dyslexia is identified, the various exclusionary and discrepancy criteria in the definitions above imply that the origin of dyslexia is constitutional, due to neurobiological factors which are intrinsic to the individual (Adams & Bruck, 1993; Bruck, 1990; Gough & Tunmer, 1986; Perfetti, 1985, 1986; Siegel, 2003; Stanovich, 1994). There is general agreement that this intrinsic impairment manifests itself in the act of single-word reading for the vast majority of individuals with dyslexia (e.g., see Adams, 1990; National Research Council, 1998; Stanovich, 1982; Vellutino, 1979). Although many individuals with dyslexia also are impaired in reading comprehension, the impaired comprehension usually is a concomitant of the primary impairment in single-word reading (Aaron, 1989; Stanovich & Siegel, 1994). Furthermore, individuals with dyslexia commonly over-rely on comprehension processes in the form of guessing the identity of a word from context in an attempt to compensate for their impaired single-word reading ability (Aaron, 1989; Bruck, 1988). Additional support for the view that the primary impairment for most individuals with dyslexia is manifest in their single-word reading is the fact that adults who have compensated for their reading difficulty and no longer are impaired at reading comprehension nevertheless continue to struggle with word recognition (Bruck, 1988, 1990, 1993; Scarborough, 1984).

For the vast majority of individuals with dyslexia, poor single-word reading derives from a deficiency that is based in the language rather than the visual system, and the problem of poor performance commonly is compounded by ineffective instruction (Spear-Swerling & Sternberg, 1996; Wagner, 2005; Wagner & Garon, 1999; Wagner & Torgesen, 1987). Compared to reading-level matched controls, most individuals with reading impairment perform poorly on measures of phonological awareness and phonological decoding, and have fewer words that can be decoded by sight (Ehri, 1998; Fox, 1994; Siegel & Faux, 1989).

Phonological awareness refers to an individual's awareness and access to the sound structure of an oral language. Phonological decoding refers to decoding words by sounding them out, as when one is asked to decode nonwords such as TANE. The underlying language problem for individuals with reading impairment is likely to be a subtle and not well-understood problem in forming accurate phonological representations, which in turn leads to poor phonological awareness and phonological decoding. Once beginning readers fall behind, they are exposed to reading instruction designed for more advanced readers, which provides little assistance, until they finally are identified as having a reading problem and more appropriate instruction is provided.

One of the hallmark manifestations of the single-word reading of individuals with dyslexia is their significant impairment at decoding pronounceable nonwords or pseudowords (see Rack, Snowling, & Olson, 1992 for review). Children with dyslexia continue to struggle to read pseudowords even once they have demonstrated knowledge of similar orthographic patterns in real words (Siegel & Faux, 1989), and the pseudoword reading deficit persists into adulthood (Bruck, 1990, 1992, 1993). The causal role of deficits in phonological skills is further supported by the multitude of intervention studies which have utilized phonological training and phonics instruction to produce gains in at-risk or dyslexic readers (e.g., Ball & Blachman, 1991; Brady, Fowler, Stone, & Winbury, 1994; Byrne & Fielding-Barnsley, 1989, 1991, 1993, 1995; Byrne, Fielding-Barnsley, & Ashley, 2000; Ehri, Nunes, Stahl, & Willows, 2001; Ehri, Nunes, Willows et al., 2001; Foorman et al., 2003; Foorman, Francis, Fletcher, Schatschneider, & Mehta, 1998; Foorman, Francis, Novy, & Liberman, 1991; Hatcher, Hulme, & Ellis, 1994; Lovett, Steinbach, & Frijters, 2000; Rashotte, MacPhee, & Torgesen, 2001; Schneider, Ennemoser, Roth, & Kuespert, 1999; Schneider, Roth, & Ennemoser, 2000; Torgesen et al., 2001; Torgesen et al., 1999; Vellutino, Scanlon, & Tanzman, 1998; Wise, Ring, & Olson, 1999; see also Adams, 1990; Bus & van Ijzendoorn, 1999; Chall, 1967/1983; National Reading Panel, 2000; National Research Council, 1998).

CLASSIFICATION OF INDIVIDUALS WITH
DEVELOPMENTAL DYSLEXIA INTO SUBTYPES

The traditional view of single-word reading has been that a reader can get from print to meaning in either of two ways (Adams, 1990; Ehri, 1997). The first, which may be termed phonological decoding, involves translating graphemes (individual letters or specific letter combinations) into phonemes (sounds) using a set of grapheme phoneme correspondence (GPC) rules. According to the traditional view, phonological decoding is what makes it possible for us to come up with a pronunciation when confronted with a word that is new to us, or even a pseudoword. The second way to get from print to meaning is a more direct, orthographic-based approach that results from repeated associations of letter strings and meanings. For example, look at the following word but don't decode it:

horseradish

Try as you might, it is just about impossible to look at the string of letters in the printed word 'horeseradish' and not to become aware of either the pronunciation "horseradish" or aspects of its meaning such as its pungency when added to food.

The traditional model stumbled over unfriendly data from carefully constructed experiments. It has been replaced by two seemingly different models that nevertheless are almost indistinguishable by the predictions they make. The first is a modification of the traditional model that improves its performance by allowing associations between graphemes and phonemes to include units larger than individual graphemes (e.g., rhymes such as the 'at' part of cat, rat, and hat), and incorporating more sophisticated rules for combining the products of phonological and visual processing. The second replacement model is a neural net based model in which both familiar words and pseudowords are decoded by associations between print and pronunciations learned from a corpus of real words (see e.g., Coltheart, Curtis, Atkins, & Haller, 1993; Coltheart, Rastle, Perry, Langdon, & Ziegler, 2001; Harm & Seidenberg, 2004; Plaut, McClelland, Seidenberg, & Patterson, 1996; Seidenberg & McClelland, 1989).

Although academic careers have been made debating seemingly subtle aspects of models that can account for reader's performance when given words and pseudowords, the basic empirical facts remain that (a) both phonological and orthographic processing or information can be useful in single-word reading, and (b) the balance of phonological and orthographic processing or knowledge required is different when we are asked to pronounce the pseudoword 'iplomaynuth' compared to the exception word "yacht."

Categories of Dyslexia

The contrast between phonological and orthographic processing or knowledge parallels the most thoroughly investigated potential categorization of individuals with developmental dyslexia into subtypes. The subtypes correspond to primary deficits in either phonological or orthographic processing. Investigation of these possible subtypes of developmental dyslexia grew out of related work in acquired dyslexia, in which formerly adequate readers acquired deficiencies after experiencing brain insult or illness.

Research on acquired dyslexia has provided examples of individuals with distinct deficits in either orthographic or phonological processing (Baddeley, Ellis, Miles, & Lewis, 1982; Bryant & Impey, 1986; Coltheart, 1983). In the acquired dyslexia literature, individuals who are unable to read pseudowords but are unimpaired in regular and exception word reading are described as phonological dyslexics; their impairment resides in phonological processing, causing them to rely on orthographic information to identify words and leaving them unable to phonologically decode words whose print forms are unfamiliar (i.e., pseudowords). Surface dyslexics, on the other hand, have a primary deficit in orthographic processing and are characterized by strong phonological decoding skills but poor exception word reading. It should be noted that the extreme examples of either phonological or surface dyslexia that have been featured prominently in the literature on acquired dyslexia are the rare exception rather than the rule. Most individuals with acquired dyslexia are properly classified as "mixed" as they exhibit some deficits in both phonological and orthographic processing.

The existence of at least some cases of individuals with acquired dyslexia whose deficits were primarily phonological or primarily orthographic motivated an exploration of whether phonological and surface dyslexia might also represent subtypes of developmental dyslexia (Baddeley et al., 1982; Bryant & Impey, 1986; Castles & Coltheart, 1993; Coltheart, 1987; Snowling, 1983). As in the literature on subtypes within acquired dyslexia, subtyping studies in developmental dyslexia categorize individuals on the basis of relative differences in performance on pseudoword and exception word reading tasks. Pseudowords should place heavy demands on phonological processing, whereas exception words (e.g., yacht, weight) should stress orthographic processing. However, the case of developmental dyslexia may differ from that of acquired dyslexia for several reasons. Difficulty in developing phonological or orthographic skill may be a quite different phenomenon from becoming selectively impaired in either skill subsequent to its acquisition (Castles & Coltheart, 1993). Furthermore, correlational studies indicate that for most individuals, including individuals with developmental dyslexia, performance on single-word reading tasks with pseudowords as stimuli is highly related to performance for reading exception words (e.g., Booth, Perfetti, & MacWhinney, 1999; Ehri, 1997, 1998; Manis, Custodio, & Szeszulski, 1993; Share, 1995, 1999).

Studies of phonological and surface categories of developmental dyslexia have used two means of classifying individuals: "hard" versus "soft" classifications (Stanovich, Siegel, & Gottardo, 1997). The hard subtype implies normal processing ability in one domain, either phonological or orthographic as measured by pseudoword or exception word reading tasks, respectively, but subnormal ability in the other domain. Identification of individuals with dyslexia meeting subtype criteria under this classification scheme, then, requires comparisons of pseudoword and exception word reading to a control group of skilled readers; an individual who meets the hard phonological subtype of dyslexia would demonstrate levels of exception word reading equivalent to that of skilled readers but significantly poorer pseudoword reading ability, whereas an individual who meets the hard surface subtype of dyslexia would show normal levels of pseudoword reading and significantly impaired exception word reading.

The soft subtype implies a relative discrepancy in phonological and orthographic abilities; it does not necessarily require development of either skill to reach the levels attained by skilled readers. The methodology required for subtyping individuals under this classification scheme is more involved than for identifying hard subtypes. First, typical relations between pseudoword and exception word reading are established by regressing performance on pseudoword reading on exception word reading, and vice versa. Then, individuals with developmental dyslexia whose pseudoword performance is poorer than would be predicted based on their exception word performance would be considered to meet criteria for a soft phonological subtype; individuals whose exception word performance is poorer than would be predicted based on their pseudoword performance would be considered to meet criteria for a soft surface subtype. Although various researchers have employed different means of computing these comparisons (e.g., regression analyses, z score cutoffs based on the population of skilled readers), all phonological versus surface subtyping studies utilize these same essential comparisons.

Evidence to support the existence of subtypes within developmental dyslexia has been sought in a number of samples of poor readers. For example, Castles and Coltheart (1993) recruited a sample of 56 males of average intelligence who were identified as dyslexic based on composite reading scores or word identification scores which were at least 1.5 years below their chronological ages (ranging from 8:6 to 14:11). This group was compared to a sample of 56 males of a similar age range (7:6 to 14:0) whose composite reading scores fell within six months of their chronological ages. The comparison of the two groups' pseudoword and exception word reading showed that 15% of dyslexic individuals met the hard classification criteria for the phonological subtype and 19% met the hard criteria for the surface subtype. Using the soft classification criteria, 54.7% and 30.2% of the sample met the requirements for phonological and surface subtypes, respectively, and 5.7% of the sample showed a dual deficit, with impairments in both phonological and orthographic processing. As 75% of the dyslexic group scored below the 90% confidence interval on the measure of exception word reading as compared to their peers of normal reading ability, Castles and Coltheart (1993) also investigated whether the dyslexic individuals' impairment in exception word reading was due to a general lack of familiarity with these words. However, the disabled readers were not impaired in their aural comprehension of the exception words. Castles and Coltheart (1993) thus concluded that their phonological and surface subtypes of developmental dyslexia were valid subtypes.

The Castles and Coltheart (1993) study has been criticized because of its reliance on a chronological-age rather than reading-age matched control group (Manis, Seidenberg, Doi, McBride-Chang, & Peterson, 1996; Stanovich, Siegel, & Gottardo, 1997; Stanovich, Siegel, Gottardo, Chiappe, & Sidhu, 1997). Because relative competence in single-word reading of pseudowords versus exception words may vary with absolute level of reading skill, a reading-age matched control group becomes important (Stanovich, 1988; Stanovich, Nathan, & Zolman, 1988).

Given the wide range in both chronological age and reading abilities within Castles and Coltheart's (1993) sample, Stanovich and colleagues (Stanovich, Siegel, Gottardo et al., 1997) were able to reanalyze the original Castles and Coltheart (1993) data using a reading-age matched control group of normal readers to establish the empirical relations between phonological and orthographic abilities. Upon reanalysis, 37.5% of the sample of poor readers met the soft phonological subtype criteria, while only two (5.0%) met the soft surface subtype criteria. Stanovich, Siegel, Gottardo, et al. (1997) concluded that while the phonological subtype represents a deviant pattern of processing consistent with conceptualizations of dyslexia, the surface subtype shows a processing pattern similar to that seen in younger normal readers, suggesting a developmental lag in these reading disabled individuals' acquisition of orthographic skill.

Several other studies have reached a similar conclusion. Manis, Seidenberg, Doi, McBride-Chang, and Peterson (1996) looked at hard and soft subtypes within a developmental dyslexic group (n = 51) as defined by a chronological-age matched (n = 51) comparison and validated the resultant subtypes based on comparisons to reading-age matched controls (n = 27). Individuals within the dyslexic group had chronological ages in the range of 9 to 15 years, IQs of at least 85, and scores at or below the 30th percentile on a measure of word identification. Comparison of these disabled readers with their chronologically age matched peers resulted in 9.8% of the sample meeting the hard classification criteria for each subtype. Using the soft classification scheme, 33.3% of the dyslexic group was categorized as the phonological subtype, 29.4% as the surface subtype, and 9.8% met the criteria for inclusion in both subtypes. When compared to the younger, reading-age matched group, dyslexic individuals meeting the phonological subtype criteria displayed significantly poorer phonological processing (phoneme segmentation) but better orthographic processing (orthographic choice) skill on validation measures. The surface subtype, on the other hand, did not differ significantly from the reading matched controls on either task. Furthermore, when analyses similar to those used to identify the subtypes within the dyslexic group were conducted to compare the pseudoword and exception word reading abilities of younger normal readers to those of the older normal readers, a pattern similar to that of the surface subtype's emerged: The younger normal readers' exception word reading tended to be poorer than would be predicted given their pseudoword reading skill. Together, the comparisons of the dyslexic subtypes with the reading level matched group suggest a model of deviance for the phonological subtype but developmental lag for the surface subtype.

Further findings by Stanovich and colleagues (Stanovich & Siegel, 1994; Stanovich, Siegel, Gottardo et al., 1997) also support the notion of deviance for the phonological subtype but delay for the surface subtype. They performed subtype analyses using the soft criteria with a sample of dyslexic readers (n = 67), normal readers matched on chronological age (n = 146), and younger normal readers matched on reading age (n = 87). The dyslexic group had reading scores below the 25th percentile and could range in chronological age from 7 to 16 years. Of this group, 23.3% met the phonological subtype criteria and 19.1% met the surface subtype criteria when compared to chronological age matched peers. Using the reading-age matched controls, 14.9% of the dyslexic group were classified as members in the phonological subtype but none met the criteria for the surface subtype.

Stanovich, Siegel, and Gottardo (1997) extended this line of research on dyslexic subtypes to a younger sample of children with dyslexia (n = 68 third grade students with reading scores below the 25th percentile) using the soft classification scheme and both chronological-age matched (n = 44) and reading-age matched (n = 23) comparisons. Using the chronological age matched controls, they found that 25.0%, 22.1%, and 27.9% of the dyslexic sample could be classified as members of the phonological subtype, surface subtype, or both subtypes, respectively. Once reading ability was controlled through comparison to the younger normal reader group, 25.0% of the dyslexic group was identified in the phonological subtype and only one disabled reader (less than 1.5% of the dyslexic sample) met the surface subtype criteria. Consistent with the notion of deviance for the phonological subtype, validation tasks showed that members in this group were significantly poorer than the reading-age matched controls on measures of pseudoword reading, phonological awareness, syntactic processing, and working memory, but that they outperformed the younger normal readers on measures of orthographic processing. In contrast, members of the surface subtype did not differ from the reading-age matched group on these measures. Furthermore, although members of the phonological subtype could be reliably identified when the actual classification measures were changed, members of the surface subtype were not, providing additional support for the pattern of developmental lag in the surface subtype.

Given the distinction between the phonological subtype and those dyslexic individuals who are best classified as exhibiting a developmental lag in reading, Manis and colleagues (Manis et al., 1999) chose to investigate these groups in a two-year longitudinal study of dyslexic subtypes. Out of their sample of 72 third grade students with dyslexia, as defined by scores of word identification at or below the 26th percentile, two subtypes were created: one group (44.4% of the total dyslexic sample, n = 32) who showed a deficit in phonological processing as compared to a reading-age matched control group (n = 33) and one developmental delay group (55.6% of the total dyslexic sample, n = 40) who showed no evidence of deviance in phonological processing (within the developmental delay group, only 12.5% met criteria for the surface subtype). Validation tasks supported the developmental lag conceptualization of impairments in orthographic processing: Although such tasks were not used when initially defining the subtypes, neither of the subtypes differed from the younger normal readers on orthographic processing measures (exception word reading and orthographic choice) in the first year of the study. Manis et al. (1999), like Stanovich, Siegel, and Gottardo (1997), analyzed the stability and reliability of the subtypes and found that although the phonological subtype and developmental delay classifications were reliable across a year's time (with 80.8% and 84.4%, respectively, reclassified in that same subtype in year two of the study), the surface subtype was an unstable means of classification (only 22.2% were reclassified in the surface subtype during year two). Thus, only deviance in phonological processing ability may be an important distinction to be made in dyslexia, as opposed to differences in orthographic processing skill.

The behavioral genetic study by Castles, Datta, Gayan, and Olson (1999) provides another means of examining the phonological versus surface subtypes in developmental dyslexia. Castles et al. (1999) studied 592 twin pairs of ages 8 to 18 in which at least one member of the pair had dyslexia (defined as scoring at least one standard deviation below what would be expected given the participant's chronological age on a composite measure of word reading). Subtypes were established via soft classification criteria and data from an unselected group of twins in the same age range. The subtypes were validated using a number of measures, with members of the phonological subtype performing more poorly than those in the surface subtype on phonological awareness and decoding tasks, while members of the surface subtype performed more poorly on a measure of orthographic processing (orthographic choice). The differences in the heritability estimates for the subtypes (H^2_g = .67 and C^2_g = .27 for the phonological subtype and H^2_g = .31 and C^2_g = .63 for the surface subtype) demonstrate the distinctiveness of the two subtypes, where the phonological subtype was accounted for primarily by genetic factors (i.e, H^2_g) while the surface subtype was accounted for primarily by environmental factors (i.e, C^2_g). Finally, the strong genetic component in the phonological subtype supports the view that this subtype may be due to an inherent and deviant impairment in phonological processing ability.

In summary, although both phonological and surface subtypes may be discriminated within the population of poor readers, only the phonological subtype is congruent with the characterization of dyslexia as an unexpected, specific impairment in word reading processes. Once reading level is controlled, the surface subtype virtually disappears, consistent with the notion that orthographic deficits are best conceptualized as the results of developmental lag.

CONCLUSIONS

The consensus view is that most individuals with dyslexia demonstrate a primary impairment that affects their single-word reading. Secondary impairments in reading comprehension also are common. These can reflect immediate or long-term sequelae of impaired single-word reading. Impaired single-word reading has an immediate effect on reading comprehension when errors are made in decoding or when decoding is so laborious that comprehension suffers. Impaired single-word reading can have longer-term effects on reading comprehension because decoding problems can limit acquisition of both vocabulary and content knowledge, both of which can impact later comprehension.

The evidence clearly supports a phonological subtype of dyslexia, characterized by poor phonological processing and impaired decoding of nonwords. The evidence in support of a surface subtype of dyslexia is mixed. In particular, surface dyslexia cannot be readily distinguished from simply a slower overall rate in reading development. Although these conclusions apply to the vast majority of individuals with dyslexia, rare peculiarities in both biological and experiential aspects of development make it possible for a given individual to deviate from these common patterns of performance.

Recognition of dyslexia as primarily a deficit in single word reading due to phonological processing deficits has implications for identification and intervention. Screening aimed at identifying very young children at risk for dyslexia should target rudimentary phonological awareness and letter knowledge. For older children, impaired decoding of nonwords is perhaps the most commonly observed limitation. Effective interventions target children's acquisition of phonological processing abilities and correspondences between letters and sounds, but also address the need for fluent recognition of common words and comprehension-related skills and knowledge including vocabulary development.

REFERENCES

Aaron, P. G. (1989). Qualitative and quantitative differences among dyslexic, normal, and nondyslexic poor readers. *Reading & Writing, 1*, 291–308.

Adams, M. J. (1990). *Beginning to read: Thinking and learning about print.* Cambridge, MA: MIT Press.

Adams, M. J., & Bruck, M. (1993). Word recognition: The interface of educational policies and scientific research. *Reading & Writing, 5*, 113–139.

Baddeley, A. D., Ellis, N. C., Miles, T. R., & Lewis, V. J. (1982). Developmental and acquired dyslexia: A comparison. *Cognition, 11*, 185–199.

Ball, E. W., & Blachman, B. A. (1991). Does phoneme awareness training in kindergarten make a difference in early word recognition and developmental spelling? *Reading Research Quarterly, 26*, 49–66.

Booth, J. R., Perfetti, C. A., & MacWhinney, B. (1999). Quick, automatic, and general activation of orthographic and phonological representations in young readers. *Developmental Psychology, 35*, 3–19.

Bradley, L., & Bryant, P. E. (1983). Categorizing sounds and learning to read: A causal connection. *Nature, 301*, 419–421.

Brady, S., Fowler, A., Stone, B., & Winbury, N. (1994). Training phonological awareness: A study with inner-city kindergarten children. *Annals of Dyslexia, 44*, 26–59.

Bruck, M. (1988). The word recognition and spelling of dyslexic children. *Reading Research Quarterly, 23*, 51–69.

Bruck, M. (1990). Word-recognition skills of adults with childhood diagnoses of dyslexia. *Developmental Psychology, 26*, 439–454.

Bruck, M. (1992). Persistence of dyslexics' phonological awareness deficits. *Developmental Psychology, 28*, 874–886.

Bruck, M. (1993). Word recognition and component phonological processing skills of adults with childhood diagnosis of dyslexia. *Developmental Review. 13*, 258–268.

Bryant, P. E., & Impey, L. (1986). The similarities between normal readers and developmental and acquired dyslexics. *Cognition. 24*, 121–137.

Bus, A. G., & van Ijzendoorn, M. H. (1999). Phonological awareness and early reading: A meta-analysis of experimental training studies. *Journal of Educational Psychology. 91*, 403–414.

Byrne, B., & Fielding-Barnsley, R. (1989). Phonemic awareness and letter knowledge in the child's acquisition of the alphabetic principle. *Journal of Educational Psychology, 81*, 313–321.

Byrne, B., & Fielding-Barnsley, R. (1991). Evaluation of a program to teach phonemic awareness to young children. *Journal of Educational Psychology, 83*, 451–455.

Byrne, B., & Fielding-Barnsley, R. (1993). Evaluation of a program to teach phonemic awareness to young children: A 1-year follow-up. *Journal of Educational Psychology, 85*(1), 104–111.

Byrne, B., & Fielding-Barnsley, R. (1995). Evaluation of a program to teach phonemic awareness to young children: A 2- and 3-year follow-up and a new preschool trial. *Journal of Educational Psychology, 87*, 488–503.

Byrne, B., Fielding-Barnsley, R., & Ashley, L. (2000). Effects of preschool phoneme identity training after six years: Outcome level distinguished from rate of response. *Journal of Educational Psychology, 92*, 659–667.

Case, L. P., Speece, D. L., & Molloy, D. E. (2003). The validity of a response-to-instruction paradigm to identify reading disabilities: A longitudinal analysis of individual difference and contextual factors. *School Psychology Review, 32*, 557–582.

Castles, A., & Coltheart, M. (1993). Varieties of developmental dyslexia. *Cognition, 47*, 149–180.

Castles, A., Datta, H., Gayan, J., & Olson, R. K. (1999). Varieties of developmental reading disorder: Genetic and environmental influences. *Journal of Experimental Child Psychology, 72*, 73–94.

Chall, J. S. (1967/1983). *Learning to read: The great debate.* New York: McGraw-Hill.

Coltheart, M. (1983). Surface dyslexia. *Quarterly Journal of Experimental Psychology: Human Experimental Psychology, 35,* 469–495.

Coltheart, M. (1987). Varieties of developmental dyslexia: A comment on Bryant and Impey. *Cognition, 27,* 97–101.

Coltheart, M., Curtis, B., Atkins, P., & Haller, M. (1993). Models of reading aloud: Dual-route and parallel-distributed-processing approaches. *Psychological Review, 100,* 589–608.

Coltheart, M., Rastle, K., Perry, C., Langdon, R., & Ziegler, J. (2001). DRC: A dual route cascaded model of visual word recognition and reading aloud. *Psychological Review, 108,* 204–256.

Crowder, R. G., & Wagner, R. K. (1992). The psychology of reading: An introduction (2nd ed.). *London, Oxford University Press, 266.*

Cunningham, A. E., Perry, K. E., & Stanovich, K. E. (2001). Converging evidence for the concept of orthographic processing. *Reading & Writing, 14,* 549–568.

Ehri, L. C. (1997). Sight word learning in normal readers and dyslexics. In B. A. Blachman (Ed.), *Foundations of reading acquisition and dyslexia: Implications for early intervention* (pp. 163–189). Mahwah, NJ: Lawrence Erlbaum Associates.

Ehri, L. C. (1998). Grapheme-phoneme knowledge is essential to learning to read words in English. In J. L. Metsala & L. C. Ehri (Eds.), *Word recognition in beginning literacy* (pp. 3–40). Mahwah, NJ,: Lawrence Erlbaum Associates.

Ehri, L. C., Nunes, S. R., Stahl, S. A., & Willows, D. M. (2001). Systematic phonics instruction helps students learn to read: Evidence from the National Reading Panel's meta-analysis. *Review of Educational Research, 71,* 393–447.

Ehri, L. C., Nunes, S. R., Willows, D. M., Schuster, B. V., Yaghoub-Zadeh, Z., & Shanahan, T. (2001). Phonemic awareness instruction helps children learn to read: Evidence from the National Reading Panel's meta-analysis. *Reading Research Quarterly, 36,* 250–287.

Fletcher, J. M., Coulter, W. A., Reschly, D. J., & Vaugh, S. (2004). Alternative approaches to the definition and identification of learning disabilities: Some questions and answers. *Annals of Dyslexia, 54,* 304–331.

Fletcher, J. M., Francis, D. J., Rourke, B. P., Shaywitz, S. E., & Shaywitz, B. A. (1992). The validity of discrepancy-based definitions of reading disabilities. *Journal of Learning Disabilities, 25,* 573–331.

Fletcher, J. M., Morris, R. D., & Lyon, G. R. (2003). Classification and definition of learning disabilities: An integrative perspective. In H. L. Swanson & K. R. Harris (Eds.), *Handbook of learning disabilities* (pp. 30–56). New York: Guilford Press.

Foorman, B. R., Chen, D.-T., Carlson, C., Moats, L., Francis, D. J., & Fletcher, J. M. (2003). The necessity of the alphabetic principle to phonemic awareness instruction. *Reading and Writing, 16,* 289–324.

Foorman, B. R., Francis, D. J., Fletcher, J. M., Schatschneider, C., & Mehta, P. (1998). The role of instruction in learning to read: Preventing reading failure in at-risk children. *Journal of Educational Psychology, 90,* 37–55.

Foorman, B. R., Francis, D. J., Novy, D. M., & Liberman, D. (1991). How letter-sound instruction mediates progress in first-grade reading and spelling. *Journal of Educational Psychology, 83,* 456–469.

Fox, E. (1994). Grapheme-phoneme correspondence in dyslexic and matched control readers. *British Journal of Psychology, 85,* 41–53.

Francis, D. J., Shaywitz, S. E., Stuebing, K. K., Shaywitz, B. A., & Fletcher, J. M. (1996). Developmental lag versus deficit models of reading disability: A longitudinal, individual growth curves analysis. *Journal of Educational Psychology, 88,* 3–17.

Fuchs, D., Deshler, D. D., & Reschly, D. J. (2004). National Research Center on Learning Disabilities: Multimethod studies of identification and classification issues. *Learning Disability Quarterly, 27,* 189–195.

Fuchs, D., Fuchs, L. S., McMaster, K. N., & Al Otaiba, S. (2003). Identifying children at risk for reading failure: Curriculum-based measurement and the dual-discrepancy approach. In H. L. Swanson & K. R. Harris (Eds.), *Handbook of learning disabilities* (pp. 431–449). New York, NY: Guilford Press.

Fuchs, D., Mock, D., Morgan, P. L., & Young, C. L. (2003). Responsiveness-to-intervention: Definitions, evidence, and implications for the learning disabilities construct. *Learning Disabilities Research & Practice, 18*, 157–171.

Fuchs, L. S., & Fuchs, D. (1998). Treatment validity: A unifying concept for reconceptualizing the identification of learning disabilities. *Learning Disabilities Research & Practice, 13*, 204–219.

Gough, P. B., & Tunmer, W. E. (1986). Decoding, reading, and reading disability. *Remedial and Special Education, 7*, 6–10.

Hallahan, D. P., & Mock, D. R. (2003). A brief history of the field of learning disabilities. In H. L. Swanson & K. R. Harris (Eds.), *Handbook of learning disabilities* (pp. 16–29). New York: Guilford Press.

Harm, M. W., & Seidenberg, M. S. (2004). Computing the meanings of words in reading: Cooperative division of labor between visual and phonological processes. *Psychological Review, 111*, 662–720.

Hatcher, P. J., Hulme, C., & Ellis, A. W. (1994). Ameliorating early reading failure by integrating the teaching of reading and phonological skills: The phonological linkage hypothesis. *Child Development. 65*, 41–57.

Individuals with Disabilities in Education Act, 20 U.S.C. §1400 *et seq.* (1999, 2005).

Joanisse, M. F., Manis, F. R., Keating, P., & Seidenberg, M. S. (2000). Language deficits in dyslexic children: Speech perception, phonology, and morphology. *Journal of Experimental Child Psychology, 77*, 30–60.

Juel, C. (1988). Learning to read and write: A longitudinal study of 54 children from first through fourth grades. *Journal of Educational Psychology, 80*, 437–447.

Lovett, M. W., Steinbach, K. A., & Frijters, J. C. (2000). Remediating the core deficits of developmental reading disability: A double-deficit perspective. *Journal of Learning Disabilities. 33*, 334–358.

Lyon, G. R., Fletcher, J. M., Shaywitz, S. E., Shaywitz, B. A., Torgesen, J. K., Wood, F. B., et al. (2001). Rethinking learning disabilities. In C. E. Finn, A. J. Rotherham & C. R. Hokanson, Jr. (Eds.), *Rethinking special education for a new century* (pp. 259–287). Washington, D. C.: Thomas B. Fordham Foundation and Progressive Policy Institute.

Lyon, G. R., Shaywitz, S. E., & Shaywitz, B. A. (2003). A definition of dyslexia. *Annals of Dyslexia, 53*, 1–14.

Manis, F. R., Custodio, R., & Szeszulski, P. A. (1993). Development of phonological and orthographic skill: A 2-year longitudinal study of dyslexic children. *Journal of Experimental Child Psychology, 56*, 64–86.

Manis, F. R., Seidenberg, M. S., Doi, L. M., McBride-Chang, C., & Peterson, A. (1996). On the bases of two subtypes of development dyslexia. *Cognition, 58*, 157–195.

Manis, F. R., Seidenberg, M. S., Stallings, L., Joanisse, M., Bailey, C., Freedman, L., et al. (1999). Development of dyslexic subgroups: A one-year follow up. *Annals of Dyslexia, 49*, 105–134.

National Reading Panel. (2000). *Report of the National Reading Panel: Teaching children to read* (No. 00–4769). Washington, D. C.: National Institute of Child Health and Human Development.

National Research Council. (1998). *Preventing reading difficulties in young children.* Washington, D. C.: National Academy Press.

No Child Left Behind Act, 20 U.S.C. § 6301 *et seq.* (2005).

Olson, R., Wise, B., Conners, F., Rack, J., & et al. (1989). Specific deficits in component reading and language skills: Genetic and environmental influences. *Journal of Learning Disabilities, 22*, 339–348.

Perfetti, C. A. (1985). *Reading ability.* New York: Oxford University Press.

Perfetti, C. A. (1986). Continuities in reading acquisition, reading skill, and reading disability. *Remedial & Special Education, 7,* 11–21.

Plaut, D. C., McClelland, J. L., Seidenberg, M. S., & Patterson, K. (1996). Understanding normal and impaired word reading: Computational principles in quasi-regular domains. *Psychological Review, 103,* 56–115.

Rack, J. P., Snowling, M. J., & Olson, R. K. (1992). The nonword reading deficit in developmental dyslexia: A review. *Reading Research Quarterly, 27,* 28–53.

Rashotte, C. A., MacPhee, K., & Torgesen, J. K. (2001). The effectiveness of a group reading instruction program with poor readers in multiple grades. *Learning Disability Quarterly. 24,* 119–134.

Rayner, K. (1998). Eye movements in reading and information processing: 20 years of research. *Psychological Bulletin, 124,* 372–422.

Scarborough, H. S. (1984). Continuity between childhood dyslexia and adult reading. *British Journal of Psychology, 75,* 329–348.

Schneider, W., Ennemoser, M., Roth, E., & Kuespert, P. (1999). Kindergarten prevention of dyslexia: Does training in phonological awareness work for everybody? *Journal of Learning Disabilities, 32,* 429–436.

Schneider, W., Roth, E., & Ennemoser, M. (2000). Training phonological skills and letter knowledge in children at risk for dyslexia: A comparison of three kindergarten intervention programs. *Journal of Educational Psychology, 92,* 284–295.

Seidenberg, M. S., & McClelland, J. L. (1989). A distributed, developmental model of word recognition and naming. *Psychological Review, 96,* 523–568.

Share, D. L. (1995). Phonological recoding and self-teaching: Sine qua non of reading acquisition. *Cognition, 55,* 151–218.

Share, D. L. (1999). Phonological recoding and orthographic learning: A direct test of the self-teaching hypothesis. *Journal of Experimental Child Psychology, 72,* 95–129.

Shaywitz, B. A., Fletcher, J. M., Holahan, J. M., & Shaywitz, S. E. (1992). Discrepancy compared to low achievement definitions of reading disability: Results from the Connecticut longitudinal study. *Journal of Learning Disabilities, 25,* 639–648.

Shaywitz, S. E., & Shaywitz, B. A. (2003). Neurobiological indices of dyslexia. In H. L. Swanson & K. R. Harris (Eds.), *Handbook of learning disabilities* (pp. 514–531). New York: Guilford Press.

Siegel, L. S. (2003). Basic cognitive processes and reading disabilities. In H. L. Swanson & K. R. Harris (Eds.), *Handbook of learning disabilities* (pp. 158–181). New York: Guilford Press.

Siegel, L. S., & Faux, D. (1989). Acquisition of certain grapheme-phoneme correspondences in normally achieving and disabled readers. *Reading & Writing, 1,* 37–52.

Snowling, M. J. (1983). The comparison of acquired and developmental disorders of reading: A discussion. *Cognition, 14,* 105–118.

Spear-Swerling, L., and Sternberg, R. (1996). *Off track: When poor readers become learning disabled,* Boulder, Colorado: Westview Press.

Stanovich, K. E. (1982). Individual differences in the cognitive processes of reading: I. Word decoding. *Journal of Learning Disabilities, 15,* 485–493.

Stanovich, K. E. (1988). Explaining the differences between the dyslexic and the garden-variety poor reader: The phonological-core variable-difference model. *Journal of Learning Disabilities, 21,* 590–604, 612.

Stanovich, K. E. (1994). Does dyslexia exist? *Journal of Child Psychology & Psychiatry & Allied Disciplines, 35,* 579–595.

Stanovich, K. E., Nathan, R. G., & Zolman, J. E. (1988). The developmental lag hypothesis in reading: Longitudinal and matched reading-level comparisons. *Child Development, 59,* 71–86.

Stanovich, K. E., & Siegel, L. S. (1994). Phenotypic performance profile of children with reading disabilities: A regression-based test of the phonological-core variable-difference model. *Journal of Educational Psychology, 86,* 24–53.

Stanovich, K. E., Siegel, L. S., & Gottardo, A. (1997). Converging evidence for phonological and surface subtypes of reading disability. *Journal of Educational Psychology, 89,* 114–127.

Stanovich, K. E., Siegel, L. S., Gottardo, A., Chiappe, P., & Sidhu, R. (1997). Subtypes of developmental dyslexia: Differences in phonological and orthographic coding. In B. A. Blachman (Ed.), *Foundations of reading acquisition and dyslexia: Implications for early intervention* (pp. 115–141). Mahwah, NJ: Lawrence Erlbaum Associates.

Torgesen, J. K., Alexander, A. W., Wagner, R. K., Rashotte, C. A., Voeller, K. K. S., & Conway, T. (2001). Intensive remedial instruction for children with severe reading disabilities: Immediate and long-term outcomes from two instructional approaches. *Journal of Learning Disabilities, 34,* 33–58.

Torgesen, J. K., Wagner, R. K., Rashotte, C. A., Rose, E., Lindamood, P., Conway, T., et al. (1999). Preventing reading failure in young children with phonological processing disabilities: Group and individual responses to instruction. *Journal of Educational Psychology, 91,* 579–593.

Vellutino, F. R. (1979). *Dyslexia: Theory and research.* Cambridge, MA: MIT Press.

Vellutino, F. R., Scanlon, D. M., & Tanzman, M. S. (1998). The case for early intervention in diagnosing specific reading disability. *Journal of School Psychology. 36,* 367–397.

Wagner, R. K. (1988). Causal relations between the development of phonological processing abilities and the acquisition of reading skills: A meta-analysis. *Merrill Palmer Quarterly, 34,* 261–279.

Wagner, R. K. (2005). Reading impairment. In P. Strazny (Ed.), *Encyclopedia of Psycholinguistics.* New York: Routledge, Taylor, and Francis.

Wagner, R. K., & Muse, A. (2006). Phonological memory and reading disability. In T. Alloway & S. Gathercole (Eds.), *Working memory in neurodevelopmental conditions.* (pp. 41–59) East Sussex, England: Psychology Press.

Wagner, R. K., & Garon, T. (1999). Learning disabilities in perspective. In R. Sternberg & L. Spear-Swerling (Eds.), *Perspectives on learning disabilities.* Boulder, CO: Westview.

Wagner, R. K., & Torgesen, J. K. (1987). The nature of phonological processing and its causal role in the acquisition of reading skills. *Psychological Bulletin, 101,* 192–212.

Werker, J. F., Bryson, S. E., & Wassenberg, K. (1989). Toward understanding the problem in severely disabled readers: II. Consonant errors. *Applied Psycholinguistics, 10,* 13–30.

Wise, B. W., Ring, J., & Olson, R. K. (1999). Training phonological awareness with and without explicit attention to articulation. *Journal of Experimental Child Psychology., 72,* 271–304.

CHAPTER SIXTEEN

Fluency Training as an Alternative Intervention for Reading-Disabled and Poor Readers

James M. Royer and Rena Walles
University of Massachusetts, Amherst

The major contribution of the article to follow is the demonstration that fluency training in single word reading can be an effective intervention for some readers who have not responded well to more conventional intervention techniques. Understanding this contribution though will require the presentation of some background information on the origins of reading difficulty and on conventional intervention techniques and their effectiveness.

ORIGINS OF READING DIFFICULTY

It is generally assumed among reading researchers and professional educators that the large majority of students with reading difficulties have difficulties at the level of reading individual words (e.g., Seidenberg, 1992; Shaywitz, 2003, Snow, Burns & Griffin, 1998; Wang, 1996). Slow and/or inaccurate word reading uses valuable cognitive resources (e.g., working memory capacity) necessary for higher level reading activities such as activation of meaning and the comprehension of connected text. Word reading difficulty does not account for all reading problems, but it certainly is a characteristic shared by many readers who fall behind their peers in reading performance.

The prevailing view is that the central cause of word reading difficulties is a core phonological processing deficit. Poor phonological processing is thought to inhibit the accurate encoding of the constituent sounds of speech (phonemes), and this in turn has consequences for both the acquisition of speech and the subsequent development of reading ability. For instance, individuals who develop reading difficulties often exhibit delays in learning to speak, and they often display articulation difficulties when they do speak (Shaywitz, 2003). Shaywitz (2003) describes poor phonological processing as resulting in the storage of "fuzzy phonemes," which subsequently inhibit normal language development and the acquisition of reading skill. More formally, Harm and Seidenberg (1999) have presented a connectionist model that shows how a phonological processing deficit can negatively impact both speech acquisition and reading acquisition.

One lingering question regarding phonological processing deficits is where they come from. One answer is that they are in part constitutional in origin. There is a large body of research showing that reading difficulties have genetic components (e.g., Olson, 2004, Shaywitz, 2003) and FMRI research has shown that the brains of individuals with dyslexia process written information differently than the brains of unimpaired readers (e.g., Salmelin & Helenius, 2004). There is also, however, evidence that phonological processing difficulties can have environmental origins (e.g., Vellutino, Scanlon & Sipay, 1997). At this point it is not possible to sort out the unique contributions of environmental and biological factors in poor reading performance but it is apparent that both can play a role.

As an aside, a particularly striking example of phonological processing difficulties arising from environmental origins comes from the first author's research with adult neoliterates (adults who have little or no formal schooling) in Burkina Faso (Royer, Abadzi & Kinda, 2004). Royer et al.'s (2004) sample of over 100 adolescents and adults who had never been to school did not include a single individual who initially could identify whether two words rhymed, started with the same phoneme, or ended with the same phoneme when the tasks were presented in the participant's mother tongue. However, exactly the same tasks were readily accomplished when administered to 3rd grade Burkina Faso children who were native speakers of the same language as spoken by the adult neoliterates. The Royer et al (2004) study showed that training in phonological awareness and training in rapid word recognition (in the students' mother tongue) significantly improved end of course literacy performance.

CONVENTIONAL INTERVENTIONS FOR READING DIFFICULTIES

Two general approaches have dominated attempts to improve word reading performance. The first is to directly tackle the source of the difficulty: poor phonological processing. One commonly used indicator of phonological processing is phonological awareness which can be defined as the ability to attend explicitly to the phonological structure of spoken words. Individuals who have phonological awareness can readily identify words that rhyme, and that start and end with the same phoneme. They can also perform phoneme manipulation tasks such as indicating what the word "cat" would sound like if the c were removed.

Many studies have attempted to improve word reading performance by explicitly teaching phonological awareness skills. Brady, Fowler, Stone and Winbury (1994), for example, showed that phonological awareness skills could be readily taught to inner-city children who were at risk for developing reading difficulties and Lundberg and her colleagues (Lundberg, 1994; Lundberg Frost and Peterson, 1988) reported research indicating that children taught phonological awareness skills prior to receiving formal reading instruction were stronger word readers that untaught controls at the end of second grade. Moreover, Lundberg (1994) showed that the improvement in word reading skills was greatest in children whose initial phonological awareness skills were lowest. The positive impact of phonological awareness training on subsequent reading performance has been shown for studies conducted in Germany (Schneider, 1997), Norway (Lie, 1991), Australia (Byrne & Fielding-Barnsley, 1991, 1995), Burkina Faso (Royer et al, 2004) and the United States (e.g., Cunningham, 1990).

Another common approach to improving single word reading is the explicit teaching of decoding strategies. Typically, explicit decoding instruction (also commonly called phonics based instruction) involves the systematic teaching of letter-sound correspondences, and sounding out and blending strategies. Foorman, Francis, Fletcher, Schatschneider and Mehta (1998), for example, implemented an intervention they called embedded phonics with grade 1 and 2 students in a school district serving a high proportion of students who were at risk for reading difficulty. They showed that students exposed to embedded phonics were better word readers than their control counterparts receiving regular instruction, and that phonics instructed students made measurable gains in reading performance over the school year whereas control students showed an essentially flat reading performance trajectory.

A third approach, perhaps more common than the previous two, is to combine aspects of phonological awareness training and decoding instruction into the same intervention package. Henceforth, this kind of intervention will be referred to as conventional intervention. One example of such an approach (Vellutino and others, 1996) involved presenting kindergarten and grade 1 children with daily tutoring sessions that were individually tailored to the instructional needs of the child. There was, however, a common core of each instructional session that included exposure to phoneme awareness training, training in letter sound correspondences, instruction in using phonics based word attack strategies, and instruction in writing. Vellutino et al. (1996) showed that their intervention procedures had a positive impact on the reading performance of most, but not all, of the students who had been identified early in the study as being at risk for reading failure. The issue of not all of the readers benefiting from what should be a particularly potent blend of intervention procedures is the starting point for the intervention strategy described later in this chapter. However, before describing that strategy, several other examples of intervention attempts that did not work for everyone should be mentioned.

Torgesen, Wagner, Rashotte, Rose, Lindamood and Conway (1999) screened approximately 1400 kindergarten students with letter naming and phonological awareness tasks and selected the 180 lowest scorers who had an IQ of at least 75. All students received approximately 80 hours of specialized reading instruction over a 2rb ½ year period beginning in the second half of their kindergarten year. Students were divided between three intervention conditions. Two of the intervention conditions varied in the intensity of their phonics based approach, and a third was designed to provide support for regular classroom reading instruction. The intervention approach that provided the most phonemically explicit instruction produced the strongest growth in word reading performance; but interestingly, the groups did not differ in reading comprehension performance at the end of the study. Also of interest was the fact that even the most successful of the intervention approaches did not produce gains in all of the students. Using a criterion which said that students scoring one standard deviation or more below the mean in word reading performance were impaired, Torgesen et al. (1999) reported that 21% of the students in their best intervention condition remained impaired at the end of the study.

Olson, Wise, Johnson, and Ring (1997) also provide evidence that interventions targeted at students lacking in phonological processing skills may not be uniformly effective. They reviewed a number of studies and concluded that some students do demonstrate improved reading performance (particularly word reading performance), but may not show consistent benefits. This latter group of students, that is, those who do not show a positive response to phonological awareness and/or systematic decoding instruction, have been referred to as "treatment resistors" (e.g., Blachman, 1997).

A meta-analysis of intervention studies (Swanson, 1999) indicated that the most effective interventions for students with reading difficulties was one that combined direct instruction (typically phonics based) with strategy instruction designed to enhance reading comprehension performance. Swanson's research showed that the combined interventions produced better learning outcomes than did interventions that used either direct instruction or strategy instruction alone, or that used procedures not including either direct instruction or strategy instruction. However, Swanson's (1999) review did not consider the issue of treatment resistors so one cannot estimate the percentage of students who did not show gains as a consequence of exposure to combined interventions.

A WORKING HYPOTHESIS OF INTERVENTION EFFECTIVENESS

As described in the above mentioned research, intervention efforts have typically targeted young children who are slow in developing letter recognition abilities, who have poor phonological awareness abilities, and who display little understanding of letter-sound correspondences. Studies have shown that some of these children respond well to interventions that train phonological awareness and/or word decoding, and others do not. The working hypothesis adopted by the authors of this chapter for why conventional intervention effectiveness is problematic for some students was alluded to earlier. The speculation is that there are two kinds of readers in the mix of students who display properties that predict reading difficulty: students whose difficulties are largely biological in origin, and students whose difficulties are largely environmental in origin. The hypothesis is that students who have biological difficulties are likely to be resistant to conventional interventions, whereas students whose difficulties are environmental in origin are likely to respond positively to conventional interventions.

The way these two explanations play out is as follows. Students who have biological problems are those who have early difficulty in identifying and separating the phonemic properties of speech (Shaywitz's fuzzy phoneme students). This may produce difficulties in early speech acquisition and the development of phonological awareness, and it delays the discovery of the alphabetic principle which allows a child to attach speech sounds to orthographic characters. This, in turn, delays reading acquisition and makes it difficult for the child to utilize sounding out strategies to assist in the word recognition process.

Students whose problems are environmental in origin are likely to come from family circumstances where there is little exposure to print materials and where the child has little practice in activities such as rhyming exposure (as in nursery rhymes), letter identification, and practice in attaching sounds to letters. This lack of exposure can produce a child who behaviorally looks very much like the child whose difficulties are biological in origin. That is, the child has difficulty in acquiring letter names upon entering school, has difficulty in successfully completing phonological awareness tasks, and who has difficulty in acquiring and using the alphabetic principle.

Cisero and Royer (1995) reported two studies with kindergarten and grade 1 students that showed the possible impact of environmental factors in the development of phonological awareness. Their studies were conducted in two Western Massachusetts communities that differed in SES status and language status. The students in the higher SES communities were all native English speakers and the students in the lower SES community were mainstream English speakers and Spanish speaking students enrolled in a transitional bilingual education program (TBE). All students were administered phonological awareness tasks (detection of rhyme, initial phoneme, ending phoneme) in both English and Spanish. The overall performance of the three groups showed that the higher SES students performed best followed by the lower SES mainstream students, with the lower SES Spanish speaking student performing the lowest. One striking aspect of the results was that the higher SES English speaking students performed better on the Spanish phonological awareness tasks than did the lower SES Spanish speaking students. In fact, the general trend in the data was that if a student could do well on the phonological awareness tasks in one language, they could also perform the tasks in the second language, even if they did not speak the language.

After the study was completed the authors surveyed stores in the community surrounding the schools enrolling the lower SES Spanish speaking students. They could not find a single alphabet book or young child's story book in Spanish.

The idea that some readers have difficulties of biological origin whereas others have difficulties that can be traced to environmental experience can perhaps be traced to a paper by Clay (1987) who argued that the only way to identify readers who were truly disabled (i.e., dyslexic) was to examine their responsiveness to effective reading instruction. Readers who appeared to be at risk for reading failure but who did respond to effective instruction were judged by Clay to not be truly disabled, but rather, she suggested that they had difficulties that could be traced to lack of early experiences necessary for the development of reading ability. In contrast, readers who did not respond to effective instruction were those that were truly disabled. As we will see later in the chapter, Clay's idea that disabled readers should be identified by responsiveness to intervention is currently at the forefront of the debate about how best to identify reading disabled students (e.g., Fuchs, Mock, Morgan, & Young, 2003).

Vellutino and his colleagues (Vellutino et al., 1996; 1997) have also written about two types of readers among those at risk for reading failure. They described readers as having difficulties attributable to "experiential" deficits or to "cognitive" deficits. They described the cognitive deficits group as likely having problems that were constitutional in nature. Vellutino and his colleagues also suggested that students with experiential deficits were likely to benefit from intervention, whereas those having cognitive deficits were likely to be resistant to interventions. A similar theme about intervention effectiveness being problematic can be found in the article by Olson et al. (1997), though Olson does not make the dichotomy made by Clay and Vellutino.

ANECDOTAL EVIDENCE REGARDING INTERVENTION EFFECTIVENESS

The first author became acutely aware of the problematic nature of reading interventions when he founded a laboratory studying reading disabilities at the University of Massachusetts in the 1980s. Initially, the laboratory, called the Laboratory for the Assessment and Training of Academic Skills (LATAS), was devoted to developing a computer-based reading diagnostic system, but it soon also began conducting research on interventions for students who were experiencing reading difficulties. LATAS is located in a building adjacent to the Psychology building at the University of Massachusetts and is staffed by the first author and by graduate students in the Department of Psychology. LATAS charges a small fee for assessment and intervention services that is used for graduate student support. All of the students participating the LATAS research were referred by professional diagnosticians, school personnel, or by parent to parent recommendations.

The impetus for moving from a sole focus on diagnostics to a focus on both diagnostics and remediation came from parents and educators who urged the first author to try and develop intervention procedures for children who had not responded well to the educational experiences they received at school and/or from tutors. The intervention experiences they had received involved a mix of the type of interventions described earlier. Some of the LATAS children who were identified in kindergarten and the first grade as being at risk for reading difficultly received training in phonological analysis followed by various forms of phonics based instruction. Other children who were identified at the third grade or later received only phonics based interventions that were often accompanied by other instructional treatments designed to improve strategic reading practices and to encourage frequent reading.

The common characteristic exhibited by all of the LATAS children with a reading disability, regardless of grade, was that they were slow and halting when they read aloud. Many of them were very successful at word identification in the sense that they could accurately identify words. However, they were slow at doing so and often had to reread several times in order to comprehend what they were reading.

Over time the first author developed the idea that there was a sense in which the instruction these children had received turned out to be as harmful as it was helpful. Children who were in the 6th grade and older may have received as much as 4 years of fairly intensive phonics based instruction as prescribed by their IEPs (Individualized Education Plans). The schools frequently touted their improved accuracy of word recognition as evidence of reading progress. However the author viewed it in many cases as evidence of increased impairment. The problem was that the students had developed sounding out of words as the strategy of first choice when reading. They sounded out virtually every word they read. As will be seen in the data to follow, this resulted in long word reading times, often accompanied by impaired comprehension of sentence and paragraph length material. Some children did not exhibit impaired comprehension if given unlimited reading time. They were willing to "grind out" the meaning of text through a laborious process of continuous rereading. But there was no sense in which their successful comprehension was a product of skilled reading.

INTERVENTION EFFECTIVENESS AND THE IDENTIFICATION OF READING DISABILITY

For many years reading disabilities were defined using a discrepancy procedure that involved administering intelligence tests and reading tests. If the child had an average or above average IQ, but below average reading performance, then the student was identified as having a reading disability. Over time evidence accumulated that there were many problems with discrepancy procedures and a number of writers called for alternatives that were more viable (e.g., Aaron, 1997).

One currently popular alternative to discrepancy formulas as a way of identifying reading disability is to implement Clay's (1987) idea of using responsiveness to intervention (RTI) as a means of identifying truly disabled students. The idea is that students who are not truly disabled will be responsive to best practice interventions but students who are truly disabled will not (e.g., Fuchs et al, 2003).

RTI as a means of identifying reading disability does, however, present an interesting paradox. Students who have a reading disability are identified by their failure to respond to effective instruction. Effective instruction is most often defined as the conventional instruction (described in an earlier section) that has proven to be effective in many previous studies. If children are unresponsive to conventional instruction, what can we offer them that will be effective? The sections to follow describe one alternative and evidence regarding the effectiveness of that alternative.

FLUENCY TRAINING AS AN ALTERNATIVE TO PHONICS BASED INTERVENTIONS

If there is a population of students for whom phonological awareness training and the teaching of systematic phonics is not successful, what might be successful for them? The answer the first author decided to try with the clinical population at LATAS was to attempt to improve the accuracy and fluency of word recognition by continuously practicing rapid word recognition.

Fluency training is an old idea in the reading research community. Wolf and Katzir-Cohen (2001) trace the history of the idea that reading problems were associated with reading fluency and they provide a review of intervention studies designed to enhance reading fluency. Wolf and Katzir-Cohen (2001) reported the characteristics of the students that were provided fluency interventions, the length of the interventions, the nature of the interventions, the impact of the interventions on the intervention materials themselves, and the extent to which the interventions transferred to untrained passages.

Most of the studies involved a relatively short intervention of several sessions, with the longest intervention period being 21 sessions over 7 days. Most of the interventions consisted of a mix of intervention procedures with the most popular of the procedures involving repeated re-readings of the same passage. In addition, most of the interventions were targeted at multiple levels of reading (e.g., orthographic patterns, words, passages) with the exceptions generally involving a sole focus on improving the fluency of passage reading. Many of the interventions showed improved fluency on the intervention material with a lesser or no impact on transfer materials.

An article not reviewed by Wolfe and Katzir-Cohen (2001) involved a longer intervention period and a primary focus on improving the fluency of word recognition (Johnson & Layng, 1992). Johnson and Layng showed that word recognition could be greatly improved in both efficiency and accuracy by practicing the rapid identification of words, and they provided some evidence that improved word recognition fluency improved overall reading performance as reflected in standardized test scores. However, it was uncertain whether this procedure would work with the type of disabled readers referred to LATAS.

The fluency training that is currently in use as LATAS has evolved as a function of trial and error. Many of the early students referred to LATAS were adolescents who had been diagnosed with an attentional disorder. Initially, the LATAS intervention consisted of training in the rapid identification of nonwords (e.g., plok). This intervention was based on the idea that the fundamental problem LATAS readers were having involved the rapid analysis of letter-sound correspondences and one way to isolate and strengthen this ability was through practice sounding out nonwords. This intervention was soon abandoned because readers were resistant to repeatedly practicing the pronunciation of nonwords, and because we saw little evidence that improvements in nonword identification was transferring to naming of real words. This failure may be attributable in part to the general resistance many attentional disorder adolescents display to academic activities and should not be taken to mean that the procedure will not work. However, our subjective impression was that the students saw little utility to practicing the recognition of nonwords, and without their buy-in to an intervention activity, whatever we did was doomed to failure.

Another aborted procedure, predicated on the same idea that led to practicing the pronunciation of nonwords, was to have readers practice the rapid naming of words that were unfamiliar to them. For instance, students in grade 3 and 4 might practice words that were at the grade 8 or 9 level, and students in grade 8 or 10 might practice vocabulary words likely to be encountered on SAT exams. This procedure turned out to be even less successful—in terms of student resistance and lack of transfer—than the practicing of nonwords. In retrospect, having students with reading difficulties practice the rapid recognition of difficult to recognize words seems like a very silly idea.

Eventually LATAS settled on the procedures to be described in the section below.

METHOD

Participants

The research described in this section took place over a period of years beginning in the mid 1990s and continuing until 2004. Since LATAS served a referred population, students varied in age, grade, time of referral, and length of intervention period. In addition, LATAS students varied in terms of the academic difficulty they were experiencing. Some had relatively mild impairments and others had very severe impairments.

The way the LATAS referral process worked was as follows. A parent would contact LATAS indicating the source of the referral. At that point or shortly thereafter they generally talked to the first author to ascertain the suitability of the child for LATAS services. On occasion the student was deemed not appropriate for LATAS and was referred elsewhere. For instance, LATAS services were seen as not being appropriate for retarded students, for autistic students and for students with emotional disturbances. Upon establishing suitability for services, the parent made three appointments. On the first appointment the child completed listening and reading comprehension assessments and the first author completed an in-take interview that collected information about birth history, early language development, incidence of learning difficulties in the family, and educational history. The parent was also instructed to bring to the first meeting copies of psych-educational evaluations and IEPs. On the second meeting the child completed the CAAS computer tasks described below. On the third meeting the first author met with the child and parent and presented a report detailing the assessment findings and suggestions for intervention activities. If the child chose to continue with intervention services, we provided a set of intervention materials (to be described) that were to be practiced at least five times per week. Most children returned to LATAS on a weekly basis to be reassessed and to receive new practice materials if they had mastered the first set.

One group referred to LATAS that will be described in this chapter was not formally diagnosed as having a learning disability. This group consisted of readers (henceforth referred to as poor readers) who were referred to LATAS because a parent, a teacher, or a clinical diagnostician believed they were not reading as well as they should have. A few of the students in this poor reading group had been through a formal diagnostic process, conducted either by a school's child study team or by a licensed diagnostician outside of the school system, and were found not to have a disability that would qualify them for special education services.

The second group of students that will be described in the chapter are students who had formally been diagnosed as having a specific reading disability (reading disabled group). On most occasions the diagnosis of reading disability was made by an outside diagnostician, but in some of the cases the diagnosis was also made by a school-based evaluation team. All of the children in the reading disabled group were either receiving or had received special education services in their schools and all had IEPs. Since we will focus our analyses on students who were in the third grade or beyond, the majority of the students in the reading disabled group had been receiving school-based intervention services for multiple years. Sometimes these school-based interventions were supplemented by private tutoring.

The nature of the special education services provided to students of varying ages is interesting. Typically the pattern is that students up to grade 5 or 6 will receive services that are designed to improve their reading skill. These services involve some variant of conventional interventions. Beyond grade 5 most schools in the LATAS area begin to substitute accommodations for intervention services. Students are given extra time for assignments and tests, they are provided with readers or books on tape, and the nature of the assignments they are expected to complete is watered down relative to assignments completed by peers. Schools seemed to have made the tacit assumption that at grade 6 or so they should give up on trying to improve reading skills and they should concentrate instead on creating an environment where students can function without reading.

WISC III Scores and Wide Range Achievement Test Scores

We will report our data in two ways. First, we will report data for students who have a WISC III (Weschler Individual Scale for Children) score sometime accompanied by reading, math and spelling scores on the WRAT (Wide Range Achievement Test). The WISC III is an individually administered test that consists of six verbal and five performance subtests. Children receive three scores: Performance IQ, Verbal IQ, and Full Scale IQ. This standardized test is used to identify learning disabled individuals as well as gifted children. The WRAT is a short, individually administered achievement test that measures performance in the areas of reading, spelling, and math. It is often used to assess the presence of a learning disability, though it can also be used to compare student performance and to aid in the design of educational programs. Like the WISC III, scores are standardized with a mean of 100 and a standard deviation of 15.

The second way that we will report our data is to report available data for all students who were either poor or disabled readers. We report the data in multiple ways to give the reader a complete picture of intervention outcomes.

CAAS Assessments

When students first begin participating in the LATAS program they are administered a battery of assessments that is contained on the Cognitive Aptitude Assessment System (CAAS). This is a computer-based assessment system that has been developed at LATAS and that has been described in a number of publications (e.g., Cisero, Royer, Marchant & Jackson, 1997; Royer, 1997; Sinatra & Royer, 1993). This system measures the speed and accuracy of performance on both reading and math tasks. The CAAS system is based on the assumption that reading can be conceptualized as involving a number of component skills that develop in sequence. If one moves from very simple skills to complicated skills it should be possible to identify the skill that is deficient relative to peer performance. That skill could then be targeted for direct intervention. The rationale for conceptualizing reading as involving component skills that have diagnostic utility is presented in Royer and Sinatra (1994). The selection of the particular skills to be evaluated in the CAAS system was based on a review of the literature on developmental reading patterns reported in Greene and Royer (1994).

The CAAS system exists in an elementary version (grades 2–5), a middle school version (grades 6-9) and an adult version (high school and adult). The data described in this report all came from the elementary version of the system. This was true even though the oldest students participating in the study were 9th graders.

In the sections to follow grade level percentiles will be reported as well as data on accuracy and speed of performance on CAAS tasks. Grade level percentiles are calculated by combining speed and accuracy into a combined index (contact the senior author for how this is done). The percentile performances are based on data from at least 20-30 students at each grade level. This data was collected by administering the CAAS battery to every student at a particular grade except for students who had an IEP. Data collection for normative purposes was completed at a school in Western Massachusetts, at several schools in the Cleveland Ohio region, and at several schools in central Connecticut. The students contributing normative data were largely Caucasian students from middle to upper middle income groups, though the Cleveland sample did come from lower income and minority households. No claim is made about the grade level percentiles of LATAS students being representative of a larger group. Rather, the percentile data is presented to simply give a rough indication of how the students in the study performed relative to other students who are comparable in background and enrolled in the same grade as study students.

All of the tasks in the CAAS system, with the exception of the listening and reading comprehension tasks, are administered by having a stimulus appear on the computer screen and the examinee then makes a response into a microphone. When the stimulus appears on the screen a clock starts in the computer and when the examinee makes a response, the clock stops. An examiner then scores the response for accuracy.

CAAS assessments provide three scores. First, overall accuracy in terms of percent correct responses is reported. Second, average response time is reported. Average response time is actually a trimmed average that is computed by first computing average response time for all items, trimming times that are either impossibly fast (below .25 seconds) or 2 standard deviations above the mean, and then recalculating mean time and standard deviations using the trimmed times. The third score that is reported for each task is a grade level percentile that is based on an index that combines speed and accuracy into a single metric. A description of each of the CAAS tasks is listed below. Examples of each of the CAAS tasks, plus examples of assessment outcomes and assessment reports can be found at www.readingsuccesslab.com. A trial version of the CAAS system can also be downloaded from the site.

DESCRIPTION OF CAAS ASSESSMENT TASKS

Simple Perception; The examinee sees 3 stars (***) or three plusses (+++) on the screen and says star or plus into the microphone and accuracy of the response is scored by a human examiner. The participant responds to 20 items that are varied randomly during each assessment. This task provides a baseline measure of student's ability to respond to simple stimuli presented via computer.

Letter Recognition: Twenty randomly selected upper or lower case letters appear on the screen and the student says the name of the letter into a microphone whereupon the examiner scores it for accuracy.

Word Naming : Forty 3, 4, 5, or 6 letter words (10 at each length) appear on the screen and the student says the name of the word into a microphone and it is then scored for accuracy. The words have been specifically chosen so that the difficulty of the words ranges from grade 2 to grade 5.

Pseudoword Naming: Pseudowords were created by changing one or two letters (typically vowels) in a word in the word task. The task is administered just like the word task. This task, in conjunction with the word task has proven to be very valuable in identifying students with a specific reading disability.

Concept Activation: The student is given a number of category names (e.g., animals, modes of transportation, furniture names) and told that two words will appear on the screen. The student is to respond "yes" if the two words belong to the same category and "no" if they belong to different categories. Twenty randomly selected items are presented during each assessment.

Sentence Understanding: Twenty cloze sentences appear on the screen (e.g., "Jill patted the cat's fur/claws") and the student says the name of the word into the microphone that best completes the sentence.

Listening comprehension. Students listen to 3 tape recorded passages that vary in difficulty. One passage is at a level below their current grade, one is at their current grade level, and one is above their grade level. After listening to a passage they complete a comprehension test that is based on Royer's SVT procedure (see Royer, Carlo & Cisero, 1992, for a review).

Reading comprehension. Students read 3 passages that are based on the same content as used in the listening comprehension tests. Again there are 3 passages varying in difficulty and the student reads a passage and then completes an SVT test that assesses the extent to which the passage was comprehended. The test is untimed, meaning that students could take as much time as they wanted to complete the three passages.

With the exception of the reading and listening comprehension tests, all of the tasks in the CAAS battery contain a large number of potential items that are randomly sampled for presentation on any given assessment. For example, the elementary version of the CAAS word assessment used in the reported research involves presenting 10 three letter words, 10 four letter words, 10 five letter words, and 10 six letter words during an assessment. These 40 presented words are randomly sampled from a pool of 60 words of each letter length (240 words total). This sampling process means that repeated assessments are different from one another and it allows for the tracking of progress without worrying about whether the examinee remembers items from a previous assessment.[1]

Characteristics of Participants and Discussion of Those Characteristics

Over the years data was collected from over 100 students referred to LATAS. Some of the referred students were diagnosed with attentional disorders or dyscalculia and their data will not be considered in this chapter. Given the nature of the referring process, many of the students had incomplete testing records and others participated only briefly in prescribed interventions. Our primary analyses will be conducted with data from poor and disabled readers for whom we at least have IQ scores and relatively complete intervention data. Students that are listed as reading disabled had a diagnosis in the files that were collected upon entry to the LATAS program. However, some of the students did not have complete reports listing IQ scores, achievement tests scores, or other testing data. Both reading disabled students and poor readers who had at least an IQ score and CAAS assessment information are listed as having complete data in the tables to follow. Students who had a diagnosis as reading disabled but did not have test data available upon entry to the LATAS program will be added to the data set for students with incomplete data.

The poor readers with incomplete data are readers who had a diagnosis that said they were *not* disabled readers or they had never gone through a diagnostic process but were referred to LATAS because a parent, teacher or diagnostician thought they might benefit from the program. All of the referred students were Caucasian and almost all of them were from middle or upper middle class households with many parents having postgraduate educational degrees.

Grade Breakdown. The breakdown of our total sample in terms of grade enrollment is presented in Table 16.1. As can be seen in the table, students who are in the poor reader group tend to be referred to LATAS at a somewhat younger age than students in the reading disabled group. This probably reflects the fact that many schools often do not initiate formal diagnostic procedures for reading delayed children until the 3rd grade. Some students in lower grades could not complete CAAS assessments beyond the letter and word level. Hence, the analyses to be reported in the sections below will focus on students in grade 3 or above.

---

[1]A commercial version of the CAAS assessment system and a version of the intervention system described in this chapter is available at: www.readingsuccesslab.com

TABLE 16.1
Number of Students Per Grade by Diagnosis
and Complete versus Incomplete Data

Diagnosis	Grade								
	1	*2*	*3*	*4*	*5*	*6*	*7*	*8*	*9*
Poor reader complete	3	3	2	4	3				
Reading disabled complete		4	4	4	3	4	1	1	3
Poor reader incomplete	3	9	3	5	4	2	1	3	
Reading disabled incomplete	1	8	8	8	10	6	2	4	

IQ and Achievement Test Performance

The mean WISC scores for the 3rd grade and beyond poor and disabled readers are presented in Figure 16.1, along with WRAT scores, when available. As per our definition in the preceding section, all of the data in Figure 16.1 comes from students who have taken the WISC III test and they have completed CAAS assessments. In several cases WISC verbal and performance scores were reported but the full scale score was not. As can be seen, the average student in both the poor reader group and the disabled reader group was above average in WISC performance (mean of WISC = 100, SD = 15). Note also that the average student in both the reading disabled and the poor reader group scored below the mean on all of the WRAT tests (mean of WRAT = 100, SD = 15). However, students in the poor reader group are only scoring slightly below the mean on all of the WRAT tests. This contrasts to the performance of the reading disabled group where there was a discrepancy of over one SD between performance on the WISC and performance on the reading and spelling sections of the WRAT. Also noteworthy is the fact that the reading disabled group scores noticeably better on the math subtest of the WRAT than they did on the spelling and reading subtest.

Patterns of Performance. The patterns of performance displayed in Figure 16.1 are consistent with what would be expected based on diagnostic classifications. The reading disabled group displays a large gap between reading and spelling WRAT performance and IQ performance, whereas the gap between IQ and

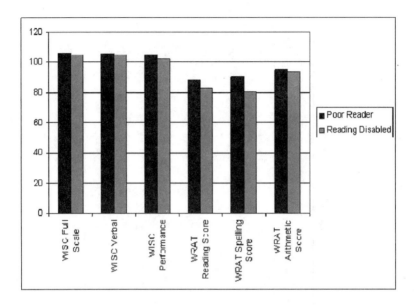

FIGURE 16.1   Mean Performance on the WISC and WRAT as a Function of Diagnosis

math WRAT performance was much smaller. In contrast, the poor reader group has much less of a gap between reading, spelling and IQ, and there is little difference in reading and math WRAT performance.

Performance on the CAAS Assessments

The grade level percentile performance on the CAAS tasks is presented in Table 16.2. The table breaks the data down in two ways. The data for poor readers and reading disabled readers labeled "complete" is for students who have WISC III data. That is, the data is from the same students who contributed data to Figure 16.1. The data from students labeled "incomplete" comes from all the students who have gone through at least four weeks of the fluency intervention. This includes students for whom WISC III scores were available plus some additional students who participated in the intervention but did not have WISC scores available upon entry to the LATAS program.

An important point to remember about percentile performance is that it has an artificial floor of one. That is, even if a student scores 3 or more standard deviations below the mean, the lowest score they can get is 1. This makes the percentiles listed in Table 16.2 deceptive. In fact, many of the students in the reading disabled group score more than 3 standard deviations below the mean on the CAAS tasks. For example, the student with the greatest disability (at least test performance wise) in the reading disabled group was a 9th grade male whose average word naming time

TABLE 16.2

Percentile Performance on the CAAS Tasks as a Function of Diagnostic Category

Diagnosis		Simple	Letter	Word	Nonword	Category	Sentence	Listening Comprehension	Reading Comprehension
Poor reader complete	Mean	67.12	65.11	28.88	31.55	26.37	22.62	53.14	42.98
	N	8	8	9	9	8	8	7	7
	SD	27.33	23.01	27.75	31.97	27.42	28.81	36.63	37.49
Reading disabled complete	Mean	68.92	58.08	11.16	9.57	17.10	9.99	40.87	23.54
	N	21	21	21	21	20	20	21	20
	SD	24.50	30.88	17.89	17.83	16.14	18.61	26.69	24.56
Poor reader incomplete	Mean	63.85	50.74	20.00	24.90	32.00	24.50	51.33	43.22
	N	10	10	11	11	10	10	9	9
	SD	30.52	33.57	19.44	28.63	28.47	22.22	33.14	30.87
Reading disabled incomplete	Mean	65.62	51.75	9.89	7.17	20.28	8.73	44.80	21.96
	N	33	33	34	34	32	31	33	32
	SD	24.23	29.42	13.79	12.29	23.08	15.55	28.96	21.89

was over 10 seconds per word. Given his age peers named words on average at .6 seconds per word with a standard deviation of .11, this student was performing at a level of over 90 standard deviations below the mean in word naming performance. This student was deleted from the intervention data to be reported. However, it should be mentioned that this student more than halved his negative Z score as a function of the fluency interventions.

Patterns of Performance. As can be seen, there is very little difference between the two data sets. In both the incomplete and complete data sets there is little difference between poor readers and reading disabled readers on the simple perception and letter naming tasks. Moreover, in both cases the students are performing at the average level or the slightly above average level on the tasks. As an aside, the average or above average performance for both of these groups speaks to a hypothesis that would suggest that disabled readers are deficient on all speeded naming tasks. Neither the disabled readers nor the poor readers showed a hint of deficiency on the simple perception and letter naming tasks.

Beyond the letter naming tasks there was clear evidence that the patterns of performance differed for the two groups. The poor reader group hovered between the 20th and 30th percentile on the word, nonword, category and sentence task. This indicates that these students were deficient in low-level reading performance relative to comparable grade peers. It is noteworthy that there was little difference between word and nonword performance for either the complete or incomplete readers. In fact, nonword performance was slightly better than word performance.

The profile of performance is different for the reading disabled group. First, they have considerably lower performance on the word, nonword, category and sentence task than does the poor reader group. Second, the pattern is different. Notice that the reading disabled group has lower performance on the nonword task than they do on the word task. As noted in the paragraph above, this pattern is reversed in the poor reader group.

Turning now to the comprehension tasks, the poor reading group has a grade percentile almost at the mean for the listening comprehension task, and slightly below the mean on the reading comprehension task. The reading disabled group is slightly below the mean on the listening comprehension task and well below the mean on the reading comprehension task. The patterns on the comprehension tests, along with the patterns on the simple perception and letter naming tasks, are consistent with the idea that the readers in the both groups have deficiencies that are specific to reading. It should also be remembered that the reading comprehension tests were administered untimed. It is likely that the performance of both the poor reading group and the reading disabled group would have been lower if the reading comprehension tests were timed.

Taken overall, the patterns of performance on the CAAS tasks are again what would be expected based on diagnostic categories. Specifically, both the poor readers and the disabled readers do not display deficiencies in perceptual responding (the simple and letter tasks) and in listening comprehension, though the disabled readers are slightly below average in listening comprehension. The groups do display deficiencies in reading with particularly striking deficiencies in the reading disabled group. In addition, the poor readers do not display a disassociation in their ability to recognize words and nonwords. In contrast, as would be expected among individuals with a phonological processing problem, the disabled readers have more difficulty with nonwords than they do with words.

THE READING INTERVENTION

Prior to describing the intervention process it should be indicated that the words that students practice during intervention and the words that are contained in the CAAS assessments are different. This was deliberately done so that CAAS assessments would provide an assessment of the degree to which word practice transfers to unpracticed words.

The LATAS intervention consisted of speeded practice at naming words for at least five days per week. The typical word practice set consists of 160 words divided into pages of 4 pages with 40 words per page. A practice session would consist of having the student look at a practice page and ask to have any word on the page pronounced if the word was not recognized. When the student was ready to be timed, he/she would name the words on a page as rapidly as possible while trying to maintain accuracy. During this naming period a parent, teacher, or peer would record time in seconds per page and would record on a separate sheet any words that were named incorrectly. The student was encouraged to guess a word if the word was not immediately recognized. After the student completed naming the words on a page the person working with the student would go back and point out words where errors occurred and indicate the error the student made and would then correctly pronounce the word. Words that were repeatedly missed over practice sessions would be isolated and would be subject to added practice before and after regular practice sessions. Practice of the remaining three pages followed the same procedure as used for the first page.

After practicing naming the four pages of words the mean time per page would be calculated and plotted on a graph. This graph was completed for each practice session so that the student would have immediate feedback on the time taken to name the words on each practice session.

Every student that participated in the LATAS process lowered average time per page within three practice sessions. Time would continue to decrease over practice sessions until it reached a low asymptote of somewhere between 30 and 40 seconds per page. There was considerable variability in the number of sessions it would take to reach low asymptote, but there was relatively little variability between students in the low asymptote point.

When time per page reached a low asymptote for four practice sessions with near perfect accuracy, the student was given a new set of 160 words and repeated the process. Practice words were divided into 4 practice sets at each grade level ranging from grade 1 to grade 8. When the 4 practice sets at a given grade were completed the student moved to practice materials at the next grade level. In addition to the graded practice sets, practice sets of words were developed from textbooks the students were currently using. These materials were often used with students in grade 6 and beyond who indicated they were having difficulty keeping up with assigned reading.

The assignment of the right set of practice materials was an important part of the intervention process. The idea was to assign practice materials that were at a level where the student could show improvement, but not so difficult so as to create frustration. The process of assigning materials at the right level involved consideration of multiple sources of information. The first source was the intake interview which involved collection of a psychological and educational history. The second source of information was records the students brought to LATAS including diagnostic reports, testing data, and copies of IEPs and school reports of progress. Finally, the CAAS assessment data also contributed to the process of material assignment.

Another practical aspect of the intervention that proved to be important was varying the order in which students named the words. It quickly became obvious that if one allowed student to name the words in the same order on every practice occasion they would memorize sequences as long as 10 words. In order to prevent responding from memory we varied the order of word naming, sometimes going from top to bottom, left to right, then varying other orders so as to prevent responding from memory.

While interventions were occurring the student returned to LATAS either once per week or once every other week. When they returned the students completed one of two versions of a CAAS reassessment consisting of the word task, the nonword task, the category task and the sentence understanding task. One version was completed upon admission to LATAS and was then repeated at 4 week intervals. This is the CAAS transfer version that was described in the earlier section of the chapter and it is the one that will provide the data to be described in the next section. A second set of CAAS materials that included some of the words the students were practicing during intervention was administered on the weeks the student was not scheduled to complete the regular CAAS assessment.

When students returned for reassessment they brought their home/school practice graphs. These graphs, along with the results of the CAAS reassessments, provided the information needed to decide if it was time to assign a new set of practice words.[2] The home graphs also provided a check on whether students were engaging in assigned practice.

Another component of the intervention process was a reward system. When students were reassessed, if they made improvements in speed and accuracy of performance on the majority of tasks (3 of the 4) without declining in either speed or accuracy, they were allowed to draw a slip from a grab bag where they could win a monetary reward ranging from 25 cents to 10 dollars. This reward system was

---

[2]All of the intervention procedures described in this section are now implemented in the commercial version of the CAAS system. Also available are all of the practice words including many sets of words drawn from subject matter textbooks at varying grade levels.

popular, but in the opinion of the authors a far more important reinforcement for continuing practice was watching the time line decrease on the practice graphs.

Finally, both parents and students were told that practice in naming words was only one part of the process of becoming a skilled reader. Another very important part was practicing their developing skills on a nightly basis by reading books, magazines or any other material they were interested in.

RESULTS OF THE READING INTERVENTION

The results of the interventions are reported in the form of changing performance on the CAAS reassessments. As indicated earlier, performance on the word, non-word, category and sentence understanding tasks was measured on the regular CAAS system at four week intervals. The speed and accuracy of performance for reading disabled and poor readers will be reported for week 0 (the week the students were initially assessed) and then at weeks 4 and 12. This data will be reported for both reading disabled (RD) and poor reading (PR) groups.

These intervention results provide indications of two kinds of transfer. First, since the words in the regular CAAS system are different than the words the students are practicing, any improvement in performance on the CAAS words represents general improvement in word naming performance. Second, the measurement of performance on the nonword, category, and sentence understanding tasks provide an indication of the extent to which word naming practice transfers to other reading tasks.

The results of the interventions are presented in Figures 16.2 and 16.3. Since students in both the reading disabled and poor reading groups vary in grade, performance for each student was converted into a grade level Z score and then Z scores were averaged across students. The means and standard deviations for grade levels were obtained from the norm groups that were mentioned previously in the chapter.

As can be seen in the figures, both the reading disabled and the poor readers improve on the CAAS tasks during the 12 weeks of interventions. The change in the reading disabled group is particularly striking with improvement of as much as four standard deviations over the intervention period.

DISCUSSION

The results reported in the above section show differential effectiveness of the fluency intervention as a function of treatment group. Looking first at accuracy, the poor reading group made little change in word performance and an initial decline in nonword accuracy followed by a subsequent improvement at the 12 week point. There was some evidence of negative change for the poor reading group in their performance on the category and sentence task in that they start at the beginning of intervention around the mean in accuracy performance and then decline to below accuracy during the intervention period. The pattern is quite different for the disabled reading group where the students made steady improvement in accuracy of performance during the intervention period.

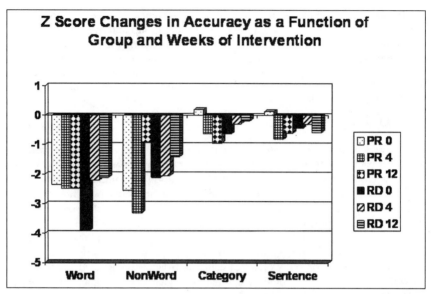

FIGURE 16.2   Z Score Changes in Accuracy as a Function of Group and Weeks of Intervention

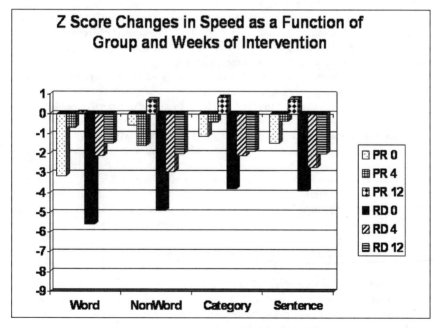

FIGURE 16.3   Z Score Changes in Speed as a Function of Group and Weeks of Intervention.

The patterns for both groups were more consistent for speed of performance. There was clear evidence in both the poor reading group and the reading disabled group that performance improved on all of the tasks during the intervention period. The only exception to this generalization occurs in the poor reading nonword task where performance declined slightly at the 4 week interval but then showed gain by the 12 week interval.

Sources of Improvement

Our sense in watching students improve their performance was that there were two factors at play. First, there was a strategy shift that occurred, particularly in the reading disabled group. Most of the reading disabled group used sounding out excessively when reading. They seemed to use sounding out as the strategy of first choice for most of the words they read. From observation we developed the sense that over time the speeded practice brought about a strategy shift where the preferred strategy was to go into the head for the word rather than sound it out. You could almost see this happen on a word by word basis. As practice with the same list continued, the student would drop out words that were immediately recognized and this group of words became larger as practice continued, ultimately creating a situation where all of the words were recognized without sounding them out.

We believe that the second source of improvement was cognitive in nature. Our thinking about cognitive improvement is influenced by Perfetti's (1992) description of the word representation that is developed in skilled readers. Perfetti argued that over time skilled readers develop cognitive representations for individual words that "bind" together orthography and phonology. The skilled reader's representation is activated by the visual form of the word and upon activation the readers hears with his or her "mind's ear" the word being pronounced. We believe that one consequence of word fluency training is the development of bound representations for words that were being practiced.

We believe that a corollary that follows from Perfetti's perspective on word representations in skilled readers is that bound representations are unlikely to be developed in readers who consistently sound out words when reading. Our perspective is that representations that bind orthography and phonology will only develop when the sound of a correctly pronounced word and visual representation of a word are in working memory simultaneously. The reader who consistently sounds out words when trying to recognize them will have a difficult time binding together orthography and phonology because the correct pronunciation of the word is only a part of sound pattern that is available in working memory.

Transfer of Fluency Training to Other Reading Activities

There is evidence for two kinds of positive transfer in our data. One kind of positive transfer involves improvements in the recognition of words that were not practiced, and a second kind of positive transfer involves improvements in reading tasks other than word recognition. Evidence for improvements in the recognition of unpracticed words is apparent in that improvements in the speed and accuracy of the recognition of practiced words was accompanied by changes in speed and accuracy of unpracticed word recognition as evidenced by the CAAS system assessments. These changes are depicted in the word recognition performance in Figures 16.2 and 16.3.

Evidence for improvements of reading performance in general can also be seen in Figures 16.2 and 16.3. The graphs in the figures show that most students made improvements in the recognition of nonwords, improvements in the ability to activate the meaning of words as indicated by performance on the category task, and in improvements in the ability to accurately and rapidly interpret sentences as evidenced by performance on the sentence comprehension task. These gains were particularly noteworthy in the reading disabled group.

Again we believe that there are two factors that are interacting to produce these improvements. First, we believe that as the efficiency of word recognition improved, more cognitive resources were available to activate meaning and to devote to comprehension processes. Students who struggle to sound out words have relatively few resources to devote to comprehension The extreme of this situation is reflected in the student who took an average of 10 seconds to decode a word, but even students who decode in ranges of 2 to 3 times slower than peers have a distinct disadvantage with respect to comprehension, particularly when comprehension is indexed by both the speed and the accuracy of performance.

The second factor is more complicated and provides a possible explanation for the curious finding that word fluency training not only positively transferred to the recognition of other words, it also positively transferred to the recognition of nonwords. We believe the explanation for this kind of transfer was proposed in an early paper by LaBerge and Samuels (1974). LaBerge and Samuels proposed that automatic word recognition is enabled by the development of a series of cognitive representations that with practice become automatically activated. The lower levels of their representation system included letters, letter sound connections, spelling patterns and words. Our hypothesis is that word fluency training produces two types of "bound representations." The end product is bound representations that bind orthography and phonology for whole words, but underneath these representations are spelling pattern representations for regular spelling patterns in English. Figure 16.4 illustrates our hypothesis. A reader who practices the rapid recognition of a word like "prepare" is forming two kinds of representations. First, the reader is forming a representation that binds the visual form and the phonology of the complete word. Second the reader is forming a spelling pattern representation corresponding to the "pre" and "pare" parts of the word. These are frequently occurring spelling and pronunciation patterns in English and the spelling pattern representations map onto words that the reader has not practiced that contain the same patterns. So, for example, the reader's ability to recognize the words "prevent" and "compare" will be facilitated due to the existence of the underlying spelling pattern representations. These spelling patterns will also facilitate the reading of nonwords that contain the patterns. Most of the nonwords in the CAAS system are created by altering the spelling of regularly pronounced words, hence a facilitation of nonword

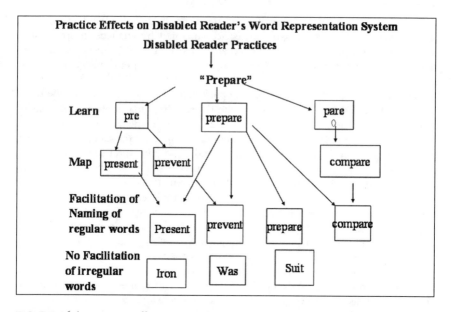

FIGURE 16.4   Practice Effects on Disabled Reader's Word Representation System.

recognition as a function of fluency training. Notice also that our hypothesis would predict that one would not get facilitation on irregularly pronounced words and nonwords. We have not systematically tested this hypothesis but we do believe we have seen evidence supporting it in our observations of reading performance.

Limitations of Our Research

There are two major limitations of our research. The first stems from the fact that it is based on a referred population in a clinical setting. We are not able to control important factors like nature of disability, comparability of students and length and adherence to an intervention process. We are also not able to offer concrete evidence that our disabled readers are treatment resistant. The evidence we have suggests that they have not optimally benefited from the instruction they have received. However, this evidence is not systematic and we are not able to document the exact interventions students received nor are we able to document the failure to benefit from those interventions. We believe the fact that our disabled readers in particular are poor readers as evidenced by our objective measures indicate that they have not made substantial gains from the interventions they have received. But an examination of their current status is not a substitute for careful experimentation that controls intervention procedures and monitors outcomes associated with those procedures.

A second major limitation of our study is that our data is based on a relatively small number of participants. We have data from more participants than we have reported but chose to only present data for the subset of participants for whom we had relatively complete data sets. The majority of students receiving the intervention who did not contribute data to this article showed gains comparable to those reported.

We also chose to limit our data reporting to students who only had reading problems. This means that we did not report data for students who had attentional disorders, or who had some combination of dyslexia, dyscalculia, attentional disorders or emotional disorders. It should be noted though that our reading intervention procedures have been successful with students who have both attentional disorders and reading problems (Royer, Rath & Tronsky, 2001). We have also reported a study showing that fluency training procedures produce math gains in students with attentional disorders (Royer & Tronsky, 1998).

This said, the reader should still be cautious about assuming the generalizability of our findings for the effectiveness of word fluency training. Additional research needs to be conducted before one can be confident that it provides an alternative to better established procedures.

Even given these cautionary notes, we believe that our research offers hope of intervention possibilities for students who seem not to have benefited from traditional interventions. Our students do improve in reading performance and some of our disabled readers improve to the point where they are reading at the level of their peers. We hope that our report encourages further research into the procedure and in so doing develops an alternative reading intervention procedure that may help readers that are not responding to conventional interventions.

REFERENCES

Aaron, P. G. (1997). The impending demise of the discrepancy formula. *Review of Educational Research, 67*, 461–502.

Blachman, B. A. (1997). Early intervention and phonological awareness: A cautionary tale. In B. Blachman (Ed), *Foundations of reading acquisition and dyslexia*. Mahwah, NJ: Lawrence Erlbaum. (pp. 305–326).

Brady, S., Fowler, A., Stone, B., and Winbury, N. (1994). Training phonological awareness: A study with inner-city kindergarten children. *Annals of Dyslexia, 44*, 27–59.

Byrne, B., & Fielding-Barnsley, R. (1991). Evaluation of a program to teach phonemic awareness to young children. *Journal of Educational Psychology, 83*, 451–455.

Byrne, B., & Fielding-Barnsley, R. (1995). Evaluation of a program to teach phonemic awareness to young children. A 2-and 3- year follow up and a new preschool trial. *Journal of Educational Psychology, 87*, 488–503.

Clay, M. M. (1987). Learning to be learning disabled. *New Zealand Journal of Educational Studies, 22*, 155–173.

Cisero, C. A., & Royer, J. M. (1995). The development and cross-language transfer of phonological awareness. *Contemporary Educational Psychology, 20*, 275–303.

Cisero, C. A., Royer, J. M., Marchant, H. G., & Jackson, S. J. (1997). Can the Computer-based Academic Assessment System (CAAS) be used to diagnose reading disability in college students? *Journal of Educational Psychology, 89*, 599–620.

Cunningham, A. E. (1990). Explicit versus implicit instruction in phonemic awareness. *Journal of Experimental Child Psychology, 50*, 429–444.

Foorman, B. R., Francis, D. J., Fletcher, J. M., Schatschneider, C., and Mehta, P. (1998). The role of instruction in learning to read: Preventing reading failure in at-risk children. *Journal of Educational Psychology, 90,* 37–55.

Fuchs, D., Mock, D., Morgan, P. L., & Young, C. L. (2003). Responsiveness-to-intervention: Evidence, and implications for the learning disabilities construct. *Learning Disabilities Research and Practice, 18,* 151–171.

Greene, B. A., & Royer, J. M. (1994). A developmental review of response time data that support a cognitive component model of reading. *Educational Psychology Review, 6,* 141–172.

Harm, M. W. and Seidenberg, M. (1999). Phonology, Reading Acquisition, and Dyslexia: Insights From Connectionist Models. *Psychological Review, 106,* 491–528.

Johnson, K. R., & Layng, T. V. (1992). Breaking the structuralist barrier: Literacy and numeracy with fluency. *American Psychologist, 47,* 1475–1490.

LaBerge, D., & Samuels, S. J. (1974). Toward a theory of automatic information process in reading. *Cognitive Psychology, 6,* 293–323.

Lie, A. (1991). Effects of a training program for stimulating skills in word analysis in first-grade children. *Reading Research Quarterly, 26,* 234–250.

Lundberg, I. (1994) Reading difficulties can be predicted and prevented: A Scandinavian perspective on phonological awareness and reading. In C. Hulme and M. Snowling (Eds.), *Reading development and dyslexia.* London: Whurr publishing. (pp. 180–199).

Lundberg, I., Frost, J., and Peterson, O.P. (1988). Effects of an extensive program for stimulating phonological awareness in preschool children. *Reading Research Quarterly, 23,* 264–284.

Olson, R. K. (2004). SSSR, environment and genes. *Scientific Studies of Reading, 8,* 111–124.

Olson, R. K., Wise, B., Johnson, M. C., & Ring, J. (1997). The etiology and remediation of phonologically based word recognition and spelling disabilities: Are phonological deficits the "hole" story. In B. Blachman (Ed), *Foundations of reading acquisition and dyslexia.* Mahwah, NJ: Lawrence Erlbaum. (pp. 305–326).

Perfetti, C. A. (1992). The representation problem in reading acquisition. In P. B. Gough, L. Ehri & R. Treiman (Eds.), Reading acquisition. Hillsdale, N.J.: Erlbaum.

Royer, J. M. (1997). A Cognitive Perspective on the Assessment, Diagnosis and Remediation of Reading Skills. In G. D. Phye (Ed.), *Handbook of academic learning.* San Diego, CA: Academic Press. (pp. 199–234).

Royer, J. M., Abadzi, H., Kinda, J. (2004). The Impact of Phonological Awareness and Rapid Reading Training on the Reading Skills of Adolescent and Adult Neoliterates, *International Review of Education, 50,* 53–71.

Royer, J. M., Carlo, M. S., & Cisero, C. A. (1992). School-based uses for the Sentence Verification Technique for measuring listening and reading comprehension. *Psychological Test Bulletin, 5,* 5–19.

Royer, J. M., Rath, K. A., & Tronsky, L. N. (2001). Automaticity training as a reading intervention for adolescents with attentional disorders. *Advances in Learning and Behavioral Disorders.* (Vol 15), 3–16. New York: JAI Press.

Royer, J. M., & Sinatra, G. M. (1994). A cognitive theoretical approach to reading diagnostics. *Educational Psychology Review, 6,* 81–114.

Royer, J. M., & Tronsky, L. N. (1998). Addition practice with math disabled students improves subtraction and multiplication performance. In T. E. Scruggs and M. A. Mastropieri (Eds.), *Advances in Learning and Behavioral Disabilities (Vol 12).* Greenwich, Conn.: JAI Press, Inc. (pp 185–218).

Salmelin, R., & Helenius, P. Functional neuroanatomy of impaired reading in dyslexia. *Scientific Studies of Reading, 8,* 257–272.

Schneider, W., Kuspert, P., Roth, H., Mechtild, V., and Marx, H. (1997). Short-and long-term effects of training phonological awareness in kindergarten: Evidence from two German studies. *Journal of Experimental Child Psychology, 66,* 311–340.

Seidenberg, M., (1992). Dyslexia in a computational model of word recognition. In P. B. Gough, L. C. Ehri, and R. Treiman (Eds), *Reading Acquisition*. Hillsdale N.J.: Lawrence Erlbaum Associates. (pp. 243–274).

Shaywitz, S. (2003). *Overcoming dyslexia*. New York: Alfred Knopf.

Sinatra, G. M., & Royer, J. M. (1993). The development of cognitive component processing skills that support skilled reading. *Journal of Educational Psychology, 85*, 509–519.

Snow, C. E., Burns, M. S., and Griffin, P. (1998). *Preventing reading difficulties in young children*. Washington, DC: National Academy Press.

Swanson, H. L. (1999). *Interventions for students with learning disabilities: A meta-analysis of Treatment Outcomes*. New York: Guilford Press.

Torgesen, J. K., Wagner, R. K., Rashotte, C. A., Rose, E., Lindamood, P., and Conway, T. (1999). Preventing reading failure in young children with phonological processing disabilities: Group and individual responses to instruction. *Journal of Educational Psychology, 91,* 579–593.

Vellutino, F. R., Scanlon, D, M,, Sipay, E. R., Small, S. G., Pratt, A., Chen, R., & Denckla, M. B. (1996). Cognitive profiles of difficult to remediate and readily remediated peer readers: Early intervention as a vehicle for distinguishing between cognitive and experiential deficits as basic cuuses of specific reading disability. *Journal of Educational Psychology, 88*, 601–638.

Vellutino, F. R., Scanlon, D. M., and Sipay, E. R. (1997). Toward distinguishing between cognitive and experiential deficits as primary sources of difficulty in learning to read: The importance of early intervention id diagnosing specific reading disability. In B. Blachman (Ed), *Foundations of reading acquisition and dyslexia*. Mahwah, NJ: Lawrence Erlbaum. (pp. 347–380).

Wang, B. Y. L. (1996). *The ABCs of learning disabilities*. San Diego: Academic Press.

Wolf, M., & Katzir-Cohen, T. (2001). Reading fluency and its intervention. *Scientific Studies of Reading, 5*, 211–239.

CHAPTER SEVENTEEN

Neurobiological and Behavioral Studies of Skilled and Impaired Word Reading

Stephen J. Frost
Rebecca Sandak
W. Einar Mencl
Nicole Landi
Haskins Laboratories
Dina Moore
Southern Connecticut State University &
Haskins Laboratories
Gina Della Porta
Yale University School of Medicine, Department of Pediatrics
Jay G. Rueckl
University of Connecticut & Haskins Laboratories
Leonard Katz
University of Connecticut & Haskins Laboratories
Kenneth R. Pugh
Yale University School of Medicine,
Department of Pediatrics & Haskins Laboratories

Extensive behavioral research over the past several decades has examined the factors that govern the successful acquisition of reading skills and identification of the cause(s) of reading failure (Grigorenko, 2001; Pugh et al., 2000a). Research on the neurobiology of reading acquisition and development in skilled and impaired readers has benefited in recent years from rapid advances in several neuroimaging technologies (e.g., Positron Emission Tomography (PET); functional Magnetic Resonance

Imaging (fMRI); Magnetoencephology (MEG)). This chapter will review behavioral studies of skilled reading and reading disability, and will describe how functional imaging methods have been used in parallel with behavioral research to examine the role of component processes and the functional brain organization for language and reading in children and adults with and without reading disability (Papanicolaou et al., 2004).

BEHAVIORAL STUDIES OF SKILLED READING

A central question in behavioral studies of skilled reading concerns the role of phonological processing in mediating lexical access. Different classes of models have been put forward to address this question. Purely orthographic access models (Baron, 1973) and phonological coherence models (Van Orden, Pennington, & Stone, 1990) each assume singular lexical access codes; graphemic in the former, and phonologically-mediated in the latter. By contrast, dual-process accounts incorporate two independent mechanisms or routes for accessing meaning: (1) by mapping from spelling to the lexicon and then obtaining phonological information through a lexical lookup procedure or (2) by mapping from spelling to a phonological code and then to the lexicon ("phonologically mediated access") (Coltheart, 1978; Coltheart, Rastle, Perry, Langdon, & Ziegler, 2001; Paap & Noel, 1991). A number of alternative models do not assume multiple independent mechanisms, but instead posit interactive bi-directional links with a cooperative division of labor between orthographic, phonological, and semantic processes to support efficient word recognition (Harm & Seidenberg, 1999; Plaut, McClelland, Seidenberg, & Patterson, 1996; Seidenberg & McClelland, 1989).

With regard to the evidence for the role of phonology in skilled word recognition, many studies have now demonstrated that phonological access is early and automatic (see R. Frost, 1998 for review). Using a semantic categorization task, Van Orden found that participants produced more false positive responses to words that were homophones or pseudohomophones of category exemplars than for spelling foils (e.g., categorizing ROWS/ROZE as a flower more often than the control foil ROBS/REEZ) (Van Orden, 1987; Van Orden et al., 1988). This effect persisted, even at brief exposure durations, indicating that phonological recoding occurred early in processing and mediated activation of meaning. Moreover, because pseudohomophones are not represented lexically, Van Orden et al. concluded that the effect must occur prior to lexical access.

Findings using brief exposure paradigms, such as backward masking and priming also point to an early and robust influence of phonology on lexical access (Lesch & Pollatsek, 1993; Lukatela, Frost, & Turvey, 1999; Lukatela & Turvey, 1994a, 1994b; Perfetti & Bell, 1991; Perfetti, Bell & Delany, 1988). For example, Perfetti and colleagues found significantly better identification rates when briefly presented target words were followed by pseudoword masks that were phonologically similar than when they were graphemically similar, suggesting that phonological information was automatically extracted from the pseudoword mask and contributed to the identification of the target (Perfetti & Bell, 1991; Perfetti et al., 1988). Furthermore,

Lukatela and Turvey (1994a; see also Lesch & Pollatsek, 1993) observed associative priming, pseudo-associative priming, and pseudohomophonic associative priming relative to matched controls. At a short prime-target interval robust priming of the target word FROG was obtained for TOAD, TOWED, and TODE. At a long interval both TOAD and TODE effects were observed, but TOWED effects were eliminated. The authors concluded that the initial access code must be phonological in nature, with orthographic constraints coming into play relatively late.

Cross-language studies have provided additional evidence indicating that lexical access is mediated by the assembly of pre-lexical phonological codes. A unique feature of Serbo-Croatian is that it has one spoken form, but two written alphabets (the Roman and Cyrillic) that share characters, some of which are pronounced the same in both alphabets (i.e., common letters) and some of which are pronounced differently in the two alphabets (i.e., phonologically ambiguous letters). This feature allows researchers to combine the characters such that letter strings have one or more phonological interpretations, depending on whether the phonologically ambiguous characters are interpreted as Cyrillic or Roman. Studies of readers who are competent in both written forms produce slower word naming and lexical decision latencies for letter strings composed of phonologically ambiguous and common letters compared to letter strings composed of phonologically unique and common letters (Lukatela, Popadic, Ognjenovic, & Turvey, 1980) and that the size of the effect is positively correlated with the number of phonologically ambiguous letters (Feldman & Turvey, 1983). Moreover, this phonological ambiguity effect can be reduced by using an alphabetic prime composed of phonologically unique letters that effectively specify the target's script (Lukatela, Feldman, et al., 1989). There is also growing evidence that readers of Mandarin are sensitive to the sub-lexical phonological information contained in the phonetic components of compound words (see Perfetti, Liu, & Tan, 2005 for review). Studies have shown that homophonic characters that are unrelated in meaning produce slower decision latencies and higher error rates than control stimuli in semantic similarity judgments (Perfetti & Zhang, 1995). Experiments in Chinese using the backward masking paradigm have shown that briefly exposed target words are better identified when a following mask is a homophone (Tan, Hoosain, & Peng, 1995), paralleling results in English (Perfetti et al., 1998). Although language differences have been reported relative to the size or type of phonological unit that governs lexical access (e.g., see the German/English comparison study of Ziegler et al., 2001; Goswami, Ziegler, et al., 2003), the key point is that the findings converge to indicate that word recognition in skilled adult readers does not appear to differ in fundamental ways across languages and orthographies despite differences in the complexity of the mapping between a language's written form and its spoken form (Carello, Turvey, & Lukatela, 1992; Perfetti, 1985).

FUNCTIONAL IMAGING STUDIES OF SKILLED READING

Given the importance of phonological information evidenced from behavioral studies of skilled reading, identifying the neuroanatomical correlates of phonology and their interaction with regions that suppot orthographic and lexico-semantic component processes represents an important step toward understanding the functional architecture of reading and reading failure. Evidence from functional imaging studies indicates that skilled word recognition requires the development of a highly organized cortical system that integrates processing of orthographic, phonological, and lexico-semantic features of words (see Pugh et al., 2000a; and Sarkari et al., 2002 for reviews). This system broadly includes two posterior sub-systems in the left hemisphere (LH): a ventral (occipitotemporal) and a dorsal (temporoparietal) system, and a third area, anterior to the other two, centered in and around the inferior frontal gyrus.

The ventral system includes a left interior occipitotemporal/fusiform area and extends anteriorly into the middle and inferior temporal gyri (MTG, ITG). The more anterior foci within the ventral system, extending into MTG and ITG appear to be semantically tuned (Fiebach et al., 2002; Simos et al., 2002; Tagamets et al., 2000). The functional specificity of the more posterior occipitotemporal (OT) region appears to be late developing and critically related to the acquisition of reading skill (Booth et al., 2001; Shaywitz et al., 2002). Moreover, the ventral system, particularly the posterior aspect, responds quickly to linguistic stimuli in skilled readers but not in RD individuals (Salmelin et al., 1996). Some researchers have suggested that the OT region functions as a per-semantic visual word form area (VWFA) (Cohen et al., 2002; but see Price et al., 2003 for an alternative account); howerver, we refer to this region more neutrally as the ventral 'skill zone' because of its critical role in skilled reading. It should be noted that there is some disagreement in the literature about the precise localization of critical sub-regions comprising the ventral system (Price et al., 2003). Nevertheless, recent studies examining both timing and stimulus-type effects suggest that, moving from posterior to anterior within the ventral, system, areas respond to word and word-like stimuli in a progressively abstracted and linguistic manner (Tagamets et al., 2000; Tarkiainen et al., 2003).

The more dorsal temporoparietal system broadly includes the angular gyrus (AG) and supramarginal gyrus (SMG) in the inferior parietal lobule, and the posterior aspect of the superior temporal gyrus (Wernicke's Area). Among their other functions (e.g., attentionally controlled processing) the areas within this system seem to be involved in mapping visual percepts of print onto the phonological and semantic structures of language (Black & Behrmann 1994). In skilled readers, certain regions within the LH temporoparietal system (particularly the SMG) respond with greater activity to pseudowords than to familiar words (Price et al., 1996; Simos et al., 2002; Xu et al., 2001). This finding, along with our developmental studies (Shaywitz et al., 2002), suggests that the temporoparietal system plays a role in the types of phonological analyses that are relevant to learning new material.

The anterior system, centered in posterior aspects of the inferior frontal gyrus (IFG), appears to be associated with phonological recoding during reading, among other functions (e.g., phonological memory, syntactic processing); the more anterior aspects of IFG seem to play a role in semantic retrieval (Poldrack et al., 1999). The phonologically relevant components of this multi-functional system have been found to function in silent reading and in naming (see Fiez and Petersen 1998 for review; Pugh et al., 1997) and like the temporoparietal system, is more strongly engaged by low-frequency words (particularly, words with irregular/inconsistent spelling-to-sound mappings) and pseudowords than by high-frequency words (Fiebach et al., 2002; Fiez and Peterson 1998). We have speculated that this anterior system operates in close conjunction with the temporoparietal system to decode new words during normal reading development (Pugh et al., 2000b).

More recently, the functional neuroanatomy of visual word recognition in reading has been investigated in mature readers in a variety of languages (which employ both alphabetic and non-alphabetic writing systems) (e.g., Chee et al., 1999; Fiebach et al., 2002; Kuo et al., 2003, 2004; Paulesu et al., 2000; Salmelin et al., 1996). Neuroimaging studies of alphabetic languages broadly implicate the same set of LH cortical regions (including occipitotemporal, temporoparietal, and inferior frontal networks) identified in English-language studies (see Pugh et al., 2005a). These networks are almost always engaged by skilled readers irrespective of the specific language and/or writing system under investigation. Language-specific differences usually appear to be a matter of degree, not of kind. That is, in one language, the reading-relevant constituents of a neural network might be more or less activated than in another language, but the general circuitry appears similar in its taxonomic organization (Paulesu et al., 2000). For example, Kuo et al. (2003) examined covert naming of high-frequency and low-frequency Chinese characters and observed greater activation in left premotor/inferior frontal regions and the left insula for low-frequency characters relative to high-frequency characters. These areas have been implicated in phonological processing in English; in particular, the inferior frontal gyrus is more strongly engaged by low-frequency words and pseudowords than by high-frequency words (Fiebach et al., 2002; Fiez & Peterson, 1998). Moreover, high-frequency characters produced greater activation in the middle temporal/angular gyrus, which have been implicated in lexical-semantic processing in neuroimaging studies of English word recognition (Fiebach et al., 2002; Price et al., 1997; Simos et al., 2002) and the precuneus, previously implicated in visual imagery (Fletcher et al., 1996). In a subsequent study, Kuo and colleagues had participants perform homophone judgments and physical judgments on real characters, pseudo-characters (novel combinations of legal semantic and phonetic radicals that follow the positional architecture of Chinese characters), and Korean Hangul-like nonsense figures (Kuo et al., 2004). A number of regions important for orthographic-to-phonological mapping in English were also more active for the homophone judgment relative to the character judgment in Chinese. These regions included the inferior frontal gyrus, inferior parietal lobule/supramarginal gyrus, and the fusiform gyrus. Note that some differences have been reported for Mandarin reading with increased reading-related activation at both superior parietal (Kuo et al., 2003), and left middle frontal regions (Tan et al., 2001); however, overall the reading networks appear to be largely similar to those observed for alphabetic writing systems (Kuo et al., 2003, 2004).

BEHAVIORAL STUDIES OF READING DISABILITY

Significant progress has been made in understanding the cognitive and linguistic skills that must be in place to insure adequate reading development in children

(Brady & Shankweiler 1991; Bruck, 1992; Fletcher et al., 1994; Liberman et al., 1974; Rieben & Perfetti 1991; Shankweiler et al., 1995; Stanovich & Siegel, 1994; see also Piasta & Wagner, this volume). With regard to reading disability, it has been argued that the reading difficulties experienced by some children may result from difficulties with processing speed (Wolf & Bowers, 1999), rapid auditory processing (Tallal, 1980), general language deficits (Scarborough & Dobrich, 1990), or visual deficits (Cornelissen & Hansen, 1998). However, there is growing consensus that for the majority of struggling readers, a core difficulty in reading manifests itself as a deficiency within the language system and, in particular, a deficiency at the level of phonological analysis (Liberman et al., 1974; Stanovich et al., 1984; Wagner & Torgesen, 1987).

Deficits in behavioral performance are most evident at the level of single word and pseudoword reading; reading disabled (RD) individuals are both slow and inaccurate relative to nonimpaired (NI) readers. Many lines of evidence converge on the conclusion that the word and pseudoword reading difficulties in RD individuals are, to a large extent, manifestations of more basic deficits at the level of rapidly assembling the phonological code represented by a token letter string (Bradley & Bryant, 1983; Liberman et al., 1989). The failure to develop efficient phonological assembly skill in word and pseudoword reading, in turn, appears to stem from difficulties – at the earliest stages of literacy training – in attaining fine-grained phonemic awareness.

As for why RD readers should have exceptional difficulty developing phonological awareness, the etiological underpinnings of this difficulty are still actively being investigated and the question of whether such language-level challenges might, in some children at least, be linked to more basic deficits in one of the above-mentioned domains is much debated. Nonetheless, a large body of evidence directly relates deficits in phonological awareness to difficulties in learning to read: phonological awareness measures predict later reading achievement (Bradley & Bryant, 1983; Stanovich et al., 1984; Torgesen et al., 1994); deficits in phonological awareness consistently separate RD and nonimpaired children (Fletcher et al., 1994; Stanovich & Siegel, 1994); phonological deficits persist into adulthood (Bruck, 1992; Felton et al., 1990; Shaywitz et al., 1999) and instruction in phonological awareness promotes the acquisition of reading skills (Ball & Blachman, 1991; Bradley & Bryant, 1983; Foorman et al., 1998; Torgesen et al., 1992; Wise & Olson, 1995). For children with adequate phonological skills, the process of phonological assembly in word and pseudoword reading becomes highly automated, efficient, and, as the evidence above suggests, continues to serve as an important component in rapid word identification even for mature skilled readers (R. Frost, 1998).

In terms of the characteristics of reading disability across languages, the extant evidence shows many similarities and few differences in profiles of RD across orthographies. Like disabled readers in English, many RD readers, specifically readers of regular orthographies with transparent spelling-to-sound correspondences:

Phonological awareness in general, is defined as the metalinguistic understanding that spoken words can be decomposed into phonological primitives, which in turn can be represented by alphabetic characters (Brady & Shankweiler, 1991; Bruck, 1992; Fletcher et al., 1994; Liberman et al., 1974; Rieben & Perfetti, 1991; Shankweiler et al., 1995; Stanovich & Siegel 1994).

(a) have a family history of RD (Lyytinen, 2004a, 2004b); (b) show larger lexicality, length, and grain-size effects relative to nonimpaired readers (Ziegler et al., 2003); and (c) exhibit signs of reduced distinctiveness (precision) in their phonological representations in the lexicon (Elbro, 1998; Elbro et al., 1998; Goswami, 2000; Ziegler & Goswami, 2005). Unlike English, in which RD readers are both slow and inaccurate, errors in regular orthographies are rare; however, wide individual differences occur in reading speed and the slowest readers are considered to have RD (Landerl et al., 1997; Wimmer & Mayringer, 2002). Nonetheless, the evidence provides some support for the hypothesis that RD is attributable to the same core phonological deficit in all languages. In line with previous theoretical work at Haskins Laboratories (Fowler, 1991), Goswami and colleagues have proposed that reduced precision in representing and processing phonological information may be the universal hallmark of RD (Goswami, 2000; Ziegler & Goswami, 2005).

In regular orthographies, the transparency of the speeling-to-sound correspondences allow the yoked processes of phonemic awareness and analysis to develop earlier and more fully (even in RD) than for readers of an irregular orthography with complex spelling-to-sound mappings. Thus, unlike English, in which RD readers are both slow and inaccurate, errors in regular orthographies are rare; however, the imprecision (and potentially reduced accessibility) of phonological knowledge about words still impedes routinization and subsequent fluency. The result is that wide individual differences in reading speed are observed in regular orthographies and the slowest are considered to have RD (Landerl et al., 1997; Wimmer & Mayringer, 2002). Although plausible and parsimonious, there is not yet sufficient evidence favoring this hypothesis over the notion that RD may have different etiologies across languages. Until longitudinal data are collected across orthographies using repeated administrations of the same array of cognitive and literacy measures (and neurobiological indices) interpretation of available cross-language comparisons will remain inconclusive.

FUNCTIONAL IMAGING STUDIES OF READING DISABILITY

Evidence for Altered Circuits in Reading Disability. There are clear functional differences between NI and RD readers with regard to activation patterns in dorsal, ventral, and anterior sites during reading tasks. In disabled readers, a number of functional imaging studies have observed LH posterior functional disruption, at both dorsal and ventral sites during phonological processing tasks (Brunswick et al., 1999; Paulesu et al., 2001; Pugh et al., 2000a, 2000b; Salmelin et al., 1996; Shaywitz et al., 1998; 2002; Temple et al., 2001). This disruption is instantiated as a relative under-engagement of these regions specifically when processing linguistic stimuli (words and pseudowords) or during tasks that require decoding. This functional anomaly in posterior LH regions has been observed consistently in children (Shaywitz et al., 2002) and adults (Salmelin et al., 1996; Shaywitz et al., 1998). Hypoactivation in three key dorsal and ventral sites, including cortex within the temporoparietal region, the angular gyrus, and the ventral OT skill zone is detectable as early as the end of kindergarten in children who have not reached important milestones in learning to read (Simos et al., 2002).

Most neuroimaging studies have attempted to isolate specific brain regions where activation patterns discriminate RD from NI readers (e.g., Rumsey et al., 1997; Shaywitz et al., 1998; Simos et al., 2002; Temple et al., 2001). However, work in reading disability (Horwitz et al., 1998; Pugh et al., 2000a, 2000b) employing functional connectivity analyses has also provided important insights into functional differences between RD and NI readers in word recognition. In this approach, the primary aim is to consider relations among distinct brain regions that function cooperatively as circuits to process information during reading (Friston, 1994). For example, Horwitz, Rumsey and Donohue (1998) examined correlations (within task/across subjects) between activation levels in the LH angular gyrus and other brain sites during two reading aloud tasks (exception word and pseudoword naming). Correlations between the LH angular gyrus and occipital and temporal lobe sites were strong and significant in NI readers but not in RD readers. Such a result suggests a breakdown in functional connectivity across the major components of the LH posterior reading system. A subsequent study by pughand colleagues (2000b) examining functional connectivity between the angular gyrus and occipital and temporal lobe sites on tasks that systematically varied demands made on phonological assembly showed that for RD readers LH functional connectivity was disrupted on word and pseudoword reading tasks as reported by Horwitz et al. (1998); however, there appeared to be no dysfunction on the tasks which tapped metaphonological judgments only (e.g., a single letter rhyme task), or complex visual-orthographic coding only (e.g., an orthographic case judgment task). The results are most consistent with a specific phonological deficit hypothesis: Our data suggest that a breakdown in functional connectivity among components of the LH posterior system manifests only when phonological assembly is required. The notion of a developmental lesion, one that would disrupt functional connectivity in this system across all types of cognitive behaviors, is not supported by this result. Moreover, Pugh et al. (2000b) found that on word and pseudoword reading tasks RH homologues appear to function in a compensatory manner for RD readers; correlations were strong and stable in this hemisphere for both reading groups with higher values in RD readers.

Because the evidence from neuroimaging studies of skilled reading indicates that different languages and orthographies engage common circuits during reading, we might expect language-invariant neurobiological signatures to be associated with reading disability as well. The evidence to date from alphabetic languages is supportive of this expectation (Paulesu et al., 2001; Salmelin et al., 1996; Shaywitz et al., 2002). Functional disruptions in LH posterior cortex (particularly the occipitotemporal region) in RD individuals performing reading tasks during neuroimaging have been found in several languages that vary in the complexity of mappings between printed and spoken forms (English, Finnish, German, French, and Italian). This common neurobiological signature, within a largely language-invariant circuitry for reading in the LH, reinforces the notion of universality in RD. A recent study of Chinese RD readers (Siok et al., 2004) reported a language-specific difference in the RD signature (specifically, diminished activation of middle frontal regions for RD readers relative to controls). This finding has not been reported in alphabetic languages. However, these authors also found diminished activation in RD readers at the same LH ventral regions previously reported by Paulesu and others in RD within alphabetic languages (Brunswick et al., 1999; Paulesu et al., 2001; Salmelin et al., 1996; Shaywitz et al., 2002).

Potentially Compensatory Processing in Reading Disability. Behaviorally, poor readers compensate for their inadequate phonological awareness and knowledge of letter-sound correspondences by over-relying on contextual cues to read individual words; their word reading errors tend to be visual or semantic rather than phonetic (see Perfetti, 1985 for review). These behavioral markers of reading impairment may be instantiated cortically by compensatory activation of frontal and RH regions. In our studies (Shaywitz et al., 1998, 2002), we observed processing in RD readers that we interpret as compensatory. We found that on tasks that made explicit demands on phonological processing (pseudoword- and word-reading tasks), RD readers showed a disproportionately greater engagement of IFG and prefrontal dorsolateral sites than did NI readers (see also Brunswick et al., 1999; Salmelin et al., 1996 for similar findings). Evidence of a second, potentially compensatory, shift – in this case to posterior RH regions – comes from several findings. Using MEG, Sarkari et al. (2002) found an increase in the apparent engagement of the RH temporoparietal region in RD children. More detailed examination of this trend, using hemodynamic measures, indicates that hemispheric asymmetries in activity in posterior temporal and temporoparietal regions (MTG and AG) vary significantly among reading groups (Shaywitz et al., 1998) there was greater right than LH activation in RD readers but greater left than RH activation in NI readers. Rumsey et al. (1999) examined the relationship between RH activation and reading performance in their adult RD and NI participants and found that RH temporoparietal activation was correlated with standard measures of reading performance only for RD readers (see also Shaywitz et al., 2002).

We hypothesize that the reason RD readers tend to strongly engage inferior frontal sites is their increased reliance on covert pronunciation (articulatory recoding) in an attempt to cope with their deficient phonological analysis of the printed word. In addition, their heightened activation of the posterior RH regions with reduced LH posterior activation suggests a process of word recognition that relies on letter-by-letter processing in accessing RH localized visuo-semantic representations (or some other compensatory process) rather than relying on phonologically structured word recognition strategies. The increased activation in frontal regions might also reflect increased effort during reading. In contrast, we believe that the under-engagement of LH posterior areas, particularly ventral sites, likely represents a failure to engage these areas.

Neurobiological Effects of Successful Reading Remediation.

Converging evidence from other studies supports the notion that gains in reading skill resulting from intense reading intervention are associated with a more "normalized" localization of reading processes in the brain. In a recent MEG study, eight young children with severe reading difficulties underwent a brief but intensive phonics-based remediation program (Simos et al., 2002). After intervention, the most salient change observed on a case-by-case basis was a robust increase in the apparent engagement of the LH temporoparietal region, accompanied by a moderate reduction in the activation of the RH temporoparietal areas. Similarly, Temple et al. (2003) used fMRI to examine the effects of an intervention (FastForword™) on the cortical circuitry of a group of 8- to 12-year-old children with reading difficulties. After intervention, increased LH temporoparietal and inferior frontal increases were observed. Moreover, the LH increases correlated significantly with increased reading scores. In another recent study, Shaywitz et al. (2004) examined three groups of young children (average age was 6.5 years at Time 1) with fMRI and behavioural indices pre-and post-intervention. A treatment RD group received nine months of an intensive phonologically-analytic intervention (Blachman et al., 1999), and there were two control groups: a typically developing and an untreated RD group. Relative to RD controls, RD treatment participants showed reliable gains on reading measures (particularly on fluency-related measures). Pre- and post-treatment fMRI employed a simple cross modal (auditory/visual) forced choice letter match task. When RD groups were compared at post-treatment (Time 2), reliably greater activation increases in LH reading related sites were seen in the treatment group. When Time 2 and Time 1 activation profiles were directly contrasted for each group it was evident that both RD treatment and typically developing, but not RD controls, showed reliable increases in LH reading related sites. Prominent differences were seen in LH IFG, and importantly in LH ventral skill zone. Importantly, the treatment group returned one year post-treatment for a follow up fMRI scan and progressive LH ventral increases along with decreasing RH activation patterns were observed even one year after treatment was concluded. All these initial neuroimaging treatment studies suggest that a critical neurobiological signature of successful intervention, at least in younger children, appears to be increased engagement of major LH reading-related circuits, and reduced reliance on RH homologues.

REFINING OUR ACCOUNT OF NEUROBIOLOGY OF SKILLED WORD RECOGNITION

In a preliminary model (Pugh et al., 2000a) we speculated that the temporoparietal and anterior systems are critical in learning to integrate orthographic, phonological, and semantic features of words, whereas the ventral system develops, as a consequence of adequate learning during reading acquisition, to support fluent word identification in normally developing, but not reading disabled, individuals (see below for relevant data). This general taxonomy however, is both coarse-grained and under-specified. To explore functional sub-specialization further we have recently conducted a series of experiments with skilled readers as participants (Frost et al., 2005; Katz et al., 2005; Mencl et al., 2005; Sandak et al., 2004). We examined: phonological priming (Mencl et al., 2005), phonological/semantic tradeoffs (Frost et al., 2005), and critical factors associated with repetition effects (Katz et al., 2005) and adaptive learning (Sandak et al, 2004). This line of research is aimed at providing more information on both sub-specialization with the major LH regions, and how different component systems modulate processing in relation to one another during learning.

Phonological Priming We have recently completed an fMRI study of phonological and orthographic priming effects in printed word recognition (Mencl et al., 2005). Participants performed a primed lexical decision task. Word prime-target pairs were either (1) both orthographically and phonologically similar (bribe-TRIBE); (2) orthographically similar but phonologically dissimilar (couch-TOUCH); or (3) unrelated (lunch-SCREEN). Results revealed that targets primed by phonologically dissimilar words evoked more activation than targets primed by phonologically similar words in several LH cortical areas hypothesized to underlie phonological processing: this modulation was seen in IFG, Wernicke's area, and the SMG. Notably, this phonological priming effect was also obtained within the early-activating LH OT skill zone, consistent with the claim that phonological coding influences lexical access at its earliest stages.

Tradeoffs Between Phonology and Semantics Many previous studies have attempted to identify the neural substrates of orthographic, phonological, and semantic processes in NI (Fiebach et al., 2002) and RD (Rumsey et al., 1997) cohorts. RD readers have acute problems in mapping from orthography to phonology and appear to rely on semantic information to supplement deficient decoding skills (Plaut & Booth, 2000). NI readers too, appear to show a trade-off between these component processes. Strain et al. (1995) provided behavioral confirmation of this, demonstrating that the standard consistency effect on low-frequency words (longer naming latencies for words with inconsistent spelling-to-sound mappings such as PINT relative to words with consistent mappings such as MILL) is attenuated for words that are highly imageable/concrete. Importantly, this interaction reveals that semantics can facilitate the processes associated with orthographic-to-phonological mapping in word recognition.

Using fMRI, we sought to identify the neurobiological correlates of this phenomenon (Frost et al., 2005). A go/no-go naming paradigm was employed in an event-related fMRI protocol with word stimuli representing the crossing of frequency, imageability, and spelling-to-sound consistency. Higher activation for high-imageable words was found in middle temporal and posterior parietal sites. In contrast, higher activation for inconsistent relative to consistent words was found in the IFG, replicating findings by Fiez et al. (1999) and Herbster et al. (1997). Critically, analyses revealed that imageability was associated with reduced consistency-related activation in IFG but increased posterior parietal activation; this appears to be the principal neural signature of the behavioral trade-off between semantics and phonology revealed by Strain and colleagues. This finiding serves to highlight the need to better understand the interactions among regions that support component processes in word recognition.

Adaptive Learning Previous studies have demonstrated that both increased familiarity with specific words and increased reading skill are associated with a shift in the relative activation of the cortical systems involved in reading, from predominantly dorsal to predominantly ventral. In another line of research, we are carrying out functional neuroimaging experiments in order to provide a more precise character-ization of the means by which practice with unfamiliar words results in this shift, and to gain insights into how these systems learn to read new words. In one study from our group (Katz et al., 2005) we found evidence for this shift as skilled read-ers acquired familiarity for words via repetition. We examined repetition effects (comparing activation for thrice repeated tokens relative to unrepeated words) in both lexical decision and overt naming. Across tasks, repetition was associated with reduced response latencies and errors. Many sites, including IFG, SMG, supplemen-tary motor area, and cerebellum, showed reduced activation for highly practiced tokens. Critically, a dissociation was observed within the ventral system: the OT skill zone showed practice-related reduction (like the SMG and IFG sites), whereas more anterior ventral sites, particularly MTG, were stable or even showed increased acti-vation with repetition. Thus, we concluded that a neural signature of increased effi-ciency in word recognition is more efficient processing in dorsal, anterior, and posterior ventral sites, with stable or increased activation in more anterior middle and inferior temporal sites.

A second experiment (Sandak et al., 2004) examined whether the type of pro-cessing engaged in when learning a new word mediates how well that word is learned, and the cortical regions engaged when that word is subsequently read. We suspected that repetition alone is not sufficient to optimize learning; rather, we hypothesized that the quality of the lexical representations established when new words are learned is affected by the type of processing engaged in during learning. Specifically, we predicted that, relative to attending to the orthographic features of novel words, learning conditions that stress phonological or semantic analysis would speed naming and, in turn, cortical activation patterns similar to those char-acteristic of increased familiarity with words (as seen in Katz et al., in press). Prior to MRI scanning, participants completed a behavioral session in which they acquired familiarity for three sets of pronounceable pseudowords while making orthographic (consonant/vowel pattern), phonological (rhyme) or semantic (cate-gory) judgments. Note that in the semantic condition, participants learned a novel semantic association for each pseudoword. Following training, participants com-pleted an event-related fMRI session in which they overtly named trained pseudo-words, untrained pseudowords, and real words.

As predicted, we found that the type of processing (orthographic, phonological, or semantic) engaged in when learning a new word influences both how well that word is learned, and the cortical regions engaged when that word is subsequently read. Behaviorally, phonological and semantic training resulted in speeded naming times relative to orthographic training. Of the three training conditions, we found that only phonological training was associated with both facilitated naming and the pattern of cortical activations previously implicated as characteristic of increased efficiency for word recognition (Katz et al., 2005). We suggest that for phonologically trained items, learning was facilitated by engaging in phonological processing during training; this in turn resulted in efficient phonological processing (instantiated cortically as relatively reduced activation in IFG and SMG) and efficient retrieval of pre-semantic lexical representations during subsequent naming (instantiated cortically as relatively reduced activation in the OT skill zone). Semantic training also facilitated naming but was associated with increased activation in areas previously implicated in semantic processing, suggesting that the establishment and retrieval of semantic representations compensated for less efficient phonological processing for these items.

IMPLICATIONS OF RECENT FINDINGS

We had initially speculated that the temporoparietal and anterior systems are critical in learning to integrate orthographic, phonological, and semantic features of words whereas the ventral system develops, as a consequence of adequate learning during reading acquisition, to support fluent word identification in normally developing, but not RD, individuals (Pugh et al., 2000a). Our recent experiments examining phonological priming, phonological/semantic tradeoffs, and critical factors associated with adaptive learning in reading have yielded findings that require us to refine our initial taxonomy. These data allow for the development of a more fine-grained picture of the functional neuroanatomy and sub-specializations within these systems, illustrated in Figure 17.1. Across these studies identical sets of voxels in the SMG (within the temporoparietal system), IFG (within the anterior system) and the OT skill zone (within the ventral system) showed (1) increased activation for pseudowords relative to words, (2) strong phonological priming effects, and (3) repetition-related reductions that were most salient in the phonologically-analytic training condition. This pattern strongly suggests a phonological "tuning" in these sub-regions. (It is particularly noteworthy that the developmentally critical OT skill zone – the putative VWFA – by these data, appears to be phonologically tuned. It makes good sense that this region should be so structured given the failure to develop this system in reading disability when phonological deficits are one of the core features of this population). By contrast, the angular gyrus (within the temporoparietal system) and the middle/inferior temporal gyri (within the ventral system) appear to have more abstract lexico-semantic functions across our studies (see Price et al., 1997 for similar claims).

From these findings, we speculate that sub-regions within SMG and IFG operate in a yoked fashion to bind orthographic and phonological features of words during learning; these systems also operate in conjunction with the AG where these features are further yoked to semantic knowledge systems distributed across several cortical regions. Adequate binding, specifically adequate orthographic/phonological integration, enables the development of the pre-semantic OT skill zone into a functional pattern identification system. As words become better learned, this area becomes capable of efficiently activating lexico-semantic subsystems in MTG/ITG, enabling the development of a rapid ventral word identification system. RD individuals, with demonstrable anomalies in temporoparietal function (and associated difficulties

Components of the Reading System

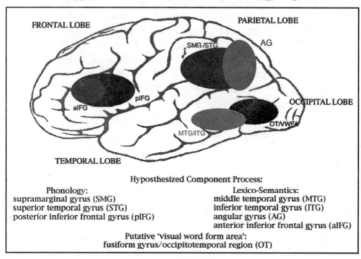

FIGURE 17.1   Components of the Reading System.

with phonologically analytic processing on behavioral tests), fail to adequately "train" ventral subsystems (particularly the OT skill zone) and thus develop compensatory responses in frontal and RH systems.

FUTURE DIRECTIONS

In recent years, significant progress has been made in the study of reading and reading disability with the use of functional neuroimaging techniques. A good deal is now known about the distributed neural circuitry for reading in skilled adult readers, the developmental trajectory toward this mature reading circuitry in normally developing children, deviations from this trajectory in reading disability, and the ways in which intensive training for struggling younger readers alters brain organization for reading. Further advancement in developing an adequate theory of the neurobiology of reading demands considerable progress in a number of domains.

One such domain is the area of functional connectivity. Studies of reading employing functional connectivity analyses of reading and reading disability have been promising (Horwitz et al., 1998; Pugh et al., 2000; Shaywitz et al., 2002). However, this approach has largely been limited to assessments of with task/across-subject connectivity; extending the approach to assessments of within-subject connectivity is still in its early stages of development. Moreover, studies using both hemodynamic and electrophysiological data to isolate correlated activation can be combined with emerging findings from diffusion weighted tensor imaging (DTI), which reveals axonal tracts connecting distributed neural subsystems across cortex.

Indeed, a recent study using diffusion-weighted imaging analysis has documented structural anomalies in white matter tracts within the LH temporoparietal region suggesting a possible neural basis for the often seen functional anomalies in disabled readers (Klingberg et al., 2000). In addition, new developments in spectroscopic imaging techniques can support more careful analyses of the basic neurochemistry of regions targeted by functional studies to investigate the etiology of abnormal development.

More deeply, while neurobiological studies of word recognition, particularly those identifying neurobiological signatures of reading disability, have generated a good deal of enthusiasm, it should be remembered that functional neuroimaging measures are not intrinsically explanatory; they simply describe brain organization at a given point in development. Links between multiple indices of reading (dis)ability, including genetic risk/protective factors, brain structure and function, and cognitive deficits promise to constitute the core scientific foundation for our understanding of neurodevelopmental disorders in the coming years; to progress from descriptive neurobiological findings to potentially explanatory models. By establishing meaningful links between behavioral/cognitive skills that must be in place to read and neuroanatomical, neurochemical, and genetic measures, projects aimed at developing an explanatory account of neurocognitive divergences in typically developing and RD children (Grigorenko 2001; Pugh et al., 2000a). That is, we believe that designs of this type will allow specifications of the biological *pathways* predisposing for risk for the development of RD and explorations of elements of these pathways that might be most suitable for pharmacological and behavioral intervention.

The neuroimaging studies of reading interventions to date indicate that the signature of successful intervention in at-risk children is an increased response in critical LH posterior regions (Shaywitz et al., 2004; Simos et al., 2002; Temple et al., 2003). Each of these studies has utilized training programs that emphasize phonological awareness training to differing degrees. However, several pressing questions remain. First, will similar remediation effects be obtained for older populations with persistent reading difficulties? Moreover, are there specific etiological factors that distinguish children who demonstrate only minimal gains with treatment from responders? If so, might alternative instructional approaches be more effective for these children? These are complex issues and demand large-scale studies that compare and contrast various interventions and examine interactions with individual difference (Simos, et al., this volume) or subtype dimensions (Piasta & Wagner, this volume). Such contrastive research will greatly extend the utility of developmental research of the neurobiology of word recognition.

In addition, there is a real need to find better markers of abnormal trajectories in very young (pre-school age) children, as well as to develop appropriate early interventions. Whereas it is known that the development of phonemic awareness is strongly and causally related to the development of reading skill (e.g., Bradley & Bryant, 1985; Wagner & Torgesen, 1987), little is known about the cognitive primitives underlying the development of phonemic awareness. Some researchers have suggested that deficits in phonemic awareness in reading impaired children may arise from a more basic deficit in speech perception (e.g., Mody et al., 1997) or auditory temporal processing (e.g., Tallal, 1980). Future behavioral and neuroimaging work needs to continue to examine the development of phonological awareness and reading in order to understand the etiology of reading disabilities at multiple levels of analysis.

Finally, much behavioral research supports the notion that word recognition engages common processes across languages and orthographies; however, at present there is much less cross-linguistic neuroimaging research on reading development, disability, and the effects of intervention. Although the initial evidence has provided support for a common neurobiological signature of both skilled and impaired reading, some differences have been observed (Siok et al., 2004). Given the significant variability in orthographic form, orthographic-to-phonological mappings, methods of reading instruction, and manifestations of reading disability across languages and cultures, more work needs to be done in the area of cross-linguistic studies of reading, both in order to identify the neurobiological universals of reading and to understand how the functional organization of reading varies with language-specific features. Additionally, few cross-linguistic studies of literacy acquisition have employed well-matched longitudinal designs and samples, and none have as yet included integrated neurobiological and behavioral measures. As a result, it has been difficult to identify universal versus language-specific aspects of skill acquisition by typically developing children and those with RD; such knowledge is crucial to a full theoretical and practical account of reading acquisition and disability. Cross-linguistic neurocognitive research has the potential we think, to enhance significantly our current understanding of universal influences on learning to read.

ACKNOWLEDGMENTS

We lost our friend and colleague, Rebecca Sandak, during the writing of this chapter. Her contributions to this research and to our lives will be felt for many years. This research was funded by NICHD grants F32-HD42391 to Rebecca Sandak, R01-HD40411 to Kenneth R. Pugh, and P01-HD01994 to Haskins Laboratories.

Portions of this chapter have appeared in: Pugh et al. (2006). Neurobiological Studies of Skilled and Impaired Reading: A Work in Progress. In G. R. Rosen (ed.), *The dyslexic brain: New pathways in neuroscience discovery.* (pp. 21–47). Mahwah, NJ: Lawrence Erlbaum; Sandak et al. (2004). The Neurobiological Basis of Skilled and Impaired Reading: Recent Findings and New Directions. *Scientific Studies of Reading. 8,* 273–292.

REFERENCES

Ball, E. W., & Blachman, B. A. (1991). Does phoneme awareness training in kindergarten make a difference in early word recognition and developmental spelling? *Reading Research Quarterly* 26:49–66.

Black, S. E., & Behrmann, M. (1994). Localization in alexia. In *Localization and neuroimaging in neuropsychology*, ed. A. Kertesz. New York: Academic Press.

Booth, J. R., Burman, D. D., Van Santen, F. W., Harasaki, Y., Gitelman, D. R., Parrish, T. B., & Mesulam, M. M. (2001). The development of specialized brain systems in reading and oral-language. *Neuropsychol Dev Cogn Sect C Child Neuropsychol* 7 (3):119–41.

Bradley, L., & Bryant, P. (1985). *Rhyme and reason in reading and spelling.* Ann Arbor: Univ. of Michigan Press.

Breier, J. I., Simos, P. G., Zouridakis, G., & Papanicolaou, A. C. (1999). Temporal course of regional brain activation associated with phonological decoding. *Journal of Clinical an Experimental Neuropsychology* 21:465–476.

Bruck, M. (1992). Persistence of dyslexics' phonological deficits. *Developmental Psychology* 28: 874–886.

Brunswick, N., McCrory, E., Price C., Frith, C. D., & Frith, U. (1999). Explicit and implicit processing of words and pseudowords by adult developmental dyslexics: A search for Wernicke's Wortschatz. *Brain* 122:1901–1917.

Chee, M.W.L., O'Craven, K.M., Bergida, R., Rosen, B.R., Savoy, R.L., 1999. Auditory and visual word processing studied with fMRI. *Hum. Brain Mapp.* 7, 15–28.

Coltheart, M. (1978). Lexical access in simple reading tasks. In G. Underwood (Ed.), *Strategies of information processing* (pp. 151–216). London: Academic Press.

Coltheart, M., Rastle, K., Perry, C., Langdon, R., & Ziegler, J. (2001). DRC: A dual route cascaded model of visual word recognition and reading aloud. *Psychological Review, 108,* 204–256.

Cohen, L., Lehericy, S., Chochon, F., Lemer, C., Rivaud, S., and Dehaene, S. (2002). Language-specific tuning of visual cortex? Functional properties of the Visual Word Form Area. *Brain* 125:1054–69.

Cornelissen, P. L. & Hansen, P. C. (1998). Motion detection, letter position encoding, and single word reading. *Annals of Dyslexia* 48:155–188.

Dale, A. M., Liu, A. K., Fiscal, B. R., Buckner, R. L., Belliveau, J. W., Lewine, J. D., & Halgren, E. (2000). Dynamic Statistical Parametric Mapping: Combining fMRI and MEG for high-resolution imaging of cortical activity. *Neuron* 26:55–67.

Eden, G. F., & Zeffiro, T. A. (1998). Neural systems affected in developmental dyslexia revealed by functional neuroimaging. *Neuron* 21:279–82.

Elbro, C., Neilsen, I., & Petersen, D.K. (1994). Dyslexia in adults: Evidence for deficits in non-word reading and in the phonological representation of lexical items. *Annals of Dyslexia, 44,* 205–226.

Elbro, C., Borstrom, I., & Petersen, D. K. (1998). Predicting dyslexia from kindergarten: The importance of distinctness of phonological representations of lexical items. *Reading Research Quarterly, 33 (1),* 36–60.

Fiebach, C. J., Friederici, A. D., Mueller, K., & von Cramon, D. Y. (2002). fMRI evidence for dual routes to the mental lexicon in visual word recognition. *Journal of Cognitive Neuroscience* 14: 11–23.

Fiez, J. A., Balota, D. A., Raichle, M. E., & Petersen, S. E. (1999). Effects of lexicality, frequency, and spelling-to-sound consistency on the functional anatomy of reading. *Neuron* 24: 205–218.

Fiez, J. A., & Peterson, S. E. (1998). Neuroimaging studies of word reading. *Proceedings of the National Academy Sciences* 95: 914–921.

Filipek P. A. (1995). Neurobiologic correlates of developmental dyslexia: How do dyslexics brains' differ from that of normal readers? *Journal of Child Neurology,* (Suppl. 1): S62–69.

Fletcher, J., Shaywitz, S. E., Shankweiler, D. P., Katz, L., Liberman, I. Y., Stuebing, K. K., Francis, D. J., Fowler, A. E., & Shaywitz, B. A. (1994). Cognitive profiles of reading disability: Comparisons of discrepancy and low achievement definitions. *Journal of Educational Psychology* 86:6–23.

Foorman, B. R., Francis, D., Fletcher, J. K., Schatschneider, C. & Mehta, P. (1998). The role of instruction in learning to reading: preventing reading failure in at-risk children. *Journal of Educational Psychology* 90:37–55.

Friston, K. (1994). Functional and effective connectivity: A synthesis. *Human Brain Mapping* 2:56–78.

Frost, R. (1998). Toward a strong phonological theory of visual word recognition: True issues and false trails. *Psychological Bulletin* 123:71–99.

Frost, S. J., Mencl, W. E., Sandak, R., Moore, D. L., Rueckl, J., Katz, L., Fulbright, R. K., & Pugh, K. R. (2005). An fMRI study of the trade-off between semantics and phonology in reading aloud. *Neuroreport, 16*, 621–624.

Galaburda A .M. (1992). Neurology of developmental dyslexia. *Current Opinion in Neurology and Neurosurgery* 5(1):71–76.

Goswami, U. (2000). Phonological representations, reading development and dyslexia: Towards a cross-linguistic theoretical framework. *Dyslexia, 6,* 133–151.

Grady, C. L., McIntosh, A. R., Beig, S., & Craik, F. I. (2001). An examination of the effects of stimulus type, encoding task, and functional connectivity on the role of right prefrontal cortex in recognition memory. *Neuroimage* 14: 556–71.

Grigorenko, E. L., Wood, F. B., Meyer, M. S., Hart, L. A., Speed, W. C., Shuster, A., & Pauls, D. L. (1997). Susceptibility loci for distinct components of developmental dyslexia on chromosomes 6 and 15. *American Journal of Human Genetics* 60: 27–39.

Grigorenko, E. L. (2001). Developmental Dyslexia: An update on genes, brain, and environments. *Journal of Child Psychology and Psychiatry* 42: 91–125.

Hampson, M., Peterson, B. S., Skudlarski, P., Gatenby, J. C., & Gore, J. C. (2002). Detection of functional connectivity using temporal correlations in MR images. *Human Brain Mapping* 15: 247-262.

Harm, M. W., & Seidenberg, M. S. (1999). Computing the meanings of words in reading: Cooperative division of labor between visual and phonological processes. *Psychological Review 106*, 491-528.

Herbster, A., Mintun, M., Nebes, R., & Becker, J. (1997). Regional cerebral blood flow during word and nonword reading. *Human Brain Mapping* 5: 84–92.

Horwitz, B., Rumsey, J. M., & Donohue, B. C. (1998). Functional connectivity of the angular gyrus in normal reading and dyslexia. *Proceedings of the National Academy Sciences, 95,* 8939–8944.

Katz, L., Lee, C. H., Tabor, W., Frost, S. J., Mencl, W. E., Sandak, R., Rueckl, J. G., & Pugh, K. R. (2005). Behavioral and neurobiological effects of printed word repetition in lexical decision and naming. *Neuropsychologia. 43*, 2068–2083.

Keller, T. A., Carpenter, P. A., & Just, M. A. (2001). The neural bases of sentence comprehension: An fMRI examination of syntactic and lexical processing. *Cerebral Cortex* 11:223–237.

Klingberg, T., Hedehus, M., Temple, E., Salz, T., Gabrieli, J. D., Moseley, M. E., & Poldrack, R. A. (2000). Microstructure of temporo-parietal white matter as a basis for reading ability: evidence from diffusion tensor magnetic resonance imaging. *Neuron* 25:493–500.

Kuo, W. J., Yeh, T. C., Lee, C. Y., Wu, Y. T., Chou, C. C., Ho, L. T., Hung, D. L., Tzeng, O. J. L., & Hsieh, J. C., (2003). Frequency effects of Chinese character processing in the brain: an event-related fMRI study. *NeuroImage 18*, 720–730.

Kuo, W. -J., Yeh, T. -C., Lee, J. -R., Chen, L. -F., Lee, P. -L., Chen, S. -S., Ho, L. -T., Hung, D. L., Tzeng, O. J .-L., & Hsieh, J. -C. (2004). Orthographic and phonological processing of Chinese characters: An fMRI study. *NeuroImage, 21*, 1721–1731.

Landerl, K., Wimmer, H., & Frith, U. (1997). The impact of orthographic consistency on dyslexia: A German-English comparison. *Cognition, 63*, 315–334

Lesch, M. F. & Pollatsek, A. (1993). Automatic access of semantic information by phonological codes in visual word recognition. *Journal of Experimental Psychology: Learning, Memory and Cognition, 19*, 285–294.

Liberman, A. M. (1992). The relation of speech to reading and writing. In *Orthography, phonology, morphology, and meaning,* eds. R. Frost and L. Katz. Amsterdam: Elsevier.

Liberman, I. Y., Shankweiler, D., Fischer, W., & Carter, B. (1974). Explicit syllable and phoneme segmentation in the young child. *Journal of Child Psychology* 18:201–212.

Lukatela, G., Frost, S. J., & Turvey, M. T. (1999). Identity priming in English is compromised by phonological ambiguity. *Journal of Experimental Psychology: Human Perception and Performance, 25,* 775–790.

Lukatela, G. & Turvey, M. T. (1994a). Visual lexical access is initially phonological: 1. Evidence from associative priming by words, homophones, and pseudohomophones. *Journal of Experimental Psychology: General, 123,* 107–128.

Lukatela, G. & Turvey, M. T. (1994b). Visual lexical access is initially phonological: 2. Evidence from phonological priming by homophones and pseudohomophones. *Journal of Experimental Psychology: General, 123,* 331–353.

Lyytinen, H. et al. (2004a). Early development of children at familial risk for dyslexia: Follow-up from birth to school age. *Dyslexia, 10,* 3, 146–178.

Lyytinen, H. et al. (2004b). The development of children at familial risk for dyslexia: Birth to school age. *Annals of Dyslexia, 54,* 185–220.

McIntosh, A. R., Bookstein, F. L., Haxby, J. V., & Grady, C. L. (1996). Spatial pattern analysis of functional brain images using partial least squares. *Neuroimage* 3:143–157.

Mencl, W. E., Frost, S. J., Sandak, R., Lee, J. R. Jenner, A. R., Mason, S., Rueckl, J. G., Katz, L., and Pugh, K. R. (2005). Effects of orthographic and phonological priming in printed word identification: An fMRI study. Under revision.

Mody, M., Studdert-Kennedy, M., & Brady, S. (1997). Speech perception deficits in poor readers: Auditory processing or phonological coding? *Journal of Experimental Child Psychology* 64:199–231.

Paap, K. R., & Noel, R. W. (1991). Dual route models of print to sound: Still a good horse race. *Psychological Research, 53,* 13–24.

Papanicolaou, A.C., Pugh, K.R., Simos, P.G., & Mencl, W.E. (2004). Functional brain imaging: An introduction to concepts and applications. In *The Voice of Evidence in Reading Research,* eds. P. McCardle and V. Chhabra. Baltimore: Paul H. Brookes Publishing Company.

Paulesu, E., Demonet, J. –F., Fazio, F., McCrory, E., Chanoine, V., Brunswick, N., Cappa, S. F., Cossu, G., Habib, M., Frith, C. D., & Frith, U. (2001). Dyslexia: Cultural diversity and biological unity. *Science* 291:2165–2167.

Pennington, B. F., Gilger, J. W., Pauls, D., Smith, S. A., Smith, S. D., & DeFries, J. C. (1991). Evidence for major gene transmission of developmental dyslexia. *Journal of the American Medical Association* 266:1527–1534.

Perfetti, C. A. (1985). *Reading Ability.* New York: Oxford University Press.

Perfetti, C. A., & Bell, L. (1991). Phonemic activation during the first 40 ms of word identification: Evidence from backward masking and priming. *Journal of Memory & Language* 30:473–485.

Perfetti, C. A., Bell, L., & Delaney, S. (1988). Automatic phonetic activation in silent word reading: Evidence from backward masking. *Journal of Memory and Language, 27,* 59–70.

Plaut, D. C. & Booth, J. R. (2000). Individual and developmental differences in semantic priming: Empirical and computational support for a single-mechanism account of lexical processing. *Psychological Review* 107:786–823.

Plaut, D. C., McClelland, J. L., Seidenberg, M., & Patterson, K. E. (1996). Understanding normal and impaired word reading: Computational principles in quasi-regular domains. *Psychological Review, 103,* 56–115.

Poldrack, R. A., Wagner, A. D., Prull, M. W., Desmond, J. E., Glover, G. H. & Gabrieli, J. D. (1999). Functional specialization for semantic and phonological processing in the left inferior prefrontal cortex. *Neuroimage* 10:15–35.

Price, C. J., More, C. J., Humphreys, G. W., & Wise, R. J. S. (1997). Segregating semantic from phonological processes during reading. *Journal of Cognitive Neuroscience* 9:727–733.

Price, C. J., Winterburn, D., Giraud, A. L., Moore, C. J., & Noppeney, U. (2003). Cortical localization of the visual and auditory word form areas: A reconsideration of the evidence. *Brain and Language* 86:272–286.

Price, C. J., Wise, R. J. S., & Frackowiak, R. S. J. (1996). Demonstrating the implicit processing of visually presented words and pseudowords. *Cerebral Cortex* 6:62–70.

Pugh, K. R., Mencl, W. E., Jenner, A. R., Katz, L., Frost, S. J., Lee, J. R., Shaywitz, S. E., & Shaywitz, B. A. (2000a). Functional neuroimaging studies of reading and reading disability (developmental dyslexia). *Mental Retardation & Developmental Disabilities Research Reviews* 6:207–213.

Pugh, K., Mencl, E. W., Shaywitz, B. A., Shaywitz, S. E., Fulbright, R. K., Skudlarski, P., Constable, R. T., Marchione, K., Jenner A.R., Shankweiler, D. P., Katz, L., Fletcher, J., Lacadie, C., & Gore, J. C. (2000b). The angular gyrus in developmental dyslexia: Task-specific differences in functional connectivity in posterior cortex. *Psychological Science* 11:51–56.

Pugh, K. R., Shaywitz, B. A., Shaywitz, S. A., Shankweiler, D. P., Katz, L., Fletcher, J. M., Skudlarski, P., Fulbright, R. K., Constable, R. T., Bronen, R. A., Lacadie, C., & Gore, J. C. (1997). Predicting reading performance from neuroimaging profiles: The cerebral basis of phonological effects in printed word identification. *Journal of Experimental Psychology: Human Perception and Performance* 2:1–20.

Rumsey J. M., Horwitz B., Donohue B. C., Nace K. L., Maisog J. M., & Andreason P. A. (1999). Functional lesion in developmental dyslexia: left angular gyral blood flow predicts severity. *Brain & Language* 70:187–204.

Rumsey, J. M., Nace, K., Donohue, B., Wise, D., Maisog, J. M., & Andreason, P. (1997). A positron emission tomographic study of impaired word recognition and phonological processing in dyslexic men. *Archives of Neurology* 54:562–573.

Salmelin R., Schnitzler A., Schmitz F., & Freund, H-J. (2000). Single word reading in developmental stutterers and fluent speakers. *Brain* 123:1184–1202.

Salmelin, R., Service, E., Kiesila, P., Uutela, K., & Salonen, O. (1996). Impaired visual word processing in dyslexia revealed with magnetoencephalography. *Annals of Neurology* 40: 157–162.

Sandak, R., Mencl, W. E., Frost, S. J., Mason, S. A., Rueckl, J. G., Katz, L., Moore, D.L., Mason, S.A., Fulbright, R., Constable, R. T., & Pugh, K. R. (2004). The neurobiology of adaptive learning in reading: A contrast of different training conditions. *Cognitive Affective and Behavioral Neuroscience* 4:67–88.

Sarkari, S., Simos, P. G., Fletcher, J. M., Castillo, E. M., Breier, J. I., & Papanicolaou, A. C. (2002). The emergence and treatment of developmental reading disability: Contributions of functional brain imaging. *Seminars in Pediatric Neurology* 9:227–236.

Scarborough, H., & Dobrich, W. (1990). Development of children with early language delay. *Journal of Speech and Hearing Research* 33:70–83.

Seidenberg, M. S., & McClelland, J. L. (1989). A distributed, developmental model of visual word recognition. *Psychological Review,* 96, 523–568.

Shankweiler, D., Crain, S., Katz, L., Fowler, A. E., Liberman, A. M., Brady, S. A., Thornton, R., Lundquist, E., Dreyer, L., Fletcher, J. M., Stuebing, K. K., Shaywitz, S. E., & Shaywitz, B. A. (1995). Cognitive profiles of reading-disabled children: Comparison of language skills in phonology, morphology, and syntax. *Psychological Science* 6:149–156.

Shankweiler, D., Lundquist, E., Katz, L., Stuebing, K. K., Fletcher, J. M., Brady, S., Fowler, A., Dreyer, L. G., Marchione, K. E., Shaywitz, S. E., & Shaywitz, B. A. (1999). Comprehension and decoding: Patterns of association in children with reading difficulties. *Scientific Studies of Reading* 3:69–94.

Shaywitz, B. A., Shaywitz, S. E., Blachman, B. A., Pugh, K. R., Fulbright, R. K., Skudlarski, P., Mencl, W. E., Constable, R.T., Holahan, J. M., Marchione, K. E., Fletcher, J. M., Lyon, G. R., & Gore, J.C. (2004). Development of left occipitotemporal systems for skiled reading in children after a phonologically-based intervention. *Biological Psychiatry, 55,* 926–933.

Shaywitz, S. E., Shaywitz, B. A., Fulbright, R. K., Skudlarski, P., Mencl, W. E., Constable, R. T., Pugh, K. R., Holahan, J. M., Marchione, K. E., Fletcher, J. M., Lyon, G. R., & Gore, J. C. (2002). Disruption of posterior brain systems for reading in children with developmental dyslexia. *Biological Psychiatry* 52:101–110.

Shaywitz, S. E., Shaywitz, B. A., Fulbright, R. K., Skudlarski, P., Mencl, W. E., Constable, R. T., Pugh, K. R., Holahan, J. M., Marchione, K. E., Fletcher, J.M., Lyon, G. R., & Gore, J. C. (2003a). Neural systems for compensation and persistence: young adult outcome of child-hood reading disability. *Biological Psychiatry* 54:25–33.

Shaywitz, S. E., Shaywitz, B. A., Pugh, K. R., Fulbright, R. K., Constable, R. T., Mencl, W. E., Shankweiler, D. P., Liberman, A. M., Skudlarski, P., Fletcher, J. M., Katz, L., Marchione, K. E., Lacadie, C., Gatenby, C., & Gore, J. C. (1998). Functional disruption in the organiza-tion of the brain for reading in dyslexia. *Proceedings of the National Academy of Sciences* 95:2636–2641.

Simos, P. G., Breier, J. I., Fletcher, J. M., Foorman, B. R., Castillo, E. M., & Papanicolaou, A. C. (2002). Brain mechanisms for reading words and pseudowords: an integrated approach. *Cerebral Cortex* 12:297–305.

Simos, P. G., Breier, J. I., Fletcher, J. M., Foorman, B. R., Mouzaki, A., & Papanicolaou, A. C. (2001). Age-related changes in regional brain activation during phonological decoding and printed word recognition. *Developmental Neuropsychology* 19:191–210.

Simos, P. G., Breier, J. I., Wheless, J. W., Maggio, W. W., Fletcher, J. M., Castillo, E., & Papanicolaou, A. C. (2000). Brain mechanisms for reading: The role of the superior tempo-ral gyrus in word and pseudoword naming. *Neuroreport* 11:2443–2447.

Simos, P. G., Fletcher, J. M., Bergman, E., Breier, J. I., Foorman, B. R., Castillo, E. M., Davis, R. N., Fitzgerald, M., & Papanicolaou, A. C. (2002). Dyslexia-specific brain activation profile becomes normal following successful remedial training. *Neurology* 58:1203–1213.

Stanovich, K. E. & Siegel, L. S. (1994). Phenotypic performance profile of children with read-ing disabilities: A regression-based test of the phonological-core variable-difference model. *Journal of Educational Psychology* 86:24–53.

Strain, E., Patterson, K., & Seidenberg, M. S. (1995). Semantic effects in single-word naming. *Journal of Experimental Psychology: Learning, Memory, and Cognition* 21:1140–1154.

Tagamets, M. A., Novick, J. M., Chalmers, M. L. & Friedman, R. B. (2000). A parametric approach of orthographic processing in the brain: an fMRI study. *Journal of Cognitive Neuroscience* 1:281–297.

Tallal, P. (1980). Auditory temporal perception, phonics, and reading disabilities in children. *Brain & Language* 9:182–198.

Tan, LH, Liu, H-L, Perfetti, CA, Spinks, JA, Fox, PT, Gao, J-H (2001). The neural system under-lying Chinese logograph reading. *NeuroImage, 13,* 836–846.

Tan, L. H., Spinks, J. A., Gao, J. H., Liu, H. L., Perfetti, C. A., Xiong, J., Stofer, K. A., Pu, Y., Liu, Y., Fox, P. T. 2000. Brain activation in the processing of Chinese characters and words: A functional MRI study. *Human Brain Mapping* 10:16–27.

Tarkiainen, A., Cornelissen, P. L., & Salmelin, R. (2003). Dynamics of visual feature analysis and object-level processing in face versus letter-string perception. *Brain* 125:1125–1136.

Temple, E., Deutsch, G. K., Poldrack, R. A., Miller, S. L., Tallal, P., Merzenich, M. M., & Gabrieli, J. D. E. (2003). Neural deficits in children with dyslexia ameliorated by behavioral remediation: Evidence from functional MRI. *Proceedings of the National Academy of Sciences* 100:2860–2865.

Temple, E., Poldrack, R. A., Salidis, J., Deutsch, G. K., Tallal, P., Merzenich, M. M. & Gabrieli, J. D. (2001). Disrupted neural responses to phonological and orthographic processing in dyslexic children: an fMRI study. *NeuroReport* 12:299–307.

Torgesen, J. K., Morgan, S. T., & Davis, C. (1992). Effects of two types of phonological awareness training on word learning in kindergarten children. *Journal of Educational Psychology* 84:364–370.

Turkeltaub, P. E., Gareau, L., Flowers, D. L., Zeffiro, T. A., & Eden, G. F. (2003). Development of neural mechanisms for reading. *Nature Neuroscience* 6:767–73.

Van Orden, G. C. (1987). A ROWS is a ROSE: Spelling, sound, and reading. *Memory and Cognition, 10,* 434–442.

Van Orden, G. C., Johnston, J. C., & Hale, B. L. (1988). Word identification in reading proceeds from the spelling to sound to meaning. *Journal of Experimental Psychology: Memory, Language and Cognition, 14,* 371–386.

Van Orden, G. C., Pennington, B. F., & Stone, G. O. (1990). Word identification in reading and the promise of subsymbolic psycholinguistics. *Psychological Review, 97,* 488–522.

Wagner, R. K. & Torgesen, J. K. (1987). The nature of phonological processing and its causal role in the acquisition of reading skills. *Psychological Bulletin* 101:192–212.

Wolf, M. & Bowers, Greig, P. (1999). The double-deficit hypothesis for the developmental dyslexias. *Journal of Educational Psychology* 91:415–438.

Xu, B., Grafman, J., Gaillard, W. D., Ishii, K., Vega-Bermudez, F., Pietrini, P., Reeves-Tyer, P., DiCamillo, P., & Theodore, W. (2001). Conjoint and extended neural networks for the computation of speech codes: The neural basis of selective impairment in reading words and pseudowords. *Cerebral Cortex* 11:267–277.

Ziegler, J. C. & Goswami, U. (2005). Reading acquisition, developmental dyslexia, and skilled reading across languages: A psycholinguistic grain size theory. *Psychological Bullitein, 131 (1),* 3–29.

Ziegler, J. C., Perry, C., Jacobs, A. M., & Braun, M. (2001). Identical words are read differently in different languages. *Psychological Science, 12,* 379–384.

Ziegler, J. C., Perry, C., Ma-Wyatt, A., Ladner, D., & Schulte-Korne, G. (2003). Developmental dyslexia in different languages: Language-specific or universal? *Journal of Experimental Child Psychology, 86,* 169–193.

CHAPTER EIGHTEEN

Nondeterminism, Pleiotropy, and Single-Word Reading: Theoretical and Practical Concerns

James S. Magnuson
University of Connecticut and Haskins Laboratories

It's daunting to be asked to write a chapter based on your lack of expertise. My primary expertise *is* in SWR – but *spoken word recognition* rather than *single word reading*. I was asked to read the chapters collected in this book, and comment from the perspective of a distinct, though closely related, field. Within this volume, rather stunning breadth and depth are represented. Consider the list:

Two chapters focus on developmental theories of literacy (Seymour) and spelling (Pollo, Treiman, & Kessler). Five chapters – two on orthographic-phonological consistency (Grainger & Ziegler; Kessler, Treiman, & Mullennix), and one each on developmental interactions between phonological and orthographic representations (Goswami), the role of semantics at the single word level (Keenan & Betjemann), and a new index of semantic richness that appears to moderate morphological effects (Feldman & Basnight-Brown) – provide landmarks for how deep and complex the questions have become in behavioral studies of single word reading. One chapter focuses on a powerful new paradigm of using artificial language materials to provide manipulations that would be virtually impossible with natural materials, and simultaneously provide a glimpse into acquisition processes (Hart & Perfetti; see also Mauer & McCandliss). Two focus on identification and remediation of dyslexia and reading disability (Piasta & Wagner; Royer & Walles). Four chapters review the remarkable progress over the past few years in mapping the brain regions and circuits that are crucial for reading (Frost, Sandak, Mencl, Landi, Moore, Della Porta,

Rueckl, Katz & Pugh; Mauer & McCandliss; Nazir & Husckauf; Simos, Billingsley-Marshall, Sarkari, & Papanicolaou). Finally, three chapters (Barr & Couto; Grigorenko; Olson) review how tantalizingly close the field is to identifying genetic and environmental influences on reading development (though Grigorenko provides some cautions about interpreting this work).

I was struck by two general themes that apply to the enterprise of studying single word reading. The first is *pleiotropy*, a theme of Grigorenko's chapter. Grigorenko introduces pleiotropy as follows: "…from the Greek *pleio*, or many, and *tropos*, manner, assumes 'multiple impact,' indicating diverse properties of a single agent, or that a single cause might have multiple outcomes." While this term is used technically to refer to effects of a single gene on multiple, possibly unrelated phenotypic characteristics, it resonates with similar notions at different levels of analysis from developmental psychology (equifinality), dynamical systems theories (coupling and emergentism), and more generally of the rampant nondeterminism, or many-to-many mappings, apparent in the information processing that underlies language understanding. The second issue is much more concrete: how to grapple empirically and theoretically with the multiple, interacting assumptions in theories of language processing.

So my chapter has two parts. In the first, I will argue that significant caution is warranted in focusing on any theorized level or stage of language processing (such as single word reading), on two bases: first, there is substantial evidence for radical interaction in language processing, and second, principles of theoretical neuroscience support the need for interaction in both processing and learning for a nondeterministic domain such as language processing. In the second part, I will argue that artificial language materials and, more importantly, computational models provide means for addressing the "material dilemma" of psycholinguistics – the ever-growing number of factors that must be controlled, which makes experimental design a truly Sisyphean task.

PART 1: PLEIOTROPY AND NONDETERMINISM

An obvious point of critique of the topic of single word reading is the focus on single words. Several chapters in this volume begin with justifications for focusing on single words. Hart and Perfetti argue that single word decoding is perhaps as close as one can come to a skill that is purely associated with reading. In contrast, there are other general cognitive traits (e.g., working memory, attention and motivation) that are argued to moderate rather than mediate broader aspects of reading, such as text comprehension. Maurer and McCandliss argue that focusing on single words makes pragmatic sense, as single word reading represents a "critical component process within reading" that can also provide a window into lower-level component processes with careful experimental designs. Olson points out that deficits in single word reading are highly correlated with deficits in reading in general, and Piasta and Wagner provide considerable support for the notion that the single word is the "nexus of … reading problem(s)" (this nexus is held to be complex, as it is the junction at which influences of auditory processing, phonology, morphology, etc., can be simultaneously observed). These "proof is in the pudding" arguments are compelling. There is no doubt that studies of single word reading have shed tremendous light on reading (indeed, studies of single word reading are arguably the source of nearly all our crucial knowledge of reading mechanisms).

In preparing to critique this focus on single words, I am reminded of a possibly apocryphal story about a prominent cognitive neuroscientist. After a conference talk about single word reading, he was asked what the impoverished, artificial tasks used in word recognition studies really have to do with reading outside the laboratory. The reply: "Nothing, unless one supposes reading involves words."

All the same, I will pursue this line of criticism. Let me reiterate that I will not challenge the usefulness of the single word level. While one might review the dangers of focusing on single words (e.g., the need for assessments of more complex reading tasks to ensure word-level findings generalize [cf. Royer & Walles, this volume, who report that word recognition can be boosted independently or even to the detriment of broader reading ability], or the fact that reading in context is demonstrably different from reading isolated words, at least for poor readers; e.g., Nicholson, 1991; see also Landi, Perfetti, Bolger, Dunlap, & Foorman, 2006), these issues are covered several times in preceding chapters. Rather, I will address two theoretical concerns for single word research. The first is that whether one considers the single word (or any other level of analysis) to be an isolable unit (a) based on theoretical principles identifying words as a discrete level of representation *or* (b) simply because it is useful pragmatically in the practice of research, the focus on a single level *functions* as a theoretical assumption and influences the types of research questions one asks. The second concern is that it may actually be the case that we can appeal to theoretical principles to assert that the single word level is discrete, or at least, not immediately subject to top-down interaction, and so can be treated as a distinct stage. I will argue that this position is untenable, based on theoretical principles that demand interaction in order to learn hierarchical representations like those involved in language processing, and based on strong evidence for early interaction in processing and learning.

First Concern: Implications of the Division of Labor in Psycholinguistics

> The second principle is that of division into species according to the natural formation, where the joint is, not breaking any part as a bad carver might. – (Plato's *Phaedrus*, 265e)

The justifications for focusing on single words offered in several chapters suggest a degree of unease with the focus on single words. There is a bit of tension on this point apparent in the chapter by Feldman and Basnight-Brown describing the impact of semantic richness in morphological characteristics, and in the arguments presented by Keenan and Betjemann against neglecting semantics and comprehension even at the single word level. Is the single word akin to a natural kind, neatly jointed and easily segmented from other aspects of language and cognition? Or is the focus a benign simplifying assumption that allows significant progress? If so, might it do so at the cost of misleading us somewhat about the larger reading and language processing systems?

Consider Marr's (1982) notion of a computational information processing theory. At the computational level of analysis, the focus is the computations performed by the system in a broad sense: what is the basic nature of the input and the output, and what general constraints can be identified in the mapping between them? Now consider a broad psycholinguistic domain, such as spoken or written language understanding. A computational theory of such a broad domain is intractable in a fairly transparent way – how do we tackle directly the problem of mapping from orthography or acoustics to message? Unsurprisingly, in the practice of psycholinguistics, we break the problem into several more tractable components. Psycholinguists working on speech perception have the job of determining how listeners achieve the mapping from the speech signal to consonants and vowels. Psycholinguists working at the level of spoken word recognition have the job of figuring out how listeners parse the phoneme stream into sound forms that provide access to the lexicon. Other psycholinguists have the jobs of figuring out how streams of word forms could be parsed into syntactic, semantic, and discourse structures.

For some researchers, these divisions correspond closely to theoretically motivated divisions of labor within the actual language processing system, in which hierarchical stages of processing provide fast, veridical perception and understanding (Norris, McQueen, & Cutler, 2000; Frazier & Fodor, 1978).

For others, the divisions are accepted as benign simplifying assumptions that have afforded progress at higher levels before all lower-level problems are solved. Proponents of highly interactive theories may find dubious the notion of discrete levels of representation and processing that correspond closely to linguistic levels of description. Rather, they might consider, for example, the assumption of phonemic input to word recognition, and even the notion of a specific mechanism that could be labeled word recognition, as useful but temporary and heuristic solutions. I will argue that it does not matter whether one adopts division of labor assumptions of convenience or principle; both reify the division of labor. That is, in spite of their obvious usefulness, division of labor assumptions are not benign fictions, but function like theoretical assumptions, constraining the sorts of research questions that are asked. To illustrate this point, consider the embedded word problem in spoken word recognition.

The division of labor assumption that we can consider a phoneme string to approximate the output of speech perception allows us to defer the perennially unsolved problems of speech perception, such as *lack of invariance* (the many-to-many mapping of acoustics to perceptual categories) and the *segmentation problem* (the lack of discrete boundaries between coarticulated phonemes). This allows research on spoken word recognition to focus on word-level problems, such as the embedding problem. McQueen, Cutler, Briscoe and Norris (1995) estimated that 84% of words in English have one or more words embedded within them (e.g., depending on dialect, *catalog* contains *cat, at, a, cattle, law* and *log*). This presents a significant theoretical challenge: how is it that all those embedded words are not recognized when we hear *catalog*? However, several recent results suggest the embedding problem is overestimated by division of labor simplifications.

While a few studies have shown that lexical access is exquisitely sensitive to fine-grained, subphonemic detail in the speech signal (Andruski, Blumstein, & Burton, 1994; Dahan, Magnuson, Tanenhaus, & Hogan, 2001; Marslen-Wilson & Warren, 1994), their focus typically has more to do with questions of how lexical competition is resolved. The larger implications were missed until quite recently. Davis, Marslen-Wilson, and Gaskell (2002) and Salverda, Dahan, and McQueen (2003) noted that vowel duration is inversely proportional to word length, such that the /ae/ in *ham* is, on average, slightly longer than that in *hamster* (by about 20 msecs at typical speaking rates; cf. Lehiste, 1972; Peterson & Lehiste, 1960; Port, 1981). Both groups found that listeners are sensitive to these subphonemic differences (Davis et al. found evidence via priming, while Salverda et al. found more direct evidence using eye tracking). This suggests the embedding problem is not so dire: goodness of fit to lexical representations is graded according to fine-grained bottom-up details of the speech signal. *Ham* and *hamster* compete, but much less than *hammer* and *hamster*, which have more similar vowels in their first syllables.

Converging evidence has been found in visual word recognition, where there is an astounding sensitivity to fine-grained *phonetic* tendencies. For example, the longer it takes to pronounce a word (e.g., the pronunciation of *plead* tends to be longer than that of *pleat* due to durational effects of voicing; Peterson & Lehiste, 1960; Port, 1981), the longer it takes to process it even in a silent reading task (Abramson & Goldginer, 1997; Lukatela, Eaton, Sabadini, & Turvey, 2004). Lukatela et al. argue that this proves not only that visual lexical access is initially phonological (Lukatela & Turvey, 1994a, 1994b), but that lexical access is organized according to reliable *phonetic* patterns.

It is noteworthy that subcategorical sensitivity had been exploited previously in service of, e.g., asking questions about lexical competition (Dahan et al., 2001; Marslen-Wilson & Warren, 1994), and the vowel duration differences described decades earlier were well-known, but the joint implications of these findings for issues like the embedding problem were not immediately apparent. This is because the simplifying assumption that *the relevant grain for thinking about the input to spoken word recognition is the phoneme* has a powerful influence on the sorts of questions one asks and the patterns of results one is prepared to discover; that is, functionally, it acts as a computational-level theoretical assumption. Specifically, division of labor assumptions reify the stage view of processing, where each step in a series of processes creates a discrete product to be passed on to the next level.

This notion of *product* calls for *bidirectional* caution. It can lead us not only to underestimate the detail of the bottom-up input still available at some mid-level of description, but also to neglect the role of top-down interaction. That is, by assuming modular organization, even temporarily, we can ironically overestimate the complexity of processing required at any hypothesized level because we neglect the possibly helpful role of top-down constraints. However, there are long-running debates in psycholinguistics between proponents of autonomous processing theories (staged processing with feedforward encapsulation, such that low-levels are protected from feedback; Frazier & Fodor, 1978; Frazier & Rayner, 1982; Norris et al., 2000) and proponents of interactive models (e.g., MacDonald, Pearlmutter, &

Seidenberg, 1994; McClelland, Mirman, & Holt, in press), as well as debates about modularity more generally. There are also well-known studies that appear to support autonomous architectures. The goal of the next section is to analyze the case against and for interaction.

Second Concern: The Need for Interaction

The preceding argument has little implication for single word reading unless there are bidirectional constraints on the single word level – that is, that there is top-down interaction. If there is not top-down interaction, context dependence at the word level would be manageable, and there would be little concern about misconstruing the problem of language understanding by focusing on the single word level. So: how can we evaluate whether there is top-down interaction?

Consider again the concepts of pleiotropy, and more generally, equifinality. When one measures the state of any component of a complex system (i.e., any system of coupled, multiple parts that interact nonlinearly) at any time scale, one cannot recover the history of the isolated component – that is, the previous set of states of this component – without referring to states of the larger system. Multiple previous states can result in a single state (equifinality), but the converse is generally true as well: multiple outcomes can follow the same initial state, at least when what is known about the initial state is limited to only a portion of the entire system. This is true at multiple scales; genetically, developmentally, and perceptually and cognitively. A familiar perceptual/cognitive example is the context dependence of the H/A ambiguity shown at the left in Figure 18.1. Perception of the figure cannot be understood at the single letter level, but instead depends on lexical context. A slightly more complex example is shown at the right in Figure 18.1 (modeled after an example used by Friston, 2003). If the sentences are presented in isolation, readers experience little ambiguity in the "Jack and Jill..." example, despite the fact that "went" has been replaced with "event." For this example, lexical and letter ambiguities are resolved at the sentence level.

These examples, by themselves, do not demonstrate on-line perceptual interaction, only that top-down and bottom-up information is integrated eventually. Whether the temporal locus of integration is "early" (perceptual) or "late" (post-perceptual) has been the subject of vigorous debate in several areas of psycholinguistics, and psychology and cognitive neuroscience more generally (e.g., Fodor, 1983), and many readers will be familiar with the logical arguments and empirical results that are typically marshaled against interaction. I will first review arguments for autonomous architectures and a pair of well-known results that are often cited in support of autonomous theories. I will provide an alternative account of the evidence, and then turn to principles of theoretical neuroscience to make a case that unsupervised learning of linguistic systems requires feedback.

Arguments Against Interaction.   There are three primary arguments made in favor of autonomous architectures. First, *interaction is inefficient*. One of the clearest versions of this argument was made by Norris et al. (2000), who argued that

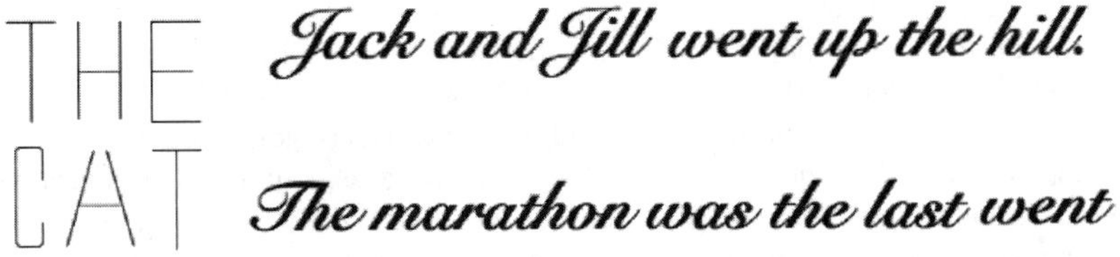

T H E   *Jack and Jill went up the hill.*

C A T   *The marathon was the last went*

FIGURE 18.1   A well-known letter ambiguity resolved at the word level (left), and a letter *and* lexical ambiguity resolved at the sentence level (right; based on an example used by Friston, 2003).

lexical-phonemic feedback could not possibly improve spoken word recognition. The logic is similar to specific principles of information theory (e.g., *law of diminishing information;* Kahre, 2002) and control theory (e.g., Ashby's [1962] *law of requisite variety*), which can be paraphrased as follows: once a signal enters a processing system, the information in the signal itself cannot be increased; at best it can remain constant. Norris et al. argue that this logic implies that a processing system with the goal of mapping, e.g., from phonemes to words, cannot improve on a direct mapping from phonemes to words. Lexical feedback might change the dynamics of processing, but it could not provide greater accuracy than a purely feedforward system, since it cannot, for example, improve the resolution of sublexical representations.

The second argument is that *interaction entails hallucination*. If interaction is permitted at low levels (i.e., perceptual levels), veridical perception by definition becomes impossible, since the information not present in the signal will be added. While one might argue that it would be possible to balance top-down and bottom-up sources of information, the typical rejoinder is that there is not a principled way to balance the two. From this perspective, attempts to quantify new sources and balances are ad-hoc and experiment-specific.

The last argument is against *radical* interaction – interaction among relatively distant representations, such as discourse and phonemes, or between modalities. The argument is that *context is infinite,* and unless interaction at low levels is prohibited or at least very tightly restricted, information processing will become intractable.

The latter two arguments are weak. Indeed, integrating top-down information will alter perception, but not randomly; as I will argue in a moment, it simply provides needed context dependence. Balancing top-down and bottom-up information is a matter of learning, for any given state of the system, the past relative reliability of sources of information. The same answer applies to the infinite context argument. We know multiple sources of information are integrated eventually (e.g., preceding context in the following sentence helps at least partially disambiguate "bank:" *John lost his money when the bank collapsed*); thus, this argument simply defers the inevitable. We must determine empirically what sorts of information are integrated and how early (potentially immediately in the previous example, but in the following case no biasing information aside from sense frequency is available except postperceptually: *when the bank collapsed, John lost his money*).

The first argument is rather more difficult. It is tempting simply to appeal to evidence of top-down effects, such as the word superiority effect (i.e., that phonemes can be detected more quickly in words than nonwords; Rubin, Turvey, & Van Gelder, 1976), or phoneme restoration (context-dependent restoration of a phoneme replaced with noise or an ambiguous sound as a function of lexical or sentential context, e.g., Warren, 1970; Samuel, 1981, 1997). Norris et al. argue most such effects are post-perceptual, and feedforward explanations are possible for others. In addition, in simulations with the TRACE model (McClelland & Elman, 1986), the premier example of an interactive activation network where lexical feedback plays an instrumental role in the system's dynamics, Frauenfelder and Peeters (1998) reported that when they turned feedback off, half the words they tested were recognized more quickly than they were with feedback on. This would seem to suggest that feedback in TRACE is simply providing a mechanism for accounting for top-down effects, but plays no functional role in the model.

However, there are two gaps in this argument. The first is noise, which is no small concern when we are talking about virtually any aspect of perception. Noise is of particular importance in the case of spoken language, given the tremendous sources of variability (phonetic context, speaking rate, talker characteristics, acoustical environment, background noise, etc.). One of the original motivations for feedback in interactive activation models was to make them robust in noise (McClelland, Rumelhart & Hinton, 1986). The second gap is context dependence. Feedback provides a basis for context-sensitive processing. In the case of lexical feedback, words provide implicit, context-sensitive prior probabilities for strings of phonemes. Consider a case where a phoneme is mispronounced, obscured by noise, or is otherwise ambiguous, with the result that the bottom-up input is slightly biased toward a nonword ("I told the poss" rather than "I told the boss"). All parties agree that eventually, top-down knowledge will resolve the ambiguity in favor of the lexical bias, but Norris et al. argue that the lexical bias should not come into play at early perceptual levels.

However, it is telling that Norris et al. are willing to accommodate any top-down knowledge that can be incorporated into feedforward connections, such as diphone transitional probabilities – their proposed solution for accommodating findings that transitional probabilities from phone A to phone B influence the processing of both (e.g., Pitt & McQueen, 1998). This appears to violate the assertion that one cannot do better than well-tuned bottom-up acoustic-phoneme and phoneme-lexical mappings, as incorporating transitional probabilities permits a small degree of context dependence. Technically, this context dependence should not be required, but it does not violate the bottom-up principle so long as the feedforward units remain sublexical and unmodulated by lexical or other top-down knowledge *during perception*. But if diphones are allowed, why not triphones, or any *n*-phone that is helpful? As it turns out, the *n*-phones required to explain the entire range of findings similar to those of Pitt and McQueen are dynamic – the length of *n* varies from context-to-context, such that the appropriate context is approximately equal to word length (Magnuson, McMurray, Tanenhaus, & Aslin, 2003). So far, no one has proposed a mechanism for instantiating dynamic contexts without appealing to feedback.

Allowing context reduces the argument from a strong position ("top-down feedback does not benefit speech recognition; it can hinder it," Norris et al., 2000, p. 299) to an assertion that context can help, but you do not need feedback to provide it; anything that can be done with feedback can be done with a purely feedforward system (and that feedforward systems are less complex than feedback systems and so should be preferred). It is well-known that for any nondeterministic system, there exists a deterministic solution (Ullman & Hopcroft, 1969; also, Minsky & Pappert, 1969, provide a related proof that for any recurrent network, there exists a feedforward network that can provide identical input-output mappings for any finite period of time).

There are three hitches, however, if one wishes to assert that a feedforward system can do anything a feedback system can. First, feedforward solutions that are equivalent to feedback solutions (e.g., feedforward networks that are behaviorally-equivalent to recurrent networks; Rumelhart, Hinton, & Williams, 1986) have to be (sometimes several times) larger, because the network must be reduplicated for every desired time step of history (violating Norris et al.'s paraphrase of Occam: "never ... multiply entities unnecessarily"). This is minor, though, compared to the second and third problems, which I will discuss in detail in the next two sections. The second problem is that while the autonomous view predicts perceptual feedback should not exist, and that it should hinder recognition if it does, there is considerable evidence for interaction. The final problem is that it is virtually impossible to learn the appropriate feedforward mapping *without supervision* (being told the correct mapping) for any system that is not "easily invertible" (Friston, 2003) – that is, for any nondeterministic many-to-many mapping from signal to percept – which we shall see is true of language.

Evidence Against Interaction?   Tanenhaus, Leiman, and Seidenberg (1979) and Swinney (1979), in very similar studies, famously demonstrated apparent evidence for staged processing of lexical access and context integration. Tanenhaus et al. presented spoken homophones (e.g., *rose*) in sentences biased towards different homophone senses (e.g., *they all rose* vs. *they all bought a rose*). The task for subjects was to name a visually presented word as quickly as possible. When visual probes were presented at the offset of the spoken homophone, priming was found for all senses (e.g., *flower* and *stand*). If the probe was delayed 200 msecs, only context-appropriate priming was found. This is consistent with staged processing, in which a word recognition system activates all form matches, and a later stage of processing selects the context-appropriate form (and this is how it is typically presented in textbooks: "Thus, context does have an effect on word meaning, but it exerts its influence only after all meanings have been briefly accessed," Goldstein, 2005, p. 356). However, the story is much more complicated.

First, even when the probe is presented at homophone offset, there is a trend towards greater priming of the context-appropriate sense. This is consistent with continuous rather than staged integration, if one assumes it takes some time for a detectable degree of integration to occur (cf. McClelland, 1987). To make this more

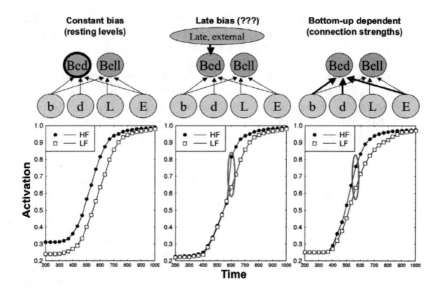

FIGURE 18.2   Schematics of three possible loci of frequency effects in spoken word recognition and predicted activation patterns.

concrete, I will use a parallel example having to do with the locus of word frequency effects. Conine, Titone, and Wang (1993) reported that frequency effects were not evident in fast responses (in a critical condition) to a lexical frequency biased stop continuum (e.g., *grass-crass*). This, among other results, led them to propose that frequency is a late-acting bias that is not an integral part of lexical representations. How else might we explain this effect?

Consider Figure 18.2, which contains schematics of three possible ways of implementing frequency in neural network models (limited for illustration to phoneme and lexical nodes). On the left, we have a constant bias, in the form of resting level bias (indicated by the bold circle around *bed*). Below the network, there is a plot comparing the resulting time course of activation for separate simulations with either *bed* (high frequency, or HF) or *bell* (LF) as the target. On this account, even if the system were forced to make a response early in the time course, there would always be a frequency effect. In the middle panels, the late-bias approach is schematized. Here, there is a constant frequency effect that kicks in at an unspecified point during processing (e.g., when lexical activations hit some threshold). If the system must respond prior to this "magical moment," no frequency effect will be observed. The oval indicates the point in time where the frequency effect can first be detected. A third possibility is shown in the right panels: making the bottom-up connection strengths proportional to frequency. The thicker lines emanating from phoneme nodes to *bed* (e.g., the thicker connection from /b/ to *bed* compared to *bell*) indicate stronger connections. Consistent with a general Hebbian learning account, these connections are proposed to be stronger because they have been used more frequently. This arrangement leads to a substantially different activation pattern compared to the other two. There is a constant frequency effect, but it is proportional to the bottom-up input, so it starts out weak, and becomes stronger. The oval in this panel indicates a hypothetical moment when the difference becomes large enough to be detected in a button-press task like that used by Connine et al. Depending on the resolution of the measurement, a weak effect can masquerade as a late effect.

Dahan, Magnuson, and Tanenhaus (2001) revisited this finding using the "visual world" eye tracking paradigm. Participants saw a display with four objects in it. On critical trials, these were a low-frequency target (e.g., *bell*), a low-frequency competitor (e.g., *bench*), a high-frequency competitor (e.g., *bed*) and an unrelated distractor (e.g., carriage). We used the interactive activation model, TRACE (McClelland & Elman, 1986), to predict the proportion of fixations to each object at a fine-grained time scale. Consistent with a connection-strength implementation of frequency, we found early, continuous effects of frequency that increased over time (analogous to the pattern in the bottom right panel of Figure 18.1, but with our more complex design).

But what about the Tanenhaus et al. (1979) and Swinney (1979) results, which suggest there is an initially encapsulated stage of form access prior to the availability of larger context? There are two further wrinkles to consider. Several studies have demonstrated that how early one detects evidence of interaction in ambiguity resolution depends on (a) the strength of any bias that may exist between possible lexical interpretations (e.g., frequency differences in *rose=flower* vs. *rose=stood*; Simpson & Burgess, 1985) and (b) the strength of the contextual bias (Duffy, Morris, & Rayner, 1988). Consistent with these general findings, Shillcock and Bard (1993) revisited the homophone issue, focusing on a single pair: *would/wood*, for which there is a very strong frequency bias for *would*, which they augmented with strong contexts (*John said he couldn't do the job but his brother would* vs. *John said he couldn't do the job with his brother's wood*). In the modal-biased condition, they found no evidence of priming for *timber* when they probed at word offset, or even if they probed prior to word offset. Similarly, Magnuson, Tanenhaus, and Aslin (2002) found no evidence for activation of adjective-noun onset competitors (analogous to *purple-purse*) given strong pragmatic and syntactic expectations for one part of speech. Thus, it is eminently plausible to attribute the 1979 results to continuous interaction that is proportional to bottom-up input, and therefore is difficult to detect early in processing.

Evidence for interaction is not limited to adjacent levels of linguistic description. Another aspect of written and spoken language where strictly staged, autonomous models have dominated is sentence processing. The Garden Path Model (Frazier & Fodor, 1978; Frazier & Rayner, 1982) provides an elegant, compact theory of human sentence parsing, in which initial syntactic structure building proceeds without consideration of the semantics of individual words nor of any larger context. Instead, the parser proposes the simplest possible structure (following a small number of clearly operationalized heuristics, such as minimal attachment and late closure), which nearly always turns out to be correct. When it is not, reanalysis is required. Proponents of the Garden Path theory claimed it was possible

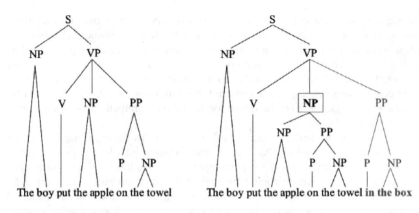

FIGURE 18.3   The simplest structure consistent with hearing *the boy put the apple on the towel* (left), and the more complex structure required to accommodate a sentence that continues ...*in the box* (the boxed NP is the additional node required to parse *the apple on the towel* as a noun phrase rather than a noun phrase and location).

to account for apparent demonstrations of strong effects of lexical semantics and context (such as those reviewed by MacDonald, Pearlmutter & Seidenberg, 1994, and Trueswell & Tanenhaus, 1994), typically by proposing that reanalysis was able to operate too quickly to be detected reliably given strong contexts.

Figure 18.3 illustrates potential syntactic structures when the sentence being heard or read is "the boy put the apple on the towel in the box." By the time you get to "towel," the simplest structure is consistent with the towel being the goal location of "put." That structure is shown on the left in Figure 18.3. When you encounter "in the box," that structure no longer works. One of multiple possibilities is shown on the right in Figure 18.3. The structures explicitly handling "in the box" are in grey. Our focus is the new NP node (shown in a box) required to make "on the towel" modify "apple" (i.e., which apple – the one on the towel) rather than specify the goal location of "put." This new structure is more complex than the one on the left, and so is initially dispreferred. On this sort of model, though, it is crucial to note that the structure on the left should always be built first given a sentence like this one, without early reference to any sort of context.

Tanenhaus, Spivey-Knowlton, Eberhard and Sedivy (1995) tested a dramatically different interactive hypothesis. They provided potentially "unhelpful" and "helpful" visual contexts for instructions like, "put the apple on the towel in the box." Schematics of example contexts are shown in Figure 18.4. In the helpful case, there are two apples, so a complex referring expression is required to disambiguate between the two; "on the towel" specifies *which* apple. In the unhelpful case, there is only one apple, which means that the instruction, with respect to the display, violates Grice's (1975) maxim of quantity (do not be overly specific): there is no need to specify the location of the apple, since "the apple" would be unambiguous. In both contexts, there is an empty towel, allowing a possible goal interpretation of

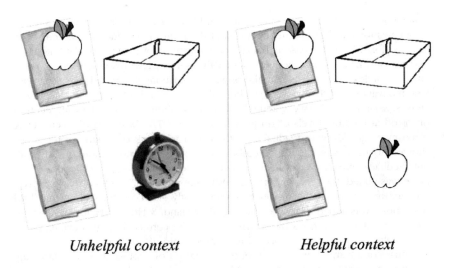

Unhelpful context   *Helpful context*

FIGURE 18.4   Schematics illustrating the helpful and unhelpful visual displays from Tanenhaus et al. (1995).

"on the towel" in either case. On the Garden Path view, there should be an initial period of linguistic processing encapsulated from the visual display, and so the visual context should not have an early impact. On a highly interactive view, linguistic processing ought to be constrained by expectations governed by potential ambiguities in the display.

Tanenhaus et al. tracked eye movements as subjects followed the spoken instructions, and found differences between the two contexts from the earliest eye movements. In the helpful context condition, upon hearing "apple" subjects were equally likely to make a saccade to either apple, and on hearing "on" they quickly settled on the correct apple. They made no looks to the empty towel, and performed the expected action quickly. In contrast, given the unhelpful context, subjects made many looks to the empty towel, and were significantly slower to perform the expected action (and in some cases, subjects actually moved the apple from one towel to the other, or even picked up the apple and towel and moved both to the box). This is an example of unequivocally non-linguistic context influencing linguistic processing as early as we can measure, and so supports radical interaction.

Later studies using this technique have shown discourse, syntax and even lexical processing are moderated by visual contexts (e.g., Chambers, Tanenhaus, Eberhard, Filip, & Carlson, 2001; Sedivy, Tanenhaus, Chambers, & Carlson, 1999), affordances of held instruments (Chambers, Tanenhaus, & Magnuson, 2004), and even momentary changes in the affordances available to an interlocutor (Hanna & Tanenhaus, 2003).

But what of the finding that feedback in TRACE does not improve processing (Frauenfelder & Peeters, 1998)? To put it simply, this result has not held up. The original simulations were conducted with a rather odd set of 21 words that were all seven phonemes long with a uniqueness point at the fourth phoneme. These items were selected for principled reasons for earlier simulations. We revisited this finding for two reasons: first, we questioned whether that set of 21 words would be represen-tative of the lexicon, and second, the original simulations did not address the impor-tant motivation for feedback of making the system robust in noise (Magnuson, Strauss, & Harris, 2005). We tested a large lexicon (about 1000 words) with feedback on or off at multiple levels of noise. Without noise, 77% of the words were recog-nized more quickly with feedback on than with feedback off (many of the others showed no advantage, though a number were recognized much more quickly with-out feedback, which we attribute to peculiarities of their neighborhoods). When noise was added, the recognition time advantage persisted, and feedback preserved accurate recognition – the model was significantly less accurate without feedback when noise was added. (See also Mirman, McClelland, & Holt, 2005, for another case where TRACE's predictions have turned out to be correct despite previous claims that feedback in TRACE was inconsistent with empirical results).

Thus, contra arguments for autonomous levels of representation in language processing, there is evidence for interaction at any level we measure as early as we can measure. Furthermore, feedback provides benefits in simulations with TRACE, speeding processing (on average) and protecting the model against noise. But Norris et al. (2000) complain in their reply to the concurrently published commen-taries on their article that no one has offered a theoretical case for the need for feed-back. I present just such an argument in the next section, by appealing to principles of theoretical neuroscience.

Interaction, Ambiguity, and Representational Learning.   In appealing to neurobiology for insight into the interaction question, we can begin by asking about the prevalence of feedback (reciprocal) connections in cortex. Not only are they plentiful, they outnumber forward connections, and span more cortical levels (Zeki & Shipp, 1988). So certainly there exist potential mechanisms for on-line inter-action in the brain. Next, we can ask whether there are any clear cases where per-ceptual processes in any domain are mediated in an on-line fashion. The answer here is "yes," from vision research, where the neural substrates are better understood than for language. For example, Rivadulla, Martinez, Varela, and Cudeiro (2002) report evidence that feedback connections modulate gain of thalamic receptive fields, Lee and Nguyen (2001) report that illusory contours activate V1 and V2 cells with timing consistent with feedback modulation, and Rao and Ballard (1999) argue that backward connections are required for a satisfactory account of dynamic con-text dependence of visual receptive fields. So there are precedents for interaction in perceptual-cognitive systems. How can we establish whether perceptual interaction underlies language processing, given that the neural basis for language remains rather sketchy? Here is where we must appeal to general learnability principles.

Again, while feedforward mappings (i.e., deterministic mappings) are possible for any nondeterministic system, the mapping cannot be learned without supervision unless it is *easily invertible*. A system that is not easily invertible is one in which forward (cause to data) and inverse (data to cause) mappings are largely distinct. Another way of putting this is that nondeterministic systems (in which there are many-to-many mappings from causes to data, or stimuli to percepts) are not easily invertible because the effects of "causes" mix nonlinearly such that one cannot unambiguously recover the source of any given "datum." To approximate an unmixing in a feedforward network, the model must be given access to context-specific prior probabilities. That is, it requires a training signal – typically the expected or correct result – which means it requires explicit access to the outcome of the mapping, rather than opportunities to discover the mapping.

For illustration, Friston (2003) uses the example of $v = u^2$. Given v, it is impossible to know the whether u is positive or negative. Such ambiguities are rampant in perception generally, and in language in particular, due to context dependence. Perceptual constancy depends upon mapping raw sensory stimulation to context-appropriate causes (e.g., attributing distinct wavelengths of light to the same color as a function of ambient illumination). In the case of speech perception, we experience phonetic constancy despite dependence on phonetic context (the same acoustic pattern signals a different consonant depending on the following vowel; Liberman, Cooper, Shankweiler, & Studdert-Kennedy, 1967), talker characteristics (two talkers' productions of different vowels may have identical formants, while their productions of the same vowel might have quite distinct formants [Peterson & Barney, 1952], and consonants are similarly talker-dependent [Dorman, Studdert-Kennedy, & Raphael, 1977]), and rate (the same acoustic pattern may be perceived as /b/ at one rate, but /w/ at another; Miller & Baer, 1983). And consider again the ambiguities in Figure 18.1, or global orthographic (*lead*), lexical (*bowl*), or sentential ambiguities (*the cop watched the spy with binoculars*). The point is that context dependency and ambiguity are *typical* of language at any level of analysis. This puts language in the domain of non-invertible mappings, and therefore, feedback is required to learn the context-dependent and ambiguous mappings required of language processing.

Friston (2003) reviews a variety of learning frameworks used in theoretical neuroscience, and compares them within an expectation maximization framework. He presents empirical Bayes as a neurobiologically plausible learning framework. This method does not require supervised learning. It does require a hierarchy of representations, however, and details of how the hierarchy itself is learned are sparse so far. We can appeal to mechanisms proposed in adaptive resonance theory (ART; e.g., Grossberg, 1986) for potential mechanisms to establish hierarchies. When a learning system is exposed to an input signal, it begins to compile recurring patterns into representational units (chunks). As patterns among chunks are discovered, compositional chunks are instantiated downstream of the smaller chunks. Empirical Bayes is a bootstrap method in which representations at level x provide estimated prior probabilities for level x-1, providing the basis for both forward and inverse models of the input, which is what is required to approximate a nondeterministic (non-invertible) mapping. Even though the representations at level x may be weak or noisy, their ability to provide additional constraint on the potential causes of the bottom-up signal is leveraged into distinct forward and inverse inferences (see

Friston, 2003, for technical details). Other frameworks have potential as well (indeed, adaptive resonance itself may be approximately equivalent), but the key point here is that feedback serves two purposes: it provides necessary information (prior probability estimates) for representational learning, and provides context-dependence for on-line processing.

Norris, McQueen, and Cutler (2003) recently reported evidence for rapid retuning of speech perception. To account for this learning without appealing to on-line feedback, they point out the logical difference between on-line feedback and what they call "feedback for learning" (e.g., the distinct step in typical connectionist models of backpropagating error). They agree feedback for learning is necessary, but deny this has any implications for their arguments against on-line feedback. They open the door to admitting evidence for on-line feedback, but only with "spandrel" status (a "spandrel" being an architectural feature that is not functionally necessary but results from combinations of necessary features, such as the spaces between joined gothic arches): on-line feedback may exist, but only because mechanisms are required for feedback for learning, and, for unknown reasons, those feedback mechanisms may operate continuously – providing useless on-line feedback as well as necessary feedback for learning. However, while spandrels in evolutionary biology typically refer to exaptions (putting the spandrel to use, such as a bird using its wings to shield its eyes, or a snail making use of its umbilicus [a groove formed incidentally in shell formation] as a brooding chamber; Gould & Lewontin, 1979), Norris et al. maintain that even if evidence of on-line feedback is found, its on-line use *logically cannot provide any benefit to language processing*.

The autonomous theory is significantly weakened by this position (cf. McClelland, Mirman, & Holt, 2006). It hedges its bets by allowing that on-line feedback may exist, but rather than offering a theoretical explanation for the large and varied number of results that support interaction reviewed in the previous section, it predicts that on-line feedback should not exist, and if it does, the theory claims it cannot serve any useful purpose and in fact should hinder speech recognition. Interactive theories explicitly predict effects of on-line feedback as well as feedback for learning, hold that feedback provides benefits (speed, accuracy, and protection against noise), and are consistent with biological evidence for the prevalence of feedback connections and their beneficial use in vision (Lee & Nguyen, 2001; Rao & Ballard, 1999; Rivadulla et al., 2002). As I have reviewed here, language falls into a class of representational learning problems that require feedback for learning (since the forward and inverse models are distinct; Friston, 2003), and for which feedback is eminently useful in on-line processing (in helping resolve nondeterminancies via context-specific prior probabilities of dynamic size).

The implication, therefore, is that a focus on any single level (such as words) must be considered provisional in two respects. First, the arguments in this section present a strong case that language is highly interactive, which limits the inferences that should be drawn when observation of the system is limited to a discrete level such as the single word. Second, as I discussed under the first concern (division of labor), the focus must be recognized as a functional theoretical assumption, capable of masking useful information available to the listener/reader because of the hypotheses it leads us to consider, as well as those it dissuades us from considering. When language is viewed developmentally, both of these concerns should be amplified, as the relative autonomy of a single level may change over development, as a function of development within the language system (cf. Seymour, this volume), as well as in other cognitive and social domains.

PART 2: THE PSYCHOLINGUIST AS SISYPHUS

Will we be able to run any psycholinguistic experiments at all in 1990? (Anne Cutler, 1981)

Every year it seems that new constraints on language processing are discovered. At the lexical level, there is a growing list of factors to be controlled that includes frequency, neighborhood, uniqueness point, word length, phonotactic probability, prosodic context – and on and on. Just when one might assume a debate is settled – e.g., that semantics influences single word naming (Strain, Patterson, & Seidenberg, 1995) – someone appeals to the growing list of lexical characteristics to find one that may provide an alternative explanation (in this case, age of acquisition; Monaghan & Ellis, 2002). Debate ensues as to the degree to which various measures can be considered independent, etc. (Strain, Patterson, & Seidenberg, 2002), and rolling a boulder up a hill for all eternity starts sounding not so bad by comparison. The ever-expanding list of factors that must be controlled led Anne Cutler to the (perhaps only somewhat) tongue-in-cheek title quoted at the beginning of this section. Two tools that can provide considerable leverage on this "material dilemma" are artificial materials and computational models.

Let's Make Stuff Up

In addition to the sheer number of lexical characteristics that have been identified, we must grapple with the fact that establishing independent influences of these factors is made very difficult because (a) subsets of them tend to be highly correlated, and (b) the degree to which they are based on strong theoretical principles varies (age of acquisition and imageability can be operationalized in a lexicon-external fashion, but metrics like neighborhood cannot, and their theoretical interpretation depends crucially on assumptions regarding lexical activation and competition). Words in natural languages do not fall into neat strata that would allow easy factorial exploration of lexical characteristics, and the facts that the characteristics tend to correlate and vary in theoretical transparency makes even regression approaches less than compelling.

Kessler, Treiman, and Mullennix (this volume) suggests a way out of this dilemma would be to train subjects on artificial linguistic materials, so as to have precise control over the materials. An additional advantage would be the fact that, in principle, individual differences in factors such as vocabulary would be somewhat mitigated. Artificial orthographies were used productively over the last few decades mainly to study acquisition processes (e.g., Byrne & Carroll, 1989; Knafle & Legenza, 1978), and this approach has been extended recently to examine neural effects of alphabeticallity and training conditions (Bitan & Karni, 2003, 2004; Bitan, Manor, Morocz, & Karni, 2005). More to the point for the 'material dilemma', this method has more recently been applied to issues of control. Two impressive uses of this approach are described in this volume in chapters by Mauer and McCandliss and Hart and Perfetti. While their results are compelling, their methods are rather daunting, as they require considerable training. For example, Mauer and McCandliss review a study by McCandliss, Posner, and Givon (1997) in which subjects were trained for 50 hours. Such a study obviously requires tremendous amounts of labor, analysis, and motivated subjects. While one can address exceedingly complex questions with this much training (and one can go quite a bit further; pairs of subjects in a study by Hudson & Eigsti [2003] spent 30 hours over 9 weeks learning 233 Farsi words and using those to communicate with each other, which allowed Hudson & Eigsti to observe analogs to Pidginization processes in the lab, as pairs developed various syntactic mechanisms), one can do quite a lot with much less training.

For example, my colleagues and I used artificial spoken materials to set up factorial comparisons of different sorts of phonological overlap, frequency, and neighborhood density (Magnuson, Tanenhaus, Aslin, & Dahan, 2003). Subjects learned 16 words that referred to novel geometric forms. After two days of training (with about 1 hour per day), performance resembled that with real words, and we were also able to track the emergence of competition dynamics as new neighborhoods of artificial words were learned.

With similar amounts of training, we were also able to address the cross-form class competition questions I discussed earlier (Magnuson et al., 2002). We wanted to test whether items like *purse* and *purple* compete when pragmatics lead to strong expectations for a noun or adjective. For example, consider Figure 18.5. In the top panel, where there are two purses and two cups (one of which is meant to be purple), if I ask you, "hand me the pur-," *purple* should be a strong pragmatic candidate at that moment, quite possibly stronger than *purse*. Given the display on the bottom, *purse* is a much better candidate than *purple*, as a simple noun is much more likely, since it would be sufficient for unambiguous reference. A crucial question regarding interaction is *when* those pragmatic influences kick in – do they constrain initial lexical activation, or do they apply post-perceptually? However, the kinds of pairs we would need, like *purple-purse*, are relatively hard to come by, and are hopelessly uncontrolled for phonological overlap, frequency, neighborhood, etc. (e.g., *tan-tambourine, dotted-dog, rough-rug*). By using an artificial lexicon where "nouns" referred to geometric shapes and "adjectives" referred to textures applied to the shapes, we had precise control over not just lexical characteristics, but also pragmatic expectations, as we determined the sets of items in the display and the regularity with which conversational norms were obeyed. We found that pragmatic constraints had immediate impact; when the display predicted adjective use, there was no competition between adjectives and nouns, and vice-versa.

Two days of training is still a lot, and impractical for many populations (such as children). We are currently exploring simplified and more engaging versions of this paradigm for use with children. However, there is a new study closer to our topic of single word reading that resolves a rather slippery debate with a design limited to one-hour, including training and testing. Trudeau (2006) re-examined the so-called

Adjective felicitous

Please hand me
the purple cup.

? Please hand me
the cup.

Adjective infelicitous (TMI)

Please hand me
the cup.

? Please hand me
the purple cup.

FIGURE 18.5   Conditions that require an adjective (or other complex referring expression) for unambiguous reference (top), versus conditions where an adjective is not required (bottom).

Strain effect (Strain et al., 1995). In the original study, an interaction of regularity and imageablity was found. This would support the "triangle" model (Harm & Seidenberg 2004; Plaut, McClelland, Seidenberg, & Patterson, 1996; Seidenberg & McClelland, 1989) over the dual route model (Coltheart, Rastle, Perry, Langdon, & Ziegler, 2001), since the former predicts an integral, low-level role for semantics in word recognition while the latter does not. Monaghan and Ellis (2002) argued that imageabiity was confounded with age of acquisition. Trudeau recognized this as a perfect opportunity for using artificial materials. He assembled a set of 60 nonwords based on real English words with irregular pronunciation (e.g., BINT and MAVE). Subjects learned high- or low-imageablity definitions for the "new" words, as well as their pronunciation. Two lists were used with different groups of subjects. Each item was trained with a regular pronunciation in one list (BINT rhymes with MINT) and irregular in the other (BINT rhymes with PINT – though note that pronunciation training was based on actual audio recordings of the pronunciations, not analogies to real words). Within the space of an hour, subjects learned the items to an 80% criterion and were given a rapid naming test. Trudeau observed an interaction of regularity and imageabiity similar to that found by Strain et al. (1995).

Caution is warranted with artificial language materials, however. The largest cause for concern is whether results with artificial materials will generalize to natural language. Frequency effects, for example, are implemented in artificial language studies by manipulating number of exposures. But it is not apparent that relatively short-term repetition frequencies are comparable to the long-term prior probabilities that underlie frequency effects with natural language materials. Another concern is that the artificial materials may interact with native language knowledge.

While there is evidence that artificial materials are largely functionally isolated from the native lexicon in typical studies (Magnuson et al., 2003, Experiment 3), the likelihood of interference will depend on tasks and the nature of the artificial materials (indeed, Ramscar [2002] exploited interaction with the native lexicon to examine past-tense inflection of novel words presented as though they were new words in English). To state these concerns broadly, effects observed under the idealized conditions of artificial language studies may not generalize back to natural language processing.

A solution is to treat artificial language studies as exercises in prototyping. With knowledge in hand of how the factors studied in an artificial language experiment interact, one can refine hypotheses of what to expect with natural language materials – and if possible, those hypotheses should be tested, rather than trusting only in the artificial language results. On the other hand, artificial language studies can be extremely helpful when results with natural materials are ambiguous or in dispute (as in Trudeau's [2006] replication of the Strain effect, i.e., the regularity by imageability interaction).

Where Are the Models?

Theories of language processing continue to grow more complex, reflecting the amazingly rich database of empirical results. Once a theory includes even a handful of interacting theoretical assumptions, the behavior of an implemented system with properties corresponding to the assumptions becomes difficult to predict, even analytically, let alone based on box-and-arrow diagrams. When a theory arrives at a fairly low level of complexity, *simulation* in an implemented model becomes the best (if not perhaps the only reliable) method of predicting the actual behavior that results from a set of theoretical assumptions. There have been several examples in spoken word recognition where quite logical inferences about what various theories or models would predict were suggested in the literature and generally accepted, only to turn out to be completely wrong when someone finally attempted to verify the predictions with an implemented model (see Magnuson, Mirman, & Harris, in press, for a review).

So it is surprising to see so little modeling work in the domain of single word reading. On the one hand, there are the familiar debates between proponents of the dual route model (Coltheart et al., 2001) and the triangle model (Harm & Seidenberg, 2004; Plaut et al., 1996; Seidenberg & McClelland, 1989), which arguably provide similar coverage for basic effects in visual word recognition, as well as for different types of dyslexia (though the mechanisms underlying the explanations are often quite dissimilar; for recent overviews, see Coltheart, 2005, and Plaut, 2005). However, the triangle model has important advantages compared to the dual route model. First, it is a learning model, which makes it amenable to testing predictions of how reading should change over time as the component skills of reading develop (Harm, McCandliss, & Seidenberg, 2003; Powell, Plaut, & Funnell, 2006), and even to testing predictions regarding the efficacy of different interventions (Harm et al., 2003). Recent work by Harm and Seidenberg (2001, 2004) has set a new standard of specificity, analyzing how cooperative and competitive elements of the model lead to efficient reading. Their 2004 paper includes an ambitious attempt to incorporate semantics into a model. Harm and Seidenberg found that the model predicts that early in training, phonological representations provided the main pathway to accessing meaning, but with expertise, the balance shifted to include more direct access from orthography (though both pathways remained instrumental).

This last finding is generally consistent with discoveries that part of the left fusiform gyrus is engaged strongly in the processing of print (Cohen et al., 2000). Three somewhat different takes on the organization of this "visual word form area" (and the areas and circuits involved in reading more generally) appear in the chapters in this volume (Frost et al.; Mauer & McCandliss; Nazir & Husckauf; Simos et al.). The behavioral and neuroimaging evidence appear to depend on expertise, tasks (including precise control and presentation of visual stimuli; Nazir & Husckauf), materials, and the transparency of subjects' native language orthography (Maurer & McCandliss). The comprehensive approaches represented in this volume present tremendous challenges for theory development. Theories must synthesize behavioral and neuroimaging studies of normal and disabled readers of various ages, reading native language or artificial language materials (and note that the VWFA may be analogous to some degree to the iconographic procedure within Seymour's theory [Seymour, this volumes). Model simulations provide partial means for bootstrapping theories from these disparate sources of data by identifying principles that govern not just visual expertise in reading, but its weight relative to phonological skill as reading develops in different populations. Models also provide a tool somewhat like artificial language material studies. One can set up idealized cases and examine what predictions emerge from the model. Then, one can observe which factors lead to significant changes in model performance as more realistic conditions and more factors are added. In particular, this approach could shed light on complex effects like the feedback consistency results described by Kessler et al. (this volume). Another case where modeling could provide true insights is in comparing the three approaches to spelling development reviewed by Pollo, Treisman, and Kessler (this volume). Pollo et al. suggest that the distinct accounts favored primarily in English-speaking countries (the phonological perspective that the child must grasp the alphabetic principle before she can master spelling) and Romance-speaking countries (the constructivist perspective, which predicts specific stages that appear not to take place in English spelling development) may be the result of distinct pressures on spelling development in the different languages. On their view, a general statistical learning account might explain both patterns as a function of language-specific features. This is an ideal question for modeling: can one model provide both developmental patterns as a function of language-specific features?

On the other hand, the range of data reported in this volume may also provide the means for distinguishing between competing models. For example, it is not clear whether current models could capture hypothesized changes in phonological and orthographic grain size as reading develops (Goswami, this volume; though one might be able to test whether an analog to grain size can be detected in hidden unit space as a connectionist model like the triangle model develops). Also, the advent of great specificity in describing brain regions and circuits, in typical and poor readers, young and old (e.g., Frost et al.) suggests this area is ripe for symbiotic model use, where models may be able to guide interpretation of neural data, and the neural data may provide the basis for pushing models from Marr's (1982) *algorithmic* level to a level somewhat closer to his *implementational* level. But for models to guide theories, or for results to test models, the models must be used.

In this volume, only one chapter makes significant reference to model predictions. Grainger and Ziegler, in their chapter on cross-code consistency, explain a series of results with reference to figures diagramming an interactive activation framework. Their explanations are compelling, and I do not doubt that actual simulations with an implemented model could come out as they predict. Indeed, their work on inter-modality neighborhood effects is truly groundbreaking (Ziegler, Muneaux, & Grainger, 2003), and their model schematics provide a convincing account of the effects. However, this falls into the domain of what Kello and Plaut (2003) call "fun-damentalist" rather than "realist" use of modeling. That is, the hypothetical model pro-vides a framework for describing a set of theoretical principles. In this case, the predictions, while complex, follow so sufficiently transparently from the model dia-grams that actual simulations may not be needed. Even if they were, though, they would provide a *fundamentalist* demonstration of the general principles of cross-code consistency. What would not be clear is whether they would hold up in a *realist* model: one with a large vocabulary, and the ability to provide broad coverage of the empir-ical findings on reading beyond cross-code consistency (and again, there is always the risk that actual simulations might diverge from the predictions).

So why is so little modeling done? One reason is that modeling is technically challenging. Even when existing models are made publicly available (e.g., the dual route model is available at: http://www.maccs.mq.edu.au/~max/DRC/), they tend to require significant computer and/or programming skill to use or modify. If model developers wish to see modeling adopted widely, one strategy would be to develop user-friendly versions, ideally with graphical user interfaces, that would make mod-eling approachable for the average researcher (cf. "jTRACE," a cross-platform, easy-to-use and modify implementation of the TRACE model [McClelland & Elman, 1986] of speech perception and spoken word recognition; Strauss, Harris, & Magnuson, in press).

CONCLUSIONS

I have addressed two distinct themes. The second was the simpler of the two: I reviewed two tools (artificial language material studies and computational models) that can be used to "prototype" experiments by setting up very clear tests of hypothe-ses. In the case of artificial language materials, the researcher has control over expe-rience with the materials to be tested, and all their properties (orthographic transparency and neighborhood, phonological neighborhood, frequency, etc.). This allows one to design studies in which dimensions hypothesized to be important (e.g., imageability and regularity; Trudeau, 2006) can be manipulated more strongly than is often possible with natural materials, and without potential interference from the numerous confounding and extraneous variables at play in typical psycholinguistic studies. Computational models can serve a similar function via idealized simulations where only the dimensions of interest vary, but also provide the means to examine how multiple theoretical assumptions will interact. Lately, models of reading have provided not just accounts of typical effects in adult reading (frequency, neighborhood, length, etc.) but also of reading development and even remediation (Harm et al., 2003; Harm & Seidenberg, 2004). I also bemoaned the absence of modeling in most work on single word reading, and advocated the development of implemented models that are easy enough to use for the average researcher.

The more complex theme was theoretical. I argued that while studies focused on single word reading have been extremely productive and provide a necessary window on many component skills of reading, as well as vital diagnostics for reading disability, caution is warranted when focusing on single words. Identifying any level of description as a discrete level of representation may overestimate the complexity of the information processing problem (by masking potentially useful bottom-up and top-down constraints) and overestimate modularity of language processing; even if one assumes discrete levels as a simplifying assumption, the questions asked and the explanations considered tend to be influenced by those assumptions. I also provided a theoretical and empirical case for the argument that language is highly interactive. The interactive nature of the language processing system implies that the focus on single words must be provisional, and the goal in developing theories of reading must be to integrate word-level theories into larger theories of comprehension.

ACKNOWLEDGMENTS

Discussions with Harlan Harris, Ted Strauss, and Dan Mirman fostered many of the ideas presented here, and Inge-Marie Eigsti's insightful comments improved this chapter considerably. Preparation of this chapter was supported by NIH grants DC005765 to James Magnuson, and HD001994 and HD40353 to Haskins Laboratories.

REFERENCES

Abramson, M., & Goldinger, S. (1997). What the reader's eye tells the mind's ear: Silent reading activates inner speech. *Perception & Psychophysics, 59*, 1059–1068.

Andruski, J. E., Blumstein, S. E. & Burton, M. (1994). The effect of subphonetic differences on lexical access. *Cognition, 52*, 163–187.

Ashby, W. R. (1962). Principles of the self-organizing system. In von Foerster, H. & G. W. Zopf, Jr. (Eds.), *Principles of Self-organization*, pp. 255–278. Pergamon Press.

Bitan, T. & Karni, A. (2003). Alphabetical knowledge from whole words training: effects of explicit instruction and implicit experience on learning script segmentation. *Cognitive Brain Research, 16*, 323–337.

Bitan, T. & Karni, A. (2004). Procedural and declarative knowledge of word recognition and letter decoding in reading an artificial script. *Cognitive Brain Research, 19*, 229–243.

Bitan, T., Manor, D., Morocz, I. A., & Karni, A. (2005). Effects of alphabeticality, practice and type of instruction on reading an artificial script: An fMRI study. *Cognitive Brain Research, 25,* 90–106.

Byrne, B., & Carroll, M. (1989). Learning artificial orthographies: Further evidence of a nonan-alytic acquisition procedure. *Memory & Cognition, 17(3),* 311–317.

Chambers, C. G., Magnuson, J. S., & Tanenhaus, M. K. (2004). Actions and affordances in syntactic ambiguity resolution. *Journal of Experimental Psychology: Learning, Memory & Cognition, 30,* 687–696.

Chambers, C.G., Tanenhaus, M.K., Eberhard, K.M., Filip, H., & Carlson, G.N. (2001). Circumscribing referential domains in real-time language comprehension. *Journal of Memory and Language. 47,* 30–49.

Cohen, L., Dehaene, S., Naccache, L., Lehericy, S., Dehaene-Lambertz, G., Henaff, M. (2000) The visual word form area: Spatial and temporal characterization of an initial stage of reading in normal subjects and posterior split-brain patients. *Brain, 123,* 291–307.

Coltheart, M. (2005). Modeling reading: The dual-route approach. In M. J. Snowling & C. Hulme (Eds.), *The Science of Reading: A Handbook,* pp. 6–23. Oxford: Blackwell.

Coltheart, M., Rastle, K., Perry, C., Langdon, R. & Ziegler, J. (2001). DRC: A Dual Route Cascaded model of visual word recognition and reading aloud. *Psychological Review, 108,* 204–256.

Connine, C. M., Titone, D., & Wang, J. (1993). Auditory word recognition: Extrinsic and intrinsic effects of word frequency. *Journal of Experimental Psychology: Learning Memory and Cognition, 19(1),* 81–94.

Cutler, A. (1981). Making up materials is a confounded nuisance: or, Will we be able to run any psycholinguistic experiments at all in 1990? *Cognition, 10,* 65–70.

Dahan, D., Magnuson, J. S., and Tanenhaus, M. K. (2001). Time course of frequency effects in spoken-word recognition: Evidence from eye movements. *Cognitive Psychology, 42,* 317–367.

Dahan, D., Magnuson, J. S., Tanenhaus, M. K., and Hogan, E. M. (2001). Tracking the time course of subcategorical mismatches: Evidence for lexical competition. *Language and Cognitive Processes, 16 (5/6),* 507–534.

Davis, M. H., Marslen-Wilson, W. D. & Gaskell. M. G. (2002). Leading up the lexical garden-path: segmentation and ambiguity in spoken word recognition. *Journal of Experimental Psychology: Human Perception and Performance, 28,* 218–244.

Dorman, M. F., Studdert-Kennedy, M., & Raphael, L. J. (1977). Stop consonant recognition: Release bursts and formant transitions as functionally equivalent, context-dependent cues. *Perception & Psychophysics, 22,* 109–122.

Duffy, S. A., Morris, R. K., Rayner, K. (1988). Lexical ambiguity and fixation times in reading. *Journal of Memory and Language, 27,* 429–446.

Fodor, J. (1983). *The Modularity of Mind.* Cambridge, MA: MIT Press.

Frazier, L. & Fodor, J.D. (1978). The sausage machine: A new two-stage parsing model. *Cognition, 6,* 1–34.

Frazier, L., & Rayner, K. (1982). Making and correcting errors during sentence comprehension: Eye movements in the analysis of structurally ambiguous sentences. *Cognitive Psychology, 14,* 178–210.

Frauenfelder, U. H. & Peeters, G. (1998). Simulating the time course of spoken word recognition: an analysis of lexical competition in TRACE. In J. Grainger and A. M. Jacobs (Eds.), Localist connectionist approaches to human cognition (pp. 101–146). Mahwah, NJ: Erlbaum.

Friston, K. (2003). Learning and inference in the brain. *Neural Networks, 16,* 1325-1352.

Goldstein, E. B. (2005). *Cognitive Psychology: Connecting Mind, Research, and Everyday Experience.* Belmont, CA: Thomson Wadsworth.

Gould, S. J., & Lewontin, R. C. (1979). The spandrels of San Marco and the Panglossian paradigm: A critique of the adaptationist programme. *Proceedings of the Royal Society of London, B 205*, 581–598.

Grice, H. P. (1975). Logic and conversation. In P. Cole & J. L. Morgan (Eds.), *Syntax and Semantics, Vol. 3, Speech Acts*, pp. 41–58. New York: Academic Press.

Grossberg, S. (1986), The adaptive self-organization of serial order in behavior: Speech, language, and motor control. In: E.C. Schwab & H.C. Nusbaum (Eds.), *Pattern recognition by humans and machines, Vol. I, Speech perception*, pp. 187-294, Orlando: Academic Press, Inc.

Hanna, J.E. & Tanenhaus, M.K. (2003). Pragmatic effects on reference resolution in a collaborative task: evidence from eye movements. *Cognitive Science, 28*, 105–115.

Harm, M., McCandliss, B.D., & Seidenberg, M.S. (2003). Modeling the successes and failures of interventions for disabled readers. *Scientific Studies of Reading, 7*, 155–182.

Harm, M., & Seidenberg, M.S. (2001). Are there orthographic impairments in phonological dyslexia? *Cognitive Neuropsychology, 18*, 71–92.

Harm, M., & Seidenberg, M.S. (2004). Computing the meanings of words in reading: cooperative division of labor between visual and phonological processes. *Psychological Review, 111*, 662–720.

Hudson, C. L., & Eigsti, I. M. (2003). The Lexical Competence Hypothesis: A cognitive account of the relationship between vernacularization and grammatical expansion in creolization. *Journal of Pidgin and Creole Languages, 18(1)*, 1–79.

Kahre, J. (2002). *The Mathematical Theory of Information*. Boston: Kluwer Academic Publishers.

Kello, C. T., & Plaut, D. C. (2003). Strategic control over rate of processing in word reading: A computational investigation of the tempo-naming task. *Journal of Memory and Language, 48*, 207–232.

Knafle, J. D., & Legenza, A. (1978). External generalizability of inquiry involving artificial orthography. *American Educational Research Journal, 15(2)*, 331–347.

Landi, N., Perfetti, C. A., Bolger, D. J., Dunlap, S., & Foorman, B. R. (2006) The role of discourse context in developing word representations: A paradoxical relation between reading and learning. *Journal of Experimental Child Psychology, 94(2)*, 114–133.

Lee, T. S. & Nguyen, M. (2001). Dynamics of subjective contour formation in early visual cortex. *Proceedings of the National Academy of Sciences, 98*, 1907–1977.

Lehiste, I. (1972). The timing of utterances and linguistic boundaries. *Journal of the Acoustical Society of America, 51*, 2018–2024.

Liberman, A.M., Cooper, F. S., Shankweiler, D. P., and Studdert-Kennedy, M. (1967). Perception of the speech code. *Psychological Review, 74*, 431–461.

Lukatela, G., Eaton, T., Sabadini, L., & Turvey, M. T. (2004). Vowel duration affects visual word identification: Evidence that the mediating phonology is phonetically informed. *Journal of Experimental Psychology: Human Perception and Performance, 30*, 151–162.

Lukatela, G., & Turvey, M. T. (1994a). Visual lexical access is initially phonological: 1. Evidence from associative priming by words, homophones, and pseudohomophones. *Journal of Experimental Psychology: General, 123*, 107–128.

Lukatela, G., & Turvey, M. T. (1994b). Visual lexical access is initially phonological: 2. Evidence from phonological priming by homophones and pseudohomophones. *Journal of Experimental Psychology: General, 123*, 331–353.

MacDonald, M. C., Pearlmutter, N. J., & Seidenberg, M. S. (1994). Lexical nature of syntactic ambiguity resolution. *Psychological Review, 101(4)*, 676–703.

Magnuson, J. S., McMurray, B., Tanenhaus, M. K., and Aslin, R. N. (2003). Lexical effects on compensation for coarticulation: A tale of two systems? *Cognitive Science, 27*, 795–799.

Magnuson, J. S., Mirman, D., & Harris, H. D. (in press). Computational models of spoken word recognition. In M. Spivey, M. Joanisse, & K. McRae (Eds.), *The Cambridge Handbook of Psycholinguistics*. Cambridge University Press.

Magnuson, J. S., Strauss, T. J. & Harris, H. D. (2005). Interaction in spoken word recognition models: Feedback helps. *Proceedings of the XXVII Annual Conference of the Cognitive Science Society*, 1379–1384. Lawrence Erlbaum Associates.

Magnuson, J. S., Tanenhaus, M. K. and Aslin, R. N. (2002). Immediate integration of syntactic and referential constraints on spoken word recognition. In W. D. Gray & C. Schunn (Eds.), *Proceedings of the 24th Annual Conference of the Cognitive Science Society*, pp. 614–619. Mahway, NJ: Erlbaum.

Magnuson, J. S., Tanenhaus, M. K., Aslin, R. N., and Dahan, D. (2003). The microstructure of spoken word recognition: Studies with artificial lexicons. *Journal of Experimental Psychology: General, 132(2)*, 202–227.

Marr, D. (1982). *Vision*. San Francisco: W.H. Freeman.

Marslen-Wilson, W., & Warren, P. (1994). Levels of Perceptual Representation and Process in Lexical Access: Words Phonemes and Features. *Psychological Review, 101*, 653–675.

McCandliss, B. D., Posner, M. I., & Givon, T. (1997). Brain plasticity in learning visual words. *Cognitive Psychology, 33*, 88–110.

McClelland, J. L. (1987). The case for interactions in language processing. In M. Coltheart (Ed.), *Attention and performance XII: The psychology of reading*, pp. 3–36). Erlbaum.

McClelland, J. L., & Elman, J. L. (1986). The TRACE model of speech perception. *Cognitive Psychology, 18*, 1–86.

McClelland, J. L., Mirman, D., & Holt, L. L. (2006). Are there interactive processes in speech perception? *Trends in Cognitive Sciences, 10*(8), 363–369.

McClelland, J. L., Rumelhart, D. E. & Hinton, G. E. (1986). The appeal of parallel distributed processing. In D. E. Rumelhart, J. L. McClelland, and the PDP research group. *Parallel distributed processing: Explorations in the microstructure of cognition. Volume I* (pp. 3–44). Cambridge, MA: MIT Press.

McQueen, J.M., Cutler, A., Briscoe, T. & Norris, D. (1995). Models of continuous speech recognition and the contents of the vocabulary. *Language and Cognitive Processes, 10*, 309–331.

Miller, J. L., & Baer, T. (1983). Some effects of speaking rate on the production of /b/ and /w/. *Journal of the Acoustical Society of America, 73*, 1751–1755.

Minsky, M. L. & Papert, S. A. (1969). *Perceptrons*. Cambridge: MIT Press.

Mirman, D., McClelland, J. L., & Holt, L. L. (2005). Computational and behavioral investigations of lexically induced delays in phoneme recognition. *Journal of Memory and Language, 52*, 424–443.

Monaghan, J., & Ellis, A.W. (2002). What, exactly, interacts with spelling-sound consistency in word naming? *Journal of Experimental Psychology: Learning, Memory & Cognition, 28*, 183–206.

Nicholson, T. (1991). Do children read words better in context or in lists? A classic study revisited. *Journal of Educational Psychology, 83*, 444–450.

Norris, D., McQueen, J.M. & Cutler, A. (2000). Merging information in speech recognition: Feedback is never necessary. *Behavioral and Brain Sciences, 23*, 299–325.

Norris, D., McQueen, J.M., & Cutler, A. (2003). Perceptual learning in speech. *Cognitive Psychology, 47*, 204–238.

Peterson, G. E. & Barney, H. L. (1952). Control methods used in a study of vowels. *Journal of the Acoustical Society of America, 24*, 175–184.

Peterson, G., & Lehiste, I. (1960). Durations of syllabic nuclei in English. *Journal of the Acoustical Society of America, 32*, 693–703.

Pitt, M. A., & McQueen, J. M. (1998). Is compensation for coarticulation mediated by the lexicon? *Journal of Memory and Language, 39*, 347–370.

Plaut, D. C. (2005). Connectionist approaches to reading. In M. J. Snowling & C. Hulme (Eds.), *The Science of Reading: A Handbook*, pp. 24–38. Oxford: Blackwell.

Plaut, D. C., McClelland, J. L., Seidenberg, M. S., & Patterson, K. (1996). Understanding normal and impaired word reading: Computational principles in quasi-regular domains. *Psychological Review, 103*, 56–115.

Port, R. (1981). Linguistic timing factors in combination. *Journal of the Acoustical Society of America, 69*, 262–274.

Powell, D., Plaut, D. C., and Funnell, E. (2006). Does the PMSP connectionist model of single word reading learn to read in the same way as a child? *Journal of Research in Reading, 29*, 299–250.

Rao, R. P., & Ballard, D. H. (1998). Predictive coding in the visual cortex: A functional interpretation of some extra-classical receptive field effects. *Nature Neuroscience, 2*, 79–87.

Rivadulla, C., Martinez, L. M., Varela, C.,&Cudeiro, J. (2002). Completing the corticofugal loop: A visual role for the corticogeniculate type 1 metabotropic glutamate receptor. *Journal of Neuroscience, 22*, 2956–2962.

Rubin, P., Turvey, M. T., & van Gelder, P. (1976). Initial phonemes are detected faster in spoken words than in spoken nonwords. *Perception & Psychophysics, 19*, 384–398.

Rumelhart, D. E., Hinton, G. E., & Williams, R. J. (1986). Learning internal representations by error propagation. In D. E.. Rumelhart & J. L. McClelland (Eds.), *Parallel and Distributed Processing: Exploration in the Microstructure of Cognition, Vol. 1*, pp. 318–362. MIT Press, Cambridge, Massachusetts.

Salverda, A. P., Dahan, D., & McQueen, J. M. (2003). The role of prosodic boundaries in the resolution of lexical embedding in speech comprehension. *Cognition, 90*, 51–89.

Samuel, A. G. (1981). Phonemic restoration: Insights from a new methodology. *Journal of Experimental Psychology: General, 110(4)*, 474–494.

Samuel, A. G. (1997). Lexical activation produces potent phonemic percepts. *Cognitive Psychology, 32(2)*, 97–127.

Sedivy, J.C., Tanenhaus, M.K., Chambers, C., & Carlson, G.N. (1999). Achieving incremental semantic interpretation through contextual representation. *Cognition, 71*, 109–147.

Seidenberg, M. S. and McClelland, J. L. (1989). A distributed, developmental model of word recognition and naming. *Psychological Review, 96*, 523–568.

Shillcock, R. C. & E. G. Bard. (1993). Modularity and the processing of closed class words. In Altmann, G.T.M. & Shillcock, R.C. (Eds.) *Cognitive models of speech processing. The Second Sperlonga Meeting*, pp. 163–185. Erlbaum.

Simpson, G. B., & Burgess, C. (1985). Activation and solution processes in the recognition of ambiguous words. *Journal of Experimental Psychology: Human Perception and Performance, 11*, 28–39.

Strain, E., Patterson, K., & Seidenberg, M. S. (1995). Semantic effects in single-word naming. *Journal of Experimental Psychology: Learning, Memory, and Cognition 21*, 1140–1154.

Strain, E., Patterson, K, Seidenberg, M. S. (2002). Theories of word naming interact with spelling-sound consistency. *Journal of Experimental Psychology: Learning, Memory, and Cognition, 28*, 207–241.

Strauss, T. J., Harris, H. D., & Magnuson, J. S. (in press). jTRACE : A reimplementation and extension of the TRACE model of speech perception and spoken word recognition. *Behavior Research Methods, Instruments & Computers.*

Swinney, D. A. (1979). Lexical access during sentence comprehension: (Re)consideration of context effects. *Journal of Verbal Learning and Verbal Behavior, 18*, 645–659.

Tanenhaus, M. K., Leiman, J. M., & Seidenberg, M. S. (1979). Evidence for multiple stages in the processing of ambiguous words in syntactic contexts. *Journal of Verbal Learning and Verbal Behavior, 18*, 427–440.

Tanenhaus, M.K., Spivey-Knowlton, M.J., Eberhard, K.M. & Sedivy, J.E. (1995). Integration of visual and linguistic information in spoken language comprehension. *Science, 268*, 1632–1634.

Trudeau, J. (2006). *Semantic Contributions to Word Naming with Artificial Lexicons.* Unpublished Ph.D. dissertation, University of Connecticut Department of Psychology.

Trueswell, J.C. & Tanenhaus, M. K. (1994). Toward a lexicalist framework of constraint-based syntactic ambiguity resolution. In Clifton, and Frazier (Eds), *Perspectives on sentence processing*, pp. 155–179. Hillsdale, NJ: Lawrence Erlbaum.

Ullman, J. & J. E. Hopcroft. (1969). *Formal Languages and Their Relation to Automata*. Reading, MA: Addison Wesley.

Warren, R. M. (1970). Restoration of missing speech sounds. *Science, 167*, 392–393.

Zeki, S., & Shipp, S. (1988). The functional logic of cortical connections. *Nature, 335*, 311–317.

Ziegler, J. C, Muneau, M. & Grainger, J. (2003). Neighborhood effects in auditory word recognition: Phonological competition and orthographic facilitation. *Journal of Memory and Language, 48*, 779–793.

Author Index

Subject Index

421